Defining the New Testament Logia
on Divorce and Remarriage in a Pluralistic Context

Defining the New Testament Logia
on Divorce and Remarriage in a Pluralistic Context

YORDAN KALEV ZHEKOV

PICKWICK *Publications* • Eugene, Oregon

DEFINING THE NEW TESTAMENT LOGIA ON DIVORCE AND REMARRIAGE IN A PLURALISTIC CONTEXT

Copyright © 2009 Yordan Kalev Zhekov. All rights reserved. Except for brief quotations in critical publications or reviews, no part of this book may be reproduced in any manner without prior written permission from the publisher. Write: Permissions, Wipf and Stock Publishers, 199 W. 8th Ave., Suite 3, Eugene, OR 97401.

ISBN 13: 978-1-55635-650-6

Cataloging-in-Publication data:

Defining the New Testament logia on divorce and remarriage in a pluralistic context / Yordan Kalev Zhekov.

Eugene, Ore.: Pickwick Publications, 2008

xii + 402 p. ; 23 cm. — Includes bibliographical references.

ISBN 13: 978-1-55635-650-6

1. Divorce—Biblical teaching. 2. Remarriage—Biblical teaching. 3. Divorce—Religious Aspects—Christianity. 4. Remarriage—Religious Aspects—Christianity. I. Title.

BS680 Z58 2009

Manufactured in the U.S.A.

To my lovely wife Monica

Contents

Abbreviations xi

one   Introduction: Establishing the Framework 1

two   The Old Testament Canonical Context 47

three   The New Testament Passages 84

four   The New Testament Canonical Context 188

five   The Context in Dogmatics 239

six   Applying the Conclusions in a Pluralistic Context 314

seven   Conclusion 349

Bibliography 355

Permissions have been obtained for the following sources:

1. Excerpt from *The New Jerusalem Bible*, copyright ©1985 by Darton, Longman & Todd, Ltd. and Doubleday, a division of Random House, Inc. Reprinted by Permission.

2. Translation of Marriage Contract, AD 66, Bacchias, Egypt (GM66 = *P.Ryl.* II.154):
David Instone-Brewer, "1 Corinthians 7 in the Light of the Graeco-Roman Marriage and Divorce Papyri." *Tyndale Bulletin* 51.2 (2001) 103, 104; and David Instone-Brewer, "1 Corinthians 7 in the Light of the Graeco-Roman Marriage and Divorce Papyri." *Tyndale Bulletin* (2001). [online]. Available at http://www.tyndale.cam.ac.uk/Brewer/MarriagePapyri/1Cor_7a.htm. Accessed on 26 August 2004.

3. Translation of Marriage Certificate, 92 BC, Tebtunis, Egypt (GM-92 = *P.Tebt.* I.104):
David Instone-Brewer, "1 Corinthians 7 in the Light of the Graeco-Roman Marriage and Divorce Papyri." *Tyndale Bulletin* 51.2 (2001) 108; and D. Instone-Brewer, "1 Corinthians 7 in the Light of the Graeco-Roman Marriage and Divorce Papyri." *Tyndale Bulletin* (2001). [online]. Available at http://www.tyndale.cam.ac.uk/Brewer/MarriagePapyri/1Cor_7a.htm. Accessed on 26 August 2004.

4. Translation of Divorce Deed, 13 BC, Alexandria, Egypt (GD-13 = BGU IV.1103):
David Instone-Brewer, "1 Corinthians 7 in the Light of the Graeco-Roman Marriage and Divorce Papyri." *Tyndale Bulletin* 51.2 (2001) 112 and D. Instone-Brewer, "1 Corinthians 7 in the Light of the Graeco-Roman Marriage and Divorce Papyri." *Tyndale Bulletin* (2001). [online]. Available at http://www.tyndale.cam.ac.uk/Brewer/MarriagePapyri/1Cor_7a.htm. Accessed on 26 August 2004.

5. Translation of Marriage Contract, AD 175, Philadelphia, Egypt (LM175 = *ChLA*.IV.249):
David Instone-Brewer, "1 Corinthians 7 in the Light of the Graeco-Roman Marriage and Divorce Papyri." *Tyndale Bulletin* 51.2 (2001) 113 and D. Instone-Brewer, "1 Corinthians 7 in the Light of the Graeco-Roman Marriage and Divorce Papyri." *Tyndale Bulletin* (2001). [online]. Available at http://www.tyndale.cam.ac.uk/Brewer/MarriagePapyri/1Cor_7a.htm. Accessed on 26 August 2004.

6. Translation of Marriage Contract, AD 128, Petra (JM128 i.e. *P.Yadin*.18):
David Instone-Brewer, "1 Corinthians 7 in the Light of the Jewish Greek and Aramaic Marriage and Divorce Papyri." *Tyndale Bulletin* 52.2 (2001) 226–27 and

D. Instone-Brewer, "1 Corinthians 7 in the Light of the Jewish Greek and Aramaic Marriage and Divorce Papyri." *Tyndale Bulletin* (2001). [online]. Available at http://www.tyndale.cam.ac.uk/Brewer/MarriagePapyri/1Cor_7b.htm. Accessed on 26 August 2004.

7. Translation of Marriage Contract, AD 126, Palestine (AM126 i.e. *P.Yad.*10): David Instone-Brewer, "1 Corinthians 7 in the Light of the Jewish Greek and Aramaic Marriage and Divorce Papyri." *Tyndale Bulletin* 52.2 (2001) 231 and D. Instone-Brewer, "1 Corinthians 7 in the Light of the Jewish Greek and Aramaic Marriage and Divorce Papyri." *Tyndale Bulletin* (2001). [online]. Available at http://www.tyndale.cam.ac.uk/Brewer/MarriagePapyri/1Cor_7b.htm. Accessed on 26 August 2004.

8. Translation of Divorce Deed, AD 72, Masada (AD72 i.e. *DJD*.II.19 = *P.Mur.*19): David Instone-Brewer, "1 Corinthians 7 in the Light of the Jewish Greek and Aramaic Marriage and Divorce Papyri." *Tyndale Bulletin* 52.2 (2001) 237 and D. Instone-Brewer, "1 Corinthians 7 in the Light of the Jewish Greek and Aramaic Marriage and Divorce Papyri." *Tyndale Bulletin* (2001). [online]. Available at http://www.tyndale.cam.ac.uk/Brewer/MarriagePapyri/1Cor_7b.htm. Accessed on 26 August 2004.

9. Pontifical Council for the Family. *Family, Marriage and "De Facto" Unions*. Libreria Editrice Vaticana. [online]. Available at http://www.vatican.va/roman_curia/pontifical_councils/family/documents/rc_pc_family_doc_20001109_de-facto-unions_en.html. Accessed on 30 August 2005.
Copyright by Libreria Editrice Vaticana.

10. Pope John Paul II. *Letter to Families from Pope John Paul II*. (1994—Year of the Family). Libreria Editrice Vaticana. [online]. Available at http://www.vatican.va/holy_father/john_paul_ii/letters/documents/hf_jp-ii_let_02021994_families_en.html. Accessed on 29 August 2005.
Copyright by Libreria Editrice Vaticana.

11. *Gaudium et Spes*, 48. Pastoral Constitution on the Church in the Modern World, Promulgated by His Holiness Pope Paul VI on December 7, 1965. Libreria Editrice Vaticana. [online]. Available at http://www.vatican.va/archive/hist_councils/ii_vatican_council/documents/vat-ii_cons_19651207_gaudium-et-spes_en.html. Accessed on 23 September 2004.
Copyright by Libreria Editrice Vaticana.

12. *Code of Canon Law, Title VII, Marriage.* Libreria Editrice Vaticana. [online]. Available at http://www.vatican.va/archive/ENG1104/__P3V.HTM. Accessed on 23 September 2004. Copyright by Libreria Editrice Vaticana.

13. Wilson Yates, "The Protestant View of Marriage." *JES* 22 (1985) 41–54. Copyright © 1985 by *Journal of Ecumenical Studies*.

14. J. M. Kuntz, "Is Marriage Indissoluble." *JES* 7 (1970) 333–37. Copyright 1970 by *Journal of Ecumenical Studies*.

15. Excerpts from *Divorce and Remarriage in the Catholic Church*, by Gerald D. Coleman, SS. Copyright © 1988 by Gerald D. Coleman. Paulist Press, Inc., New York/Mahwah, NJ. Reprinted by permission of Paulist Press, Inc. www.paulist press.com.

Abbreviations

AB	Anchor Bible
ABD	*The Anchor Bible Dictionary.* 6 vols. Edited by David Noel Freedman. New York: Doubleday, 1992
Bib	*Biblica*
BNTC	Black's New Testament Commentaries
CBQ	*Catholic Biblical Quarterly*
CH	*Church History*
ChrTo	*Christianity Today*
CTJ	*Conservative Theological Journal*
CTM	*Concordia Theological Monthly*
DJG	*Dictionary of Jesus and the Gospels.* Edited by Joel B. Green, Scot McKnight, and I. Howard Marshall. Downers Grove, IL: InterVarsity, 1992
DPHL	*Dictionary of Paul and His Letters.* Edited by Gerald F. Hawthorne, Ralph P. Martin, and Daniel G. Reid. Downers Grove, IL: InterVarsity, 1993
EvQ	*Evangelical Quarterly*
GOTR	*The Greek Orthodox Theological Review*
GTJ	*Grace Theological Journal*
HUCA	*Hebrew Union College Annual*
IBC	Interpretation: A Bible Commentary for Teaching and Preaching
ICC	International Critical Commentary
IDB	*The Interpreter's Dictionary of the Bible.* 4 vols. Edited by George A. Buttrick. Nashville: Abingdon, 1962
IEJ	*Israel Exploration Journal*
Int	*Interpretation*
JBL	*Journal of Biblical Literature*
JES	*Journal of Ecumenical Studies*

JETS	*Journal of the Evangelical Theological Society*
JFM	*Journal of Family Ministry*
JP	*Journal for Preachers*
JPC	*Journal of Pastoral Care*
JRE	*Journal of Religious Education*
JSNT	*Journal for the Study of the New Testament*
JSOT	*Journal for the Study of the Old Testament*
LCL	Loeb Classical Library
MFBW	*Marriage and Family in the Biblical World*. Edited by Ken M. Campbell. Downers Grove, IL: InterVarsity, 2003
NCBC	The New Century Bible Commentary
NICNT	New International Commentary on the New Testament
NIDNTT	*New International Dictionary of New Testament Theology*. Edited by Colin Brown. Grand Rapids: Zondervan, 1999. Zondervan Reference Software V. 2.7
NIGTC	The New International Greek Testament Commentary
NovT	*Novum Testamentum*
NTCI	*New Testament Criticism and Interpretation*. Edited by David Alan Black and David S. Dockery. Grand Rapids: Zondervan, 1991
NTS	*New Testament Studies*
OBT	Overtures to Biblical Theology
RevExp	*Review and Expositor*
SVSQ	*St Vladimir's Seminary Quarterly*
TDNT	*Theological Dictionary of the New Testament*. 10 vols. Edited by Gerhard Kittel and Gerhard Friedrich. Translated by Geoffrey W. Bromiley. Grand Rapids: Eerdmans, 1964–1976
TDOT	*Theological Dictionary of the Old Testament*. 14 vols. Edited by Johannes Botterweck, Helmer Ringgren, and Heinz-Josef Fabry. Grand Rapids: Eerdmans, 1974–
ThDig	*Theology Digest*
TrinJ	*Trinity Journal*
TS	*Theological Studies*
TynBul	*Tyndale Bulletin*
VT	*Vetus Testamentum*
WBC	Word Biblical Commentary

one

Introduction: Establishing the Framework

THE UNSTOPPABLE CONSTANT INCREASE OF MARITAL BREAKDOWN, THE globalisation of our world, the pluralisation of our cultures, and the liberalisation of Christianity require a fresh answer to the issues of divorce and remarriage. That answer needs to be biblically grounded, pluralistically applicable, and ecumenically valuable. Toward such an endeavor I will devote the present research.

DIVORCE AND REMARRIAGE DILEMMA DEFINED

The problem, which is the core of the divorce and remarriage dilemma, might be defined as the multiplicity of incoherent, one-sided, and self-centered methodologies of different scholars in dealing with the New Testament (NT) teaching on divorce and remarriage which has led them to fourfold inaccuracy in defining the NT logia on divorce and remarriage.

First, some scholars have produced inadequate exegetical analyses of the relevant NT texts. An example in this respect might be offered in relation to the misunderstanding of Paul's view on marriage, divorce, and remarriage based on 1 Cor 7:12-16.[1] Scholars' misinterpretation of 1 Cor 7:15, 16 as part of 1 Cor 7:12-16 led them to remarkably different conclusions. Some scholars argue that Paul allows divorce but does not speak about remarriage at all.[2] Others claim that Paul does not allow either di-

---

1. That problem might be easily detected in the scholarly debates presented in H. Wayne House, ed., *Divorce and Remarriage: Four Christians Views* (Downers Grove, IL: InterVarsity, 1990).

2. Gordon D. Fee, *The First Epistle to the Corinthians* (Grand Rapids: Eerdmans, 1987) 303; I. H. Marshall, "Divorce," in *New International Dictionary of New Testament Theology*, ed. Collin Brown (Grand Rapids: Zondervan, 1999) Zondervan Reference Software V. 2.7.

vorce or remarriage for the deserted Christian spouse.³ Some others even maintain that Paul allows divorce but disallows remarriage.⁴ The problem, according to the present author, is primarily related to the scholars' attempt to combat the so called "Erasmian View" of marriage, divorce and remarriage,⁵ which, according to them, is expressed in the writings of some contemporary protestant authors.⁶ That struggle led these scholars to compromise the solid exegetical reading of the text and to offer suggestions which distort both Paul's view on marriage, divorce, and remarriage and the nature of the NT teaching on these matters.

Second, inadequate methodologies have led some scholars to fractional and imbalanced theological integration of the exegetical conclusions into the canonical biblical literature. An example of such a matter might be presented in the misinterpretation of the passage of Deut 24:1–4 which led to an improper understanding of the Old Testament (OT) view on marriage, divorce, and remarriage.⁷ The problem is primarily related to the scholars' misunderstanding of the NT concepts of marriage, divorce, and remarriage which they read into the Deuteronomy text.⁸ If one

---

3. J. Carl Laney, "No Divorce & No Remarriage," in *Divorce and Remarriage: Four Christian Views*, ed. H. Wayne House (Downers Grove, IL: InterVarsity, 1990) 43; C. Burns, *Divorce and Remarriage* [online], Available at http://www.utdallas.edu/~michaelh/christian/message/divorce.html, Accessed on 7 December 2000; C. Smith, *Divorce and Remarriage* [online], Available at http://members.aol.com/cbsmith/TheWord.html, Accessed on 8 December 2000.

4. William A. Heth, "Divorce, but No Remarriage," in *Divorce and Remarriage: Four Christian Views*, ed. H. Wayne House (Downers Grove, IL: InterVersity, 1990) 113, 114.

5. Desiderius Erasmus (1466–1536) rejected the Catholic view of indissolubility of marriage and argued that divorce and remarriage should be allowed on the basis of Jesus' exception for adultery (Matt 5:32; 19:9) and Paul's exception for desertion (1 Cor 7:15). (See Joseph Sauer, "Desiderius Erasmus," in *The Catholic Encyclopedia*, vol. V, trans. W. G. Kofron [online], Available at http://www.newadvent.org/cathen/05510b.htm, Accessed on 7 December 2000; David Instone-Brewer, *Biblical Divorce and Remarriage: History of Divorce*, ch.9 [online], Available at http://www.tyndale.cam.ac.uk/Brewer/Academic/Chap_09.htm, Accessed on 26 November 2000; David Smith, *Divorce and Remarriage in Church History* [online], Available at http://www.providence.mb.ca/didcurar.htm, Accessed on 8 December 2000.)

6. See also William A. Heth, "Another Look at the Erasmian View of Divorce and Remarriage," *Journal of the Evangelical Theological Society* 25 (September 1982) 269, 270. Electronic edition by Galaxie Software, 1998; J. C. Laney, *No Divorce & No Remarriage*, 38; C. Burns, *Divorce and Remarriage* [online]; C. Smith, *Divorce and Remarriage* [online].

7. Also presented in H. Wayne House, ed. *Divorce and Remarriage*.

8. This might be clearly seen in such works as J. Carl. Laney, "Deuteronomy 24:1–4 and the Issue of Divorce," *Bibliotheca Sacra* 149/593 (January 1992) 4–16. Electronic

accepts the understanding of these scholars that Jesus condemned every second marriage as adulterous and embraces their claim that Deut 24:1–4 expresses the same view, then the question arises, "Why did Jesus refer to Gen 1:27; 2:24 to prove his argument?" If Deut 24:1–4 clearly speaks about the second marriage as adulterous, Jesus could have based his argument entirely on an explanation of this text without referring to Genesis (See Mark 10:2–12; Matt 19:3–12). Actually, these scholars understood neither Jesus' teaching on marriage, divorce, and remarriage (not every second marriage is adulterous, see exceptions in Matt 5:32 and 19:9) nor the Deut 24:1–4 view on these matters (if Deut 24:1–4 understood the second marriage as adulterous then it should have introduced a death punishment for the adulterous wife, cf. Lev 20:10).[9]

Third, while reading through the works of scholars from different Christian traditions it might be observed an incomplete interrelation of the theological conclusions in the dogmatic bodies within the traditions themselves, and lack of establishing a justifiable ecumenical view of the NT teaching on divorce and remarriage. On the one hand, some Catholic scholars argue that the church's teaching on these issues is ecumenically tolerable but it does not resolve its inner tensions. The Council of Trent (1545–1563) combated Luther's view which disqualified the authority of the church over matrimonial matters. Thus, in regard to Luther's view, the decision of the council affirmed the indissolubility of marriage even in the case of adultery and the church's control over matrimonial matters due to the sacramental nature of marriage. However, the Council did not engage in resolving the inner tension of the church in relation to these matters even though it attempted to smoothen its decision in relation to some of the church politics in respect to the Orthodox Church.[10] Furthermore, even though the absolute indissolubility of marriage is clearly stated in Canon 1118 in light of the Decree on Ecumenism paragraph 16 (Vatican II), it is argued that the Catholic Church approves the practices of the

---

edition by Galaxie Software, 1999; Jack Ford & A. R. G. Deasley, "Deuteronomy," in *Beacon Bible Commentary*, vol. 1 (Kansas City: Beacon Hill, 1969) 581; S. R. Driver, *Deuteronomy*, ICC (Edinburgh: T. & T. Clark, 1986) 272; P. C. Craigie, *The Book of Deuteronomy*, NICOT (Grand Rapids: Eerdmans, 1976) 305.

9. See also Joe M. Sprinkle, "Old Testament Perspectives on Divorce and Remarriage," *JETS* 40 (1997) footnote 4.

10. Walter Kasper, *Theology of Christian Marriage* (London: Burns & Oates, 1980) 59–62.

Orthodox churches related to dissolution of sacramental marriages but still keeps such practices prohibited within its own structures.[11] On the other hand, one may see the lack of Ecumenical tolerance on the matrimonial issues by the Orthodox Church. The canons of the Orthodox Church (10 and 31 of Laodicea, 21 of Carthage, 14 of Chalcedon, 72 of the Sixth Ecumenical Council) prohibit mixed marriages between Orthodox and non-Orthodox Christians.[12] Even though the church adapts more lenient politics due to the continuing increase of mixed marriages, it is always in a way which meets the conditions of the Orthodox Church.[13] Thus, the sacrament of marriage as understood by the Orthodox Church needs to be shared by non-Orthodox churches if a mixed marriage performed by the latter might be recognized.[14] Protestant scholars, representing a third position, show in their writings both a lack of dogmatical interrelation and ecumenical dialog. They labelled their views either as Roman Catholic or Protestant with the purpose to disqualify the validity of their conclusions. On the one hand, Thomas R. Edgar states that those scholars who stay behind the view of "no divorce and no remarriage" and "divorce, but no remarriage" are dogmatically shaped according to the Roman Catholic sacramental view of marriage.[15] William A. Heth disagrees with Edgar and insists that the author misrepresented his argument intentionally so that he might engage in refuting the presuppositions of his view but not its content.[16] On the other hand, J. Carl Laney argues that Edgar's view is only an expression of the Protestant viewpoint on these issues, and as such, it is primary engaged in refutation of other views but not of its substantiation.[17] However, Edgar maintains that his view should not be

---

11. J. M. Kuntz, "Is Marriage Indissoluble," *JES* 7 (1970) 333–37.

12. Lewis J. Patsavos, "Mixed Marriages and the Canonical Tradition of the Orthodox Church," *GOTR* 23 (1978) 244.

13. Ibid., 247.

14. Ibid., 254, 255.

15. Thomas R. Edgar, "Response to No Divorce & No Remarriage," by J. Carl Laney, in *Divorce and Remarriage: Four Christian Views*, ed. H. Wayne House (Downers Grove, IL: InterVarsity, 1990) 66.

16. William A. Heth, "Response to Divorce & Remarriage for Adultery or Desertion," by Thomas R. Edgar, in *Divorce and Remarriage: Four Christian Views*, ed. H. Wayne House (Downers Grove, IL: InterVarsity, 1990) 205, 206.

17. J. Carl Laney, "Response to Divorce & Remarriage for Adultery or Desertion," by Thomas R. Edgar, in *Divorce and Remarriage: Four Christian Views*, ed. H. Wayne House (Downers Grove, IL: InterVarsity, 1990) 198.

based on the Protestant traditional understanding of the matter but on the analysis of the relevant biblical texts.[18]

Fourth, some scholars have proposed an inadequate practical implementation of their established understanding of NT divorce and remarriage passages into the ecclesiastical communities within the present pluralistic societies. This problem has two aspects, namely, lack of consideration of the biblical teaching on the discussed matters and deficient analysis of the social context of the ecclesiastical communities. In relation to the first aspect, Hays gives an example with the American Christian community which has established its ethical standards not on a close reading of the Bible but on the categories derived from the popular national discourse.[19] The second aspect might be seen in the work of exegetes who have disregarded the complexities of the pluralistic contexts of the church communities. They followed their views into applications that shape their arguments with impractical subjectivity and practical inadequacy. While trying to apply his view of "no divorce & no remarriage"[20] Laney reaches the point where he does not have practical solutions, and as such, shifts his argument to a subjective appeal to God's grace and faithfulness.[21] The fluidity of such argumentation might be recognized through Larry Richards' appeal to the same reasoning, God's grace and forgiveness, but in order to oppose Laney's view.[22] Heth, who criticizes Laney's view as impractical and rigid[23] when he needs to defend his view

---

18. Thomas R. Edgar, "Divorce & Remarriage for Adultery or Desertion," in *Divorce and Remarriage: Four Christians Views*, ed. H. Wayne House (Downers Grove, IL: InterVarsity, 1990) 151. Idem, "Response to Divorce, but No Remarriage," by William A. Heth, in *Divorce and Remarriage: Four Christian Views*, ed. H. Wayne House (Downers Grove, IL: InterVarsity, 1990) 141.

19. Richard B. Hays, *The Moral Vision of the New Testament* (New York: HarperSanFrancisco, 1996) 2.

20. J. C. Laney, *No Divorce & No Remarriage*, 15–54.

21. Ibid., 48, 49.

22. How one needs to look at people who have suffered divorce. How God's grace and forgiveness relate to those who want to remarry after the divorce. (Larry Richards, "Response to No Divorce & No Remarriage," by J. Carl Laney, in *Divorce and Remarriage: Four Christian Views*, ed. H. Wayne House [Downers Grove, IL: InterVarsity, 1990] 69.)

23. Hays states: "I do not know how strictly Laney would apply this prohibition, but I doubt that he would insist that a wife remain in a home where the husband beat her, or committed incest with the children or was promiscuously adulterous (that is, in which case his wife becomes just another one of his 'flings.') My own view would not prohibit separation or legal divorce in these situations." (William A. Heth, "Response to No

of no remarriage under any circumstances,[24] also exhausts his practical argumentation and appeals to God's empowering grace, which will help those who have suffered divorce to commit themselves to single life.[25] Edgar, on the other hand, attempting to apply his view of divorce and remarriage only for adultery and desertion,[26] faces a level of absurdity in relation to some cases of marriage, which suffer incredibly not because of adultery or desertion, but because of other matters of abuse.

The fourfold inaccuracy in defining the NT logia on divorce and remarriage by the scholarship from different Christian traditions presents grounds for improvement in these four areas. The present work will attempt to provide a methodological framework which will facilitate development of an argument to resolve the fourfold inaccuracy. Hence, the four main parts of the study will pursue a clear exegetical analysis of the important NT texts; balanced theological integration of the exegetical conclusions into the canonical biblical literature; complete interrelation of the theological conclusions in the dogmatic bodies within the traditions themselves with establishing a justifiable ecumenical view; and sufficient practical implementation of the exegetical, theological, dogmatical, and ecumenical conclusions into the ecclesiastical communities within the present pluralistic societies.

BIBLICAL AND THEOLOGICAL STARTING POINTS

Establishing grounds for ecumenical discussion related to the matrimonial teachings of the main Christian traditions is a difficult task which necessitates formulation of the main standpoints of the author as well as of the traditions themselves. The author, understanding the role which his primarily Protestant background plays in shaping his thought, finds important for the successful development of the present work to define the concepts of marriage, sex, divorce, remarriage, ministry of divorced and remarried believers, celibacy, and widowhood. Lucid and accurate presentation is the only way to express the author's position and to clarify his possible presuppositions. Hence, the concepts will be expressed with

---

Divorce & No Remarriage," by J. Carl Laney, in *Divorce and Remarriage: Four Christian Views*, ed. H. Wayne House (Downers Grove, IL: InterVarsity, 1990) 59.

24. W. A. Heth, *Divorce, but No Remarriage*, 73–129.
25. Ibid., 115.
26. T. R. Edgar, *Divorce & Remarriage for Adultery or Desertion*, 151–96.

a straightforward language and without the support of the secondary sources.

Marriage, to start with, is a permanent, lifelong, covenantal union between a man and a woman who are testified by the proper institutions as physically and psychologically capable of establishing a marital relationship. A valid marriage is established when both parties agree to it, the church witnesses and blesses it, and the legal authorities legalize it. A valid marital union is the one established between one man and one woman. All other relationships, e.g. polygamy (one man many wives), polyandry (one woman many husbands), homosexual unions (marriages between two men or two women) cannot be treated as valid marital institutions. Any self-gratification marriage, e.g. "open marriage," "conditioned marriage," or cohabitation, is considered invalid and against the biblical standards for holy matrimony (Gen 1:27; 2:24; Mark 10: 6–9; Matt 19:4–6; Eph 5:25–32; Rom 7:2, 3; 1 Cor 7:10, 11).

Marriage is sustained by the mutual love of the spouses and its climactic expression is found in their sexual relationship. Sex is God's gift to the married couple. Marriage provides security for completeness of the sexual activity between the spouses. No cessation of sexual activity in the marriage is to be applied for any reason, except for spiritual purposes for a short period of time. All premarital and extramarital sexual activity is condemned as sinful and destructive for the person and for the society. Believers who are caught in premarital or extramarital sexual activities should be admonished and led to repentance. Believers who are caught in any kind of sexual promiscuity should be rebuked and led to repentance. If there is no repentance shown, and after a period of counseling there is no change of attitude and behavior, those believers may be excommunicated from the church. If after that action a change appears, they should be accepted back and restored into the body of Christ (Exod 20:14; Lev 20:10; Deut 5:18; Prov 6:32; Matt 5:32; 19:9; Mark 10:11, 12; Luke 16:18; 1 Cor 6:9, 15–18; 7:1–6; Heb 13:4).

Marriage is encouraged only between believers. Marriage should provide an atmosphere for the mutual edification of the spouses helping them to accomplish God's standards of life and the raising of children with Christian virtues and values. That is possible only when both parties, husband and wife, are fully converted, faithful, and devoted members of the body of Christ (1 Cor 7:39). Marriage between believer and unbeliever is discouraged. The church may not approve nor bless such a marriage. This kind of marriage may be regarded as a failure from the very beginning, since faith in Christ is considered foundational for establishing one's proper standards of life. A man and woman with different standards of life may not provide an atmosphere of unity and mutual spiritual edification in their marriage. Also, they cannot provide a proper spiritual environment for raising their children. Marriage is not arranged as a missionary tool even though it serves as such when one of the spouses becomes Christian. When mixed marriages appear due to the conversion of one of the spouses then, in accordance with the willingness of the unbeliever, the believer is encouraged to sustain the marital bond in every possible way (2 Cor 6:15; 1 Cor 7:12–16).

Divorce is not an option for marital crises, but may be conceived as a solution for marital breakdown. Lack of fulfillment of the stipulations of the marriage covenant by any of the spouses destroys the marital union. Any abuse of the spouse's marital rights and privileges destroys the marital bond. In such cases divorce is granted for the purpose of providing the innocent party with a healthier way of living. No limitations are established on the number of times a believer may divorce. However any divorce is considered in a sense a failure to reach God's standards for marriage (Exod 21:10–11; Deut 24:1–4; Ezek 9:9; 16:15–26; Jer 3:8–10; 5:11; Hos 8:14; Matt 19:9; 5:32; 1 Cor 7:15, 16).

It may be argued that there are proper grounds for divorce. The two biblical grounds for divorce are adultery or inappropriate sexual conduct and desertion. However, since these grounds are contextually rooted in the first century Christian communities and do not express ultimate undefined legalistic codes but rather an interpretation of Jesus' teaching, any other abuse or lack of fulfillment of the marriage obligations might be considered satisfactory for providing proper biblical grounds for divorce. When there is sufficient evidence for adultery committed by one of the spouses, then he/she should be admonished by the church community and led to repentance. If repentance is reached, then reconciliation and the continuation of the marriage is encouraged. If repentance is not reached and the adulterous behavior continues, then divorce may be considered an option. This pattern applies to any other marital abuse or failure in fulfillment of the marriage covenant stipulations. There are also grounds which may be considered improper for initiating divorce. When there is no abuse of any kind and no failure in fulfillment of the marriage covenant stipulations of one of the spouses then there are not sufficient grounds for divorce. Any mutual agreement for divorce by the spouses based on financial, physical or other reasons for their mutual benefit may be treated as unbiblical and improper. If a believer initiates divorce for improper, unbiblical reasons he/she needs to be encouraged to reconcile with the spouse and stop the divorce process. If a divorce is obtained in spite of the church's counsel, the believer needs to be admonished and led to repentance. If a level of repentance is reached, then every attempt for reconciliation with the former spouse is to be encouraged. If all attempts for reconciliation are exhausted, then a celibate lifestyle may be recommended. If the ability for this kind of life does not exist, then remarriage may be allowed (Deut 22:13-19, 28-29; Mal 2:10-16; Matt 5:32; 19:9; Mark 10:11-12; Luke 16:18; 1 Cor 7:1-7, 10, 11, 12-16).

It is very important to consider the relations with the children after divorce. Children are a crucial part of the family and require the necessary attention and care by their parents for their healthy and morally sound growth. When divorce takes place children are as traumatized as their parents. However, the children are not part of the divorce in the sense that the leaving parent does not divorce himself/herself from them. Hence, special attention should be given to them by both parents in order that the pain of losing a parent is softened as much as possible. Financial, physical, and spiritual support should be given to them by both parents (Matt 19:13-15; Mark 10:13-16; 1 Cor 7:12-14).

It is also very important to formulate the relations to one's former spouse. A peaceful and loving relationship should be established between the divorced parties in spite of the divorce. Until there is no involvement of a third party the possibility for reconciliation always exists. In the case of an unbiblical, improper divorce, reconciliation is to be considered mandatory and both spouses should make every effort toward this. In the case of a biblical, proper divorce, attempts at reconciliation need to be limited according to the nature of the marital breakdown. Even after remarriage peaceful communication between the former spouses should continue, especially when they have children (Matt 5:44; Luke 6:27, 35; Rom 12:18; 1 Cor 7:10, 11, 16).

Remarriage should not be always considered a failure from the biblical standards. Any believer who is divorced on proper biblical grounds has a right to remarry. Remarriage should follow the same principles as any normal first marriage. Remarriage which follows immediately after divorce may be discouraged due to the necessity of time for the divorced believer to be healed from the wounds of divorce, to think about reconciliation, a life of celibacy, or subsequent remarriage. Remarriage is encouraged only between believers. If a believer marries an unbeliever in spite of the church's counsel, he/she is to be admonished and led to repentance. If a divorce is obtained on improper, unbiblical grounds, then remarriage is to be discouraged and even prohibited. However, if remarriage is pursued in spite of the church's counsel the divorced believer should be admonished and led to repentance. If repentance is not reached and remarriage is established through secular institutions, then the ministry of the remarried believer in the Christian community is to be suspended and he/she may be even excommunicated. After a period of time and sufficient evidence that the believer has regretted his/her actions, he/she should be restored both in membership and ministry. The church hates sin and it is intolerant to sinful actions, but it loves the sinners and always forgives when there is sincere repentance (Deut 24:1–4; Matt 19:9; 5:32; 1 Cor 5:5; 7:8, 9, 15, 16).

Ministry is not only the responsibility of any believer but also part of a believer's search for spiritual identity on the basis of his/her spiritual gifts and abilities. Hence, any believer who has been divorced or/and remarried on biblical grounds should not be removed from his/her public ministry in the church, but encouraged and helped to continue his/her service to God according to his/her gifts and abilities. However, any believer who has been divorced or/and remarried on improper, unbiblical grounds should be removed from his/her public ministry for a period of time, during which a sincere repentance and appropriate conduct should be expected from him/her in order that he/she might be restored into the ministry. The duration of the period of penance should depend on the positive changes in the believer's behavior (John 4:1–42; 1 Cor 12:1–10; 28–31; Rom 12:4–8).

Since the concept of celibacy has been mentioned as a choice of a lifestyle of the divorced believer in the previous discussions it is beneficial to be elaborated further. Celibacy is considered a gift of God. It is neither emasculation, nor unhealthy, nor a fragmented sexual life. Celibacy is a healthy spiritual and physical condition of the believer in which, with the supernatural help of God, the believer is able to abstain from any kind of sexual activity and marriage. Some biblical examples for people leading this kind of life are Jesus and Paul. In relation to the believer's status, celibacy is considered to have an equal value with marriage. In relation to the ministry, celibacy is defined as being in a better position to devote more time to the ministry than marriage. However, it is the personal decision of the believer which places him/her in the condition he/she chooses. The exception to the latter are the cases when divorce on improper grounds is obtained and the ways of reconciliation with the former spouse are exhausted. In such cases the church leadership may insist on a celibate lifestyle (Matt 19:11, 12; 1 Cor 7:7, 8, 32–38).

The concept of widowhood needs some clarification as it bears some importance to the concepts of remarriage and celibacy. After the death of a spouse the living party is allowed to decide his/her marital status, i.e. celibacy or remarriage. Celibacy is encouraged if the believer considers himself/herself equipped by God's gift for this lifestyle. Remarriage is allowed, and if chosen, all the characteristics of a proper marital union are expected to be preserved. Thus, only a believer should be chosen for a new marriage partner (Rom 7:2, 3; 1 Cor 7:39; 1 Tim 5:14).

The presentation of the author's standpoints does not attempt to be exhaustive, covering all the dimensions of the concepts and all the possible cases in relation to marriage breakdown, divorce, and remarriage. It, however, looks to establish the author's understanding of the main biblical principles related to these concepts. The following presentations of the scholars from the main Christian traditions may also be considered limited due to the author's own premises and the introductory nature of this chapter.

The Catholic Church formulates marriage as a covenant relationship between man and woman for theirs and their children's mutual good throughout their entire life, which is established by Christ as a sacrament.[27] The church as well as some Catholic scholars argue that due to its sacramental nature marriage should be understood as a permanent, indissoluble institution and, as such, maintain that the acts of divorce and remarriage should not be allowed for any reason.[28] The institution of mar-

27. *Catechism of the Catholic Church*. Article 7: The Sacrament of Matrimony, 1601 (London: Chapman, 1994) 358.

28. "The Church does not allow divorce any more than she allows sin." (Encyclical Letter of the Holy Synod of Bishops, *On Marriage* [online], Available at http://www.holy-trinity.org/morality/synod-marriage.html, Accessed on 02 November 2000; Norbert Greinacher, "The Problem of Divorce and Remarriage," *Theology Digest* 35/3 [Fall 1988] 221–26; Denis O'Callaghan, "Marriage as Sacrament," *Concilium* 5/6 [May 1970] 102, 103, 106; C. Jaime Snoek, "Marriage and the Institutionalisation of Sexual Relations," *Concilium* 5/6 [May 1970] 118.)

riage is defined as a covenant union between man and woman primarily for the purpose of mutual edification, sexual realisation, and natural procreation.[29] Every canonically valid marriage, i.e. an officially established union between a baptised man and woman, is a sacrament because of its redemptive potential[30] and resemblance of the relationship between Christ and his church.[31] This holy matrimony is formulated as an indissoluble bond between the spouses finalized by their consent and sexual consummation and as a covenant is assured by God's fidelity.[32] Thus, the actions of divorce and remarriage have been defined as entirely inappropriate and sinful and their application to any canonically valid marriage institution has been prohibited.[33] In this respect both Matthew's exception clause[34] and Pauline privilege are treated not as justifiable grounds for divorce and remarriage, but either as reasons for separation from "bed and board" of the adulterous party or for marital annulment.[35] The latter is considered the only possible way of lawful cessation of a marital bond or attestation of a never existing one.[36]

Some Protestant scholars[37] maintain the indissolubility of marriage understanding the nature of union as a covenant relationship depicted

---

29. D. O'Callaghan, *Marriage as Sacrament*, 103; Petar Čalić, *Brak u procijepu: oženjan-rastavljen-ponovno vjenčan* (Zagreb: Glas Koncila, 1995) 59, 61, 62.

30. All dimensions of the healthy marital relationship are empowered with a redemptive potential for building the Kingdom of God. (See D. O'Callaghan, *Marriage as Sacrament*, 102, 103.)

31. Leonardo Boff, "The Sacrament of Marriage," *Concilium* 7/9 (September 1973) 22, 23; Richard M. Hogan, *John Paul II's New Vision of Human Sexuality, Marriage and Family Life* [online], Available at http://nfpoutreach.org/Hogan_New_Vision_marriage.htm, Accessed on 19 April 2001.

32. *Catechism of the Catholic Church*. Article 7: The Sacrament of Matrimony, 1639–1640, pp. 366–67.

33. N. Greinacher, *The Problem of Divorce and Remarriage*, 221–26.

34. "*Propter adulterium alterius coniugum matrimonii vinculum non posse dissolvi*." Piet Fransen, "Divorce on the Ground of Adultery-The Council of Trent (1563)," *Concilium* 5/6 (1970) 95, 96.

35. Dave Armstrong and William Klimon, *Dialogue: Annulment vs. Divorce* [online], Available at http://ic.net/~erasmus/RAZ150.HTM, Accessed on 19 April 2001.

36. *Divorce & Remarriage* [online], Available at http://www.catholic.com/answers/tracts/_divorce.htm, Accessed on 02 November 2000; Fr. Bob Pinkston, "When A Marriage Fails," [online], Available at http://www.rc.net/org/paulist/cicdoc6.htm, Accessed on 02 November 2000. Also Roderick Phillips, *Untying the Knot: A Short History of Divorce* (Cambridge: Cambridge University Press, 1991) 5.

37. J. C. Laney, *No Divorce & No Remarriage*, 15–54. Stephen Wilcox, *The Restoration*

through the terminology of the first marriage in the creation account (Gen 2:24).[38] Thus, they condemn divorce and remarriage as entirely sinful and completely unbiblical. According to them, both the teachings of Jesus (Mark 10:11, 12; Luke 16:18) and Paul (1 Cor 7:10, 11) express this understanding and neither the exception clause of Matthew[39] nor Pauline privilege[40] justify divorce and remarriage for any reason.

Other Protestant scholars[41] define the nature of marriage on the basis of the creation account (Gen 1:27; 2:23, 24) as a covenant kinship union[42] which makes the marital bond absolutely indissoluble, the act of divorce possible but ineffective in relation to the indissolubility of marriage, and the act of remarriage impossible and completely sinful. Thus, the teachings of Jesus and Paul are interpreted as expressing complete indissolubility of marriage. The exceptions which appear in both of them are ineffective in dissolving the marital bond and providing legitimate grounds for remarriage.[43]

---

of *Christian Marriage: A Call for Repentance and Reformation* [online], Available at http://www.mastershelp.com/wwwboard/divorceforum/messages/35.html, Accessed on 25 April 2001; Charles C. Ryrie, "Biblical Teaching on Divorce and Remarriage," *Grace Theological Journal* 3/2 (Fall 1982) 178–93. Electronic edition by Galaxie Software, 1999; Neels Smit, "Why May a Marriage not be Dissolved," *Orientation* 58–62 (December 1990–1991) 111–17; Harry G. Coiner, "Divorce and Remarriage: Toward Pastoral Practice," *CTM* 34 (1963) 541–55; John J. Kilgallen, "To What are the Matthean Exception-Texts (5,32 and 19,9) an Exception?" *Bib* 61 (1980) 102–5.

38. The terms "leaving," "cleaving," and "one flesh" signify the strong, unbreakable relationship established between the first husband and wife.

39. Matthew's exception clause is treated as related only to the incestuous Gentile marriages in Matthew's community.

40. Pauline privilege is understood as exemption of the believer from preserving the marriage.

41. W. A. Heth, *Divorce, but No Remarriage*, 73–129. William A. Heth and Gordon J. Wenham, *Jesus and Divorce: The Problem with the Evangelical Consensus* (London: Hodder and Stoughton, 1984); David Engelsma, *The Remarriage of the Guilty Party* [online], Available at http://www.rsglh.org/remarriage_of_the_guilty_party.htm, Accessed on 25 April 2001.

42. The terminology used to depict the process of the first marriage, i.e. "forsake," "cleave," "one flesh," "bone and flesh," is understood to establish covenant kinship relationship.

43. Both Matthew's exception clause and Pauline privilege are interpreted under the influence of their contexts (Matt 19:9, 12; 1 Cor 7:10–16) as allowing illegitimate divorce and not referring to remarriage at all.

Some other representatives of Protestant scholarship[44] maintain the permanent nature of marriage but not to the extent of indissoluble union due to the exceptions of adultery and desertion, which legitimize a legal divorce and remarriage for the innocent party. Hence, the marriage covenant terminology of the creation account is not understood as making the marital bond indissoluble,[45] and the teaching of Jesus used by Paul is not perceived as establishing a legal code, but an ethical imperative which justifies the force of Matthew's exception and Pauline privilege as appropriate grounds for divorce and remarriage.[46]

Other Protestant scholars[47] understand marriage as ordained by God to be a permanent covenant union between husband and wife, but due to the fallen human nature, they allow divorce and remarriage for

---

44. T. R. Edgar, *Divorce & Remarriage for Adultery or Desertion*, 151–96. Craig Keener, *Free to Remarry* [online], Available at http://www.christianitytoday.com/ct/2000/135/48.0.html, Accessed on 25 April, 2001; John MacArthur, *Divorce and Remarriage* [online], Available at http://www.webzonecom.com/ccn/bible-s/divorce.txtm, Accessed on 25 April 2001; J. K. Manful, *Divorce* [online], Available at http://home.freeuk.net/otchereh/divorce.htm, Accessed on 25 April 2001; Timothy S. Morton, *From Marriage to Remarriage: Has a Remarried Christian Commited an "Unpardonable Sin?"* [online], Available at http://members.citynet.net/morton/marriage.htm, Accessed on 25 April 2001; David J. Macleod, *The Problem of Divorce: the Teaching of Paul* [online], Available at http://www.emmaus.edu/ej_div.html, Accessed on 25 April 2001; J. David Hoke, *Thinking Biblically About . . . Divorce & Remarriage: Matthew 19:1–10* [online], Available at http://www.horizonsnet.org/sermons/tba04.html, Accessed on 25 April 2001.

45. The expression "one flesh" should not be defined as signifying indissoluble union since it is also used to designate tentative sexual relationships (1 Cor 6:6).

46. The grammatical and syntactical nature of Matthew's exception clause guided by the meaning of πορνεία shape it as a real exception in a case of adultery. Due to that understanding of the exception clause in the teaching of Jesus by Paul, he interpreted the latter in relation to the new situations of mixed marriages in the Corinthian church as allowing divorce and remarriage for the deserted believer.

47. L. Richards, "Divorce & Remarriage under a Variety of Circumstances," in *Divorce and Remarriage: Four Christians Views*, ed. H. Wayne House (Downers Grove, IL: InterVarsity, 1990) 215–48. Olan Hicks, *Bible Solutions to Divorce Problems* [online], Available at http://www.theophilus.org/divorce.html, Accessed on 25 April 2001; Graeme Codrington, *Marriage, Divorce and Remarriage in the Light of the Teaching of Jesus* [online], Available at http://www.youth.co.za/papers/divorce.htm, Accessed on 25 April 2001; Zenith Harris Merrill, *Marriage, Divorce, Remarriage: What Does the Bible Allow?* [online], Available at http://www.bloomington.in.us/~lgthscac/marriagedivorce.htm#marriage,%20divorce,%20remarriage:%20what%20does%20the%20bible%20allow?, Accessed on 25 April 2001; Gary D. Collier, *Rethinking Jesus on Divorce* [online], Available at http://www.rq.acu.edu/Volume_037/rq03702collier.htm, Accessed on 25 April 2001.

any reason. However, they define these as sinful actions requiring repentance and do not see any legitimate biblical grounds for them except for the Pauline privilege because the believer's active participation is not involved. In this view even Matthew's exception clause does not establish proper grounds for divorce and remarriage. There the correct response is forgiveness and reconciliation.[48]

Finally, the Eastern Orthodox Church in general and some of its scholars define marriage as a lifelong sacramental institution established on the basis of the mutual consent of the spouses and the blessing of the church. They argue that the vulnerability of this institution in respect to the sinful human nature might be resolved through the acts of divorce and remarriage. The permanent character of marriage is sustained by its sacramental and covenant nature depicted through the teachings of Jesus, Paul and the holy fathers.[49] The covenant relationship between the husband and wife is personified through their mutual love and God's grace, which makes it a sacramental embodiment of the mysterious union between Christ and the church.[50] The solemnity of that relationship requires specific characteristics for its verification. No marriage is validated apart from those which are performed in the church and do not suffer impediments of blood relations, marital attachments, and baptismal or spiritual inadequacy.[51] However, due to human failure to achieve God's standards

48. Understanding God's attitude towards the adulterous spouse in the story of Hosea (Hos 1, 11) as establishing reconciliation and forgiveness, not divorce, as the appropriate action of the innocent party determines the interpretation of Matthew's exception clause not as a real exception in the case of adultery.

49. Fr. Ted, *What is the Orthodox Position on Divorce and Remarriage?* [online], Available at http://www.beliefnet.com/story/15/story_1595_1.html, Accessed on 21 April 2001; Constas H. Demetry, *Catechism of the Eastern Orthodox Church* [online], Available at http://www.christusrex.org/www1/CDHN/catechis.html, Accessed on 21 April 2001; Sotirios, "Matrimony," in *Orthodox Catechism: Basic Teachings of the Orthodox Faith* [online], Available at http://www.gocanada.org/Catechism/catmatri.htm, Accessed on 21 April 2001.

50. Michel Najim, *The Theology of the Orthodox Sacrament of Matrimony and Its Implications in our Family Life* [online], Available at http://www.antiochian.org/theology/theology_of_the_orthodox_marriage.htm, Accessed on 22 April 2001; Encyclical Letter of the Holy Synod of Bishops, *On Marriage* [online], Available at http://www.holy-trinity.org/morality/synod-marriage.html, Accessed on 21 April 2001; Hicolass Van Der Wal, "Secular Law and The Eastern Church's Concept of Marriage," *Concilium* 5/6 (1970) 81.

51. C. H. Demetry, *Catechism of the Eastern Orthodox Church* [online]; Sotirios, *Matrimony* [online]; H. Van Der Wal, *Secular Law and The Eastern Church's Concept of*

of marriage and the paradoxical nature of the biblical teaching on divorce and remarriage, the church also recognizes, accepts, and treats the marriage breakdown in a threefold manner.[52] First, using the exception clause of Matthew and Pauline privilege, the church allows divorce and subsequent remarriage on the grounds of adultery,[53] permanent insanity, desertion, forcing the spouse into prostitution, and endangering the life of the spouse.[54] Second, the church accepts divorce and remarriage recognising the dissolution of some dead marriages.[55] Third, when improper divorce and remarriage are performed the church offers forgiveness to the repentant sinners.[56]

The views expressed by the scholars of different Christian traditions are widely diverse. They have various formulations of marriage and cover all possible interpretations of the biblical texts from complete prohibition of divorce and remarriage to permission for both on various grounds. The author's own standpoints also express various dissimilarities with the traditions in understanding the main matrimonial concepts. The central problem of the present discussion may be established as whether unity is to be found in the diversity of Christian views of understanding the ex-

Marriage, 82; Encyclical Letter of the Holy Synod of Bishops, *On Marriage* [online].

52. C. H. Demetry, *Orthodox Creed* [online], Available at http://www.bible.ca/cr-Orthodox.htm, Accessed on 21 April 2001; Fr. Ted, *What is the Orthodox Position on Divorce and Remarriage?* [online]; Stanley S. Harakas, *The Orthodox Church: 455 Questions and Answers* (Minneapolis: Light & Life, 1987) 107; Orthodox Church in America Tenth All-American Council, *Synodal Affirmations On Marriage, Family, Sexuality, and the Sanctity of Life* [online], Available at http://www.oca.org/pages/ocaadmin/documents/All-American-Council/10-Miami-1992/Synodal-Affirmations.html, Accessed on 22 April 2001.

53. Sotirios, *Matrimony* [online].

54. Fr. Ted, *What Is the Orthodox Position on Divorce and Remarriage?* [online].

55. Eastern Orthodox Church recognizes three types of marital death: moral, psychological, and political. The moral death relates to the cessation of the mutual love between the spouses due to different kinds of moral abuse such as incest, murder, violence, homosexual activities, etc. The psychological death is established when one of the parties experiences a certain psychological condition which is unbearable by the other party. The political death designates the withdrawal of one of the parties from marriage due to political reasons like imprisonment or going for a political career. See Gwenda Callaghan, *Annulment Process. Remarriage in the Church: Pastoral Solutions. A Statement by the Board Members of the Association for the Rights of Catholics in the Church (ARCC)* [online], Available at http://astro.temple.edu/~arcc/marriage.htm, Accessed on 19 April 2001.

56. C. H. Demetry, *Orthodox Creed* [online].

act biblical teaching on marriage, divorce, and remarriage in general and the NT teaching on these issues in particular. Also, if the main question derived from the previous presentations may be formulated as whether Christians may legitimately divorce and remarry and on what grounds then a further issue to be considered is whether an ecumenical answer of this question is possible. In the present work I will attempt to provide answers to these questions.

PRESENTATION OF THE WORKING HYPOTHESIS

The presentation of the author's standpoint and various theories of the scholarship from different Christian traditions in relation to the concepts of marriage, divorce, and remarriage leads one to find some lines of continuity and some of discontinuity between different views. The former might be defined as the overall understanding of marriage, divorce, and remarriage as a twofold biblical concept. As such, scholarship agrees that there are two dimensions to be considered, one which relates to the nature of marriage itself and the other to the nature of marital breakdown and its postulates. As far as the nature of marriage is concerned, the theories explored previously reach a mutual ground on the fact that marital union is a lasting institution which requires the partnership of the spouses for its lifelong preservation. However, the failure of the latter is the point of disagreement among theologians and creates the discontinuity of their theories. Thus, the second dimension represents the treatment of sick marriages and encompasses concepts like indissolubility of the marital bond, separation from bed and board, annulment, divorce, and remarriage. It is this part of the twofold concept which requires possible solution, which, according to the present author, is found in the understanding of marriage as a covenant relationship. This would establish the marital union as an institution with a permanent character and divorce and remarriage only as an exceptional solution for relationships which being corrupted by the sinful human nature lack the fulfillment of the covenant responsibilities by the spouses. From that standpoint derives the main hypothesis of the present work.

The NT teaching on divorce and remarriage should be understood as a twofold concept which stresses the permanence of the marriage covenant and provides exceptional permission for divorce and remarriage only in the case of a spouse's failure to fulfill the covenant stipulations.

The emphasis clearly stays on the permanent, lifelong, and lasting bond of the marriage covenant which excludes divorce and remarriage actions against one's spouse limiting these in only exceptional cases when the sinful behavior of one of the spouses has endangered the moral integrity and life of the other. Thus, the twofold concept would appear to be an attempt not only to present the author's view of the NT teaching on divorce and remarriage, but also to balance the extremes in different Christian understandings of the latter and to provide an alternative answer, one which is theoretically sound, ecumenically adequate, and practically relevant. Acceptance of that proposal by the whole church will both preserve the biblical view of marriage, divorce, and remarriage in our pluralistic society and help to reduce all theological, dogmatical, and practical abuses of marital issues.

METHODOLOGICAL DESIGN OF THE WORK

General Overview of the Methodology

The methods which will be used for conducting the study might be defined as a revised combination of the methods for doing NT ethics presented by Richard B. Hays in "The Moral Vision of the NT: A Contemporary Introduction to the NT Ethics,"[57] and for doing NT exegesis presented by Gordon D. Fee in "NT Exegesis: A Handbook for Students and Pastors."[58] Hays' methodology includes four levels of developing an ethical argument: descriptive, synthetic, hermeneutical, and pragmatic. These levels institute for the researcher the task of exegeting all the relevant passages in relation to the subject, the task of analyzing the canonical biblical literature and its contribution to the subject, the task of interpreting the exegeted passages within the present context, and the task of applying these interpretations in the Christian communities and the society at large. The modifications to Hays' methodology are based on a twofold correction in relation to the present theme of marriage, divorce, and remarriage. Firstly, the suggested threefold guidance for the synthetic task, community, cross, and new creation is too restrictive and does not do justice to all the NT and OT data. Moreover, the Old Testament canonical writings

---

57. Hays, *The Moral Vision of the New Testament*.

58. Gordon D. Fee, *New Testament Exegesis* (Lousville: Westminster John Knox, 1993).

are not allowed to contribute to the synthetic analysis[59] even though they have been evaluated in general[60] and engaged in pursuing the descriptive and pragmatic tasks. Hence, guidance is found more specific to the issues of marriage, divorce, and remarriage in the concept of marriage covenant and the whole canonical corpus of the OT is allowed to participate in developing the synthetic task. Secondly, due to the insignificant contribution for the subject of divorce and remarriage of the pre-formulated modes[61] of the hermeneutical task, the latter should be concentrated on analysis of the main Christian traditions with an attempt for an ecumenical proposal.

Fee's methodology of doing NT exegesis has been established around these four areas of research.[62] The exegetical analysis of the specific passages in all its dimensions is foundational. Its conclusions are established against the biblical and theological contexts and the results produced from the process are applied into the interpreter's ecclesiastical context. Fee's methodology is more integrated into the descriptive level of Hays' approach. The latter is further presented by the present author as a compilation of the historical-critical and narrative-critical methods for biblical analysis. These both are modified with each other in relation to their limitations. Historical-critical approach tends to destroy the unity of the text through its source, form, tradition, and redaction critical analyses, and it is balanced with the unifying narrative-critical approach. The narrative-critical approach disregards the historical roots of the text and as such it makes its relationship to the original context so loose that the exegete's understanding of the story becomes a canon within the canon. Hence, that understanding shapes the meaning of the text and disrupts the dis-

---

59. Hays, *The Moral Vision of the New Testament*, 9.

60. Ibid., 307–9.

61. In his discussion on "the mode of hermeneutical appropriation" on divorce and remarriage Hays argues that both "principle" and "paradigm" modes have little role to play if at all in regard to the issue of divorce and remarriage. Furthermore, having in consideration the complex relationship between the other two modes "rules" and "a symbolic world" Hays concludes that the hermeneutical discussion in relation to the issues of divorce and remarriage needs to be conducted primarily through the analysis of the "other authorities." (See Hays, *The Moral Vision of the New Testament*, 367, 368.)

62. Fee's analysis does include the characteristics of the four main tasks of Hays' approach but he integrates the synthetic, hermeneutical, and pragmatic tasks into two levels, namely, consideration of broader biblical and theological contexts and application. (G. D. Fee, *New Testament Exegesis*, 54–55, 60–61, 160–61.

closure of the author's original intentions. The historical-critical approach in this regard keeps the narrative analysis strongly grounded to the historical foundations of the text.[63] Therefore, the methodology which I will use for developing the present work includes five levels of research.

First, in order to establish proper contextual grounds for the analysis of the NT texts and holistic canonical environment for the NT conclusions I will formulate the OT perspective on marriage covenant with its fundamental characteristics as related to the nature of marriage, divorce, and remarriage. Second, I will analyze exegetically the NT passages related to the subjects of divorce and remarriage (Mark 10:2–12 and Matt 19:3–12; Matt 5:31, 32 and Luke 16:18; 1 Cor 7:12–16). Third, the exegetical conclusions will be examined in relation to their broader NT context. Hence, the whole body of NT canonical literature will be allowed to contribute to the understanding reached from the exegesis with the input from the previously established OT perspective. Fourth, the conclusions drawn from the first three levels of research will be examined dogmatically through the analysis of different Christian traditions. The goal of this section is to establish an ecumenical view of the New Testament teaching on divorce and remarriage. Finally, I will attempt to offer some proposals for applying the NT teaching on divorce and remarriage in the ecclesiastical communities considering the complexities of our pluralistic society.

63. The following scholars have contributed to this critique in different ways: William Baird, "New Testament Criticism," in *The Anchor Bible Dictionary*, ed. David Noel Freedman, electronic ed. (New York: Doubleday, 1996, c1992) 6 volumes.—[Logos Library System]; Robert H. Stein, "Redaction Criticism (NT)," in *The Anchor Bible Dictionary*, electronic ed.; Grant R. Osborne, "Redaction Criticism," in *Dictionary of Jesus and the Gospels*, eds. Joel B. Green, Scot McKnight, and I. Howard Marshall (Downers Grove, IL: InterVarsity, 1992) 669; idem. "Preaching the Gospels: Methodology and Contextualization," *JETS* 27 (1984) 27–42. Electronic Edition by Galaxie Software, 1998. Maurice Casey, "Where Wright is Wrong: A Critical Review of N. T. Wright's Jesus and the Victory of God," *JSNT* 69 (1998) 99, 100; Douglas J. Moo, review of *The Climax of the Covenant: Christ and the Law in Pauline Theology*, by N. T. Wright, in *JETS* 39 (1996) 664; Michael W. Nicholson, "Abusing Wittgenstein: The Misuse of the Concept of Language Games in Contemporary Theology—A Critique of the Appropriation of Wittgenstein's Philosophy in the Works of George Lindbeck, Anthony Thiselton and N. T. Wright," *JETS* 39 (1996) 628. Electronic edition by Galaxie Software, 1999; Pieter F. Craffert, review of *Paul's Narrative Thought World: the Tapestry of Tragedy and Triumph*, by Ben Witherington III, in *CBQ* 58 (1996) 177; Bruce N. Fisk, review of *Paul's Narrative Thought World: The Tapestry of Tragedy and Triumph*, by Ben Witherington III, in *JBL* 115 (1996) 554; Dale B. Martin, review of *The Moral Vision of the New Testament: A Contemporary Introduction to New Testament Ethics*, by Richard B. Hays, in *JBL* 117 (1998) 359.

Detailed Analysis of the Methodology

A comprehensive analysis of the methodology is offered in the present section. An attempt will be made to define Hays' four tasks for doing NT ethics and further elaborate and critically assess them in relation to the present work. Fee's approach of analysing the NT texts will be presented with the intention of underlining the basic aspects of doing biblical exegesis. Due to the specific goal of the present research and the broad character of the topics which will be discussed, the analysis might suffer some limitations though not affecting the conclusions in relation to the methods employed in this work.

OVERALL NATURE OF RICHARD HAYS' APPROACH TO NEW TESTAMENT ETHICS

Richard Hays is a defender of the narrative approach in doing NT Ethics and Theology. In his most significant work, *The Moral Vision of the New Testament*, he argues that within the diversity of the NT writings a "loose unity"[64] emerges in the form of a "single fundamental story."[65] A short summary of that story would suffice for our purposes. In the person of Jesus Christ through his death and resurrection, the God of Israel reconciles to himself the alienated humanity which he created perfect but was lost due to its rebellious disobedience. However, the full consummation of that process is not yet completed. God created the church, a witness of that good news of salvation and liberation through Jesus Christ. The church empowered by the Holy Spirit, lives the teachings of its Lord and declares God's eternal purposes for the world in this present time before the final realization of the story.[66]

The story, according to Hays, is established on three focal images: community, cross, and new creation. The order in which the three images appear is very significant for the author since it establishes the main plot of the story. Hence, the community institutes the continuity with Israel. The cross, defines the pivot-point of the plot, Jesus. And the new cre-

---

64. Hays, *The Moral Vision of the New Testament*, 193.

65. Ibid. In agreement with him Robin Parry argues that the unity of the NT is not contained in a dogmatic system but in the story of God's saving act in Jesus Christ. (Robin Parry, Review of *The Moral Vision of the New Testament*, by R. B. Hays, In *European Journal of Theology* 7/2 [1998] 134.)

66. Hays, *The Moral Vision of the New Testament*, 193.

ation closes the story with the expectation of God's final redemptive act in history.[67] Hays concludes that through using imaginative analogies and metaphorical juxtaposition the believers engage in reading the story in a way which reshapes their lives forming accordingly their own stories.[68]

In relation to Paul, Hays uses the same narrative approach. He argues that Paul's thought is shaped by the story, whose three focal points are community, cross, and new creation.[69] For Paul the plot develops in the same manner as presented before. The community consists of the redeemed followers of Christ, who live in unity and "in Christ," using the diversity of their gifts in the attitude of love toward each other.[70] The cross signifies the death of Jesus as the unique event of reconciliation between man and God, presenting the obedience of the Son of God and prompting the same of his followers, and pointing to the hope of resurrection, the act of believers' final deliverance by God.[71] The new creation is the result of the inauguration of the new age in the old one. That fact should be the moving conscience of the church in time of tension between the inauguration and the consummation of the new aeon.[72]

Following his conviction that the moral judgments of the Christian community must be established on Scripture, Hays undertakes the task to articulate a methodology for defining NT Ethics as "a normative theological discipline."[73] The purpose is to bring the church to constant engagement with Scripture so that it might influence the life of the community of faith.[74] Hays accomplishes this project through establishing four different but overlapping analytical operations, namely, descriptive, synthetic, hermeneutical, and pragmatic.[75] This division is an attempt for shaping our engagements with Scripture in a systematic way.[76] Hence, in the following chapters I would like to present and evaluate the four tasks

---

67. Ibid., 194–204.
68. Ibid., 298–304.
69. Ibid., 36.
70. Ibid., 32–36.
71. Ibid., 27–32.
72. Ibid., 19–32.
73. Ibid., 3.
74. Ibid., 3.
75. Ibid., 3, 7, 8.
76. Ibid., 8.

for doing NT Ethics and reshape them in relation to the methodology of the present work.

THE DESCRIPTIVE TASK

The descriptive task as explained by Hays is an attempt to analyze the major NT canonical writings with the purpose to establish their main ethical message for the Christian communities. The texts are analyzed critically accepting their historical nature but focusing on their final literary forms for understanding of their message.[77] The latter is not only expressed in the form of teachings, but also as "stories, symbols, social structures and practices that shape the community's ethos."[78] Hays favors and encourages a systematic exegetical approach for analysis[79] but due to the extensiveness of such a task he limits himself to the major elements of the text which underline the author's moral logic.[80] The NT biblical scholarship considers Hays' exegetical work solid and fare in relation to the selection of the significant texts, the depth of the analysis, and consideration of the scholarly opinions.[81] However, due to the nature of the narrative approach, Hays' descriptive task might be evaluated as being under the influence of his synthetic task.[82] Thus, he not only underlines the main elements of coherence between the individual texts, using as guidance the three focal images,[83] but also attempts to deduct the main themes and motives of the texts into specific moral imperatives.[84] Hence, in order to balance the predominantly narrative nature of Hays' descriptive task in the following chapter, I would like to present, evaluate, and integrate narrative-critical and historical-critical approaches for biblical analysis in their most essential forms.

77. Ibid., 9.
78. Ibid., 4.
79. Ibid., 3, 47.
80. Ibid., 13, 14.
81. Douglas J. Moo, review of *The Moral Vision of the New Testament: Community, Cross, New Creation. A Contemporary Introduction to New Testament Ethics*, by Richard B. Hays, in *Bulletin for Biblical Research* 9 (1999) 272. Richard A. Young, review of *The Moral Vision of the New Testament: Community, Cross, New Creation. A Contemporary Introduction to New Testament Ethics*, by Richard B. Hays, in *JETS* 42 (1999) 138.
82. Also R. A. Young, review of *The Moral Vision of the New Testament*, 137.
83. Hays, *The Moral Vision of the New Testament*, 19, 80.
84. R. A. Young, review of *The Moral Vision of the New Testament*, 137.

*Analysis and Evaluation of the Narrative-Critical
and Historical-Critical Approaches to the Biblical Text*

The descriptive level of Hays' approach is presented as a compilation of the historical-critical and narrative-critical methods for biblical analysis. These two critical methods require further and more detailed presentation before they are actually applied to the text analysis. Hence, in the following chapters I will lay down the most significant characteristics related to both methods beginning with the narrative-critical approach.

Narrative-Critical Method for Biblical Analysis. My attempt at the present section of the work is to establish the narrative-critical method for New Testament studies as essential for providing a holistic approach to analysis of the biblical texts. With the view of integrating this method into the methodology of the present work I will limit myself to providing a working definition of the discipline underlining its main elements. I will evaluate the method in relation to historical criticism and present its advantages and disadvantages for biblical analysis.

Narrative criticism is defined in a broader sense as discipline which has ontological significance. Narrative is not just a literary expression of a text but an overreaching category which defines human existence. An individual comprehends his world as a story which is part of the global narrative which embraces the whole universe. Hence, with such description narrative criticism becomes normative for nonnarrative or discursive texts since it presupposes a narrative substructure. Paul's letters, for example, are understood as an expression of his religious narrative perception based on the story of God's relationship with man with climax in Jesus in regard to the churches' problems and needs he dealt with.[85] In a more narrow sense narrative criticism is defined as the discipline which deals primarily with the stories found in the biblical literature using the insights of the broader field of modern literary criticism with an attempt to identify their effect on the reader.[86] The basic framework of narrative criticism is established by three major elements: narrative, implied author, and implied reader.

---

85. W. Baird, "New Testament Criticism" (Logos Library System).

86. Mark Allan Powell, "Narrative Criticism," in *Hearing the New Testament: Strategies for Interpretation*, ed. Joel B. Green (Grand Rapids: Eerdmans, 1995) 239.

Generally, narrative should be defined as any literary work which is expressed in terms of a story.[87] Particularly, NT narratives are understood as stories with plots, characters, and outcomes.[88] Their literary analysis, according to Howell, should be underlined by two axiomatic presuppositions. First, the narrative should be comprehended as one whole unit undermining the fragmentary results of the source critical theories. Second, the meanings derived from the small units of the narrative are guided by the meaning of the whole narrative.[89] In their relation to the reader the biblical stories become a foundation of one's life and personal story. Thus, in the very fact of the reality of the story of Jesus Christ the believer makes the story his own story of Christian journey from justification through sanctification to perfection.[90]

The implied author is the writer of the narrative who emerges from a narrative analysis by the reader without any extrinsic help and apart from the evidence or assumptions related to the historical author. Due to the fact that these two might be different, the relevance of the narrative in terms of values, beliefs, and perceptions is not dependent on historical time. Hence, neither the lack of a clear image of the historical author nor the length of historical time passed from the original writing diminishes the relevance of the narrative for the reader.[91]

The implied reader is different from the historical reader and is presupposed by the narrative. Due to the fact that narrative criticism attempts to understand the text through the eyes of the implied reader, the relationship between the two becomes very significant. The text provides the framework in which the implied reader's comprehension of the narrative should be viewed. Nothing from what the text does not specify, imply or presuppose about the implied reader should be identified as a characteristic of the latter.[92] Within this framework narrative critics accept the possibility of broadening the range of meanings of the text within

---

87. Idem, *What is Narrative Criticism?* (Minneapolis: Fortress, 1990) 23.

88. William Baird, "New Testament Criticism," in *ABD* 1:735.

89. David B. Howell, *Mathew's Inclusive Story: A Study in the Narrative Rhetoric of the First Gospel*, JSNTSup 42 (Sheffield: JSOT Press, 1990) 33.

90. Hans Frei, "Apologetics, Criticism, and the Loss of Narrative Interpretation," in *Why Narrative? Readings in Narrative Theology*, eds. Stanley Hauerwas and L. Gregory Jones (Grand Rapids: Eerdmans, 1989) 45–64.

91. Powell, *Narrative Criticism*, 240, 241.

92. Powell, *What is Narrative Criticism*, 19, 20.

different contexts. In such a way narrative criticism establishes itself between the historical criticism, which attempts to define the meaning of the text as related to its original readers, and reader-response criticism, which deals with the text as appealing to different groups of readers in their contexts.[93]

The method of the narrative criticism needs to be evaluated in relation to its benefits and limitations for the analysis of the biblical texts. First, with the presentation of its benefits to the historical-critical method I would justify its contribution to the exegetical analysis of the NT texts. Narrative criticism deals primarily with the biblical text itself but it does assume knowledge of the social and historical contexts.[94] However, it does not depend entirely on the results of the historical criticism and, as such, goes beyond the points of uncertainty reached by the latter and even brings some helpful insights to them on the basis of its analysis of the text.[95] Further, in its relation to the historical-critical method narrative criticism serves as indicator for accuracy of the interpretations of the traditional method by paralleling or contrasting the results of the latter from text-centered analysis and does help the historical critics to reevaluate their conclusions.[96] With its emphasis on the text and its literary effects on the readers the narrative criticism balances the results of the historical criticism, which in its process of reconstruction of the text leaves some skepticism about its meaning.[97] The method also appears to be ecumenically supportive due to its provision of grounds for agreement between different Christian traditions on the basis of the text apart from the historical disagreements of the scholars and on the basis of possibility for multiple interpretations within the parameters established by the text itself.[98] It is important to underline the essential role of narrative for "proper moral reasoning."[99] And finally, narrative criticism makes the ap-

---

93. Powell, *Narrative Criticism*, 242.
94. Powell, *What is Narrative Criticism*, 85, 86.
95. Ibid., 86.
96. Ibid., 86, 87.
97. Ibid., 88, 89.
98. Ibid., 89.
99. Wayne A. Meeks, *The Origins of Christian Morality* (New Haven: Yale Univesity Press, 1993) 189.

plication of the text's principles in the life of the reader easier due to the personal involvement of the latter in the plot of the text.[100]

Second, the exposition of the limitations of narrative criticism in regard to the historical-critical method would propose its improvement through an integration of both methods for the purpose of more holistic analysis of the NT texts. It is argued that while the main goal of the historical-critical method is to use the texts for understanding the nature of their times, narrative criticism is more interested in the stories which shape the text and to define their effects upon their interpreters in their present situation.[101] Due to this primary interest, the method is criticized as losing the historical foundation of the text and the importance of its elements for defining the meaning which the text conveys.[102] Such a movement from the historical foundations of the text to the solely literary expression of the latter brings disharmony in the holistic approach to textual analysis. Hence, other elements which occupy significant place in this process are rejected as unimportant for uncovering the meaning of the text. The role of the original author in the process is completely ignored and the text is argued to become autonomous after being written. In such a way the author's intended meaning is neglected and his sources are not considered as significant.[103] Furthermore, without relying on the historical background of the text the openness of narrative criticism for multiple meanings of the text creates the danger of manipulating the text according to the reader's agenda.[104] Finally, loosing the historical grounds has created the danger of turning the use of the story into a canon within the canon.[105]

---

100. Ibid., 90, 91.

101. Powell, *Narrative Criticism*, 239, 240.

102. Ibid., 253.

103. Grant R. Osborne, *The Hermeneutical Spiral: A Comprehensive Introduction to Biblical Interpretation* (Downers Grove, IL: InterVarsity, 1991) 164–68.

104. This is possible even in spite of the attempted restrictions offered through the limitations posed by the text itself. (Powell, *What is Narrative Criticism*, 95, 96.)

105. The following scholars have touched on this critique in different ways. For N. T. Wright see M. Casey, *Where Wright is Wrong: A Critical Review of N. T. Wright's Jesus and the Victory of God*, 99, 100; D. J. Moo, review of *The Climax of the Covenant: Christ and the Law in Pauline Theology*, 664; M. W. Nicholson, *Abusing Wittgenstein*, 628. Electronic edition by Galaxie Software, 1999. For Ben Witherington III see P. F. Craffert, review of *Paul's Narrative Thought World: the Tapestry of Tragedy and Triumph*, 177; B. N. Fisk, review of *Paul's Narrative Thought World: The Tapestry of Tragedy and Triumph*, 554. For

Historical-Critical Method for Biblical Analysis. Historical-critical method for biblical analysis has endured much criticism, but it has survived to be acknowledged as establishing foundational guidance for biblical studies. One of its strong sides is its capability to respond to criticism and reshape its nature accordingly.[106] Thus, in the present section I will attempt to define the discipline, establishing its continuity and discontinuity with the literary criticism, and describe further the main parts of the method in relation to their nature and use. I will modify and attempt to improve the historical-critical method for the purposes of the methodology of the present work with input from the grammatical-historical method.

Due to the complex nature of the historical-critical method it is difficult to express all its elements in a single definition.[107] In general historical criticism might be defined as a method which attempts to analyze historical events on the basis of specific objective criteria based on the assumption that reality is suitable for examination.[108] To narrow further the definition, the method might be defined as an endeavor for providing, analyzing, and comparing all the valuable witnesses to a particular historical event and establishing on their basis coherent presentation with conclusive evidence for the latter.[109] As a biblical discipline historical criticism is dealing with the history of the biblical text[110] and as such it is devoted to furnishing the historical, social, and cultural contexts of a text and analyzing the latter in two dimensions. First, the document's historical content is established in parallel to the contemporary literature and religious atmosphere. Second, the text's historical background should be analyzed in relation to its dimensions, namely, author, recipients, genre, date, and place of writing.[111]

Richard B. Hays see D. B. Martin, review of *The Moral Vision of the New Testament*, 359.

106. Francis Watson, "Biblical Criticism and Interpretation 2: New Testament," in *The Blackwell Encyclopedia of Modern Christian Thought*, ed. Alister E. McGrath (Oxford: Blackwell, 1993) 41.

107. F. Watson, *Biblical Criticism and Interpretation 2: New Testament*, 41; Edgar Krentz, *The Historical-Critical Method* (Philadelphia: Fortress, 1975) 33.

108. Richard N. Soulen, *Handbook of Biblical Criticism*, 2nd ed. (Atlanta: John Knox, 1981) 78.

109. Krentz, *The Historical-Critical Method*, 41.

110. Mike Stallard, "An Essay on Liberal Hermeneutics," *CTJ* 3 (1999) 293–95.

111. Also Baird, *New Testament Criticism*, 732; Watson, *Biblical Criticism and Interpretation 2: New Testament*, 41, 46, 47; Soulen, *Handbook of Biblical Criticism*, 78.

Introduction: Establishing the Framework   29

The task for identifying the main disciplines of the historical-critical method is as difficult as the attempt to define the method since three of the four disciplines which are suggested (source, form, tradition, and redaction criticisms) due to their preoccupation with different aspects of the history of the text are also identified as literary criticisms. Thus, in order to establish the main disciplines of the historical-critical method, I need to define the method of literary criticism and establish its discontinuity with the historical criticism.

The term "literary criticism," which has been originally related to source criticism,[112] should either refer to the analysis of the text which involves entirely literary issues[113] or needs to be directed to refer to new types of criticisms which deal exclusively with the literary nature of the text, such as rhetorical or narrative criticisms.[114] However, the scholarship has not reached consensus on the exact nature of literary criticism. That leads to disagreement in defining the method's main disciplines. Hence, some scholars define source and redaction criticisms as literary methods.[115] Others argue that form and redaction criticisms might be viewed as grounds for the development of the literary approaches.[116] Others include any of the source,[117] form,[118] or redaction criticisms[119] as part of the literary criticism. In spite of the different emphasis of these three critical disciplines, they all deal with the issues related to the history of the text, issues which lay outside of the text itself.[120] The traditional literary criticism, on the other hand, is defined as a method which concentrates on

112. Baird, *New Testament Criticism*, 733.
113. Soulen, *Handbook of Biblical Criticism*, 78.
114. Stallard, *An Essay on Liberal Hermeneutics*, 298.
115. See Baird, *New Testament Criticism*, 733, 734.
116. Powell, *What is Narrative Criticism*, 6, 7.
117. Werner Georg Kümmel, *Introduction to the New Testament*, trans. Howard Clark Kee, 17th ed. (Nashville: Abingdon, 1975) 33, quoted in Aida Besancon Spencer, "Literary Criticism," in *New Testament Criticism and Interpretation*, eds. David Alan Black and David S. Dockery (Grand Rapids: Zondervan, 1991) 236.
118. Rudolf Bultmann, *Form Criticism: Two Essays on New Testament Research*, trans. F. C. Grant (New York: Harper, 1962), quoted in A. B. Spencer, *Literary Criticism*, 236.
119. Donald Guthrie includes under the literary criticism all three disciplines, source, form, and redaction criticisms. R. K. Harrison, B. K. Waltke, D. Guthrie, and G. D. Fee, *Biblical Criticism: Historical, Literary and Textual* (Grand Rapids: Zondervan, 1978) 98–110.
120. Spencer, *Literary Criticism*, 237.

the final form of the text disregarding its historical characteristics.[121] It is engaged to define the meaning of the text and how it is expressed by the author and communicated to the readers through the particular style expressed in the text.[122] Furthermore, the so-called new literary approaches disregard the historical-critical analysis as important for the understanding of the texts and associate closely with the methodologies from the secular literary criticism.[123] Hence, on the basis of the definitions presented so far of the historical and literary critical disciplines, the main elements of the historical-critical method might be defined as source, form, tradition, and redaction criticisms.[124] As their names suggest they deal with different aspects of the history of the text such as the original sources of the text, the background oral forms of the text, the tradition of the textual development of the oral forms, and the redactional activities of the authors.[125] A short description of each of these criticisms will suffice the purposes of this presentation.

Source criticism might be defined in general as "tradition" behind the text apart from its history. In particular, the discipline examines biblical texts in order to find their sources, different texts than the author's but used by the author for developing his writing.[126] The results from source criticism in regard to the relationship between the synoptic gospels are established by the generally accepted and least problematic[127] "Two-Source theory," or "the Oxford four-documents hypothesis."[128] This theory de-

---

121. G. R. Osborne, "Redaction Criticism," in *Dictionary of Jesus and the Gospels*, 662.

122. Spencer, *Literary Criticism*, 238.

123. Powell, *What is Narrative Criticism*, 7.

124. See also Susan E. Gillingham, *One Bible, Many Voices: Different Approaches to the Biblical Studies* (London: SPCK, 1998) 157–68. Gerald Sheppard, "Canon Criticism: The Proposal of Brevard Childs and an Assessment for Evangelical Hermeneutics," *Studia Biblica et Theologica* (October 1974) 10, quoted in John Piper, "The Authority and Meaning of The Christian Canon: A Response to Gerald Sheppard on Canon Criticism," *JETS* 19 (1976) 92; and John Piper, "The Authority and Meaning of The Christian Canon: A Response to Gerald Sheppard on Canon Criticism," *JETS* 19 (1976) 92.

125. M. Stallard, *An Essay on Liberal Hermeneutics*, 293–95.

126. Dietrich-Alex Koch, "Source Criticism (New Testament)," in *ABD*, 6:165.

127. Grant R. Osborne, "Redaction Criticism," in *New Testament Criticism & Interpretation*, eds. David Alan Black and David S. Dockery (Grand Rapids: Zondervan, 1991) 213.

128. There are 3 main theories which attempt to give solution to the Synoptic Problem, namely Augustinian Hypothesis (defining the interdependence of the synoptic gospels

fines Mark as the primary source for both Matthew and Luke, both of whom further used another primary source "Q" (materials found in both Matthew and Luke but not found in Mark) and each of them independently used their own sources called "M" for Matthew and "L" for Luke.[129] Going beyond the source critical studies, form criticism examines the texts in order to identify different literary forms of the material, to find their authentic traditional forms, and to describe their theological development by the early Christian communities.[130] Closely related to form criticism, tradition criticism studies the history of the oral traditions from their origins until their final presentation in the literary texts.[131] Using specific criteria the discipline attempts to define the authentic traditions and the relation between tradition and Christian community in respect to the rise and development of the former and the historical situation of the latter.[132] Using the results of these three criticisms, redaction criticism develops its studies beyond their limitations. It might be defined as a historical and literary discipline which attempts to discover how the authors used their sources in editing and arranging them.[133] Focusing upon the comparative analysis of the gospels the discipline examines the unique theological contributions of the evangelists to their sources,[134] the main theological

---

placing them in the following chronological order, Matthew, Mark, and Luke); Griesbach Hypothesis (chronological priority is given to Matthew used by Luke, both conflated by Mark); Oxford Hypothesis (priority is attributed to Mark and Q used by Matthew and Luke who have used their independent sources "M" and "L"). (Scot McKnight, "Source Criticism," in *New Testament Criticism & Interpretation*, eds. David Alan Black and David S. Dockery [Grand Rapids: Zondervan, 1991] 141)

129. D. A. Koch, *Source Criticism*, 165, 169. Robert H. Stein, "Synoptic Problem," in *Dictionary of Jesus and the Gospels*, eds. Joel B. Green, Scot McKnight, I. Howard Marshall (Downers Grove, IL: InterVarsity, 1992) 791; S. McKnight, *Source Criticism*, 143, 144.

130. Darrell L. Bock, "Form Criticism," in *New Testament Criticism & Interpretation*, eds. David Alan Black and David S. Dockery (Grand Rapids: Zondervan, 1991) 176–78; Vernon K. Robbins, "Form Criticism: New Testament," in *ABD* 2:841; Baird, *New Testament Criticism*, 732.

131. G. R. Osborne, "Redaction Criticism," in *Dictionary of Jesus and the Gospels*, 662. Soulen, *Handbook of Biblical Criticism*, 165.

132. Peter H. Davids, "Tradition Criticism," in *Dictionary of Jesus and the Gospels*, eds. Joel B. Green, Scot McKnight, and I. Howard Marshall (Downers Grove, IL: InterVarsity, 1992) 831.

133. Osborne, "Redaction Criticism," 662.

134. Robert H. Stein, *Gospel and Tradition* (Grand Rapids: Baker, 1991) 17.

purpose of the evangelists which stands behind their gospels,[135] and the particular *Sitz im Leben* of the evangelists.[136]

The historical-critical method needs to be assessed in relation to its benefits and limitations to the analysis of the biblical texts. A review of biblical scholarship would justify the claim that historical-critical method stays in the foundation of the contemporary biblical interpretation.[137] Thus, every study of the biblical texts which attempts to be holistic requires an involvement of the historical-critical method. On the one hand, the legitimacy of the method might be approved by the historical nature of the texts. The historical statements of the texts require historical means for analysis.[138] On the other hand, the necessity of the method is affirmed by the nature of the truth which is conveyed by the biblical texts. Analysis which leads to establishing whether the text is intended to convey historical truth takes in consideration both the form of the narrative and the purpose of the author.[139] Therefore, due to the fact that the historical-critical method, one which recognizes the supernatural phenomena as part of the historical process, is established as essential for proper understanding of the biblical texts,[140] I would implement in the methodology of the present work a modified version of the method in relation to its improved limitations.

The historical-critical method is generally criticized due to its working assumption that the texts lack historical validity[141] (i.e. they do not re-

135. Ibid., 32.

136. Briggs, *Interpreting the New Testament Today*, 111, 112; Stein, *Gospel and Tradition*, 32.

137. Briggs, *Interpreting the New Testament Today*, 19.

138. Ibid., 19, 20.

139. I. Howard Marshall, "Historical Criticism," in *New Testament Interpretation: Essays on Principles and Methods*, ed. I. Howard Marshall (Exeter: Paternoster, 1977) 130–32.

140. Donald A. Hagner, "The New Testament, History, and the Historical-Critical Method," in *New Testament Criticism & Interpretation*, eds. David Alan Black and David S. Dockery (Grand Rapids: Zondervan, 1991) 88.

141. Due to this objection to the method, scholarship is divided into two groups. Some argue for complete rejection of the historical-critical method as a result of its assumptions of lack of historical validity of the text. (F. David Farnell and Robert L. Thomas, eds., *The Jesus Crisis: The Inroads of Historical Criticism into Evangelical Scholarship* [Grand Rapids: Kregel, 1998] and Robert L. Thomas, "The 'Jesus Crisis:' What is It?" in *The Jesus Crisis* [Grand Rapids: Kregel, 1998] 13, quoted in M. Stallard, *An Essay on Liberal Hermeneutics*, 296. See also Gary North, *The Hoax of Higher Criticism* [Tyler, TX:

fer to actual historical happenings).[142] The method is evaluated as giving more attention to the historical issues behind the text than to the nature of the text itself and in the case of the gospels, their narrative character. It missed reading them as whole units of literature which tell stories about Jesus.[143] The discipline is defined as incomplete in light of literary criticism since it disregards the text,[144] its message,[145] its narratives,[146] and its literary context.[147] While looking at the nature of these limitations of the historical-critical method their improvement might occur through the contribution of the grammatical-historical method and integration with the narrative-critical method.

Historical-critical method should be modified and improved by grammatical-historical method both in relation to its presuppositions and goals. First, the working assumption of some of the historical critics that the biblical text has no historical value should be completely rejected and abandoned and thus, biblical texts should be accepted as authentic in

---

Institute for Christian Economics, 1989].) Others maintain that only the assumptions of the method should be rejected but the valuable analysis from its different elements should be accepted. (Grant Osborne, "Historical Criticism and the Evangelical," *JETS* 42 [1999] 208 and Moises Silva, "Has the Church Misread the Bible?" in *Foundations of Contemporary Interpretation*, Moises Silva ed. [Grand Rapids: Zondervan, 1996] 25–27, quoted in M. Stallard, *An Essay on Liberal Hermeneutics*, 297. And M. Stallard, *An Essay on Liberal Hermeneutics*, 297, 303.)

142. Stallard, *An Essay on Liberal Hermeneutics*, 293–95.

143. Powell, *What is Narrative Criticism*, 2.

144. Historical criticism focuses on the levels of the development of the text accepting its historicity but disregarding the text itself, while literary criticism engages in interpretation of the finished form of the text. For historical criticism the text is a tool for obtaining knowledge about the events, characters, and situations which are attested by the text but stay in its historical background, while for the literary criticism the goal is to understand the text itself; to analyze and describe the narratives of the text (ibid., 7, 8).

145. Historical criticism deals with the text in a vertical dimension (i.e. it looks for different evolutionary stages of the development of the text) while literary criticism uses the text in a horizontal dimension (i.e. the text is understood as the vehicle of a message communicated from the author to the reader) (ibid., 8, 9).

146. Historical criticism examines the gospel texts to obtain historical and theological information, ignoring their narrative capacity, in the contrary literary criticism engages exactly in studying the narratives and the effects they have upon their readers (Howell, *Mathew's Inclusive Story*, 24, 25).

147. Historical criticism engages in analysis of the individual units of the work apart from their literary context, while for literary criticism different textual units are analyzed in the light of their contribution to the whole story (Powell, *What is Narrative Criticism*, 7).

their final form and analyzed with the view of their historical nature.[148] Second, due to the fact that the text is understood as conveying meaning in its present form, the analysis should be expanded to include literary and grammatical issues which the text raises.[149] A method for textual analysis which integrates both historical and grammatical tools for the study of the biblical text is the proposed model for NT exegesis by Gordon D. Fee.[150] A short synthesis of the method with a modified format[151] might suffice for the purpose of methodological layout of the present work.

Taking in consideration the genre differences and the specific attention they require, the NT literature might be analyzed in respect to two main dimensions: content and context. The latter investigates both historical and literary contexts of the text.[152] The historical context establishes the text in its historical, cultural, social, and religious backgrounds, discussing their characteristics in general and specific in order to contribute to the understanding of the intended meaning by the author.[153] The literary context, on the other hand, deals with the inner environment of the text in relation to the whole document looking to establish the most probable explanation in relation to the flow of the author's argument, its structure and logic, and the role of the passage in it.[154] The content engages in development of textual-critical analysis, word studies, and defining the grammatical relations.[155] The discipline of textual criticism[156]

---

148. Stallard, *An Essay on Liberal Hermeneutics*, 293, 294, 303.

149. Baird, *New Testament Criticism*, 730; M. Stallard, *An Essay on Liberal Hermeneutics*, 292, 293; Sheppard, *Canon Criticism*, 10, quoted in Piper, *The Authority and Meaning of The Christian Canon*, 92; and idem, *The Authority and Meaning of The Christian Canon*, 92.

150. Fee, *New Testament Exegesis*.

151. The format of the book appears to be slightly confusing and complicated due to some repetitions, overlaps, and insertions. (Also David L. Turner, review of *New Testament Exegesis: A Handbook for Students and Pastors*, by Gordon D. Fee, in *GTJ* 6 [1985] 127 and 128.)

152. Fee, *New Testament Exegesis*, 31.

153. Ibid., 34, 41, 114–23.

154. Ibid., 44–45, 48–52, 54.

155. Ibid., 31, 32.

156. I am aware of the fact that the goal of textual criticism to restore the original text of the NT is problematic since there are no available original manuscripts written by the NT authors. Thus, the conclusion based on analyses of different variant readings of the text should never claim final authority.

evaluates the manuscript traditions in relation to the four kinds of variations: interpolation, omission, transposition, and substitution, with the purpose to establish the actual words of the author.[157] The lexical analysis deals with diachronic and/or synchronic study of the significant words for understanding the meaning of the text.[158] And, finally, the grammatical analysis of the text establishes the sentence structures and syntactical relations with the help of sentence flow and diagrammatical methods that attempt to define all the important grammatical relationships between words, clauses, sentences, and paragraphs.[159] After historical criticism is enriched with the contributions of the grammatical-historical method only one further final step is required for completing the descriptive task as part of the methodology of the present work. Thus, in the following conclusive section of this chapter I will integrate the historical-critical and narrative-critical methods presented above for analysis of the biblical text.

Integration between Narrative-Critical and Historical-Critical Approaches

Narrative-critical and historical-critical approaches should be used in a complementary fashion.[160] The narrative and historical criticisms "might even be viewed as necessary complements, each providing information that is beneficial to the exercise of the other."[161]

The nature of narrative criticism may stay in contrast to the historical-critical method but it is inclusive of its elements. Hence, on the one hand, it is primarily concerned with the narrative nature of the biblical text whose main features are defined as plot, characters, and outcome. On the other hand, the discipline does not ignore the historical nature of the biblical texts. It assumes their historical background but goes further in arguing that history should be understood as story. "The writing of history is not the exact reiteration of the past but a process which involves

---

157. Fee, *New Testament Exegesis*, 81–91.

158. Ibid., 100–113.

159. Ibid., 65–80, 92–99.

160. Mark Allan Powell, "Toward a Narrative-Critical Understanding of Mark," *Int* 47 (1993) 345.

161. Powell, *What is Narrative Criticism*, 98.

selection, plotting, and interpretation."[162] Paul Ricoeur finds this connection as well arguing that both historical and fictional narratives share the common form of a story with a structural similarity in the concept of a plot and even though they refer to the events in a different manner,[163] they both deal with historicity as part of human nature.[164]

> ... histories which deal with the unification or the disintegration of an empire, the rise and fall of a class, social movement, religious sect, or literary style, *are* narratives. And the *reading* of such histories derives from our competence in following stories. If histories are rooted in this way in stories, the distinctive traits of historical explanation must be considered as expansions ancillary to the 'follow-ability' of the basic story.[165] (italics his)

Furthermore, the complementary use of the two methods establishes the movement of the critics not from historical to literary criticism, but using them in an incorporated fashion. Thus, the narrative approach to the biblical text should be firmly established on the historical analysis of the latter. There are at least two indispensable contributions of the historical-critical method which need to be considered. First, the contextual awareness offered by historical criticism is fundamental for providing the proper first century context of the NT text with its elements and, as such, laying the bridge over the hermeneutical gap of the interpreter. Second, affirming and analyzing the historical nature of the biblical narratives protects the interpreter from misusing the text by projection of his beliefs onto it.[166] Therefore, in the light of the practice of many contemporary interpreters[167] I would argue that an eclectic method, which incorporates both historical and narrative criticisms, should be applied for analysis of the NT texts.[168]

---

162. Baird, *New Testament Criticism*.

163. Historical narratives engage in defining events outside their texts while the fictional narratives do not.

164. Paul Ricoeur, "The Narrative Function," in *Semeia 13* [online], Available at http://shemesh.scholar.emory.edu:6336/dynaweb/Semeia/Semeia_13/@Generic__BookView, Accessed on 23 October 1999.

165. Ibid.

166. Howell, *Mathew's Inclusive Story*, 28, 29.

167. As argued by Baird, *New Testament Criticism*.

168. Also Osborne, *The Hermeneutical Spiral*, 165.

THE SYNTHETIC TASK

The synthetic task deals with the relationship between the individuality and the coherence of the texts.[169] On the one hand, each text should be allowed to express its unique message clearly as intended and shaped by the author's intentions without cross reference obscurity. On the other hand, the whole canonical corpus of the NT should be understood as playing a role of establishing the voice of every individual text as part of the message of the entire NT. Hays is convinced that only in this way one may attempt to formulate the NT ethics as "normative theological discipline."[170] The proper formulation of the synthetic task establishes a movement from descriptive analysis of every important text to synthetic evaluation of the whole body of NT texts. Hence, every individual text is searched for repetitive moral patterns and designs with the purpose to establish the main model of reading the whole of the NT ethical teaching. However, the idea of a single unifying principle such as "love" is refused as inadequate for accomplishing the synthetic task.[171] Hays also expresses his awareness of the fact that every approach of establishing a guidance for synthesis of the NT teaching is going to be imperfect and strongly influenced by interpreters' assumptions.[172] Thus, he attempts to lay some ground rules on which basis he formulates the frame of the synthetic task, namely the three focal images.[173] The grounds, as Hays sees them, are three-dimensional. In order to establish a solid synthetic guidance one should analyze all of the relevant texts, allow them to express their unique message in spite of the tensions between them, and attend to their specific genre. Thus, Hays argues that the unifying element of the NT is that of a story, which, on the other hand, is narrated around three focal images: community, cross, and new creation. Community is "the concrete social manifestation of the people of God"[174] to whom his imperatives are primary directed. The cross is a dynamic presentation of Jesus' death as an act of God's love for the world. It has two basic elements: Jesus' sufferings that point to the sufferings of his followers, and the promise of Jesus'

---

169. Hays, *The Moral Vision of the New Testament*, 188.
170. Ibid., 188.
171. Ibid., 5.
172. Ibid., 189.
173. Ibid., 189–91.
174. Ibid., 196.

resurrection that leads the believers to rely only upon God's power.[175] The new creation is found in the community of the redeemed who live in a not-yet-redeemed world. Thus, it expresses the fact that the church is living in between the times of Jesus' resurrection and *parousia*. The new creation has already appeared and God's power is already active but the old age and its powers of darkness are not yet completely over.[176]

In order to integrate the synthetic task into the present methodology I will modify it in relation to its weaknesses. Four areas of the task require improvement, namely, its qualitative and quantitative nature, its subjectivism, and its lack of OT involvement.

First, the qualitative character of Hays' synthetic method needs to be modified. The danger of selecting focal images as guidance for the understanding of every text is that not all the texts will fit into such a framework. Thus, it is suggested that in relation to some topics in the NT some further focal images should be added to those three. Judith Gundry-Volf argues that the NT themes about sexuality and gender need two further guiding images, namely, creation and culture. The former plays the important role of continuity with the new creation in relation to the equality of man and woman. The latter points to Paul's enculturation of the gospel with the purpose of transforming the culture.[177] In his reply to Gundry-Volf, Hays agrees with her critique partly. He acknowledges the lack of discussing the creation as part of the focal images creating the story, but disagrees that the culture should play the same role.[178] This discussion presupposes that different NT themes would require different and better-defined guidance in relation to their nature. Hence, I would suggest that individual ethical matters require specific images of guidance. It is safer and more precise to establish a guiding image or concept in relation to specific theme than to attempt to encompass the whole of the NT teaching.

Second, the quantitative nature of the synthetic method requires modification. Thus, multiplicity of images makes their relations difficult and their order questionable. The image of community is almost identical with the image of the new creation. In both of them the church plays the

---

175. Ibid., 197.

176. Ibid., 198.

177. Judith Gundry-Volf, "Putting the Moral Vision of the New Testament into Focus: A Review," *Bulletin for Biblical Research* 9 (1999) 282–86.

178. Richard B. Hays, "The Gospel, Narrative, and Culture: A Response to Douglas J. Moo and Judith Gundry-Volf," *Bulletin for Biblical Research* 9 (1999) 296.

main role, although the image of the new creation is more eschatologically founded. Hence, one may argue to make one image from those two. Moreover, it might be argued that the image of the new creation is not so central and emphatically expressed in the NT writings in order to be placed in the same line with the other two images. In addition, the image is not so accumulative in order to provide guidance to all the eschatological images in the NT.[179] The significance of the order of the three focal images might also be criticized due to the problem of speaking about a redeemed community, which is the church, without speaking first about the Redeemer and his redeeming act on the cross. As some scholars argue the main continuity between the people of God, Israel, and the church is established by Jesus.[180] Finally, the multiplicity of guiding images opens the possibility for inner contradictions among themselves and leads to compromising exegesis.[181] Therefore, I would propose that the synthetic task needs to be guided by a single image or concept which is related to a specific ethical matter of consideration and as such does not exhaust its limits in relation to the whole body of canonical literature as in the case of the concept of love.[182]

Third, the subjective factor in Hays' synthetic task plays a significant role in the process of synthesis. Hays allows his presuppositions to influence the process, not the texts to shape them. He confesses that the three focal images are not a product of thorough exegetical analysis of the biblical text but mostly a result of his teaching experience being under "the influence by community traditions of interpretation and practice."[183] Furthermore Hays acknowledges the fact that the focal images appear to

179. See also C. Freeman Sleeper, review of *The Moral Vision of the New Testament: A Contemporary Introduction to New Testament Ethics*, by R. B. Hays, in *Int* 52 (1998) 202.

180. In temptation stories in the wilderness, narrated both by Matthew (Matt 4:1–11) and Luke (Luke 4:1–13) just mentioned by Mark (Mark 1:13) it is Jesus who is presented as the one who succeeded where Israel failed. (William Richard Stegner, *Narrative Theology in Early Jewish Christianity* [Louisville: Westminster John Knox, 1989] 110.) N. T. Wright bases his main thesis on the argument that Jesus is retelling and reenacting the story of Israel and as such he is the new Israel. (N. T. Wright, *Jesus and the Victory of God* [Minneapolis: Fortress, 1996] 243, 348).

181. D. B. Martin, review of *The Moral Vision of the New Testament*, 359.

182. According to Hays, "love" does not receive equal treatment of importance by all NT authors and its meaning has become very obscure in relation to its role as a guiding principle for the understanding of the biblical texts (See Hays, *The Moral Vision*, 84, 139, 200–203).

183. Hays, *The Moral Vision of the New Testament*, 199.

be "a canon within the canon."[184] However he does not recognize the fact that this certainly will lead one to become very selective in reading the canonical writings of the NT as some scholars argue that Hays actually did.[185] Thus, the unifying synthesis based on the three focal images leads Hays into the trap of establishing "a canon within the canon" and, thus, his treatment of the individual texts suffers from lack of consideration of their diversity and place in the entire canon.[186] It is undeniable that presuppositions are part of any exegetical process but they need to be defined as the general framework of knowledge which the interpreter has in relation to the particular subject matter of the text.[187] It is the text which should be allowed to reshape the knowledge of the interpreter. Therefore, I would argue that the synthetic image or concept needs to be derived from the biblical text which plays a crucial part in defining a specific moral theme and is engaged in establishing the relation between other biblical texts on the basis of this concept.

Fourth, the OT role in the synthetic task as presented by Hays needs to be improved. The OT canonical literature needs to be allowed to contribute to the synthetic analysis.[188] Thus, the most significant OT passages related to the particular theme need to be examined and their contribution to the synthetic process recognized. The knowledge derived from the OT articulation of a particular ethical theme may establish a solid and indispensable background for the understanding of the NT texts. The conclusions formulated on the basis of OT analysis will enlighten the NT texts under consideration and together with the NT conclusions will provide a holistic biblical view of the ethical theme. Hence, I would argue that the role of the OT in the synthetic level of the work should be strongly affirmed.

As a result of this fourfold modification of the synthetic task, I would propose a single concept as guidance for synthesis for the specific NT theme under investigation, which should be established on the basis of

---

184. Ibid.

185. See D. B. Martin, review of *The Moral Vision of the New Testament*, 359.

186. R. A. Young, review of *The Moral Vision of the New Testament*, 137.

187. Rudolf Bultmann, *Existence and Faith: Short Writings of Rudolf Bultmann*, trans. Schubert M. Ogden (London: Hoddder and Stoughton, 1961) 289, 294. Edgar V. McKnight, "Presuppositions in New Testament Study," in *Hearing the New Testament: Strategies for Interpretation*, ed. Joel B. Green (Grand Rapids: Eerdmans, 1995) 289.

188. Fee, *New Testament Exegesis*, 54.

examples from the NT text with OT involvement. Thus, in relation to the subject of marriage, divorce, and remarriage two NT texts appear as underlying such a concept. Both Matthew (19:3-9) and Mark (10:2-8) present Jesus' interpretation of Deut 24:1-4 through the perspective of Gen 1:27 and 2:24. Guided by the question of what concept has been discerned in order to establish such interpretation I will consider Matthew's account due to its Jewish-Christian character.[189]

Matthew's discussion of Deut 24:1 is part of a passage (Matt 19:3-9) conducted for the purpose of establishing Jesus' view on marriage, divorce, and remarriage as based entirely upon God's intentions which are found in the Torah. Matthew establishes that purpose, substantiating it with a twofold conclusion. First, the understanding of marriage, divorce, and remarriage should be established on the basis of the entire Torah, not only on the single passage of Deut 24:1.[190] Thus, the only normative reading of Deut 24:1 is through the perspective of Gen 1:27 and 2:24.[191] Identifying the covenantal language which depicts the process and the nature of the relationship of the first couple in the creation account[192] and

---

189. There is a tendency for a general agreement among scholars that the gospel of Matthew was written by a Greek-speaking Jewish Christian (See Raymond E. Brown, *The Birth of the Messiah: A Commentary on the Infancy Narratives in Matthew and Luke*. The Anchor Bible Reference Library [New York: Doubleday, 1993] 45.) and addressed to a Jewish-Christian audience (Eusebius Pamphilus, *The Church History of Eusebius* 6.25.4, in *Nicene and Post-Nicene Fathers*, eds. Philip Schaff and Henry Wace, series II, vol. I, *Christian Classics Ethereal Library*, v.2, CD-ROM, ed. Harry Plantinga [Wheaton, IL: Wheaton College, 1998]; R. T. France, *Matthew: Evangelist and Teacher* [Grand Rapids: Zondervan, 1989] 96-102; Dorothy A. Lee, *Matthew's Gospel and Judaism* [online], Available at http://www.jcrelations.net/articl1/lee.htm, Accessed on 24 November 2000.)

190. Matt 19:3-8 cf. Mark 10:2-8.

191. Matt 19:3-8 cf. Matt 5:31, 32.

192. See also Mal 2:14; Prov 2:17; Samuele Bacchiocchi, *The Marriage Covenant: A Biblical Study on Marriage, Divorce, and Remarriage* [online], Available at http://www2.andrews.edu/~samuele/books/marriage/1.html, Accessed on 13 August 2004; Walter Brueggemann, *Genesis*. Interpretation: A Bible Commentary for Teaching and Preaching (Atlanta: John Knox, 1982) 47; W. J. Dumbrell, *Covenant & Creation: A Theology of the Old Testament Covenants* (Grand Rapids: Baker, 1984) 36; Kenneth A. Mathews, *Genesis 1—11:26*. The New American Commentary: An Exegetical and Theological Exposition of the Holy Scripture NIV Text, ed. E. Ray Clendenen (Nashville: Broadman & Holman, 1996) 222; J. M. Sprinkle, *Old Testament Perspectives on Divorce and Remarriage*. Electronic edition by Galaxie Software; Jay E. Adams, *Marriage Divorce & Remarriage in the Bible* (Grand Rapids: Baker, 1980) 16, 17.

considering the function of covenants during the OT times[193] one may see how the concept of marriage covenant guides the interpretation of Deut 24:1. The conditional law treats marriage as a permanent covenant relationship which should be protected from the act of divorce for which serious grounds should exist and proper documentation should be always provided.[194] Second, for Matthew such a reading argues for the permanent nature of marriage, excluding the possibility of divorce and remarriage unless on exceptionally serious grounds (Matt 5:32; 19:6, 9).[195]

193. The function of the covenant might be described as a permanent relationship between two parties which nevertheless might be broken if one of the parties does not follow the basic covenant requirements. (Lev 24:8; Num 18:19; 1 Chr 16:15; 2 Chr 13:5; 21:7; Ps 89:28; 105:8; 111:9; Isa 55:3; 61:8; Sir 45:24; Lev 26:44; Jer 31:32; Ezek 17:16, 18, 19; Zech 11:10; Prayer of Azariah 1:11; See also Elmer A. Martens, *God's Design: A Focus on Old Testament Theology* [Grand Rapids: Baker, 1981] 73; W. J. Dumbrell, *Covenant & Creation*, 96, 99.)

194. See also G. Ernest Wright, Henry H. Shires and Pierson Parker, "The Book of Deuteronomy," in *The Interpreters' Bible*, vol. 2 (New York: Abingdon, 1953) 473-74; D. Instone-Brewer, *Biblical Divorce and Remarriage: The Jewish Background to the New Testament Teaching on Divorce*, ch. 2 [online], Available at http://www.tyndale.cam.ac.uk/brewer/Academic/Chap_02.htm, Accessed on 26 November 2000; J. M. Sprinkle, *Old Testament Perspectives on Divorce and Remarriage*. Electronic edition by Galaxie Software; David Instone-Brewer, *Three Weddings and a Divorce: God's Covenant with Israel, Judah and the Church* [online], Available at http://www.tyndale.cam.ac.uk/brewer/3Weddings.htm, Accessed on 11 August 2004.

195. Cf. Mark 10:9; Luke 16:18; 1 Cor 7:10, 11, 15, 16. Marriage is understood as a lifelong union by most scholars (See Craig L. Blomberg, "Marriage, Divorce, Remarriage, and Celibacy: An Exegesis of Matthew 19:3–12," *Trinity Journal* 11/2 [Fall 1990]: 162–97. Electronic edition by Galaxie Software, 1999; R. C. H. Lenski, *The Interpretation of St. Matthew's Gospel* [Minneapolis: Augsburg, 1943] 730; R. V. G. Tasker, *Matthew: An Introduction and Commentary*. Tyndale New Testament Commentaries, ed. R. V. G. Tasker [London: Tyndale, 1961] 182.). Marriage may suffer dissolution only in exceptional cases ("μὴ ἐπὶ πορνείᾳ," Matt 19:9; and "παρεκτὸς λόγου πορνείας," Matt 5:32). The role and the nature of the exceptional clause as permission for divorce and remarriage in a case of adultery and other related sexual misconduct is substantiated by textually-critical (not a single witness lacks it), etymological (the alternative views of the meaning of πορνεία as related to kinship marriages prohibited in Lev 18:6–18 and to premarital unchastity do not do justice to the primary sources which demand divorce for adultery; See *Mishnah, Yebam* 2:8; *Mishnah, Sota* 5:1; Paul, *Opinions* 2.26.1–8, 10–12, 14–17. L) and syntactical (the least ambiguous position of the clause in which it modifies both verbs [ἀπολύσῃ, γαμήσῃ] is in the middle of the sentence) evidence. (Paul, *Opinions* 2.26.1–8, 10–12, 14–17. L, trans. Mary R. Lefkowitz and Maureen B. Fant [online], Available at http://www.uky.edu/ArtsSciences/Classics/wlgr/wlgr-romanlegal120.html, Accessed on 16 October 2000.) See also St. Aurelius Augustin, *Our Lord's Sermon on the Mount* 1.16.46, in *Nicene and Post-Nicene Fathers*, ed. Philip Schaff, Series 1, vol. 6, *Christian Classics Ethereal Library*, v.2, CD-ROM, ed. Harry Plantinga (Wheaton, IL:

Therefore, I would argue that the concept of covenantal marital relationship establishes the proper understanding of the passage of Deut 24:1-4 through the perspective of the creation account of the first human couple (Gen 1:27; 2:24). This unifying concept for the subject of marriage, divorce, and remarriage has served Matthew in his presentation of Jesus' teaching on these issues. Hence, I would propose the covenantal nature of marriage as the basic concept for conducting the synthetic task of my research. In addition in order to establish the necessary background of the NT passages I will present the OT understanding of marriage covenant relationship and its dynamics related to divorce and remarriage prior to the NT exegetical analysis.

THE HERMENEUTICAL TASK

The hermeneutical task engages the reader in an attempt to make Scripture communicate its message to his own life situation. It is the way in which the reader appeals to Scripture for moral guidance. Thus, Hays lists four modes of appeal to the biblical texts, namely rules, principles, paradigms, and a symbolic world. The rules are understood as transmitting to the reader a commandment for a moral action. The principles, on the other hand, tend to establish a general moral framework for building proper behavior. Paradigms are going further in offering an exemplary model of behavior through different narratives. Broadening the perspective, Scripture expresses a symbolic world which molds the reader's view of reality. In the NT its two aspects are articulated through the presentation and the relation between human condition and God's character.[196]

Hays further attempts to define the framework for interpretation of Scripture. He defines three authoritative elements whose relation to the bible should prove essential for establishing the proper environment for interpretation. The tradition of the church in general and the traditions of different Christian communities in particular are to be characterized as crucial but not determinative for defining the proper approach to Scripture.

Wheaton College, 1998); R. C. H. Lenski, *The Interpretation of St. Matthew's Gospel*, 734, 735; William Hendriksen, *The Gospel of Luke* (Grand Rapids: Baker, 1978) 781. David Hill, *The Gospel of Matthew*, NCBC (Grand Rapids: Eerdmans, 1972) 279; W. D. Davies and Dale C. Allison Jr., *A Critical and Exegetical Commentary on the Gospel according to Saint Matthew* (Edinburgh: T. & T. Clark, 1988) 1:529-31.

196. Hays, *The Moral Vision of the New Testament*, 208, 209.

The priority of the latter should be always a guiding supervision for the theologian. The classical formula should be kept in mind, "Scripture is *norma normans* ("the norming norm"), while tradition is *norma normata* ("the normed norm")."[197] Reason appears to play a significant part in creating the proper framework for sufficient hermeneutics by appealing to the interpreter's capacity of philosophical thinking and scientific analysis. Due to the cultural grounding of every process of reasoning, its relationship with Scripture is defined as "cultural logic." Experience completes the framework for biblical interpretation. The interpreter's understanding of the meaning of the text is further enlightened and authenticated through the various life situations. It involves both individual and community experience although it is the latter which validates the former.[198] Therefore, the hermeneutical task requires a balanced treatment of the four modes of appeal to the biblical texts within the threefold hermeneutical framework. The accuracy of the hermeneutical task might be assessed through the evaluation of its embodiment into community life.[199]

Hays further establishes the relevance and the relation between the four modes and their hermeneutical framework in regard to the subjects of divorce and remarriage. He evaluates the contributions of the modes of "principle" and "paradigm" to the hermeneutical task as insignificant. This is due to the lack of textual support from the NT. The only clearly identifiable principle: "Therefore what God has joined together, let no one separate," (Mark 10:9, Matt 19:6b) might be ruled out due to its logical implication such as "if it is believed that God has not joined together, divorce can be obtained." The only obtainable NT paradigm of divorced and remarried couple (Herod and Herodias, Mark 6:17–29; Matt 14:1–12) is clearly defined as a negative example in both Jewish and Christian terms. Hays does maintain that the other two modes might be used for the hermeneutical task in relation to divorce and remarriage issues. The nature of the divorce statements as expressed in the NT writings might be clearly defined as "rule," which functions as such only in the "symbolic world" established in the NT. The latter might be clearly depicted in the light of the creation story, used by Jesus in the divorce discussions (Matt 19:3–9; Mark 10:2–8), as God's plan for devoted marital commitment

---

197. Ibid., 210.
198. Ibid., 210, 211.
199. Ibid., 212.

between the spouses which should resolve in lifelong union. However, due to their complex relation in the light of argumentation derived from principles based on different life situations, the role of those two modes have been established by Hays as secondary to the place which needs to be given to the three authoritative elements: church traditions, reason, and experience.[200] Therefore, I will modify the hermeneutical task for the purpose of the present methodology by directing the research at this level toward analysis of the main Christian traditions (Catholic, Orthodox, and Protestant) in regard to their view of marriage, divorce, and remarriage with an attempt to establish an ecumenical understanding of these issues. Within the framework of these discussions I will integrate, when appropriate, the use of the hermeneutical modes and authorities.

THE PRAGMATIC TASK

It is difficult to separate the pragmatic task from the hermeneutical task since both of them refer to the application of the message of the NT into the readers' lives. Nevertheless, a place of distinction is found in the preoccupation of the hermeneutical task with the conceptual nature of application and of the pragmatic task with the practical nature of the latter.[201] Hence, the pragmatic task leads the interpreter toward practical implementation of the ethical vision established through the descriptive, synthetic, and hermeneutical tasks into the everyday life of the community of faith in general and his life as part of this community in particular.[202] This task requires constant decisions in response to the various and continuously changing circumstances of the Christian community and its social environment. The decisions using the normative moral vision of Scripture should attempt to give a relevant answer to the individual situations which may involve the same strategies used by the NT writers.[203] Hays concludes that "the task of NT ethics is to perform an integrative

---

200. Ibid., 367–72.
201. Ibid., 7.
202. Also Fee, *New Testament Exegesis*, 161.
203. Hays, *The Moral Vision of the New Testament*, 313. Also Fee, *New Testament Exegesis*, 60.

act of the imagination[204] that will bring the world of the NT together with our world."[205]

Therefore, the pragmatic task formulates four methodological moves for finalising the thesis. First, it necessitates an examination of the contemporary context in relation to its social, cultural, religious, and philosophical dimensions. Second, it expects formulation of the contemporary notion of marriage and consideration of its inner dynamics. Third, it facilitates a discussion of the thesis' applicability to all levels of different Christian communities. Fourth, it forms the challenging task of constructive social impact. This completes the methodological part of the introduction and places the discussion on the level of argumentative substantiation of the thesis.

---

204. Fee also encourages the use of imagination by the exegete during the application process. (Fee, *New Testament Exegesis*, 60.)

205. Hays, *The Moral Vision of the New Testament*, 374.

two

The Old Testament Canonical Context

THE ROLE OF OLD TESTAMENT CANONICAL LITERATURE IN THE SYNthetic task has been affirmed in the methodology of the present work as essential for understanding not only the biblical perspective of marriage, divorce, and remarriage but also for understanding the New Testament view on these issues.[1] This contribution might be described as twofold. On the one hand, defining the relationship between the ancient Near East and OT authors and its dynamics in regard to the concept of marriage covenant and its characteristics will provide an indispensable background knowledge and understanding of the relationship between Greco-Roman and Jewish contexts and NT authors in respect to this concept. On the other hand, the understanding of the interrelation between some significant OT texts which deal with the issues of marriage, divorce, and remarriage through the concept of marriage covenant within the OT canonical corpus will provide a holistic framework for understanding the NT texts.

The concept of covenant supplied with its proper terminology[2] refers to a widespread practice in ancient Near East related to different agreements, including business, political, religious, and marital. The ba-

---

1. In my exegetical discussions I strive to keep the integrity of the OT and NT texts, i.e. I attempt to hear them in their own terms, but at the same time I insist that neither the OT might be understood apart from it relation to the NT nor the NT might be comprehended apart form the OT. (See also Brevard S. Childs, *Biblical Theology of the Old and New Testaments: Theological Reflection on the Christian Bible* [Minneapolis: Fortress, 1992] 77; idem, *Introduction to the Old Testament as Scripture* [Philadelphia: Fortress, 1979] 671.)

2. As terminology covenant was expressed with different words in different ANE languages (e.g. Akkadian - *riksu* and in Hittite - *ishiul*) which did not change the common understanding of the concept in these societies. Also David Instone-Brewer, *Divorce and Remarriage in the Bible: The Social and Literary Context* (Cambridge: Eerdmans, 2002) 3.

sic understanding of the concept might be defined as a mutually binding agreement between two parties based on stipulations and sanctions accepted by both sides. The legal nature of the covenant was established through ceremony or document and implied initiation, preservation, and dissolution in a case of failure to fulfill its stipulations by one or both of the parties. The marriage covenant conveyed the same meaning of a mutually binding agreement between two parties including payments, sanctions, and specific stipulations. This understanding of the concept with its practices and legal language was shared by Israel and presented in the Old Testament literature. The usual initiation of the marriage covenant was done through a legally binding ceremony with the pronunciation of a verbal oath (*verba solemnia*)[3] in the presence of witnesses[4] and in some cases officiated with a document[5] narrating its nature. The marriage covenant relationship[6] was sustained by the keeping of its stipulations but

---

3. This is the oral declaration of both husband and wife of the covenant commitment being undertaken. It is found both in ANE marriage covenant agreements (MAL A §41; OB marriage document CT 48:50; Porten-Yardeni, B3.8, lines 21–22) and OT (Gen 2:23; Hos 2:4, 17–19 [2:2, 15–17]; Prov 7:4f.; and Tob 7:12,). (Also Gordon Paul Hugenberger, *Marriage as a Covenant: A Study of Biblical Law and Ethics Governing Marriage Developed from the Perspective of Malachi* [Leiden: Brill, 1994] 216–39). Instone-Brewer finds similarity between the OT expression of the covenantal oath between Yahweh and Israel "I will be your God and you shall be my people" (Lev 26:12; Deut 29:13 [29:12]; etc.) and the ANE marriage covenant oath reflected in Hosea 2:2 [2:4]. (D. Instone-Brewer, *Divorce and Remarriage in the Bible*, 2.) The verbal oath, as it is argued, has been supplemented with the nonverbal oath-sign (*copula carnalis*) which has been used as "the constitutive instrument for effecting a desired legal outcome." (Hugenberger, *Marriage as a Covenant*, 240) This is the consensual sexual union between the husband and wife acted as a sign for initiation of the marriage covenant, which also formed the marriage union and established its consummation. In a different way of depiction this sign might be identified in both ANE (CH §§155–156, quoted in Hugenberger, *Marriage as a Covenant*, 248) and OT (Exod 22:15, 16 [16, 17]; Deut 22:28–29; Gen 2:24; 34; and 2 Sam 13; Genesis 29 cf. Joshua 9) subject related literature. (Hugenberger, *Marriage as a Covenant*, 240–79.)

4. Also Hugenberger, *Marriage as a Covenant*, 223

5. Also Daniel I. Block, "Marriage and Family in Ancient Israel," in *Marriage and Family in the Biblical World*, ed. Ken M. Campbell (Downers Grove, IL: InterVarsity, 2003) 45.

6. The most obvious characteristic of the covenant in general and marriage covenant in particular is that of a relationship. The latter is established between two parties which are not relatives but which covenant obligations toward each other resemble that of relatives (Gen 2:24). Hence, some of the characteristics of this relationship between the two parties might be defined as "love," (cf. Deut 6:5; 7:8, 13; 23:6 [5]; 30:6, 15, 16, 20), "brotherhood," (Zech 11:14), and "peace," (Num 25:12; Isa 54:10; Ezek 34:25; 37:26). The relationship is further grounded on the free will of both parties and it is not naturally

could have been broken by the failure to keep them, which would result in the application of sanctions.[7] This twofold nature of the marriage covenant can be further elaborated through analysis of its basic elements, payments, sanctions, and stipulations.

The crucial role of payments in relation to the covenant of marriage is twofold: it acts as a legal seal of the marriage covenant and underlines the nature of the latter as stable and secure.[8] Hence, on the one hand, the groom paid to the bride's father (her family) a brideprice[9] constituted of the sum of many months wages to ensure the bride's family that he had entered the marriage covenant with serious convictions.[10] On the other hand, the father of the bride provided her with a dowry[11] which was

---

developed but specially established. The varieties of the two parties which the OT offers might be represented with several examples such as lord and servant (Gen 50:18; Josh 9:8; 1 Sam 25:8; 27:12; 2 Kgs 10:5-6; 16:7; 24:1; and Ps 116:16), God and individual (Yahweh and Noah, Gen 6:18; 9:9-17; Yahweh and Abraham, Gen 15:8-18; 17:1-4; Yahweh and Israel, Exod 19:5; etc.), two individuals (Gen 21:22f.; 26:23ff.; 31:44ff.; 47:29; 1 Sam 18:3; 20:8; 22:8; 23:18; 2 Sam 3:12f.; 1 Kgs 2:42-46; etc.), two people groups (Josh 9:6, 11, 151), and leaders and their groups (2 Sam 5:3//1 Chr 11:3; 2 Kgs 11:17//2 Chr 23:16, 3; Hos 6:7; 10:3-4). The two parties in a marriage covenant and the relational character of their covenantal bond expressed through feelings, attitudes, and actions is best reflected in the marriage metaphor of Yahweh's marriage to Israel (and Judah) employed by the later prophets (Hosea 1, 3; Isaiah 43, 49, 51, 62, 63; Jeremiah 2, 3, 30; Ezekiel 16, and 23). (Hugenberger, *Marriage as a Covenant*, 176-81.)

7. D. Instone-Brewer, *Divorce and Remarriage in the Bible*, 3, 4.

8. It has been a usual practice both for Nuzi in particular and Mesopotamia in general that the institutions of brideprice and the dowry are part of the same marriage, (the Code of Hammurapi §§ 163 and 164). (Katarzyna Grosz, "Dowry and Brideprice in Nuzi," in *Studies on the Civilization and Culture of Nuzi and the Hurrians*, eds. M. A. Morrison and D. I. Owen [Winona Lake, IN: Eisenbrauns, 1981] 179.)

9. The institution of the brideprice in Nuzi might be defined as a material transaction between the families of the bride and of the groom given by the groom himself or with the support of his family to the bride's family, (Nuzi texts for brideprice: AASOR 16. 54, 55; HSS 5. 13, 16; 25; 80; HSS 9. 111; HSS 19. 75, 80, 83, 84, 96, 99, 134, 144; RA 23. 12; JEN 186). This marriage prestation establishes strong connection between the two families and serves to provide resources for the marriages of the wife's brothers. While the entire dowry has to be given at the time of marriage, the brideprice was possible to be paid in installments over a period of time (K. Grosz, *Dowry and Brideprice in Nuzi*, 163, 177, 178).

10. See Gen 24:53; 29:18; Exod 22:16-17; Hos 3:2. Also Edwin M. Yamauchi, "Cultural Aspects of Marriage in the Ancient World," *BibSac* 135/539 (1978) 243; D. Instone-Brewer, *Divorce and Remarriage in the Bible*, 4, 6.

11. The institution of dowry in Nuzi might be defined as a marriage prestation according to which the bride receives from the father her share of the inheritance during

usually her share of the family estate in order to secure the new family materially.[12] Marriages between gods and humans in Ugaritic literature and Yahweh and Israel in the OT also reflect the groom payment.[13] The significant role of the payments in the marriage covenant is also underlined by the sanctions at the time of divorce. Thus, if the wife is guilty for the divorce she loses her dowry.[14] When the husband bares the guilt or divorces the wife without reason he is obliged to return the full amount of dowry to the wife.[15]

The stipulations of marriage covenants of ancient Near East nations had primarily a verbal nature due to the oral character of the marriage ceremony as a whole.[16] The basic stipulations of the covenantal union were well known and on different occasions their recitation in front of witnesses during the marriage ceremony well preserved. The need for providing a written form of the covenant including some of its stipulations depended on the variations from the normal marital union. Thus, one of the stipulations found in several covenant documents is the prohibition to the husband of taking a wife whom he would treat as senior to the first

---

the time of marriage with the purpose to help the independent economical existence of the young family, (Nuzi texts for daughters' share given as their dowry: HSS 19. 1, 7, 12, 17, 20, 21, HSS 5. 59; JEN 443; RA 23. 5). In some cases even a part of the brideprice might be given as dowry. This institution might be defined as "indirect dowry," (AASOR 16. 55; HSS 13. 263; HSS 5. 80; HSS 19. 144). The role of the dowry to secure the position of the wife in the marriage is underlined by the fact that even the husband who was allowed to administer the dowry was prohibited of disposing of it without wife's consent. Selling the dowry was considered a shameful act. (K. Grosz, *Dowry and Brideprice in Nuzi*, 162, 163, 179)

12. See Judg 1:14–15; 1 Kgs 9:16; Tob 7:14; 8:21; Assuan papyri (Cowley nos. 15, 18). Also D. Instone-Brewer, *Divorce and Remarriage in the Bible*, 4.

13. Hos 2:19. Also D. Instone-Brewer, *Divorce and Remarriage in the Bible*, 5.

14. "(31–35) And should Nahdi-Esu release Harri-menna her husband, she will forfeit (?) her entire dowry in favour of Harri-menna, and thereby she will relinquish her means of support (?)." (Marriage Agreement No. 34 TBER 93f. [Susa, n.d.] in Martha T. Roth, *Babylonian Marriage Agreements 7th–3rd Centuries B.C.* [Kevelaer: Butzon & Bercker, 1989] 110; Also Hugenberger, *Marriage as a Covenant*, 227.

15. "(28–31) Should Harri-menna release Nahdi-Esu his wife, and have another wife live (in the house) in preference to her, he will give her five minas of silver in addition to her dowry." (Marriage Agreement No. 34 TBER 93f. [Susa, n.d.] in M. T. Roth, *Babylonian Marriage Agreements*, 110.) Also D. Instone-Brewer, *Divorce and Remarriage in the Bible*, 6; and Hugenberger, *Marriage as a Covenant*, 227.

16. M. T. Roth, *Babylonian Marriage Agreements*, 1–2. Also D. Instone-Brewer, *Divorce and Remarriage in the Bible*, 8.

wife which would result in lack of support of the latter.[17] Another more elaborate form of the stipulations is found in the context of marriages which include a second wife. The husband is not to withdraw support in the form of "food, anointing oil and clothing" from the first wife.[18] In a similar marital situation,[19] Exodus 21:10 lists three stipulations, "food, clothing, and marriage rights," which the husband should fulfill toward his first wife even if she is taken as a slave-wife.[20]

One of the most common unwritten stipulations both in the ancient Near East and the OT marriage covenants is sexual faithfulness. The ANE documents which deal with the issue of divorce for adultery stipulate capital punishment for the guilty party.[21] The fact that in some cases the

---

17. Marriage Agreement No. 17: "(22–26) Should Nabu-ah-asur bring (?) a woman of senior status(?) into his house as a wife, he will give six minas of silver to Tala-Uruk (and) she may go to the house of a mar bani." (Marriage Agreement No. 17, YOS 6 188 (YBC 3732), Alu-la-Lane, 27–IX-14 Nabonidus [542 B.C.] in M. T. Roth, *Babylonian Marriage Agreements*, 70.) This as Roth and Instone-Brewer observe is not a statement against polygamy but against unequal treatment of the wives. (See M. T. Roth, *Babylonian Marriage Agreements*, 13. D. Instone-Brewer, *Divorce and Remarriage in the Bible*, 8.) Lipit-Ishtar Lawcode #28: "If a man has turned his face away from his first wife . . . (but) she has not gone out of the [house], his wife which he married as his favourite is a second wife; he shall continue to support his first wife" (Lipit-Ishtar Lawcode in James B. Pritchard, ed., *Ancient Near Eastern Texts Relating to the Old Testament*, 3rd ed. [Princeton: Princeton University Press, 1978, 1992] 190. Also D. Instone-Brewer, *Divorce and Remarriage in the Bible*, 8.)

18. D. Instone-Brewer, *Divorce and Remarriage in the Bible*, 9.

19. Appearance of a second wife: "And if a man sells his daughter to be a female slave, she shall not go out as the male slaves do. If she does not please her master, who has betrothed her to himself, then he shall let her be redeemed. He shall have no right to sell her to a foreign people, since he has dealt deceitfully with her. And if he has betrothed her to his son, he shall deal with her according to the custom of daughters. If he takes another wife, he shall not diminish her food, her clothing, and her marriage rights. And if he does not do these three for her, then she shall go out free, without paying money" (Exod 21:7–11, NKJ).

20. Also D. Instone-Brewer, *Divorce and Remarriage in the Bible*, 9. If the husband does not keep the covenant stipulations to the slave wife expressed in Exod 21:10 he is commanded to release her without any requirement of payment toward her freedom (Exod 21:11) which underlines his guilt and the wife's freedom to remarry. (Also D. Instone-Brewer, *Divorce and Remarriage in the Bible*, 23.)

21. E.g., Laws of Eshnunna #28; Code of Hammurabi #129; Middle Assyrian laws #13–14; Hittite laws #189–91, 195, in J. B. Pritchard, *Ancient Near Eastern Texts*, 160–98. See also Victor H. Matthews, "Marriage and Family in the Ancient Near East," in *Marriage and Family in the Biblical World*, ed. Ken M. Campbell (Downers Grove, IL: InterVarsity, 2003) 27–29.

king is involved in exercising authority to spare the guilty party[22] suggests that the lack of keeping this stipulation affected the society as a whole.[23] The OT expresses the same attitude against adultery, treating it as a crime against the innocent party (Lev 20:10, 22), society (Deut 22:22, 24), and God (Gen 20:6; 26:10; 39:9), and as such underlines the importance of the stipulation of sexual faithfulness for the marriage covenant.[24] The attempts to undermine the importance of the husband's sexual fidelity in the marriage covenant due to cases of polygamy in Jewish society[25] and the emphasis on man's property rights in marriage in Semitic legal systems[26] cannot be justified. There are clear cases in which polygamy has been forbidden.[27] There are also no texts which tolerate sexual unfaithfulness of the husband.[28] Finally, there are texts which clearly underline the importance of the sexual fidelity of the husband and discourage sexual promiscuity (1 Sam 2:22; Job 31:1; Hos 4:14; Prov 5:15–23).[29] The close resemblance of the stipulations and their marital context in the OT and ANE suggests a continuation of the understanding of the nature and functions of the marriage covenant in both of them.[30] The basic elements of marriage covenants discussed so far lead to a further consideration of the contractual nature of marriage covenants.

The contractual nature of ANE and OT marriage covenants needs to be clarified in light of the attempts made by some scholars to make a distinction between contract and covenant in relation to marriage. These scholars defined marriage as a covenant but reject or underestimate its contractual character. Paul F. Palmer maintains that the concepts of covenant and contract are completely irreconcilable.[31] Covenant is based on

---

22. See Code of Hammurabi §129.

23. D. Instone-Brewer, *Divorce and Remarriage in the Bible*, 9–10. See also V. H. Matthews, *Marriage and Family in the Ancient Near East*, 27.

24. D. Instone-Brewer, *Divorce and Remarriage in the Bible*, 9–10.

25. Idem, *Three Weddings and a Divorce: God's Covenant with Israel, Judah and the Church* [online].

26. E. Neufeld, *Ancient Hebrew Marriage Laws. With Special References to General Semitic Laws and Customs* (London: Longmans, Green, 1944), 163.

27. Lev 18:18 cf. 11 QTemple 57:17–19; 66:15–17; Lev 18:17; 20:14; Deut 17:17.

28. Hugenberger, *Marriage as a Covenant*, 323–326, 338.

29. Ibid., 327–338.

30. D. Instone-Brewer, *Divorce and Remarriage in the Bible*, 12.

31. S. Bacchiocchi agrees with Palmer using his conclusions without defending or

trust and faith whose nature is that of fidelity. It is further initiated through the exchange of vows, a fact which underlines its indissoluble nature.[32] Thus, covenant cannot be broken but can be violated due to lack of faith and trust.[33] Contract, on the other hand, is based on a personal agreement between parties, but its continuation is limited by the preservation of its terms.[34] Thus, Palmer negates the existence of any contractual element in the marriage covenant.[35] On the contrary, this attempt to exclude any contractual element from the marriage covenant cannot be sustained in light of the ANE and OT evidence.[36] G. P. Hugenberger also argues that a distinction should be made between the marriage covenant and the marriage contract due to the requirement of an oath in the former and the importance of witnesses in the latter as well as the predominantly commercial nature of the contract and its subsequent appearance to the marriage covenant.[37] However, Hugenberger's distinction cannot be maintained since all three elements: oath, witnesses, and financial stipulations, appear in some of the ANE marriage contractual documents.[38] Further, the time difference between the marriage covenant and its contractual documentation in relation to their characteristics is proved irrelevant.[39] Dennis J.

---

questioning them with any further argumentation. (Samuele Bacchiocchi, *The Marriage Covenant: A Biblical Study on Marriage, Divorce, and Remarriage* [Berrien Springs, MI: Biblical Perspectives, 1991] 25.)

32. Paul F. Palmer, "Christian Marriage: Contract or Covenant?" *TS* 33 (1972) 663.

33. Ibid., 619.

34. Ibid.

35. Ibid., 627–29. However, he contradicts himself making the written contract as one of the forms for the expression of the marriage covenant and at the same time not considering it "the actual" representation of the covenant agreement between the spouses. (Ibid., 627)

36. Also D. Instone-Brewer, *Divorce and Remarriage in the Bible*, 17, 18.

37. Hugenberger, *Marriage as a Covenant*, 191, 192, 215.

38. Marriage Agreements No. 6, 16 in M. T. Roth, *Babylonian Marriage Agreements*, 19. Also Instone-Brewer, *Divorce and Remarriage in the Bible*, 18. Even Hugenberger himself argues for the presence of oath as *verba solemnia* of the marriage covenant in the ANE marriage documents which is paralleled by the OT language. (Hugenberger, *Marriage as a Covenant*, 217–39)

39. Hugenberger defines marriage as a covenant and engages in refuting the arguments of the scholars (Jacob Milgrom, *Cult and Conscience: The Asham and the Priestly Doctrine of Repentance*, Studies in Judaism in Late Antiquity 18 [Leiden: Brill, 1976] 134 and Moshe Greenberg, *Ezekiel 1–20* [Garden City, NY: Doubleday, 1983] 278, quoted in Hugenberger, *Marriage as a Covenant*, 168.) who argue against a covenantal definition of marriage. The main argument of these scholars is that a ratifying oath is indispensable

McCarthy, similarly to Hugenberger, argues that covenant and contract are agreements which belong to two different genres. The main difference according to him is the relational character of covenant based on an oath and as such, requiring no witnesses to ensure its fulfillment. Contract, on the other hand, is defined by reward and punishment in relation to the fulfillment of its stipulations by the parties.[40] However, McCarthy maintains that covenant is also based on blessings and curses in relation to the fulfillment of its stipulations.[41] Moreover the covenant relationship between the two parties is defined through their mutual obligations which are based on the covenant stipulations.[42] He himself places covenant under the general category of contracts,[43] defines the marriage covenant as a contractual relationship,[44] and refers to the relationship between the two

---

for establishing a covenant relationship and since they found no evidence for the presence of such oaths in the marriage contracts they negate the understanding of marriage as covenant. (Hugenberger, *Marriage as a Covenant*, 168, 214) Hugenberger considers it of crucial importance for substantiating his argument to make a distinction between covenant and contract. Thus, he states that the marriage contract is different than the marriage covenant due to the fact that it has served the needs for various secondary agreements related to the already established marriage covenant. (Hugenberger, *Marriage as a Covenant*, 191, 192, 215) However, Hugenberger's argumentation has shown that such distinction is not only unnecessary but also inadequate. First, Hugenberger has expressed an agreement with Milgrom and Greenberg about the covenant elements of marriage apart from that of oath. Elements which they have found in the ANE marriage contracts (Hugenberger, *Marriage as a Covenant*, 4), obvious from his critique, (Hugenberger, *Marriage as a Covenant*, 215) he has described using the OT. (Hugenberger, *Marriage as a Covenant*, 168–185) Second, Hugenberger himself has underlined the presence of oaths in the Babylonian marriage agreements (Marriage Agreements No. 6, 16 in M. T. Roth, *Babylonian Marriage Agreements*, 19.) as an argument against Milgrom and Greenberg. (Hugenberger, *Marriage as a Covenant*, 187) Third, Hugenberger himself presents examples of overlap between covenant and contract (1 Kgs 5:15ff; Nehemiah 8–10) (Hugenberger, *Marriage as a Covenant*, 192). Hence, if covenant and contract share the same elements and samples of such overlaps are found, the time of the appearance of the written contractual document in relation to marriage covenant is not essential.

40. Dennis J. McCarthy, *Treaty and Covenant: A Study in Form in the Ancient Oriental Documents and in the Old Testament* (Rome: Biblical Institute Press, 1978), 17, 41, 297.

41. Ibid., 51, 52.

42. Ibid., 51; Also Paul Kalluveettil, *Declaration and Covenant: A Comprehensive Review of Covenant Formulae from the Old Testament and the Ancient Near East* (Rome: Biblical Institute Press, 1982), 91 and Hugenberger, *Marriage as a Covenant*, 179.

43. McCarthy, *Old Testament Covenant* (Oxford: Basil Blackwell, 1973), 34.

44. Ibid., 33.

parties within the covenant as an act of contracting.⁴⁵ Finally McCarthy, contrary to Palmer, for whom oath makes the covenant an indissoluble agreement, defines the breakdown of both covenant and contractual agreements in a similar way with only a quantitative difference.⁴⁶

ANE marriage records as well as OT references to the legal nature of the marriage institution do not make a difference between contract and covenant in relation to marriage agreements.⁴⁷ The concept of covenant contains contractual characteristics and is expressed with a single terminology.⁴⁸ Marriage covenants in the ANE were made within the framework of the general covenant structure used in all spheres of life (e.g. business, diplomatic). This is also reflected in the OT language and Law. The latter might be clearly observed in the covenant between Yahweh and Israel (Exod 19–24) which is analogous⁴⁹ to the model of a treaty

---

45. D. J. McCarthy, *Treaty and Covenant*, 47, 94.

46. While contract is defined as "an impersonal instrument which goes into effect automatically as though simple infidelity must mean everlasting alienation," the covenant breakdown is based on "persistent infidelity, a state which mocks the commitment which is the heart of covenant, that effectively ends it because it effectively denies it any real existence." (D. J. McCarthy, *Treaty and Covenant*, 297)

47. The significant role of the marriage contract for the institution of marriage might be observed in its centrality among the ceremonies for marriage initiation in the marriages of the contemporary Palestinian villages. (Hilma Granqvist, *Marriage Conditions in a Palestinian Village II*. Societas Scientarum Fennica, Commentationes Humanarum Litterarum, VI [Helsingfors: Centraltryckeriet, 1935] 28)

48. OT has only one word for both contract and covenant (בְּרִית). Also D. Instone-Brewer, *Divorce and Remarriage in the Bible*, 17.

49. Even though scholars disagree on the quantity and quality of the resemblance between the Sinai covenant and ANE treaties, they come to an understanding of the existence of continuity between them. McCarthy defines the genre of the Sinai covenant as more complex than that of the ANE treaty tradition. However, he finds a clear resemblance between the stipulations of the treaty tradition and the nature of the covenant expressed in the commands which manifest the divine will. He also defines some of the contextual elements and accomplished purposes of the treaty tradition as paralleling the Sinai covenant such as the need for a mediator, provision of a written document, and the establishment of peace, brotherhood, and loyal friendship between the parties. Finally McCarty defines the Sinai covenant as being one of the various OT covenant formulations which find their full expression with a clear resemblance with the treaty tradition in Urdt (Deuteronomy 5–28) (D. J. McCarthy, *Treaty and Covenant*, 253, 255, 256, 276, 293) Ernest W. Nicholson understands the covenant between Yahweh and Israel more like "an ideal rather than a social reality" (p.82) which makes him diminish the social aspect of the covenant for the sake of its theological aspect. Hence, he argues that any attempt of looking for a relation between the Hittite treaty texts and the covenant of Yahweh with Israel is damned. However, even he acknowledges the terminological resemblance

covenant between an empire and a vassal state.[50] The main structure of the covenant included basic stipulations (cf. Exod 20:3–17), divine witness (cf. Exod 24:4 or Exod 24:4–8), and the outcome from keeping the stipulations as expressed in the blessings and curses (cf. Deut 28).[51] The only difference between ANE covenants and the one at Sinai is that in the latter God is both witness and party to the covenant.[52] Thus, the marriage covenant included both trust and stipulations followed by penalties.[53] Hence, in order to function the covenant required the mutual trust of both parties that they would keep its stipulations. The penalties existed to provide justice by preserving the dignity and financial status of the innocent party, and as such they involved different financial charges to the guilty party.[54] That understanding of marriage covenant extends to the NT as well.[55]

The contractual nature of the marriage covenant was defined by its stipulations which established the legal relationship between the two par-

---

between the treaty texts and some Deuteronomy texts. Moreover he maintains that not the Hittite but the neo-Assyrian treaties should be seen as the model for the covenant between Yahweh and Israel. (Ernest W. Nicholson, *God and His People* [Oxford: Clarendon, 1986] 81, 82.) However, McCarthy argues that the treaty tradition finds its roots in the ancient Mesopotamian legal tradition which reached both Israel and Hatti through their sharing of the mutual cultural area of Canaan and Palestine and through the Assyrian political role in it in regard to Israel. (D. J. McCarthy, *Treaty and Covenant*, 286, 287) In the same light Dumbrell clearly states that Hittite state treaties have preserved their form for a long period of time and the treaties from later Assyrian period have used the same basic structure with just a small elaboration of some elements. (W. J. Dumbrell, *Covenant and Creation*, 95)

50. For an example of the summary of such treaties based on the classic juristic analysis of a group found in the archives of the ancient Hittite capital (XV and XIV centuries B.C.) see Delbert R. Hillers, *Covenant: The History of a Biblical Idea* (Maryland: Johns Hopkins University Press, 1969), 28–45.

51. Also D. Instone-Brewer, *Divorce and Remarriage in the Bible*, 17, 18; E. A. Martens, *God's Design*, 69–70; W. J. Dumbrell, *Covenant and Creation*, 94–99.

52. Also D. Instone-Brewer, *Divorce and Remarriage in the Bible*, 17, 18.

53. Dumbrell also sees the relation between the covenant at Sinai and the marriage covenant presented by the prophets based primarily on the similar dynamics of the relationship between Yahweh and Israel expressed in both of them. (W. J. Dumbrell, *Covenant and Creation*, 99)

54. Also D. Instone-Brewer, *Divorce and Remarriage in the Bible*, 15–19.

55. D. Instone-Brewer, *Divorce and Remarriage in the Bible*, 17. Pope Paul VI uses the words contract and covenant interchangeably. (See Pope Paul VI, "The Marriage Bond," *The Pope Speaks* 21[1976] 152–53, quoted in Gerald D. Coleman, *Divorce and Remarriage in the Catholic Church* [Mahwah, NJ: Paulist, 1988] 40.)

ties on mutual obligations. The characterising place of the concept of obligation to the nature of the covenant in the OT is clearly attested through the study of the syntagms of בְּרִית.

> ... among its 283 occurrences in 263 verses some sense of obligation typically attends the presence of a covenant. For this reason covenants are said to be kept (שׁמר - 15x, נצד - 2x), commanded (צוה - 7x), remembered (זכר - 14x), or confirmed (העמיר - 3x), and one is to be faithful in a covenant (נאמן - 1x) or to hold fast a covenant (החזיק - 1x). Alternatively, covenants are said to be broken (הפר - 20x), transgressed (עבר - 9x), forgotten (שׁכח - 4x), forsaken (עזב - 5x), profaned (חלל - 3x), despised (נאר - 1x), acted falsely against (שׁקר - 1x), or violated (שׁחת - 1x).[56]

It might be even argued that there is a scholarly consensus that obligations are an essential part of every covenant.[57] The matter of further debate, however, rests on the issue of the mutuality of the obligations in all covenants. In this respect, some have argued that several of the covenants between Yahweh and his people are based on promises which leaves the whole weight of the obligations resting only on Yahweh's side.[58] However,

---

56. Hugenberger, *Marriage as a Covenant*, 169.

57. Ibid., 181.

58. G. E. Mendenhall defines such covenants as "patron" or promissory. (G. E. Mendenhall, "Covenant," in *IDB* 1: 717, quoted in Hugenberger, *Marriage as a Covenant*, 181.) Instone-Brewer maintains the view that the ANE and overall OT concept of marriage covenant is based on mutual obligation of both parties to fulfill the necessary stipulations. However he finds another covenant concept which he argues developed "entirely separate" (D. Instone-Brewer, *Divorce and Remarriage in the Bible*, 17.) from the usual marriage covenant and is defined as "new covenant." The latter signifies the ultimate faithfulness to the covenant of one of the parties in spite of the unfaithfulness of the other party which does not preserve its stipulations. This concept expresses the relationship between Yahweh and Israel by later prophets, with Yahweh as ultimately faithful to Israel in spite of her attitude and actions, (Ezekiel 36–37, Jeremiah 31). (D. Instone-Brewer, *Divorce and Remarriage in the Bible*, 17). In presentation of the marriage covenant in the later prophets, however, Instone-Brewer does not only lack definition and explanation of this new unconditional covenant but also contradicts himself defining the new covenant marriage relation between Yahweh and the united nation of Israel and Judah as remarriage. (D. Instone-Brewer, *Divorce and Remarriage in the Bible*, 52, 53, 58). The later definition presupposes the divorce status of Israel and establishes the connection with the previous covenant marriage relationship between Yahweh and Israel presented in the prophetic writings. The writings of Hosea, Ezekiel, Jeremiah, and Isaiah, as Instone-Brewer argues, offer a very consistent presentation of God's divorce from Israel and separation of Judah due to marital unfaithfulness of both Israel and Judah. (D. Instone-Brewer, *Divorce and Remarriage in the Bible*, 34, 51–54, 58.) Moreover the new

it is more convincingly argued that all covenants have a degree of mutual obligations for both parties and the covenant of marriage shares this feature.[59]

The mutuality of obligations and the indispensability of stipulations for the very definition of the nature of every covenant relationship are clearly demonstrated in the extensive study offered by Paul Kalluveettil of the metonymic synonyms for covenant and its stipulations in ANE and OT literature. Kalluveettil defines the OT terms 'ēdût,[60] ḥōzeh, ḥāzût,[61] nāḥah,[62] and dābār[63] as characterizing the very nature of covenant and

---

moral posture of the bride who is going to be remarried to Yahweh presupposes a proper fulfillment of her obligations in the new marriage covenant. (D. Instone-Brewer, *Divorce and Remarriage in the Bible*, 53.)

59. M. G. Kline argues for mutual covenant obligations of both parties. (Kline, *The Structure of Biblical Authority*, 2nd ed. [Grand Rapids, MI: Eerdmans, 1975] 125f., 14Sf, quoted in Hugenberger, *Marriage as a Covenant*, 181.) D. J. McCarthy even defines the very nature of covenant as based on conditions or stipulations arguing against the concept of covenant as "taken in an absolute sense, as though the unconditioned covenant were the normal, 'pure' form of covenant." (McCarthy, *Old Testament Covenant*, 3.) Hugenberger also stresses the obligations of both partners in the covenant of marriage. (Hugenberger, *Marriage as a Covenant*, 182.) In her critique of Eugene B. Borowitz's view of Jewish marriage covenant Laura S. Levitt maintains that a covenant understanding which does not allow mutual contractual obligation might turn the relationship between the spouses into an abusive manipulation hidden behind the model of loving submission of the wife to the authority of the husband. She critiques severely Borowitz's model of covenant relationship which allows domination of the husband over the wife and justifies suffering in the name of loving submission. (Laura S. Levitt, "Covenant or Contract? Marriage as Theology," *Cross Currents* 48/2 [Sum 1998] 172–80.)

60. The Neo-Assyrian word *adê* for treaty refers both to the pact as well as to its obligations.
The Aramaic term *'dn/'dy'*, part of the Sefire inscriptions, denotes stipulations and refers to treaty as the Akkadian *adê*. The OT *'ēdût* in the light of Akkadian *adê* and Aramaic *'dn/'dy'* usage refers to the stipulations of the covenant and is also used as synonym of the latter (2 Kgs 11:12). (P. Kalluveettil, *Declaration and Covenant*, 30, 31.)

61. The words *ḥōzeh, ḥāzût* are used with the meaning "provision of the pact, stipulations" in Isa 28:15, 18 and at the same time they signify covenant since they have been placed in parallel to *bᵉrît*. (P. Kalluveettil, *Declaration and Covenant*, 32.)

62. The word which refers to treaty in the Idrimi Inscription is *mānaḥtu* which is used as equivalent and synonym of *riksu* which denotes stipulation, (lines 41.46–48.54 and 51–52). In a parallel usage the author of Isaiah implements the term *nāḥah* (Isa 7:2). (P. Kalluveettil, *Declaration and Covenant*, 32.)

63. In light of some terms used to denote both a single stipulation and the treaty itself in Ancient Orient vassal treaties (*ka.meš, inim.meš*, [Sum.]; *awâte*, [Akk.]; *memijaš; uttar*, [Hitt.]) the OT term *dābār* is well attested as referring to both covenant (Hag 2:5; Deut 9:5 [cf. 8:18]; Ps 105:8, 42; Hos 10:4; 1 Kgs 12:7; 2 Chr 10:7) and its stipulations,

substantiating its very stipulations at the same time through their usage in the OT and their background links in the ANE sources. Furthermore Kalluveettil offers some OT words, namely, šālôm, ṭôb/ṭôbâ, ḥesed, and 'mnh whose usage leads to the conclusion that every covenant relationship is firmly based on mutual obligations for fulfillment of the covenant stipulations. This conclusion furnishes the argument that no covenant might be defined as such without mutually shared obligations of its parties based on particular stipulations.

The usage of the words salīmum/šulmum and slm/šlm in some Akkadian texts prepares a good background for the similar use of šālôm in the OT literature. The word salīmum/šulmum denotes treaty (ARMT 1,8: 6.8; 11,50: 15; 1,71:13; ARMT II,37:11–14) and refers to the mutual friendship and peace of the two parties (the Chronicles of Chaldaean Kings, B.M. 21901, obv. 29). The term slm/šlm is used to refer both to formalizing a treaty and making a friendship between the two parties (ARMT II,40:5–6) as well as establishing peace between them (ABL 129: 5–10). The OT authors use šālôm in a similar way. The word defines the very nature of the covenant as relationship between two parties based on peace (Judg 4:17; 21:13; 2 Sam 10:19 = 1 Chr 19:19; 1 Kgs 20:18; 22:45; Isa 27:5; Job 5:23; 22:21) and friendship (Deut 2:26; 20:10, 11, 12; 23:7 = Ezra 9:12; Josh 9:15; 10:1, 4; 11:19; 1 Sam 7:14; 1 Kgs 5:26; 1 Chr 12:18). It appears as a synonym for covenant (Deut 2:26; 20:10, 11, 12; Josh 9:15; 10:1, 4; 11:19; 2 Sam 10:19 = 1 Chr 19:19; 1 Kgs 20:18; 22:45; 1 Chr 12:18; Job 5:23) and leads to establishing the obligations of both parties in a set of stipulations such as preserving the peace by mutual non-aggression (covenants between Abimelech and Abraham, Abimelech and Isaac, Laban and Jacob), through military assistance (Josh 10:6ff; 1 Kgs 15:20; 22:4, 29–33; 2 Kgs 3:9–27), and mutual support for prosperous life (Josh 2:13; 6:25; 9:15, 18, 19; 1 Kgs 20:31–32; 2 Kgs 18:32; 25:24; Jer 27:12, 17).[64]

The OT word ṭôb/ṭôbâ should be understood as covenant, a pact of amity which refers to the relationship between two parties in terms of friendship both in its totality and its inner dynamics (Deut 23:7[65]= Ezra 9:12). This meaning of the word is established in relation to the use of its cognate ṭūbtu/tābūtu (in Hittite texts atterūtu) in Akkadian treaty litera-

---

(Exod 34:28; Deut 28:69; 29:8; 2 Kgs 23:3; Jer 11:2, 6, 8; 2 Chr 34:31; Josh 24:26; Josh 21:45; 23:14, 15; 1 Kgs 8:56). Kalluveettil, *Declaration and Covenant*, 32, 33, 34.

64. Kalluveettil, *Declaration and Covenant*, 34–42.

65. Deut 23:5a cf. Deut 2:26; Kalluveettil, *Declaration and Covenant*, 46, 47.

ture. The word *ṭūbtu/tābūtu* is used to refer to the act of treaty as establishing "good relations" (The Aramaic letter of king Adon to his Egyptian overlord, line 8). It also appears in combination with *epēšu* as a reference to the act of treaty in the sense of "enacting a pact of amity," (a letter of Rib-Adda of Biblos to the Pharaoh, EA 136: 8–32). In this construction, in semantic parallel to *ṭūbtu*, the word *damqātum* appears as referring to the act of treaty and also as closely related to its stipulations (A Mari text, ARMT II, 24: 21–24). Moreover, in combination with *sulummû* the word *ṭūbtu/tābūtu* refers to the treaty itself (B.M. 21901.obv.29; B.M. 92701.II.ii: 27; iii: 18.24 King, *Chronicles*, 58:6). The OT expression *'śh ṭôbâ* parallels the Akkadian *ṭūbtu/tābūtu/damqātum epēšu* and is found in the words of David to the men of Jabesh-gilead, (2 Sam 2:6). It refers to establishing a relationship formally understood as a treaty which underlines the use of the word *ṭôbâ* as a synonym for covenant. This same expression appears in another OT text where it refers to the stipulations of the formal covenant agreement (Gen 26:29). With the similar meaning, "agreeable covenant stipulations," the word appears in combination with *dᵉbārîm* (*dᵉbārîm ṭôbîm*) (1 Kgs 12:7 = 2 Chr 10:7). Another OT text also confirms the use of *ṭôb/ṭôbâ* as covenant in the sense of friendly relationship between two parties, here God and his people (2 Chr 24:16).[66]

The OT term *ḥesed* appears in the covenant context carrying the idea of loyalty "to the terms and spirit of the pact."[67] The word should be understood as referring to *bᵉrît* both by synecdoche (1 Sam 20:15; 2 Sam 10:2; 1 Kgs 20:31; 2 Chr 24:22 and 1 Sam 15:6) and as a synonym (1 Kgs 20:31). This usage of the OT term is firmly established in the parallel use of the word *kittu* in some Akkadian texts (*epēšu kittu*, "make an agreement," EA 83: 24–25; 125:39; 132:33–35; 138:53).[68] In light of these references another OT word *'mnh* (built upon the stem *'mn* = to be firm, to be true) is used as a close parallel to *ḥesed* and in the covenant context denotes fidelity and loyalty to the agreement as a whole and to its stipulations and as such should be understood as a term for covenant by synecdoche (Neh 10:1; 11:23).[69]

---

66. Kalluveettil, *Declaration and Covenant*, 42–47.
67. Ibid., 48.
68. Ibid., 47–50.
69. Ibid., 50–51.

The essential role and mutuality of the obligations furnished through stipulations for the marriage covenant is well established in the paradigmatic marriage of Adam and Eve narrated in the creation account and well attested by Malachi in his discussion of the dynamics of the marriage covenant. The mutuality of obligations is clearly stated in both of these accounts. The emphasis is placed on the man's fulfillment of the covenantal stipulations. The creation account underlines the prioritizing shift of the most crucial responsibilities of love and loyalty which the son owed to his parents, now owed to his covenantal partner, his wife (Gen 2:24). The prophet stresses the fidelity of the husband toward his wife as so crucial that failure from this obligation threatens his own life (Mal 2:14–16). The wife's covenant responsibility toward her husband is clearly stated as well. She is identified as man's helper and partner in both accounts (Gen 2:18; 20;[70] Mal 2:14[71]).[72]

The development of the present discussion requires examining the content of the legal records of one of the most common forms of Babylonian marriage covenants and establishing clear parallels with the OT marriage covenants.

> (1–4) [. . .]-su, son of Nādinu spoke to Qunnabātu, daughter of Nabû-zēr-lišir, as follows: (4–6) "Cut yourself off from any other man. Be my wife."
>
> (7) Qunnabātu consented (to his proposal), and
>
> (8–9) she will(?) cut herself off from any other man.
>
> (9–12) Should Qunnabātu be discovered with another man, she will die [by the iron] dagger.
>
> (12–17) Should [. . .]-su marry another wife in preference to Qunnabātu, he will give [Qunnabātu] six minas of silver, and she may go [wherever she] wishes.
>
> (18–19) May Nabû and Marduk decree the destruction of whoever contravenes this agreement.

---

70. עֵזֶר כְּנֶגְדּוֹ, "helper as his partner," NRS, "a helper corresponding to him," Hugenberger, *Marriage as a Covenant*, 182, "a help *corresponding to* him i.e. equal and adequate to himself," WTM Morphology and Abridged BDB Lexicon in *Bible Works* version 5.0.020w, LLC, 2001.

71. חֲבֶרְתֶּךָ, "your partner," NIV, Hugenberger, *Marriage as a Covenant*, 182.

72. Hugenberger, *Marriage as a Covenant*, 182.

(20) At the sealing of this agreement,

(21–28) before: x-x-a-..., [son of...], descendant of A-...; Aplā, son of Nabû-...; Bēl-apla-usur, son of Nabû-...; Kuna, son of Nabû-...; Nabû-šarrani, son of...; and the scribe Bēl-..., son of šangû Sippar.

(29–31) Sippar, month IX, day 2(?), year 2 of Sîn-šar-iškun king of Aššur.[73]

In lines 4 to 9 is found the usual initiation formula for the marriage covenant. It stays in the core of the general model for such marital initiation in the ANE.[74] The formula which consists of two statements given respectively by each party according to their individual consent,[75] "You are my husband" and "You are my wife," might be considered as *verba solemnia*, "the requisite covenant-ratifying oath for marriage."[76] The counterstatements of the two phrases,[77] on the other hand, provide the declarations of both parties for the breakdown of covenant and assure the divorce state.[78] These two statements and their counterstatements in their various modifications appear in the ANE marriage documents.[79] The formulas are well attested in the OT as well. Two examples should suffice the present argument. The *verba solemnia* of marriage covenant is clearly identified in

---

73. Marriage Agreement No. 2, BM 50149 (82-3-23, 1140); Sippar, 2(?)-IX-2 Sîn-šar-iškun (ca. 625–23 B.C.) in M. T. Roth, *Babylonian Marriage Agreements*, 39, 40.

74. Husband: "Cut yourself off from any other man. Be a wife."
"Wife consented, and she will cut herself off from any other man."
Husband: "Come to me. You will be a wife."
"Wife consented. She will live in [marriage (?)] with Husband." (M. T. Roth, *Babylonian Marriage Agreements*, 6. Also D. Instone-Brewer, *Divorce and Remarriage in the Bible*, 12.)

75. The usual style of the written form of the marriage covenant expressing the groom's point of view does not underestimate the importance of the bride's consent for initiation of the marriage covenant. (Also D. Instone-Brewer, *Divorce and Remarriage in the Bible*, 12, 13.)

76. Hugenberger, *Marriage as a Covenant*, 216.

77. "You are not my husband" and "you are not my wife;" or "she is not my wife," "he is not my husband." Also Hugenberger, *Marriage as a Covenant*, 231.

78. Also D. I. Block, *Marriage and Family in Ancient Israel*, 49.

79. Marriage Agreement No. 5, BM 61176 (82-9-18, 1152) and dupl. BM 67388 (82-9-18, 7384), Sippar, 4-XII-20 Nebuchadnezzar 11 (584 B.C.) in M. T. Roth, *Babylonian Marriage Agreements*, 39, 44, 45, 46. MAL A §41; OB marriage document CT 48:50; Porten-Yardeni, B3.8, lines 21–22; Also Hugenberger, *Marriage as a Covenant*, 216–225; P. Kalluveettil, *Declaration and Covenant*, 111.

Adam's words in relation to the initiation of his marriage covenant with Eve. "This is now bone of my bones and flesh of my flesh; she shall be called 'woman,' for she was taken out of man," (Gen 2:23, NIV). In light of other OT parallels of the so called "relationship formula"[80] ("bone of my bones and flesh of my flesh," Gen 29:14; 2 Sam 5:1; 19:13f. [12f.]; and 1 Chr 11:1 cf. also Judg 9:2),[81] Adam's statement given before God serves as a covenant oath through which he as a husband declares his marital commitments to Eve.[82] The negative form of the *verba solemnia* which serves as a disavowal of the marriage covenant, i.e. for divorce or dissolution of the marriage, is used by Hosea for presenting the divorce statement[83] of the husband Yahweh to the wife Israel. The statement "for she is not my wife, and I am not her husband," (NIV, Hos 2:2 [MT 2:4]) which is part of the marriage metaphor which Hosea uses to narrate the relationship between Yahweh and Israel, is understood as a divorce formula due to the following arguments. First, it appears to be a parallel to the statement for the covenant dissolution between Yahweh and Israel in Hosea 1:9, "for you are not my people, and I am not your God," (NIV). Second, the promise for remarriage given by Yahweh to his people (Hos 2:16–25) in which the positive form of the covenant *verba solemnia* appears,[84] presupposes the dissolution of the previous marriage. Third, the statement of divorce in Hos 2:2 [MT 2:4] is followed by vivid pictorial language (Hos 2:3),[85] which presents the striping of the wife by the husband, a symbolic ac-

---

80. Also Hugenberger, *Marriage as a Covenant*, 165.

81. These examples present establishment of covenantal relationship which defines Adam's statement as attestation of Eve's family status of wife. (Also Hugenberger, *Marriage as a Covenant*, 164, 165.)

82. Also Hugenberger, *Marriage as a Covenant*, 165, 230, 231.

83. Whether divorce here is not finalised and appears just as threat from the husband, since Israel's actions in Hos 2:2–15 are defined as "adultery," not just "promiscuity," does not affect the understanding of the divorce formula (Hos 2:2) since the intention of the author until v 15 is to present the complete breakdown of the marriage of Yahweh and Israel so that he may introduce the promise of remarriage in v16 which extends to v23. (Also Hugenberger, *Marriage as a Covenant*, 232, 233.)

84. "I will plant her for myself in the land; I will show my love to the one I called 'Not my loved one.' I will say to those called 'Not my people,' '*You are my people*'; and they will say, '*You are my God*'" (italics mine, Hos 2:23).

85. "Otherwise I will strip her naked and make her as bare as on the day she was born; I will make her like a desert, turn her into a parched land, and slay her with thirst" (NIV).

tion pointing to the dissolution of the relationship. Fourth, Jeremiah (3:8) reads Hosea's text[86] as Yahweh's divorce from Israel.

Lines 4 to 9 of the Babylonian marriage covenant under analysis also express clear resemblance with the covenant language used for the first marriage initiation narrated in Genesis 2:24, where forsaking (יַעֲזָב־אִישׁ)[87] one's former relationships is for the purpose of establishing a new one by cleaving (וְדָבַק)[88] to the new partner.[89] Lines 9-12 define the capital punishment for adultery which underlines the stipulation of marital faithfulness. The OT expresses an equal attitude toward both adultery and marital faithfulness (Gen 20:6; 26:10; 39:9; Lev 20:10, 22; Deut 22:22, 24). Lines 12-17 serve as a warning to the husband in the potential case of abuse of his wife. The latter might be identified as the diminishing of the husband's support to his first wife with the coming of a second wife. The new wife has been treated with preference to the first by the husband and as such she has obtained superior status which resolved in the inferiority of the first wife leading to the diminishing of her support. Hence, the failure of the husband to keep the stipulations of the covenant toward his first wife is to be punished with divorce which resolves in returning the dowry to her.[90] The divorced status of the wife is clearly defined in the expression which underlines her freedom from marital obligations and suggests remarriage as an option. The OT expresses a warning[91] to the husband not to divorce

---

86. The assumption that Jeremiah's writing has been influenced by Hosea's message is widely accepted. (J. A. Thompson, *The Book of Jeremiah*, NICOT [Grand Rapids, MI: Eerdmans, 1980] 81–87; John Skinner, *Prophecy and Religion*, 2nd ed. [Cambridge: Cambridge University Press, 1922] 21; Hans Jurgens Hendricks, "Juridical Aspects of the Marriage Metaphor in Hosea and Jeremiah," D. Lit. diss. [University of Stellenhosch, South Africa, nd. 1974] 182–186, quoted in Hugenberger, *Marriage as a Covenant*, 234.)

87. Cf. Exod 23:32; 34:15; Deut 31:16; 31:20; Josh 23:16; 2 Kgs 17:35, 38; Jer 11:10; 22:9. See also Gordon J. Wenham, *Genesis 1–15*. Word Biblical Commentary, eds. David A. Hubbard, Glenn W. Baker, John D. Watts and Ralph P. Martin, electronic ed. (Dallas: Word, 1998), 352—Logos Library System 2.1g.

88. See Deut 4:4; 10:20; 11:22; 13:4; 30:20; Josh 23:8; 1 Kgs 11:2. See also Nahum M. Sarna, *Genesis* (Jerusalem: The Jewish Publication Society, 1989), 23; S. Bacchiocchi, *The Marriage Covenant* [online]; Wallis, "Dābhaq," in *TDOT* 3:80–84; G. J. Wenham, *Genesis 1–15*, 352.

89. Also D. Instone-Brewer, *Divorce and Remarriage in the Bible*, 14.

90. Also M. T. Roth, *Babylonian Marriage Agreements*, 12–14.

91. See also *What Does the Bible Teach: The Divine Permission* [online], Available at http://www.gospelcom.net/rbc/ds/q0806/point1.html, Accessed on 20 November

his wife without serious legitimate grounds (עֶרְוַת דָּבָר,[92] Deut 24:1). Such an illegitimate divorce action underlines the husband's failure to fulfill the covenant stipulations and places him in a situation of covenant breakdown with irreversible consequences (Deut 24:4[93]). The latter are clearly substantiated with the divorce certificate (סֵפֶר כְּרִיתֻת) which affirms the wife's freedom, especially in giving her a possibility for remarriage (Deut 24:1, 3). The significance of this document was clearly understood by the rabbinic interpreters (see *The Mishnah, Gittin* 9:3).[94] Lines 18–19 reveal the negative attitude of the Babylonian gods[95] toward the person who breaks the narrated marriage covenant by acting against its clearly stated nature. The same attitude is shown by Malachi (2:14–16).[96] The God of

---

2000; Herbert W. Armstrong, *Marriage and Divorce* [online], Available at http://www.icgno.org/hwa/BA/MD73.HTM, Accessed on 20 November 2000; David E. Garland, "A Biblical View of Divorce," *Review and Expositor* LXXXIV/3 (Summer 1987): 419; Earl S. Kalland, "Deuteronomy," in *Expositor's Bible Commentary: Old Testament* (Grand Rapids, MI: Zondervan, 1999), Zondervan Reference Software [32-bit edition], Version 2.7.; Christopher Wright, *Deuteronomy*. NIBC (Peabody: Hendrickson, 1996), 255.

92. The phrase עֶרְוַת דָּבָר constitutes legitimate grounds for divorce and its meaning in Deut 24:1 might be defined as shameful behavior with sexual implications (cf. Gen 9:22; Exod 20:26; Lev 18:6; Deut 23:15; Lam 1:8; Ezek 16:36; *The Mishnah, Ketub.* 7:6; See also *Whittaker's Revised BDB* and *TWOT Hebrew Lexicon in BibleWorks for Windows*. Version 4.0.026e (4000). Cambridge, MA: Lotus Development Corporation, 1998; J. M. Sprinkle, *Old Testament Perspectives on Divorce and Remarriage*. Electronic edition by Galaxie Software; D. E. Garland, *A Biblical View of Divorce*, 422; S. R. Driver, *Deuteronomy*, 270, 271). The inclusion of adultery as part of the suggested meaning due to some prophetic texts (Hos 2:2 [MT, v4]; Jer 3:8, See also R. F. Collins, *Sexual Ethics and the New Testament: Behavior and Belief*, 2, 3), which imply that in the actual practice the death penalty was replaced with divorce, might be favored to its exclusion due to the law of capital punishment. (Lev 20:10, Deut 22:22; See also J. C. Laney, *Deuteronomy 24:1–4 and the Issue of Divorce*. Electronic edition by Galaxie Software; J. M. Sprinkle, *Old Testament Perspectives on Divorce and Remarriage*. Electronic edition by Galaxie Software.)

93. Close association between עֶרְוַת דָּבָר, (Deut 24:1) and הֻטַּמָּאָה, (Deut 24:4) would lead to the conclusion that once the wife has been pronounced unclean (הֻטַּמָּאָה) by the husband he is forbidden to remarry her when she is free from other marriages. (See also B. Ward Powers, *Marriage and Divorce: The New Testament Teaching* [Petersham: I. M. P. A. C. T., 1987] 159, 160; Andrew Cornes, *Divorce and Remarriage* [Grand Rapids, MI: Eerdmans, 1993] 135.)

94. Also D. Instone-Brewer, *Divorce and Remarriage* in the Bible, 14.

95. Mentioning of Nabu and Marduk is a reference to the Babylonian gods. See Marriage Agreement No.6 Strassmaier Liverpool 8 (29–11–77,4), Opis, 13–11–41 Nebuchadnezzar II (564 B.C.) #17–19 in M. T. Roth, *Babylonian Marriage Agreements*, 48.

96. "You ask, 'Why?' It is because the LORD is acting as the witness between you

Israel expresses his anger against the sin of treachery (בָּגַד) of those who were breaking their marriage covenants on unlawful grounds.[97] The last several lines of the marriage covenant (20–31) establish the legal nature of the document by listing the names of the witnesses. The importance of witnesses for the validation of the marriage covenant is also expressed in the OT (Ruth 4:9–11). Even God himself is referred to as one of the witnesses of any marriage covenant (Mal 2:14).[98] Having established a clear resemblance between ANE and OT marriage covenants I would like to continue the present discussion by offering an explicit example of the dynamics of the marriage covenant relationship in the OT literature.

First, I will offer an analysis of Deut 24:1–4 from the perspective of Gen 1:27 and 2:24 arguing that the dynamics of the concept of marriage covenant establish the grounds for such a reading. Second, I will present the most explicit OT example of the dynamics of the marriage covenant relationship that between God and Israel from the perspective of the prophetic writings.

The creation account related to humankind (Gen 1:26, 27) has several unique features in comparison with the rest of the creation (Gen 1:1–25). The most important for my discussion is that only human crea-

---

and the wife of your youth, because you have broken faith with her, though she is your partner, the wife of your marriage covenant. Has not the LORD made them one? In flesh and spirit they are his. And why one? Because he was seeking godly offspring. So guard yourself in your spirit, and do not break faith with the wife of your youth. 'I hate divorce,' says the LORD God of Israel, 'and I hate a man's covering himself with violence as well as with his garment,' says the LORD Almighty. So guard yourself in your spirit, and do not break faith." (Mal 2:14–16, NIV)

97. The negative attitude of Yahweh related to divorce should be understood within the context of the marriage covenant violation by his people. Malachi deals with cases of marriage covenant abuse by the people from Judah most probably due to remarriage to foreign women (Mal 2:11). He uses frequently (2: 10, 11, 14, 15, and 16) the word בָּגַד (bāḡaḏ) in order to underline such a violation of the marriage covenant relationships. The meaning of the word in this context (*act* or *deal treacherously, faithlessly, deceitfully*, in the marriage covenant relation, in *Abridged BDB Lexicon*, p.93, in Bible Works for Windows, version 5.0.020w), clearly underlines the abuse of one's spouse through the unlawful breaking of the marriage covenant by the other spouse. The word is used in the same way in Jeremiah 3:8, 11, 20 as an act of Israel's spiritual adultery. Thus, God's negative attitude is not toward divorce in general but toward the act of the unlawful breaking of the marriage covenant by his people and as such abusing of their spouses. (Also D. Instone-Brewer, *Divorce and Remarriage in the Bible*, 14, 15; Hugenberger, *Marriage as a Covenant*, 82, 83.)

98. Also D. Instone-Brewer, *Divorce and Remarriage in the Bible*, 1.

tures were made in the image of God and this was particularly related to human sexuality, ἄρσεν καὶ θῆλυ ἐποίησεν αὐτούς (Gen 1:27, LXX).[99] The change of the personal pronouns referring to God and man from singular to plural in vv 26[100] and 27[101] emphasizes the unity in the plurality for both the divine being and human creatures.[102] God, on the one hand, is presented as the unique being experiencing the freedom of varieties in his oneness. Man, on the other hand, reflects that uniqueness in the varieties of the two genders, male and female (1:27), who are going to be united in "one flesh" (2:24).[103] Thus, the second narration of the creation account of humankind goes into detail to present the creation of woman from man's body and their coming together in "one flesh" through the act of marriage (2:21–24).

Man's loneliness and need of a partner was not provided through animals but through someone special (2:20). The Creator God made another human being, the woman from the body of Adam (2:21). The result of God's action was a climactic one for the whole of creation, the

---

99. See also LeRoy S. Capper, "The *Imago Dei* and Its Implications for Order in the Church," Πρεσβυτέριον: *A Journal of The Eldership* 11/1 (1985) 21–33. In this respect Barth says: "Men are simply male and female. Whatever else they may be, it is only in this differentiation and relationship. This is the particular dignity ascribed to the sex relationship. . . . But as the only real principle of differentiation and relationship, as the original form not only of man's confrontation of God but also of all intercourse between man and man, it is the true humanum and therefore the true creaturely image of God. Man can and will always be man before God and among his fellows only as he is man in relationship to woman and woman in relationship to man." (Karl Barth, *Church Dogmatics*, vol. III, *The Doctrine of Creation*, part 1 [Edinburgh: T. & T. Clark, 1958] 186). See also W. Brueggemann, *Genesis*, 33, who clarifies that sexuality is not a characteristic of the divine being but it is ordained by God for the goodness of the creation. Sexuality in this verse does not relate to procreation, which is a mark shared by both humans and animals (1:22, 28). (See also Phyllis Trible, *God and the Rhetoric of Sexuality* [Philadelphia: Fortress, 1978] 12–23.) To be sure there are some other suggestions (See Henri Blocher, *In the Beginning: The Opening Chapters of Genesis*, trans. David G. Preston [Downers Grove, IL: InterVarsity, 1984] 80–82.) for the interpretation of the image of God in man but because of the limitations in space and subject-matter, I will not discuss them.

100. καὶ εἶπεν ὁ θεός ποιήσωμεν ἄνθρωπον . . . cf. καὶ ἀρχέτωσαν . . . (LXX)

101. ἐποίησεν ὁ θεὸς τὸν ἄνθρωπον cf. ἄρσεν καὶ θῆλυ ἐποίησεν αὐτούς. (LXX)

102. Cf. Gen 5:1. See also P. Trible, *God and the Rhetoric of Sexuality*, 21; John H. Sailhamer, "Genesis," in *Expositor's Bible Commentary: Old Testament*, ed. Frank E. Gaebelein (Grand Rapids, MI: Zondervan, 1999), Zondervan Reference Software [32-bit edition], Version 2.7.; K. Barth, *Church Dogmatics*, vol.III, *The Doctrine of Creation*, part 1, 195–196.

103. LXX, ἔσονται οἱ δύο εἰς σάρκα μίαν; WTT, לְבָשָׂר אֶחָד.

appearance of the genders, i.e. for the first time the man (הָאָדָם) referred to himself as man (אִישׁ) and he called his partner woman (אִשָּׁה) (2:23).[104] The uniqueness of this variety coming from the unity is underlined by Adam's words, "Then the man (הָאָדָם) said, 'This at last is bone of my bones and flesh of my flesh; this one shall be called Woman (אִשָּׁה), for out of Man (אִישׁ) this one was taken'" (Gen 2:23, NRS). The climax is completed when the variety, the male and the female, come back to their original unity through the "one flesh" relationship in the marriage (2:24).[105]

The phrase לְבָשָׂר אֶחָד underlines the threefold character of the husband–wife relationship, i.e. social, domestic, and physical.[106] The husband is no more associated with his parents but with his wife, who is now the object of his allegiance and with whom he is bound physically through sexual intercourse.[107] That relationship is reached through the two steps of leaving one's parents (2:24a) and cleaving to one's spouse (2:24b).[108] Considering this process and the nature of that relationship one may argue that the narrator has depicted the picture of a covenant relation-

---

104. See also P. Trible, *God and the Rhetoric of Sexuality*, 98; Sarna, *Genesis*, 23; Theodore W. Jennings, "Theological Perspectives on Sexuality," *JPC* 33 (1979): 3–6.

105. See also Trible, *God and the Rhetoric of Sexuality*, 94–105; Sarna, *Genesis*, 23; K. Barth, *Church Dogmatics*, vol.III, *The Doctrine of Creation*, part 1, 304–6. Contra Gunkel who argues that the text here does not refer to marriage but to sexual attraction of the man to the woman which resolves in an act of procreating the rest of the human kind. (See Hermann Gunkel, *Genesis*, trans. Mark E. Biddle [Macon: Mercer University Press, 1997] 13)

106. See also H. Blocher, *In the Beginning*, 106; H. C. Leupold, *Exposition of Genesis*, vol.1 (Grand Rapids, MI: Baker, 1942), 137; Steve Zeisler, *What Is Marriage?* [online], Available at http://www.pbc.org/dp/zeisler/4556.html, Accessed on 19 November 2000; Contra Laney, (J. C. Laney, *No Divorce and No Remarriage*, 17, 19 and W. A. Heth, *Divorce, but No Remarriage*, 76, 77) who argue for different meanings of "one flesh" which nevertheless read too much into the phrase without considering its context (2:24). (See also J. M. Sprinkle, *Old Testament Perspectives on Divorce and Remarriage*, footnote 4. Electronic edition by Galaxie Software.)

107. See also S. Bacchiocchi, *The Marriage Covenant* [online].

108. "Therefore a man leaves his father and his mother and cleaves to his wife, and they become one flesh." (Gen 2:24, RSV) This process might be observed even in a physical way in the Erēbu Marriages illustrated in some Nuzi tablets where the husband is depicted as going to live with his wife in her father's domain for unlimited time. However, this has not been the normal ANE practice. (Cyrus H. Gordon, "Erēbu Marriage," in *Studies on the Civilization and Culture of Nuzi and the Hurrians*, eds. M. A. Morrison and D. I. Owen [Winona Lake, IN: Eisenbrauns, 1981] 155–60.)

ship.¹⁰⁹ On the one hand, the process of abandoning (יַעֲזָב־אִישׁ)¹¹⁰ one's former relationships in order to establish a new one and cleaving (וְדָבַק)¹¹¹ to the new partner is covenant language, used to express the covenant relationship between Yahweh and Israel.¹¹² On the other hand, the threefold nature of marriage is reflected in Exod 21:10 in the form of three specific stipulations, food, clothing, and love (conjugal rights), which establish the ground for a marital covenant relationship as based on spouses' obligations to each other.¹¹³

109. See also Mal 2:14; Prov 2:17; Bacchiocchi, *The Marriage Covenant* [online]; W. Brueggemann, *Genesis*, 47; W. J. Dumbrell, *Covenant and Creation*, 36; K. A. Mathews, *Genesis 1–11:26*. The New American Commentary, 222; J. M. Sprinkle, *Old Testament Perspectives on Divorce and Remarriage*. Electronic edition by Galaxie Software; J. E. Adams, *Marriage Divorce and Remarriage in the Bible*, 16, 17.

110. The notion of leaving, abandoning one's relationships for the purpose of establishing a new one might not be directly related to the covenant between Israel and God but it echoes the commandments of God that the people of Israel should have a covenant only with him and with no other gods. (Exod 23:32; 34:15; Deut 31:16; 31:20; Josh 23:16; 2 Kgs 17:35, 38; Jer 11:10; 22:9) See also G. J. Wenham, *Genesis 1–15*, 352.

111. The notion of cleaving expresses a covenant relationship of Israel to God. See Deut 4:4; 10:20; 11:22; 13:4; 30:20; Josh 23:8; 1 Kgs 11:2. See also Sarna, *Genesis*, 23; Bacchiocchi, *The Marriage Covenant* [online]; Wallis, "Dābhaq," in TDOT, 80–84; G. J. Wenham, *Genesis 1–15*, 352.

112. The clearest example for the covenant relationship between Yahweh and Israel is found in Exod 19–24. The Sinai covenant followed the general structure of the treaty between the Hittite king and his vassal (cf. *Akkadian-Hittite Treaty*, ed. Daniel Bellissimo [online], Available at http://ccat.sas.upenn.edu/~humm/Topics/Contracts/treato1.html, Accessed on 26 November 2000). Its main characteristics were the friendship and mutual faithfulness between the two partners based on keeping specific stipulations (cf. Exod 20:3–17). The main stipulation pointed to the break with other relationships and the establishment of the new one through the means of the covenant (Exod 20:2–6 cf. Exod 23:22–25). Keeping the covenant resolved into blessings and its breaking into curses (cf. Deut 28). The legitimacy of the covenant was established by the presence of witnesses (cf. Exod 24:4 or Exod 24:4–8). (See also E. A. Martens, *God's Design*, 66–75; W. J. Dumbrell, *Covenant and Creation*, 94–99; Mathews, *Genesis 1–11:26*, The New American Commentary, 222, 223.)

113. The law offered in Exod 21:10 relates to the provision of the wife by the husband of three things "food, clothing, and marital rights (conjugal rights)" (NRS, NAS). This law has served to establish the three most basic stipulations of the Jewish marriage covenants in the Jewish Bible (Ps 132; Hos 2:3–13; Ezek 16:1–13), the Mishnah, and in latter Judaism as found in the marriage contracts in the Geniza collection. (See *The Mishnah: Ketubot* 5:1–9, A New Translation by Jacob Neusner [New Haven: Yale University Press, 1988] 387–90; Jewish Marriage Contracts in *The Princeton Geniza Project* [online], Available at http://www.princeton.edu/~geniza/, Accessed on 19 November 2000, See also E. M. Yamauchi, *Cultural Aspects of Marriage in the Ancient World*, 245, 246). The third obliga-

If the nature of marriage is perceived as a covenant relationship between husband and wife, then two conclusions can be drawn on the basis of understanding the function of covenants during the OT times.[114] First, the marriage covenant establishes a permanent relationship between the two spouses.[115] Second, the marriage covenant is weakened through the human sinful nature and may suffer dissolution if the stipulations are not fulfilled and, thus, allegiance and faithfulness have not been given to one's partner.[116] The appropriateness of these two claims might be seen in

---

tion of the man and the woman to give each other and nobody else his/her love (conjugal rights) has been confirmed by a death penalty (Lev 20:10; See also *Hammurabi's Code of Laws*, #129, #130, trans. L. W. King [online], Available at http://www.fordham.edu/halsall/ancient/hamcode.html#text, Accessed on 26 November 2000) or divorce (as some prophetic texts suggest in regard to the actual practice, Hos 2:2 [MT, v4]; Jer 3:8; See also R. F. Collins, *Sexual Ethics and the New Testament: Behavior and Belief*, 2, 3) in a case of adultery. Thus, the importance of sexual fidelity of both husband and wife for sustaining the marriage covenant has been well established. Even in the light of a more relaxed attitude toward polygamy (Gen 4:19, 23; Deut 21:15–17) although in some cases clearly forbidden (Lev 18:17; 20:14; Deut 17:17, Lev 18:18 cf. 11 QTemple 57:17–19; 66:15–17, *The Dead Sea Scrolls Translated: 11QTemple*, trans. Florentino Garcia Martinez [Netherlands: Copyright Bruce and Kenneth Zuckerman, 1992], In *Dead See Scrolls Electronic Reference Library*, v 5.3 [Provo, Utah: Brigam Young University; Leiden: Brill, 1999].), or higher concern of the property rights in marriage on the side of the man in Semitic legal systems (Lev 18:20, See also E. Neufeld, *Ancient Hebrew Marriage Laws*, 163.) husband's marital fidelity has not been disregarded as some argue (D. Instone-Brewer, *Three Weddings and a Divorce: God's Covenant with Israel, Judah and the Church* [online], Neufeld, *Ancient Hebrew Marriage Laws*, 163) but has been clearly affirmed (1 Sam 2:22; Job 3 1:1; Hos 4:14; and especially Proverbs 5, See also Hugenberger, *Marriage as a Covenant*, 313–38).

114. The function of the covenant might be described as a permanent relationship between two parties which nevertheless might be broken if one of the parties does not follow the basic covenant requirements. (Lev 24:8; Num 18:19; 1 Chr 16:15; 2 Chr 13:5; 21:7; Ps 89:28; 105:8; 111:9; Isa 55:3; 61:8; Sir 45:24; Lev 26:44; Jer 31:32; Ezek 17:16, 18, 19; Zec 11:10; Prayer of Azariah 1:11; See also E. A. Martens, *God's Design*, 73; W. J. Dumbrell, *Covenant and Creation*, 96, 99.)

115. This statement is strongly confirmed by the nature of the Image of God in man as referring to human sexuality.

116. This claim does not assert that with the termination of the marriage covenant the image of God in man is destroyed. On the contrary, this statement implies that since the termination of the marriage covenant is always a result of a sinful action of one of the spouses, it does not obliterate the image of God in man but recognizes the effect of sin on the marriage covenant, and eliminates sin from the relationship by dissolving the covenant. Hence, keeping the covenant under the conditions of serious abuse of the convenantal rights of one of the spouses is what may disrupt God's image in man. Official abolishment of the marriage covenant due to the serious violation of one's marital rights

the marriage covenantal relationship between God and Israel expressed through the Israelite prophets. Even though God was entirely faithful to his people Israel fulfilling all the stipulations of their covenant relationship Israel did not respond in the same way being under the influence of sin and broke the marriage covenant.[117] Therefore, I would argue that these two assertions derived from the creation account of man and woman establish the proper grounds for understanding any marriage, divorce, and remarriage text in the OT in general and for reading Deut 24:1-4 in particular.

The passage of Deut 24:1-4 is part of the book of Deuteronomy which restates the Mosaic covenant for the new generation of Israelites.[118] The passage appears in a section (12-26) which is an expansion and implementation of the basic stipulations of the covenant (5:6-21).[119] Hence, the passage should be interpreted within the framework of the covenant between Yahweh and Israel.[120] The nature of the passage is a conditional law, i.e. the law is applicable only when certain conditions exist.[121] Hence,

---

is what will save God's image since a freedom for subsequent remarriage is granted and a potential for new "one flesh" relationship in harmony and peace is established. (See also Rudolf J. Ehrilich, "The Indissolubility of Marriage as a Theological Problem," *SJT* 23 [1970] 309-10.)

117. The prophets understood the covenant relations between Yahweh and Israel in terms of marriage covenant. God made a marriage covenant with Israel (Hos 2:15; Jer 2:2; Ezek 16:3) and according to its stipulations he provided her with clothes, food, and love (Ezek 16:1-14; Hos 2:3-13). However, Israel, now split into Israel and Judah, did not keep the marriage covenant but instead, gave her allegiance to the gods of the nations (Ezek 9:9; 16:15-26; Jer 3:8-10; 5:11; Hos 8:14) and for this reason Israel was given the bill of divorce (Jer 3:8) and Judah was abandoned (Isa 54:6, 7). K. Barth argues in this respect that: "Numerous direct and indirect references remind us again and again that the covenant which is the prototype of human love and marriage is the covenant which in its historical reality was broken by Israel; the covenant in which, as is re-echoed even in the New Testament, Israel, Judah, and Jerusalem showed themselves to be 'an evil and adulterous generation,' a nation which could only ignore, despise and ridicule the grace of God addressed to it" (Barth, *Church Dogmatics*, III: *The Doctrine of Creation*, part 1, 316). See also D. Instone-Brewer, *Three Weddings and a Divorce: God's Covenant with Israel, Judah and the Church* [online]; W. J. Dumbrell, *Covenant and Creation*, 99.

118. See also Terence E. Fretheim, *The Pentateuch* (Nashville: Abingdon, 1996) 155.

119. J. C. Laney, *Deuteronomy 24:1-4 and the Issue of Divorce*. Electronic edition by Galaxie Software; E. S. Kalland, "Deuteronomy," in *Expositor's Bible Commentary: Old Testament*, Zondervan Reference Software; T. E. Fretheim, *The Pentateuch*, 158.

120. E. S. Kalland, "Deuteronomy," in *Expositor's Bible Commentary: Old Testament*, Zondervan Reference Software.

121. See also B. W. Powers, *Marriage and Divorce*, 156.

both the conditions and the law are important. Thus, since the structure of the passage is a conditional clause with protasis and apodosis, they should both be analyzed and considered as significant for the original reader.

There is general agreement among the present scholarship that the protasis of the conditional clause (Deut 24:1-4) expends until the end of v3 and the apodosis is expressed in v4.[122] Hence, the protasis is understood as expressing the conditions of the law offered through the apodosis in v4. The latter includes the consequences if the law is not kept. The analysis of the protasis shows that it presents five different conditions and four of them are placed in parallel for both the first and the second husbands.

The first condition states the act of marriage or remarriage ("When a man takes a wife and marries her," v1 NAS cf. "and she leaves his house and goes and becomes another man's *wife*," v2 NAS). It determines that a legal marital union is in view. In both cases, the first and the second marriage, a marriage covenant relationship is established and confirmed with a marriage contract between the husband and the wife.[123] The sec-

---

122. See also J. M. Sprinkle, *Old Testament Perspectives on Divorce and Remarriage*. Electronic edition by Galaxie Software; *What Does the Bible Teach: The Divine Permission* [online]. J. C. Laney, *Deuteronomy 24:1-4 and the Issue of Divorce*. Electronic edition by Galaxie Software; Gundry, *Mark*, 539; E. S. Kalland, "Deuteronomy," in *Expositor's Bible Commentary: Old Testament*, Zondervan Reference Software; S. R. Driver, *Deuteronomy*, 269; J. H. Sailhamer, *The Pentateuch as Narrative*, 465.

123. Marriage contracts were part of Israelite legislation (See Jewish-Aramaic marriage and divorce contracts from Elephantine: *Aramaic Papyri from Elephantine*, trans. H. L. Ginsberg [online], Available at http://ccat.sas.upenn.edu/~humm/Topics/Contracts/marrio1.html#M1Mo, Accessed on 26 November 2000). They were important for formalising the marriage covenants. This claim is substantiated by the significance of the rules related to "bride price" and "dowry" which marriage contracts established (See Exod 22:15-16; Deut 22:28-29; Gen 24:53; 29:18-20 cf. *Marriage Contract of a Former Slave Girl Who is Subject to Paramoné*, 420 BC, trans. H. L. Ginsberg [online], Available at http://ccat.sas.upenn.edu/~humm/Topics/Contracts/marrio5.html, Accessed on 25 November 2000; See also J. M. Sprinkle, *Old Testament Perspectives on Divorce and Remarriage*. Electronic edition by Galaxie Software). See Tobit 7:13 (NRS) and Code of Hammurabi # 128 in which the word *riksātu* is translated by most of the scholars as "contract." (*Hammurabi's Code of Laws*, trans. L. W. King [online], Available at http://www.fordham.edu/halsall/ancient/hamcode.html#text, Accessed on 26 November 2000.) Marriage contracts were the usual practice for Greek as well as Roman cultures. Greeks have used marriage contracts as early as the fourth century BC. In the Roman society the earliest form of marriage contract (prior to the fifth century BC) may be associated with the legal form of transaction *manus* or "putting the wife 'in her husband's hand,' *in manu mariti*." (Susan Treggiari, "Marriage and Family in Roman Society," in *Marriage*

ond condition presents the ground for divorce or the reason for breaking the marriage covenant ("and it happens that she finds no favor in his eyes because he has found some indecency in her," v1, NAS cf. "and if the latter husband turns against her," v3 NAS). That condition determines that a particularly serious reason should exist in order to break the marriage covenant.[124] That reason is presented with the phrase עֶרְוַת דָּבָר, which cannot be defined exactly, but in the most general sense implies shameful behavior with sexual implications.[125] Hence, on such grounds the mar-

---

and Family in the Biblical World, ed. Ken M. Campbell [Downers Grove, IL: InterVarsity, 2003] 138, 137-39; D. Instone-Brewer, *Divorce and Remarriage in the Bible*, 233; E. M. Yamauchi, *Cultural Aspects of Marriage in the Ancient World*, 245, 246. See also *Marriage and Divorce Papyri of the Ancient Greek, Roman and Jewish World*, ed. D. Instone-Brewer [online], Available at http://www.tyndale.cam.ac.uk/brewer/MarriagePapyri/Index.htm, Accessed on 26 November 2000.)

124. B. W. Powers, *Marriage and Divorce*, 157.

125. Cf. Gen 9:22; Exod 20:26; Lev 18:6; Deut 23:15; Lam 1:8; Ezek 16:36; *The Mishnah*, Ketub. 7:6; See also *Whittaker's Revised BDB* and *TWOT Hebrew Lexicon in BibleWorks for Windows*. Version 4.0.026e (4000), 1998; J. M. Sprinkle, *Old Testament Perspectives on Divorce and Remarriage*. Electronic edition by Galaxie Software; D. E. Garland, *A Biblical View of Divorce*, 422; S. R. Driver, *Deuteronomy*, 270, 271. The inclusion of adultery in the suggested meaning might be more acceptable than its exclusion. Even though the punishment for adultery stipulated by the law was death (Lev 20:10; Deut 22:22) which is not in view in the present context (See also J. C. Laney, *Deuteronomy 24:1-4 and the Issue of Divorce*. Electronic edition by Galaxie Software; J. M. Sprinkle, *Old Testament Perspectives on Divorce and Remarriage*. Electronic edition by Galaxie Software) there are texts which suggest that in the actual practice the capital punishment was replaced with divorce (Hos 2:2 [MT, v4]; Jer 3:8, See also Raymond F. Collins, *Sexual Ethics and the New Testament: Behavior and Belief* [New York: A Herder and Herder Book, Crossroad, 2000] 2, 3). Furthermore, the debate between the schools of Hillel and Shammai about the exact meaning of the phrase עֶרְוַת דָּבָר in Deut 24:1 considered adultery as possible meaning. The school of Hillel interpreted the phrase to include many aspects of the wife's relationship with the husband, even the spoiling of his dish. (*The Mishnah Gittin* 9:10, Cf. Josephus, *The Antiquities of the Jews*, 4.8.23.253, Flavius Josephus, *The Works of Josephus* [computer file]: complete and unabridged/ trans. William Whiston — electronic ed. of the new updated ed. — Peabody: Hendrickson, 1996, c1987. [Oak Harbor, WA: Logos Research Systems, 1997]. The school of Shammai interpreted the phrase as "unchastity" or "adultery." (*The Mishnah*, *Gittin* 9:10; Cf. Philo, *The Special Laws* III.XIV.80, Philo, *The Special Laws*, [computer file]: complete and unabridged/ trans. William Whiston — electronic ed. of the new updated ed. — Oak Harbor, WA: Logos Research Systems, 1997.) This interpretation was maintained on the grounds that in Palestine during Roman times compulsory divorce was practiced instead of the death penalty stipulated by the law. (Halacha, 26, *Adultery - Sotah* [online], Available at http://www.torah.org/learning/halacha-overview/chapter26.html?print=1, Accessed on 18 October 2000; Also Hays, *The Moral Vision*, 354.) See also Rabinowithz (Jacob J. Rabinowitz, "The 'Great Sin' in Ancient Egyptian Marriage Contracts," *Journal of Near Eastern Studies* 18 [1959] 73.)

riage covenant could be broken and the marriage completely dissolved.¹²⁶ The third condition points to the legal procedure of divorce or the legal termination of the marriage contract ("and he writes her a certificate of divorce and puts *it* in her hand," v1 NAS cf. "and writes her a certificate of divorce and puts *it* in her hand," v3 NAS). After the grounds for divorce are established the latter proceeds by issuing a bill of divorce, a document through which the marriage contract was nullified and the marriage covenant broken.¹²⁷ The general content of this certificate pointed to the wife's detachment from the husband and her freedom to remarry anyone she wishes.¹²⁸ The fourth condition shows the end of the marriage covenant ("and sends her out from his house," v1 NAS cf. "and sends her out of his house," v3 NAS). After the divorce bill is issued and given to the woman she should not expect the stipulations from the marriage contract to be in force anymore, i.e. no more support from her former husband by way of food, clothing, and love.¹²⁹ The fifth condition refers to the end of marriage because of the death of the second husband ("or if the latter husband dies who took her to be his wife," v3 NAS).

It is only after all these conditions are fulfilled that the law could be applied, "then her former husband who sent her away is not allowed to take her again to be his wife, since she has been defiled," (v4 NAS). The reason for a prohibition of remarriage between the wife and her first husband is that she is defiled (הֻטַּמָּאָה). The exact meaning of that word is hard to establish but in the context of עֶרְוַת דָּבָר, v1 it should be associated with uncleanliness produced by the loose sexual behavior of the woman which was the ground for her first husband's divorce.¹³⁰ Hence, since the first

---

who argues that עֶרְוַת דָּבָר means adultery.

126. J. M. Sprinkle, *Old Testament Perspectives on Divorce and Remarriage*. Electronic edition by Galaxie Software.

127. Idem, *Old Testament Perspectives on Divorce and Remarriage*. Electronic edition by Galaxie Software; B. W. Powers, *Marriage and Divorce*, 160; J. E. Adams, *Marriage Divorce and Remarriage in the Bible*, 29, 30.

128. See Hos 2:2; *The Mishnah, Gittin* 9:3. See also B. W. Powers, *Marriage and Divorce*, 157; A. Cornes, *Divorce and Remarriage*, 133.

129. Cf. Exod 21:10, 11. See also J. E. Adams, *Marriage Divorce and Remarriage in the Bible*, 29.

130. Cf. Lev 15:18, 24; 18: 19, 20; 21:3. Uncleanness related to sexual issues is one of the meanings proposed by both *Whittaker's Revised BDB* and *TWOT Hebrew Lexicon in BibleWorks for Windows*. Version 4.0.026e (4000), 1998. Consideration of adultery as included into the suggested meaning might have grounds even in light of the law

husband legally broke his marriage covenant with the wife on the grounds of עֶרְוַת דָּבָר, he cannot marry her again if she is free from other marriages because he has already pronounced her unclean (הֻטַּמָּאָה) through the bill of divorce and she is still considered as such for him. Thus, in such a way the law was impelling the husband to consider the ground for divorce seriously before taking any legal steps for divorce.[131]

In a case where the law is not applied, there are consequences which are related to disruption of the covenant between Yahweh and Israel ("for that is an abomination before the LORD, and you shall not bring sin on the land which the LORD your God gives you as an inheritance," v4 NAS). Thus, not fulfilling this law brings sin on the promised land and, in such

---

stipulation of death punishment which is not in view in the present context (Lev 20:10, Deut 22:22; See also B. W. Powers, *Marriage and Divorce*, 159, 160; A. Cornes, *Divorce and Remarriage*, 135.) since some prophetic texts (Hos 2:2 [MT, v4]; Jer 3:8; See also R. F. Collins, *Sexual Ethics and the New Testament: Behavior and Belief*, 2, 3) suggest that in the actual practice the capital punishment was replaced with divorce. (See also Laney [J. C. Laney, *Deuteronomy 24:1–4 and the Issue of Divorce*. Electronic edition by Galaxie Software.] and H. Camping [Harold Camping, *What God Hath Joined Together* [online], Available at http://www.lmsusa.com/Scripts/Job1/H%20Camping%20items/What%20God%20Hath%20Joined.html, Accessed on 27 November 2000.] who argue that the word relates to adultery.) The other major views related to the meaning of הֻטַּמָּאָה in Deut 24:4 have been found unsatisfactory by the author due to their improper reading of its context. On the one hand, R. Yaron failed to consider the death of the second husband (Deut 24:3), which invalidates his view of the legislative attempt for protecting the second marriage. (R. Yaron, "The Restoration of Marriage," *JJS* 17 [1966] 1–11, quoted in Raymond Westbrook, "The Prohibition on Restoration of Marriage in Deuteronomy 24:1–4," in *Studies in Bible*, vol. XXXI, ed. Sara Japhet [Jerusalem: Magnes, 1986] 390) On the other hand, G. J. Wenham's view of incest between the wife and the former husband as being brother and sister (Lev 18, 20 cf. Gen 2:24) and R. Westbrook's view of attempted financial benefits by the first husband to profit from the wife's new financial status read too much additional data into the context of the word. (G. J. Wenham, "The Restoration of Marriage Reconsidered," *Journal of Jewish Studies* XXX/1 [Spring 1979]: 36–40, quoted in J. M. Sprinkle, *Old Testament Perspectives on Divorce and Remarriage*, footnote 4. Electronic edition by Galaxie Software; R. Westbrook, *The Prohibition on Restoration of Marriage in Deuteronomy 24:1–4*, pp. 387–405; See also J. M. Sprinkle, *Old Testament Perspectives on Divorce and Remarriage*, footnote 4. Electronic edition by Galaxie Software.)

131. See also *What Does the Bible Teach: The Divine Permission* [online]; H. W. Armstrong, *Marriage and Divorce* [online]; D. E. Garland, *A Biblical View of Divorce*, 419; E. S. Kalland, "Deuteronomy," in *Expositor's Bible Commentary: Old Testament*, Zondervan Reference Software; C. Wright, *Deuteronomy*, 255.

a way, Israel violates her covenant with Yahweh and brings curses upon herself.[132]

To conclude the exegetical analysis of Deut 24:1–4 I would argue that the passage presents the matter of marriage, divorce, and remarriage as firmly established upon the principles of the marriage covenant, a relationship originating in the creation account of the first couple. Hence, on the one hand, marriage is treated as a permanent covenant relationship, no easy divorce is allowed without grounds, divorce certificate, and nullification of the marriage contract.[133] On the other hand, when serious grounds for divorce exist the marriage covenant could be broken, the divorce can be obtained, and legalized through the proper documentation, i.e. the bill of divorce.[134] This nature of the marriage covenant relationship may be closely observed in the relationship between Yahweh and Israel depicted in the prophetic writings.

The later prophets, Hosea, Jeremiah, Ezekiel, and Isaiah, presented the relationship between Yahweh and his people using the marriage metaphor but exhausted its literary limitations by tackling its different conceptual dimensions and by treating the issues related to the relationship between the two parties as a real covenant marriage. Developed against the ANE background concept of marriage between god as husband and the personified city as wife,[135] the marriage covenant between Yahweh and his nation has found a consistent presentation in the writings of the prophets. With different emphases and individually shaped concerns, the prophetic writings underline three main dimensions of the relationship: the attitude of the husband and the wife toward the marriage covenant, its consequences, and the future of the relationship.

First, the attitude of the husband Yahweh toward his wife the nation of Israel and Judah had been according to the stipulations of the marriage

---

132. Deut 29:1–29.

133. See also G. E. Wright, H. H. Shires and P. Parker, *The Book of Deuteronomy*, 2:473–74; D. Instone-Brewer, *Biblical Divorce and Remarriage: The Jewish Background to the New Testament Teaching on Divorce*, ch.2 [online].

134. See also J. M. Sprinkle, *Old Testament Perspectives on Divorce and Remarriage*. Electronic edition by Galaxie Software; D. Instone-Brewer, *Three Weddings and a Divorce: God's Covenant with Israel, Judah and the Church* [online].

135. For multiple examples see Julie Galambush, *Jerusalem in the Book of Ezekiel: The City as Yahweh's Wife*, Society for Biblical Literature Dissertation Series 130 (Atlanta: Scholars, 1992), 20–22, quoted in Instone-Brewer, *Divorce and Remarriage in the Bible*, 35.

covenant. God, as a faithful husband, had acted with love and faithfulness toward his wife, his nation, supplying her with the necessary material provisions for an abundant marriage life (Hos 2:8a, b, MT v10). However, the attitude of the wife had been totally against the proper functioning of the marriage covenant, failing to fulfill its stipulations. Israel had been unfaithful and living in continuous adultery with other gods (Hos 1:2; 2:2). She had received the provisions of the husband but did not act according to the marriage covenant stipulations[136] and instead of looking after her husband's supplies for their mutual benefit, she used them as offerings to other gods (Hos 2:8c).[137] While Hosea depicts the picture of the unfaithful wife referring only to Israel, Jeremiah goes further to include Judah due to historical developments. The attitude of Judah expressed in her actions toward the marriage covenant with Yahweh had become even worse than that of Israel. She had acted unfaithfully, committing adultery with other gods (Jer 2:27-28; 5:7) and abandoning her covenantal responsibilities, she had forsaken her husband (Jer 2:32-37).[138] Ezekiel also presents the failure of Judah to fulfill the marriage covenant stipulations toward her husband (Ezek 16:16-19). In contrast to Judah's attitude and actions, Yahweh had not only fulfilled them according to the law of Exod 21:10 but also exceeded abundantly the usual requirements (Ezek 16:9-12[139]).[140] Isaiah also agrees with the understanding of the wife's failure to be faithful to her husband (Isa 1:21).[141]

Second, the consequences of the stand and actions of both Yahweh and his people have been presented as the breakdown of the marriage covenant, the state of divorce for Israel and separation of Judah, and the status of divorcee of both the husband and the wife. Hosea shows that due to Israel's faithlessness to the marriage covenant, Yahweh is forced

---

136. The usual expectations from the wife were related to household management for family's sake, and making meals and clothes. (Instone-Brewer, *Divorce and Remarriage in the Bible*, 38.)

137. D. Instone-Brewer, *Divorce and Remarriage in the Bible*, 38.

138. Ibid., 40.

139. "Then I bathed you with water and washed off the blood from you, and anointed you with oil. I clothed you with embroidered cloth and with sandals of fine leather; I bound you in fine linen and covered you with rich fabric. I adorned you with ornaments: I put bracelets on your arms, a chain on your neck, a ring on your nose, earrings in your ears, and a beautiful crown upon your head." (NRS)

140. D. Instone-Brewer, *Divorce and Remarriage in the Bible*, 45, 46.

141. Ibid., 48.

to divorce her and give her the divorce certificate (Hos 2:2, MT v4). The divorce status of Israel is further confirmed by her reference to Yahweh as "the first husband," (Hos 2:7, MT v9) and the extinguishing of his supplies to her (Hos 2:3, 5, 9).[142] Jeremiah substantiates Israel's position of divorcee and clearly states that she has obtained the divorce certificate, (Jer 3:8). He has depicted the way Israel has obtained this position in order to show to Judah that she is following in her steps. Judah is threatened with divorce (Jer 3:1–20).[143] Ezekiel goes further to describe the exact stipulations which Judah failed to fulfill and deserved to be divorced. She has not devoted herself to giving reciprocal support to her husband according to the requirements expressed in Exod 21:10 (Ezek 16:16–19). Instead, she was unfaithful to her husband becoming a harlot (Ezek 16:15), and she committed deliberate childlessness (Ezek 16:20–21[144]).[145] Isaiah completes the argument with a clear presentation of the fact that Judah[146] had been abandoned by Yahweh in an action which might be treated as divorce[147] but not yet legalized since she had not been given the certificate of divorce (Isa 50:1; 54:4–7).[148]

142. Ibid., 37, 38.

143. Ibid., 40, 41.

144. Within the marital context of the chapter these verses are best understood as a refusal to raise heirs. (See M. Yebam. 6.6, Also D. Instone-Brewer, *Divorce and Remarriage in the Bible*, 46).

145. D. Instone-Brewer, *Divorce and Remarriage in the Bible*, 45, 46, 47.

146. The object of Lord's words in Isa 50:1 and the surrounding context should be identified as Judah due to the author's interchangeable use of the terms "Israel," "Jacob," "Judah," "Jerusalem," and "Zion" (e.g. Isa 48:1; 59:20) and his preoccupation with the exiles in Babylon (e.g. 40:3–4; 41:25–27; 44:28; 45:1; 43:14; 48:20) after chapter 40. (Also D. Instone-Brewer, *Divorce and Remarriage in the Bible*, 48.)

147. The word שלח ("put away," "send away") used in Isa 50:1 within a context of marital breakdown might be identified as a technical term for divorce. (Also Richard Whitaker, ed. "Whitaker's Revised BDB Hebrew-English Lexicon," in *Bible Works*, version 5.0.020w [Bigfork: Hermeneutika Computer Bible Research Software, L.L.C, 2001] 1018 and D. Instone-Brewer, *Divorce and Remarriage in the Bible*, 50)

148. The author enters into such a detailed analysis of the breakdown of the relationship between Yahweh and Judah in order to make a case that since Judah has not received a certificate of divorce as Israel did (Hos 2:2), even though abandoned, she has not been divorced. This argument has been shaped by his desire to encourage those in exile in Babylon who, being aware of Israel's destiny, viewed themselves in the same light as being completely abandoned by God. The goal of the author was reached in presenting the condition of God's people as temporal and their upcoming reconciliation completely secure (Isa 54:4–7; 62:4, 5). (Also D. Instone-Brewer, *Divorce and Remarriage in the Bible*, 50, 51).

Third, the future of the relationship has been viewed as remarriage, depicted in such bright terms as to compare to a new marriage between Yahweh and his bride. The bride has been presented in a new light as the united nation of Israel and Judah, who have changed their previous attitude toward the marriage covenant. Hosea provides the solution for Israel through her unification with the nation of Judah who, according to him, has remained faithful to God (Hos 11:12).[149] The image of the bride is presented in a new positive light in order to underline her different stand and attitude toward the covenant of marriage to which she is led by Yahweh (Hos 2:14–23). Her devotion is to her husband only (Hos 2:17) in "... righteousness and justice, in love and compassion ..., in faithfulness ...," and acknowledgement of the Lord (Hos 2:19, 20, NIV). It is Yahweh who has made this total change possible (Hos 2:14, 23). Jeremiah follows Hosea's understanding of establishing a new covenant relationship between Yahweh and his new bride, the nation consisting of Israel and Judah (Jer 31:31–34).[150] Jeremiah, however, tackles the matter differently, evaluating the condition of Judah as worse then Israel (Jer 3:11) and dealing with the possibility for remarriage in light of the law in Deuteronomy 24:1–4, (Jer 3:1).[151] Thus, he concludes that the remarriage is possible without breaking the law due to the complete renewal of the bride ("the virgin Israel," Jer 31:3–5) through her repentance (Jer 31:19) and God's mercy and forgiveness (Jer 31:20). Ezekiel (Ezek 16:60–62) and Isaiah (Isa 62:4, 5) also support Hosea's vision for the new marriage covenant.[152]

The later prophets have presented the present stage of the covenant relationship between Yahweh and his people as suffering a severe breakdown. The guilt for this has been clearly associated with the wife's attitude and actions toward the marriage covenant, the fulfillment of its stipulations, and the preservation of its oaths.[153] Malachi, tackling the issue of marriage covenant on a human level, reflects this referring it indirectly to the covenant relationship between Yahweh and Judah. The prophet deals with the issue of breaking the marriage covenant on illegitimate grounds. The argument is gradually built to present the treacherous attitude of

---

149. D. Instone-Brewer, *Divorce and Remarriage in the Bible*, 52.
150. Ibid., 42.
151. Ibid., 41, 42.
152. Ibid., 51, 52.
153. Ibid., 53, 54.

God's people toward their covenant with Yahweh[154] and finds its climax in the passage 2:10–16 where the word בגד is repeated 5 times. The latter underlines the breakdown of the covenant relationship due to such a treacherous, faithless, deceitful attitude and actions toward the covenant partner by one of the parties.[155] The culmination is reached with Yahweh's warning toward those people, "If one hates and divorces [that is, if one divorces merely on the ground of aversion][156], says Yahweh, God of Israel, he covers his garment with violence [i.e. such a man visibly defiles himself with violence], says Yahweh of hosts. Therefore, take heed to yourselves and do not be faithless [against your wife]," (Mal 2:16).[157] The words of

---

154. Malachi shows Judas' failure to keep their covenant with Yahweh due to their sinful actions and behavior (1:6–14; 2:5; 2:10–16; 3:5, 8–10) and despite of his love (Mal 1:2). (Also D. Instone-Brewer, *Divorce and Remarriage in the Bible*, 54.)

155. The word בגד is used in this passage (2:10–16) to depict covenant breakdown by the actions of one of the parties. This meaning of the word is paralleled in several places in the OT related to the break of the Sinai covenant (1 Sam 14:33; Ps 119:158), betrothal covenant (Exod 21:8), marriage covenant (Jer 3:20; 9:2). (Also D. Instone-Brewer, *Divorce and Remarriage in the Bible*, 57.)

156. The subject of the verb hate (שָׂנֵא) may not be Yahweh due to the lack of grammatical justification in the presence of third person verb and in the clear reference to the divorcing husband in the subsequently appearing word "he covers" (וְכִסָּה). The subject should be identified as an indefinite pronoun "one" or more precisely in Malachi's context (2:10–16) as the divorcing husband in the light of association of hatred with the husband's attitude toward his wife in the context of marriage (Gen 29:31; Deut 21:15–17; 22:13, 16; 24:3; Judg 15:2; Prov 30:23; and Isa 60:15) and the relationship between the attitude of hatred and the usual divorce formula in the context of divorce "if H . . . says 'I hate my wife W, she shall not be my wife'" (Kraeling 7 lines 21–22 [= PY B3.8]). Hence, the translation of the whole phrase כִּי־שָׂנֵא שַׁלַּח (2:16a) as "if one hates and divorces" should be understood as divorce on illegal or inadequate grounds without justification and might be paraphrased as "if one divorces merely on the ground of aversion." This is further supported by the most probable association of the word "his garments" (עַל־לְבוּשׁוֹ) with either one's covenantal partner, his wife (Deut 22:30 [23:1], Ruth 3:9, Ezek 16:8), or a metaphorical expression of one's inner state (Jer 2:34; Ps 73:6; Ps 109:18) which both lead to express in the phrase חָמָס עַל־לְבוּשׁוֹ וְכִסָּה (he covers his garment with violence) the sinful act of unjustifiable marriage covenant breakdown by the husband. (Hugenberger, *Marriage as a Covenant*, 67–76. Also D. Instone-Brewer, *Divorce and Remarriage in the Bible*, 56, 57.)

157. This translation of Mal 2:16 is offered by Hugenberger who has done the most extensive up to date study of the history of the interpretation of this verse. Analyzing its different grammatical, syntactical, and semantic issues, he has reached this variant of the text which he believes is the most faithful presentation of its meaning without emendation of the MT and is best incorporated in the context of Mal 2:10–16. (Hugenberger, *Marriage as a Covenant*, 67, 76; Also John T. Strong, review of *Marriage as a Covenant: A Study of Biblical Law and Ethics Governing Marriage Developed from the Perspective*

the prophet show that the husband who divorces his wife on illegitimate, illegal grounds, mistreats and abuses her, acting with violence against her. This act of faithlessness against the covenant partner and the covenant itself is condemned by Yahweh.[158]

In conclusion, the predominant OT view of marriage is that of a covenant relationship (Mal 2:10-16; Prov 2:17).[159] The dynamics of this relationship may be observed even in the creation account of the first marriage which establishes the foundations of the marriage institution (Gen 2:24).[160] The nature of the marriage covenant is defined as twofold, permanent and dissoluble, in light of the general understanding of the covenant during OT times and marriage covenantal and contractual agreements in the ANE.[161] The marriage covenant relationship is characterised by the mutual obligation of the spouses for preserving it through keeping its particular stipulations. Thus, even though the nature of the marriage covenant is viewed as twofold, perpetual and vulnerable to abuses, its preservation is emphatically depicted through the sanctions and penalties stipulated to the offender of the covenant. The permanent nature of the covenant relationship between the two parties is based on

---

of Malachi, by Gordon Paul Hugenberger, in *Catholic Biblical Quarterly* 57/3 [July 95]: 557.)

158. D. Instone-Brewer, *Divorce and Remarriage in the Bible*, 54-58.

159. Also Bacchiocchi, *The Marriage Covenant* [online]; W. Brueggemann, *Genesis*, 47; W. J. Dumbrell, *Covenant and Creation*, 36; K. A. Mathews, *Genesis 1-11:26*. The New American Commentary, 222; J. M. Sprinkle, *Old Testament Perspectives on Divorce and Remarriage*. Electronic edition by Galaxie Software; J. E. Adams, *Marriage Divorce and Remarriage in the Bible*, 16, 17.

160. It is depicted by the author of Genesis through defining the marital relationship with the phrase לְבָשָׂר אֶחָד, 2:24 (Also H. Blocher, *In the Beginning*, 106; H. C. Leupold, *Exposition of Genesis*, vol. 1, 137; S. Zeisler, *What Is Marriage?* [online]; J. M. Sprinkle, *Old Testament Perspectives on Divorce and Remarriage*, footnote 4. Electronic edition by Galaxie Software.) and using covenant terminology for its establishment (abandoning [וְיַעֲזָב־אִישׁ], [cf. Exod 23:32; 34:15; Deut 31:16; 31:20] of one's former relationships, i.e. with the father and the mother, in order to establish a new one, i.e. with the wife, and cleaving [וְדָבַק] to the new partner, [cf. Deut 4:4; 10:20; 11:22; 13:4; 30:20; Josh 23:8; 1 Kgs 11:2]). Also G. J. Wenham, *Genesis 1-15*, 352; Wallis, "Dābhaq," in TDOT 3:80-84; N. M. Sarna, *Genesis*, 23; S. Bacchiocchi, *The Marriage Covenant* [online].

161. Permanent: Lev 24:8; Num 18:19; 1 Chr 16:15; 2 Chr 13:5; 21:7; Ps 89:28; 105:8; 111:9; Isa 55:3; 61:8; Sir 45:24. Dissoluble: Lev 26:44; Jer 31:32; Ezek 17:16, 18, 19; Zec 11:10; Prayer of Azariah 1:11; Also E. A. Martens, *God's Design*, 73; W. J. Dumbrell, *Covenant and Creation*, 96, 99.

the mutual fulfillment of the covenant stipulations.¹⁶² Thus, attempts to break the covenant relationship without proper grounds are condemned and prohibited (Deut 22:13–19, 28–29; Mal 2:10–16).¹⁶³ The vulnerability of the marriage covenant may be defined as the failure of one of the spouses to fulfill his/her obligations neglecting the preservation of the covenant stipulations which constitutes legitimate grounds for divorce and covenant dissolution (Exod 21:10–11; Ezek 9:9; 16:15–26; Jer 3:8–10; 5:11; Hos 8:14).¹⁶⁴ Nevertheless, even this aspect of the marriage covenant, which is entirely determined by the sinful human nature, is controlled by the covenant endurance. Hence, when there are no serious

---

162. In Exod 21:10 three specific stipulations are mentioned: provision of food, clothing, and love (conjugal rights). (Also D. Instone-Brewer, *Three Weddings and a Divorce* [online]; E. M. Yamauchi, *Cultural Aspects of Marriage in the Ancient World*, 245, 246.) See Ps 132; Hos 2:3–13; Ezek 16:1–13; *Mishnah, Ketubot 5:1–9*; Jewish Marriage contracts in *The Princeton Geniza Project* [online], Available at http://www.princeton.edu/~geniza/, Accessed on 19 November 2000.

163. Also J. M. Sprinkle, *Old Testament Perspectives on Divorce and Remarriage*. Electronic edition by Galaxie Software; D. Instone-Brewer, Biblical Divorce and Remarriage, ch.2, 3 [online], Available at http://www.tyndale.cam.ac.uk/brewer/Academic/Chap_02.htm, Accessed on 26 November 2000; David Clyde Jones, "Malachi on Divorce," *Presbyterion* XV/1 (Spring 1989):16–22. The proper understanding of Deut 24:1–4 signifies no easy divorce without particular grounds (עֶרְוַת דָּבָר), divorce certificate and nullification of the marriage contract (סֵפֶר כְּרִיתֻת). Also G. E. Wright, H. H. Shires and P. Parker, *The Book of Deuteronomy*, 2:473–74; D. Instone-Brewer, *Biblical Divorce and Remarriage*, ch.2 [online].

164. With an understanding of the phrase עֶרְוַת דָּבָר as shameful behavior with sexual implications (cf. Gen 9:22; Exod 20:26; Lev 18:6; Deut 23:15; Lam 1:8; Ezek 16:36; *Mishnah, Ketub.* 7:6; Also *Whittaker's Revised BDB* and *TWOT Hebrew Lexicon in BibleWorks for Windows*. Version 4.0.026e [4000] 1998; J. M. Sprinkle, *Old Testament Perspectives on Divorce and Remarriage*. Electronic edition by Galaxie Software; *The Divine Permission* [online]; D. E. Garland, *A Biblical View of Divorce*, 422; S. R. Driver, *Deuteronomy*, 270, 271; D. Instone-Brewer, *Biblical Divorce and Remarriage: The Jewish Background to the New Testament Teaching on Divorce*, ch.2 [online]; idem, *Three Weddings and a Divorce* [online].) the text of Deut 24:1 is perceived as expressing such a covenant breakdown. Even a wife who could not initiate divorce according to Jewish Law (See Josephus, *Ant.* 15.7.10. 259; *Mishnah, Yebamot* 14.1.III L; Also Gundry, *Mark*, 543; C. L. Blomberg, *Marriage, Divorce, Remarriage, and Celibacy*. Electronic edition by Galaxie Software; Tracey R. Rich, ed. *Divorce: Inequality of the Sexes* [online], Available at http://www.jewfaq.org/divorce.htm, Accessed on 08 October 2000) was able to plead for such an act before the rabbinic court for unfulfillment of the covenant stipulations by the husband (*Mishnah, Ketub.*5.6; *Mishnah, Ketub.*77a; cf. Philo, *The Special Laws* III. XIV.82; *Hammurabi's Code of Laws*, #142, #143; Also D. Instone-Brewer, "Jewish Women Divorcing Their Husbands in Early Judaism: The Background to Papyrus Se'elim 13," *HTR* 92 [1999] 352–53; idem, *Biblical Divorce and Remarriage*, ch.2 [online]).

grounds for divorce but an attempt to manipulate the Law is made with a selfish purpose for divorce by one of the partners (basically man) then divorce is forbidden in order that the permanent nature of the marriage covenant be preserved (Deut 22:13-19, 28-29; Mal 2:10-16).[165] Further emphases on the permanency of the marriage covenant may be observed in the seriousness of divorce, the legitimacy of its grounds, and the vital importance of the proper documentation for the legal termination of the marriage covenant (obtaining the bill of divorce by the woman) which establishes the freedom for remarriage (Deut 24:1-4).[166] The most explicit OT example of the dynamics of the marriage covenant relationship is that between God and Israel.[167]

---

165. See also J. M. Sprinkle, *Old Testament Perspectives on Divorce and Remarriage*. Electronic edition by Galaxie Software; See also D. Instone-Brewer, *Biblical Divorce and Remarriage*, ch. 2, 3 [online]; D. C. Jones, *Malachi on Divorce*, 16–22.

166. Cf. *The Mishnah Gittin* 9:10; See also D. Instone-Brewer, *Biblical Divorce and Remarriage*, ch.2 [online].

167. God established his relationship with Israel as a marriage covenant between husband and wife (Hos 2:15; Jer 2:2; Ezek 16:3). According to the demands of the covenant God provided Israel with clothes, food, and love (Ezek 16:1-14; Hos 2:3-13). However since Israel, split into Israel and Judah, did not keep the stipulations of the covenant relationship giving her allegiance to other gods (Ezek 9:9; 16:15-26; Jer 3:8-10; 5:11; Hos 8:14), God broke his covenant with her, i.e. Israel was given the bill of divorce (Jer 3:8) and Judah was abandoned (Isa 54:6, 7). Also K. Barth, *Church Dogmatics*, vol.III, *The Doctrine of Creation*, part 1, 316; D. Instone-Brewer, *Three Weddings and a Divorce* [online]; W. J. Dumbrell, *Covenant and Creation*, 99.

three

The New Testament Passages

IT IS A GENERALLY ACCEPTED FACT THAT THE MOST RELEVANT NT passages that deal with the matters of divorce and remarriage are Mark 10:2–12; Matt 5:31, 32; 19:3–12; Luke 16:18; and 1 Cor 7:12–16. That the roots of these scriptures are firmly grounded in Jesus' tradition is a proposition established through defining the sources used by the evangelists by means of a comparative analysis of their texts. The format of this proposition should be best determined, in the light of the most widely accepted two-document hypothesis,[1] as Mark 10:2–12 being the source of Matt 19:3–12 and both texts plus Q being the sources for Matt 5:31–32 and Luke 16:18. First, Mark's sources[2] might be identified as the oral tradition,[3] tradition

---

1. This theory establishes Mark as the primary source for both Matthew and Luke who used it independently of each other. The latter two further used another source Q, and each of them used his own independent source, M (for Matthew) and L (for Luke). Also R. H. Stein, "Redaction Criticism (NT)," in *ABD* (Logos Library System); idem, "Synoptic Problem," in *Dictionary of Jesus and the Gospels*, 787–92; G. R. Osborne, "Redaction Criticism," in *Dictionary of Jesus and the Gospels*, 662–69; D. A. Koch, *Source Criticism (NT)*, (Logos Library System); Robert A. Guelich, *Mark 1–8:26* (Dallas: Word, 1989), xxxiii.

2. One should acknowledge the fact that it is often impossible and speculative to separate the sources from Mark's own words. Also Guelich, *Mark*, xxxv.

3. The oral tradition finds its roots in the words of Peter and Paul with whom Mark has been very closely connected. Mark has been recognized as Peter's ἑρμηνευτής by Papias (Eusebius Pamphilus, *The Church History of Eusebius*, 3.39.15; Also idem, *The Church History of Eusebius*, 2.15.1.) a testimony somehow confirmed by Peter himself (1 Peter 5:13), and his relations to Paul have been testified by both Luke and Paul. (Acts 12:25; 13:5, 13; 2 Tim 4:11; Col 4:10; Philemon 24). Also Ralph Martin, *Mark* (Grand Rapids: Zondervan, 1973), 51–61; John Wenham, *Redating Matthew, Mark and Luke* (Downers Grove, IL: InterVarsity, 1992), 173–82.

part of which is Q,[4] and written tradition.[5] Second, the numerous parallels between Mark 10:2-12 and Matt 19:3-12 establish the former as the source of the latter.[6] Third, the role of Mark 10:2-12 as a source could further be identified through distinguishing a close relationship between Luke 16:18 and Mark 10:11[7] and between Matt 5:31 and Mark 10:2-10.[8] Fourth, some parallels might be found between Matt 5:32 and Luke 16:18 which do not follow Mark 10:11, 12, and as such are associated with Q.[9] Fifth, Matt 5:32 and Luke 16:18 have some dissimilarities which suggest different sources or editorial moves.[10] Finally, 1 Cor 7:10-11[11] is closely related to Luke 16:18[12] and it still has some parallels with Mark

---

4. Some parallels between Mark, Matthew, and Luke (e.g. the Temptation, 1:12-13; the Beelzebul incident, 3:22-30) and Mark and John (e.g. Feeding of the five thousand and walking on the water, 6:34-52 cf. 8:1-9) show that Mark is using a tradition from which Q is an older witness.

5. This might be detected behind some passages as a collection of controversies (2:15-28); Kingdom parables (4:1-34); passion narrative (14:1-16:8) etc. Also Guelich, *Mark*, xxxiii-xxxv.

6. Mark 10:2 cf. Matt 19:3; Mark 10:4 cf. Matt 19:7; Mark 10:5 cf. Matt 19:8; Mark 10:6 cf. Matt 19:4; Mark 10:7 cf. Matt 19:5; Mark 10:8 cf. Matt 19:6; Mark 10:9 cf. Matt 19:6; Mark 10:11, 12 cf. Matt 19:9.

7. Cf. Luke's καὶ γαμῶν ἑτέραν μοιχεύει with Mark's καὶ γαμήσῃ ἄλλην μοιχᾶται. Also Davies and Allison, *The Gospel according to Saint Matthew*, 1:528.

8. Two elements establish that relationship. On the one hand, Matt 5:31 assumes a background discussion which appears in Matt19:3-8 and the later uses Mark 10:2-10. On the other hand, Matt 5:31 has a different introductory formula than the other antithesis (ἐρρέθη δέ [Matt 5:31] cf. ἠκούσατε ὅτι ἐρρέθη [Matt 5:21, 27, 33, 38, 43]) which suggests that it does not derive from the oral tradition but from the material used in Matt 19:7 and 9 which source is Mark 10:11. Also Donald A. Hagner, *Matthew 1-13* (Dallas: Word, 1993), 123.

9. Matt 5:32, ὁ ἀπολύων τὴν γυναῖκα αὐτοῦ = Luke 16:18, ὁ ἀπολύων τὴν γυναῖκα αὐτοῦ; Matt 5:32, ὃς ἐὰν ἀπολελυμένην γαμήσῃ μοιχᾶται = Luke 16:18, ὁ ἀπολελυμένην ἀπὸ ἀνδρὸς γαμῶν μοιχεύει. Also W. D. Davies and Dale C. Allison, Jr., *The Gospel according to Saint Matthew*, 1:527.

10. Luke 16:18 lacks Matthew's exception clause παρεκτὸς λόγου πορνείας and Matt 5:32 lacks Luke's καὶ γαμῶν ἑτέραν μοιχεύει and ἀπὸ ἀνδρὸς.

11. This passage plays a significant role in Paul's exposition of Jesus' teaching on divorce and remarriage presented in 1 Cor 7:12-16.

12. Also Joseph A. Fitzmyer, *Luke X-XXIV* (New York: Doubleday, 1985), 1120; G. F. Hawthorne, "Marriage and Divorce, Adultery and Incest," in *Dictionary of Paul and His Letters*, eds. Gerald F. Hawthorne and Ralph P. Martin (Leicester: InterVarsity, 1993), 598.

10:9 and Matt 19:6.¹³ The source and other historical-critical analyses will be balanced through consideration of each of the Synoptic gospels as a narrative,¹⁴ a complete unit which establishes the gospel's coherence and confirms the validity of the present literary form of the texts. Thus, each of the evangelists wrote a story about Jesus the Christ with different major characters¹⁵ and a plot.¹⁶ The narrative approach contributes as well to the analysis of 1 Cor 7:12–16, looking at it through the perspective of the unity of Paul's thought based on the story of Christ.¹⁷

---

13. 1 Cor 7:10 ἀνδρὸς μὴ χωρισθῆναι cf. Mark 10:9 ἄνθρωπος μὴ χωριζέτω and Matt 19:6 ἄνθρωπος μὴ χωριζέτω. Also Gundry, *Mark*, 533.

14. Mark Allen Powell, *What is Narrative Criticism*, 23.

15. The main characters of the stories of all three evangelists are basically the same, Jesus, the disciples, and Israel. Jesus, Messiah, the Son of God who came to bring the salvation history to its climax bringing salvation to Israel and the Gentiles (Matt 1:21; 20:28; 26:27–28; Mark 2:23; 3:16; 12:29; 15:32, 39; Luke 1:13–17, 30–35, 77; 3:6) is depicted as the main figure of the stories. The disciples are the ones who are following him and share his life and experiences (Matt 5:10–12; 9:15, 19; 12:30; 20:25–28; 26:38–40; Mark 1:16–20, 3:13–18, 4:10–12, 6:7–13; Luke 5:11, 28; 9:23; 14:27; 18:28) but they also are the ones who failed in all respects to be the true disciples, reaching even the point of denial (Matt 15:15–16; 16:5–12; 26:30–46, 56, 69–75; Mark 8:31–10:45; Luke 9:43–45; 18:31–34; 22:57). The Israel consists from the crowds and Jewish religious leaders. The former group is initially sympathetic toward Jesus (Matt 14:5; 15:31–35; 21:26; Mark 2:12; 12:12; Luke 8:40; 13:17) but later on joins the religious leaders in their battle against Jesus (Matt 26:47, 56; 27:15–26; Mark 3:6; 11:18; 14:43; 15:15; Luke 4:31–8:40; 18:36–39 cf. 19:39; 23:21). See also David R. Bauer, "The Major Characters of Matthew's Story," *Int* 46 (1992) 357–67; Jack Dean Kingsbury, "The Place, Structure, and Meaning of the Sermon on the Mount within Matthew," *Int* 41 (1987) 132, 133; Robert C. Tannehill, *The Narrative Unity of Luke-Acts* (Philadelphia: Fortress, 1991) 1:1; idem, "The Gospel of Mark as Narrative Christology" [online], Available at http://shemesh.scholar.emory.edu:6336/dynaweb/Semeia/Semeia_16/@Generic__BookView. Accessed on 23 October 1999.

16. The plot of the Evangelists' story in general is based on the conflict between Jewish leaders and Jesus which unfolds in a progressive manner (Matt 9:9–13; 14–17 cf. 12:15; 38–45; Mark 2:16, 18; 2:24 cf. 3:6; 11:18; 12:13; Luke 5:17, 21, 30, 33 cf. 11:53; 19:47) throughout the gospels. The conflict reaches its climax in the passion narrative where the religious authorities are presented as "dominating" over Jesus in his death on the cross (Matt 27:41–43; Mark 15:16–20, 29–32; Luke 23:13–25). The resolution of the plot is presented by God's vindication of Jesus through his resurrection (Matt 16:32; 27:64; 28:6; Mark 16:6; Luke 9:22; 24:5, 7). See also D. R. Bauer, *The Major Characters of Matthew's Story*, 357–367; Kingsbury, "The Place, Structure, and Meaning of the Sermon on the Mount within Matthew," 132, 133; Tannehill, *The Narrative Unity of Luke-Acts*; idem, "The Gospel of Mark as Narrative Christology" [online].

17. Ben Witherington III, *The Paul Quest: The Renewed Search for the Jew of Tarsus* (Downers Grove, IL: InterVarsity, 1998), 302.

This understanding of the discussed passages and the lines of their relationship will further establish the individuality and order of their presentation. The exegetical analyses will begin with discussions of Mark 10:2–12 and Matt 19:3–12, whose interrelations will be established within the individual analysis and summarised in a coherent conclusion. The analyses of the other synoptic passages will continue in the same manner, first exegeting Matt 5:31–32 and Luke 16:18 individually and then concluding with an integrating summary. Finally, the descriptive task will be completed with an analysis of 1 Cor 7:12–16 and a comprehensive conclusion.

MARK 10:2–12

In this chapter I will engage in a thorough analysis of Mark 10:2–12 using a method which combines both historical and narrative critical approaches to the biblical text.[18] Thus, on the one hand, I will conduct the analysis of Mark's divorce text considering also its usage by other NT authors, of whom the primary one is Matthew.[19] That restricting of the historical-critical analysis is based on two considerations. First, it is due to the very speculative nature of the process of identification of Mark's sources,[20] the tracing of their developments, establishing their forms, and determining Mark's redaction activity.[21] Second, it is in agreement

---

18. See also Norman R. Petersen, *Semeia 16* [online], Available at http://shemesh.scholar.emory.edu:6336/dynaweb/Semeia/Semeia_16/@Generic__BookView, Accessed on 23 October 1999.

19. See also Gundry, *Mark*, 22, 533; Robert M. Fowler, *Let the Reader Understand* (Minneapolis: Fortress, 1991), 237; Davies and Allison, *The Gospel according to Saint Matthew*, 1:527, 528; G. F. Hawthorne, *Marriage and Divorce, Adultery and Incest*, 598; Joseph A. Fitzmyer, "Matthean Divorce Texts and Some New Palestinian Evidence," *TS* 37 (1976) 200; Hagner, *Matthew 1–13*, 123; R. C. H. Lenski, *The Interpretation of St. Matthew's Gospel*, 230; D. Martyn Lloyd-Jones, *Studies in the Sermon on the Mount* (Grand Rapids: Eerdmans, 1993), 257; Douglas R. A. Hare, *Matthew* (Louisville: John Knox, 1993), 53; William Hendriksen, *Matthew* (Edinburgh: The Banner of Truth Trust, 1989), 304; John Nolland, *Luke 9:21—18:34* (Dallas: Word, 1993), 816, 819; Fitzmyer, *Luke X–XXIV*, 1120.

20. One may detect three possible sources, i.e. oral tradition, tradition part of which is Q, and written tradition. (See also Guelich, *Mark*, xxxiii–xxxv.) However one should maintain a humble attitude in this process due to the understanding that it is many times impossible and most speculative to separate the sources from Mark's own words. (See also Guelich, *Mark*, xxxv.)

21. See also Gundry, *Mark*, 1026–45.

with the most widely accepted two-document hypothesis.[22] On the other hand, I will balance the fractural nature of historical-critical analysis with a narrative, holistic understanding of Mark's gospel. Thus, Mark's gospel is understood as a narrative with main characters and a plot with a leading theme, culmination, and resolution.

The overreaching theme of Mark's story is Jesus' acquirement and fulfillment of God's commission to inaugurate his Kingdom (1:11; 9:1; 10:14, 17–27; 12:34) and administer his plan for the salvation of mankind through his death on the cross (2:10; 8:31; 10:45; 15:31).[23] Two other commissions interwoven with the main one establish the main plot of the story. The first is Jesus' call and commission to his disciples (1:16–20; 3:14) to be sharers of his mission and work on a subordinate level, resembling his character and reshaping their behavior according to his teachings (3:13–19, 6:7–13, 8:34–38; 8:31–10:45). This is further understood within the unfolding of the plot as the narrator's blueprint for assessing the disciples' behavior in order to provide guidance for the reader (4:10–12, 35–41; 6:45–52; 8:14–21). The second is the self-commitment of Jesus' opponents to destroy him, expressed through their constant desire and attempts to kill him (3:6; 11:18).[24]

The main character of Mark's story is Jesus, who is marked by several titles: Son of God, Son of David, Son of the Blessed One, Christ (1:1; 8:29; 12:35; 13:21; 14:61; 15:39). He is the one who has been commissioned to fulfill God's saving purposes. The rest of the characters of the gospel's narrative are depicted through their relationship with the main character. These are Jesus' disciples,[25] his opponents,[26] the demons,[27] and the supplicants who ask for healing.[28]

---

22. See R. H. Stein, "Synoptic Problem," in *Dictionary of Jesus and the Gospels*, 787–92; G. R. Osborne, "Redaction Criticism," in *Dictionary of Jesus and the Gospels*, 662–69; R. H. Stein, "Redaction Criticism (NT)," in *ABD* (Logos Library System); D. A. Koch, *Source Criticism (NT)*, (Logos Library System); Guelich, *Mark*, xxxiii.

23. There are some other themes (faith, Christopher D. Marshall, *Faith as a Theme in Mark's Narrative* [Cambridge: Cambridge University Press, 1989]; predestination, Fowler, *Let the Reader Understand*, 138) which are part of Mark's narrative as being incorporated in the main theme.

24. R. C. Tannehill, "The Gospel of Mark as Narrative Christology" [online].

25. See Mark 9:28, 31; 10:10, 13, 23, 24, 46; 11:1, 14, 19; 12:43; 13:1; 14:12–14, 16, 32; 16:7.

26. See Mark 2:6, 16, 18; 2:24; 3:6, 22; 7:1, 3, 5; 8:11, 15, 31; 9:11, 14; 10:2, 33; 11:18, 27; 12:13, 18; 14:1, 43, 53, 15:1; 15:31.

27. See Mark 1:32, 34, 39; 3:15, 22; 5:18; 6:13; 9:38; 7:26, 29, 30.

28. See Mark 5:23; 6:55, 56; 7:26; 7:32; 8:22.

The plot of Mark's story unfolds with a presentation of Jesus' mission to the disciples and to the needy people (1:29-31, 40-45; 9:14-27), of his controversy with his opponents (2:1-3:6; 10:2-12; 11:27-12:37), and of his exorcism of the demonic powers (1:34, 39; 3:20-27; 5:1-20; 6:13). The relationship between Jesus and these groups intensifies until the plot reaches its climax in the passion narrative. The latter presents all the opponents of Jesus at the peak of their antagonistic reaction, mocking Jesus in his agony on the cross (15:16-20, 29-32). Even the disciples, who in the beginning of the plot are presented in very positive light (1:16-20, 3:13-18, 4:10-12, 6:7-13), became part of Jesus' opposition, not understanding his commission (8:31-10:45) and not willing to suffer with him (chapter 14). The climax of the story is reached in the passion narrative, when it becomes clear that Jesus is fulfilling his commission through death on the cross. This is depicted very vividly by the narrator through the centurion's confession at the cross (15:39). The resolution of the story is given in advance, on the one hand, through Jesus' foretelling of his resurrection (8:31; 9:31; 10:34; 14:58) and his presentation of a picture of the disciples' positive future role (10:39; 13:3, 9) and it is expressed, on the other hand, as a fulfillment of Jesus' predictions in the act of his resurrection (16:6).[29]

The pericope of divorce (Mark 10:2-12) stays in the context of Mark's gospel[30] (8:27-10:52), which underlines the theme of Jesus' role in the life of his disciples, and discloses Mark's presentation of the standards for being Jesus' disciple.[31] This is the reason why the pericope is placed here even though it is a controversy material and as such should stay among other

---

29. See also Tannehill, "The Gospel of Mark as Narrative Christology" [online]; Guelich, *Mark*, xxii-xxv; idem, "Mark, Gospel of," in *Dictionary of Jesus and the Gospels*, eds. Joel B. Green, Scot McKnight, I. Howard Marshall (Downers Grove, IL: InterVarsity, 1992), 523-24; Powell, *Toward a Narrative-Critical Understanding of Mark*, 341-46.

30. In agreement with Papias' elder that Mark "did not write in order the things either said or done by the Lord" (οὐ μέντοι τάξει τὰ ὑπὸ τοῦ κυρίου ἢ λεχθέντα ἢ πραχθέντα . . . , Eusebius Pamphilus, *The Church History of Eusebius*, 3.39.15) and apart from the failure of the numerous attempts of the scholars to establish topographical, thematic or other divisions of Mark's gospel one may attempt to comprehend the structure of the latter as three parts loosely related to each other, namely John the Baptist's ministry, 1:1-15; Jesus' public ministry, 1:16-10:52; the passion narrative, 11:1-16:8. (See also Gundry, *Mark*, 1045-49; Guelich, *Mark*, xxxv-xxxvii; R. C. Tannehill, "The Gospel of Mark as Narrative Christology" [online].).

31. See also Tannehill, "The Gospel of Mark as Narrative Christology" [online]; Hays, *The Moral Vision of the New Testament*, 349, 350.

controversy pericopes, (2:1–3:6 and 11:27–12:37).³² The whole of chapter 10 is a clear example of reforming the disciples' attitude towards different ways of life³³ and the section under consideration (vv2–12) covers a very crucial part of human life related to marital issues.³⁴ Jesus raises the standard for marriage held by the Jews and as such he makes it part of his disciples' sacrificial life for the Kingdom.³⁵ Thus, the life of the disciples is glorious, blessed, and rewarded (10:30a, c), but it requires their sacrificial endeavor (10:29) and has to pass through times of hardship (10:30b). This thrust of Mark's narrative is part of his purpose to qualify glory by suffering through the portrait of Jesus for the Christian community.³⁶

32. See also Hays, *The Moral Vision of the New Testament*, 349, 350; Tannehill, "The Gospel of Mark as Narrative Christology" [online].

33. Toward marriage, divorce, and remarriage (1–12); children (13–16); rich people (17–27); ministry (28–31); power (35–45). See also Robert W. Herron, Jr "Mark's Jesus on Divorce: Mark 10:1–12 Reconsidered," *JETS* 25 (1982) 274–83. Electronic edition by Galaxie Software, 1998.

34. See also Tannehill, "The Gospel of Mark as Narrative Christology" [online]. Paul J. Achtemeier, "Mark, Gospel of," in *ABD* 4:546.

35. See also Hays, *The Moral Vision of the New Testament*, 349, 350.

36. Mark's purpose should be defined as a collateral process of qualifying glory by suffering and suffering by glory through the portrait of Jesus for Christian and non-Christian readers. That claim is established on the basis of the holistic comprehension of Mark's gospel (other numerous attempts to define Mark's purpose fell under the criticism of subjectivity due to the lack of holistic textual support, See also Guelich, *Mark*, xli; Gundry, *Mark*, 1024). Thus, the holistic reading of the latter reaches a threefold portrait of Jesus Christ, the Son of God (1:1) which is directed to a twofold audience. On the one hand, Jesus is depicted by the evangelist as a three-dimensional character: he is a human being who lives a life within his limitations and weaknesses (11:12) and dies suffering, being rejected even by his close ones (9:32; 14:66–72; 15:21–39); he is the divine Son of God exercising unlimited power and authority in his deeds (1:32–34; 3:7–12; 6:53–56; exorcisms, 1:27, 39; 5:1–20; 7:24–30; miracles, 1:40–41; 2:11–12; 3:5, 9–10; 4:35–41; 5:27–34; 6:35–44; 45–52; 10:52) and words (he spoke with authority, 1:22, 27; 2:10; he predicted the future, 10:32–34; 11:1–6; ch 13; 14:17–25; he silenced the religious authorities, 2:23–28; 7:1–13; 10:2–9); and he is the envoy of God who fulfills through his life, death, and resurrection God's saving purposes for humanity in inaugurating God's Kingdom on earth (9:1) and proclaiming its full consummation in the coming future (13:26–27). (See also Martin, *Mark*, 144) On the other hand, Mark addresses his message to both Christians and non-Christians. Before the latter he attempts to defend the cross from its shame in order to convert them to Christianity. He accomplishes this in a process of qualification of suffering by glory. The heart of this process is the passage 8:34–9:8 (See also Martin, *Mark*, 141). Mark starts with the call for suffering, moves through the prophesy of seeing the Kingdom of God by some who are present there, and ends in its fulfillment in the Transfiguration. (See also Gundry, *Mark*, 1022–26) Before the former, he attempts to point to the real cost of discipleship. Through the threefold portrait of

Mark establishes the *Sitz im Leben Jesu* for introducing the pericope of divorce and remarriage as the Transjordan tradition of Jesus ministry.³⁷ After Jesus leaves the house (9:33) he goes "to the region of Judea and beyond the Jordan." (10:1, NRS) With such a move Jesus is presented as fulfilling his predictions about the coming time of passion (8:31; 9:31; 10:33). He is traveling to Jerusalem for the Passover Festival and many pilgrims from Judea and Transjordan are doing the same (συμπορεύονται). They are not ignorant of each other, and the crowds once again are showing great interest in Jesus and his teaching.³⁸ Thus, by using a verb in durative imperfect (ἐδίδασκεν),³⁹ Mark emphasizes Jesus' common approach to the crowds in his own style,⁴⁰ "as He was accustomed, He taught them again" (10:1, NKJ). Matthew, however, using a verb in a constative aorist (ἐθεράπευσεν), stresses another aspect of Jesus' ministry to the crowds, i.e. the miraculous instant healing of the sick, "he healed them there" (NAS, NIV). Due to his previous emphasis on Jesus' teaching,⁴¹ the evangelist having just finished the fourth discourse of his gospel, Matthew adds that nuance to Mark's account by pointing to the other significant part of Jesus' ministry to the crowds (διδάσκων . . . καὶ κηρύσσων . . . καὶ θεραπεύων, Matt 4:23).⁴²

Mark does not mention the content of Jesus' teaching of the crowds, since he wants to bring the attention of his readers to the content of the teaching which Jesus will deliver to the Pharisees.⁴³ The latter are brought

---

Jesus, the evangelist approaches his community with a message that the way of glory goes through sufferings (8:27—10:52). Thus, the true disciples of Jesus should follow the steps of their teacher and Lord. (See also Guelich, *Mark*, xlii, xliii; Gundry, *Mark*, 2, 3.)

37. See also Gundry, *Mark*, 529.

38. See also ibid.

39. See also Lenski, *The Interpretation of St. Mark's Gospel* (Minneapolis: Augsburg, 1961), 413.

40. Previous references to this custom of Jesus justify Mark's comment (1:21, 22; 2:13; 4:1, 2; 6:2, 6; 8:31; 11:17; 12:14, 35; 14:49).

41. See also Hagner, *Matthew 14-28*, 542.

42. See also William Hendriksen, *The Gospel of Mark*. New Testament Commentary (Edinburgh: The Banner of Truth Trust, 1975), 375.

43. The textual problem with the exclusion of the Pharisees in v2 is insignificant since both internal (the context does not allow for exclusion of the Pharisees because then the crowds will be the ones who ask the question being referred to with the third person plural verb [ἐπηρώτων] in v2. This is very unlikely for Mark who has not done this anywhere else. See also Gundry, *Mark*, 535. Contra Morna D. Hooker, *The Gospel according to Saint Mark*. Black's New Testament Commentary, Henry Ghadwick, ed. [Peabody:

by Mark on the scene (v2) as part of the crowd, but who have a special approach to Jesus' teaching. This approach is clearly expressed by the evangelist's comment that the Pharisees asked Jesus a question with the purpose of testing him (πειράζοντες αὐτόν). Such an attitude towards Jesus was usual for the Jewish authorities (Mark 7:5; 8:11; 12:13–15). The most probable reason for this approach is that they wanted to "catch him in his words," (Mark 12:13, NIV) disgrace him in front of the crowd as heretic, and eventually justify their plans to kill him (Mark 11:18).[44] Moreover such an attitude should have been expected, since the Pharisees were "the literate local village leaders"[45] who were fighting for influence over the nonelite community of the villages. Thus, the question posed to Jesus, "εἰ ἔξεστιν ἀνδρὶ γυναῖκα ἀπολῦσαι," was a provocative device intended to test the expected answer of Jesus against the Pharisees' understanding of the Law of Moses. That Mark did not see the question as based on the Jewish debate[46] about the grounds for divorce between the schools of Hillel[47] and Shammai[48] is evident from the absence of a clause which

---

Hendrickson, 1991] 235) and external (A B K L Γ Δ Ψ f[13] 28. 700. 892. 1010 pm bo; other MSS which include the Pharisees just changing the word order, W Θ 565 pc sa[ms (s)]; ℵ C N [f[1]] 1241. 1424 pm. The external evidence for omission of the phrase is very weak [D it sy[s] (sa[mss])]. See also Gundry, Mark, 535 and the preference of NA[26]. Contra William L. Lane, The Gospel of Mark. NICNT [Grand Rapids: Eerdmans, 1974] 351 who argues that those MSS which included the phrase have been influenced by Matt 19:3. Such an argument does not have strong grounds since Matthew used Mark not vice versa. See also Guelich, Mark, xxxiii) evidence favor their inclusion.

44. See also William Hendriksen, Mark. New Testament Commentary (Edinburgh: The Banner of Truth Trust, 1975), 375; John Paul Heil, The Gospel of Mark as a Model for Action (New York: Paulist, 1992), 203. Even though Mark does not have a previous teaching on divorce like Matthew (Matt 5: 31, 32) the attempt of the Pharisees to expose Jesus' teaching on divorce and remarriage as inconsistent with the Law of Moses might be understood in the light of other issues discussed by Jesus and condemned by the Jewish leaders as "heretical" (Mark 2:5–7; 16–19; 23–28 etc.). See also Hays, The Moral Vision of the New Testament, 350; Gundry, Mark, 534.

45. Richard L. Rohrbaugh, "The Social Location of the Markan Audience," Int 47 (1993) 386.

46. The debate between the schools of Hillel and Shammai was about the grounds for divorce based on the interpretation of the phrase עֶרְוַת דָּבָר, ἄσχημον πρᾶγμα, (something objectionable) in Deut 24:1.

47. The school of Hillel allowed divorce on multiple grounds. See Mishnah Gittin 9:10 (The Mishnah, A New Translation by Jacob Neusner, 487.); Cf. Josephus, The Antiquities of the Jews, 4.8.23.253.

48. The position held by the school of Shammai in regard to the interpretation of Deut 24:1 considered only adultery as grounds for divorce. (See Mishnah, Gittin 9:10; Cf.

appears in Matthew's version of the question, ("κατὰ πᾶσαν αἰτίαν," Matt 19:3).⁴⁹ The clause underlines clearly the question's provocative nature within the framework of Matthew's exception clause ("μὴ ἐπὶ πορνείᾳ" Matt 19:9), as offered from Hillel's liberal perspective.⁵⁰ Nevertheless five essential arguments support the legitimacy of Mark's question as asked by the Pharisees and the subsequent editorial work of Matthew.⁵¹ First, the Pharisees may not have established the question on the basis of the Hillel and Shammai debate at all, but on the basis of some challenges to their understanding of the Law of Moses in relation to divorce coming from the more conservative Jewish circle of the Qumran Community (11 QTemple 57:17-19;⁵² CD 4:21⁵³). Second, the preference of Mark for such a version of the question might have been determined by the

---

Philo, *The Special Laws* III.XIV.80; See also Hagner, *Matthew 14-28*, 547.)

49. Contra Lenski, (*The Interpretation of St. Mark's Gospel*, 414) who argues that Mark's version of the question posed to Jesus was mainly whether he agrees with Hillel's exposition of Deut 24:1 or not.

50. Even though both schools had equal support for the large period of time of their existence (flourished at the end of 1 BC) the sources (*b. Erub.* 13b; *j. Sota* 3.4 19a; *Zohar, Rava Mehemna* 3:245a) suggest that the school of Hillel eventually gained preeminence over its opponents. (See also Robert Goldenberg, "Shammai, School of," in *ABD* 5:1158; Larry W. Hurtado, *Mark*. New International Biblical Commentary [Peabody: Hendrickson, 1993] 159.)

51. See also Gundry, *Mark*, 536; Fitzmyer, *Matthean Divorce Texts and Some New Palestinian Evidence*, 213-21. Contra R. B. Hays, *The Moral Vision of the New Testament*, 350; Hugh Anderson, *The Gospel of Mark*. The New Century Bible Commentary, ed. Matthew Black (Grand Rapids: Eerdmans, 1981), 240.

52. "From his father's family. He shall take no other wife apart from her because only she will be with him all the days of her life. If she dies, he shall take for himself another from his father's house, from his family. He shall not pervert justice, . . . " (*The Dead Sea Scrolls Translated: 11QTemple*, trans. Florentino Garcia Martinez.)

53. ". . . are caught twice in fornication: by taking two wives in their lives, even though the principle of creation is Gen 1:27 'male and female he created them.'" (*The Dead Sea Scrolls Translated: The Damascus Document*, trans. Wilfred G. E. Watson [Netherlands: Copyright Bruce and Kenneth Zuckerman, 1992] In *Dead See Scrolls Electronic Reference Library*, v 5.3, [Provo, Utah: Brigam Young University; Leiden and Boston (MA): Brill, 1999].) Here the text might not refer to polygamy because it is mentioned particularly in CD 5:2. If the text is interpreted as stating a general condemnation of divorce it should be viewed as establishing a specific prohibition to a king in 11 QTemple 51:17-19. (See Gundry, *Mark*, 537.) However some scholars maintain that condemnation of polygamy is the proper interpretation of CD 4:21 (See Kenneth J. Thomas, "Torah Citations in the Synoptics," *NTS* 24 [1977] 86, 87; D. Instone-Brewer, *Divorce and Remarriage in the Bible*, 61-72).

unacquaintedness of his Gentile-Christian audience[54] with the Jewish debate. Third, one may easily argue that Matthew edited Mark's question due to his Jewish-Christian audience.[55] Fourth, the most widely accepted two-source hypothesis determines Matthew as the user of Mark, not vice versa. Fifth, the clash between Herod and John the Baptist also supports

---

54. The Markan scholarship agrees that both external and internal evidence supports the understanding of Mark's audience as predominantly Gentile, most probably situated in Rome. The following arguments establish the grounds for that view. First, from the testimonies of the church fathers one may receive the impression that Mark wrote in Rome. (Irenaeus, *Against Heresies* 3.1.2 [online], Available at http://www.ccel.org/fathers2/ANF-01/anf01-60.htm#P7297_1937859, Accessed on 14 March 2001; Clement of Alexandria, *From the Books of the Hypotyposes* 6.14 [online], Available at http://www.ccel.org/fathers2/ANF-02/anf02-77.htm#P10243_2869382, Accessed on 14 March 2001.). That notion is substantiated by some Latinisms used (e.g., Gk. *modios* = Lat. *modius* [Mark 4:21] [measure]; Gk. *legion* = Lat. *legio* [legion] [Mark 5:9, 15]) and some Latin translations of the Greek terms (e.g., ὅ ἐστιν πραιτώριον = Lat. *praetorium* [Mark 15:16]). Second, Mark offers an explanation of the Jewish customs: Pharisaic purification practices Mark 7:3–4 cf. Matt 15:1–11; Passover procedures Mark 14:12 cf. Matt 26:17; notifying the day of preparation Mark 15:42 cf. Matt 27:62. Third, the evangelist translates his Aramaic terminology into Greek (e.g., Mark 3:17; 5:41; 7:11, 34; 10:46; 15:22). Fourth, in contrast with Matthew and Luke, Mark is not interested in including a genealogy in his gospel. Fifth, Mark is using Roman measures for time rather than Hebrew (Mark 6:48 cf. Matt 14:22–33; Mark 13:35). See also Donald Guthrie, "New Testament Study Helps: Mark's Gospel," in *Theology Website* [online], Available at http://www.theologywebsite.com/nt/mark.shtml, Accessed on 13 March 2001; Barry D. Smith, *The Gospel of Mark: Introduction and Outline* [online], Available at http://www.abu.nb.ca/courses/NTIntro/Mark.htm, Accessed on 13 March 2001; Martin, *Mark*, 60, 61; Daniel B. Wallace, *Mark: Introduction, Argument, and Outline* [online], Available at http://www.bible.org/docs/soapbox/markotl.htm, Accessed on 14 March 2001; David Malick, *An Introduction to the Gospel of Mark* [online], Available at http://www.bible.org/docs/nt/books/mar/mrk_intr.htm, Accessed on 14 March 2001; J. Julius Scott, Jr., "The Synoptic Gospels," in *Expositor's Bible Commentary: Old Testament*, ed. Frank E. Gaebelein (Grand Rapids: Zondervan, 1999). Zondervan Reference Software (32-bit edition) Version 2.7.

55. Both primary (Origen's witness concerning Matthew's gospel documented by Eusebius testifies that ". . . it [the gospel of Matthew] was prepared for the converts from Judaism, ..." (Eusebius Pamphilus, *The Church History of Eusebius* 6.25.4.) and secondary sources (David C. Sim, "The Gospel of Matthew and the Gentiles," *JSNT* 57 [1995]: 36, 37; Graham N. Stanton, "The Communities of Matthew," *Int* 46 [1992] 379–91; R. T. France, *Matthew: Evangelist and Teacher*, 96–102.) agree that Matthew's audience was predominately Jewish. Thus, Matthew introduces the phrase κατὰ πᾶσαν αἰτίαν (v3) into Mark's version of the question (Mark 10:2). The question is what is/are the juridical reason/s for divorce. In this way the Pharisees related the question to the debate between the schools of Hillel and Shammai about the grounds for divorce based on the interpretation of the phrase עֶרְוַת דָּבָר, ἄσχημον πρᾶγμα, (something objectionable) in Deut 24:1.

the relevance of Mark's version of the question in the first century Jewish context.[56]

The provocative question from the Pharisees was answered by Jesus with a challenging reply, τί ὑμῖν ἐνετείλατο Μωϋσῆς; (v3). The purpose of the latter might be defined as threefold. First, Jesus underlined his awareness of the Pharisees' understanding of divorce and remarriage issues. Second, he attempted to challenge the Pharisees' interpretation of Deut 24:1 as commanding divorce. And third, his intention was to prompt his opponents to think holistically about the Torah, i.e. how should Deut 24:1 be understood in the light of Gen 1:27; 2:24.[57] The following discussion (vv4–9) fulfills the threefold purpose of Jesus' question.

The Pharisees replied with their understanding of Deut 24:1 that, "Moses allowed *us* to write a writ of dismissal and to divorce *her*," (v4), according to Jesus' expectations. It becomes clear that, in his question (v3), Jesus did not use the impersonal noun, ἀνδρὶ, to whose advantage the divorce action is performed according to the Pharisees' question (v2), but intentionally made Moses' command relate to the Pharisees themselves by using the personal pronoun ὑμῖν. Thus, according to Jesus' question, Moses' command is expected to benefit the Pharisees. Hence, the answer of the Pharisees loses the undefined figure of the man from their initial question (v2) and leaves the object of Moses' command to be supplied by the reader, 'ἐπέτρεψεν Μωϋσῆς βιβλίον ἀποστασίου γράψαι καὶ ἀπολῦσαι. The most probable object to supply is the personal pronoun ὑμῖν from Jesus' question.[58] In such a way the Pharisees showed their understanding of Deut 24:1 that they are the ones to whom the advantage

---

56. Because of John the Baptist's destiny due to his criticism of Herod's marriage with Herodias (Mark 6:17–28), the Pharisees' expectation of Jesus' eventual reply on the issue of divorce and remarriage, and the ground on which they were seating, i.e. Herod's territory, one may analyze the Pharisees' question as an attempt to place Jesus against Herod. They hoped that Jesus' destiny might follow that of John and in such a way their plans to kill Jesus might be easily fulfilled (Mark 11:18).

57. See also W. L. Lane, *The Gospel of Mark*, 354.

58. Many translations do not grasp the dynamic in the relationship between the Pharisees' and Jesus' questions and the Pharisees' reply and supply the object from the Pharisees' question, ἀνδρὶ, v2, (NIV, NIB, NAS, NAU, RSV, NRS, NKJ). However some translations (BBE, NJB) do grasp the dynamic and supply the object from Jesus' question, ὑμῖν. Some of the translations leave the reply without an object leaving the choice to the reader (KJV, ASV, WEB, DRA, RWB, DBY, YLT). (BibleWorks for Windows 95/NT v.4.0.025e [o]. Lotus Development Corporation, 1996).

of divorce has been given by Moses.⁵⁹ This clearly demonstrates Jesus' awareness of the Pharisees' attitude about divorce and remarriage, which has also determined Jesus' differentiation from the Jewish religious leaders in relation to the receiver of Moses' law as interpreted in this way. Jesus used the personal pronoun ὑμῖν rather than ἡμῖν (v3) in his question to the Pharisees, clearly underlining the difference between his and the Pharisees' understanding of Deut 24:1.⁶⁰

In the statement following the Pharisees' answer, Jesus condemns their understanding of Deut 24:1, πρὸς τὴν σκληροκαρδίαν ὑμῶν ἔγραψεν ὑμῖν τὴν ἐντολὴν ταύτην, (v5). Mark expresses Jesus' judgment of the Pharisees' interpretation by introducing his reply in an emphatic way with an adverbial prepositional clause in accusative of reference, πρὸς τὴν σκληροκαρδίαν ὑμῶν, establishing the limits of the action of the main verb ἔγραψεν.⁶¹ Within that syntactical construction the meaning of σκληροκαρδίαν intended by Mark should be defined as the intentional refusal of the Pharisees to properly understand God's commandment in Deut 24:1-4.⁶² Moreover, by using the personal pronoun ὑμῖν, Jesus refers

---

59. See Sirach 25:26; Josephus, *The Antiquities of the Jews*, 4.8.23.253; Josephus, *The Life of Flavius Josephus*, 76. 426.

60. See also Gundry, *Mark*, 529, 530.

61. Understanding the clause "πρὸς τὴν σκληροκαρδίαν ὑμῶν" as expressing a purpose (the preposition πρὸς establishes the role of the following accusative noun as telic, Gundry, *Mark*, 530) or hostile relationship (the preposition πρὸς establishes the role of the following accusative noun as accusative of relationship, Gundry, *Mark*, 538) satisfies its syntax but does not do justice to the meaning of the word σκληροκαρδίαν.

62. Due to the fact that the word does not appear in Classical Greek literature, the word's etymological construction might be established as based on the use of σκληρός/σκληρότης/σκληρύνω and καρδία in biblical literature. Thus, on the one hand, the word καρδία is used to designate man's center of thought and intellectual life (Gen 6:5; Exod 35:10; 1 Kgs 3:12; Mark 7:21; Matt 13:15; 15:19; 24:28; Luke 2:51; John 12:40). On the other hand, the verb σκληρύνω is used to refer to an intentional refusal to understand the teaching about Jesus (Acts 19:9). (See also Johannes Behm, "Καρδία among the Greeks," in *TDNT*, ed. Gerhard Kittel, trans. Geoffrey W. Bromiley—electronic ed.—Grand Rapids: Eerdmans, 2000, c1964. Logos Library System 2.1g.; T. Sorg, "Heart," in *NIDTT* (Zondervan Reference Software V. 2.7); Walter Bauer, *A Greek-English Lexicon of the New Testament and Other Early Christian Literature*, trans. William F. Arndt and F. Wilbur Gingrich [Chicago: University of Chicago Press, 1957], 763). The verb πωρόω is also used together with the noun καρδία, even though not in the form of a compound word, to express the concept of hardening one's heart in relation to the understanding of the divine message (Mark 6:52; 8:17; Eph 4:18). (See also J. Behm, "Καρδία among the Greeks," in *TDNT* (Logos Library System 2.1g); T. Sorg, *Heart*. Zondervan Reference Software v. 2.7; W. Bauer, *A Greek-English Lexicon of the New Testament and Other Early Christian*

Moses' command (τὴν ἐντολὴν ταύτην) only to the Pharisees. Hence, as far as the Pharisees' misunderstanding of the law is concerned, Moses wrote this command to them. Therefore Jesus challenges the Pharisees' intentional misunderstanding of Deut 24:1–4 which they used to justify their loose attitude towards divorce and remarriage.[63] Jesus did not diminish the validity of Deut 24:1–4 as a casuistic law, which includes legal divorce procedures, but he condemned the Pharisees' understanding of it as commanding these procedures.[64] Jesus went further, explaining

---

Literature, 763). However, the concept of hardening one's heart appears in nonbiblical literature and it parallels the concept of hardening one's mind which expresses the intentional ignorance of men to God's Law. (Philo, *Spec. Leg.*, I, 304 f.; See also Karl Ludwig Schmidt & Martin Anton Schmidt, "Σκληρότης," in *TDNT*—electronic ed.—Grand Rapids: Eerdmans, 2000, c1964. Logos Library System 2.1g.). In the OT the concept of hardening one's heart includes lack of understanding (Isaiah 6:10; Jer 31:33) or intentional refusal to understand the divine word (Exod 7:13, 14, 22). In the NT the word σκληροκαρδία is used only once (Mark 16:14) apart from the divorce texts (Mark 10:5 and Matt 19:8) with the meaning of an intentional refusal to understand and receive the testimony of the eyewitnesses to Jesus' appearance after the resurrection. Σκληροκαρδία is also used analogously to σκληροτράχηλος (Exod 33:3, 5; Deut 9:6, 13; Prov 29:1 etc.; Acts 7:51. Philo, *Spec. Leg.*, I, 305 adduces Deut 10:16; See also Behm, "Σκληροκαρδία," in *TDNT*—electronic ed.—Grand Rapids: Eerdmans, 2000, c1964. Logos Library System 2.1g). Σκληροτράχηλος, on the other hand, is a hapax-legomena in the NT and it is only used in Ac 7:51 as the stubbornness of the Jewish religious leaders in their thinking and understanding the teaching about Jesus. (See also *Louw-Nida Lexicon* in BibleWorks for Windows 95/NT v.4.0.025e [o]. Lotus Development Corporation, 1996; Becker, "Hard, Hardened," in *NIDTT* (Zondervan Reference Software V. 2.7); Behm, "Σκληροκαρδία," in *TDNT*, Logos Library System 2.1g; Paul T. Eckel, "Mark 10:1–16," *Int* 42 [1988] 287).

63. Philo, *The Special Laws* III.XIV.80; See also Lenski, *The Interpretation of St. Mark's Gospel*, 415.

64. The text of Deut 24:1–4 is clearly established as a casuistic law based on a conditional grammatical construction. Thus, even though both the conditions, i.e. the protasis, and the law, i.e. the apodosis, are important the conditions cannot be mixed with the law. Due to the function of the future verbs (γράψει, δώσει, ἐξαποστελεῖ) as aorist subjunctives and the presence of the conjunction καὶ throughout vv1–3 until the start of v4 the grammatical construction of Deut 24:1–4 might be established as an extended protasis (vv1–3) governed by the conjunction ἐὰν and the apodosis as expressing the command in v4. Hence, what is prohibited is the remarriage of the divorced woman to her former husband after she has been married to another one (v4). (See also Gundry, *Mark*, 539; J. M. Sprinkle, *Old Testament Perspectives on Divorce and Remarriage*. Electronic edition by Galaxie Software; *What Does the Bible Teach: The Divine Permission* [online]; J. C. Laney, *Deuteronomy 24:1–4 and the Issue of Divorce*. Electronic edition by Galaxie Software; Gundry, *Mark*, 539; E. S. Kalland, "Deuteronomy," in *Expositor's Bible Commentary: Old Testament*, Zondervan Reference Software; S. R. Driver, *Deuteronomy*, 269; J. H. Sailhamer, *The Pentateuch as Narrative*, 465.)

his understanding of the Law as related to divorce and remarriage matters, arguing that the only legitimate reading of Deut 24:1-4 is through the perspective of Gen 1:27 and 2:24.[65] The Pharisees already knew the hermeneutics which related these two places of the Torah (Genesis Rabbah XVIII:V[66]; CD 4:21), but intentionally disregarded it. Hence, Mark makes the contrast between Jesus' and the Pharisees' interpretation of Deut 24:1-4, clearly establishing the beginning of Jesus' argument with the postpositive adversative conjunction δέ.

Firstly, Jesus establishes the grounds for marital union between husband and wife through the creation account of male and female, ἀπὸ ἀρχῆς κτίσεως ἄρσεν καὶ θῆλυ ἐποίησεν αὐτούς, v6. Thus, the diversity in the creation of the two genders has been made by the Creator, who reflected the richness of his unity by making man according to his image and likeness as male and female (Gen 1:27, LXX, καὶ ἐποίησεν ὁ θεὸς τὸν ἄνθρωπον κατ' εἰκόνα θεοῦ ἐποίησεν αὐτόν ἄρσεν καὶ θῆλυ ἐποίησεν αὐτούς). For this reason the act of marriage confirms the unity of the va-

---

65. Understanding the nature of marriage as a covenant relationship establishes the grounds for a legitimate reading of Deut 24:1-4 through Gen 1:27; 2:24. On the one hand, Gen 1:27; 2:24 presents marriage as a covenant relationship, which in the light of the whole OT is viewed as having a twofold nature, namely emphasizing the permanence of marriage and providing possibility of legal divorce if there is failure to fulfill the basic covenant stipulations (Lev 24:8; Num 18:19; 1 Chr 16:15; 2 Chr 13:5; 21:7; Ps 89:28; 105:8; 111:9; Isa 54:6, 7; 55:3; 61:8; Sir 45:24; Lev 26:44; Jer 3:8-10; 5:11; 31:32; Ezek 9:9; 16:16-26; 17:16, 18, 19; Zec 11:10; Hos 8:14; Prayer of Azariah 1:11; See also E. A. Martens, *God's Design*, 73; Dumbrell, *Covenant and Creation*, 96, 99). On the other hand, the passage of Deut 24:1-4 read through this perspective is understood as emphasizing the permanence of marriage; discouraging an easy divorce without particular grounds attributed to עֶרְוַת דָּבָר, shameful behavior with sexual implications (cf. Gen 9:22; Exod 20:26; Lev 18:6; Deut 23:15; Lam 1:8; Ezek 16:36; *Mishnah, Ketub.* 7:6), divorce certificate, and nullification of the marriage contract (Exod 21:10, 11 cf. Ps 132; Hos 2:3-13; Ezek 16:1-13; *Mishnah, Ketubot* 5:1-9; Tobit 7:13; *Marriage Contract of a Former Slave Girl Who is Subject to Paramoné*, 420 B.C, trans. H. L. Ginsberg [online]); but granting divorce and remarriage when serious grounds for such an action exist. (עֶרְוַת דָּבָר, Deut 24:1. See also J. M. Sprinkle, *Old Testament Perspectives on Divorce and Remarriage*. Electronic edition by Galaxie Software; D. Instone Brewer, *Three Weddings and a Divorce: God's Covenant with Israel, Judah and the Church* [online].)

66. Apart from the difficulty of establishing the exact interpretation of Genesis Rabbah XVIII:V (*Genesis Rabbah: The Judaic Commentary to the Book of Genesis. A New American Translation*, vol.1, trans. Jacob Neusner [Atlanta: Scholars, 1985] 193-96) among several possible options, one will certainly notice the attempt of the Jewish interpreters to relate the matters of divorce (Deut 24:4; Mal 2:16) to the text of Gen 2:24. See also Gundry, *Mark*, 540; K. J. Thomas, *Torah Citations in the Synoptics*, 87.

rieties established as God's image in man in the creation account.⁶⁷ Thus, Jesus could explain the process of marriage as an act of uniting man and woman, which is firmly based on God's intention in the creation of two genders.⁶⁸ This is clearly expressed by Mark with the phrase ἕνεκεν τούτου (v7a) which in a causal way links the two clauses (vv6, 7). The establishment of the first marriage is depicted by Jesus using three verbs in the future tense with imperatival force (καταλείψει, προσκολληθήσεται, and ἔσονται), corresponding to three basic stages of marriage as commanded by the Creator.

The first step, καταλείψει ἄνθρωπος τὸν πατέρα αὐτοῦ καὶ τὴν μητέρα, v7b does not refer to the physical leaving of the man's family, since this was not Jewish practice,⁶⁹ but to the relocation of loyalties from the parents to the wife. The second step, καὶ προσκολληθήσεται πρὸς τὴν γυναῖκα αὐτοῦ, v7c⁷⁰ depicts the act of establishing the marriage from a

---

67. The question of God's image and likeness in man has never been satisfactorily resolved by scholarly agreement (See H. Blocher, *In the Beginning*, 80–82). Thus, I argue that to consider the image of God in man as primarily related to human sexuality, ἄρσεν καὶ θῆλυ ἐποίησεν αὐτούς (LXX, 1:27), is one of the legitimate readings of Gen 1:26, 27 and 2:24. It is based not only on the parallel reading of the two creation passages in their contexts, as shown by Jesus, but also on the understanding of the grammar of Gen 1:26, 27 (The change of the numbers of the substantives and the verbs referring to God and man from singular to plural and vice versa in vv 26 [καὶ εἶπεν ὁ θεὸς ποιήσωμεν ἄνθρωπον κατ' εἰκόνα ἡμετέραν καὶ καθ' ὁμοίωσιν καὶ ἀρχέτωσαν .... LXX] and 27 [καὶ ἐποίησεν ὁ θεὸς τὸν ἄνθρωπον κατ' εἰκόνα θεοῦ ἐποίησεν αὐτόν ἄρσεν καὶ θῆλυ ἐποίησεν αὐτούς, LXX] underlines a characteristic of unity in the plurality shared by both the divine being and the human creatures. Cf. Gen 5:1. See also Trible, *God and the Rhetoric of Sexuality*, 21; J. H. Sailhamer, *Genesis*, Zondervan Reference Software [32-bit edition], Version 2.7; K. Barth, *Church Dogmatics*, vol. III, *The Doctrine of Creation*, part 1, 195–96]) and the issue of human sexuality as ordained by God for the goodness of the creation, not as his characteristic (See also Brueggemann, *Genesis*, 33) and as a mark shared just partly with the animals in relation to the ability of procreation (Gen 1:22, 28; See also Trible, *God and the Rhetoric of Sexuality*, 12–23). See also L. S. Capper, *The Imago Dei and Its Implications for Order in the Church*, 21–33; Barth, *Church Dogmatics*, vol.III, *The Doctrine of Creation*, part 1, 186.

68. See also Gundry, *Mark*, 531; W. L. Lane, *The Gospel of Mark*, 356.

69. Gen 24:67; Tob 6:13; 7:12; 2 Sam 17:3.

70. There are some external and internal arguments for omission of the clause καὶ προσκολληθήσεται πρὸς τὴν γυναῖκα αὐτου. First, some MSS (א B Ψ 892 sy^s) have dropped it. Second, the question raised by the Pharisees relates only to the husband (v2). Third, including the clause would destroy the balance created by excluding the references to the wife from Deut 24:1 in Mark 10:4. However there is a strong external support, i.e. D W Θ f¹³ Majority Text lat sy^p.h co (A C L N f¹ al: τη γυναικι), for inclusion of the clause. One may argue that the context also supports the longer reading of v7 because

social point of view. That is basically the process of formalizing the marriage through Israel's legislation by a marriage contract.⁷¹ The third step, καὶ ἔσονται οἱ δύο⁷² εἰς σάρκα μίαν, v8a expresses the culmination in the marriage relationship, its sexual consummation (cf. 1 Cor 6:16). Thus, the unity which both man and woman originally had before the creation of genders in the body of Adam⁷³ has been restored in a new and unique way through a "one flesh" relationship between man and woman in marriage.⁷⁴ That is why the phrase in v8a is repeated in order to emphasize by the temporal negative adverb οὐκέτι, the end of the singleness, "they are no longer two" (8a, NRS); and by the adversative conjunction ἀλλὰ, the establishment of the relation between the two as one flesh, "but one flesh"

---

without the discussed clause the phrase καὶ ἔσονται οἱ δύο εἰς σάρκα μίαν will point to τὸν πατέρα . . . καὶ τὴν μητέρα instead of ἄνθρωπος . . . καὶ . . . τὴν γυναῖκα αὐτοῦ. Even if the phrase from v8 οἱ δύο might be referred to ἄρσεν καὶ θῆλυ and in such a way one may argue for more difficult reading it is less probable since such a relation will be very awkward. Moreover one may easily explain the scribal removal of the clause as based on the two coordinative conjunctions καὶ appearing at the beginning of the phrase and in the beginning of v8. Thus, the inclusion of the clause should be preferred. (See also NA²⁶, Gundry, *Mark*, 531)

71. Marriage contracts were an essential part of Israelite legislation and were mandatory for formalising marriages (See Jewish-Aramaic marriage and divorce contracts from Elephantine: *Aramaic Papyri from Elephantine*, trans. H. L. Ginsberg [online].). That might be clearly seen by analysing the significance of the rules related to "bride price" and the "dowry" which marriage contracts established (See Exod 22:15–16; Deut 22:28–29; Gen 24:53; 29:18–20 cf. *Marriage Contract of a Former Slave Girl*, trans. H. L. Ginsberg.) See also J. M. Sprinkle, *Old Testament Perspectives on Divorce and Remarriage*. Electronic edition by Galaxie Software. See Tobit 7:13 (NRS) and Code of Hammurabi # 128 in which the word *riksātu* is translated by most of the scholars as "contract." Marriage contracts were usual practice for Greek as well as Roman cultures, as early as 4 BC. (See *Marriage & Divorce Papyri of the Ancient Greek, Roman and Jewish World*, ed. David Instone-Brewer [online].) See also E. M. Yamauchi, *Cultural Aspects of Marriage in the Ancient World*, 245, 246.

72. Even though the MT does not have a Hebrew equivalent for οἱ δύο there are many other MSS which support the fact that LXX has been using other Hebrew text than MT. (See also Gundry, *Mark*, 539; M. D. Hooker, *The Gospel according to Saint Mark*, 236.)

73. Through Adam's words, "'this at last is bone of my bones and flesh of my flesh; this one shall be called Woman ['iššâ], for out of Man ['îš] this one was taken,'" (Gen 2:23, NRS), the two genders coming from the unity of his body are emphasized. For the first time the man [hā-'ādām] referred to himself as man ['îš] and called his partner woman ['iššâ]. (See also P. Trible, *God and the Rhetoric of Sexuality*, 98; N. M. Sarna, *Genesis*, 23; T. W. Jennings, *Theological Perspectives on Sexuality*, 3–6.).

74. Gen 2:24: LXX ἔσονται οἱ δύο εἰς σάρκα μίαν, WTT לְבָשָׂר אֶחָד. (See also P. Trible, *God and the Rhetoric of Sexuality*, 94–105; N. M. Sarna, *Genesis*, 23; K. Barth, *Church Dogmatics*, vol.III, *The Doctrine of Creation*, part 1, 304–306.)

(8b, NRS). The kind of relationship the two spouses have in the marriage, as presented by Jesus on the basis of the creation account, might be defined as that of a covenant.[75]

With such a clarification of the proper understanding of Deut 24:1–4 in the light of Gen 1:27; 2:24, Jesus reached the conclusion of his argument, depicted by Mark through the inferential conjunction οὖν, "therefore what God has joined together let no man separate" (10:9, NKJ) (ὃ οὖν ὁ θεὸς συνέζευξεν ἄνθρωπος μὴ χωριζέτω). In the latter, the antithetical parallelism between the subjects (ὁ θεὸς, ἄνθρωπος) and their related verbs (συνέζευξεν, χωριζέτω) is complete. On the one hand, God, the Creator of man and woman, has established the first family and presented it as a model of unity for future marriages,[76] an action depicted with a

---

75. Cf. Mal 2:14; Prov 2:17; See also S. Bacchiocchi, *The Marriage Covenant* [online]; W. Brueggemann, *Genesis*, 47; Dumbrell, *Covenant and Creation*, 36; K. A. Mathews, *Genesis 1–11:26*. The New American Commentary, 222; J. M. Sprinkle, *Old Testament Perspectives on Divorce and Remarriage*. Electronic edition by Galaxie Software; J. E. Adams, *Marriage Divorce & Remarriage in the Bible*, 16, 17. The covenant terminology used in Gen 2:24 to depict the process of marriage suggests this conclusion, i.e. abandoning (יַעֲזָב־אִישׁ, cf. Exod 23:32; 34:15; Deut 31:16; 31:20; See also G. J. Wenham, *Genesis 1–15*. Word Biblical Commentary, 352) and cleaving (וְדָבַק, cf. Deut 4:4; 10:20; 11:22; 13:4; 30:20; Josh 23:8; 1 Kgs 11:2; See also N. M. Sarna, *Genesis*, 23; S. Bacchiocchi, *The Marriage Covenant* [online]; Wallis, "Dābhaq," in *Theological Dictionary of the Old Testament*, 80–84; G. J. Wenham, *Genesis 1–15*, Word Biblical Commentary, 352.). That language is used by the prophets as well to express the covenant relationship between Yahweh and Israel. (Exod 19–24 cf. *Akkadian-Hittite Treaty*, ed. Daniel Bellissimo; See also Marterns, *God's Design*, 66–75; Dumbrell, *Covenant and Creation*, 94–99; Mathews, *Genesis 1–11:26*, The New American Commentary, 222, 223.) The covenant relationship was based on the loyalty between the two parties through fulfillment of particular stipulations. If the latter have not been kept the covenant could be broken. (Lev 24:8; Num 18:19; 1 Chr 16:15; 2 Chr 13:5; 21:7; Ps 89:28; 105:8; 111:9; Isa 55:3; 61:8; Sir 45:24; Lev 26:44; Jer 31:32; Ezek 17:16, 18, 19; Zec 11:10; Prayer of Azariah 1:11; See also E. A. Martens, *God's Design*, 73; Dumbrell, *Covenant and Creation*, 96, 99.). Thus, the view of marriage as an indissoluble institution may not be sustained (See also C. L. Blomberg, *Marriage, Divorce, Remarriage, and Celibacy*, 162–197. Electronic edition by Galaxie Software, 1999. Contra Hays, *The Moral Vision of the New Testament*, 351 and Lenski, *The Interpretation of St. Mark's Gospel*, 419).

76. See Tertullian, *Exhortation to Chastity*, V "Unity of Marriage."
"And accordingly the man of God, Adam, and the woman of God, Eve, discharging mutually (the duties of) a marriage, sanctioned for mankind a type by the considerations of the authoritative precedent of their origin and the primal will of God." (Tertullian, *Exhortation to Chastity*, trans. S. Thelwall, in *Ante-Nicene Fathers: Translations of The Writings of the Fathers Down to A.D. 325*, eds. Alexander Roberts & James Donaldson, vol.4. *Christian Classics Ethereal Library*, vol.2, CD-ROM, ed. Harry Plantinga [Wheaton, IL: Wheaton College, 1998]).

consummative aorist verb συνέζευξεν.⁷⁷ On the other hand, the man, who under the pressure of his fallen nature wishes to serve his selfish desires and purposes, is prohibited from destroying God's creation of marriage as perfect unity by divorce⁷⁸ through the imperative of prohibition μὴ χωριζέτω.⁷⁹ Thus, with that conclusion, Jesus establishes the proper understanding of divorce and remarriage based on the holistic reading of the Torah and places the ones who look for divorce and remarriage on the basis of an intentional misunderstanding of the Law, i.e. the Pharisees, under God's judgment.⁸⁰

77. See also Lenski, *The Interpretation of St. Mark's Gospel*, 419.

78. The word χωριζέτω here (Mark 10:9) should be understood as a synonym of the word used for divorce ἀπολῦσαι in vv2, 4 since χωρίζω in the context of marriage and divorce is understood as a technical term referring to a divorce action. (In the papyri: PS 166, II [II BC]; BGU 1101, 5; 1102, 8; 1103 [I BC] [BGU IV.1103, The Duke Databank of Documentary Papyri [online], Available at http://www.perseus.tufts.edu/cgi-bin/ptext?doc=Perseus%3Atext%3A1999.05.0001&layout=&loc=1103, Accessed on 22 August 2000; BGU IV.1102, The Duke Databank of Documentary Papyri [online], Available at http://www.perseus.tufts.edu/cgi-bin/ptext?doc=Perseus%3Atext%3A1999.05.0001&layout=&loc=1102, Accessed on 22 August 2000; BGU IV.1101, The Duke Databank of Documentary Papyri [online], Available at http://www.perseus.tufts.edu/cgi-bin/ptext?doc=Perseus%3Atext%3A1999.05.0001&layout=&loc=1101, Accessed on 22 August 2000]; See also W. Bauer, *A Greek-English Lexicon of the New Testament and Other Early Christian Literature*, 898; P Ryl II. 154²⁵ [AD 66]; BGU 1.251⁶ [AD 81]; ib. IV. 1045²² [AD 154]; P. Ryl II. 154³⁰ [AD 66]; See also James Hope Moulton and George Millgan, *The Vocabulary of the Greek Testament. Illustrated from the Papyri and Other Non-Literary Sources* [Grand Rapids: Eerdmans, 1976] 696. In other nonbiblical literature: Polyb., 32, 12, 6. In LXX: 1 Esd 9:9; 1 Esd 9:36. In the NT: Matt 19:6; 1 Cor 7:10; Matt 1:19; Luke 16:18.) The word refers to "separation, desertion," within the context of divorce and remarriage only when it expresses an action of the wife, since the wife could not initiate divorce according to Jewish Law. (See Josephus, *Ant.* 15.7.10. 259). Hence, when Mark refers to the divorce action initiated by the wife he uses the word ἀπολύω, v12. However the context of Mark 10:9 suggests that the husband is in view not the wife, since the question of the Pharisees was particularly related to him (Mark 10:2). See also Vincent Taylor, *The Gospel according to St Mark: The Greek Text With Introduction, Notes and Indexes* (London & Basingstonke: Macmillan, 1974), 419; Gundry, *Mark*, 540; M. D. Hooker, *The Gospel according to Saint Mark*, 236; M. J. Harris, "Χωρίζω," in *New International Dictionary of New Testament Theology*, Collin Brown, ed. (Grand Rapids: Zondervan, 1999) as Zondervan Reference Software V. 2.7; C. Brown, "Χωρίζω," in *New International Dictionary of New Testament Theology*, ed. Collin Brown (Grand Rapids: Zondervan, 1999) as Zondervan Reference Software V. 2.7.

79. See also Gundry, *Mark*, 531. This prohibition against destroying a marital union goes contrary to the view of indissolubility of marriage. See also C. Brown, Χωρίζω. Zondervan Reference Software V. 2.7; W. Hendriksen, *The Gospel of Mark*, 379.

80. See also W. L. Lane, *The Gospel of Mark*, 356.

Matthew (vv4-8) reverses Mark's order (vv3-9), presenting first Jesus' creation argument and then the Pharisees' contra argument based on their understanding of Deut 24:1. Immediately after the Pharisees' question (Matt 19:3), Jesus presents his creation argument (19:4-6). In the form of a rhetorical question introduced by the formula "οὐκ ἀνέγνωτε,"[81] which, as a culminative aorist, underlines the result of the completed action and, due to the negative particle οὐκ, expects an affirmative answer, Jesus challenges the Pharisees' intentional refusal to consider the creation passages (Gen 1:27; 2:24) as part of the divorce debate.[82] Jesus' creation argument is presented by Matthew along the same lines as Mark's presentation.[83] After Jesus concludes his argument with a general prohibition of divorce (Matt 19:6b) based on God's involvement in establishing the marriage as a perfect unity, Jesus' creation argument is challenged by the Pharisees' question referring to Deut 24:1 (19:7). Jewish religious leaders attempted to disprove the validity of Jesus' statement by showing that he places Moses (Gen 1:27; 2:24) against Moses (Deut 24:1-4). Thus, Matthew has placed the verb ἐνετείλατο, which is used by Jesus according to Mark's account (Mark 10:3), at the disposal of the Pharisees (Matt 19:7) in order to define their understanding of Deut 24:1 as commanding divorce. Jesus replies to this challenge by correcting the Pharisees' view of the nature of Deut 24:1. Using the verb ἐπέτρεψεν (19:8) and condemning their intentional misunderstanding of the latter (19:8a), he leads them back to his creation argument (19:8b). The repositioning of Mark's verbs

---

81. In relation to the rabbinic understanding of the difference between 'reading' and 'understanding' (*Mishnah, Shegalim* 1.4; *Genesis Rabbah* IX:26; *Babylonian Moed Qatan* 16b; *Berakoth* 18a; *Palestinian Berakoth* 4d) and considering the style of Matthew (it makes a difference between Jesus' addressing of the crowd with ἠκούσατε [Matt 5:21; 21:16] and his addressing of its leaders with οὐκ ἀνέγνωτε [Matt 19:4; 21:42; 22:31]), the formula might be paraphrased in the following way: "Surely you have read this/that text but you do not seem to understand its import." Cf. Matt 12:3, 5; 21:16, 42; 22:31; Mark 2:25; 12:10, 26; Luke 6:3; 10:26; Acts 8:30; 2 Cor 3:14; Rev 13:18; Neh 8:3, 8; Amos 4:5; Josephus, *Ant.* 4.8.209; See also W. D. Davies and Dale C. Allison, Jr., *The Gospel according to Saint Matthew: A Critical and Exegetical Commentary*, vol. 3 (Edinburg: T&T Clark, 1991), 9, 10; W. D. Davies and Dale C. Allison, Jr., *The Gospel according to Saint Matthew: A Critical and Exegetical Commentary*, vol. 2 (Edinburg: T&T Clark, 1991), 313, 314; David Daube, *The New Testament and Rabbinic Judaism* (New York: Arno, 1973), 422-37; C. L. Blomberg, *Marriage, Divorce, Remarriage, and Celibacy*. Electronic edition by Galaxie Software.

82. The Pharisees were aware of such an understanding of divorce matters based on the creation account (CD 4:21, Genesis Rabbah XVIII:V).

83. Matt 19:4-6 cf Mark 10:6-9.

ἐνετείλατο and ἐπέτρεψεν by Matthew shows that Mark used the verb ἐνετείλατο as part of Jesus' provocative question to the Pharisees only as a reference to the Pharisees' false hermeneutics of Deut 24:1 and not as expressing Jesus' understanding of that text. Thus, the Pharisees tried to get around Jesus' provocation by using the verb ἐπέτρεψεν (Mark 10:4).[84] Therefore, while Mark's intention is to present to his Gentile-Christian audience Jesus' challenge and correction of the Pharisees' false hermeneutics of Deut 24:1–4, Matthew's intention is to show his Jewish-Christian audience the Pharisees' challenge to Jesus' creation argument and their complete failure to disprove it.[85]

In v10 Mark presents Jesus as being in the house, making a topographical shift from the previous discussion (vv2–9) with the spatial preposition εἰς. He also makes a shift in relation to Jesus' audience, i.e. from the Pharisees to the disciples. This perfectly fits Mark's style according to which Jesus' usual habit is to speak to his disciples in private.[86] However the subject under discussion stays the same, "περὶ τούτου," though Jesus' answer is expanded to include the issue of remarriage. The inclusion of remarriage is a natural continuation of the previous discussion related to divorce and not a redactional act[87] of the author, since in the

---

84. Any different understanding of the issue will present the Pharisees as contradicting themselves asking about man's rights (Mark 10:2) and at the same time referring to Moses' command as permission (Mark 10:4). Thus, neither Hays' argument that the change of verbs helps Jesus to escape opposing the Law of Moses (Hays, *The Moral Vision of the New Testament*, 350) nor Gundry's claim that Jesus had the supernatural knowledge about Moses' reason to give such a command (Moses instigated that vice of the Pharisees which Jesus exposed, Gundry, *Mark*, 530) could satisfy one's accurate reading of the text.

85. Contra Ezra P. Gould (*Critical and Exegetical Commentary on the Gospel according to St. Mark*. The International Critical Commentary, eds. S. R. Driver, A. Plummer, C. A. Briggs [Edinburgh: T. & T. Clark, 1969] 184.) who failed to identify the exchange of the verbs ἐνετείλατο and ἐπέτρεψεν in Matthew and Mark and claimed that the change of Mark's order by Matthew does not have any significance.

86. Cf. Mark 9:28–29. See also Gundry, *Mark*, 541.

87. The claim that Mark has used a source which contained the traditional saying of Jesus about remarriage expressed by Matthew (Matt 5:31–32) and Luke (Luke 16:18) using Q and placed it next to his teaching of divorce (vv1–9) for the purpose of uniting both subjects because of their close content and to radicalize them further (Hays, *The Moral Vision of the New Testament*, 352) cannot be sustained due to the unity of the two subjects of divorce and remarriage which is supported by the first century context in which remarriage was assumed after divorce. Moreover to argue that Mark joined the two passages (2–9 and 10–12) in order to make the connection made by the Jewish

first century context divorce was usually followed by remarriage.[88] Hence, both passages (vv2–9 and vv10–12) support each other in understanding the matter related to divorce and remarriage. If a division is applied, the first passage (vv2–9) would allow remarriage since it is assumed to be not explicitly forbidden and the second passage (vv10–12) would not disallow divorce but only remarriage as an act of adultery.[89] Apart from questioning the unity of the whole passage (vv2–12) one should consider the special attention the evangelist pays to Jesus' disciples. They were a group of people, who where made transparent by Mark in his descriptions of their unstable behavior towards their teacher. Although closest to Jesus, the disciples were troubled with fear and unbelief which finally resulted in desertion of their teacher.[90] In the present pericope, the disciples are once again close to Jesus, but, in the same manner as the Pharisees, they think about divorce in terms of their benefit from it through subsequent remarriage.[91] Hence, their question reflects the unexpectedness of his an-

---

author of CD 4:21 who used a quotation of Gen 1:27 to express a prohibition of remarriage (Hays, *The Moral Vision of the New Testament*, 352) would diminish Mark's general redactional approach to his sources in regard to his Gentile audience.

88. *The Mishnah Gittin* 9:3. Remarriage was even mandatory: "No man should live without a wife lest he be tempted to sin, and no woman should live without a husband lest she be suspected of sin...." (Halacha, *Women – Nashim*, 22. Marriage – *Ishus* [online] Available at http://www.torah.org/learning/halacha-overview/chapter22.html. Accessed on 19 October 2000.) See also W. A. Heth, *Another Look at the Erasmian View of Divorce and Remarriage*, 269, 270. Gundry, *Mark*, 541. Contra Hooker, (M. D. Hooker, *The Gospel according to Saint Mark*, 237) who argues that vv10–12 is Mark's interpretation of vv2–9 using a church maxim.

89. See also Gundry, *Mark*, 541; Contra C. S. Mann (*Mark: A New Translation With Introduction and Commentary*. The Anchor Bible, eds. William Foxwell Albright & David Noel Freedman, vol 27 [New York: Doubleday, 1986] 392) who argues that the section about divorce is completed in v9 and the section about remarriage 10–12 is just an appendix to it.

90. Mark 6:45–52; 8:14–21; 8:33; 14:50.

91. The most widely spread reason for divorce among Jewish men was their desire for subsequent remarriage. "A. Just as the water puts her to the proof, so the water puts him [the lover] to the proof. B. 'since it is said, And it shall come . . . , And it shall come . . . (Num 5:22, 24).' C. 'Just as she is prohibited to the husband, so she is prohibited to the lover, ...'" (*Mishnah, Sotah* 5:1). (See also Nolland, *Luke 9:21–18:34*, 819; I. Howard Marshall, *The Gospel of Luke: A Commentary on the Greek Text*. The New International Greek Testament Commentary, eds. I. Howard Marshall and W. Ward Gasque [Exeter: Paternoster, 1978] 631.) In some specific cases Jewish women also fell in this category. ". . . but Herodias, their sister, was married to Herod [Philip], the son of Herod the Great, who was born of Mariamne, the daughter of Simon the high priest, who had a daughter,

swer to the Pharisees.[92] With such an emphasis, Mark attempts to help his Christian community to identify itself with the group of disciples and to respond in a proper way to Jesus' teaching.[93]

Mark underlines Jesus' answer to the disciples for his audience by using the historical present tense of the verb λέγω. The first part of Jesus' answer casts a new light on the subject of adultery in Jewish and Greco-Roman contexts. Jesus states that "whoever divorces his wife and marries another commits adultery against her" (10:11, NRS).[94] The fact that the phrase γυναῖκα αὐτοῦ is the antecedent of ἐπ' αὐτήν leads to two conclusions. First, it is clear that a legal action of divorce is not in view here, since the marital bond is still in place, i.e. the woman is still defined as "his wife." Hence, divorce and remarriage lead to adultery. Second, the identity of the offended party is changed. The prevailing notion in the Jewish[95] and Greco-Roman[96] world was that the man commits adultery

---

Salome; after whose birth Herodias took upon her to confound the laws of our country, *and divorce herself from her husband while he was alive, and was married to Herod* [Antipas], her husband's brother by the father's side; he was tetrarch of Galilee." Josephus, *The Antiquities of the Jews*, 18.5.4.136; (See also Josephus, *The Antiquities of the Jews*, 15.7.10.259. The same was true for the Gentiles, both men and women, and even on a larger scale: See Diodorus Siculus, *Library*, 12.18.1.XVIII, trans. C. H. Oldfather [online], Available at http://www.perseus.tufts.edu/cgi-bin/ptext?lookup=Diod.+12.18.1, Accessed on 25 December 2000; M. Tullius Cicero, *Letters*, ed. Evelyn Shuckburgh [online], Available at http://perseus.csad.ox.ac.uk/cgi-bin/ptext?lookup=Cic.+Fam.+13.10, Accessed on 21 December 2000.)

92. See also R. L. Rohrbaugh, *The Social Location of the Markan Audience*, 390.

93. See also R. W. Herron, Jr *Mark's Jesus on Divorce: Mark 10:1–12 Reconsidered*. Electronic edition by Galaxie Software.

94. Lenski (*The Interpretation of St. Mark's Gospel*, 419, 421) suggests a translation as "Whoever . . . is made adulterous in regard to her" on the basis of the passive voice of the verb μοιχᾶται and the relation of the preposition ἐπί to the accusative αὐτήν as accusative of relationship. However his argument cannot be sustained because the verb μοιχᾶται is deponent (See also *GNM Morphology* and *Barclay-Newman Greek Dictionary* in BibleWorks for Windows 95/NT v.4.0.025e [o]. Lotus Development Corporation, 1996) and the nature of the accusative of relationship of αὐτήν should be defined further as a hostile one. (See also Gundry, *Mark*, 541; NIV; NAS; NRS; NKJ).

95. Josephus, *The Antiquities of the Jews*, 4.8.23.244 ". . . And he that does not marry a virgin, let him not corrupt another man's wife, and marry her, *nor grieve her former husband*; . . . ." See also Josephus, *The Antiquities of the Jews*, 4.8.23.(251, 252).

96. For the liberty of man, in contrast to woman, according to the law to have extramarital sexual activities in the Greco-Roman world see Antiphon, *Speeches* 1.13, ed. K. J. Maidment [online], Available at http://perseus.csad.ox.ac.uk/cgi-bin/ptext?lookup=Antiph.+1+13, Accessed on 21 December 2000; Demosthenes, *Speeches 51–61: Apollodorus*

against the man whose wife he slept with but not against his wife.⁹⁷ The grounds for this widespread notion might be found in the well established authoritative position of the husband in relation to his wife and its potential for abuse.⁹⁸ Thus, the fact that the husband is accused of committing

Against Neaera 59.17, trans. A. T. Murray, Norman W. DeWitt, and Norman J. DeWitt [online], Available at http://perseus.csad.ox.ac.uk/cgi-bin/ptext?lookup=Dem.+59+17, Accessed on 21 December 2000; See also Thomas R. Martin, *An Overview of Classical Greek History from Homer to Alexander* [online], Available at http://perseus.csad.ox.ac.uk/cgi-bin/ptext?doc=Perseus:text:1999.04.0009:head%3D%23197, Accessed on 21 December 2000; Aulus Gellius, *Avli Gelli Noctes Atticae*, 10, 23, 5 [online], Available at http://www.gmu.edu/departments/fld/CLASSICS/gellius10.html#23m, Accessed on 19 March 2001.

97. See also Friedrich Hauck, "Μοιχεύω," in *TDNT*, eds. Gerhard Kittel & Gerhard Friedrich, trans. Geoffrey W. Bromiley (Grand Rapids: Eerdmans, 1964)—electronic ed. 10 v.—(Logos Library System); Gundry, *Mark*, 533; W. L. Lane, *The Gospel of Mark*, 357; L. W. Hurtado, *Mark*, 161; Walter W. Wessel, "Mark," in *Expositor's Bible Commentary: New Testament*, ed. Frank E. Gaebelein (Grand Rapids: Zondervan, 1999). Zondervan Reference Software (32-bit edition) Version 2.7.

98. The leadership of the husband over his household and his dominion over his wife is well attested in the second Temple Jewish literature and might be traced in the OT as well. (Josephus, *Against Apion* 2.25.(201); 4 Q416.2.IV; CD XVI, 10-12; Philo, *The Special Laws* II.VI.24; Sirach 25:13-26; Gen 20:3; Deut 22:22; Exod 21:3, 22; Lev 21:4; 2 Sam 11:26; Prov 12:4; 31:11, 23, 28; Hos 2:18; Num 30:2-15; See also D. I. Block, *Marriage and Family in Ancient Israel*, 64-66; David W. Chapman, "Marriage and Family in Second Temple Judaism," in *Marriage and Family in the Biblical World*, ed. Ken M. Campbell [Downers Grove, IL: InterVarsity, 2003] 207-210). The cases of male authority abuse against the wife (as D. I. Block argues, texts as Gen 3:16 might have been easily misused by authoritarian husbands [D. I. Block, *Marriage and Family in Ancient Israel*, 65]; see also Judg 19:24; Gen 12:11-20; 20:2; 26:7-10; Gen 38:6-26) as well as the emphatic expressions of this authority in some of the previously mentioned texts have led some scholars to conclude that "in much Jewish tradition the woman is often spoken of as though she were here husband's chattel or property." (Davies and Allison, *The Gospel according to Saint Matthew*, vol. 1, 527; See also William L. Countryman, *Dirt, Greed and Sex: Sexual Ethics in the New Testament and Their Implications for Today* [London: SCM, 1989] 155, 147-234; F. Hauck, "Μοιχεύω," in *TDNT*, Logos Library System; Hays, *The Moral Vision of the New Testament*, 352; L. W. Hurtado, *Mark*, 161.) However, others argue that this position does not reflect all the evidence from the second Temple Jewish literature and overlooks the difference between "authority and ownership, legal dependence and servitude, functional subordination and possession" in the OT passages. (D. I. Block, *Marriage and Family in Ancient Israel*, 64) The Jewish ideal expressed in the OT (kings - Deut 17:14-20; judges - Exod 18:13-27; cf. Deut 10:17-19; priest - Num 6:24-27; Deut 10:8-9; prophets - Deut 18:14-22; 2 Kgs 17:13-23) defines the role of the leader including that of the husband in relation to his household as being performed for the benefit of those under his authority. (D. I. Block, *Marriage and Family in Ancient Israel*, 64; 61-70; See also D. W. Chapman, *Marriage and Family in Second Temple Judaism*, 207-210; D. Instone-Brewer, *Divorce and Remarriage in the Bible*, 98) Nevertheless, it

adultery against his own wife by marrying another does not share the overall Jewish and Greco-Roman understanding of the matter.[99] By placing the woman in her rightful place next to her husband, Jesus forced a shift in the disciples' marital ethics and made them an integral part of the high Kingdom standards that required their sacrificial endeavor.[100] Thus,

---

is acknowledged that the actual experience of many Jewish women might have been contrary to the biblical norms. (D. I. Block, *Marriage and Family in Ancient Israel*, 65).

The family in the Greco-Roman world reflects more egalitarian structure in which husband and wife are seen as partners. (*Tebtunis papyrus I 104. G*, in *Women's Life in Greece & Rome*, trans. Mary R. Lefkowitz and Maureen B. Fant [online], Available at http://www.stoa.org/diotima/anthology/wlgr/wlgr-greeklegal101.shtml, Accessed on 24 December 2004; Dio Cassius, *History of Rome* 56.3.3-4, Loeb Classical Library, No. 175; See also S. M. Baugh, "Marriage and Family in Ancient Greek Society," in *Marriage and Family in the Biblical World*, ed. Ken M. Campbell [Downers Grove, IL: InterVarsity, 2003] 119; S. Treggiari, *Marriage and Family in Roman Society*, 177–82) Yet the leadership role of the man over his household and his wife is clearly defined (Cicero *De officiis* 1.54, quoted in S. Treggiari, *Marriage and Family in Roman Society*, 145; Gaius, *Institutes* 1.108-118, 136-137a, trans. Gordon and Robinson L., in *Women's Life in Greece & Rome*, eds. Mary R. Lefkowitz and Maureen B. Fant [online], Available at http://www.stoa.org/diotima/anthology/wlgr/wlgr-romanlegal132.shtml, Accessed on 24 December 2004; Plutarch, *Lives*, Alcibiades 8.3-5, in *Plutarch's Lives*, trans. Bernadotte Perrin [Cambridge, MA: Harvard University Press, 1914] [online], Available at http://www.perseus.tufts.edu/cgi-bin/ptext?lookup=Plut.+Alc.+8.1, Accessed on 23 December 2004; Plutarch, *Moralia* 138a-146a, trans. R. Warner G., in *Women's Life in Greece & Rome*, eds. Mary R. Lefkowitz and Maureen B. Fant [online], Available at http://www.stoa.org/diotima/anthology/wlgr/wlgr-privatelife242.shtml, Accessed on 24 December 2004; Aulus Gellius, *Attic Nights* 10.23, in *Women's Life in Greece & Rome*, trans. Mary R. Lefkowitz and Maureen B. Fant [online], Available at http://www.stoa.org/diotima/anthology/wlgr/wlgr-romanlegal111.shtml, Accessed on 24 December 2004; See also S. M. Baugh, *Marriage and Family in Ancient Greek Society*, 119–20, 126; S. Treggiari, *Marriage and Family in Roman Society*, 137, 145]). Misuses of husband's authority may also be noticed. (Valerius Maximus, *Memorable Deeds and Sayings* 6.3.9-12, in *Women's Life in Greece & Rome*, trans. Mary R. Lefkowitz and Maureen B. Fant [online], Available at http://www.stoa.org/diotima/anthology/wlgr/wlgr-romanlegal109.shtml, Accessed on 24 December 2004).

99. See also W. L. Countryman, *Dirt, Greed and Sex*, 180–81.

100. For the positive side of the argument see Tertullian, *To His Wife* 2.8. "What kind of yoke is that of two believers, (partakers) of one hope, one desire, one discipline, one and the same service? Both (are) brethren, both fellow servants, no difference of spirit or of flesh; nay, (they are) truly 'two in one flesh.' Where the flesh is one, one is the spirit. Together they pray, together prostrate themselves, together perform their fasts; mutually teaching, mutually exhorting, mutually sustaining. Equally (are they) both (found) in the Church of God; equally at the banquet of God; equally in straits, in persecutions, in refreshments." (Tertullian, *To His Wife*, trans. S. Thelwall, in *Ante-Nicene Fathers: Translations of The Writings of the Fathers Down to A.D. 325*, eds. Alexander Roberts and

even though the text of Mark 10:11 might be considered closer to the tradition of Jesus' teaching than the Q source of Matt 5:32 and Luke 16:18,[101] the redactional activity of Mark in relation to the phrase ἐπ' αὐτήν may not be disregarded.

The next part of Jesus' answer (10:12) is parallel to the first one (10:11), but it relates to the woman's divorce activity καὶ ἐὰν αὐτὴ ἀπολύσασα τὸν ἄνδρα αὐτῆς γαμήσῃ ἄλλον μοιχᾶται. Its construction might be defined as a fifth class conditional statement due to the presence of the particle ἐὰν followed by the verb in the subjunctive mood γαμήσῃ in the protasis and the present indicative verb μοιχᾶται in the apodosis.[102] Following the formula of the fifth class conditional statement (if A then B) with an emphasis on its present generic nature, one may argue that the result of the woman's action of divorcing[103] her husband and marrying another equals

---

James Donaldson, vol.4. *Christian Classics Ethereal Library*, vol.2, CD-ROM, ed. Harry Plantinga [Wheaton, IL: Wheaton College, 1998].) For the negative side see St. Basil, *Letter* 188.9. "The sentence of the Lord that it is unlawful to withdraw from wedlock, save on account of fornication, applies, according to the argument, to men and women alike." (St. Basil, *Letter 188: To Amphilochius, Concerning the Canons* 9, in *Early Church Fathers: Nicene and Post-Nicene Fathers*, eds. Philip Schaff & Henry Wace, Series II, vol. VIII, *Christian Classics Ethereal Library*, vol.2, CD-ROM, ed. Harry Plantinga [Wheaton, IL: Wheaton College, 1998].) See also I. Howard Marshall, "Ἀπολύω," in *New International Dictionary of New Testament Theology*, Collin Brown, ed. (Grand Rapids: Zondervan, 1999) as Zondervan Reference Software V. 2.7; idem, *Understanding the New Testament: Mark* (London: Scripture Union, 1978), 37; Thomas C. Oden & Christopher A. Hall, eds. *Mark. Ancient Christian Commentary on Scripture. New Testament II*, ed. Thomas C. Oden (Downers Grove, IL: InterVarsity, 1998), 134–36.

101. The text of Mark 10:11, which is in agreement with Luke 16:18a stays closer to the original tradition than Matt 5:32a, which is in agreement with Luke 16:18b because of the detected redactional emphasis of Matthew on social justice already shown in places like Matt 5:21–48; 6:14–15; 7:1–5, 12. Hence, Matthew stresses the outcome from the action of the leaving husband for the divorced wife. Due to the economic dependence of the women, such an action by the husband will push her to remarry and cause her to commit adultery. Thus, Matt 5:32a stays against Mark 10:11 which highlights the fact that the husband commits adultery against his wife. That leads to the conclusion that Luke 16:18a presents a purer version of Q than Matt 5:32a even without considering the exception clause (See also Gundry, *Mark*, 533, 542). However the relative pronominal construction of Mark "ὃς ἂν ἀπολύσῃ goes closer to the original Aramaic language which most probably was used by Jesus rather than the substantival participle ὁ ἀπολύων introduced by πᾶς used by Matthew (5:32a) and Luke (16:18a).

102. See also Daniel B. Wallace, *Greek Grammar Beyond the Basics: An Exegetical Syntax of the New Testament* (Grand Rapids: Zondervan, 1996), 696, 697.

103. The change of ἀπολύω to ἐξέλθῃ in some of the MSS might be defined as a major textual problem with the text of Mark 10:12 (there are three variants supported by dif-

adultery. That saying of Jesus is adapted by Mark to suit his Gentile audience,[104] which accepted that women could divorce their husbands,[105] and

---

ferent witnesses but the major issue is whether the wife divorces [ἀπολύσῃ, A Majority text vg sy$^{p.h}$ or ἀπολύσασα, ℵ B (C) (Δ, Ψ) 892 pc co] or she deserts [ἐξέλθῃ, D (Θ) f^{13} (28). 565. (700) it] her husband). That variation appeared most probably because of the difficulty in understanding the right of a woman to divorce her husband in a Jewish context (See also M. D. Hooker, *The Gospel according to Saint Mark*, 237). Apart from some exceptions, Jewish women were not allowed to divorce their husbands (Josephus, *Ant.* 15.7.10.259). Hence, the copyists introduced a word which pointed to a woman who leaves her husband who has already divorced her or who deserts her husband without divorcing him. The arguments for selection of the alternative reading with ἐξέλθῃ lack satisfactory explanation (To read ἐξέλθῃ in the light of Herodias' desertion of her husband [V. Taylor, *The Gospel according to St Mark*, 420, 421; R. W. Herron, Jr *Mark's Jesus on Divorce* (Electronic edition by Galaxie Software); W. L. Lane, *The Gospel of Mark*, 352; C. S. Mann, *Mark*, 392, 393] does not do favor to the fact that the issue with Herodias' desertion has been neither raised by John the Baptist nor by Jesus. What was condemned by John was the action of Herod [Mark 6:18]. Moreover to argue that the reading with ἐξέλθῃ establishes a parallel to Paul's words in 1 Cor 7:10, 11 is to overlook the meaning of the word χωρίζω which Paul uses in relation to divorce not to desertion. [See also Gundry, *Mark*, 543] And finally arguing for desertion instead of divorce would expose a misunderstanding of the first century context in which on many occasions divorce was established simply by separation. [See also G. D. Fee, *The First Epistle to the Corinthians*, 293-94; Gundry, *Mark*, 536; David Field, "Talking Points: The Divorce Debate-Where are we Now?" *Themelios* 8/3 [April 1983] 29.) and disregard the quality and multiplicity of the external evidence. (See also Gundry, *Mark*, 543; NA^{26}, 1993; NIV, 1984; NAS, 1977; NRS, 1989; NKJ, 1982.)

104. In general within Judaism women were not allowed to divorce their husbands (Josephus, *Ant.* 15.7.10.259; 18.9.6; *Mishnah Yebam.* 14:1; Str-B 1.318-19). Even though a woman might appeal for divorce before the rabbinic court when she suffers at the hand of her husband, in the area of her conjugal rights (*m.Ketub.*5.6); lack of support (*m.Ketub.*77a); abuse of her freedom (*m.Ketub.*7.2-5) etc, (cf. Philo, *The Special Laws* III.XIV.82.) and in some sections of early Judaism she might have had equal rights to man in relation to divorce (See also D. Instone-Brewer, *Jewish Women Divorcing Their Husbands in Early Judaism*, 352-53) the majority of scholars agree that woman's legal action could not have initiated divorce but eventually prompted the man to divorce her (See Gundry, *Mark*, 543; C. L. Blomberg, *Marriage, Divorce, Remarriage, and Celibacy*. Electronic edition by Galaxie Software; T. R. Rich, ed. *Divorce: Inequality of the Sexes* [online].). The argument derived from Papyrus Se'elim 13 will not be included because the reading of its text is very debatable. For the development of the debate see D. Instone-Brewer, *Papyrus Se'elim 13*, 349-57; Adiel Schremer, "Divorce in Papyrus Se'elim 13 Once Again: A Reply to Tal Ilan," *Harvard Theological Review* 91/2 (April 1998): 191-202; Tal Ilan, "The Provocative Approach Once Again: A Response to Adiel Schremer," *Harvard Theological Review* 2 (1998): 203-4.

105. This was a common practice in the Greco-Roman culture (cf. 1 Cor 7:10, 13). (See Gaius, *Institutes* 137a; Diodorus Siculus, *Library*, 12.18.1, XVIII; See also W. Hendriksen, *Mark*, 380; G. D. Fee, *The First Epistle to the Corinthians*, 294; Ben

it differs from Q in several details. First, the main difference is that Mark changes the woman from subject to object. In Mark she is divorcing her husband; in Q she is divorced by her husband (ὁ ἀπολύων τὴν γυναῖκα αὐτοῦ, Matt 5:32; Luke 16:18). Thus, ὃς ἐὰν in Matt 5:32 becomes ἐὰν αὐτὴ in Mark 10:12. Second, the voice of the verbs is changed from passive in Q (ἀπολελυμένην ἀπὸ ἀνδρὸς, Luke 16:18) (ἀπολελυμένην, Matt 5:32) to active in Mark 10:12 (αὐτὴ ἀπολύσασα τὸν ἄνδρα αὐτῆς). Third, the husband (ἀνδρὸς, Luke 18:32) becomes her husband (ἄνδρα αὐτῆς, Mark 10:12). And finally in Mark 10:12 the inclusion of another man (ἄλλον) becomes necessary. In this way, Mark attempts to correct women's abuse of freedom in the Greco-Roman world in relation to matters of divorce and remarriage.[106]

Mark's primary interest in the position of women in divorce and remarriage matters shapes his presentation of Jesus' prohibition of divorce and remarriage in its present absolute and rigorous form which allows no exceptions. On the one hand, Mark defends the equality of the wife's place in marriage to that of her husband, condemning the husband's licentious view of marriage in the light of the Pharisees' selfish misunderstanding of the Law related to divorce and remarriage matters. On the other hand, Mark condemns the women's excesses in exercising their freedom to divorce their husbands and remarry.

MATTHEW 19:3–12

In the present chapter I will devote myself to exegetical analysis of Matt 19:3–12, using a method which combines both narrative-critical and historical-critical approaches to the biblical text. First, the passage will be established within the context of the whole gospel and its place defined in the light of the gospel narrative. Second, a detailed analysis will be conducted through the use of the historical-critical method.

The narrative character of Matthew's gospel is expressed in the form of a story about Jesus the Christ with different major characters and a plot with culmination, resolution and leading theme. Three major characters are clearly defined in the story, Jesus, his disciples, and Israel. Jesus is depicted by the narrator as the main figure of the story. He is the Messiah,

---

Witherington III, *Conflict and Community in Corinth: A Socio-Rhetorical Commentary on 1 and 2 Corinthians* [Grand Rapids: Eerdmans, 1995] 171.)

106. See also Wessel, *Mark*. Zondervan Reference Software.

the Son of God who came to bring the salvation history to its climax by bringing salvation to Israel and the Gentiles (1:21; 20:28; 26:27–28). Jesus' disciples are the ones who follow him and share his life experiences (Matt 5:10–12; 9:15, 19; 12:30; 20:25–28; 26:38–40) but they are also the ones who failed in all respects to be the true disciples due to misunderstanding (15:15–16; 16:5–12), little faith (6:30; 8:26; 14:31; 16:8; 17:20), and even denial (26:30–46, 56, 69–75). In spite of this, Jesus did not forsake them, but helped them overcome their weaknesses. Another major character of the story is Israel, which consists of two groups of people, the crowds (14:5; 15:31–35; 21:26) and the Jewish leaders (9:11, 34; 12:14; 27:20). The former group is initially sympathetic toward Jesus, but later on joins the religious leaders in their battle against Jesus (26:47, 56; 27:15–26). The latter were associated by the narrator with the powers of evil or Satan (13:38–39) and were mainly interested in having authority over the people and receiving their praise (6:1–18; 23:1–36).[107]

The plot of the gospel's story is based on the conflict between Jewish leaders and Jesus related to the question of authority (21:23; 22:17, 24, 36, 43–45).[108] It unfolds in a progressive manner as the conflict between the religious leaders and Jesus intensifies throughout the gospel. In the beginning the leaders opposed Jesus through his disciples (9:9–13; 14–17), but soon they faced him themselves and turned the clash into a mortal one (12:14; 38–45). The conflict reaches its climax in the passion narrative, where the religious authorities are represented as seeing Jesus in his death on the cross as stripped of all the authority he previously exercised (27:41–43).[109] The resolution of the plot comes in the form of God's vindication of Jesus through his resurrection (16:21; 27:53; 28:6).[110] Jesus' death and resurrection bring salvation and forgiveness to all people (1:23; 20:28; 26:28; 28:19) and result in his empowerment with all authority on heaven and earth (28:18).[111]

The leading theme of Matthew's gospel might be summarized as the vindication[112] of Jesus as the expected King, the anointed one, the

---

107. See also D. R. Bauer, *The Major Characters of Matthew's Story*, 357–67.

108. Jack Dean Kingsbury, "The Plot of Matthew's Story," *Int* 46 (1992) 353.

109. Idem, *The Plot of Matthew's Story*, 354, 355.

110. See also idem, *The Place, Structure, and Meaning of the Sermon on the Mount within Matthew*, 132, 133.

111. Idem, *The Plot of Matthew's Story*, 347–356.

112. John Henry Bennet, "Matthew: An Apologetic," *BibSac* 103/412 (1946) 477–84.

Messiah and his Kingdom over Israel in fulfillment of the Old Testament prophecies. This theme might be elaborated by following some of the main developments of the gospel story. It begins with the presentation of the King and his ancestry (1:1–17), developing through his preparation and establishment (1:18–4:11), the disclosure of the Kingdom principles (4:12–7:29), the King's power and authority (8:1–11:1), and his new program (11:2–13:53). The thematic flow continues with the rejection of the King and his Kingdom (13:54–26:1),[113] goes through his passion (26:2–27:66), and is completed in his resurrection and triumph (28:1–20).[114] It is through the event of the cross and the resurrection that the theme of Matthew's gospel receives its full expression in the accomplishment of universal salvation for "all nations," including those who have rejected the King and his Kingdom (28:19).[115] Another major concern of Matthew's gospel, which is interwoven with the main theme, is the character of the citizens of the Kingdom in the light of the coming King. The gospel defines the community of those who have accepted Jesus as a household with kinship relationships, where God is the Father (6:9; 12:46–50; 18:1–4; 23:8, 9). The relationships in the family are established on the basis of high moral principles (5:27–30; 31–32; 19:3–9, 19).[116] Taking into consideration the main purpose of Matthew's gospel, which is defined as the apology of Jesus as the expected Messiah[117] in the light of the previously depicted themes, the place of the divorce pericopes in the gospel can be clearly established. In both of the divorce sayings Matthew underlines Jesus' authority as above that of the Law (5:31, 32)[118] and the Pharisees

113. John F. Walvoord, "Interpreting Prophecy Today. Part 3: The New Testament Doctrine of the Kingdom," *BibSac* 139/555 (1982) 213, 214.

114. S. Lewis Johnson, Jr. "The Argument of Matthew," *BibSac* 112/446 (1955) 143–54. Mal Couch, "The Importance of the Book of Matthew," *CTJ* 3 (1999) 224.

115. J. D. Kingsbury, "The Plot of Matthew's Story," 355.

116. S. C. Barton, "Family," in *Dictionary of Jesus and the Gospels*, eds. Joel B. Green, Scot McKnight, and I. Howard Marshall (Downers Grove, IL: InterVarsity, 1992), 227.

117. *The Purpose of Matthew* [online], Available at http://www-relg-studies.scu.edu/netcours/nt/synoptic/mthwprp.htm, Accessed on 5 November 2000. Charles Dailey, *Internal Evidence of Inspiration of the Four Gospels* [online], Available at http://charlesdailey.net/4gospels.html, Accessed on 5 November 2000. Luis J. Avila, *The Biblical and Theological Understanding of the Gospel of the Kingdom* [online], Available at http://www.jps.net/jehu/chapterone.html, Accessed on 5 November 2000. Mike Randall, ed. *The Gospel of Matthew* [online], Available at http://www.dabar.org/NewTestament/Berkhof/matthew.html, Accessed on 5 November 2000.

118. He starts with the introductory formula, ἐγὼ δὲ λέγω ὑμῖν expressing his un-

(19:3–9).[119] Hence, the teacher established new ethical standards of the Kingdom of God which are fundamental for his followers.[120]

Matthew establishes the *Sitz im Leben Jesu* to introduce the pericope of divorce and remarriage in the way Mark does, but according to his own style,[121] using two transitional verses (19:1, 2), which conclude the fourth main discourse (ch 18)[122] and begin the fifth narrative section (chs 19–22) of his gospel.[123] Both Matthew and Mark present Jesus' journey to

---

paralleled authority and objecting the Law (an adversative δέ). (See also Kingsbury, "The Place, Structure, and Meaning of the Sermon on the Mount within Matthew," 139.)

119. Jesus disregarded Pharisees' understanding of the Law (19:4–6) and established a new understanding (19:7–9).

120. For Jesus' followers, righteousness, which exceeds that of the scribes and the Pharisees, was mandatory in order to be part of God's Kingdom (Matt 5:20; 6:33). (See also Hagner, *Matthew 1–13*, 103, 550; Kingsbury, "The Place, Structure, and Meaning of the Sermon on the Mount within Matthew," 137.)

121. Based on the parallels between the synoptic divorce passages and in agreement with the most widely accepted theory, the two-document hypothesis, Matthew's sources for 19:1–12 might be defined as Mark and "M," but not "Q." First, Mark 2–12 is used by Matt 19:3–12 (Mark 10:2 cf. Matt 19:3; Mark 10:4 cf. Matt 19:7; Mark 10:5 cf. Matt 19:8; Mark 10:6 cf. Matt 19:4; Mark 10:7 cf. Matt 19:5; Mark 10:8 cf. Matt 19:6; Mark 10:9 cf. Matt 19:6; Mark 10:11, 12 cf. Matt 19:9.). Second, "M" might be the source of Matthew's part of the divorce pericope (19:10–12) which is not paralleled in any way by the rest of the Evangelists. Third, "Q" might not be a direct source of Matt 19:1–12 due to its association with parallels between Matt 5:32 and Luke 16:18 which do not follow Mark 10:11, 12, which is used by Matt 19:9 (Matt 5:32, ὁ ἀπολύων τὴν γυναῖκα αὐτοῦ = Luke 16:18, ὁ ἀπολύων τὴν γυναῖκα αὐτοῦ; Matt 5:32, ὃς ἐὰν ἀπολελυμένην γαμήσῃ μοιχᾶται = Luke 16:18, ὁ ἀπολελυμένην ἀπὸ ἀνδρὸς γαμῶν μοιχεύει.). See also Gundry, *Mark*, 533; Davies and Allison, *Matthew*, 1:527, 528; G. F. Hawthorne, *Marriage and Divorce, Adultery and Incest*, 598; Fitzmyer, *Matthean Divorce Texts and Some New Palestinian Evidence*, 200; Hagner, *Matthew 1–13*, 123; Lenski, *The Interpretation of St. Matthew's Gospel*, 230; Lloyd-Jones, *Studies in the Sermon on the Mount*, 257; Hare, *Matthew*, 53; Hendriksen, *Matthew*, 304; Nolland, *Luke 9:21–18:34*, 816, 819; Fitzmyer, *Luke X–XXIV*, 1120.

122. Matthew uses the phrase "καὶ ἐγένετο ὅτε ἐτέλεσεν ὁ Ἰησοῦς τοὺς λόγους τούτους" with some variations as a formula in order to conclude his five main discourses (19: 1a cf. 7:28; 11:1; 13:53; 26:1). See also Hagner, *Matthew 14–28*, 542.

123. No consensus has been reached among the Matthean scholarship in relation to the structure of his gospel. The fallibility of most of the suggested theories is due to the large variety of structural elements in the text which do not allow any superficial structure to be imposed upon the text without diminishing some aspects of the latter or leaving aside some of its crucial portions. Thus, the geographical-biographical proposal does not take into consideration the narrative-discourse literary aspect of the gospel; the chiastic/concentric and fivefold discourse theories do not provide an appropriate place for the birth and the passion narratives; the biographical and theological proposal

Jerusalem, but, while Mark emphasizes the massive pilgrimage of people going for the Passover,[124] Matthew, in his usual way, presents the crowds as following Jesus.[125] The two evangelists see Jesus' ministry to the crowds in two different ways. Mark, on the one hand, puts forward Jesus' teaching, which will be tested later by the Jewish Scriptures.[126] Matthew, on the other hand, after recording his fourth discourse, turns to the other aspect of Jesus' ministry to the crowds, that of healing.[127] The teacher's relationship with the crowds appeared to be the evangelist's pursuit and the pericope of divorce and remarriage was his starting point in presenting the series of meetings Jesus had with different people from the mob.[128] The

---

gives too much weight to the repeated phrase in 4:17 and 16:21. Therefore I will neither attempt to embrace any of the proposed theories nor try to develop any new theory, but allow the text to underline its structural signals and shape its own structure. In such a way I pay attention to all structural elements which different theories emphasized without losing the perspective of the gospel as a complete unit, i.e. story with main characters (Jesus, the disciples, and Israel: the crowds and the religious leaders), plot (the conflict between Jesus and the Jewish leaders), culmination (the passion narrative), and resolution (Jesus' resurrection). Hence, the pericope of divorce in its context focuses readers' attention on the geographical/biographical shift in Jesus' ministry (beginning of Judean ministry–journey to Jerusalem, 19:1–20:34), discourse-narrative shift in Matthew's writing (19:1 uses the formula for concluding the main discourses), and Matthew's thematic arrangement presenting the Lord's instructions to his followers for sacrificial life (disciples are led to understand the sacrificial nature of one's life for the Kingdom of God, 19:10–12 cf. 16:21–20:34). See also Scot McKnight, "Matthew, Gospel of," in *Dictionary of Jesus and the Gospels*, eds. Joel B. Green, Scot McKnight, I. Howard Marshall (Downers Grove, IL: InterVarsity, 1992), 529–532; John P. Meier, "Matthew, Gospel of," in *ABD* 4:627–37; Ulrich Luz, *The Theology of the Gospel of Matthew*, trans. J. Bradford Robinson (Cambridge: Cambridge University Press, 1995), 101–16; Hagner, *Matthew 1–13*, l–liii; idem, *Matthew 14–28*, 550; D. R. Bauer, *The Major Characters of Matthew's Story*, 357–67; Kingsbury, "The Place, Structure, and Meaning of the Sermon on the Mount within Matthew," 132, 133; idem, *Matthew as Story*, 2nd ed. (Philadelphia: Fortress, 1988); R. T. France, *Matthew: Evangelist and Teacher*, 141–53.

124. συμπορεύονται πάλιν ὄχλοι πρὸς αὐτόν, Mark 10:1. See also Gundry, *Mark*, 529.

125. Matt 19:2 cf. Matt 4:25; 8:1; 12:15; 14:13. Matthew adds the phrase, μετῆρεν ἀπὸ τῆς Γαλιλαίας to Mark's account in order to underline the fact that a crucial part of Jesus' ministry in this region is completed.

126. Mark 10:1 ἐδίδασκεν αὐτούς. That has been also the teacher's custom of dealing with the crowds (See Mark 1:21, 22; 2:13; 4:1, 2; 6:2, 6; 8:31; 11:17; 12:14, 35; 14:49).

127. Matt 19:2 ἐθεράπευσεν αὐτούς. See also Hagner, *Matthew 14–28*, 542; W. Hendriksen, *Mark*, 375.

128. In Matt 19:3–12 with the Pharisees (3–9) and his disciples (10–12); in 19:13–15 with the little children; in Matt 19:16–20:16 with the rich young man. See also C. L.

teaching of Jesus continues to have preeminence in this narrative section and, in each of the meetings, it underlines different aspects of discipleship.[129] Thus, Jesus' meeting with the Pharisees (3–9) and later his private conversation with his disciples (10–12) resulted in underlining the high ethical standards related to the marital aspect of life which the disciples should strive to reach, even through sacrificial endeavor.

Matthew, using Mark's account, presents the approach of the Pharisees to Jesus in the same way (Matt 19:3). The group of Jewish religious leaders wanted to test the teacher (πειράζοντες αὐτὸν). The three fundamental reasons for this attitude of the Pharisees might be considered the same as in Mark's account, i.e. Jesus' previous teaching on divorce and remarriage (Matt 5:32, 33),[130] the clash between Herod and John the Baptist,[131] and their intention to expose Jesus before the crowd as heretic.[132] However, unlike Mark, Matthew puts the question of the Pharisees within the frame of the Jewish debate about the grounds for divorce.[133]

Blomberg, *Marriage, Divorce, Remarriage, and Celibacy*, 162–97 (Electronic edition by Galaxie Software.)

129. See also Warren Carter, *Matthew* (Peabody: Hendrickson, 1996) 168, 169, 249–51.

130. The Pharisees' attempts to expose Jesus' teaching as inconsistent with the Law of Moses has reached the issue of divorce and remarriage. Mark does not have a previous teaching on divorce like Matthew but might express the same notion in the light of other issues discussed by Jesus and condemned by the Jewish leaders as "heretical" (Mark 2:5–7; 16–19; 23–28 etc.). See also Hays, *The Moral Vision of the New Testament*, 350; Alfred Plummer, *An Exegetical Commentary on the Gospel according to S. Matthew* (Grand Rapids: Eerdmans, 1956) 259.

131. Due to Jesus' present location (the territory where Herod imprisoned John, Mark 10:1; Matt 19:1) and their desire to see Jesus killed, the Pharisees attempted to make him criticize Herod on account of his marriage with Herodias and thus follow the destiny of John the Baptist (Matt 14:2–11 cf. Mark 6:14–28). See also Blomberg, *Marriage, Divorce, Remarriage, and Celibacy*; idem, *Matthew*, The New American Commentary: An Exegetical and Theological Exposition of Holy Scripture, ed. David S. Dockery, vol. 22 (Nashville: Broadman, 1992) 289.

132. The Jewish leaders usually approached Jesus with an opposing attitude (Matt 16:1–4; 12:38; 22:15 cf. Mark 7:5; 8:11; 12:13–15) prompted by their desire "to trap him in his words" (NIV, Matt 22:15 cf. Mark 12:13), convict him before the crowd as heretic, and carryout their plans to kill him (Matt 12:14 cf. Mark 3:6).

133. The Jewish debate about the proper grounds of divorce was between the two main schools (houses) of Hillel and Shammai. Even though both schools had equal support for the large period of time of their existence (flourished at the end of 1 BC) the sources (*b. Erub.* 13b; *j. Sota* 3.4 19a; *Zohar, Rava Mehemna* 3:245a) suggest that the school of Hillel eventually gained preeminence over its opponents. See also R. Goldenberg, "Shammai,

This editorial addition is due to the Jewish character of the evangelist's audience.¹³⁴ Hence, he introduces the phrase κατὰ πᾶσαν αἰτίαν (v3) into Mark's version of the question (Mark 10:2).¹³⁵ The clause is led by the

---

School of," in *ABD* 5:1158.

134. There is an overwhelming amount of proof and overall agreement among the Matthean scholarship that Matthew's audience was predominately Jewish. The early church fathers' tradition supports this conclusion: Origen's witness concerning Matthew's gospel documented by Eusebius testifies that "... it [the gospel of Matthew] was prepared for the converts from Judaism, ..." (Eusebius Pamphilus, *The Church History of Eusebius* 6.25.4.) The comments of Origen and Papias (Eusebius Pamphilus, *The Church History of Eusebius* 6.25.4; 3.39.16) that Matthew wrote in Hebrew language is a remark which in its literary and social context refers to Matthew's style not to the exact language of the gospel. The latter confirms the overwhelming linguistic evidence that the gospel is originally composed in Greek. The language issue, however, does not contradict the suggested audience but clarifies its nature as Jews of the Diaspora. The latter proposes an origin of the gospel outside the Palestine. The language does not contradict Matthew's authorship either, but suggests a latter Hellenistic Jewish Christian editorial work. (See also Hagner, *Matthew 1–13*, lxiv-lxxvii; S. McKnight, *Matthew*, 526-28; J. P. Meier, "Matthew, Gospel of," in *ABD* 4:623-27.) From a sociological point of view there is strong evidence that Matthew's community was primarily Jewish. The formalising of Judaism in the postwar period brought it into conflict with Jewish-Christianity. Thus, the latter parted from the former and attempted to prove its independence and legitimacy as a divinely based community which traced its roots back to Jesus the Messiah. In this respect Matthew's gospel shows both sides of the community: on the one hand, it has mutual beliefs with the Jewish synagogue; and, on the other hand, it criticizes the scribes and Pharisees for their religious practices and other matters of religious life on the basis of Jesus' teaching (Matt 4:23; 9:35; 10: 17; 12:9; 13:54; 23:4). (See also D. C. Sim, *The Gospel of Matthew and the Gentiles*, 36, 37; Stanton, "The Communities of Matthew," 379-91.) Finally, there is enormous amount of textual evidence for predominantly Jewish audience of the gospel. For a discussion of Jewish characteristics of Matthew's gospel, see R. T. France, *Matthew: Evangelist and Teacher*, 96-102.

135. There is a debate relating to the exclusion/inclusion of the phrase "κατὰ πᾶσαν αἰτίαν" by the two evangelists. The problem is whether Matthew judiazed the question of the Pharisees adding the phrase or Mark christianised it by removing the phrase. There are good arguments on both sides. The supporters of Mark's editorial activity argue that the only possible question which the Pharisees should have asked is about the grounds of divorce, the form seen in Matt 19:3. Thus, on the one hand, in Mark, Jesus' answer (missing the exception clause) required a question in which the grounds for divorce are not mentioned. On the other hand, the predominantly gentile audience of Mark did not need to be exposed to Jewish discussion of the grounds for divorce, since divorce is presented as having never been part of God's plan, (Hays, *The Moral Vision of the New Testament*, 350, 351; V. Taylor, *The Gospel according to St Mark*, 417). The proponents of Matthew's editorial work argue that in Mark (10:2) the Pharisees' question goes beyond the reasons for divorce to its lawfulness and as such parallels the challenge of some religious groups in the fist century to that issue, (see 11 QTemple 57:17-19; CD 4:21). (Gundry, *Mark*, 536; Fitzmyer, *Matthean Divorce Texts and Some New Palestinian Evidence*, 213-221).

preposition κατὰ which identifies the function of the accusative αἰτίαν as that of reference, indicating what limits/restricts the action of the verb, i.e. What is/are the juridical reason/s for divorce?[136] The adjective πᾶσαν adds the dimension of quantity. In this way, the Pharisees were asking Jesus whether he agreed with the school of Hillel, which allowed divorce on multiple grounds,[137] or the school of Shammai, which permitted divorce on the grounds of adultery.[138] Thus, according to the Jewish debate, the whole issue is related to the interpretation of the phrase עֶרְוַת דָּבָר, "ἄσχημον πρᾶγμα," (something objectionable) in Deut 24:1. However, according to Matthew, who changes the order of Mark,[139] Jesus is not willing to discuss that issue, but establishes the original will of God as presented in Gen 1:27; 2:24 (Matt 19:4, 5). The evangelist introduces Jesus' response to the leaders and teachers of the Law with the formula "οὐκ ἀνέγνωτε."[140] The emphasis falls on their erudition, the culminative aorist pointing to the result of the completed action and the negative particle calling to an affirmative answer, i.e. the Pharisees knew the Scriptures, they had read them. And at the same time, introduced in such a way, the rhetorical question implies their ignorance of its true meaning, i.e. they have not really

---

This is a more convincing theory, taking into consideration its fundamental assumptions that Matthew used Mark as his source, which fits the most widely accepted theory by the scholars, the Oxford four-documents hypothesis established by B. H. Streeter.

136. Contra Kilcallen who argues that Matthew's formulation of the Pharisees' question is equal to Mark's, i.e. they both refer to the lawfulness of divorce. (J. J. Kilgallen, *To What are the Matthean Exception-Texts [5,32 and 19,9] an Exception?* 104.)

137. "C. And the House of Hillel say, Even if she spoiled his dish,
D. 'since it is said, Because he has found in her indecency in anything.'
E. R. Aquba says, Even if he found someone else prettier than she,
F. 'since it is said, And it shall be if she find no favour in his eyes (Dt. 24:1).'" *Mishnah Gittin* 9:10 (*The Mishnah*, A New Translation by Jacob Neusner, 487.); Cf. Josephus, *The Antiquities of the Jews*, 4.8.23.253.

138. "A. The House of Shammai say, A man should divorce his wife only because he has found grounds for it in unchastity, B. 'since it is said, Because he has found in her indecency in anything (Dt. 24:1).'" *Mishnah, Gittin* 9:10; Cf. Philo, *The Special Laws* III. XIV.80; See also Hagner, *Matthew 14–28*, 547.

139. Matthew (vv4–7) reverses Mark's order which presents first the Pharisees' argument and than Jesus' contra-argument of creation (vv3–9).

140. Matthew makes a difference in presenting Jesus' addressing to the crowd with ἠκούσατε (Matt 5:21; 21:16) and his addressing to its leaders with οὐκ ἀνέγνωτε (Matt 19:4; 21:42; 22:31).

understood it.[141] While the Pharisees did not fully understand the implications of Gen 1:27 and 2:24 as related to divorce matters, to think about divorce in terms of these verses was not totally new for them. There were teachers who considered the issues of divorce in the light of the creation account (CD 4:21[142], Genesis Rabbah XVIII:V[143]), so it is reasonable to assume that the Pharisees intentionally refused to consider these creation passages as part of the divorce debate.

Jesus' analysis of divorce through the perspective of the creation of man and the first family goes beyond any such interpretation which existed during his time. He establishes the grounds for reading Gen 1:27 together with Gen 2:24 as the relation between unity and variety found in the divine image of man (Matt 19:4). The Creator God, who in the oneness of his being expresses the riches of varieties, created man in his own image to reflect that uniqueness in the diversity of the two genders, male and female (Gen 1:27),[144] who are brought into the oneness through

---

141. A reasonable paraphrase of that formula based on the rabbinic understanding of the difference between 'reading' and 'understanding' (*Mishnah, Shegalim* 1.4; *Genesis Rabbah* IX:26; *Babylonian Moed Qatan* 16b; *Berakoth* 18a; *Palestinian Berakoth* 4d) might be the following: "Surely you have read this/that text but you do not seem to understand its import." Cf. Matt 12:3, 5; 21:16, 42; 22:31; Mark 2:25; 12:10, 26; Luke 6:3; 10:26; Acts 8:30; 2 Cor 3:14; Rev 13:18; Neh 8:3, 8; Amos 4:5; Josephus, *Ant.* 4.8.209; See also Davies and Allison, *The Gospel according to Saint Matthew*, 3:9, 10; Davies and Allison, *The Gospel according to Saint Matthew*, 2:313, 314; D. Daube, *The New Testament and Rabbinic Judaism*, 422–37; C. L. Blomberg, *Marriage, Divorce, Remarriage, and Celibacy*. Electronic edition by Galaxie Software.

142. ". . . are caught twice in fornication: by taking two wives in their lives, even though the principle of creation is Gen 1:27 'male and female he created them.'" (*The Dead Sea Scrolls Translated: The Damascus Document*, trans. Wilfred G. E. Watson, [electronic version].)

143. Apart from the difficulty to establish the exact interpretation of Genesis Rabbah XVIII:V (*Genesis Rabbah: The Judaic Commentary to the Book of Genesis. A New American Translation*, vol.1, trans. Jacob Neusner, 193–196) among several possible options one will certainly notice the attempt of the Jewish interpreters to relate the matters of divorce (Deut 24:4; Mal 2:16) to the text of Gen 2:24. See also Gundry, *Mark*, 540; K. J. Thomas, *Torah Citations in the Synoptics*, 87.

144. The unique characteristic of man in relation to the rest of creation (Gen 1:1–25) which might be considered as God's image in man is related to human sexuality, not in a sense of procreation, but as an unique gender variety, "ἄρσεν καὶ θῆλυ ἐποίησεν αὐτούς" (LXX, Gen 1:27). (See also L. S. Capper, *The Imago Dei and Its Implications for Order in the Church*, 21–33; K. Barth, *Church Dogmatics*, vol.III, *The Doctrine of Creation*, part 1, 186; W. Brueggemann, *Genesis*, 33; See also P. Trible, *God and the Rhetoric of Sexuality*, 12–23.) That understanding of the image of God in man is underlined by the change of

the "one flesh" marriage union (Gen 2:24).¹⁴⁵ Thus, Jesus clearly states that the creation of man and woman is the basis for man's separation from his parents and uniting with his wife (Matt 19:4, 5).¹⁴⁶ The emphasis lies

the personal pronouns referring to God and man from singular to plural in vv 26 (καὶ εἶπεν ὁ θεός ποιήσωμεν ἄνθρωπον ... cf. καὶ ἀρχέτωσαν.... LXX) and 27 (LXX ἔσονται οἱ δύο εἰς σάρκα μίαν, WTT לְבָשָׂ֣ר אֶחָֽד). (cf. Gen 5:1. See also P. Trible, *God and the Rhetoric of Sexuality*, 21; J. H. Sailhamer, *Genesis*, Zondervan Reference Software (32-bit edition) Version 2.7.; K. Barth, *Church Dogmatics*, vol.III, *The Doctrine of Creation*, part 1, 195–196).

145. The relationship between variety and unity is underlined, on the one hand by Adam's words ("'This at last is bone of my bones and flesh of my flesh; this one shall be called Woman ['iššâ], for out of Man ['iš] this one was taken,'" [Gen 2:23, NRS]) through which he emphasized the variety of genders coming from the unity of his body (See also P. Trible, *God and the Rhetoric of Sexuality*, 98; N. M. Sarna, *Genesis*, 23; T. W. Jennings, *Theological Perspectives on Sexuality*, 3–6.); and on the other hand, it is underlined by the "one flesh" language of marriage (Gen 2:24: LXX ἔσονται οἱ δύο εἰς σάρκα μίαν, WTT לְבָשָׂ֣ר אֶחָֽד.) which points to the process in which the variety of the two genders, male and female, come back to their original unity. (See also P. Trible, *God and the Rhetoric of Sexuality*, 94–105; N. M. Sarna, *Genesis*, 23; K. Barth, *Church Dogmatics*, vol. III, *The Doctrine of Creation*, part 1, 304–6.)

146. The statement of Jesus starts with a prepositional clause (ἕνεκα τούτου) which pronoun refers to the act of creation of man and woman (v4). The statement (v5) expresses clearly the three basic stages of marriage. The first step, καταλείψει ἄνθρωπος τὸν πατέρα καὶ τὴν μητέρα, v5a does not primarily refer to the physical leaving of one's family, since this was not the Jewish practice, but to replacement of loyalties from the parents to the wife. Thus, the second step, κολληθήσεται τῇ γυναικὶ αὐτοῦ, v5b expresses the fact that the man unites with his wife giving her the prior place of his allegiance. That step anticipates the third one, ἔσονται οἱ δύο εἰς σάρκα μίαν, v5c which expresses the final result of the process of marriage, i.e. becoming one flesh. The latter focuses primarily on the columniation of the marriage, its sexual consummation (cf. 1 Cor 6:16) but it is also inclusive in regard to the spiritual unity of the two spouses. However in the present context "one flesh" primarily refers to the unity which both partners have in the marital bond, unity which echoes the original unity of Adam's body before the creation of the woman (Gen 2:21–24). The best way to express the kind of relationship the two spouses have in the marriage is that of a covenant (cf. Mal 2:14; Prov 2:17; See also S. Bacchiocchi, *The Marriage Covenant* [online]; W. Brueggemann, *Genesis*, 47; Dumbrell, *Covenant and Creation*, 36; K. A. Mathews, *Genesis 1–11:26*. The New American Commentary, 222; J. M. Sprinkle, *Old Testament Perspectives an Divorce and Remarriage*. Electronic edition by Galaxie Software; J. E. Adams, *Marriage Divorce & Remarriage in the Bible*, 16, 17). In Gen 2:24 this is suggested by the covenant terminology used to depict the process of marriage, i.e. abandoning (יַעֲזָב־אִישׁ, cf. Exod 23:32; 34:15; Deut 31:16; 31:20; See also G. J. Wenham, *Genesis 1–15*. Word Biblical Commentary, 352) one's former relationships (leaving father and mother) and cleaving (וְדָבַק, cf. Deut 4:4; 10:20; 11:22; 13:4; 30:20; Josh 23:8; 1 Kgs 11:2; See also N. M. Sarna, *Genesis*, 23; S. Bacchiocchi, *The Marriage Covenant* [online]; Wallis, "Dābhaq," in *Theological Dictionary of the Old Testament*,

in the fact that in marriage man and woman are no more two, but one flesh (ὥστε οὐκέτι εἰσὶν δύο ἀλλὰ σὰρξ μία). The temporal negative adverb οὐκέτι points to the end of singleness, "they are no longer two" (6a, NRS) and the adversative conjunction ἀλλὰ determines the relation between the two as one flesh, "but one flesh" (6a, NRS). It is on these grounds that Jesus concludes his answer to the Pharisees' question. This is made clear by Matthew through the inferential conjunction οὖν, "therefore what God has joined together let no man separate," (19:6, NKJ), (ὃ οὖν ὁ θεὸς συνέζευξεν ἄνθρωπος μὴ χωριζέτω). In this statement, the antithetical parallelism between the subjects (ὁ θεὸς, ἄνθρωπος) and their related verbs (συνέζευξεν, χωριζέτω) is complete. On the one hand, God, the infinite model of justice and righteousness, is contrasted to man, his fallen creation. On the other hand, God's action is depicted with a consummative aorist verb συνέζευξεν as already accomplished in the joining of the first family and presenting it as a model of unity for all future marriages.[147] The emphasis lies on the lasting results from the action of the Creator. Contrary to this, the human action of separation is prohibited by the imperative of prohibition, μὴ χωριζέτω. It is God who is the

---

80–84; G. J. Wenham, *Genesis 1–15*, Word Biblical Commentary, 352.) to the new one (the marriage partner), which is used by the prophets to express the covenant relationship between Yahweh and Israel. (Exod 19–24 cf. *Akkadian-Hittite Treaty*, ed. Daniel Bellissimo; See also E. A. Marterns, *God's Design: A Focus on Old Testament Theology*, 66–75; Dumbrell, *Covenant and Creation*, 94–99; Mathews, *Genesis 1–11:26*, The New American Commentary, 222, 223.) Due to the fact that covenant relations were based on loyalty between the two parties through fulfillment of particular stipulations the covenant could break if these conditions were not fulfilled (Lev 24:8; Num 18:19; 1 Chr 16:15; 2 Chr 13:5; 21:7; Ps 89:28; 105:8; 111:9; Isa 55:3; 61:8; Sir 45:24; Lev 26:44; Jer 31:32; Ezek 17:16, 18, 19; Zec 11:10; Prayer of Azariah 1:11; See also E. A. Martens, *God's Design*, 73; Dumbrell, *Covenant and Creation*, 96, 99.). Thus, the view of marriage as indissoluble is not sustainable on the grounds of "one flesh" union. (See also C. L. Blomberg, *Marriage, Divorce, Remarriage, and Celibacy*. Electronic edition by Galaxie Software. Contra Hays, *The Moral Vision of the New Testament*, 351; and Lenski, *The Interpretation of St. Matthew's Gospel*, 730.)

147. See Tertullian, *Exhortation to Chastity*, V "Unity of Marriage."
"And accordingly the man of God, Adam, and the woman of God, Eve, discharging mutually (the duties of) a marriage, sanctioned for mankind a type by the considerations of the authoritative precedent of their origin and the primal will of God." (Tertullian, *Exhortation to Chastity*, trans. S. Thelwall, in *Ante-Nicene Fathers: Translations of The Writings of the Fathers Down to A.D. 325*, eds. Alexander Roberts, & James Donaldson, vol.4. *Christian Classics Ethereal Library*, vol.2, CD-ROM, ed. Harry Plantinga [Wheaton, IL: Wheaton College, 1998].)

Master and the Lord of marriage, not man. Hence, man should not put aside his wife as Jews used to do (cf. Sirach 25:26).[148] With such a claim Jesus expresses God's prohibition of divorce.[149] However because the word χωριζέτω refers to divorce here[150] one may argue against the view of indissolubility of marriage since ἄνθρωπος may destroy the marital bond which ὁ θεὸς initiated.[151]

The Pharisees responded to Jesus' answer with a question "τί οὖν Μωϋσῆς ἐνετείλατο δοῦναι βιβλίον ἀποστασίου καὶ ἀπολῦσαι [αὐτήν], Matt 19:7." That question shows that the Pharisees were not willing to discuss the creation passages (Gen 1:27; 2:24) as related to the matters of divorce, but attempted to disprove Jesus' argument by showing that he places Moses (Gen 1:27; 2:24) against Moses (Deut 24:1-4). Thus, according to Matthew, they emphasized the nature of Moses' words as a command (ἐνετείλατο) to them. Understanding the nature of Deut 24:1-4 as a command, which includes legal divorce procedures but does

---

148. See also David E. Garland, *Reading Matthew: A Literary and Theological Commentary on the First Gospel* (New York: Crossroad, 1993), 199.

149. See also Hagner, *Matthew 14-28*, 548.

150. The word χωριζέτω here should be understood as a synonym of the word used for divorce ἀπολῦσαι in vv3, 7, 9 since χωρίζω in the context of marriage and divorce is understood as a technical term referring to a divorce action. (In the papyri: PS 166, II [II BC]; BGU 1101, 5; 1102, 8; 1103 [I BC] [BGU IV.1103, The Duke Databank of Documentary Papyri [online]; BGU IV.1102, The Duke Databank of Documentary Papyri [online]; BGU IV.1101, The Duke Databank of Documentary Papyri [online].]; See also W. Bauer, *A Greek-English Lexicon of the New Testament and Other Early Christian Literature*, 898; P Ryl II. 154^{25} [AD 66]; BGU 1.251^{6} [AD 81]; ib. IV. 1045^{22} [AD 154]; P. Ryl II. 154^{30} [AD 66]; See also J. H. Moulton and G. Millgan, *The Vocabulary of the Greek Testament. Illustrated from the Papyri and Other Non-Literary Sources*, 696. In other non-biblical literature: Polyb., 32, 12, 6. In LXX: 1 Esd 9:9; 1 Esd 9:36. In the NT: Matt 19:6; 1 Cor 7:10; Matt 1:19; Luke 16:18.) An exception might be when the word is used in the Jewish context of divorce, referring to the wife, than it carries the meaning of "separation, desertion," since the wife could not initiate divorce according to Jewish Law. (See Josephus, *Ant.* 15.7.10. 259). However here in Matt 19:6 the context refers to the husband not to the wife, since the question of the Pharisees was particularly related to him (Matt 19:3) and thus the exception related to the meaning of χωρίζω is not applicable.

151. As Blomberg states that "the only way to maintain an indissolubilist view of marriage and to make sense of v6b is to argue that Jesus is commanding people not to do in appearance that which in fact they cannot do in reality." (See C. L. Blomberg, *Marriage, Divorce, Remarriage, and Celibacy*. Electronic edition by Galaxie Software.) Contra Kilgallen (J. J. Kilgallen, *To What are the Matthean Exception-Texts [5,32 and 19,9] an Exception?* 104) who attempts to argue that man's inability to separate (divorce) what God united is the "fundamental and primary reason" for indissolubility of marriage.

not command them,¹⁵² Jesus affirms the law¹⁵³ but exposes the Pharisees' intentional misunderstanding of it. Four significant details of Jesus' reply lead to that conclusion. First, he uses the verb ἐπέτρεψεν to refer to Moses' words related to divorce (Deut 24:1).¹⁵⁴ Second, he relates Moses' words directly to the Pharisees by using the personal pronoun ὑμῖν. Third, Jesus exposes the Pharisees' attitude towards the law (Deut 24:1-4) as intentional ignorance based on their selfish desires¹⁵⁵ (πρὸς¹⁵⁶ τὴν σκληροκαρδίαν¹⁵⁷

152. An analysis of the text of Deut 24:1-4 makes it clear that what should be understood as a command is the remarriage of the divorced woman to her former husband after she has been married to another one (v4). However the command does not exclude divorce but assumes it to include the act of giving a divorce bill (vv1-3). See also Gundry, *Mark*, 539; J. M. Sprinkle, *Old Testament Perspectives on Divorce and Remarriage*. Electronic edition by Galaxie Software; *What Does the Bible Teach: The Divine Permission* [online]; J. C. Laney, *Deuteronomy 24:1-4 and the Issue of Divorce*. Electronic edition by Galaxie Software; Gundry, *Mark*, 539; J. H. Sailhamer, *Genesis*, Zondervan Reference Software [32-bit edition], Version 2.7; S. R. Driver, *Deuteronomy*, 269; J. H. Sailhamer, *The Pentateuch as Narrative*, 465.

153. Apart from scholarly attempts to find a proper reason (Gerhard Barth, "Matthew's Understanding of the Law," in *The New Testament Library: Tradition and Interpretation in Matthew* [Philadelphia: Westminster, 1976] 65, 93; Donald Senior, C. P., *What Are They Saying About Matthew?* [New York: Paulist, 1983] 52 searches for a group of Christian antinomians who required Matthew's defending of the Law) or proper perspective (Robert Banks, "Matthew's Understanding of the Law: Authenticity and Interpretations in Matthew 5:17-20," *JBL* 93/2 [June 1974]: 226-242, argues that the Law's affirmative attitude towards Jesus' authoritative teaching and position is most important) for interpreting Matthew's understanding of Jesus' attitude towards the Law, it is hard and even impossible for an exegete to read many Matthean texts (5:17-19, 23, 24; 6:1-4, 16, 18; 8:4; 19:17; 23:2-3, 23; 24:20) in any other way but as presenting Jesus' affirmation of the Law (See also Davies and Allison, *The Gospel according to Saint Matthew*, 1:501-2; Klyne R. Snodgrass, "Matthew's Understanding of the Law," *Int* 46 (1992) 369, 374; D. J. Moo, "Law," in *Dictionary of Jesus and the Gospels*, eds. Joel B. Green, Scot McKnight, I. Howard Marshall (Downers Grove, IL: InterVarsity, 1992), 459.

154. Matthew's change of the verbs (ἐπιτρέπω and ἐντέλλομαι Matt 19:7, 8 cf. Mark 10:3, 4) and the order of Pharisees' and Jesus' arguments found in Mark (10:3-9) is related to his intention to underline from one side the Pharisees' attempt to undermine Jesus' creation argument by pointing to Moses' command (Deut 24:1) and from the other side to emphasize once again (see Matthew's formula "οὐκ ἀνέγνωτε," in 19:4) the Pharisees' intentional ignorance in interpreting Deut 24:1-4 apart from Gen 1:27; 2:24 and in accordance with their selfish attitude toward marriage, divorce, and remarriage.

155. See Philo, *The Special Laws* III.XIV.80.

156. Here the preposition πρὸς introduces an adverbial prepositional clause as accusative of reference which establishes the limits of the action of the main verb. Thus, I propose the following translation: he said to them, "Moses allowed you to divorce your wives as far as your intentional misunderstanding of the law is concerned...."

157. Σκληροκαρδία is used in Matt 19:8 in the same way as in Mark 10:5 as an in-

ὑμῶν, Matt 19:8). Fourth, he leads them to the proper understanding of Deut 24:1–4 through the perspective of the creation accounts of man and woman (ἀπ' ἀρχῆς δὲ οὐ γέγονεν οὕτως, Matt 19:8) which he presented at the beginning of the discussion (Matt 19: 4–6 cf. Gen 1:27; 2:24).[158] With this clarification of the Pharisees' understanding, Jesus is ready to conclude his answer to them. Matthew introduces this conclusion in an emphatic way with λέγω δὲ ὑμῖν, "I say to you" (v9).

Jesus concludes the discussion with the Pharisees with a general prohibition of divorce and remarriage (v9). It is the same prohibition with which Mark finishes his discussion of divorce and remarriage, but has three redactional changes which relate to Matthew's Jewish-Christian audience. First, Matthew drops the phrase ἐπ' αὐτήν (Mark 10:11), because it is contrary to the common Jewish understanding. According to the latter, the victim of divorce is not the woman, but always the man, in this case the one whose wife is defiled.[159] Second, Matthew removes the whole saying of Mark which relates to the wife's act of divorce and remarriage, since such an issue bears minor significance in his Jewish context.[160]

---

tentional refusal of the Pharisees to understand properly God's commandment of Deut 24:1–4.

158. A legitimate reading of Deut 24:1–4, as a conditional law in which both the protasis and the apodosis are important, through the perspective of the creation account of the man and the first family (Gen 1:27; 2:24) is established on the basis of understanding the nature of marriage as covenant relationship. See also E. A. Martens, *God's Design*, 73; Dumbrell, *Covenant and Creation*, 96, 99; *Marriage Contract of a Former Slave Girl Who is Subject to Paramoné*, 420 B.C, trans. H. L. Ginsberg [online], J. M. Sprinkle, *Old Testament Perspectives on Divorce and Remarriage*. Electronic edition by Galaxie Software; D. Instone-Brewer, *Three Weddings and a Divorce: God's Covenant with Israel, Judah and the Church* [online].)

159. See Josephus, *The Antiquities of the Jews*, 4.8.23.

160. According to Jewish Law (See Josephus, *The Antiquities of the Jews*, 15.7.10. 259) Jewish women were not allowed to divorce their husbands. A woman might appeal for divorce before the rabbinic court when she suffers abuse from the husband, in the area of her conjugal rights (*Mishnah, Ketub*.5.6), lack of support (*Mishnah, Ketub*.77a), abuse of her freedom (*Mishnah, Ketub.* 7.2–5) etc. cf. Philo, *The Special Laws* III.XIV.82. (See also D. Instone-Brewer, *Jewish Women Divorcing Their Husbands in Early Judaism*, 352–353. Brewer even argues that women had equal rights to men in relation to divorce in some sections of early Judaism. D. Instone-Brewer, *Jewish Women*, 349.) However Gundry insists that a woman's legal action might not initiate divorce but eventually prompt the man to divorce her. (Josephus *Ant*. 15.7.10; 18.9.6; *Mishnah, Yebamot* 14.1.III L. "'The man who divorces his wife is not equivalent to a woman who receives a divorce.' M. 'For a woman goes forth willingly or unwillingly.' N. 'But a man puts his wife away only willingly;'" Str-B 1.318–19), (See R. H. Gudnry, *Mark*, 543; See also C. L. Blomberg,

Third, Matthew introduces the exception clause μὴ ἐπὶ πορνείᾳ.[161] Due to the importance of its proper understanding, I will analyze the clause in relation to its three main aspects, i.e. textually-critical, semantic, and syntactical.[162]

In relation to the variant readings of the exception clause, there is not a single witness which lacks it. However some of the MSS[163] have a version which follows the reading of Matt 5:32 (παρεκτὸς λόγου πορνείας). It is very likely that the copyists have tried to synchronize both versions through the perspective of that in Matt 5:32. However the variant μὴ ἐπὶ πορνείᾳ is preferable because of the quantity and quality of the witnesses (ℵ C³ K L (W) Z Θ Π 078. 28. 69. 157. 209. 565. 700. 892. 1006. 1010. 1071. 1241. (1342) 1424. 1506. m lat sy$^{s.p.h}$).[164]

The semantic analysis of the word πορνεία divides scholars into three main groups. Some scholars[165] argue that πορνεία means adultery, i.e. sexual activity of the wife with a man other than her husband, or various acts of sexual immodesty or misconduct. On this basis Jesus' words are in line with the school of Shammai,[166] which brings an objection from some

---

Marriage, Divorce, Remarriage, and Celibacy. Electronic edition by Galaxie Software; T. R. Rich, ed., *Divorce: Inequality of the Sexes* [online].) The argument based on the reading of papyrus Seʾelim 13 will not be included due to its very debatable nature. For the debate see D. Instone-Brewer, *Jewish Women*, 349–357; A. Schremer, *Divorce in Papyrus Seʾelim 13 Once Again: A Reply to Tal Ilan*, 191–202; T. Ilan, *The Provocative Approach Once Again: A Response to Adiel Schremer*, 203–4.

161. That editorial comment is made in Matthew 5:32 as well.

162. Stanley E. Porter and Paul Buchanan proved that any attempt to solve the problems with the proper understanding of the exception clause by appealing to a logical solution is inadequate. See Stanley E. Porter and Paul Buchanan, "On the Logical Structure of Matt 19:9," *Journal of the Evangelical Theological Society* 34/3 (September 1991): 336–341. Electronic edition by Galaxie Software, 1998.

163. D f¹³ 33 pc it (sy^c) sa mae. Critical Apparatus NA²⁶ (Kurt and Barbara Aland, eds. *Critical Apparatuses of NA²⁶* [Munster/Westphalia: Deutsche Bibelgesellschaft, 1993]).

164. Also NA²⁶; Hagner, *Matthew 14–28*, 545; Michael W. Holmes, "The Text of the Matthean Divorce Passages: A Comment on the Appeal to Harmonization in Textual Decisions," *JBL* 109 (1990) 651.

165. David Hill, *The Gospel of Matthew*, 279; Davies and Allison, *The Gospel according to Saint Matthew*, 1:529–31; Andreas Köstenberger, "Marriage and Family in the New Testament," in *Marriage and Family in the Biblical World*, ed. Ken M. Campbell (Downers Grove, IL: InterVarsity, 2003), 260, 261.

166. See also W. F. Albright and C. S. Mann, *Matthew* (New York: Doubleday, 1971), 225, 226; Floyd V. Filson, *The Gospel according to St. Matthew*. BNTC (London: A. & C. Black, 1975), 206, 207.

scholars that, if this meaning of the word is accepted, the distinctiveness of Jesus' teaching on divorce and remarriage is lost.[167] However, as stated above, Jesus' teaching was not completely unique (cf. CD 4:21; Genesis Rabbah XVIII:V) and Matthew edited the question of the Pharisees with the phrase "κατὰ πᾶσαν αἰτίαν" in order to prepare for Jesus' agreement with one of the schools in the debate. Nevertheless, even Jesus' prohibition of divorce and remarriage except for πορνεία exceeds that of the school of Shammai, since the former just allows divorce and remarriage for πορνεία, but the latter requires it.[168] Thus, on the grounds of Moses' command (Deut 24:1–4), the school of Shammai emphasized the necessity of divorce when the issue of adultery is involved, but Jesus emphasized the permanence of marriage based on God's original intention (Gen 1:27; 2:28).[169] Another objection relates to the use of the term πορνεία instead of μοιχεία, a term used with specific reference to adultery.[170] However, the verbal form of the word μοιχεία appears in the same verse (μοιχάομαι, v9) and it would have been redundant if repeated in the exception clause. Contrary to μοιχεία, the term πορνεία is more inclusive and as such it better serves Matthew's purposes, covering all the main areas of sexual misconduct which were known in Jewish and Hellenistic cultures.[171] The

---

167. J. C. Laney, *No Divorce and No Remarriage*, 34; John L. McKenzie, "The Gospel according to Matthew," in *The Jerome Biblical Commentary*, eds. Raymond E. Brown, S. S. et.al., vol.2., The New Testament and Topical Articles (Norwich: Fletcher & Son, 1977), 96; D. A. Carson, "Matthew," in *The Expositor's Bible Commentary*, ed. F. E. Gabelein, vol.8 (Grand Rapids: Zondervan, 1984), 415.

168. See also C. L. Blomberg, *Marriage, Divorce, Remarriage, and Celibacy*. Electronic edition by Galaxie Software; idem, *Matthew*, 110, 111; R. V. G. Tasker, *Matthew*, 184.

169. See also W. Hendriksen, *Matthew*, 714, 715.

170. The term μοιχεία is used in biblical and nonbiblical literature with the meaning of adultery (Wis 14:26; Hos 4:2; Jer 13:27; Matt 15:19; Mark 7:22; John 8:3; Philo, *Spec. Leg.* 2.13; Josephus, *Ant.* 16.340). See also W. Bauer, *A Greek-English Lexicon of the New Testament and Other Early Christian Literature*, 528.

171. πορνεία covers "every kind of extramarital, unlawful, or unnatural sexual intercourse fornication, sexual immorality, prostitution" (Timothy and Barbara Friberg, *Analytical Lexicon to the Greek New Testament*, 2000 edition. [electronic edition], BibleWorks v. 5.0.020w, 2001). Apart from its figurative usage in the OT and Revelation of John (it expresses the apostasy of Israel from God in Hos 6:10; Jer 3:2, 9; in Revelation 19:2 it is used for presenting the misconduct of the city of Babylon) the term refers to all kinds of unlawful sexual intercourse including adultery, and as such is used by nonbiblical (Philo, *Mos.* 1.300 slightly different from μοιχεία), biblical and extra-biblical authors (In LXX, Sir 23:23, and in Hermas, *Commandment* 4.1 as synonym of μοιχεία; *The Shepherd of Hermas*, in Ante-Nicene Fathers: Translations of The Writings of the Fathers Down to A.

last objection relates to the punishment of adultery according to Jewish Law, which was death, not divorce (Lev 20:10; Deut 22:22). In response to this objection, the evidence shows that during the time of Jesus compulsory divorce was practiced instead of death penalty.[172] Thus, Matthew offered the exception clause for his Jewish-Christian audience for whom the matter of adultery was a serious offense to marriage.[173]

Some scholars[174] maintain that the proper meaning of πορνεία is that of premarital unchastity, and the ground for understanding πορνεία is the text of Deut 22:13–21, which speaks about the adultery of the wife before her marriage. During the time of Jesus, the punishment for such sin was changed from death to desertion of the wife by the husband (cf. Matt 1:19). This view may not be sustained, however, since the arguments from both sides in the debate presented in Matt 19:3–12 assumed married couples, not just engaged partners.[175]

D. 325, eds. Alexander Roberts & James Donaldson, vol. 2. [Grand Rapids: Eerdmans, 1973], *Christian Classics Ethereal Library*, v.2, CD-ROM, ed. Harry Plantinga [Wheaton, IL: Wheaton College, 1998]; Mark 7:21; John 8:41; Acts 15:20; 1 Cor 5:1), and Matthew in particular (Matt 5:32; 15:19; 19:9). See also W. Bauer, *A Greek-English Lexicon of the New Testament and Other Early Christian Literature*, 698; Hagner, *Matthew 14–28*, 549; H. Reisser, "Discipline, Prudence, Immorality, Prostitute," in *New International Dictionary of New Testament Theology*, ed. Collin Brown (Grand Rapids: Zondervan, 1999). Zondervan Reference Software V. 2.7; C. Brown, Χωρίζω. Zondervan Reference Software V. 2.7.

172. "If a woman is deliberately unfaithful to her husband she becomes forbidden to him and he must divorce her, as it says 'Her first husband . . . cannot take her again to be his wife after she has been defiled'; and she is also forbidden to marry the man with whom she was unfaithful. If a man tells his wife before witnesses that she must not be alone with someone and she disobeys, she also becomes forbidden to both of them." (Halacha, 26, *Adultery – Sotah* [online], Available at http://www.torah.org/learning/halacha-overview/chapter26.html?print=1, Accessed on 18 October 2000; See also Hays, *The Moral Vision*, 354.)

173. Rabbinic Judaism provided divorce as an action against the unfaithful wife (*Mishnah, Sotah* 5:1; *Mishnah, Yebamot* 2:8 "F. He who is suspected [of having intercourse] with a married woman, and they [the court] dissolved the marriage with her husband, G. even though he [the suspect] married [the woman], H. he must put her out." 1 QapGen 20:15) See also Hagner, *Matthew 14–28*, 549; Hays, *The Moral Vision of the New Testament*, 354.

174. Mark Geldard, "Jesus' Teaching on Divorce," *Churchman* 92 (1978) 134–43; A. Isaksson, *Marriage and Ministry in the New Testament* (Lund: C. W. K. Geerup, 1965), 135.

175. Laney, *No Divorce and No Remarriage*, 35.

A good number of scholars[176] support the view that πορνεία refers to kinship marriages prohibited in Lev 18:6–18. Due to the fact that this was an issue in Gentile communities, some of their members had a difficult time in communicating with Christian-Jews after their conversion. Hence, in agreement with the decision of the apostolic decree (Acts 15:28–29), these Gentile-Christians were allowed to end their incestuous marriages by divorce. Accordingly, these scholars argue that since Matthew's community appeared to be one of that kind, such an exception was necessary.[177] Moreover, according to them, with this understanding, the high standard of the Kingdom ethics has been successfully preserved. There are several problems with this view. Firstly, it is selective to read the text of Lev 18:6–18 as extending its prohibition only to incestuous marriages. The text refers to other sexual misconduct, which might also be part of the apostolic creed given in Acts 15. Secondly, it is hard to base the meaning of πορνεία on a passage (Lev 18:6–18) in which the word does not appear at all. Thirdly, a strong reason to reject such an interpretation of the word is the fact that kinship marriages were not even recognized as true marriages within the boundaries of Judaism and as such did not require divorce.[178] Fourthly, to argue that the meaning of πορνεία established by

---

176. See Fitzmyer, *Matthean Divorce Texts and Some New Palestinian Evidence*, 211; Ben Witherington III, "Matthew 5:32 and 19:9 – Exception or Exceptional Situation?" *NTS* 31 (1985) 571–76; J. C. Laney, *No Divorce and No Remarriage*, 35–37; Kingsbury, "The Place, Structure, and Meaning of the Sermon on the Mount within Matthew," 140; Leopold Sabourin, S.J., *The Gospel according to St. Matthew* (Bandra: St. Paul, 1982), 2:734–35.

177. Witherington argues (*Matthew 5:32 and 19:9*, 573.) that Jesus was using the texts from Genesis (Matt 19:4, 5, 6) as a maneuver to bring Rabbis to their normal understanding of Gen 2:28 as prohibiting incestuous marriages (Witherington quotes R. Akiba exegesis on Gen 2:28 cited in B. T. Sanhedrin 58a) and just after that to point to the absolute prohibition of divorce and remarriage including the exception clause which refers to incestuous relationships (Matt 19:9). This logic creates few problems for proper understanding of the passage and the role of the exception clause. The interpretation of Gen 2:28 suggested by Witherington was not the only interpretation by Jewish exegetes of the passage and other interpretations of the verse might fit much better in the context of divorce (cf. CD 4:21; Genesis Rabah XVIII:V; See also Gundry, *Mark*, 540.). If one accepts that Jesus used Genesis passages in the way suggested by Witherington here in Matthew 19:3–12, one's whole logic collapses when he meets the same passages used by Jesus in Mark 10:2–12 but without the appearance of the exception clause.

178. Mitzvot 86–100. (Rambam, "List of 613 Mitzvot," in *Halakhah*, ed. Tracey R. Rich [online], Available at http://www.jewfaq.org/613.htm, Accessed on 08 October 2000.) See also Tracey R. Rich, ed., *Marriage: The Marital Relationship* [online], Available at http://www.jewfaq.org/marriage.htm#Relationship, Accessed on 08 October 2000;

DSS relates only to incest is inadequate in relation to all the evidence.[179] Finally, one last objection to the last two views should be provided. It is illogical and contextually weak to suggest the permissibility of divorce on the grounds of premarital unfaithfulness and incest and not to allow it on the grounds of adultery.[180] Thus, it is hard to understand the ethics of the Kingdom as intolerant of these two kinds of marital abuse, but tolerant of adultery or other sexual misconduct. Therefore, the first view should be accepted as the least problematic, inclusive in relation to the second and third views, and best fitting Matthew's intentions, context, and audience, since it includes a variety of immoral sexual activities.[181]

Syntactically, the function of the exception clause as such has been challenged by some scholars, who argue that it should be understood as absolute prohibition, i.e. "not even in the case of."[182] That argument, how-

---

Hagner, *Matthew 1-13*, 124.

179. One might be quite sure that πορνεία is a translation of the Hebrew זְנוּת (Sir 23:23; 26:9; Nah 3:4; Isa 47:10; Jer 2:20; Ezek 16:25) on the basis of LXX. And also that DSS relates זְנוּת to the matters of incest, polygamy, and divorce (11 QT; Zodokite Document 4-5). (See John Kampen, "A Reexamination of the Relationship Between Matthew 5:21-48 and the Dead Sea Scrolls," *SBL Seminar Papers* [1990] 51-54.) But one should also recognize the fact that זְנוּת does not refer only to polygamy, divorce, and incest in DSS but also to the matter of fornication. That becomes clear by the consideration of a parallel between Jubilees 20:3-6, and 11 QT 59:13-14, which underlines the matter of fornication as related to the issues of uncleanness. (See also J. Kampen, *A Reexamination of the Relationship Between Matthew 5:21-48 and the Dead Sea Scrolls*, 51, 52.)

180. Divorce was mandatory in the case of adultery according to Jewish legislation: See *Mishnah, Yebam* 2:8; *Mishnah, Sota* 5:1, Roman's legislation: "(6) After having killed the adulterer, the husband should at once dismiss his wife, and publicly declare within the next three days with what adulterer, and in what place he found his wife. . . . (8) It has been decided that a husband who does not at once dismiss his wife whom he has taken in adultery can be prosecuted as a pimp." (Paul, *Opinions* 2.26.1-8, 10-12, 14-17. L.), and Greek legislation: "When he has caught the adulterer, it shall not be lawful for the one who has caught him to continue living with his wife, and if he does so, he shall lose his civic rights and it shall not be lawful for the woman who is taken in adultery to attend public sacrifices; and if she does attend them, she may be made to suffer any punishment whatsoever, short of death, and that with impunity."(Demosthenes, *Speeches* 51-61: speech 59, section 87 [*Apollodorus Against Neaera*], trans. A. T. Murray & Norman W. DeWitt [online], Available at http://www.perseus.tufts.edu/cgi-bin/ptext?lookup=Dem.+59+86, Accessed on 16 October 2000)

181. See also Hays, *The Moral Vision of the New Testament*, 353; C. L. Blomberg, *Marriage, Divorce, Remarriage, and Celibacy*. Electronic edition by Galaxie Software; Köstenberger, *Marriage and Family in the New Testament*, 258-261.

182. Maximilian Zerwick, *Biblical Greek*, Eng. ed. (Rome: Scripta Pontificii Instituti Biblici, 1963), 43/128; Michael Brunec, "Tertio de clausulis divortii Mt 5, 32 et 19, 9," in

ever, cannot be sustained in the light of the evangelist's use of the negative particle μή. In order to make the exception clause absolute another negative particle should have been used, i.e. μηδέ.[183] A different syntactical debate concerning the relation of the exception clause to the rest of the sentence should be exposed as well. Does the exception clause modify the divorce part of the sentence, the remarriage part, or both parts? This issue is resolved by defining the exact position of the clause in the sentence. It has three possible positions, at the beginning, in the middle, and at the end. If it had been placed at the beginning of the sentence, the emphasis would have been on the exception clause itself, but this was not Jesus' intention. If it had been placed at the end of the sentence, it would have limited the saying (v9) to only the cases which are directly linked to divorce and remarriage because of adultery. Thus, the least ambiguous position of the clause is in the middle and from this position it modifies both verbs (ἀπολύσῃ, γαμήσῃ).[184] Moreover, from the logical perspective, the place of the exception clause in the sentence does not make any difference to its relation to both verbs.[185]

Therefore, on the basis of the textually-critical, semantic, and syntactical arguments presented so far, I conclude that the exception clause stays firmly in Matthew's text as permission for divorce and eventual remarriage on the basis of adultery and other related sexual misconduct.[186]

Verbum Domini 27 (1949): 3-16; See also D. A. Carson, "Matthew," in *Expositor's Bible Commentary: New Testament*. Zondervan Reference Software (32-bit edition) Version 2.7.

183. See also Hagner, *Matthew 14-28*, 549; C. L. Blomberg, *Marriage, Divorce, Remarriage, and Celibacy*. Electronic edition by Galaxie Software.

184. See also Nolland, *Luke 9:21—18:34*, 816. If Jesus wanted to relate the exception clause only to divorce in the fist century context where remarriage was automatically assumed after divorce, he should have done it much more clearly. (See also C. L. Blomberg, *Marriage, Divorce, Remarriage, and Celibacy*. Electronic edition by Galaxie Software.) Contra Heth who argues that the meaning of the exception clause should be restricted to permission of divorce for Jesus' disciples from their adulterous wives without a chance for remarriage. (William A. Heth, "The Meaning of Divorce in Matthew 19:3-9," *Churchman* 98/2 [1984] 146) Heth disregarded the context which clearly points that the answer of Jesus in Matt 19:9 is related to the Pharisees' question, not to the disciples.

185. Phillip H. Wiebe, "Jesus' Divorce Exception," *Journal of the Evangelical Theological Society* 32/3 (September 1989) 328-335. Electronic edition by Galaxie Software, 1998.

186. See also St. Aurelius Augustin, *Our Lord's Sermon on the Mount* 1.16.46; Lenski, *The Interpretation of St. Matthew's Gospel*, 734, 735; W. Hendriksen, *The Gospel of Luke*, 781; David Janzen, "The Meaning of *Porneia* in Matthew 5:32 and 19:9: An Approach from the Study of Ancient Near Eastern Culture," *JSNT* 80 (2000) 67.

Having compared Matthew 19:9 with Matthew 5:32; Mark 10:11–12; Luke 16:18; and 1 Cor 7:10–11, one may easily grasp the fact that the exception clause is Matthew's editorial addition to the saying of Jesus.[187] By means of this addition, Matthew attempts to bring the absolute, rigorous, idealistic saying of Jesus into the everyday life of his Jewish-Christian community whose members had problems in living with an adulterous partner.[188] By using the exception clause, Matthew does not contradict Jesus' proclamation, but defines it in relation to his community.[189] Jesus' answer to the Pharisees is clear: "whoever divorces his wife, except for unchastity, and marries another commits adultery." (NRS) Hence, any other reason[190] to divorce one's wife than πορνεία is illegal[191] and results in adultery. Jesus referred to the normal divorce procedure in the first century[192] and did

---

187. Contra Blomberg (C. L. Blomberg, *Marriage, Divorce, Remarriage, and Celibacy*. Electronic edition by Galaxie Software.) and Witherington (*Matthew 5:32 and 19:9*, 580) who argue that the exception clause is an authentic saying of Jesus. Blomberg's arguments are too general and do not include a discussion of Mark as Matthew's source and the lack of an exception clause in the former. Witherington assumes Mark's, Paul's, and Luke's omission of the exception clause without discussing his argument from source-critical point of view.

188. *Mishnah, Sotah* 5:1; See also Hays, *The Moral Vision of the New Testament*, 356; Hagner, *Matthew 14–28*, 549; Dale C. Allison, Jr. "Divorce, Celibacy and Joseph (Matthew 1.18–25 and 19.1–12)," *JSNT* 49 (March 1993) 3.

189. See also C. Brown, Χωρίζω. Zondervan Reference Software V. 2.7.

190. The limits of the present debate related to the grounds of disagreement between the opposite sides (Jesus versus the popular liberal position of the school of Hillel) do not require exposition of all their mutual grounds which extend the legitimate reasons for legal divorce to these violations of the marriage covenant based on Exodus 21:10–11. (See also D. Instone-Brewer, *Divorce and Remarriage in the Bible*, 166)

191. A legal divorce based on a just cause was a very significant matter in first-century Judaism and the ancient Near East, since it determined who could possess the woman's dowry after the divorce (*Mishnah, Ketubot* 7:1–5, 6, *Nedarim* 11:12, *Makkot* 1:1, *Arakhin* 6:1–2, *Yebamot* 15:7; *Code of Hammurabi* 139, 141; See also Janzen, *The Meaning of Porneia*, 72–78).

192. Heth argues that ἀπολύσῃ in Matt 19:3, 7, 8, 9 refers to "simple separation." (W. A. Heth, *The Meaning of Divorce in Matthew 19:3–9*, 141) Hence, he claims that the word means "separate without the right of remarriage" (p.141) in Matt 19:9. Heth bases his argument on a logical deduction dividing v9 into two statements arranged around the exception clause and on an interpretation of "one flesh" in Gen 2:24 as "kin or blood relations."(p.142) However his argument suffers in its both statements: it presents a meaning of "one flesh" which contradicts Paul's understanding of the concept expressed in 1 Cor 6:16 and it suggests unique meaning of ἀπολύσῃ not attested anywhere in the biblical and nonbiblical literature. (See W. Bauer, *A Greek-English Lexicon of the New Testament and Other Early Christian Literature*, 96; Procksch, "Λύω and Compounds," in

not condemn all remarriages,¹⁹³ but only the ones following an illegal divorce.

When Jesus' conversation with the Pharisees is over, leaving them without a single reply, his disciples come onto the scene (Matt 19:10). The place of the following dialog and the response of the disciples to Jesus' teaching is probably the same as in Mark 10:10.¹⁹⁴ The disciples' reaction to Jesus' words is extremely negative. They presented celibacy as a better option to a lifelong marriage (οὐ συμφέρει γαμῆσαι). To place celibacy in a better position than marriage for Jewish men was an unthinkable argument.¹⁹⁵ From the disciples' reaction, one might easily conclude that they

---

TDNT, ed. Gerhard Kittel, trans. Geoffrey W. Bromiley—electronic ed.—Grand Rapids: Eerdmans, c1964–c1976. Logos Library System 2.1g; Johannes P. Louw and Eugene A. Nida, eds., *Greek-English Lexicon of the New Testament: Based on Semantic Domains* [New York: United Bible societies, c1989]. Logos Library System 2.1g)

193. Cf. Rom 7:3. ἄρα οὖν ζῶντος τοῦ ἀνδρὸς μοιχαλὶς χρηματίσει ἐὰν γένηται ἀνδρὶ ἑτέρῳ· ἐὰν δὲ ἀποθάνῃ ὁ ἀνήρ, ἐλευθέρα ἐστὶν ἀπὸ τοῦ νόμου, τοῦ μὴ εἶναι αὐτὴν μοιχαλίδα γενομένην ἀνδρὶ ἑτέρῳ. Contra Heth who argues that with his claim in Matt 19:9 Jesus condemned any remarriage as adultery. (William A. Heth, "Unmarried 'For the Sake of the Kingdom' [Matthew 19:12] in the Early Church Unmarried," *Grace Theological Journal* 8/1 [Spring 1987] 56–87. Electronic edition by Galaxie Software, 1999.)

194. This claim is established on the assumption that Matthew used Mark and the disciples' reply relates to the previous debate (λέγουσιν αὐτῷ οἱ μαθηταὶ [αὐτοῦ], Εἰ οὕτως ἐστὶν ἡ αἰτία τοῦ ἀνθρώπου μετὰ τῆς γυναικός, Matt 19:10 cf. οἱ μαθηταὶ περὶ τούτου ἐπηρώτων αὐτόν, Mark 10:10). However, neither does Matthew mention the place of the conversation between Jesus and his disciples, nor does Mark mention the exact question of the disciples.

195. On the one hand, for a Jewish man, marriage was of crucial significance, since it provided for his proper treatment in the Jewish community and his personal benefits, and it affirmed God's image through the procreation. ("Whoever has no wife lives without good, without help, without joy, without blessing, without atonement. . . . if he cannot make atonement for his wife, he cannot make atonement for himself (Lev 16:11). . . . 'Also he is not a complete man (Gen 5:2)'. . . . 'Such a person also diminishes the image of God (Gen 9:6, 7)'. . . ." [*Genesis Rabbah* XVII:II]; "Every man is required to have children (at least one son and one daughter), as it says 'Be fruitful and increase.' A man should not marry a woman who cannot bear children unless he has already fulfilled this commandment; if his wife has not conceived after ten years or if she miscarries repeatedly he should take another wife." [Halacha, *Women - Nashim*, 22, Procreation [online], Available at http://www.torah.org/learning/halacha-overview/chapter22.html. Accessed on 19 October 2000]; Gen 1:28; *Mishnah, Yebamot* 6:6). On the other hand, the Jewish attitude toward eunuchs was negative. The latter were not allowed to join the people of Israel (Deut 23:1; *Mishnah, Yebamot* 8:4–6). There were some exceptions in the Essenes communities but they did not find any acceptance in the main stream of Judaism. (1 QRule of the Congregation 2.1–4; Josephus, *Bell.*, 2, 120; *Ant.*, 18, 21; Philo,

had the same attitude toward marriage as the Pharisees did. However a question arises, why did not the Pharisees use the same argument and point to the deficiency of Jesus' statement from the viewpoint of the absurdness of celibacy for Jewish men? And moreover, why did not Jesus defend his divorce and remarriage argument against the disciples' comment, rather than attempting to approve celibacy on religious grounds (vv11–12)? Perhaps the best answer to these questions might be that this whole section (vv10–12) is Matthew's additional comment for the purpose of offering a defense of celibacy.[196] Furthermore, neither Mark nor Luke mention anything related to the issue of celibacy. Thus, it might be assumed that there was an issue in Matthew's community related to the place of eunuchs in it and especially those who renounced marriage for the sake of the Kingdom of Heaven (v12). Hence, on the ground of such an assumption, one may easily understand why the disciples made such a claim and why Jesus shifted the conversation to an explanation of celibacy as an alternative to marriage.

In comparison with Mark's account (10:10–12), one may expect here in Matthew 19:10–12 that Jesus should challenge the disciples to build sound lifelong marital relationships.[197] Jesus, however, replies to them in a restrictive manner that they cannot rule out marriage completely, since celibacy is an option only available for some (οὐ πάντες χωροῦσιν τὸν λόγον [τοῦτον][198]).[199] He explains that the ones who are qualified for such a life are the ones to whom that ability is given. Jesus implies that a third party is responsible for granting such an ability. Matthew expresses this

---

Apol. pro Iudaeis in *Eus. Praep. Ev.*, 8, 11, 14 and 1OS; See also Gustav Stählin, "Φίλος," in *TDNT*—electronic ed.—Grand Rapids: Eerdmans, c1964–c1976. Logos Library System 2.1g; *Where We Stand on Jewish Marriage* [online], Available at http://www.fishponds.freeserve.co.uk/where_we_stand/marriage.html, Accessed on 6 October 2000.)

196. See also Allison, *Divorce, Celibacy and Joseph*, 5; Davies and Allison, *The Gospel according to Saint Matthew*, 3:19; C. L. Blomberg, *Marriage, Divorce, Remarriage, and Celibacy*. Electronic edition by Galaxie Software.

197. See also Hagner, *Matthew 14–28*, 549.

198. τὸν λόγον [τοῦτον] refers to the disciples' claim in v10 (οὐ συμφέρει γαμῆσαι). (See also Hagner, *Matthew 14–28*, 550). Contra Sabourin who argues that the phrase refers to the matter discussed in v9 and as such rules out Jesus' whole argument presented in vv3–9 as reply to Pharisees' loose attitude toward lifelong marriage. (L. Sabourin, S.J., *The Gospel according to St. Matthew*, 736.)

199. Contra Schick who argues that celibacy is an offer for all by God but chosen only by few. (Ludwig Schick, "Marriage and Celibacy for the Sake of the Kingdom of Heaven," *Theology Digest* 36/2 [Summer 1989] 139, 140.)

through his use of a verb in third person singular passive form (δέδοται), most probably referring to God as the giver.[200] The evangelist also uses a consummative perfect tense for the verb in order to emphasize the past completed action of giving. Hence, God has already given to some Christians the ability to stay single. This ability might be seen as a gift using the language of Paul in 1 Cor 7:7 (χάρισμα).[201] However, in the community of Israel, celibacy was not considered a gift from God prior to this time, so Jesus needed to clarify the issue further.

Jesus presents three groups of eunuchs (v12). The first group includes people who are eunuchs from birth (εὐνοῦχοι οἵτινες ἐκ κοιλίας μητρὸς ἐγεννήθησαν οὕτως). The second group includes people who are made eunuchs by other men (εὐνοῦχοι οἵτινες εὐνουχίσθησαν ὑπὸ τῶν ἀνθρώπων). And in the third group are the people who have made themselves eunuchs (εὐνοῦχοι οἵτινες εὐνούχισαν ἑαυτοὺς). The first two groups did not need further explanation since the disciples already knew people like these.[202] The third group, though, needed more clarification since it was not a widespread practice for Israelites to abstain from marriage for religious purposes.[203] Hence, Matthew introduces an explanatory, prepositional phrase by which Jesus presented the cause of such an action, i.e. on account of the Kingdom of Heaven (διὰ τὴν βασιλείαν τῶν οὐρανῶν). And he concluded with a challenging statement that "he who is able to accept *it*, let him accept *it*" (v12, NKJ). That final clause

---

200. The word δέδοται in its present form appears 6 times in the NT (Matt 13:11; 19:11; Mark 4:11; Luke 8:10; 1 Cor 11:15) and in all of them it refers to God as a hidden subject. The clarification for the second group (v12) that some are made eunuchs by man (ὑπὸ τῶν ἀνθρώπων) also underlines the fact that the third group are eunuchs because of their gift from God. See also C. L. Blomberg, *Marriage, Divorce, Remarriage, and Celibacy*. Electronic edition by Galaxie Software.

201. "Let him that is pure in the flesh not grow proud of it, and boast, knowing that it was another who bestowed on him the gift of continence." (Clement of Rome, *The First Epistle of Clement to the Corinthians* 38, in *Ante-Nicene Fathers: Translations of The Writings of the Fathers Down to A. D. 325*, eds. Alexander Roberts and James Donaldson, vol.1. Christian Classics Ethereal Library, v.2, CD-ROM, ed. Harry Plantinga [Wheaton, IL: Wheaton College, 1998].) See also Douglas, *Matthew*, 223; Contra Heth who argues that 1 Cor 7:7 is the only passage in the NT which describes celibacy as a gift. (W. A. Heth, *Unmarried 'For the Sake of the Kingdom.'*)

202. Deut 23:1; *Mishnah, Yebam* 8:4-6.

203. For the exception in the Essenes communities see *1QRule of the Congregation* 2.1-4; Josephus, *Bell.*, 2, 120; *Ant.*, 18, 21; Philo, *Apol. pro Iudaeis* in Eus. *Praep. Ev.*, 8, 11, 14 and 1QS.

makes it clear once again that the one qualified for such an action is the one to whom such an ability has been given (ὁ δυνάμενος). It must also be noticed that there is a difference in the nature of celibacy between the first two groups and the third group. The first two groups of eunuchs were not able to have family, since they were literally castrated. The third group of "eunuchs" were able to have a family, since they were not literally castrated, but acted as such due to the fact that they had the ability to abstain from marriage. There are four lines of argument which lead to this conclusion. First, the eunuchs from the third group made themselves eunuchs, which cannot be understood literally, since such an act is hardly possible.[204] Second, this group is defined by an abstract category, i.e. the Kingdom of Heaven. Third, Paul refers to such individuals who renounced marriage in order to have an "unhindered devotion to the Lord" (1 Cor 7:35, NRV). These people have not been literally castrated since Paul never mentioned such a thing but they were able to abstain from marriage because of having such a gift (1 Cor 7:7, 32–35).[205] Fourth, the church fathers understood celibacy figuratively.[206] Therefore it is possible to abstain from marriage for those who have been gifted for it and Matthew's Christian community should respect them for sacrificing their marriage opportunities by making themselves eunuchs for the sake of the Kingdom of Heaven. For the disciples, on the one hand, the issue of celibacy was influenced by their selfish desire to defend divorce in keeping with their loose attitude to marriage. Jesus, on the other hand, argued

---

204. One may attempt to understand Paul's words in Gal 5:12 referring to such an action but not after careful syntactical analysis of the word used. Paul addresses his opponents in Gal 5:12 using the word ἀποκόψονται which should be understood as permissive or causative middle and translated accordingly in a sense of "to let themselves be emasculated." See also F. Blass and A. Debrunner, *A Greek Grammar of the New Testament and Other Early Christian Literature*, trans. Robert W. Funk (Chicago: University of Chicago Press, 1961), 166; James A. Brooks and Carlton L. Winbery, *Syntax of New Testament Greek* (Lanham, MD: University Press of America, 1979), 112.

205. In this group of people we can put John the Baptist, Jesus, and Paul. See also Hagner, *Matthew 14–28*, 550.

206. "But a true eunuch is not one who is unable, but one who is unwilling, to indulge in pleasure." Clement of Alexandria, *The Instructor* 3.4; See also Athenagoras, *Plea for the Christians* 33; Justin Martyr, *1Apol.*19, in *Ante-Nicene Fathers: Translations of The Writings of the Fathers Down to A. D. 325*, eds. Alexander Roberts and James Donaldson, vol.1 and vol.2, *Christian Classics Ethereal Library*, v.2, CD-ROM, ed. Harry Plantinga [Wheaton, IL: Wheaton College, 1998]; W. A. Heth, *Unmarried 'For the Sake of the Kingdom'* (*Matthew 19:12*) *in the Early Church Unmarried*. Electronic edition by Galaxie Software, 1999.

that the true eunuchs are the ones who were gifted, who became eunuchs for the sake of the Kingdom of Heaven. This conclusion relating to the issue of divorce and remarriage clarifies the position of those in Matthew's community who divorced their spouses on the grounds of πορνεία. Thus, they might enter the state of celibacy for the sake of the Kingdom if they regarded themselves equiped with that particular gift, or they might remarry if such a gift was not part of their life.[207]

Therefore Matthew, due to his Jewish-Christian audience, presents Jesus' teaching on divorce and remarriage as a twofold concept: on the one hand, it emphasizes the permanence of the marital union and, on the other hand, it provides exceptional grounds for proper divorce and remarriage in the case of serious sexual misconduct. The emphasis which underlines the very nature of the marriage covenant stands on the permanence of marriage which formulates divorce action as entirely exceptional. The exceptional grounds, on the other hand, may only be understood as Matthew's attempt to preserve the lifelong nature of marital union. His intention is to protect the permanent nature of marriage both from the intentional misuse of the Scriptures by Jewish authorities to dissolve the marriage covenant guided by their sinful selfish behavior and from the sinful adulterous behavior of the abuser with the support of the community which judges severely any sexual misconduct.

MARK 10:2-12 AND MATTHEW 19:3-12: CONCLUSIONS

The divorce pericopes have a clear and well-established nature and role within the framework of both gospels. On the one hand, due to their mutual source, the nature of both pericopes might be defined as "controversy" material that underlines the conflict between Jesus and the Jewish leaders and as such furnishes the unfolding of the gospels' scenario. On the other hand, both pericopes are firmly incorporated into the evangelists' overall

---

207. Here should be considered the fact that in Jewish community remarriage was automatically assumed after divorce. "A. The text of the writ of divorce [is as follows]: B. Lo, you are permitted to any man. G. R. Judah says, [in Aramaic]: Let this be from me your writ of divorce, letter of dismissal, and deed of liberation, that you may marry anyone you want. D. The text of a writ of emancipation [is as follows]: E. Lo, you are a free girl, lo, you are your own [possession]." *Mishnah, Gittin* 9:3; Halacha, 23, *Divorce - Geirushin* [online], Available at http://www.torah.org/learning/halacha-overview/chapter23.html, Accessed on 03 December 2000. Cf. Deut 24:1-4.

purposes and serve as grounds for establishing the high ethical standards of the Kingdom for Jesus' disciples.

Within these literary boundaries, firmly based on the *Sitz im Leben Jesu*, and related to their different audiences, the evangelists construct the divorce pericopes in a threefold manner. First, they expose the challenging questions of the Pharisees (πειράζοντες αὐτόν) which represent their attempt to disprove Jesus' teaching on the matters of marriage in the light of the Law, to disgrace him in front of the crowd as a heretic, and eventually to justify their plans to kill him (Matt 12:14 cf. Mark 3:6). The first question is presented by both Matthew and Mark at the beginning of the discussion. Thus Mark, in respect to his Gentile-Christian audience, shapes the Pharisees' question to refer to the lawfulness of divorce, εἰ ἔξεστιν ἀνδρὶ γυναῖκα ἀπολῦσαι (v2). Matthew edits Mark's version of the question to fit his Jewish-Christian audience by introducing the phrase κατὰ πᾶσαν αἰτίαν (v3). Understanding the force of αἰτίαν as an accusative of reference underlined by the use of the preposition κατὰ and the quantitative nature of the adjective πᾶσαν, the main emphasis of the question becomes clear, what limits/restricts the action of the verb, i.e. what is/are the juridical reason/s for divorce. In this way, Matthew presents the Pharisees as asking Jesus whether he agrees with the school of Hillel, which allowed divorce on multiple grounds, or the school of Shammai, which permitted divorce on the grounds of adultery. The second question of the Pharisees is stated by each of the evangelists in a different way and place in the debate due to the nature of their intentions. Mark shapes the question as a statement (v4) given in reply to Jesus' provocative question (v3) in order to underline Jesus' awareness of the Pharisees' understanding of the divorce issue based entirely upon Deut 24:1. Matthew places the Pharisees' second question after the presentation of Jesus' creation argument (v7), since his intention was to present the Pharisees' attempt to disprove Jesus' argument by showing that he places Moses (Gen 1:27; 2:24) against Moses (Deut 24:1). Hence, Matthew takes the verb "ἐντέλλομαι," associated by Mark with Jesus (Mark 10:3), and places it at the disposal of the Pharisees in order to show their strong affirmation of the nature of Moses' statement in Deut 24:1 as commanding divorce.

The second way the evangelists construct the divorce pericopes is by presenting Jesus' challenging reply to the Pharisees, a reply which highlights their wrong interpretation of the Law and establishes the proper holistic understanding of the Torah on the issue of divorce. The two provocative questions of the Pharisees are balanced by both evangelists with the twofold challenging reply of Jesus. Mark presents the first reply of Jesus in the form of a question (v3) given in response to the Pharisees' initial question (v2). The reference to Moses in general, the usage of the verb ἐντέλλομαι by Jesus in combination with the personal pronoun ὑμῖν, which refers to the Pharisees but does not include Jesus himself, and the most probable object in the Pharisees' reply (ὑμῖν) determine two things. On the one hand, Jesus' intention was to prompt his opponents to think holistically about the Torah, i.e. how should Deut 24:1 be understood in the light of Gen 1:27; 2:24. On the other hand, the teacher shows that Deut 24:1 is understood by the Pharisees in a way that benefits them, i.e. the ones to whom the advantage of divorce has been given by Moses, and he distances himself from such an interpretation. Matthew, like Mark, shapes Jesus' first reply to the initial question of the Pharisees as a question (v4), but offers it rhetorically with an introductory formula "οὐκ ἀνέγνωτε," which syntactical form presents at the same time both the erudition of the Jewish leaders with the Scriptures and their intentional ignorance of their meaning. Hence, even though there were teachers who considered the issues of divorce in the light of the creation account (CD 4:21, Genesis Rabbah XVIII:V), the Pharisees refused to understand the implications of Gen 1:27 and 2:24 as related to divorce matters. Both evangelists present Jesus' second reply to the Pharisees' second challenging question (Mark 10: 5; Matt 19:8) in almost the same way, using the same key phrase πρὸς τὴν σκληροκαρδίαν ὑμῶν, which syntactical construction and the meaning of the noun underline the intentional refusal of the Pharisees to understand correctly God's commandment of Deut 24:1–4. The use of the personal pronoun "ὑμῖν" and the presentation of Deut 24:1–4 as a command (Mark 10:5) point to the fact that Jesus did not diminish the validity of Deut 24:1–4 as a casuistic law, which includes legal divorce procedures, but he condemned the Pharisees' understanding of it as commanding them. According to both evangelists (Mark 10:6–9; Matt 19:4–6), Jesus offers a holistic understanding of the divorce issue, which does not stop with the interpretation of Deut 24:1–4, but also includes an understanding of God's purposes in the creation account (Gen 1:27; 2:24).

The core of Jesus' creation argument is that the abundant unity of God's image in the varieties of human gender is the foundation of the lifelong nature of marriage which settles the issue of divorce. Thus, with the help of a causal prepositional phrase (ἕνεκα τούτου), both evangelists establish the fact that marital unity resolves the diversity of the two genders by reaffirming the original unity they had in the body of Adam and thus fully reflecting God's image in man. God's intention for all marriages is revealed in the model of the first marriage, which was established, according to Jesus' argument, with three verbs in the future tense with imperative force (καταλείψει, προσκολληθήσεται/κολληθήσεται, and ἔσονται). The first verb does not refer to the physical leaving of the man's family, since this was not Jewish practice, but to the replacement of loyalties from the parents to the wife. The second verb depicts the act of establishing the marriage from a social point of view. The third verb expresses the culmination of the marriage relationship in its sexual consummation (cf. 1 Cor 6:16). This model expresses God's plan for the lifelong character of all marriages, which is finally affirmed with Jesus' conclusion, ὃ οὖν ὁ θεὸς συνέζευξεν ἄνθρωπος μὴ χωριζέτω (Mark 10:9; Matt 19:6).

The evangelists' third manner of constructing the divorce pericopes is to elaborate Jesus' conclusion on the matters of divorce, including the issue of remarriage, in relation to his disciples. With the intention of helping their audiences to associate with Jesus' disciples and guided by their context, which naturally connected remarriage to divorce, Matthew and Mark used the same setting to express one significant fact, namely that the disciples had the same attitude to the issues of divorce and remarriage as the Pharisees. That attitude is resolved with a statement based on the previous discussion and shaped differently according to the nature of the authors' audiences. Mark, on the one hand, who is preoccupied with the position of the woman in the divorce and remarriage actions, uses the saying of Jesus in its absolute and most rigorous form. Hence, the licentious divorce and remarriage action of the husband is prohibited due to its abusive nature with respect to the wife (v11). And the libertine divorce and remarriage action of the wife is prohibited due to its adulterous nature (v12). Matthew, on the other hand, following his intention to offer a defense of celibacy, changes the topic of the discussion completely. Due to the minor bearing of this topic on the issues of divorce and remarriage and the relocation of Mark's statement by Matthew (19:9), the latter should be considered as related also to the discussion between Jesus and his disciples. The evangelist, led by the Jewish character of his audience, edits Mark's rigorous portrayal of Jesus' saying in a twofold manner: first, he drops the issue of the woman as insignificant for his Jewish-Christian context; and second, he introduces an exception clause whose textually-critical, semantic, and syntactical nature establish it as legitimate permission for divorce and remarriage on the basis of adultery and other related sexual misconduct.

MATTHEW 5:31–32

The exegetical analysis conducted in the present chapter will mainly follow a method in which narrative-critical and historical-critical disciplines are combined. Since the narrative character of Matthew's gospel has already been presented, the introductory section will present only the context of the present passage (5:31–32) and its relation to Matthew's second text dealing with divorce and remarriage issues (19:3–12). The historical-critical method will contribute to the analysis of the text, emphasizing the sources of the author in keeping with the extensive treatment of the discussed matters in the later divorce pericope of Matthew's gospel.[208]

Matthew 5:31–32 contains the first mention of divorce and remarriage subject in Matthew's gospel. The evangelist places it in the body of the Sermon on the Mount (5:17–7:12), which expresses Jesus' correction[209] of the wrong interpretations of the Torah and its intensification.[210] The Sermon on the Mount is that part (4:17–11:1) of Matthew's story which presents the teaching element of Jesus' ministry (4:23; 9:35; 11:1; 5:1–2; 7:28–29) of offering salvation to Israel.[211] This ethical teaching shows Jesus' full loyalty to the Law, an essential attitude for the first century Jewish-Christian audience, and expresses Jesus' high Kingdom ethics, which are

---

208. The fact that Matthew is the only evangelist who deals with divorce and remarriage matters twice in his gospel is significant in relation to the importance of this subject for his community. (See also Hays, *The Moral Vision of the New Testament*, 356)

209. See also Hagner, *Matthew 1–13*, 103; Roger D. Congdon, "Did Jesus Sustain the Law in Matthew 5?" *BibSac* 135/538 (1978) 118–26.

210. Davies and Allison, *The Gospel according to Saint Matthew*, 1:8; Draper argues that the Sermon on the Mount draws "on the Sinai symbolism to legitimate the teaching and to indicate its continuity with the Torah." Thus, according to him, the central idea of the Sermon is to assure a faithfulness to the Torah as understood through the perspective of Matthew's Christian community in terms of the righteousness of the Kingdom. The latter is given to Christian leaders to safeguard its observation in the community. (Jonathan A. Draper, "The Genesis and Narrative Thrust of the Paraenesis in the Sermon on the Mount," *JSNT* 75 [1999] 31–34.)

211. See also Kingsbury, "The Place, Structure, and Meaning of the Sermon on the Mount within Matthew," 132, 133.

fundamental for his followers.²¹² As part of the plot of the gospel, the first divorce passage presents Jesus' opposition to the understanding of divorce held by the religious authorities. In this passage the conflict between Jesus and Jewish leaders is in its embrionic form.²¹³ In the second divorce passage, Matthew shows that the conflict has progressed further.²¹⁴ The form of Matthew's saying in 5:31, 32 is that of antithesis,²¹⁵ like the rest of the Sermon on the Mount. As with the other antitheses, Matthew's purpose here is to present Jesus' teaching as correcting the misinterpretations of the Law and presenting high Kingdom standards for his followers.²¹⁶ The

212. For Jesus' followers, righteousness which exceeds that of the scribes and Pharisees was mandatory in order to be part of God's Kingdom (5:20; 6:33). See also Hagner, *Matthew 1–13*, 103; Kingsbury, "The Place, Structure, and Meaning of the Sermon on the Mount within Matthew," 137.

213. Kingsbury calls this stage of the conflict as a one with "preliminary" quality. (Kingsbury, *The Plot of Matthew's Story*, 353.)

214. Ibid., 353.

215. See also Hagner, *Matthew 1–13*, 122; Kingsbury, "The Place, Structure, and Meaning of the Sermon on the Mount within Matthew," 139. Draper argues that the passage is an intensification of the Torah built in well-known rabbinic principle, "adding to the righteousness" which is an action of building a fence around the Torah. Draper's main support comes from *Didache* ch3 where the early Christian "intensification" of Torah is found. (J. A. Draper, *The Genesis and Narrative Thrust of the Paraenesis in the Sermon on the Mount*, 38, 39.) However there is nothing in *Didache* about the matter of divorce and remarriage. (See *Didache: The Teaching of the Twelve Apostles*, Apostolic Fathers, Kirsopp Lake, 1912 [online], Available at http://www.stmichael.org/Didache.html, Accessed on 17 October 2000). Contrary to this, John Kampen argues for the form of Matt 5:31, 32 as antithesis on a basis of a parallel between the use of the introductory formula in Matthew 5:21–48 ἠκούσατε; ἐγὼ δὲ λέγω and the similar formula appeared in 4QMMT within the context of polemical exchange of arguments. Even though the introductory formula for the saying of divorce is a bit different (ἐρρέθη) it preserves very well the parallel with the Qumran work. And furthermore Kampen's argument should be preferred over the Draper's since there are clear references to the subject of divorce in the manner of Matthew's passage in 11 QT 57:17–19 and CD 4:12–5:14. (See J. Kampen, *A Reexamination of the Relationship Between Matthew 5:21–48 and the Dead Sea Scrolls*, 39.)

216. On the one hand, Jesus' disciples were part of Jesus' audience (Matt 4:18–22). They are mentioned together with other listeners, the people from the crowd (Matt 4: 25–5:2). On the other hand, Matthew's community was the "implied readers" (Matt 5:11–12 and 7:15–23 cf. 24:15; 27:8, 15) of the Sermon on the Mount. See also Kingsbury, "The Place, Structure, and Meaning of the Sermon on the Mount within Matthew," 134–136. The "implied readers" consist of, on one side, Matthew's community, a small Jewish-Christian group parted from the synagogue and, on the other side, all those people who will respond to the story from their particular situation and background. (See D. C. Sim, *The Gospel of Matthew and the Gentiles*, 36, 37; Stanton, "The Communities of Matthew,"

antithesis is closely related to the previous one because of the subject of adultery (μοιχάομαι, 5:32; μοιχεύω, 5:27) which appears in both of them. However, it is an independent statement of which the main subject is divorce and remarriage.[217]

It is difficult to establish the exact source of Matt 5:32.[218] On the one hand, Matt 5:32 has close parallels with Luke 16:18, which do not follow Mark 10:11, 12.[219] This may suggest that Matt 5:32 follows the "Q" source. On the other hand, Matt 5:32 is not completely identical with Luke 16:18, since Luke 16:18b follows Mark 10:11[220] and Matt 5:32 lacks[221] and adds[222] some clauses. Moreover it should be noticed that this third antithesis in the Sermon on the Mount differs from the other antitheses in the use of the introductory formula ἐρρέθη δέ (Matt 5:31),[223] leading one to conclude that its origin is not the oral tradition, as the rest of the antithesis, but the material used in Matt 19:7 and 9, the source of which is Mark

---

379-91; Mark Allan Powell, "Toward a Narrative-Critical Understanding of Matthew," *Int* 46 [1992] 343.)

217. Contra John J. Kilgallen who argues that the conjunction δέ (v31) links vv31, 32 with the previous section (28-30) making vv31, 32 subordinate to its subject. That, however, is too weak link since both sections deal with different matters. The saying of adultery (vv28-30) deals with one's thoughts. On the contrary the saying of divorce (vv31-32) deals with one's actions. (See also Hagner, *Matthew 1-13*, 122, 123.) Moreover even if one allows this subordination and accepts Kilgallen's argument related to Matt 5:31, 32, it is totally unacceptable for Matt 19:9 where it is thoroughly clear that the main subject is not adultery but divorce. (p.104) Hence, it is easy to regard Kilgallen's claim as false and little more than a wordplay. (J. J. Kilgallen, *To What are the Matthean Exception-Texts [5,32 and 19,9] an Exception?* 102-105.)

218. Some argue that the source of Matt 5:32 is Mark 10:10, 11 because of some close parallels between Matt 5:32 and Mark 10:10 (Matt 19:9) and insufficiency of the parallels between Matt 5:32 and Luke 16:18 (Hagner, *Matthew 1-13*, 123). Others argue that the source of Matt 5:32 is "Q" since Matt 5:32 has some parallels with Luke 16:18 which do not appear in Mark 10:10, 11 (Davies and Allison, *The Gospel according to Saint Matthew*, 1:527).

219. Matt 5:32, ὁ ἀπολύων τὴν γυναῖκα αὐτοῦ = Luke 16:18, ὁ ἀπολύων τὴν γυναῖκα αὐτοῦ; Matt 5:32, ὃς ἐὰν ἀπολελυμένην γαμήσῃ μοιχᾶται = Luke 16:18, ὁ ἀπολελυμένην ἀπὸ ἀνδρὸς γαμῶν μοιχεύει.

220. Mark 10:11, καὶ γαμήσῃ ἄλλην μοιχᾶται = Luke 16:18, καὶ γαμῶν ἑτέραν μοιχεύει. See also Davies and Allison, *The Gospel according to Saint Matthew*, 1:528.

221. Matt 5:32 lacks Luke's καὶ γαμῶν ἑτέραν μοιχεύει.

222. Mattew adds the exception clause παρεκτὸς λόγου πορνείας.

223. Cf. ἠκούσατε ὅτι ἐρρέθη (Matt. 5:21, 27, 33, 38, 43).

10:10.²²⁴ Furthermore, the statement of Matt 5:31 assumes a background discussion which appears in Matt 19:3–8. Even some of the textual variants for Matt 5:32 represent an attempt of the copyists to follow Matt 19:9 and Mark 10:10 wording.²²⁵ Thus, the safest and the most satisfactory way to resolve the matter is to maintain that Matthew (5:31, 32) used "Q" as his source, but also relied on Mark through his use of Mark in his later pericope, Matt 19:3–12. Hence, Jesus' saying in Matt 5:31, 32 should be understood in the light of Jesus' discussion with the Pharisees in Matt 19:3–12.²²⁶

The antithesis is built upon the fact that Moses allowed divorce in Deut 24:1, which served the Jewish leaders as sufficient grounds for divorce and remarriage (Matt 19:3; Mark 10:2). Matthew (5:31) presents a paraphrase of Moses' words in Deut 24:1, with emphasis on Moses' command that, when divorce is carried through, a bill of divorce should be given to the wife. The stress on the imperative of command δότω points to the unimportance of the reasons for divorce, which relates the statement in v31 to the school of Hillel.²²⁷ The fact that anyone may divorce his wife (ὃς ἂν ἀπολύσῃ τὴν γυναῖκα αὐτοῦ) is placed before Jesus, whose answer to that statement appears as a parallel to the previous antithetical interpretations of the Law (ἐγὼ δὲ λέγω, Matt 5:22, 28). He starts with the introductory formula, ἐγὼ δὲ λέγω ὑμῖν, expressing his unparalleled authority and objecting to the previously stated misinterpretation of the Law (an adversative δέ).²²⁸ Jesus disallows divorce because it leads to the sin of adultery: both the divorced woman and the man marrying her commit adultery (. . . ποιεῖ αὐτὴν μοιχευθῆναι, καὶ ὃς ἐὰν ἀπολελυμένην γαμήσῃ μοιχᾶται). On the one hand, it is assumed that the divorced

---

224. See also Hagner, *Matthew 1–13*, 123.

225. πᾶς ὁ ἀπολύων is replaced by some of the witnesses with ὃς ἂν ἀπολύσῃ D (0250).28.1010 pm it sy^{s.c.} sa^{ms} bo.

226. See also Hagner, *Matthew 1–13*, 123–25; Lenski, *The Interpretation of St. Matthew's Gospel*, 230; Lloyd-Jones, *Studies in the Sermon on the Mount*, 257; Hare, *Matthew*, 53; Hendriksen, *Matthew*, 304.

227. During the time Matthew wrote his gospel, the teaching of the school of Hillel became widespread and gained ground against the teaching of Shammai school, which had minority support. (See Davies and Allison, *The Gospel according to Saint Matthew*, 1:530.) See also Congdon, "Did Jesus Sustain the Law in Matthew 5," 118–26.

228. See also Kingsbury, "The Place, Structure, and Meaning of the Sermon on the Mount within Matthew," 139.

woman is going to remarry, primarily because of financial reasons.[229] On the other hand, the second husband is seen as committing adultery against the former husband by marrying his wife since there has been no legal divorce. The final victim of divorce thus appears to be the first husband, i.e. the initiator of the divorce (ὃς ἂν ἀπολύσῃ . . . .). This follows closely Matthew's redaction of Mark in Matt 19:9,[230] made in the light of the Jewish culture in which the offended party is only the man whose wife has committed adultery.[231] Therefore, on the basis of these arguments, a twofold conclusion might be deduced. First, the logic in relation to the statement in v31 is that the certificate of divorce (ἀποστάσιον) does not have any effect since divorce is not lawful and the marriage remains in force. Second, the consequences of such divorce are disadvantageous for the initiator of the divorce (ὃς ἂν ἀπολύσῃ . . . .). From this conclusion, it follows that the divorce which is desirable for the purpose of subsequent remarriage[232] turns out to be destructive for the initiator as well.

The full force of the antithesis[233] now becomes clear: Moses allowed divorce for any reason, according to the school of Hillel,[234] but Jesus disallows it. What Jesus allows, according to Matthew, comes into view with his editorial inclusion of the exception clause (παρεκτὸς λόγου πορνείας, v32). The latter renders literally the idiom from Hebrew עֶרְוַת דָּבָר (Deut 24:1) and when compared with Matt 19:9 in its context (19:3–12), suggests a clear parallel between Jesus' teaching and the Shammai tradition.[235]

---

229. Financial independence for a first century Jewish woman was very rare. Thus, during those times, a single woman could hardly survive, except through prostitution, so the preferred alternative was to remarry. See also Hagner, *Matthew 1–13*, 125.

230. Matthew drops the phrase ἐπ' αὐτήν from Mark 10:11. See also Hays, *The Moral Vision of the New Testament*, 356.

231. Josephus, *The Antiquities of the Jews*, 4.8.23.

232. This was usually the reason why Jews sought divorce. See also Lenski, *The Interpretation of St. Matthew's Gospel*, 733; Nolland, *Luke 9:21–18:34*, 819.

233. If one adapts Draper's principal of "intensification" of the Torah, Matthew's point becomes clear in the sense that Jesus intensifies the Torah for his followers. (See J. A. Draper, *The Genesis and Narrative Thrust of the Paraenesis in the Sermon on the Mount*, 38, 39).The antithesis might be understood even if a parallel between the teaching of Jesus and that of the school of Shammai is considered, since Jesus' disciples might be viewed as proponents of Hillel's teaching. See Davies and Allison, *The Gospel according to Saint Matthew*, 1:530.) See also Congdon, "Did Jesus Sustain the Law in Matthew 5," 118–26.

234. See also R. D. Congdon, "Did Jesus Sustain the Law in Matthew 5," 118–26.

235. See also Hays, *The Moral Vision of the New Testament*, 356; Davies and Allison,

The difference between the two exception clauses Matthew uses (παρεκτὸς λόγου versus μὴ ἐπὶ) is unimportant to their meaning and their effect on the rest of the statements. Also, since Matthew formulates 5:32 in the light of his material presented in 19:9, the meaning of the exception clause here in 5:32 is the same as that in 19:9.[236] Hence, the exception on the basis of which divorce and remarriage is lawful is that of πορνεία, i.e. adultery and other related sexual misconduct.[237] Therefore, a man who divorces his wife on the ground of πορνεία does not make her commit adultery since she has already done it,[238] and he is free to remarry.[239] The freedom of remarriage might be inferred from the understanding that such action was logical and appropriate after a legal divorce in the first century[240] and

---

The Gospel according to Saint Matthew, 1:528; R. D. Congdon, "Did Jesus Sustain the Law in Matthew 5," 118–26.

236. See also Lenski, *The Interpretation of St. Matthew's Gospel*, 733; A. Plummer, *An Exegetical Commentary on the Gospel according to S. Matthew*, 81.

237. See the discussion of the meaning of the exception clause in Matthew 19:9. (See also Hagner, *Matthew 1–13*, 124) In the first century context divorce for adultery was mandatory for Jews (*Mishnah, Yebam* 2:8; *Mishnah, Sota* 5:1), Romans (Paul, *Opinions* 2.26.1–8, 10–12, 14–17. L), and Greeks (Demosthenes, *Speeches* 51–61: speech 59, section 87). The early Christians practiced divorce for πορνεία. See Hermas, *The Pastor of Hermas: Commandment Fourth* and Justin Martyr, *The Second Apology of Justin*, ch. 2, in *Ante-Nicene Fathers: Translations of The Writings of the Fathers Down to A. D. 325*, eds. Alexander Roberts and James Donaldson, vol.1 and 2, prepared as *Christian Classics Ethereal Library*, v.2, CD-ROM, ed. Harry Plantinga [Wheaton, IL: Wheaton College, 1998]. See also D. Hill, *The Gospel of Matthew*, 124; C. L. Blomberg, *Matthew: An Exegetical and Theological Exposition of Holy Scripture NIV Text*, 110.

238. See also Lenski, *The Interpretation of St. Matthew's Gospel*, 231; D. Martyn Lloyd-Jones, *Studies in the Sermon on the Mount*, 260; D. E. Garland, *Reading Matthew: A Literary and Theological Commentary on the First Gospel*, 68.

239. See also Hays, *The Moral Vision of the New Testament*, 357; Lenski, *The Interpretation of St. Matthew's Gospel*, 233, 734; D. Martyn Lloyd-Jones, *Studies in the Sermon on the Mount*, 261.

240. See *Mishnah, Gittin* 9:3 (*The Mishnah*, A New Translation by Jacob Neusner, 485); Josephus, *The Antiquities of the Jews*, 18.5.1. "No man should live without a wife lest he be tempted to sin, and no woman should live without a husband lest she be suspected of sin...." (Halacha, *Women – Nashim, 22. Marriage – Ishus* [online], Available at http://www.torah.org/learning/halacha-overview/chapter22.html, Accessed on 19 October 2000). One should consider also the fact that Augustus' marriage law, which was still in power during Nero's time, gave an ultimate period before remarriage with which it enforced remarriage to the divorcee for the purpose of procreation. See Suetonius, *Life of Augustus* 34. L "Having shown greater severity in the emendation of this last than the others, as a result of the agitation of its opponents he [Augustus] was unable to get it approved except by abolishing or mitigating part of the penalty, conceding a three-year grace-period

also from the lack of any specific prohibition in the words of Jesus. In this way Matthew reaches his main goal with the antithesis. Jesus corrects the erroneous understanding of the Torah in relation to divorce and remarriage with a demand to his disciples that they follow the ethical standards of the Kingdom by committing themselves to lifelong marriages, except for divorce and remarriage in the case of πορνεία.[241]

LUKE 16:18

The present chapter will present an exegetical analysis of Luke 16:18 by means of the previously presented method which uses the tools of narrative-critical and historical-critical approaches to the biblical text. The narrative approach to Luke's two volume work will be used to establish the place of the passage in the narrative flow of the work, leading to the analysis of the text within this framework. Historical-critical tools, on the other hand, will be used according to their significance and due to the quantitative limitations of the text, the importance of defining Luke's sources will occupy a crucial place in its analysis.

As in the case of Matthew, the narrative unity of Luke's gospel might be understood in terms of a story with its plot and major characters.[242] The plot of Luke's gospel has a twofold goal, to present the story of Jesus and to present God's act of salvation in human history. The former is developed within the framework of the gospel, while the latter extends to the book of Acts as well. The main characters of Luke's story are Jesus, his disciples, the crowds, the oppressed and excluded, and the authorities. The central character, Jesus, is God's Messiah who is sent by God to bring salvation

---

(before remarriage) and increasing the rewards (for having children)." (Suetonius, *Life of Augustus* 34 L, trans. Mary R. Lefkowitz and Maureen B. Fant [online], Available at http://www.uky.edu/ArtsSciences/Classics/wlgr/wlgr-romanlegal120.html, Accessed on 14 October 2000.) Such witness related to the Greek world appears in Plutarch's *Lives*. "For there was, as it appears, a penalty at Sparta not only for not marrying at all, and for a late marriage, but also for a bad marriage and to this last they subjected those especially who sought alliance with the rich, instead of with the good and with their own associates." (*Lys.* 30.5, trans. Bernadotte Perrin [online], Available at http://www.perseus.tufts.edu/cgi-bin/ptext?lookup=Plut.+Lys.+30.1, Accessed on 16 October 2000). See also Everett Ferguson, *Backgrounds of Early Christianity* (Grand Rapids: Eerdmans, 1993) 69.

241. See also Hagner, *Matthew 1–13*, 125.

242. R. C. Tannehill, *The Narrative Unity of Luke-Acts*, 1–9.

to Israel and the rest of the world (Luke 1:13–17, 30–35, 77; 3:6). The plot unfolds as Jesus interacts with the different main characters of the story.

Jesus' ministry might generally be defined as twofold. At its heart, Jesus helps and offers salvation to the poor, sinners, tax collectors, women, Samaritans, and Gentiles (Luke 4:18; 5:29, 30, 32; 7:34; 8:2).[243] In addition, there is Jesus' work of training his disciples to continue his mission (8:1–3; 9:51–12:53). This preparation is seen as a hard task which goes through a long and difficult process, from walking and sharing one's life with Jesus (5:11, 28; 9:23; 14:27; 18:28), to misunderstanding and even denying him (9:43–45; 18:31–34; 22:57).[244] The negative attitude toward Jesus which basically brings the plot to its culmination is understood as the reaction of the crowds and the authorities. The former group is initially positively inclined toward Jesus and his ministry, but later joins the authorities in their antagonism against him (4:31–8:40; 18:36–39 cf. 19:39; 23:21).[245] The authorities, represented by different groups of Pharisees, scribes, chief priests, elders, and the Sanhedrin, are constantly involved in opposing Jesus and his teaching, but their antagonism grows gradually until it reaches its climax in giving over Jesus to die on the cross (Luke 23:13–25).[246] The resolution of the story comes with the resurrection of Jesus but it has its roots in the reaction of different main characters at the time of his death. Most of the main characters are presented by the narrator as regretting their involvement in the killing of Jesus (Peter [22:62], the crowd [18:3], the centurion [23:47]). However, some of his adversaries' rejection of Jesus and his teaching still remains in force, a fact that becomes clear in Acts. This completes the story of Jesus; his mission of bringing salvation to the people and training his disciples has been accomplished; but it leaves the door open for the further development of God's story of salvation in Acts.[247]

Within this narrative flow, the saying about divorce appears in a section where the conflict of Jesus and the religious leaders is addressed through parables (Luke 14–16). The basic point of the parables is the contrast between the rich and the poor, the upright and the sinner. The

---

243. Ibid., 101–32.
244. Ibid., 201–62.
245. Ibid., 141–64.
246. Ibid., 167–87.
247. Ibid., 301.

Pharisees and the scribes are in the group of the rich and upright, but because their attitude toward their riches and uprightness is wrong, they are replaced in the Kingdom of God by the ones whom they consider unworthy of it (14:18–21; 15:1–32; 16:14–31).[248] Hence, the divorce saying in its broader context might be understood as a part of the warning to the scribes and the Pharisees. Within the framework of that controversy, Luke places the divorce passage in a section (16:1–18) that deals with matters related to the Jewish Law, as seen in a parallel found in Deut 23:15–24:4.[249] With the help of that parallel, a threefold basic division of Luke's section (16:1–18) might be established. First, Luke deals with the issue of the relation between lord and servant (Luke 16:1–13). Second, he presents a rebuke of the Pharisees' greed (Luke 16:14–15). And finally, the Law and its implications are directed toward Jesus' disciples (Luke 16:16–18).[250] In this last section, which presents Jesus' affirmation of the high ethical demands of the Law and the Prophets (especially v17), the divorce saying plays a twofold role.[251] First, it is used in order to establish a contrast with the Pharisees' misunderstanding of the Law as viewed in the light of their refusal to accept the Law-based testimony of John the Baptist about Jesus (Luke 16:16 cf. Luke 7:30). Second, its presentation also underlines the high ethical standards of the Kingdom in relation to marriage for Jesus' disciples.[252]

The exegetical analysis of Jesus' divorce saying requires an attempt to establish Luke's sources. The lack of complete certainty in such a task might be overlooked due to the limitations of the text, especially to the lack of a broader discussion of the issues of divorce and remarriage in Luke's work. Hence, such a background needs to be provided from Luke's sources, whose content will be established on the basis of comparative

---

248. Ibid., 185.

249. It is established on the basis of dictional, thematic, and exegetical coherence. For the details in relation to this discussion see Graig A. Evans, "Luke 16:1–18 and the Deuteronomy Hypothesis," in *Luke and Scripture: The Function of Sacred Tradition in Luke-Acts*, eds. Graig A. Evans and James A. Sanders (Minneapolis: Fortress, 1993) 121–39. Without considering that parallel, the unity of Luke's section 16:1–18 falls apart. To see the perplexity of the scholars who do not see that parallel: Fitzmyer, *Luke X–XXIV*, 1095.

250. See also G. A. Evans, *Luke 16:1–18 and the Deuteronomy Hypothesis*, 133–36.

251. Also J. Nolland, *Luke 9:21–18:34*, 822; I. H. Marshall, *The Gospel of Luke*, 626, 627, 630.

252. Also G. A. Evans, *Luke 16:1–18 and the Deuteronomy Hypothesis*, 133–36.

analysis of the available NT divorce material in Matt 5:32; 19:9; Mark 10:9, 11–12, and 1 Cor 7:10–11.

A comparison between Luke's text and Matthew's first appearance of Jesus' divorce saying leads to identifying two close parallels[253] that are not followed by the rest of the divorce passages and thus suggest a mutual source, "Q." On the other hand, two dissimilarities[254] between these texts lead one to consider an additional source for both authors in general and Luke in particular. In the case of the latter, the text of Mark 10:11 might be suggested due to its close parallel with Luke's text.[255] Considering the relationship between Luke's text and Paul's account in 1 Cor 7:10–11,[256] one may observe that the order of the latter is reversed, giving more attention to the woman who is willing to divorce. Due to this fact, Mark 10:12 comes closer to 1 Cor 7:10 than Luke 16:18.[257] Furthermore Paul's prohibition in v11 related to the man is absolute and therefore parallels best the prohibitions listed in Mark 10:9 and Matt 19:6. On this basis I would conclude that Luke uses two sources for his text, namely "Q" and Mark 10:11.

Two implications might be derived from that conclusion. First, Luke is aware of Mark's background debate between Jesus and the Pharisees which stays in the foundation of Jesus' divorce saying. Hence, all the issues debated in Mark (10:2–12) in relation to Deut 24:1 and Gen 1:27 and 2:24 shaped Jesus' saying in Luke as well.[258] Second, the nature of the saying in Luke is more absolute than that of Matt 5:32, since the latter

---

253. Luke's πᾶς ὁ ἀπολύων τὴν γυναῖκα αὐτοῦ is identical with Matthew's πᾶς ὁ ἀπολύων τὴν γυναῖκα αὐτοῦ and Matthew's ὃς ἐὰν ἀπολελυμένην γαμήσῃ μοιχᾶται resembles Luke's ὁ ἀπολελυμένην ἀπὸ ἀνδρὸς γαμῶν μοιχεύει.

254. Luke's passage lacks the exception clause of Matt 5:32, παρεκτὸς λόγου πορνείας. The latter should be best defined as Matthean later addition not as Luke's omission on the basis of Matthew's community concerns. (See also J. Nolland, *Luke 9:21–18:34*, 816). And Matthew's passage (5:32) lacks Luke's καὶ γαμῶν ἑτέραν μοιχεύει.

255. Luke's καὶ γαμῶν ἑτέραν μοιχεύει parallels Mark's καὶ γαμήσῃ ἄλλην μοιχᾶται. (See also Davies and Allison, *The Gospel according to Saint Matthew*, 1:528).

256. Some correspondence between the two texts should be acknowledged. (See Fitzmyer, *Luke X–XXIV*, 1120.)

257. See also G. F. Hawthorne, *Marriage and Divorce, Adultery and Incest*, 598; Fitzmyer, *Matthean Divorce Texts and Some New Palestinian Evidence*, 200; Gundry, *Mark*, 533.

258. See the discussions of Mark 10:2–12.

introduces the exception clause. Thus, one should be interested in Luke's motive for establishing the saying in its present form.

The most convincing argument for the absolute prohibition of divorce and remarriage in Luke's passage, taking into consideration his predominantly Gentile-Christian community,[259] is the reason for divorce, i.e. the subsequent remarriage. That argument is established on a threefold ground. First, any question related to divorce and remarriage discussed within the geographical setting of Palestine was assumed to be a response to the Herod's marriage with Herodias. This marriage was not approved by the Jewish community, since it broke the law of incest (Lev 18:13, 16; 20:21), and it was severely criticized by John the Baptist (Luke 3:19; Matt 14:4; Mark 6:18), because it was not only incestuous but also prearranged while both Herod and Herodias were married to their former spouses.[260] Thus, according to Luke, Jesus stresses this sinful aspect of marriage. Second, one of the common reasons for the breakdown of Gentile and Jewish marriages in Jesus' and Luke's contexts was an affair of one of the partners outside the marriage or the possibility of such an affair followed by subsequent remarriage.[261] Third, the coordinate conjunction καὶ which links the clause πᾶς ὁ ἀπολύων τὴν γυναῖκα αὐτοῦ with γαμῶν ἑτέραν suggests a finality of the following clause or expresses a semantic notion

---

259. There is an agreement among the Lucan scholarship that Luke's audience is "an urban church community in the Hellenistic world." See I. H. Marshall, *The Gospel of Luke*, 33.

260. Josephus, *Antiquities of the Jews* 18:109–115. (Flavius Josephus, *Antiquities of the Jews*, ed. William Whiston [online], Available at http://www.perseus.tufts.edu/cgi-bin/ptext?lookup=J.+AJ+18.109, Accessed on 20 January 2001.) See also Ben Witherington III, "Herodias," in *ABD* 3:174–76; David C. Braund, "Herod Antipas," in *ABD* 3:160.

261. "A. Just as the water puts her to the proof, so the water puts him [the lover] to the proof. B. 'since it is said, And it shall come . . . , And it shall come . . . (Num 5:22, 24).' C. Just as she is prohibited to the husband, so she is prohibited to the lover, ..." (*Mishnah, Sotah* 5:1. (*The Mishnah*, A New Translation by Jacob Neusner, 454.); "If a woman is *deliberately* unfaithful to her husband . . . ." (Halacha, 26, *Adultery – Sotah* [online], Available at http://www.torah.org/learning/halacha-overview/chapter26.html?print=1, Accessed on 18 October 2000.);

". . . [2] The elderly man won his proposal and set at naught the former law, also escaping the peril of the noose which threatened him; and his wife, who had thus been prevented from living with a younger husband, married again the man she had left." (Diodorus Siculus, *Library* 12.18.1.XVIII, trans. C. H. Oldfather [online], Available at http://www.perseus.tufts.edu/cgi-bin/ptext?lookup=Diod.+12.18.1, Accessed on 17 April 2004.); Also M. Tullius Cicero, *Letters*, ed. Evelyn Shuckburgh [online]. See also Nolland, *Luke 9:21–18:34*, 819; I. H. Marshall, *The Gospel of Luke*, 631.

of its subordination to the first clause.[262] Hence, both clauses should be read, "everyone who divorces his wife in order to marry another commits adultery" (Luke 16:18a). The second part of the verse (16:18b) is also primarily oriented to the act of remarriage, but now seen from the side of the woman (καὶ ὁ ἀπολελυμένην ἀπὸ ἀνδρὸς γαμῶν μοιχεύει).[263] That understanding might be discerned in the background of Jesus' explanation to the disciples in Mark 10:10–12.[264] Therefore, Luke's presentation of Jesus' absolute prohibition of divorce and remarriage should be seen in the light of one's desire for divorce, namely, the opportunity of subsequent remarriage.

MATTHEW 5:31, 32 AND LUKE 16:18: CONCLUSIONS

The divorce passages that have been shaped by their mutual sources and the specific intentions of the evangelists are a crucial part of both gospels. They play a significant role in the development of the gospels' plots and are an integral part of the contexts that deal with the issue of the Law. Matthew shapes the form of the divorce passage as an antithesis to the misinterpretations of the Law, which underlines the conflict between Jesus and the Jewish leaders. And as such he places it in the body of the Sermon on the Mount (5:17–7:12) which expresses Jesus' correction of the misinterpretations of the Torah and his intensification of its provisions. Thus, the text underlines both Jesus' full loyalty to the Law, important for the Jewish-Christian community, as well as his high Kingdom ethics which were essential for his disciples. Luke makes the divorce say-

---

262. For a discussion of that issue see D. B. Wallace, *Greek Grammar Beyond the Basics: An Exegetical Syntax of the New Testament*, 667, f.2. For that function of the conjunction in the Patristic literature see Alber-Louis Descamps, "The New Testament Doctrine on Marriage," in *Contemporary Perspectives on Christian Marriage*, ed. R. Malone and J. R. Connery (Chicago: Loyola University Press, 1984), 217–73, 347–63; Also Nolland, *Luke 9:21–18:34*, 821, 822.

263. Luke edits Q (cf. Matt 5:32) introducing the phrase "ἀπὸ ἀνδρὸς" which is used in the divorce tradition presented by Paul (1 Cor 7:10) to express a divorce action performed by the wife. For the spatial meaning of ἀπὸ which expresses an idea of separation see William Arndt, *A Greek-English Lexicon of the New Testament and Other Early Christian Literature*. [computer file]. Logos Library System 2.1g. and Louw, Johannes P. and Nida, Eugene A., *Greek-English Lexicon of the New Testament Based on Semantic Domains* (New York: United Bible Societies, 1988, 1989). Logos Library System 2.1g. Also J. Nolland, *Luke 9:21–18:34*, 819, 822.

264. Also Nolland, *Luke 9:21–18:34*, 822.

ing part of the conflict between Jesus and the religious leaders, placing it in the part of his gospel which elaborates on matters dealt with in the Jewish Law (16:1–18). Thus, on the one hand, within its narrow context (16:16–18) which establishes the high ethical demands of the Law and the Prophets (especially v17), the divorce saying contrasts with the Pharisees' misunderstanding of the Law. And on the other hand, it defines the marital standards for Jesus' disciples in relation to the high Kingdom ethics.

Within this framework, the evangelists are presenting Jesus' teaching on divorce and remarriage to their particular Christian communities. Matthew, with respect to his predominantly Jewish-Christian audience, underlines two aspects of Jesus' teaching. First, he places Jesus' teaching against the understanding of Moses' command (Deut 24:1) by the school of Hillel. The view of this liberal school is emphasized by two details in the text, namely, the fact that anyone may divorce his wife and the fact that the reasons for divorce are unimportant. Jesus replies antithetically to this understanding by stating that divorce and remarriage lead to the sin of adultery for both the divorced woman and the man she marries. His statement is based on the understanding that the divorced woman is going to remarry and the second husband offends the former husband due to the lack of a legal divorce.

Second, Matthew provides lawful divorce grounds for his Jewish-Christian audience by introducing an exception clause. The grounds in this clause are the same as in Matthew 19:9, adultery and other related sexual misconduct, allowing for the insignificance of different wording and Matthew's use of his later pericope. Within the first century context, which assumes remarriage after a legal divorce and without any stated prohibition in this respect, the exception clause provides the grounds for both actions. Hence, a man who divorces his wife on the grounds of the exception does not expose her to adultery since she has already committed it and, obtaining a legal divorce, is free to remarry. Matthew, using the antithesis, accomplishes his intention to present Jesus' teaching on the matters of divorce against the misunderstanding of the Torah and to underline his demand to the disciples for lifelong marriages with the exception of divorce and remarriage in a case of πορνεία.

Luke, on the other hand, because of his predominantly Gentile-Christian community, presents Jesus' teaching in its absolute form. This exposition of the evangelist might be defined as shaped by his perspective on divorce related to the desire for subsequent remarriage. Three arguments substantiate this conclusion. First, Jesus' teaching on divorce and remarriage responded to the sinful marriage of Herod and Herodias, which was based on divorce and remarriage that was prearranged during the time of their former marriages. Second, the rigorous form of Jesus' statement fights the most common reason for divorce, which was subsequent remarriage among both Jews and Gentiles in Luke's social context. Third, the syntactical nature of the saying (Luke 16:18a) determines a semantic notion of subordination which underlines the reason of divorce as the desire for subsequent remarriage. The second part of text (16:18b) expresses the same notion, but changes the point of view to that of the woman. Therefore, on this basis, there is no contradiction between Luke's divorce saying and Matthew's divorce sayings in relation to the exception clause. When divorce and subsequent remarriage are on the grounds of πορνεία, then they are not based on a desire for remarriage but on marital unfaithfulness.

1 CORINTHIANS 7:12-16

In this chapter I will analyze Paul's exposition of Jesus' teaching on divorce and remarriage as found in 1 Cor 7:12-16. The selection of this text for defining Paul's view on divorce and remarriage is due to the significant place it occupies in the discussions of the relevant NT scholarship and to noteworthy concepts it encompasses.[265] Nevertheless, the contribution of all the relevant parts for the issues of divorce and remarriage of 1 Cor 7 is considered, giving a prominent place to the explicit mention of Jesus' tradition on the subjects (1 Cor 7:10-11). The method which will be used for conducting the exegetical analysis of the selected passage is the previously established combination of narrative-critical and historical-critical approaches in which a predominant place will be given to the grammatical-historical approach.[266]

---

265. See J. C. Laney, *No Divorce & No Remarriage*, 42-45; W. A. Heth, *Divorce, but No Remarriage*, 109-14; T. R. Edgar, *Divorce & Remarriage for Adultery or Desertion*, 187-191; L. Richards, *Divorce & Remarriage under a Variety of Circumstances*, 238-42.

266. For using this approach to analyze NT and Pauline texts see W. Baird, *New Testament Criticism*, (Logos Library System); Grant R. Osborne, "Hermeneutics/Interpreting Paul," in *Dictionary of Paul and His Letters*, eds. Gerald F. Hawthorne, Ralph P. Martin, Daniel G. Reid (Downers Grove, IL: InterVarsity, 1993), 388-97.

The successful analysis of 1 Cor 7:12–16 requires an understanding of Paul's narrative thought.[267] The narrative approach takes the view that the main attempts of the Pauline scholarship to understand Paul's thought, i.e. the relation between contingency and coherence, the quest for center, and construction of a static system, lack an understanding of the first century culture with its narrative thinking and grasp of reality.[268] Paul did not depend on situations in order to construct his theology, but through a firm grasp of the story and its climax in Christ, he approached different problems in Christian communities.[269] Furthermore, the story of Christ, the gospel, plays a fundamental role in Paul's ethics, not only as a way of understanding Paul's teaching in relation to different situations, but also as establishing a model for Christian living.[270] Understanding of Paul's narrative thought begins with consideration of Paul's interpretation of the Jewish Scriptures (OT).

Paul's reading of the OT might not be defined as a "systematic exegetical" method of interpretation,[271] but as a narrative approach to the Jewish Scriptures. The narrative of God's righteousness, whose plot follows the path from promise to fulfillment, is the tool by which Paul is interpreting the OT. This narrative is presented in its final form in the

---

267. Two levels of narrative analysis are proposed by Norman R. Petersen in relation to Paul's letters. The first is the "poetic sequence," in which the analysis follows the natural reading of the text itself; the second is a "referential sequence," which attempts to reconstruct the larger story of the letter itself. The latter should be seen within the narrative world of public history. N. T. Wright goes further, maintaining that the analyses of Paul's letters should be placed in the framework of Paul's narrative thought world. (N. T. Wright, *The New Testament and the People of God* [Great Britain: Biddles, Guildford and King's Lynn, 1992] 403, 404. Cf. Norman R. Petersen, *Rediscovering Paul* [Philadelphia: Fortress, 1985] 47–49). Thus, Ben Witherington states that "Paul's letters theologize on the basis of a symbolic universe and the stories within that universe, particularly the story of Christ, the gospel." (*The Paul Quest*, 302.)

268. The relationship between coherence and contingency in Paul's thought is not understood as "a coherent core of Paul's thought is surrounded by a contingent fringe of his thought." Ben Witherington III, *Paul's Narrative Thought World* (Louisville: Westminster John Knox, 1994), 3, 4; Witherington III, *The Paul Quest*, 301, 302.

269. Witherington III, *The Paul Quest*, 302. Paul's hermeneutic is christologically based but ecclesiologically directed. Everything is seen through the perspective of Christ event. (Ibid., 262.) However, "the centre of Paul's story is christological, not ecclesiological or 'Israelogical . . . .'" (Ibid., 253.)

270. Witherington III, *The Paul Quest*, 302.

271. Hays, *Echoes of Scripture in the Letters of Paul* (London: Yale University Press, 1989) 160.

gospel, which narrates the story of Jesus the Messiah with culmination and resolution in his death and resurrection. It is shaped by Paul's understanding that he, together with the redeemed community, lives in the overlap of the ages.[272] By this tool, the unity between Law and gospel is established, and even the Law with its temporal nature is shown to lead to the fulfillment of God's redemptive purposes.[273] Paul is using such a narrative hermeneutic through the means of typology, which is the "framework of literary-historical sensibility"[274] by which he applies the Word of God to contemporary situations. Paul's narrative thought needs to be analyzed in relation to its main parts and their interaction within the framework of its plot.

Paul's narrative thought world is based on the understanding of a drama (mega story) consisting of five stories[275], i.e. (1) the story of God; (2) the story of the world and its fall in Adam; (3) the story of God's people–Israel; (4) the story of Christ; and (5) the story of Christians, including Paul's own story.[276] The primary place in this drama is given to the story of Christ, which is based on the OT, but is derived from the kerygma of the early church.[277]

In the story of God, Paul presents him as the Creator of the world and human beings. He is the only God and in his great goodness and kindness he has created a wonderful and perfect creation and as its crowning feature he has made the human being as man and woman according to his divine image (Rom 1:19–20; 1 Cor 11:18–12). God is not alienated from his creation, but he sustains it and interacts with it. Paul understands God's work with the world in a manifold manner. God has acted in the resurrection of Jesus (1 Cor 15:15) and he is reconciling the world to himself through Christ (2 Cor 5:18–19). For those who have accepted Christ and received his Spirit, God becomes Father and they may turn to him with the cry, "Abba" (Gal 4:6), expecting his answer to their prayers and his salvation and comfort (Rom 8:15). Thus, the story of God is one with the story of Christ and the Spirit, (2 Cor 3:17–18). Paul sees

---

272. Ibid., 185.
273. Rom 3:21.
274. Hays, *Echoes of Scripture in the Letters of Paul*, 161.
275. Witherington agrees with Wright about the five parts of the story. See N. T. Wright, *The New Testament and the People of God*, 141, 142.
276. Witherington III, *Paul's Narrative Thought World*, 5. Idem, *The Paul Quest*, 230.
277. Witherington III, *The Paul Quest*, 252.

God's work in his own life as well, having been set apart and called by him through the revelation of Jesus Christ his Son (Gal 1:15-16).[278]

The story of the world and its fall in Adam depicts three main modes in which unredeemed humanity lives i.e. the world (with its sin, sickness, and death), the flesh, and the devil. This situation has began with the fall of Adam (Rom 5:12; 1 Cor 15:21-22), including the deception of Eve (2 Cor 11:2), and was passed on to all their progeny. It is clear that Paul knows the story of creation and the condition of humanity before the fall (1 Cor 11: 7-12; 15: 47-48), but his purpose is to present the present condition of the world and its relation to Adam (1 Cor 7:31; Rom 5:12-21; 2 Cor 11:3). The human plight is portrayed in its fullness in Rom 7:7-13, where the original sin might be viewed as related to the violation of the Tenth Commandment (Rom 7:7), since the place of the Law is established in relation to the sin, the flesh, and Christ. Paul depicts the story of Adam and his seduction by the sin which is personified in the form of "the serpent," (Rom 7:8-11). The story that follows presents the whole of humanity continuing to live in the condition of its forefather (Rom 7:14-25). Thus, because of the fall, sin infected the whole creation (Rom 8:21) and all humanity was subjected to the devil and his evil powers of darkness (2 Cor 4:4). Even though the Law is good, it is because of sin that humanity is enslaved in its present condition (Rom 7:14-25). Thus, the only way out which Paul sees is deliverance in Christ (Rom 8:1-15).[279]

The story of God's people starts with Abraham (Rom 4; 9:6-15; 11:1; Gal 3:6-18; 4:21-31), whose importance for Paul exceeds that of Moses, because the former is the prototype of Christian faith, to whom the promises were made and with whom God made his covenant. He becomes the father of both Jewish and Gentiles believers (Rom 4:1, 16; Gal 3:14). Hence, the true descendants of Abraham are not those who are his physical descendants (Israel), but all who follow his faith and God's promise to him (Rom 9:6-7). Christ is presented as the seed of Abraham in both a particular and a collective sense (Gal 3:16). Thus, the Abrahamic covenant is fulfilled in Christ and as such it gives a parenthetical sense of the Mosaic covenant and a temporal role for the Law. The Law given to Moses is good and holy (Rom 7:12, 14), but it has a deadly effect upon sinful humanity in contrast to that of the Spirit who gives life (Gal 3:19).

---

278. Ibid., 237-39.

279. Witherington III, *The Paul Quest*, 239-42. Idem, *Paul's Narrative Thought World*, 9-35.

Thus, the Law has become obsolete (2 Cor 3) and the Mosaic covenant has been annulled (2 Cor 3:11) by the coming of Christ, who is the seed of Abraham (Gal 3:16) and who makes new covenant (2 Cor 3:6) with those who are in him and who as such also become seeds of Abraham (Rom 9:6–7 cf. Gen 17).[280]

The story of Christ is based on pre-Pauline Christological hymns (Philippians 2, Colossians 1, Hebrews 1, and also John 1) whose background might be defined as the early Jews' understanding of personified Wisdom. The story of Christ is also grounded in the story of Israel, God's elected people to whom the promise of the Messiah has been given (cf. Rom 9:5).[281] One of the summaries of Christ's story appears in Philippians 2:5–11. This hymn has two main parts, namely, the three modes of existence of Christ (preexistence, earthly existence, and heavenly existence) and God's reward for his life and death. The story presents Christ as the pre-existent Son of God who shares full equality with God (ὃς ἐν μορφῇ θεοῦ) but who took human likeness (ἐν ὁμοιώματι ἀνθρώπων) without taking advantage of his divine attributes and status during his earthly life (ἁρπαγμὸν). Christ became a servant and lived among the people, relying fully on God's Word and Spirit through prayer. Humbling himself even more, he gave himself to death on the cross. The story continues with God's vindication (through the resurrection, Rom 1:3–4) and exaltation of Christ because of his sacrifice and his giving him the divine name (cf. Isaiah 45:21–25) of honor and worship. This brings Christ to his present heavenly existence of divine glory and power. The sequel to the story is Christ's Second Advent, which gives the church a twofold eschatological perspective, i.e. looking upon the two advents and thus living in an "already but not yet" fashion. The present life of Christ's followers, with the help of the Holy Spirit, needs to follow the self-sacrificial example of Christ, which Paul also imitates (Phil 2:5). Thus, firmly established in the apostle's experience with the risen Lord and shaped by his understanding of the relationship between the Father, the Son, and the Spirit, the story of Christ becomes Paul's glasses through which he sees all the parts of the mega story.[282]

---

280. Witherington III, *The Paul Quest*, 242–45. Idem, *Paul's Narrative Thought World*, 37–72.

281. Idem, *Paul's Narrative Thought World*, 83, 84.

282. Idem, *The Paul Quest*, 245–48. Idem, *Paul's Narrative Thought World*, 81–205.

The story of Christians narrated by Paul includes its author and is established on the story of Christ. The emphasis made in Christ's story, his death, resurrection, exaltation, and second coming, set up the main dimensions of the believers' story. First, the sacrament of baptism signifies the death of the believer with Christ to sin and the old life in the flesh and his resurrection with Christ to a new life guided by God's Spirit and shaped by Christ's high moral standards (Rom 6:1–14). The concept of "new creation" (2 Cor 5:17) emphasizes the total detachment from the old life and the complete new beginning of the believer's life. Second, the sacrament of the Lord Supper (1 Cor 11:17–34) underlines the corporate character of the Christians' story (1 Cor 10:17). With the new creation, the believer has become part of Christ's body (1 Cor 12:13), the church, and as such the ongoing relationship which he/she experiences in the church leads to continuous sanctification. The latter concept suggests that Christians live between the times of Christ's first and his second coming. They have experienced the act of justification by grace through faith, but are still living in the world of sin and death. They need to subdue their fleshly bodies by imitating Christ (Gal 5) and expecting his second coming, when they will receive their new glorious bodies and thus become fully conformed to his image (Rom 8:29). Hence, the story of the Christians like the story of Paul (Phil 3:4–10), follows the same model of Christ's story in his death, resurrection, and exaltation (Phil 2).[283]

Paul's narrative thought world is both a continuation of the Jewish narrative and twist of the Jewish story at virtually every point.[284] It starts with the creation, goes through the fall of man, and focuses on the story of Abraham as the beginning of the answer to Adam's problem.[285] Thus, Abraham is promised not only Israel's land but also the whole cosmos.[286] The plot develops with the other key points of the deliverance of Israel from Egypt and the giving of the Torah.[287] The latter is seen as gift that determines the special status and vocation of Israel, but only to the extent

---

283. Idem, *The Paul Quest*, 248–52; idem, *Paul's Narrative Thought World*, 213–351.

284. N. T. Wright, *The New Testament and the People of God*, 405. The differences between Ben Witherington's and N. T. Wright's understanding of Paul's narrative thought will not be discussed due to author's understanding of their lack of significance for the purposes of the present work.

285. N. T. Wright, *The New Testament and the People of God*, 405.

286. Ibid.

287. Ibid.

of exposing her guilt and pointing to her abandonment by God for the sake of the salvation of the whole world.[288] Hence Israel, because of her sins, is still seen as being in exile. The culmination of the story comes with the ending of the exile through the death of Jesus the Messiah. Thus, for Paul the culmination, the turning point and the center of the story is Jesus. The story of Jesus "fulfils, subverts, and transforms" the story of Israel and the stories of the rest of humanity.[289] Jesus is viewed as the climax of the covenant between God and Abraham (Israel) because those blessings intended for the whole creation and being prevented by the Torah have been released through the death of Christ.[290] Thus, in Jesus and only in him, Israel finds and fulfills its true vocation and the Torah reaches its goal.[291] What follows next in natural sequence is the return of Israel from exile, which begins with Jesus' resurrection and develops through the formation of a new covenant people of God from all nations.[292] Within this referential sequence Paul places his own story as the apostle to the Gentiles.[293] This is not the end of the story, however, but the beginning of the end. That is to say that Christians are called to imitate Christ by following his ethical standards as Paul has done in expectation of the end, which is anticipated as the liberation of the whole cosmos from its captivity of sin and despair with Christ's second coming. With this understanding of Paul's narrative thought, I can turn to the analysis of 1 Cor 7:12–16, which first step requires a comprehensive study of its context, considering two crucial factors[294]: Who are Paul's addressees and how does he address them?

---

288. Ibid., 405, 406.

289. Ibid., 403–9.

290. N. T. Wright, *The Climax of the Covenant: Christ and the Law in Pauline Theology* (Minneapolis: Fortress, 1991), 144.

291. N. T. Wright, *The Climax of the Covenant*, 40, 241. Also cf. J. Gerald Janzen, review of *The Climax of the Covenant: Christ and the Law in Pauline Theology* by N. T. Wright, *Theology Today* L/4 (January 1994): 647.

292. N. T. Wright, *The New Testament and the People of God*, 403–6.

293. Ibid., 406.

294. The context of 1 Cor 7:12–16 might be defined as a section of Paul's letter to the Corinthian church (ch 7) in which he deals with the problems of marriage that have been raised by Corinthians' letter (περὶ δὲ ὧν ἐγράψατε, 1 Cor 7:1) brought to Paul by a delegation of Corinthian believers (Stephanas, Fortunatus and Achaicus 1 Cor 16:17). See also G. D. Fee, *The First Epistle to the Corinthians*, 6, 7; W. Harold Mare, *I Corinthians*. The Expositor's Bible Commentary, ed. Frank E. Gabelien, vol. 10 (Grand

It is clear from the text that the addressees are the believers in the Corinthian church, both men and women (ἀνήρ, ἄνθρωπος, γυνή), who are further defined according to their marital status (γεγαμηκόσιν, ἄγαμος, χήραις, παρθένων). Due to the fact that the issues raised for discussion by the Corinthians' letter (περὶ δὲ ὧν ἐγράψατε, v1a)[295] relate to the inner dynamics of the marital state (καλὸν ἀνθρώπῳ γυναικὸς μὴ ἅπτεσθαι,[296] v1b), as well as to its social dimension, the nature of the addressed groups should be established on the basis of these two dimensions, i.e. social and intimate. Hence, different groups being referred to by Paul with different titles should be analyzed in regard to their social status and sexual life as far as the text permits.[297] In order to identify the sections in which these different groups of people are addressed, one should locate the titles of designation and follow Paul's introductory words such as περὶ in v1, λέγω

Rapids: Zondervan, 1976), 180; D. Edmond Hiebert, *An Introduction to the Pauline Epistles* (Chicago: Moody, 1954), 111, 112.

295. I accept the view which maintains that Paul quotes in v1b a phrase or general idea from the Corinthians' letter. This is convincingly argued considering the structural similarity between 7:1 and 8:1, the latter being accepted by majority of biblical scholars as a quotation from Corinth. (See also Anthony C. Thiselton, *The First Epistle to the Corinthians*. The New International Greek Testament Commentary, eds. I. Howard Marshall and Donald A. Hagner [Grand Rapids: Eerdmans, 2000] 498.) The alternative view that the quotation is Paul's own belief contradicts his non-ascetic claims in some of his letters (non-ascetic approach to food and drink [1 Cor 9:19-23; 10: 25-26, 29b-30; Rom 14]; positive view of marriage [Eph 5:25-33]; condemning asceticism in general [Col 2:20-21, 1 Tim 4:3]). See also G. D. Fee, *The First Epistle to the Corinthians*, 276.

296. The word here means "sexual intercourse" in the light of widespread euphemism, ἅπτω, referring to sexual intercourse in the literature of the first century AD and before. See Plato, *Laws* 8.840a, "οὔτε τίνος πώποτε γυναικὸς ἅπσατο οὐδ' αὖ παιδός." Plato, *Platonis Opera*, ed. John Burnet. Oxford University Press, 1903 [online], Available at http://www.perseus.tufts.edu/cgi-bin/ptext?lookup=Plat.+Laws+840a, Accessed on 28 October 2000; Gen 20:6, LXX: "ἕνεκεν τούτου οὐκ ἀφῆκά σε ἅψασθαι αὐτῆς;" Ruth 2:9, LXX: "ἰδοὺ ἐνετειλάμην τοῖς παιδαρίοις τοῦ μὴ ἅψασθαί σου;" Flavius Josephus, *Antiquitates Judaicae* 1.163: "... καὶ θεάσασθαι σπουδάσας οἷος τε ὑν ἅπσαστηναι τύς Σάρρας." Flavius Josephus, *Antiquitates Judaicae*, ed. B. Niese [online], Available at http://www.perseus.tufts.edu/cgi-bin/ptext?lookup=J.+AJ+1.161, Accessed on 28 October 2000; See also G. D. Fee, *The First Epistle to the Corinthians*, 275; William F. Orr and James Arthur Walther, *I Corinthians*, AB (New York: Doubleday, 1976) 206; A. C. Thiselton, *The First Epistle to the Corinthians*, 500.

297. Thus, the nature of the text should determine whether it is necessary to discuss both dimensions or only one of them.

in v8, παραγγέλλω in v10, λέγω ἐγώ in v12, and περὶ in v25. On this basis, in chapter 7 Paul addresses five or even six groups of people.[298]

The first group of believers is addressed in vv1–7. Here there is no particular title used as for the rest of the groups, but from the issues discussed it becomes clear who Paul is speaking about. This group might be defined as married believers who attempt to live an ascetic life by abstaining from a sexual relationship with their partners (v1b). Paul prohibits such a style of life (v5), arguing that sexual intercourse is a gift from God for the married couple (v7, χάρισμα ἐκ θεοῦ)[299] and both partners should have their conjugal rights from their spouses (vv2, 3, 4).[300]

The second group is addressed in vv8–9 with two titles defining their marital status, τοῖς ἀγάμοις καὶ ταῖς χήραις. The first title creates great difficulty for the scholars in establishing its proper content.[301] The second title creates difficulty in relation to its exact gender. Due to the fact that the *koine* period does not give us any evidence for the meaning of ἄγαμος apart from the NT,[302] its meaning should primarily be established from its

---

298. See also G. D. Fee, *The First Epistle to the Corinthians*, 268.

299. See also ibid., 285.

300. Most probably Paul is thinking about one of the foundational stipulations of the Jewish marriage contracts, i.e. provision of conjugal rights. See Exod 21:10 where the law obligated the husband to provide the wife with three things "food, clothing, and marital rights (conjugal rights)" (NRS, NAS). This law has served to establish the three most basic stipulations of the Jewish marriage covenants (contracts) in the Jewish Bible (Ps 132; Hos 2:3–13; Ezek 16:1–13; Tobit 7:13), in the Mishnah, and in the latter Judaism as found in the marriage contracts in the Geniza collection. (See *The Mishnah: Ketubot 5:1–9*; Jewish Marriage contracts in *The Princeton Geniza Project* [online], Available at http://www.princeton.edu/~geniza/, Accessed on 19 November 2000). See also D. Instone-Brewer, *Three Weddings and a Divorce: God's Covenant with Israel, Judah and the Church* [online]; E. M. Yamauchi, *Cultural Aspects of Marriage in the Ancient World*, 245, 246.

301. Some scholars (those who stand behind the translation of RSV, against whom Fee is arguing, G. D. Fee, *The First Epistle to the Corinthians*, 287) argue that in vv8, 32, 34 ἄγαμος refers to those who have never been married, and as such they treated the word as synonym of παρθένων. Others (G. D. Fee, *The First Epistle to the Corinthians*, 287; J. M. Ford, *A Trilogy on Wisdom and Celibacy* [Sound Bend, 1967], 82–84; E. Arens, "Was St. Paul Married?" *Bible Today* 66 [1973] 1188–91; J. Moiser, "A Reassessment of Paul's View of Marriage with Reference to 1 Cor 7," *JSNT* 18 [1983] 108; Orr and Walther, *I Corinthians*, 210.) argue that in v8 ἄγαμος denotes only widowers. A good number of scholars (B. W. Powers, *Marriage and Divorce*, 182; C. Brown, Χωρίζω. Zondervan Reference Software V. 2.7.) argue that ἄγαμος should be interpreted as including all unmarried people who have had sexual intercourse and all de-married people (divorcee, widows, and widowers).

302. The word does not appear in LXX.

NT usage.³⁰³ The word ἄγαμος appears four times in the NT, all of them in 1 Cor 7 (vv8, 11, 32, 34). The clearest definition of the word according to its context appears in v11. Here, with the word ἄγαμος, Paul addresses a divorced woman. First, he prohibits her from divorcing her husband (γυναῖκα ἀπὸ ἀνδρὸς μὴ χωρισθῆναι, v10). Second, he makes an exception by saying that, if she divorces (ἐὰν δὲ καὶ χωρισθῇ),³⁰⁴ she should remain ἄγαμος, v11. Hence, it is thoroughly clear that to remain ἄγαμος means to remain divorced.³⁰⁵ This establishes the usage of the word ἄγαμος as designating the social status of a divorced or de-married person with an inner dynamic as someone who has had sexual relations. The other two uses of the word ἄγαμος, except for 1 Cor 7:8, are in vv32, 34. This is the section in which Paul addresses the group of παρθένων, v25, i.e. the ones who have never been married and who have never had any sexual relations. In v34, ἄγαμος is distinguished from παρθένος with a continuative conjunction καὶ.³⁰⁶ Hence, ὁ ἄγαμος in v32 cannot denote a male virgin since it is parallel to ἡ ἄγαμος in v34, but not to ἡ παρθένος in that

---

303. The classical Greek usage of the word is related to four possible meanings, namely never married, ones in widowhood, divorced, and never married but who have experienced sexual intercourse, from which the predominant one is that of never married. Never married: Plato, *Laws* 774a; Aeschylus, *Suppliant Women* 141, ed. Herbert Weir Smyth [online], Available at http://www.perseus.tufts.edu/cgi-bin/ptext?lookup=Aesch.+Supp.+141, Accessed on 29 October 2000. Widows and Widowers: Sophocles, *Oedipus Tyrannus*, 1212, ed. Sir Richard Jebb [online], Available at http://www.perseus.tufts.edu/cgi-bin/ptext?lookup=Soph.+OT+1212, Accessed on 29 October 2000; Euripides, *Helen*, 690, ed. Gilbert Murray [online], Available at http://www.perseus.tufts.edu/cgi-bin/ptext?lookup=Eur.+Hel.+666, Accessed on 29 October 2000. Divorced: Euripides, *Iphigenia in Tauris*, 215-220, ed. Robert Potter [online], Available at http://www.perseus.tufts.edu/cgi-bin/ptext?lookup=Eur.+IT+203, Accessed on 29 October 2000. Unmarried but experienced sexual intercourse: Plutarch, *Lives*, 4.3-5, ed. Bernadotte Perrin, Available at http://www.perseus.tufts.edu/cgi-bin/ptext?lookup=Plut.+Cim.+4.1, Accessed on 29 October 2000; Homer, *The Iliad* 3.39, ed. Samuel Butler, Available at http://www.perseus.tufts.edu/cgi-bin/ptext?lookup=Hom.+Il.+3.1, Accessed on 29 October 2000.

304. I argue that in this context the meaning of χωρίζω should be established as a technical term signifying a divorce action. See the discussion on 1 Cor 7:15.

305. See also W. Bauer, *A Greek-English Lexicon of the New Testament and Other Early Christian Literature*, 4; G. D. Fee, *The First Epistle to the Corinthians*, 288; B. W. Powers, *Marriage and Divorce*, 179; C. Brown, Χωρίζω. Zondervan Reference Software V. 2.7.

306. See also G. D. Fee, *The First Epistle to the Corinthians*, 288; Gustav Stählin, "Χήρα," in *TDNT*, eds. Gerhard Kittel & Gerhard Friedrich, trans. Geoffrey W. Bromiley (Grand Rapids: Eerdmans, 1964) – electronic ed. 10 v. – (Logos Library System).

verse, because the latter two are distinguished from each other.³⁰⁷ In the section vv32–35 Paul builds an argument with regard to the benefits to the Lord's service of the ones who are not married. Thus, he makes a contrast between the ones who are in a present state of marriage (ὁ γαμήσας, ἡ γαμήσασα, vv33, 34b) and the ones who are not presently involved in a marital relationship (ὁ ἄγαμος, ἡ γυνὴ ἡ ἄγαμος καὶ ἡ παρθένος, vv32, 34a). Due to the fact that ἡ παρθένος clearly denotes the ones who have never had sexual relations and have never been married, the meaning of ἄγαμος, in the light of Paul's contrast in vv32–35, should be established as the ones who are not in a present marital condition, but who have had sexual relations, i.e. all those who have been fornicators (1 Cor 6:9) and all those who are divorced and in widowhood.³⁰⁸

The context of vv8, 9 does not give us any hint as to the nature of the group represented by τοῖς ἀγάμοις. However, since Paul has the same advice for the people designated by the two titles, they must have something in common. From the closer (v11) and wider contexts (vv32, 34), the group of τοῖς ἀγάμοις is defined as the ones who are not presently married, but who have had sexual relations (thus former fornicators, divorcees, widowers, and widows). The group of ταῖς χήραις consists of people who are not presently married and who have had sexual relations.³⁰⁹ Thus, it is clear that the equal social status and former sexual life are the grounds for Paul to give the same piece of advice to these people addressed with two different titles. Therefore, the group of τοῖς ἀγάμοις in v8 should be defined as former fornicators and divorced people since ταῖς χήραις defines the ones in widowhood.³¹⁰ Solving the problem of the

307. See also G. D. Fee, *The First Epistle to the Corinthians*, 288; G. Stählin, "Χήρα," in *TDNT*, Logos Library System; Johannes Weiss, *Kommentar z. 1. Korintherbrief*, 1910 and J. Jeremias, "War Pls. Witwer?" *ZNW* 25 (1926) 310–12, quoted in G. Stählin, "Χήρα," in *TDNT*, Logos Library System; A. C. Thiselton, *The First Epistle to the Corinthians*, 590.

308. See also A. C. Thiselton, *The First Epistle to the Corinthians*, 590.

309. With the meaning of a woman whose husband died after they had lived together and had sexual relations which resulted in having children the word χήρα is used in nonbiblical (Lysias, *Speeches*, 2.71 in Lysias with an English translation by W.R.M. Lamb, Cambridge, MA: Harvard University Press; London: William Heinemann, 1930 [online], Available at http://www.perseus.tufts.edu/cgi-bin/ptext?lookup=Lys.+2+69, Accessed on 29 October 2000; Flavius Josephus, *Antiquitates Judaicae*, 16.221) and biblical literature (LXX, Lev 22:13; 2 Sam 14:5; 1 Kgs 17:9–12; NT, Luke 2:36, 37; 7:12). Paul is also using the word with the same meaning in his writings (1 Tim 5:4, 5, 9).

310. The view that in v8 ἄγαμος denotes only widowers is difficult to sustain because

gender of ταῖς χήραις will finally clarify the exact people who are behind these two titles. On the basis of the masculine form of the personal pronoun αὐτοῖς, for which both titles, i.e. τοῖς ἀγάμοις and ταῖς χήραις, are antecedents, I argue that Paul addresses in this paragraph (vv8, 9) only male individuals.[311] Hence, ταῖς χήραις should be considered as a primitive corruption of τοῖς χήροις.[312] Moreover, since Paul is giving the same advice specifically to widows in vv39–40, why should he address them here in vv8, 9 as well.[313] Nor does Paul address here those women who are divorced, since he addresses them in v11.

---

of the following problems. First, in the immediate context (v11a) ἄγαμος is used to refer to a divorced person, not to a widower. Second, there is no strong evidence that the word was used with such a meaning in the first century AD. Fee argues that the regular word for male widow "is never used in the *koine* period, in which ἄγαμος served in its place." (G. D. Fee, *The First Epistle to the Corinthians*, 288) However his source for establishing this argument, Liddell and Scott, does not prove anything like this (Liddell-Scott-Jones Lexicon of Classical Greek [online], Available at http://www.perseus.tufts.edu/cgi-bin/lexindex?entry=a)/gamos, Accessed on 29 October 2000.). The Lexicon does not explicitly say that the word ἄγαμος replaced ὁ χῆρος in the first century AD. There is usage of ἄγαμος in a sense of ὁ χῆρος but it appears in a document from 5 BC and may not serve as an argument for Fee's claim related to the *koine* period. (See Euripides, *Helen* 690, Euripides, *Helen*, ed. Gilbert Murray [online], Available at http://www.perseus.tufts.edu/cgi-bin/ptext?lookup=Eur.+Hel.+666, Accessed on 29 October 2000.) Moreover even though ὁ χῆρος appears later than ἡ χήρα (the latter is used first by Homer [VIII–VI BC], e.g., II, 6, 408f; the former is used first by Callimachus [III BC], Epigr., 15,4) and is used much more rarely, it might be argued as Stählin (G. Stählin, "Χήρα," in *TDNT*, Logos Library System) and Timothy and Barbara Friberg ("ὁ χῆρος # 28614b," in *Friberg Analytical Lexicon to the Greek New Testament*, 2000 edition. [electronic edition], *BibleWorks for Windows*. Windows 98/XP Release. Version 6.0.005y, BibleWorks, LLC, 2003.) that it appears in the NT (1 Cor.7:8b). Also Bauer does not say anything about the usage of ἄγαμος on the place of ὁ χῆρος. However the ὁ ἄγαμος in v32 may denote widower but since it appears in v34 in feminine gender, ἡ ἄγαμος, it also may denote widow. Even though both ὁ ἄγαμος and ἡ ἄγαμος in vv32 and 34 may denote those in widowhood they may also denote those who are divorced, because there is no hint in the context of the exclusion of divorced people from the term ἄγαμος in vv32, 34.

311. Also G. Stählin, "Χήρα," in *TDNT*, Logos Library System; J. Weiss, *Kommentar z. 1. Korintherbrief*, 1910 and J. Jeremias, *War Pls. Witwer?*, 310–312, quoted in G. Stählin, "Χήρα," in *TDNT*, Logos Library System; Timothy and Barbara Friberg "ὁ χῆρος # 28614b," in *Friberg Analytical Lexicon to the Greek New Testament*.

312. See also Bois who argues that the word is a primitive corruption for τοῖς χήροις and Holsten who omits ταῖς χήραις completely. (G. G. Findlay, "St. Paul's First Epistle to the Corinthians," in *the Expositor's Greek Testament*, ed. W. Robertso Nicoll, vol.II [Grand Rapids: Eerdmans, 1979] 825; K. & B. Aland, eds. *Critical Apparatuses of NA*[26], 450.)

313. G. Stählin, "Χήρα," in *TDNT*, Logos Library System.

Therefore Paul is giving advice to the former fornicators, divorced men (τοῖς ἀγάμοις),[314] and widowers (τοῖς χήροις), that it is well for them to remain as he is (καλὸν αὐτοῖς ἐὰν μένωσιν ὡς κἀγώ, v8), namely de-married.[315] But then he gives a command for remarriage because of their lack of self-control[316] (εἰ δὲ οὐκ ἐγκρατεύονται, γαμησάτωσαν,[317] κρεῖττον γάρ ἐστιν γαμῆσαι ἢ πυροῦσθαι, v9).

314. See also Hays, *The Moral Vision of the New Testament*, 373.

315. See also B. W. Powers, *Marriage and Divorce*, 182; C. Brown, Χωρίζω. Zondervan Reference Software V. 2.7.

316. It is wrong to translate v9 as RSV does it: "But if they *cannot* exercise self-control . . . ." The first class conditional statement does not need "cannot" since it "emphasizes the reality of the assumption." (See also G. D. Fee, *The First Epistle to the Corinthians*, 289, f. 9) The phrase should be translated "But if they do not exercise self-control . . . ." That presupposes that the Christian men had a problem going to the prostitutes (1 Cor 6:9–20), (See also G. D. Fee, *The First Epistle to the Corinthians*, 289; B. W. Powers, *Marriage and Divorce*, 182). Corinth was famous for the numerous prostitutes and the loose sexual life of its citizens (See Strabo, *Geography* 8.6.20, ed. H. L. Jones [online], Available at http://perseus.csad.ox.ac.uk/cgi-bin/ptext?lookup=Strab.+8.6.1, Accessed on 21 December 2000; See also S. J. Hafemann, "Corinthians, Letters to the," in *Dictionary of Paul and His Letters*, eds. Gerald F. Hawthorne, Ralph P. Martin, and Daniel G. Reid (Downers Grove, IL: InterVarsity, 1993), 173; Christopher Lane, *ΡΗΥΞ ΗΑΠΑΞ* [online], Available at http://home1.gte.net/zzyzlane/write/poetry/rhapax06.html, Accessed on 21 December 2000). Moreover Greek culture was very tolerant of the promiscuous sexual life of men. Greek men, unlike women, could have sex outside of marriage with different kinds of prostitutes without being charged with any penalties. (See Antiphon, *Speeches* 1.13, ed. K. J. Maidment [online], Available at http://perseus.csad.ox.ac.uk/cgi-bin/ptext?lookup=Antiph.+1+13, Accessed on 21 December 2000; Demosthenes, *Speeches 51–61: Apollodorus Against Neaera* 59.17, trans. A. T. Murray, Norman W. DeWitt, and Norman J. DeWitt [online], Available at http://perseus.csad.ox.ac.uk/cgi-bin/ptext?lookup=Dem.+59+17, Accessed on 21 December 2000; See also T. R. Martin, *An Overview of Classical Greek History from Homer to Alexander* [online].) Christian men with a Jewish background from the Corinthian church were not saved from the temptations of the prostitutes either. Reisser argues that in the first century AD Jews encouraged early marriages in order to avoid fornication. (H. Reisser, "*Discipline, Prudence, Immorality, Prostitute*," in The New International Dictionary of New Testament Theology. Zondervan Reference Software V. 2.7.) Here is part of Zorobabel's speech about the seductive power of women over men: "Wine is strong, as is the king also, whom all men obey, *but women are superior to them in power*; . . . (51) nor can we live separate from women; and when we have gotten a great deal of gold, and silver, and any other thing that is of great value, and deserving regard, *and see a beautiful woman, we leave all these things, and with open mouth fix our eyes upon her countenance*, and are willing to forsake what we have, that we may enjoy her beauty, and procure it to ourselves." (Josephus, *The Antiquities of the Jews*, 11.3.5)

317. Imperative of command.

The third group is addressed as τοῖς γεγαμηκόσιν (vv10–11). Here Paul addresses the ones who are in Christian marriages, i.e. where both partners are Christians. This might be concluded on the basis of the silence in relation to their religious status, in contrast to the next section (vv12–16) where Paul addresses the ones in mixed marriages, i.e. believers with unbelievers, with the phrase τοῖς λοιποῖς.[318] Thus, Paul is giving a command to married believers on the basis of Jesus' divorce tradition[319] that they should not divorce (vv10–11). Paul's emphasis, however, is on the part of the women, since in the Greco-Roman Corinth women were free to divorce their husbands.[320] The main reason for the divorce action could be anything other than their desire to stay unmarried since that is what Paul commands them to do in v11 (μενέτω ἄγαμος[321]).[322] I would argue that the main reason for divorce seen here is that of subsequent

---

318. See also G. D. Fee, *The First Epistle to the Corinthians*, 291.

319. Cf. Mark 10:9, 11; Matt 19:6, 9 and Luke 16:18; Matt 5:32.

320. See Gaius, *Institutes* 137a, trans. Gordon and Robinson [online], Available at http://www.stoa.org/diotima/anthology/wlgr/wlgr-romanlegal132.shtml, Accessed on 25 December 2000; Diodorus Siculus, *Library*, 12.18.1, XVIII, trans. C. H. Oldfather [online], Available at http://www.perseus.tufts.edu/cgi-bin/ptext?lookup=Diod.+12.18.1, Accessed on 25 December 2000; See also G. D. Fee, *The First Epistle to the Corinthians*, 294; Ben Witherington III, *Conflict and Community in Corinth: A Socio-Rhetorical Commentary on 1 and 2 Corinthians* (Grand Rapids: Eerdmans, 1995), 171. This was not true for Jewish women. Gundry insists that woman's legal action might not initiate divorce but eventually prompt the man to divorce her. (Josephus *Ant*. 15.7.10; 18.9.6; *m. Yebam.* 14:1; Str-B 1.318–19), (See Gundry, *Mark*, 543; See C. L. Blomberg, *Marriage, Divorce, Remarriage, and Celibacy*. Electronic edition by Galaxie Software; T. R. Rich, ed. *Divorce: Inequality of the Sexes* [online].) For tracing further the debate about the rights of Jewish women to divorce their husbands see W. Hendriksen, *Mark*, 380; V. Taylor, *The Gospel according to St Mark*, 420; D. Instone-Brewer, *Jewish Women Divorcing Their Husbands in Early Judaism: The Background to Papyrus Se'elim 13*, 349–357; A. Schremer, *Divorce in Papyrus Se'elim 13 Once Again: A Reply to Tal Ilan*, 191–202; T. Ilan, *The Provocative Approach Once Again: A Response to Adiel Schremer*, 203–4; G. F. Hawthorne, *Marriage and Divorce, Adultery and Incest*, 598; Fitzmyer, *The Matthean Divorce Texts and Some New Palestinian Evidence*, 200.

321. This is the apodosis in imperative of command of the third class conditional statement which presupposes a more probable future occurrence of the divorce action.

322. Contra Fee (*The First Epistle to the Corinthians*, 290, 269–70), who argues that the main reason for divorce was their ascetic desires. Contra Ben Witherington III who argues (Witherington III, *Conflict and Community in Corinth*, 16) that the reason for divorce of Christian women was primarily religious. Witherington states that a previous sacred marriage with goddess Hera Argaea prevented Corinthian women from keeping their marriages since they did not want to defile their former sacred sexual union by a human one.

remarriage. That is the reason why Paul prohibits the subsequent remarriage of the woman, but commands reconciliation with the first husband (ἢ τῷ ἀνδρὶ καταλλαγήτω³²³). This may be the motive of Paul to use the teaching of Jesus in its unchanged form as being pronounced in a Jewish context and delivered by Mark and Luke to Gentile Christian audience, and even to stress that fact (οὐκ ἐγὼ ἀλλὰ ὁ κύριος, v10).³²⁴ For the same attitude toward remarriage, Paul also prohibits the husband to divorce his wife (καὶ ἄνδρα γυναῖκα μὴ ἀφιέναι, v11). Therefore, in this section Paul addresses the married believers with the prohibition of divorce. Moreover, he forbids remarriage of the divorced women because of their pre-divorce desire for subsequent remarriage, a prohibition that does not contradict the command for remarriage of the divorced man in v9. The former were disobeying Jesus' divorce teaching by looking for divorce for the purpose of remarriage³²⁵; the latter, after being divorced, were falling prey to the sexual sin of πορνεία while attempting to stay ἄγαμος.

The fourth group is addressed as τοῖς λοιποῖς in vv12–16. The content of the passage defines this group as consisting of Christians who are married to unbelievers.³²⁶ Their attitude toward marriage depends on the

323. This is also part of the apodosis in imperative of command.

324. One of the usual reasons for divorce for Jewish men was their desire for subsequent remarriage. *Mishnah, Sotah* 5:1. See also Nolland, *Luke 9:21–18:34*, 819; I. H. Marshall, *The Gospel of Luke*, 631. That was also true for Jewish women but in some specific cases. "... but Herodias, their sister, was married to Herod [Philip], the son of Herod the Great, who was born of Mariamne, the daughter of Simon the high priest, who had a daughter, Salome; after whose birth Herodias took upon her to confound the laws of our country, *and divorce herself from her husband while he was alive, and was married to Herod* [Antipas], her husband's brother by the father's side; he was tetrarch of Galilee." Josephus, *The Antiquities of the Jews*, 18.5.4.136; See also Josephus, *The Antiquities of the Jews*, 15.7.10.259. That was exactly what was happening among Gentiles and even in larger scale: See Diodorus Siculus, *Library* 12.18.1.XVIII; M. Tullius Cicero, *Letters*, ed. Evelyn Shuckburgh [online].

325. That is exactly what Jesus prohibited from Luke's point of view. If one understands the force of the coordinate conjunction καί which connects the two clauses of Luke 16:18a as suggesting a finality of the subsequent clause or expressing a semantic notion of its subordination then the sentence built by the clauses should be translated as such: "everyone who divorces his wife in order to marry another commits adultery" For discussion of such force of καί see D. B. Wallace, *Greek Grammar Beyond the Basics*, 667, f. 2. For that function of the conjunction in the Patristic literature see Alber-Louis Descamps, *The New Testament Doctrine on Marriage*, 217–73, 347–63; See also Nolland, *Luke 9:21–18:34*, 821, 822.

326. ἄπιστον, v12; ἄνδρα ἄπιστον, v13; ὁ ἀνὴρ ὁ ἄπιστος, ἡ γυνὴ ἡ ἄπιστος, v14; ὁ ἄπιστος, v15 cf. τις ἀδελφὸς, v12; γυνή, v13; τῷ ἀδελφῷ, v14; ὁ ἀδελφὸς ἢ ἡ ἀδελφὴ, v15.

willingness of the unbelieving partners to stay in the marriage.³²⁷ If the unbeliever is willing to stay in the marriage with the believer, then the believer should not divorce (vv12–14). But if the unbeliever is not willing to stay and deserts the believer, then the latter is free to divorce and remarry (vv15, 16).

The fifth group is addressed as τῶν παρθένων in vv25–38. The plural form of the noun does not confirm a particular gender, suggesting that with this title Paul most probably addresses both men and women who have never had sexual relations.³²⁸ Paul is giving them his advice (γνώμην δὲ δίδωμι, v25) that it is better for them to stay unmarried (καλὸν ἀνθρώπῳ τὸ οὕτως εἶναι, v26). However if a virgin, man or woman, marries he/she does not sin (ἐὰν δὲ καὶ γαμήσῃς, οὐχ ἥμαρτες· καὶ ἐὰν γήμῃ ἡ παρθένος, οὐχ ἥμαρτεν, v28). In vv32–35 Paul is saying the same thing, but from a different perspective (in relation to the ministry for the Lord) and here he is also including those who are not married, but who have had sexual relations, ὁ ἄγαμος, ἡ γυνὴ ἡ ἄγαμος (vv32, 34).³²⁹ In the rest of the passage (vv36–38), Paul is repeating the same advice from a third perspective (in relation to the ones who are at a potential stage for marriage³³⁰).

Finally Paul addresses the widows by way of conclusion in vv39–40. He argues that it is better for the widow to remain as she is (μακαριωτέρα δέ ἐστιν ἐὰν οὕτως μείνῃ, v40), i.e. de-married, but if she wishes to marry she is free to do so, but only in the Lord (ἐλευθέρα ἐστὶν ᾧ θέλει γαμηθῆναι, μόνον ἐν κυρίῳ, v39).

The way Paul addresses all these groups plays a significant role in defining the context of 1 Cor 7:12–14. Established against the Corinthians'

327. See also Ethelbert Stauffer, "Γαμέω, γάμος," in *TDNT* ed. Gerhard Kittel, trans. Geoffrey W. Bromiley—electronic ed.—Grand Rapids: Eerdmans, c1964–c1976. Logos Library System 2.1g.

328. The meaning of the word as a person, man or woman, who have never had any sexual intercourse in their life is confirmed in the literature contemporary to the NT (Flavius Josephus, *Antiquitates Judaicae*, 4.8.23.244.) and from the biblical literature both OT (Judges 21:12; Leviticus 21:14, LXX) and NT (Acts 21:9; Rev 14:4). Paul is using the word with the same meaning in 1 Cor 7: 25, 28, 34, 36, 37, 38.

329. See also G. Stählin, "Χήρα," in *TDNT*, Logos Library System.

330. My conclusion that this group of Paul's addressees consists of virgins who have never been married and have never had sexual relations does not require a particular acquiescence to any of the proposed views for understanding of vv36–38 (father-daughter; man-fiancée; spiritual marriages; levirate marriages, See the discussion in Orr and Walther, *I Corinthians*, 223–225).

perspective of life,[331] and within the framework of Paul's narrative thought world, the apostle's overall approach[332] might be defined as based on the principle of God's call[333] (1 Cor 7:17–24) and shaped by the apostle's eschatological perspective (vv26a, 29a).[334] Thus, Paul argues that it is not a change of one's social setting but a change of one's perspective of life with respect to that setting that carries spiritual significance. The former proves that God's call makes all the settings irrelevant to one's spirituality.[335] Thus, one should stay in the setting where God's call found him/her (v20), although a positive change is also acceptable (δοῦλος – ἐλεύθερος vv21–22). The latter (vv26, 29) confirms that the perspective from which the believer sees his/her life in the particular social setting is the key to one's spiritual condition (vv29–31). Thus, Paul's twofold eschatological point of view maintains that the Corinthian believers should view their relationship to the passing world (v31c) in the light of "the present distress" (τὴν ἐνεστῶσαν ἀνάγκην, v26)[336] and through the perspective of the

---

331. Corinthians' main problem was that under the influence of Hellenistic dualism they put a greater value on everything related to the sphere of spirituality and knowledge than on the matters related to the physical and material world. Hence, they considered themselves highly spiritual (1 Cor 14:37) due to their spiritual gifts (1 Cor 1:7; 4:7; especially the gift of tongues, 1 Cor 14:18, 19, 22, 23), wisdom, and knowledge (1 Cor 1:17, 19–22; 2:1, 4–7; 3:19; 1:5; 8:1, 10, 11; 13:2, 8). From that perspective, Corinthian believers maintained that a new social status must be obtained which would fit their present high spiritual condition (1 Cor 7:1). See also James D. Tabor, *The Jewish Roman World of Jesus* [online], Available at http://www.uncc.edu/jdtabor/overview-roman-world.html, Accessed on 19 December 2000; G. D. Fee, *The First Epistle to the Corinthians*, 10, 11, 307; Hafemann, *Corinthians*, 174.

332. Other features which shape Paul's approach are the "temptation to immorality," (NRS, v2) and the existence of particular χάρισμα ἐκ θεοῦ, v7 in one's personal life. The former serves as grounds for the apostles' argument for preserving sexual life in the marriage (vv2–6) and for encouraging remarriage of the unmarried and de-married (v9). The latter serves the apostle as grounds for arguing that one should live according to God's gift whether in celibacy or marriage (v7).

333. Paul's understanding of God's call in 1 Corinthians may be defined as the act of Christian conversion (1 Cor 1:9).

334. "Already" and "not yet" eschatological perspective of Paul is fundamental to his thinking not only in 1 Corinthians (1 Cor 1:20; 10:11) but also in his whole corpus (Gal 1:4; Rom 8:18–20; 2 Cor 5:17; Eph 1:16; 21). See the lists of proponents of this understanding provided by Don N. Howell Jr., "Pauline Eschatological Dualism and Its Resulting Tensions," *Trinity Journal* 14 (Spring 1993) 7. See also G. D. Fee, *The First Epistle to the Corinthians*, 342.

335. See also G. D. Fee, *The First Epistle to the Corinthians*, 307.

336. This phrase echoes the "not yet" dimension of Paul's eschatological thinking.

time as having been shortened, (ὁ καιρὸς συνεσταλμένος ἐστίν, v29).[337] Hence, they should not seek to change their present social setting (vv26b, 27), but even if this happens (v29) they should strive to live their life in the light of the coming glorious future (vv29–31).[338]

Therefore Paul is addressing different groups of believers, advising them to preserve their present social status of virginity (vv26, 32–34, 37–38b), marriage (vv12–14), divorce (v8), or widowhood (vv8, 40), but if the ones who are not married or are de-married do not have the χάρισμα (v7) for keeping this status and wish to marry, then they can do so without committing sin (vv9, 28, 35, 36, 38a, 39). No change of status is approved, however, for the purpose of benefiting one's spirituality (vv12–14). On the contrary, a change of status is prohibited when it contradicts the Lord's teaching (vv10–11).

Exegetical analysis of 1 Cor 7:12–16 should be based on confirmation of the exact nature of the passage as one unit.[339] Thus, I would argue

---

Although the church has already had a foretaste of the "new age" of God's glorious Kingdom, she is still living in the "present evil age" and thus the believers will still experience distress and troubles (cf. Rom 8:18; 1 Thess 3:3–4). See also G. D. Fee, *The First Epistle to the Corinthians*, 329, 330; Frederic Louis Godet, *Commentary on First Corinthians* (Grand Rapids: Kregel, 1977), 371.

337. This phrase echoes the "already" dimension of Paul's eschatological thinking. The believers had already entered the "new age" of God's Kingdom through the act of conversion (1 Cor 7:9–11) and thus have a clear view of the coming glorious future, i.e. the day of Parousia, when a full consummation of that salvation will be experienced (1 Cor 7:14, cf. 1 Cor 15:23). Hence, any relation to the world should be established on the basis of that perspective (1 Cor 7:30–31, cf. 4:1–5 and 6:1–6). See also G. D. Fee, *The First Epistle to the Corinthians*, 335–342; Godet, *Corinthians*, 376, 377.

338. Corinthians' "over-realized eschatology" did not have a place for such a clear perspective of the coming glorious future. See also G. D. Fee, *The First Epistle to the Corinthians*, 339; Hafemann, *Corinthians*, 175.

339. Thus, I join the general agreement of the scholars that the passage is a unit which discusses the subject of mixed marriages, namely marriages between believers and unbelievers (See G. D. Fee, *The First Epistle to the Corinthians*, 297). I disagree with Elliott's argument for dividing the passage into two sections (12–14 and 15, 16) on the basis of his misunderstanding of the meaning of the verb χωρίζω used in v15 as different from that of ἀφίημι used in vv12–14. (J. K. Elliott, "Paul's Teaching on Marriage in I Corinthians: Some Problems Considered," *New Testament Studies* 19 [1972–1973] 225.) The verb χωρίζω is a synonym of ἀφίημι in the context of vv12–16 since it is very well attested as a technical term for divorce in a strict sense in the Greek literature of the Classical and Hellenistic periods (Isaeus, *Speeches* 8.36; Isaeus, *Speeches* [online], Available at http://perseus.csad.ox.ac.uk/cgi-bin/ptext?lookup=Isaeus+8+35, Accessed on 02 December 2000; Herodotus, *Hist.* 5.39.2; Herodotus, *The Histories* [online], Available at http://perseus.csad.ox.ac.uk/cgi-bin/ptext?lookup=Hdt.+5.39.1, Accessed

that Paul deals primarily with one case, that of believers who want to divorce their unbelieving spouses (vv12–14).[340] At the same time, he deals with another case as well, namely that of the believers in the process of being divorced by the unbelievers (vv15, 16), but he does this in a secondary manner as an exception to the whole argument.[341] Obviously, the main problem in the Corinthian church was not the unbelievers' desire to separate, but the believers' desire to separate.[342] This does not exclude the

---

on 02 December 2000; Euripides. *Andromache* 973; Euripides. *Andromache*, ed. David Kovacs [online], Available at http://perseus.csad.ox.ac.uk/cgi-bin/ptext?lookup=Eur.+Andr.+957, Accessed on 02 December 2000) and by the NT authors when it appears in the context of marriage (Mark 10:9 and Matt 19:6). See also Fitzmyer, *Matthean Divorce Texts and Some New Palestinian Evidence*, 211, 212; Jerome Murphy-O'Connor, "The Divorced Woman in I Cor 7:10–11," *JBL* 100 (1981) 605.

340. See also G. D. Fee, *The First Epistle to the Corinthians*, 297, 298.

341. I argue against Fee's strong restriction of the exception only to v15ab on the basis of his misapplication of Paul's fundamental principle (v17) which guided the apostle's argument (vv12–16). The principle relates to two basic features of one's Christian life, namely God's call and one's social setting. If Fee's conclusion about the relationship between these two features is correct one may clearly see where Paul's emphasis lies (*The First Epistle to the Corinthians*, 310, 311). A life according to God's call is what matters to Paul not whether one will retain or change one's social setting, since both the settings themselves (vv18–19, 22) and the changes are irrelevant (p. 311). Hence, when Paul is speaking to those in mixed marriages his emphasis is that one should continue to live according to God's call in the situation in which he was called and should not desert the unbelieving spouse. But even if the situation changes and the unbeliever leaves (v15ab), the believer should continue to live according to God's call in the new social setting (that of divorce) to which he belongs. (See also Witherington III, *Conflict and Community in Corinth*, 178.) The change of the situation, which appears to be the exception to Paul's principle, does not go against Paul's principle but modifies it (G. D. Fee, *The First Epistle to the Corinthians*, 302). Therefore the exception as such has an important place in Paul's argument as a whole. Through the exception Paul approaches the group of believers in the Corinthian church who were in the process of being divorced by the unbelievers. Thus, v15c and v16 as parts of Paul's main argument relate not only to vv12–14 but also to the exception v15ab. (Contra G. D. Fee, *The First Epistle to the Corinthians*, 303–5). This is the reason why both v15c and v16 are so ambiguous. That ambiguity is seen basically by all the scholars. For example: Archibald Robertson and Alfred Plummer, *A Critical and Exegetical Commentary on the First Epistle of St. Paul to the Corinthians*. The International Critical Commentary (Edinburgh: T. and T. Clark, 1911), 143, 144; G. D. Fee, *The First Epistle to the Corinthians*, 305, footnote 48; Hans Conzelmann, *A Commentary on the First Epistle to the Corinthians*. Hermeneia - A Critical and Historical Commentary on the Bible, trans. James W. Leitch (Philadelphia: Fortress, 1975), 123.

342. That is clear on two grounds. First, the Corinthians' statement presented by Paul in 7:1 clearly determines their ascetic notion within Christian marriages. Second, the Corinthians' misunderstanding of Paul's previous letter that they should not have relations with the immoral pagans (5:9–11) determines in the first place that in mixed mar-

group of believers, however, who suffered desertion by their unbelieving spouses.[343] Therefore the perspective of the particular first century reader should determine the relative significance of the main argument of the apostle (vv12–14) or his exception (vv15, 16) for the Corinthian audience. If the reader is a brother or sister in the process of being divorced by the unbeliever, then the exception should gain greater significance. If the reader is a believer who desires to divorce the unbeliever then the main argument becomes more important.

In the usual way for this part of his letter (7:1–40) Paul is addressing a group of Christians who have unbelieving partners, "τοῖς λοιποῖς," v12. That mixed marriages are in view here is determined by the titles with which Paul refers to both partners[344] and by the Christian nature of the marriages discussed in the previous section (vv10–11).[345] Paul is introducing his instructions with the words "I say, not the Lord" (RSV). They are in contrast to those which he used for introducing his commandment in v10 "not I but the Lord" (RSV). Paul's point is not that he does not have any connection with Jesus' teaching on divorce and remarriage, which he used in v10, but that now he is using his own authority, since Jesus did not particularly speak about mixed marriages.[346] Actually, using the Lord's teaching, Paul is addressing a new situation in the Corinthian church.[347] Hence, the apostle prohibits divorce between believers and unbelievers

---

riages the Christians would attempt to divorce the unbelievers. (See also G. D. Fee, *The First Epistle to the Corinthians*, 300; J. Carl Laney, "Paul and the Permanence of Marriage in I Corinthians 7," *Journal of the Evangelical Theological Society* 25/3 [September 1982]: 286; Witherington III, *Conflict and Community in Corinth*, 178.).

343. Mixed marriages were a place where the danger of divorce was present all the time. The tensions of such marriages were very well depicted by Tertullian. (Tertullian, *To His Wife* II.4., trans. S. Thelwall, in *Ante-Nicene Fathers: Translations of The Writings of the Fathers Down to A. D. 325*, eds. Alexander Roberts and James Donaldson, vol. 4. Christian Classics Ethereal Library. Vol.2, CD-ROM, ed. Harry Plantinga [Wheaton, IL: Wheaton College, 1998].) Thus, it is illogical to think that there were no real cases in the Corinthian church of believers who were in the process of divorce by the unbelievers.

344. The unbelieving partner, husband or wife, is defined with the adjective ἄπιστος, ον (vv12–15). (See also Friberg Greek Lexicon; UBS Greek Dictionary; Louw-Nida Lexicon in *BibleWorks for Windows*. Version 4.0.026e [4000]. Cambridge, MA: Lotus Development Corporation, 1998.) And the believer is defined with the nouns ἀδελφός, οῦ; ἀδελφή, ῆς (vv12, 14, 15) or just with γυνή, αικός; ἀνήρ, ἀνδρός (vv13, 16).

345. See also Orr and Walther, *I Corinthians*, 212.

346. See also G. D. Fee, *The First Epistle to the Corinthians*, 292.

347. That situation developed after the conversion of one of the spouses in pagan marriages to Christianity.

which has already been started by the believers.³⁴⁸ Paul addresses equally Christian wives and husbands, saying that they should not divorce unbelieving spouses who are willing to live with them (vv12–13). The apostle introduces the reason for this prohibition in v14 by a causal γάρ.³⁴⁹ The reason appears to be twofold in regard to the unbelieving spouse and the children. On the one hand, the believer is urged to consider the unbelieving partner as "ἁγιάζω," i.e. set apart by the believer's influence through his/her testimony and deeds, which may lead the unbeliever to salvation.³⁵⁰ On the other hand, the believer is compelled to consider the state of his/her children within the frame of a preserved marriage, or what their state might be if such a marriage broke. If the marriage continues the children are considered ἅγια, i.e. open to Christian influence with the possibility of being raised apart from pagan worship and evil practices.³⁵¹ If a divorce is obtained the children will be ἀκάθαρτα, i.e. they will lose the Christian influence and fall under the pagan one.³⁵² Two further implications should be noticed on the basis of Paul's argument. First, the passage vv12–14 should not be used by believers as grounds for justification of marriage to an unbeliever.³⁵³ Second, marriage should not be treated as a

---

348. μή + present imperative prohibits an action already in progress (vv12, 13).

349. Through a sentence flow analysis of the passage it becomes clear that here by using this inferential conjunction (γάρ) Paul is giving the reason for his previous statements. The fact that the unbelieving partner is set apart for the gospel by the believer and that the children of such marriages are holy, gives a strong argument for preserving one's marriage with the unbelieving spouse.

350. Here the meaning of ἁγιάζω should be stripped from its usual moral sense (1 Thess 5:23; 2 Tim 2:21) and relation to salvation (Rom 15:16; 1 Cor 6:11) because of the limitation in the context (1 Cor 7:16) and it should be restricted to Paul's analogy presented in Rom 11:16 where he expresses the idea that "if the part of the dough is holy . . . than the whole batch is holy," (NRS). This understanding helped Paul to keep his hope for the future salvation of Israel alive. (See also G. D. Fee, *The First Epistle to the Corinthians*, 301; J. C. Laney, *Paul and the Permanence of Marriage in I Corinthians 7*, 286.)

351. This understanding of ἁγιάζω is in parallel to the previous one. The idea also parallels the Jewish designation of the children in proselytes' marriages as part of the Israel's nation. (*The Mishnah, Yebam* 11.2; *The Mishnah, Ketubot* 4.3; See also G. D. Fee, *The First Epistle to the Corinthians*, 302.)

352. The word ἀκάθαρτος, ον carries with it connotations from Jewish ritual language and suggests that people in that condition stood outside the covenant relationship of Israel with Yahweh (Lev 11:24–28, 31, 36, 39, 40; Num 19:7, 8, 10; Deut 12:15, 22 etc). (See also G. D. Fee, *The First Epistle to the Corinthians*, 301.)

353. Tertullian dealt with such an abuse of the meaning of the passage (vv12–14). See Tertullian, *To His Wife* II.3.

tool for personal evangelism nor should this be used to justify marrying an unbeliever.[354]

In v15ab Paul introduces an exception to his main argument (vv12–14) answering the questions of Corinthian believers[355] concerning whether they may allow their unbelieving spouses who do not agree to live with them to divorce. Paul starts the exception by the adversative conjunction δὲ which establishes the contrast between his previous argument and this one. Previously the apostle addressed those whose unbelieving spouses were willing to live with them, but now he speaks to those whose unbelieving spouses are not willing to live with them. The exact meaning of the exception (v15ab) should be established on the grounds of the usage of the verbs χωρίζω and δουλόω. Thus, I will analyze these verbs in relation to their semantic and syntactical natures.

Semantically, the verb χωρίζω in its present context should be understood as divorce with the right of remarriage. That conclusion is established on twofold grounds. First, in relation to divorce, the verb is understood by the first century reader within the context of marital issues as a technical term expressing the act of divorce.[356] Second, in relation to

354. See 2 Cor 6:14–18; Eph 5:31–33; See also J. C. Laney, *Paul and the Permanence of Marriage in I Corinthians 7*, 286.

355. The references of Paul to both brother and sister in vv12–13 and v15 plus the apostle's reference in plural τοῖς τοιούτοις in v15c suggest that even though Paul speaks in singular forms for the persons throughout the whole passage in vv12–16 he has in mind not a single case but several cases of mixed marriages of both kinds (vv12–13 and v15).

356. The word χωρίζω in the context of marriage and divorce is understood as a technical term referring to a divorce action. (In the papyri: PS 166, II [II BC]; BGU 1101, 5; 1102, 8; 1103 [I BC] [BGU IV.1103, The Duke Databank of Documentary Papyri [online]; BGU IV.1102, The Duke Databank of Documentary Papyri [online]; BGU IV.1101, The Duke Databank of Documentary Papyri [online].]; [See also W. Bauer, *A Greek-English Lexicon of the New Testament and Other Early Christian Literature*, 898]; P Ryl II. 154²⁵ [AD 66]; BGU 1.251⁶ [AD 81]; ib. IV. 1045²² [AD 154]; P. Ryl II. 154³⁰ [AD 66], [See also J. H. Moulton and G. Millgan, *The Vocabulary of the Greek Testament. Illustrated from the Papyri and Other Non-Literary Sources*, 696.] In other nonbiblical literature: Polyb., 32, 12, 6. In the LXX: 1 Esd 9:9; 1 Esd 9:36. In the NT: Matt 19:6; Matt 1:19.) An exception might be when the word is used in a Jewish context of divorce referring to the wife, then it carries the meaning of "separation, desertion," since the wife could not initiate divorce according to Jewish Law. (See Josephus, *The Antiquities of the Jews*, 15.7.10.259). However here the context is Greco-Roman where the wife could initiate divorce. (See Gaius, *Institutes* 137a; Diodorus Siculus, *Library*, 12.18.1, XVIII; See also G. D. Fee, *The First Epistle to the Corinthians*, 294; Witherington III, *Conflict and Community in Corinth*, 171.) For the approval of this understanding of χωρίζω in 1 Cor 7: 10, 11, 15 see also Moulton and Millgan, *The Vocabulary of the Greek Testament*, 696 and Bauer, *A Greek-English Lexicon of the New Testament and Other Early Christian Literature*, 898.

remarriage, in both Jewish and Greco-Roman cultures the act of divorce was automatically associated with subsequent remarriage. Hence, on the one hand, in Judaism the right of remarriage was granted to a woman within the legal divorce document and it was assumed for the man who conducted a legal divorce.[357] On the other hand, the Greco-Roman culture not only made provision for remarriage of the divorcee but also insisted on their remarriage within the limited period.[358] The secondary sources also agree with this understanding of the verb χωρίζω.[359]

357. "A. The text of the writ of divorce [is as follows]: B. Lo, you are permitted to any man. G. R. Judah says, [in Aramaic]: Let this be from me your writ of divorce, letter of dismissal, and deed of liberation, that you may marry anyone you want. D. The text of a writ of emancipation [is as follows]: E. Lo, you are a free girl, lo, you are your own [possession]." *The Mishnah, Gittin* 9:3; Halacha, 23, *Divorce - Geirushin* [online], Available at http://www.torah.org/learning/halacha-overview/chapter23.html, Accessed on 03 December 2000. Cf. Deut 24:1–4.

358. One should consider Augustus' law related to the family issued in 19, 18 BC. Since there was no evidence that this law was no longer practiced during the time of Nero, it might be argued that it was still in effect in Greco-Roman Corinth during Paul's time. Through this law Augustus gave a limited period before remarriage of the divorcee when he enforced remarriage on them for the purpose of increasing the birth rate. (See Suetonius, *Life of Augustus* 34. L "Having shown greater severity in the emendation of this last than the others, as a result of the agitation of its opponents he [Augustus] was unable to get it approved except by abolishing or mitigating part of the penalty, conceding a three-year grace-period [before remarriage] and increasing the rewards [for having children]." Suetonius, *Life of Augustus* 34 L, trans. Mary R. Lefkowitz and Maureen B. Fant [online], Available at http://www.uky.edu/ArtsSciences/Classics/wlgr/wlgr-romanlegal120 .html, Accessed on 14 October 2000. See also Everett Ferguson, *Backgrounds of Early Christianity* [Grand Rapids: Eerdmans, 1993] 69.) Moreover unmarried Romans were exposed to severe penalties if they continued to stay in this condition beyond a particular age. (See Dio Cassius, *History of Rome* 54.16.1–2. "[Augustus] assessed heavier taxes on unmarried men and women without husbands, and by contrast offered awards for marriage and childbearing. And since there were more males than females among the nobility, he permitted anyone who wished [except for senators] to marry freedwomen, and decreed that children of such marriages be legitimate." Dio Cassius, *History of Rome* 54.16.1–2. trans. Mary R. Lefkowitz and Maureen B. Fant [online], Available at http://www.uky.edu/ArtsSciences/Classics/wlgr/wlgr-romanlegal120.html, Accessed on 14 October 2000. See also Plato, *Laws*, 774a. "All this and more one might say in a proper prelude concerning marriage and the duty of marrying. Should any man, however, refuse to obey willingly, and keep himself aloof and unpartnered in the State, and reach the age of thirty-five unmarried, an annual fine shall be imposed upon him, of a hundred drachmae if he be of the highest property-class, if of the second, seventy, if of the third, sixty, if of the fourth, thirty." Plato, *Plato in Twelve Volumes*, vols. 10 & 11 trans. R. G. Bury. Cambridge, MA: Harvard University Press; London: William Heinemann, 1967 & 1968 [online], Available at http://www.perseus.tufts.edu/cgi-bin/ptext?lookup=Plat.+Laws+774a, Accessed on 29 October 2000.)

359. Margaret S. Schatkin, "Divorce," in *Encyclopedia of Early Christianity*, ed. Everett

Syntactically, the verb χωρίζω should be analyzed in relation to its two grammatical forms in which it appears in v15a, i.e. χωρίζεται and χωριζέσθω. The first form of the verb, i.e. present middle indicative (v15a), in relation to the subordinate conjunction εἰ forms the protasis of a first class conditional statement. This structure is in parallel with that in vv12 and 13. Thus, considering the effect of the declarative indicative mood of the verb and the nature of the first class condition, one may argue that Paul had in mind real cases in the Corinthian church.[360] The exact development of the divorce process, however, might not be established with certainty due to different options in defining the exact syntax of the tense of the verb.[361] Nevertheless, since the syntax allows one to be more inclusive than exclusive, I would argue for defining the verb tense in a more general sense as carrying the notions of both tendential and descriptive present. Thus, Paul is addressing believers who are in the process of divorce by the unbelievers.

The second form in which the verb χωρίζω appears (v15a) might be defined syntactically as an imperative of permission. Three factors establish that this permission is granted primarily to the believers (ὁ ἀδελφὸς ἢ ἡ ἀδελφή) and not to the unbelievers (ὁ ἄπιστος). First, the passive voice of the verb suggests that conclusion. Second, the nature of the divorce process[362] in the first century indicates that the believers were asking Paul whether they could allow the unbelieving spouse to divorce since he/she

---

Ferguson (New York: Garland, ICG, 1977) 271, 272; C. S. Keener, . . . *And Marries Another: Divorce and Remarriage in the Teaching of the New Testament*, 72, quoted in W. A. Heth, *Divorce and Remarriage: The Search for an Evangelical Hermeneutic*, 97; C. L. Blomberg, *Matthew: An Exegetical and Theological Exposition of Holy Scripture NIV Text*, 111; Harrell, "Divorce and Remarriage in the Early Church," 71, quoted in W. A. Heth, *Divorce and Remarriage: The Search for an Evangelical Hermeneutic*, 85.

360. See also Lenski, *The Interpretation of I and II Corinthians* (Minneapolis: Augsburg, 1937) 294; G. D. Fee, *The First Epistle to the Corinthians*, 298.

361. Two options are possible: First, the tense might be defined as a descriptive present, expressing the action of divorce as being in progress ("but if the unbeliever is divorcing, let him continue to divorce . . . ."). Second, it is also possible to define the verb as tendential present with an emphasis on the action of divorce as being attempted but has not actually taken place ("but if the unbeliever attempts to divorce, let him divorce . . . .").

362. "It should be noted that 'divorce' was not a court proceeding with lawyers, etc., but essentially an agreement between two people, frequently legalized by a document of divorce." G. D. Fee, *The First Epistle to the Corinthians*, 303, footnote 37. See also Witherington III, *Conflict and Community in Corinth*, 171.

was willing to do it. Third, the addressees of Paul's letter were believers, not unbelievers.[363] Thus, on the basis of the semantic and the syntactical evidence Paul's answer to the believers' request should be read as affirmative. The believer may permit the unbeliever to divorce, which establishes the marriage as legally dissolved and the believer, as every divorced person in the first century to whom remarriage is not specially forbidden, (as in 1 Cor.7:11a) is free to remarry.[364]

The verb δουλόω together with the negative particle οὐ establishes a phrase which is well known among the scholars as the Pauline privilege. That phrase creates a significant controversy around its exact meaning.[365] The latter should be established on the basis of the semantic and

---

363. See also Godet, *Corinthians*, 336.

364. Contra Heth who introduces a foreign idea to the text arguing that the marriage is dissolved but not in the eyes of God, (W. A. Heth, *Another Look at the Erasmian View of Divorce and Remarriage*, 269, 270). Fee (*The First Epistle to the Corinthians*, 302) agrees that v15a affirms the dissolution of marriage but despite this he claims that according to Paul "one is bound to a marriage until death breaks the bond (7:39)," (G. D. Fee, *The First Epistle to the Corinthians*, 303). If the marital bond is dissolved then why should it still be argued that one is under its bondage? Furthermore Fee (*The First Epistle to the Corinthians*, 302, 303, 306) compares the exceptions regarding divorce in v11 and v15 and concludes that they are similar. Hence, due to the fact that in the first one Paul disallows remarriage Fee argues that in the second exception Paul forbids remarriage too. Fee is mistaken for two basic reasons. First, the exceptions are not similar because the first is related to the believer who wants to separate and the second is related to the unbeliever who wants to separate. Second, one should not interpret the instructions of the apostle in the same way on the basis of the verb χωρίζω (vv11, 15). To the contrary, due to the fact that the verb χωρίζω does not have further restriction in v15 as in v11 (μενέτω ἄγαμος ἢ τῷ ἀνδρὶ καταλλαγήτω) it might be properly interpreted as allowing remarriage on the basis of its meaning. However it might also be argued that there is further qualification of the verb by the phrase "not bound." Then in the light of the verb χωρίζω the phrase "οὐ δεδούλωται" may be interpreted as testifying the freedom of the believer to remarry. Furthermore if one notices the contrast between the words of Paul in vv10, 11 "Let not the wife divorce" and "Let her remain unmarried" and those in v15 "Let him/her (the unbeliever) divorce" and "a brother or sister is not under bondage in such cases" then he may interpret the latter as implying the total liberty of the deserted believer from the marriage bond. (See also G. W. Peters, *Divorce & Remarriage* [Chicago: Moody, 1972] 14–19; P. H. Wiebe, "The New Testament on Divorce and Remarriage: Some Logical Implications," *JETS* 24 (1981) 137; and Fitzmyer, *Matthean Divorce Texts and Some New Palestinian Evidence*, 200.) Contra Wenham whose argument that not a full divorce is in view in v15a and no permission of remarriage is given contradicts both the meaning of the verb χωρίζω in v15ab and understanding the nature of divorce in the first century. (See Gordon Wenham, "May Divorced Christians Remarry?" *Churchman* 95 [2, 1981] 158, 159.)

365. The understanding of this phrase divides the scholars basically into two groups.

syntactical analysis of the verb δουλόω and its relation to the previous clause. Semantically, the verb δουλόω is used in v15b figuratively with the meaning "total binding to another."[366] Thus, a strong binding relationship between the believing and unbelieving spouses is in view. Syntactically δεδούλωται is defined as an intensive perfect and, together with the negative particle οὐ, it expresses the idea that the believer is in a complete state of freedom from the marital bond. Due to the fact that this is the result of the action of the unbeliever, the freedom of the believer is not threatened by any further obligations toward the unbeliever. Hence, Paul is adding the verb δουλόω to the conditional clause guided by the role of the verb χωρίζω with the purpose of affirming that the believer who is divorced by the unbeliever is free from the apostle's previous command (vv12–14) and may consider a subsequent remarriage.[367]

The first group argues that Paul is saying that the deserted believer "is not bound to the ruling given above (vv12–14) about maintaining the marriage." Paul does not either speak or assume remarriage here. (G. D. Fee, *The First Epistle to the Corinthians*, 302; Robertson and Plummer, *Corinthians*, 143). The other group claims that by "not bound" Paul is giving a green light to the deserted believer to remarry. (H. Conzelmann, *Corinthians*, 123; T. R. Edgar, *Divorce & Remarriage for Adultery or Desertion*, 190; Larry Richards, "Divorce and Remarriage Under a Variety of Circumstances," in *Divorce and Remarriage: Four Christian Views*, ed. H. Wayne House [Downers Grove, IL: InterVarsity, 1990] 240; St. Basil, *Letter 188: To Amphilochius, Concerning the Canons* 9, in *Early Church Fathers: Nicene and Post-Nicene Fathers*, eds. Philip Schaff and Henry Wace, series II, vol. VIII, *Christian Classics Ethereal Library*, vol.2, CD-ROM, ed. Harry Plantinga.)

366. The word is used figuratively in that sense (total binding by/to something/someone) in both Classical and Hellenistic periods (Plato, *Laws* 698c; Isocrates, *Speeches and Letters* 12.78, ed. George Norlin [online], Available at http://perseus.csad.ox.ac.uk/cgi-bin/ptext?lookup=Isoc.+12+76, Accessed on 4 December 2000; Barnabas, *The Epistle of Barnabas*, XVI, in *Ante-Nicene Fathers: Translations of The Writings of the Fathers Down to A. D. 325*, ed. Alexander Roberts and James Donaldson, vol.1, *Christian Classics Ethereal Library*, v.2, CD-ROM, ed. Harry Plantinga [Wheaton, IL: Wheaton College, 1998]). In the LXX the word is used in the same sense (4 Macc 3:2, 13:2). That meaning appears in the NT (2 Pet 2:19) and in the writings of apostle Paul as well (Gal 4:3; Rom 6:22; Rom 6:18, Tit 2:3). In 1 Cor 9:19 the verb is used in the same figurative way. (See also Karl Heinrich Rengstorf, "Δουλόω, καταδουλόω," in *TDNT*, trans. and ed. Geoffrey W. Bromiley—electronic ed.—10 v.—Logos Library System 2.1g; Bauer, *A Greek-English Lexicon of the New Testament and Other Early Christian Literature*, 205.)

367. Contra Wenham who does not allow the text to prove its meaning within its context, but using other NT divorce and remarriage passages and the witness of the church fathers, argues that Paul does not approve remarriage through the phrase "not bound." (See G. Wenham, *May Divorced Christians Remarry*, 158, 159.); Contra Fee who argues that the proper understanding of the phrase "not bound" should exclude any relation to remarriage. According to him neither Paul nor the Corinthians were concerned

Paul continues his argument with the phrase "δὲ in peace God has called us[368]," (v15c). Two issues make this phrase a center of enormous debates, namely what the nature is of the concept of peace and to which part of Paul's argument it relates, to vv12–14 or to v15ab.[369] I would ar-

with remarriage since they were dealing with ascetic reasons for divorce. However Fee's argument is in contradiction to his previous conclusion related to the exception in v11a where he later disregards the primary ascetic reason for Corinthians' desire to divorce, (See G. D. Fee, *The First Epistle to the Corinthians*, 295). Contra Laney who on the basis of equalizing both exceptions of Paul in v11a and v15ab argues that "not under bondage" does not allow remarriage but just confirms the permission for divorce. (J. C. Laney, *Paul and the Permanence of Marriage in I Corinthians 7*, 287) Laney's argument is unacceptable due to the different nature and recipients of the exceptions clauses in v11 and v15. The following scholars argue that the phrase "not bound" carries the idea of permission for remarriage. D. Atkinson, *To Have and to Hold* (Grand Rapids: Eerdmans, 1979), 124; C. R. Swindoll, *Strike the Original Match* (Portland: Multnomah, 1970), 145–146, quoted in J. C. Laney, *Paul and the Permanence of Marriage in I Corinthians 7*, 288; Wiebe, *Divorce and Remarriage*, 137; J. E. Adams, *Marriage, Divorce and Remarriage* (Phillipsburg, NJ: Presbyterian and Reformed, 1980), 48, quoted in J. C. Laney, *Paul and the Permanence of Marriage in I Corinthians 7*, 287; Orr and Walther, *I Corinthians*, 214; D. Instone-Brewer, *Divorce and Remarriage in the Bible*, 201–203.

368. Even though NA^{26} prefers ὑμᾶς instead of ἡμᾶς the quality and the multiplicity of the external evidence (P^{46} ℵ^2 B D F G Ψ M latt sy sa) plus the appropriate explanation that the change of ἡμᾶς with ὑμᾶς might be a scribal attempt to fit the context (ὑμῶν, v14) should incline one to decide for ἡμᾶς. See also G. D. Fee, *The First Epistle to the Corinthians*, 297; Findlay, *Corinthians*, 827; NIV; NAS; NKJ.

369. There are three basic views about the meaning and construction of this phrase.
The proponents of the first view understand the concept of peace either as the inner condition of the believer or as his passivity toward the unbeliever who is leaving. Hence, they argue that the phrase relates to the previous two sentences of v15ab. Thus, the believer should allow the unbeliever to leave peacefully without contesting the divorce. After such an action marriage is dissolved. (Orr and Walther, *I Corinthians*, 212; Robertson and Plummer, *Corinthians*, 143; Elliott, *Teaching*, 224; S. Kubo, 1 Corinthians 7:16: Optimistic or Pessimistic?" NTS 24 [1078] 534–44; Paul A. Hamar, *The Book of First Corinthians*. The Radiant Commentary of the New Testament [Springfiled: Gospel, 1980] 60, 61; F. W. Grosheide, *Commentary on the First Epistle to the Corinthians: The English Text With Introduction, Exposition and Notes* [Grand Rapids: Eerdmans, 1953] 166, 167). Hence, they treat the coordinative conjunction δὲ as causal or consecutive. (R. N. Soulen, *Marriage and Divorce*, 447, 448; Godet, *Corinthians*, 349, 350). This view has two main problems. First, it disregards the nature of Paul's main argument (vv12–14) as attempting to preserve the mixed marriages against the Corinthians' ascetic tendencies. (See also G. D. Fee, *The First Epistle to the Corinthians*, 302; Charles Hodge, *An Exposition of 1 and 2 Corinthians* [Wilmington, Delaware: Sovereign Grace, 1972] 73.) Second, it disregards the active nature of Paul's concept of peace. (See also G. D. Fee, *The First Epistle to the Corinthians*, 304, 305.) The proponents of the second view understand the concept of peace as the believers' actions to continue the marriage and as such the phrase (v15c) relates to Paul's main argument (vv12–14). (G. D. Fee, *The First Epistle to*

gue for the most balanced solution which does not introduce any major problems in the understanding of the passage. I perceive the concept of peace as based on Paul's Jewish heritage in the sense that one should help the less favored, i.e. the Gentiles, for the sake of peace in order to gain them for Judaism.[370] That reflects the nature of the concept as both passive[371] and active.[372] Hence the believer, for the sake of peace,[373] should actively preserve the marriage with the unbeliever who is willing to live with him/her and passively allow the unbeliever to leave if he/she is not willing to preserve the marriage in order to win him/her for the Christian faith. Thus, with such a nature the concept of peace is easily understood as related to both the main part of Paul's argument (vv12-14) and to the exception (v15ab).[374]

Paul completes his discussion about believers who are in mixed marriages with a provocative rhetorical device (v16) whose nature and relations are so ambiguous that it establishes once again grounds for rigorous

---

the Corinthians, 304; C. K. Barrett, *A Commentary on the First Epistle to the Corinthians* [London: Adam and Charles Black, 1968] 166.) Hence, Paul is commanding the believer to keep his/her marriage with the unbelieving partner who is willing to preserve it. The phrase, they believe, may be understood as related to v15ab but only in a secondary manner as urging the believer to protect the marriage against the unbeliever who attempts to separate. Thus, they either leave δὲ untranslated or translate it as adversative coordinator. Several problems related to this view should be underlined. First, it overlooks the exegetical principle that the relation to the closer part of the passage should be preferred. Hence, the last phrase of v15 should be related primarily to the previous sentence (v15ab), not to those of vv12-14. Second, the view disregards the passive nature of Paul's concept of peace. Third, it neglects the importance of Paul's exception offered in v15ab related to the Corinthian believers who have been in the process of desertion by their unbelieving spouses. The proponents of the third view understand the concept of peace as the believer's attempt to live with the unbeliever who is willing to sustain the marriage and the believer's refusal to force preservation of the marital bond to the unbeliever who is not willing to stay in the marriage. Thus, they relate the phrase both to Paul's main argument (vv12-14) and to his exception (v15ab). (F. F. Bruce, ed., *1 and 2 Corinthians*, New Century Bible Series [Greenwood: Attic, 1971] 70; NRS, 1989). Δὲ is left untranslated. This view solves all the problems created by the other two views and does not bring foreign ideas into Paul's argument.

370. See also G. D. Fee, *The First Epistle to the Corinthians*, 304, 305.

371. "They do not try to prevent the poor among the gentiles from gathering gleanings, in the interests of peace." - Passive concept (*The Mishnah, Git.* 5:8)

372. "Moreover greetings [meaning 'Shalom'] may be offered to gentiles in the interests of peace" - Active concept. (*The Mishnah, Git.*5:9)

373. Cf. Rom 12:18; 14:19.

374. See also F. F. Bruce, ed., *1 and 2 Corinthians*, 70; NRS, 1989.

debate among the scholars.[375] However the grammar and the context provide some clues for a proper understanding of Paul's conclusion. Three significant grammatical features should be underlined. The indicative mood of the verb οἶδας suggests that the expected answer ought to provide factual information.[376] The indirect interrogative particle εἰ introduces an indirect discourse for which the direct equivalent are two rhetorical questions from the author by which he challenges reader's judgment.[377] Finally the deliberate future nature of the verbs from these questions (σώσεις) suggests that the result of the readers' actions is in view.[378] Thus, Paul is concluding his argument (vv12–15) in which he addresses both the believers who desire to divorce the unbelievers (vv12–14) and those who are in the process of being divorced by the unbelievers (v15ab). His rhetorical questions carry both optimistic and pessimistic connotations, depending on which of the previously mentioned groups is in view. Paul wants a factual answer about the possibility of the believer "saving" his unbelieving partner. This answer is determined by the willingness of the unbeliever to live with the believer. If the unbeliever is willing to stay with the believer, then there is a big chance that he might be saved. If the unbeliever is not willing to live with the believer, then the chance of salvation is minimal.

---

375. There are two views concerning the meaning and the relations of v16, i.e. optimistic and pessimistic. The optimistic view presents the questions of Paul as optimistic, namely, he says that there is a big chance for salvation of the heathen partner. The proponents of this view (G. D. Fee, *The First Epistle to the Corinthians*, 305; F. F. Bruce, *1 and 2 Corinthians*, 70) argue that Paul is introducing another reason for preservation of mixed marriages. Hence, the questions (v16) should be understood as linked to Paul's main argument (vv12–14). The main difficulty of this view is that it overlooks the relation of the questions to the exception (v15ab) and as such does not do favor to the ambiguity of their nature. The pessimistic view presents the questions of Paul as indicating that the chances for salvation of the heathen partner through the Christian spouse are small. The supporters of this view (H. Conzelmann, *Corinthians*, 124; Elliott, *Teaching*, 225; Godet, *Corinthians*, 350, 351.) argue that v16 covers only the case presented by v15ab. Two major problems of these view should be underlined. First, it overlooks Paul's emphasis in the passage (vv12–16), which is to preserve mixed marriages. Second, it presents Paul as contradicting himself by being too optimistic in v14 and too pessimistic in v16.

376. See J. A. Brooks and C. L. Winbery, *Syntax of New Testament Greek*, 115 (interrogative indicative). See also Lenski, *The Interpretation of I and II Corinthians*, 297.

377. See Max Zerwick and Mary Grosvenor, *A Grammatical Analysis of the Greek New Testament* (Rome: Biblical Institute Press, 1981), 510.

378. See J. A. Brooks and C. L. Winbery, *Syntax of New Testament Greek*, 97.

Therefore in this part of his letter to the Corinthian church Paul is addressing believers who are in mixed marriages with unbelievers. He deals with two groups of believers, one which desires to divorce unbelieving spouses who are willing to live with them (vv12–14) and the other which is in the process of being divorced by their unbelieving spouses (v15ab). Because the former group is more outspoken than the latter, Paul is primarily responding to it, but he still provides an exception for the other group. The apostle counsels the first group to preserve their marriages, an act which will open up the possibility for salvation for the unbelieving spouses and the children. He also instructs the second group to allow the unbeliever to separate and confirms the freedom of the believer to divorce and remarry. The context in which the passage (vv12–16) is located supports this conclusion. On the one hand, Paul is arguing that the married should preserve their marriages (vv1–6, 10–11, 12–14) and the unmarried and de-married should preserve their status as single (vv8, 32–35, 38). On the other hand, he states that if the latter do not have the gift for staying single (v7), they are free to remarry (vv9, 39).

1 CORINTHIANS 7:12–16: CONCLUSIONS

The passage (1 Cor 7:12–16) is part of the section (ch 7) which deals with marriage issues raised by the Corinthians' letter within the framework of their main problem and it is shaped by its context as the apostle's counsel to believers who are married to unbelievers. Paul's approach in this section of the epistle is shaped by his narrative thought and is established on the basis of his understanding of the role of God's call in a believer's life and of the nature of the groups addressed. Hence, the apostle admonishes the believers from the different groups to preserve their social status of virginity (vv26, 32–34, 37–38b), marriage (vv12–14), divorce (v8), or widowhood (vv8, 40). He allows and even encourages the ones who are not married or are de-married and do not have the χάρισμα (v7) of this status to marry (vv9, 28, 36, 38a, 39). He discourages and even forbids a change of status for the purpose of benefiting one's spirituality (vv12–14) and when it contradicts the Lord's teaching (vv10–11).

In the usual way of identifying the spouses in mixed marriages Paul answers the two probable questions raised by the two opposite sides of this group in a twofold manner supplying each answer with two grounds of justification. Paul first addresses the more problematic part of the group, which consisted of believers who were in the process of divorcing their unbelieving partners (vv12–14). The problem of these believers was that, due to their desire to raise their marital status to the level of their new Christian status, they wanted to divorce their non-Christian partners. Paul prohibits this action on the part of both men and women using two reasons to justify his argument. On the one hand, he argues that maintaining the marriage will create an environment where the believer's presence, expressed in action and words, might lead to the salvation of the unbeliever. On the other hand, the apostle maintains that the presence of the Christian parent will influence the spiritual condition of the children. They will be raised apart from pagan worship and evil practices and be prepared for their eventual salvation. The most significant factor that shapes this part of Paul's argument is the attitude of the non-Christian spouse, who was willing to preserve the marriage (vv13, 14). The change of this attitude in relation to the second part of the group establishes Paul's argument towards it as completely opposite to his first argument. In this second part of the group are the believers who were in the process of being divorced by their unbelieving partners, who were not willing to preserve the marriage (ὁ ἄπιστος χωρίζεται, v15a). The contrast between the two parts of the group of mixed marriages and the change of Paul's argument is designated further with the adversative conjunction δέ (v15a). The apostle permits the believers to divorce their non-Christian spouses (χωριζέσθω, v15a), releases them from his previous command (vv12–14), and affirms their freedom for subsequent remarriage (οὐ δεδούλωται ὁ ἀδελφὸς ἢ ἡ ἀδελφή, v15b). He supplies two reasons for justification of his argument. On the one hand, Paul underlines the importance of living in peace with the unbeliever under any circumstances, including divorce, due to the potential of such behavior to establish the grounds for eventual salvation (v15c). On the other hand, the apostle rhetorically expresses his pessimism about the positive influence of the believer upon the unbeliever when this is against the latter's will (v16). These two reasons could not be understood by the first part of the group as justifying their divorce actions since, due to the different attitude of the unbelievers to the marriage, the concept of peace would be seen as supporting an active preservation of the marital bond and the rhetorical questions as conveying an optimistic notion concerning the salvation of the unbelieving spouse.

The solution offered by Paul to both sides of the group of mixed marriages might be perceived as Paul's interpretation of Jesus' teaching on divorce and remarriage in relation to the new situation of the Corinthian church. He stays firmly in the context of his discussions with other groups, in which he allows remarriage of the de-married (vv9, 39) when there is lack of χάρισμα (v7) and no contradiction of the Lord's command (vv10–11).

MARK 10:2–12; MATTHEW 5:31, 32; 19:3–12; LUKE 16:18; AND 1 CORINTHIANS 7:12–16: CONCLUSIONS

The New Testament writers used the teaching of Jesus related to the issues of divorce and remarriage in a similar way, editing it in accordance with the *Sitz im Leben* of their communities. In relation to the narrative flow of their writings, the evangelists placed the sayings among the controversy material and as such furnished them in the most rigorous form possible.

On the one hand, Jesus' teaching on divorce and remarriage challenged and corrected the teaching of the religious authorities on these matters. The teachers of the Law guided by their sinful and selfish desires intentionally misinterpreted it in order to be able to dissolve any marriage according to their will. Their intentions to manipulate God's word for their benefit have been easily detected and condemned by Jesus as being based on sinful human ambitions for liberation from ones' obligations and responsibilities in a lifelong marital relationship. On the other hand, Jesus' teaching defended the vulnerable spouse within the institution of the covenant marital relationship. The essence of the marital union is to provide mutual commitment between the spouses based on love and self-giving service which is to reflect God's intentions in creating this institution. This union between man and woman which reflects the image of God in its closeness and unity may only be sustained through lifelong devotion of the spouses to each other. Hence, the covenant relationship cannot tolerate any libertine behavior against itself. Both the sinful, licentious divorce actions and the adulterous behavior against one spouse are entirely condemned.

Mark (10:10–12) shapes the saying of Jesus in its present unexceptional form in regard to his Gentile-Christian audience in order to protect the position of the wife in marriage against the abusive licentious divorce and remarriage action of the husband as well as to protect marriage from the adulterous libertine divorce and remarriage action of the women in the Greco-Roman world. The Evangelist's primary interest in the position of women in marriage as well as in divorce and remarriage matters shapes entirely his presentation of Jesus' prohibition of divorce and remarriage in its present absolute and rigorous form which allows no exceptions. His defense of the equality of the wife's place in marriage to that of her husband is focused on a condemnation of the husband's licentious view of marriage in light of the Pharisees' selfish misunderstanding of the Law related to divorce and remarriage matters. No justifying argumentation may be provided which goes against the permanent nature of marital union. The very lifelong nature of the union is grounded on God's intentions expressed in the creation account of the first marriage and God's Law does not go against these intentions but even underlines them. The divine formulation of marital union is not to be disregarded by different mores of human societies. Hence, Mark entirely condemns the women's excesses in exercising their freedom to divorce their husbands and remarry. His understanding of Jesus' teaching on divorce and remarriage does not contradict Matthew's understanding of that teaching (Matt 19:9; 5:32).

Because of his Jewish-Christian audience, for whom it was impossible to live with an adulterous partner, Matthew introduces an exception clause and thus makes a provision for proper divorce and remarriage in a case of πορνεία. The exceptional grounds do not contradict the permanence of marital union which has been stressed by the evangelist but even underline it. Divorce may only be understood as an exception to the perpetual nature of marriage which is the normative of every marital union. The exception is further limited to strictly formulated sinful and adulterous behavior which may not be tolerated neither by God's Law nor by the community which is defined by this Law. Hence, the exceptional divorce grounds may only be understood as Matthew's attempt to preserve the lifelong nature of marital union. He firmly protects the permanent nature of marriage against the intentional misuse of the Scriptures by Jewish authorities to dissolve marriage covenant guided by their sinful and selfish desires and against the sinful behavior of the adulterer with the support of the community which judges severely any sexual misconduct. In both of his accounts Matthew presents the teaching of Jesus as defining marriage covenant relationship as permanent union between a man and a woman which is based on God's intentions in the creation and is protected by his Law from abuses. Marriage perceived as a lifelong union is the only way to understand this institution both by Jewish authorities and Jesus' disciples. The exceptional formulations of divorce and remarriage grounds may only be regarded as a way to interpret Jesus' teaching for protecting the lifelong institution of marriage and the spouses who attempt to fulfill it within the hostile environment of human sinful nature which expressions attempt to pervert God's intentions.

Luke (16:18) adds a new nuance to Jesus' teaching on divorce and remarriage due to his primary concern with the issue of a pre-divorce arranged remarriage established against the background of the Herod and Herodias' case. The remarriage of Herod and Herodias becomes a prototype for establishing relationship which is entirely based on the sinful human desire for self-indulgence in one's selfish intentions and goals. Its very existence points to the vulnerability of the permanent nature of marriage to sinful human intentions and calls for divine judgment. Hence, the evangelist leaves Jesus' saying in its absolute and unexceptional form, in order to condemn divorce and remarriage on the basis of prearranged plans for subsequent remarriage.

Paul, on the one hand, facing the same situation as Mark in relation to the freedom of women to divorce and as Luke in relation to the wrong attitude toward remarriage, shapes Jesus' tradition in this respect prohibiting divorce firmly and remarriage totally in the case of divorce (1 Cor 7:10–11). This teaching of Paul is grounded on Jesus' teaching on marriage, divorce, and remarriage presented by the evangelists. The apostle's main intention is to preserve the permanent nature of marital union from two types of offenses. First, Paul fights against the libertine behavior of some wives toward their marriages being under the influence of sinful social dynamics. Second, the apostle prohibits divorce and remarriage based on the sinful personal desire of a spouse for forming a new union in spite of the existing one. On the other hand, when he deals with a different situation, i.e. the desertion of the believer by the unbeliever in mixed marriages (1 Cor 7:12–16), he introduces an exception to Jesus' teaching that allows for proper divorce and remarriage of the deserted partner (1 Cor 7:15, 16). This interpretation of Jesus' tradition comes closer to the teaching presented by the evangelists even though it deals with a new type of situation. Once again Paul's emphasis falls on preservation of marriage. He focuses on changing believer's attitude to their marital union with an unbelieving spouse providing convincing argumentation for preservation of the marriage. Only when the unbelieving spouse has become the initiating divorce party does Paul provide an exception to the permanency of marriage allowing the deserted spouse to divorce and remarry. Even under such circumstances the apostle does not lose focus from the lifelong marital commitment of the spouses providing an encouragement for marriage preservation in his conclusive statements in order to reach back to those marriages which have this potential due to the desire of the unbelieving party to continue them.

four

The New Testament Canonical Context

THE RESULTS FROM THE EXEGETICAL ANALYSES OF THE NT DIVORCE and remarriage passages might be summarized as a twofold concept offered as a presentation of Jesus' teaching on these issues through the editorial works of the evangelists and Paul. All four writers express a general prohibition of divorce and remarriage (Mark 10:9; Matt 19:6; Luke 16:18; 1 Cor 7:12–14) emphasizing the permanent nature of marriage covenant union and all four provide a place for exceptional permission of both actions interpreting Jesus' words according to the *Sitz im Leben* of their communities. Two of them, Matthew and Paul, offer explicit grounds for divorce and remarriage (Matt 5:32; 19:9; 1 Cor 7:15). The other two, Mark and Luke, furnish implicit grounds for both actions by not contradicting the interpretations of Matthew and Paul. This twofold exegetical conclusion is firmly established on the covenant understanding of marriage presented by the whole canonical corpus of NT literature.[1]

The covenant concept of marriage with its contractual nature, main constitutive elements and realization dynamics formulated in the OT is articulated in the NT as well. The NT authors expressed the concept of marriage in continuity with the view of the OT writings and in regard to the marriage and divorce contracts of the contemporaneous culture. On the one hand, the same nature, features, and functions of the marriage covenant which have been established as depicted by the OT authors are understood and utilized by the NT writers for defining the NT perspective of marriage, divorce, and remarriage. On the other hand, as in the case of OT marriage covenant formulated in relation with the marriage contracts of the ANE literature, the NT authors established their discussions and

---

1. Also Alex R. G. Deasley, *Marriage and Divorce in the Bible and the Church* (Kansas City: Beacon Hill, 2000) 40.

views in close connection with the marriage dynamics expressed in the specific literature of the Jewish and Greco-Roman societies. Within this framework the leading force for the development of their arguments is to be attributed to the teachings of Jesus on these matters.

Matthew, Mark, and Luke have followed closely the nature of their communities and, revisiting the expressions of the matrimonial matters in them, formulated their own views on marital issues through the teaching of their Lord. Paul's overall teaching on the matters of marriage, divorce, and remarriage might be also clearly understood only if the social background of his readers related to these matters is examined and its language and concepts are used to illuminate the apostle's discussions. The legal papyri regarding marriage and divorce might be considered as establishing the framework of Paul's discussions on these matters in general and its most extensive development in 1 Cor 7 in particular. Paul, of course, as well as the other NT writers, is not interested in formulating the totality of Christian teaching on the matters of marriage, divorce, and remarriage but is dealing with different marital problems related to his readers. Hence, he is expected to engage in debates which are needed to deal with different legal concepts which are found in the marriage and divorce documents used by his readers.[2] Within this framework Paul is using Jesus' tradition related to the issues of marriage and expresses his own opinion based on his apostolic authority and the guidance of the Holy Spirit (1 Cor 7:40).

The core of the Jewish marriage covenant, well supported in the specific literature contemporaneous to the NT, is the law of the slave wife recorded in Exod 21:10–11. The lack of specific relation to a marriage covenant in this text leads one to consider the development of the understanding of this text at the level of not only becoming part of the model for Jewish marriage covenant, but also the most essential part. The method which led the ancient Jewish scholars to this conclusion might be defined as "qol vahomer." This has been considered one of the most com-

---

2. The legal framework of Paul's readers established through the rulings of the various authorities does not bring such a significant contribution to the discussion due to its lack of widespread influence on the common people and lack of widespread documentary support. (David Instone-Brewer, "1 Corinthians 7 in the Light of the Graeco-Roman Marriage and Divorce Papyri," *TynBul* (2001) [online], Available at http://www.tyndale.cam.ac.uk/Brewer/MarriagePapyri/1Cor_7a.htm, Accessed on 26 August 2004.)

mon exegetical rules among Jewish interpreters before AD 70.[3] It might be summarised as an intercultural logical deduction from major to minor matters of consideration.[4] Hence, if the passage lists the foundational marital rights of a slave wife how much more should it be applicable for defining the basic marriage rights of a free wife and even more of a free husband.[5] With this logical deduction the first century Jewish interpreters unanimously established the core of the Jewish marriage contract and the grounds for the legitimate Jewish divorce on Exod 21:10–11.[6]

The text of Exod 21:10–11 does create some difficulties in terms of the proper wording of the stipulations listed but it might be resolved in the light of the agreement between early and later Jewish interpreters.

> If he marries another woman, he must not deprive the first one of her food, clothing and marital rights. If he does not provide her with these three things, she is to go free, without any payment of money. (Ex 21:10–11, NIB)

The three words which form the basic stipulations of the marriage contract are translated here as "food, clothing and marital rights." Even though there are various suggestions as to the first[7] and the last[8] words, the meaning which has been accepted by the translators of LXX and Targums,[9] the

---

3. Also Instone-Brewer, *Divorce and Remarriage in the Bible*, 100.

4. Instone-Brewer, *Divorce and Remarriage in the Bible*, 100, 101. In relation to the value of the subjects involved in the argumentation it might be expressed as "from the lesser to the greater (if the lesser is true, how much more the greater)." This argumentation is used in the NT by Jesus (Matt 6:28–30; 7:9–11; 12:12; 20:28; Luke 11:11–13; 13:15–16; 18:6–7; John 10:35–36), Peter (Acts 1:20; 2:16–18), Paul (Rom 5:16–21; 1 Cor 9:8–10; 2 Cor 3:9–11), and the author of Hebrews (Heb 2:5; 12:25). (See Craig S. Keener, *The IVP Bible Background Commentary: New Testament* [Downers Grove, IL: InterVarsity, 1993].)

5. See also D. I. Block, *Marriage and Family in Ancient Israel*, 48.

6. Instone-Brewer, *Divorce and Remarriage in the Bible*, 100, 101.

7. The word שְׁאֵרָהּ literary "flesh" is discussed as referring to rich meal (meat) not being part of everyday menu, "portion," "sexual satisfaction" (b. Ketub. 48a), (Instone-Brewer, *Divorce and Remarriage in the Bible*, 99) and "physical well-being" (R. North, "Flesh, Covering, and Response, Ex. XXI:10," VT 5 [1955] 204–6, quoted in John I. Durham, *Exodus* [Waco: Word, 1987] 312.).

8. The meanings of the word עֹנָתָהּ in its present context which have been offered encompasses a wide variety of options such as "her abode," "her right of parenthood," "her nuptial gift," "her food," and "her ointment." (Instone-Brewer, *Divorce and Remarriage in the Bible*, 100.)

9. See *Targum Onqelos* and *Jerusalem Targum* at Exod 21:10–11.

rabbis[10] and Talmudic commentators[11] is "food, clothing, and conjugal rights."[12] Thus, the law states that the slave wife should be provided for by the husband with food, clothing, and conjugal rights in spite of the appearance of the second wife. If these three stipulations are not fulfilled the slave wife must be freed without the usually required payment. The slave wife gains her freedom from the bondage of marriage and slavery at the same time. The implications for the free man and woman would be that if these stipulations are not fulfilled by one of the parties the other is freed from the marriage without payment or forfeiture of the *ketubah*.[13] This

---

10. See discussions between the schools of Hillel and Shammai. (Also Instone-Brewer, *Divorce and Remarriage in the Bible*, 100.)

11. There is a discussion between the Talmudic commentators about the exact meaning of the three words in Exod 20:10 but they come to an agreement that the overall support should include all the elements of "food, clothing, and conjugal rights." ". . . For it was taught: She'erah (Her food, שארה, Ex 21:10) refers to maintenance, for so it is said in Scripture, Who also eat the she'er (flesh, שאר) of my people; Her raiment [is to be understood] according to its ordinary meaning; Onatha (עונתה, R.V., Her duty of marriage; A.J.V., Her conjugal rights, Ex 21:10 עונתה) refers to the time for conjugal duty prescribed in the Torah, for so it is said in Scripture, ..." (*Talmud - Mas. Kethuboth* 47b, The Soncino Talmud, 1973, Davka Corporation's Judaic Classics Library, Version IIf by David Kantrowitz. Institute for Computers in Jewish Life. Davka Corporation & Judaica, 1999.)

"R. Eliezer b. Jacob interpreted: [The expressions] She'erah kesutha, (שארה כסותה [Ex 21:10], 'her age, her raiment'. שאר = flesh, hence 'body', 'age'.) [imply]: Provide her with raiment according to her age, viz. that a man shall not provide his old wife [with the raiment] of a young one nor his young wife with that of an old one. [The expressions], Kesutha we-'Onatha (כסותה ועונתה [Ex 21:10], 'her raiment and her time' עונה = 'time', 'season'.) [imply.] Provide her with raiment according to the season of the year, viz. that he shall not give her new raiment in the summer nor worn out raiment in the winter. R. Joseph learnt: Her flesh implies close bodily contact, viz, that he must not treat her in the manner of the Persians who perform their conjugal duties in their clothes. This provides support for [a ruling of] R. Huna who laid down that a husband who said, 'I will not [perform conjugal duties] unless she wears her clothes and I mine', must divorce her and give her also her *ketubah*. R. JUDAH RULED: EVEN THE POOREST MAN IN ISRAEL etc . . . ." (*Talmud - Mas. Kethuboth* 48a, The Sonico Talmud, 1973, Davka Corporation's Judaic Classics Library)

12. Also Instone-Brewer, *Divorce and Remarriage in the Bible*, 100.

13. During the intertestamental period the financial settlement of the Jewish marriage contract (*ketubah*) was developed to comprise both the brideprice and the dowry. The function of the latter continued to be the same as a gift of the father to the bride, remaining her possession, but also used to support the new family. The former, however, changed its role from being actually paid to the bride's father (family) to just being acknowledged by the husband as financial installment toward the *ketubah* in case of death or divorce. This resulted in making marriages less costly and divorces more costly. (See *t.*

understanding of the text by the rabbis provided them with the formulation of legitimate grounds for divorce as well as for emancipation. These two have found numerous grounds for comparison in the discussions of the rabbis.[14] The text of Exod 21:10–11 and its further interpretation as the core for the Jewish marriage contract and divorce certificate provides a very close relationship between the basic stipulations of the marriage and the basic grounds for divorce. Hence, the discussions of the Jewish writers related to any of these matters brought the necessity of consideration of the other. The divorce grounds could not be established without consideration of the stipulations which had not been fulfilled. The discussions of the stipulations arose due to the cases of marriage breakdown which required consideration and a clear formulation of the divorce grounds. The unity of argumentation[15] related to these stipulations and the grounds for divorce and more convenient classification of different cases[16] led to their organization by the Jewish writers in two main groups, material and emotional neglect. Early rabbinic legislation placed the rulings related to food and clothes under the category of material neglect and conjugal rights under the category of emotional neglect.[17]

The discussion related to material neglect conducted by rabbinic courts necessitated a clear formulation of the stipulations related to them. The basic stipulations defined through the interpretation of Exod 21:10, the provision of food and clothing, have been equally addressed to both spouses but characterised in relation to their roles in marriage. The man was required to bring to the family finances for obtaining food and ma-

---

Ketub. 12.1; Instone-Brewer, *Divorce and Remarriage in the Bible*, 81–84.)

14. *m. Git.* 1:4 ("C. This is one of the way in which writs of divorce for women and writs of emancipation for slaves are treated as equivalent."), *m. Git.* 1:5, 6; 9.3 (*The Mishnah*, A New Translation by Jacob Neusner, 467, 468, 485; Also Instone-Brewer, *Divorce and Remarriage in the Bible*, 101.)

15. There has been no disagreement between the schools of Hillel and Shammai related to the three grounds for divorce based on the understanding of Exod 21:10–11 but only about the extent of their quantitative application in a matter of details. The main disagreement between the schools was related to the grounds for divorce based on the interpretation of Deut 24:1. (Also Instone-Brewer, *Divorce and Remarriage in the Bible*, 111, 112.)

16. Different discussions on various divorce cases have found better treatment through their grouping in the two main categories. (See also Instone-Brewer, *Divorce and Remarriage in the Bible*, 102)

17. See *m. Ketub.* 5.5, 6, 7, 8. (Instone-Brewer, *Divorce and Remarriage in the Bible*, 102, 103.)

terials for clothes while the wife was expected to prepare the meals and the clothes.

> A. These are the kinds of labour which a woman performs for her husband:
> B. she (1) grinds flour, (2) bakes bread, (3) does laundry, (4) prepares meals, (5) feeds her child, (6) makes the bed, (7) works in wool.
> C. [If] she brought with her a single slave girl, she does not (1) grind, (2) bake bread, or (3) do laundry.
> D. [If she brought] two, she does not (4) prepare meals and does (5) not feed her child.
> E. [If she brought] three, she does not (6) make the bed for him and does not (7) work in wool.
> F. If she brought four, she sits on a throne.
> G. R. Eliezer says, 'Even if she brought him a hundred slave girls, he forces her to work in wool,
> H. 'for idleness leads to unchastity.'
> I. Rabban Simeon b. Gamaliel says, 'Also: He who prohibits his wife by a vow from performing any labour puts her away and pays off her marriage contract.
> J. 'For idleness leads to boredom.' (*m. Ketub.* 5.5)[18]

From this text it is clear that the wife is required to fulfill her marriage obligations or otherwise she is to be divorced. The main stipulations from Exod 21:10 of food, clothing, and conjugal rights are related here to the specific responsibilities of the wife. The preparation of the food was depicted as (1) grinding flour, (2) baking bread, and (4) preparing meals. The preparation of clothing was addressed as (3) doing laundry, (6) making the bed, and (7) working with wool. The reference to conjugal rights was given with the mentioning of (5) her child. The latter might be referred to as the command "fill the earth" (Gen 1:28).[19]

The marriage stipulations related to the man have been further elaborated as well. In the following text these are well attested within the specific context of provision through a third person in case of the husband's absence for a period of time. The necessity of the appearing of this ruling

---

18. *The Mishnah*, A New Translation by Jacob Neusner, 388. Mentioning of the name of Eliezer ben Hyrcanus (80–120 AD), as its commentator, establishes this tradition before 70 AD.

19. See also Instone-Brewer, *Divorce and Remarriage in the Bible*, 103.

might be understood in light of a specific case of complaint brought to the court by the wife who has not been satisfied with the support offered to her in the previously stated circumstances.

> A. He who maintains his wife by a third party may not provide for her less than two *qabs* of wheat or four *qabs* of barley [per week].
>
> B. (Said R. Yose, 'Only Ishmael ruled that barley may be given her for he was near Edom.')
>
> C. And one pays over to her a half-*qab* of pulse, a half-*log* of oil, and a *qab* of dried figs or a *maneh* of fig cake.
>
> D. And if he does not have it, he provides instead fruit of some other type.
>
> E. And he gives her a bed, a cover and a mat.
>
> F. And he gives her a cap for her head, and a girdle for her loins, and shoes from one festival season to the next, and clothing worth fifty *zuz* from one year to the next.
>
> G. And they do not give her either new ones in the sunny season or old ones in the rainy season.
>
> H. But they provide for her clothing for fifty *zuz* in the rainy season and she clothes herself with the remnants in the sunny season.
>
> I. And the rags remain hers. (*m. Ketub.* 5.8)[20]

These detailed specifications of the wife's maintenance by the husband are further elaborated in the continuing paragraph in *Mishnah Ketuboth* 5.9. The text refers to some further financial provisions for the wife's other needs. The provision of a particular amount of wool is defined according to the wife's engagement with the child. The latter also influences the increase of the amount of food which the husband needs to supply. The text makes clear that the material support of the husband is related to his financial capacity. The wealthier the husband, the better material support to be expected by the wife. Some further texts referring to material support other than food and clothes suggest that even though these two have been treated as foundational stipulations of the marriage contract, they have not been defined as the only obligations of the spouses. The

---

20. *The Mishnah*, A New Translation by Jacob Neusner, 389. This tradition should be dated as belonging to the 1 century AD due to the mentioning of the practice of giving shoes at the festivals which points to the usual festival pilgrimages to Jerusalem before 70 AD.

standard of life which the wife had before the marriage was not to be diminished after it, but even improved if possible.[21] The wife or husband who lived in Jerusalem before the marriage would not be expected to go to the Diaspora although the reverse situation was possible.[22] The material stipulations related to both husband and wife required their devotion in fulfilling them in order to sustain the marital union. The material neglect was caused by the lack of fulfillment of these stipulations and facilitated the grounds for legal divorce.[23]

The approach of the rabbis followed in their discussions related to the material neglect as being based on clear formulation of the equivalent stipulations has been paralleled with their approach to the maters of emotional neglect. The core of the tradition which furnished the development of the emotional stipulations and neglect is found in Exod 21:10, 11 expressed with the term marital or conjugal rights. The fulfillment of these stipulations has been equally related to both spouses. Their detailed prescription is well attested in relation to man, (*m. Ketub* 5:6) and penalties are specified in relation to both man and woman due to the lack of fulfillment of the stipulations or establishment of the emotional neglect, (*m. Ketub* 5:7). The form in which the details are presented is related to defining the limits for abstinence from sexual intercourse for the husband. The following text lists them with a careful precision.

    A. He who takes a vow not to have sexual relations with his wife:

    B. The House of Shammai says, '[He may allow this situation to continue] for two weeks.'

    C. And the House of Hillel says, 'For one week.'

    D. Disciples go forth for Torah study without [the wife's] consent for 30 days.

    E. Workers go for one week.

    F. 'The sexual duty of which the Torah speaks [Ex 21:10]: (1) those without work [of independent means] – every day; (2)

---

21. "She rises with him [in his dignity] but does not go down with him [to a lower status]." (*Talmud - Mas. Kethuboth* 48a, The Sonico Talmud, 1973, Davka Corporation's Judaic Classics Library)

22. "A. All have the right to bring up [his or her family] to the Land of Israel, but none has the right to remove [his or her family] therefrom. B. All have the right to bring up to Jerusalem, but none has the right to bring down – C. all the same are men and women. " (*m. Ketub.* 13.11; *The Mishnah*, A New Translation by Jacob Neusner, 405.)

23. See also Instone-Brewer, *Divorce and Remarriage in the Bible*, 104, 105.

workers – twice a week; (3) ass drivers – once a week; (4) camel drivers – once in thirty days; (5) sailors – once in six months,' the words of R. Eliezer. (*m. Ketub.* 5.6)[24]

The periods of abstinence from sexual intercourse with the wife were defined according to the husband's engagements. Husbands with less time consuming engagements were expected to have more sexual intercourse. Thus, those without work or rich men were required to spend more time with their wives. The wife is not approached in the same way with the exact limitations of abstinence from sexual intercourse with the husband perhaps due to a lack of such complaints, but the penalties related to such abuses by the wife suggest that she carried the same responsibility as the husband. The following text defines the penalties for not fulfilling the stipulation of conjugal rights for both husband and wife.

> A. She who rebels against her husband [sexual duty, declining to perform wifely services] –
>
> B. they deduct from her marriage contract seven *denars* a week.
>
> C. R. Judah says 'Seven *tropaics*.'
>
> D. How long does one continue to deduct?
>
> E. Until her entire marriage contract [has been voided].
>
> F. R. Yose says, 'He continues to deduct [even beyond the value of the marriage contract], for an inheritance may come [to her] from some other source, from which he will collect what is due him.'
>
> G. And similarly the rule for the man who rebels against his wife [sexual duty, declining to do the husband's duties] —
>
> H. they add three *denars* a week to her marriage contract.
>
> I. R. Judah says, 'Three *tropaics*.' (*m. Ketub.* 5.7)[25]

---

24. *The Mishnah, A New Translation* by Jacob Neusner, 388, 398. This tradition is dated before 70 AD due to its mentioning by Eliezer ben Hyrcanus (80-120 AD) and its nature as a school debate between the schools of Shammai and Hillel which had not continued after 70 AD since the surmount of the Hillelites over the Shammaites. (Also Instone-Brewer, *Divorce and Remarriage in the Bible*, 106)

25. *The Mishnah, A New Translation* by Jacob Neusner, 389. This tradition might not be dated before 70 AD due to the mentioning of R. Judah b. Ilai and Yose b. Halafta (active during 140-165 AD) but since its rulings are very well defined in light of the practised financial penalties, it should be understood as having a long history which reaches back to the first century.

This tradition of the penalties related to both husband and wife in failing to fulfill their conjugal rights as expected suggests that they are constituted of financial charges not divorce. The financial charges had no immediate effect to the financial status of the husband or the wife since they were reflected through the decrease or increase of the *ketubah*. Hence, the effect could be experienced on the time of death or divorce when the *ketubah* might be lost either for the wife or for the husband according to their previous faults.[26] The preference of financial penalties in a case of conjugal failure to a divorce solution might have been based on a threefold understanding of the matter by the rabbis. First, the establishment of every individual penalty due to lack of fulfillment of the conjugal obligation required the presence of both spouses in front of a court which might have acted as persuasive measure. Second, the financial punishment which had a much lesser degree of effect to the spouses than divorce might have decreased the danger of forcing conjugal rights on one of the spouses by the other.[27] Third, the stipulation of conjugal rights had become a foundation for other matters of emotional neglect which led to establishing grounds for divorce.[28]

Different kinds of improper attitudes of the husband to the wife which might be characterised as emotional neglect due to their abusive or offensive nature are listed in the Mishnah under the topic of vows. In some cases it was required by the husband to refuse acceptance of some vows from the wife. If the latter was not done divorce was prescribed (*m. Ketub.* 7:2, 3). When the husband demanded from the wife to make an unbearable vow which was abuse to her, divorce was demanded with the return of the *ketubah* to the wife (*m. Ketub.* 7.5a). If the husband required the wife to perform a humiliating act he was required to divorce her and return to her the *ketubah* (*m. Ketub.* 7.5b). Physical abuse might also be considered grounds for divorce.[29] Matters related to a wife's improper attitude to her husband which might be described as emotional neglect have been also clearly defined (*m. Ketub.* 7.6). These are related to the transgression of the Law of Moses and Jewish custom. These two references are presented

---

26. Instone-Brewer, *Divorce and Remarriage in the Bible*, 106, 107.

27. Marital rape has been considered as crime in Judaism in relatively early stage (*b. Erub.* 100b, 3rd century AD).

28. Instone-Brewer, *Divorce and Remarriage in the Bible*, 107, 108.

29. *Eben ha-'Ezer* 154.3, quoted in Instone-Brewer, *Divorce and Remarriage in the Bible*, 109.

in Jewish marriage contracts (P.Yad. 10) where they serve as establishing the foundational stipulations of the marriage covenant and for securing the marriage as a lifelong union. Thus, the violation of matters related to these two institutions brought shame on the husband and destroyed the marriage. Furthermore the wife was thought to abuse the husband if she made him unclean whether through food or through improper sexual intercourse.[30] She may have also offended or humiliated him through her domestic and social misconduct.[31] These matters of emotional neglect of the husband established grounds for divorce with the wife as the guilty party and prescribed no return of the *ketubah* (*m. Ketub.* 7.6).[32]

The stipulation of conjugal rights (Exod 21:10, 11) framed in the larger topic of emotional neglect might have been related to the topic of marital faithfulness whose dynamics might be considered as referring to the whole group under consideration. Marital faithfulness is an expected stipulation of both parties for the fulfillment of the marriage contract and the preservation of the marital bond.[33] The failure in regard to this respon-

---

30. "... And what is meant by the Law of Moses [which she has transgressed]? — [If] (1) she feeds him food which has not been tithed, or (2) has sexual relations with him while she is menstruating, or [if] (3) she does not cut off her dough offering, or (4) [if] she vows and does not carry out her vow." (*m. Ketub.* 7.6c; *The Mishnah*, A New Translation by Jacob Neusner, 392)

31. "... And what is the Jewish law? If (1) she goes out with her hair flowing loose, or (2) she spins in the marketplace, or (3) she conversed with all men. Abba Saul says, 'Also: if she cursed his parents in his presence.' R. Tarfon says, 'Also if she is a loudmouth.' What is a loudmouth? When she talks in her own house, her neighbours can hear her voice." (*m. Ketub.* 7.6d-g; *The Mishnah*, A New Translation by Jacob Neusner, 392)

32. Also Instone-Brewer, *Divorce and Remarriage in the Bible*, 109, 110.

33. "There are two types of people who commit sin after sin and a third who attracts retribution—desire, blazing like a furnace, will not die down until it has been sated—the man who lusts after members of his own family is not going to stop until he is quite burnt out; every food is sweet to the promiscuous, and he will not desist until he dies; and *the man who sins against the marriage bed* and says to himself, 'Who can see me? There is darkness all round me, the walls hide me, no one can see me, why should I worry? The Most High will not remember my sins.' What he fears are human eyes, he does not realise that the eyes of the Lord are ten thousand times brighter than the sun, observing every aspect of human behaviour, seeing into the most secret corners. All things were known to him before they were created, and are still, now that they are finished. This man will be punished in view of the whole town, and will be seized when he least expects it. Similarly *the woman unfaithful to her husband*, who provides him with an heir by another man: first, she has disobeyed the Law of the Most High; secondly, she has been false to her husband; and thirdly, she has gone whoring in adultery and conceived children by another man. She will be led before the assembly, an enquiry will be held about her children. Her

sibility of either spouse, was regarded as a legitimate ground for divorce. The mutual liability of both partners in regard to marital unfaithfulness is hard to substantiate on the side of the man due to a lenient attitude toward polygamy[34] and the understanding of the object of the offense not as the wife but her father or the husband of the adulteress.[35] However, polygamy was looked down upon[36] and the first century records show that it was not a wide spread practice.[37] Furthermore, there is evidence which suggests that both man and woman are guilty when caught in adultery.[38] Even some antiadultery texts refer only to man.[39] Man's virginity when

---

children will strike no root, her branches will bear no fruit. She will leave an accursed memory behind her, her shame will never be wiped out. And those who survive her will recognise that nothing is better than fearing the Lord, and nothing sweeter than adherence to the Lord's commandments." (Sirach 23:16–27, NJB, italics mine) (*BibleWorks for Windows*.) For married man see also Josephus, *The Antiquities of the Jews*, 3.12.1.274 and Josephus, *Against Apion* 2.25.201; for married women see Josephus, *The Antiquities of the Jews*, 4.8.23.251; for the Greco-Roman context cf. P. Tebt. I. 104. ". . . It shall not be lawful for H to bring in any other wife but W, nor to keep a concubine or boy . . . . In the same way it shall not be lawful for W . . . to have intercourse with another man . . . ." (*P. Tebt.* I. 104; *Marriage contract*. The Duke Databank of Documentary Papyri. P.Tebt.: The Tebtunis Papyri [online], Available at http://www.perseus.tufts.edu/cgi-bin/ptext?doc=P erseus%3Aabo%3Apap%2CP.Tebt.&query=1%3A104, Accessed on 26 August 2004.)

34. Josephus, *Ant.* 17.14; *b. Yoma* 18b.

35. Josephus, *The Antiquities of the Jews*, 4.8.23.(251, 252). See also David Instone-Brewer, "Jesus' Old Testament Basis for Monogamy," in *The Old Testament in the New Testament: Essays in Honour of J. L. North*, ed. Steve Moyise, JNTSSup 189 (Sheffield: Sheffield Academic, 2000) 75–105 [online], Available at http://www.tyndale.cam.ac.uk/Tyndale/PDF%20files/Monogamy.pdf, Accessed on 2 September 2004, p. 21.

36. *b. Abot* 2.5; *b. Yebam.* 44. (See also Instone-Brewer, "Jesus' Old Testament Basis for Monogamy," [online] 3–5.)

37. Instone-Brewer, *Divorce and Remarriage in the Bible*, 60, 61.

38. *m. Sota* 5.1; "(251) He that hath corrupted a damsel espoused to another man, in case he had her consent, let both him and her be put to death, for they are both equally guilty; the man because he persuaded the woman willingly to submit to a most impure action, and to prefer it to lawful wedlock; the woman because she was persuaded to yield herself to be corrupted, either for pleasure or for gain. (252) However, if a man light on a woman when she is alone, and forces her, where nobody was present to come to her assistance, let him only be put to death. Let him that hath corrupted a virgin not yet espoused, marry her; but if the father of the damsel be not willing that she should be his wife, let him pay fifty shekels as the price of her prostitution." (Josephus, *The Antiquities of the Jews*, 4.8.23.); See also Instone-Brewer, *Divorce and Remarriage in the Bible*, 96.

39. "(8) Now on the second table this is the first commandment, 'Thou shalt not commit adultery,' because, I imagine, in every part of the world pleasure is of great power,

entering marriage was also considered important next to that of woman even though the latter was much more widely emphasized.[40] Finally, a man is identified as an adulterer even when he has looked at a woman's sexual organs.[41] Thus, the husband in spite of the first century generally relaxed understanding of his sexual purity might be considered as being liable for his sexual conduct in marriage and in case of adultery he might have been required to divorce his wife with the return of the *ketubah*.[42] In the case of the wife being an adulteress the situation is much clearer but still contains matters which obscure the exact action being undertaken by the husband. Adultery was hard to prove and the rule of suspected adultery was introduced.[43] In the latter case even the slightest possibility

---

. . . (9) Therefore, even that pleasure which is in accordance with nature is often open to blame, when any one indulges in it immoderately and insatiably, as men who are unappeasably voracious in respect of eating, even if they take no kind of forbidden or unwholesome food; and as men who are madly devoted to association with women, and who commit themselves to an immoderate degree not with other men's wives, but with their own." (Philo, *The Special Laws* III.II.8-9); "(274) As for adultery, Moses forbade it entirely, as esteeming it a happy thing that men should be wise in the affairs of wedlock; and that it was profitable both to cities and families that children should be known to be genuine. He also abhorred men's lying with their mothers, as one of the greatest crimes; and the like for lying with the father's wife, and with aunts, and sisters, and sons' wives, as all instances of abominable wickedness." (Josephus, *The Antiquities of the Jews*, 3.12.1.); "(201) for, saith the Scripture, 'A woman is inferior to her husband in all things.' Let her, therefore, be obedient to him; not so, that he should abuse her, but that she may acknowledge her duty to her husband; for God hath given the authority to the husband. A husband, therefore, is to lie only with his wife whom he hath married; but to have to do with another man's wife is a wicked thing; which, if any one venture upon, death is inevitably his punishment: no more can he avoid the same who forces a virgin betrothed to another man, or entices another man's wife." (Josephus, *Against Apion* 2.25.) See also D. W. Chapman, *Marriage and Family in Second Temple Judaism*, 222.

40. *Jos. Asen.* 4:9; 7:3–5 cf. *Jos. Asen.* 2:1–16; 7:8–10 ("Joseph & Aseneth," trans. David Cook, in *The Apocryphal Old Testament*, ed. H. F. D. Sparks [Oxford: Oxford University Press, 1984] 473–503 [online], Available at http://www.bham.ac.uk/theology/goodacre/aseneth/translat.htm, [9/7/2004 12:01:10 PM], Accessed on 22 December 2004.); 11 QTemple LXV, 7–15; Josephus, *The Antiquities of the Jews*, 4.8.23.(246–248); *m. Ketub.* 1:1. See also Chapman, *Marriage and Family in Second Temple Judaism*, 222.

41. "He who looks at a woman's heel, it is as if he looked at the place of her pudenda, and if he looks there, it is as if he had intercourse with her." (*y. Hal.* 2.4, 58c; translated by Instone-Brewer, *Divorce and Remarriage in the Bible*, 98.)

42. See also Instone-Brewer, *Jesus' Old Testament Basis for Monogamy* [online] 22.

43. "(52) The law has pronounced all acts of adultery, if detected in the fact, or if proved by undeniable evidence, liable to the punishment of death; but cases in which guilt is only suspected, it does not choose who should be investigated by men, but it brings them before the tribunal of nature; since men are able to judge of what is vis-

of interpretation that an act of adultery might have happened when the wife has been alone with other man would have been suspected as adultery and proven through the rite of Bitter Water.[44] This rite was to prove the wife's guilt or her innocence with the consequences of bringing her to death or leaving her alive (Num 5:23). However, it is not clear whether it was widely practiced during the first century[45] and its effects were not always the same.[46] Also, the rite had been suspended from practice on pregnant women or those who had had sexual intercourse with their husbands after the suspected act of adultery (*m. Sota* 4.2, 3). Further obscuring the act of suspected adultery by the wife was the false accusation of the husband in order to enrich himself through withholding the *ketubah* in an eventual divorce.[47] However, the general Jewish position in the first

---

ible, but God can judge also of what is unseen, since he alone is able to behold the soul distinctly, (53) therefore he says to the man who suspects such a thing, 'Write an accusation, and go up to the holy city with thy wife, and standing before the judges, lay bare the passion of suspicion which affects you, not like a false accuser or treacherous enemy, seeking to gain the victory by any means whatever, but as a man may do who wishes accurately to ascertain the truth without any sophistry. (54) And the woman, having incurred two dangers, one of her life, and the other of her reputation, the loss of which last is more grievous than any kind of death, shall judge the matter with herself; and if she be pure, let her make her defence with confidence; but if she be convicted by her own conscience, let her cover her face, making her modesty the veil for her iniquities, for to persist in her impudence is the very extravagance of wickedness." (Philo, *The Special Laws*, III 52–54, C. D. Yonge, trans. *The Works of Philo: Complete and Unabridged* [Peabody: Hendrickson, 1996]).

44. "A. He who expressed jealousy to his wife, B. but she went aside in secret, C. even if he heard [that she had done so] from a bird flying by – D. he puts her away but pays off her marriage contract, the words of R. Eliezer." (*m. Sota* 6.1; *The Mishnah*, A New Translation by Jacob Neusner, 456)

45. This rite could not have been practiced after 70 AD due to the lack of temple. (Also Instone-Brewer, *Divorce and Remarriage in the Bible*, 95.

46. When the woman who has taken the bitter water did not die and later evidence against her was found it has been explained that her good deeds have prolonged her life. (*m. Sota* 3.4)

47. "There was a man who wanted to divorce his wife, but hesitated because she had a big marriage settlement. He accordingly invited his friends 16 and gave them a good feast and made them drunk and put them all in one bed. He then brought the white of an egg and scattered it among them and brought witnesses 17 and appealed to the Beth din. There was a certain elder there of the disciples of Shammai the Elder, named Baba b. Buta, who said: This is what I have been taught by Shammai the Elder, that the white of an egg contracts when brought near the fire, but semen becomes faint from the fire. They tested it and found that it was so, and they brought the man to the rabbinic court and flogged him and made him pay her Kethubah." (Talmud - *Mas. Gittin* 57a, The Sonico Talmud, 1973.)

century might have been in favor of divorce in the case of adultery by the wife (*m. Sota* 5.1[48]). This was the exact practice referred to by some later texts (*m. Sota* 4.3; 6.1; *m Ketub.* 2.9; 5.1) which defined the act of adultery as a violation not only of the marriage but also of the betrothal. Thus, they legitimate divorce with keeping the *ketubah* by the groom even during the time of betrothal. Even matters related to implicit adulterous behavior[49] had to be treated as adultery with the divorce of the wife and the keeping of her *ketubah* by the husband (*m. Ketub.* 7:6d-g).[50] Therefore marital faithfulness was treated as one of the fundamental stipulations of the marriage contract, and adultery by either of the spouses as breaking the marital bond and establishing legitimate grounds for divorce with the withholding of the *ketubah* from the guilty party.

A further reference to the stipulation of conjugal rights in particular and emotional neglect in general might be the obligation of the spouses to have children. Failing to fulfill this obligation might have resulted in establishing legitimate grounds for divorce. The main reason for this expectation from each family was related to the command found in the Torah (Gen 1:28). The command, "be fruitful and multiply, and fill the earth," (NRS) was understood as the main role of the marriage.[51] The importance of children for each family was generally accepted by the whole first century Jewish community and its religious authorities.[52] Furthermore,

---

48. "A. Just as the water puts her to the proof, so the water puts him [the lover] to the proof, B. 'since it is said, And it shall come . . . , And it shall come . . . (Num 5:22, 5:24).' C. Just as she is prohibited to the husband, so she is prohibited to the lover, D. 'since it is said, And she will be unclean . . . , And she will be unclean . . . (Num 5:27, 29),' the words of R. Aqiba. E. Said R. Joshua, 'Thus did Zekhariah b. Haqqassab expound [the scripture].' F. Rabbi says, 'The two times at which, If she is made unclean . . . , She is made unclean . . . are stated in the pericope refer, one to the husband and one to the lover.'" (*m. Sota* 5.1; *The Mishnah*, A New Translation by Jacob Neusner, 454, 455.)

49. See the discussion about the damaging effects of implicit adulterous behavior on marital relationships and the marriage covenant in Thomas M. Olshewsky, "A Christian Understanding of Divorce," *JRE* 7 (1979) 124–26.

50. Instone-Brewer, *Divorce and Remarriage in the Bible*, 97–99.

51. Also Block, *Marriage and Family in Ancient Israel*, 72.

52. The schools of Shammai and Hillel agreed on this matter: "A. A man should not give up having sexual relations unless he has children. B. The House of Shammai say, 'Two boys.' C. And the House of Hillel say, 'A boy and a girl,' D. 'since it is said, Male and female he created them (Gen 5:2).' E. [If] a man married a woman and lived with her for ten years and she did not give birth, he has not right to desist from having sexual relations with her. F. [if] he divorced her, she is permitted to marry someone else. G. The second husband is allowed to live with her for ten years. H. And if she miscarried, she counts the ten years form the time that she miscarried. I. The man is required to be

obstacles to performing this role of marriage were treated as legitimate grounds for divorce.[53] However, attitudes against the manipulation of the practice for personal benefit[54] and tolerance to the inability of some families to produce children in the required timeframe[55] were crucial for restricting the practice of divorce in such cases.[56]

---

fruitful and multiply but not the woman. J. R. Yohanan b. Beroqah says, 'Concerning both of them does Scripture say, And God blessed them and said to them, Be fruitful and multiply' (Gen 1:28)." (*m. Yabamot* 6.6; *The Mishnah*, A New Translation by Jacob Neusner, 352); Josephus and the Essenes also recognized this (Josephus, *Ag. Ap.* 2.199; *J.W.* 2.160-61).

53. Impotence: "A . . . Three sorts of women go forth and collect their marriage contract: . . . (2) 'Heaven [knows] what is between you and me [namely, your impotence],' . . ." (*m. Nedarim* 11.12.a; *The Mishnah*, A New Translation by Jacob Neusner, 430); Different conditions of the husband which prevented the wife to have sexual relations with him: "A. And these are the ones whom they force to put her away: (1) he who is afflicted with boils, or (2) who has a polypus, or (3) who collects [dog excrement], or (4) a coppersmith, or (5) a tanner . . ." (*m. Ketubot* 7.10; *The Mishnah*, A New Translation by Jacob Neusner, 393).

54. "A. He who divorces his wife because of sterility – B. R. Judah says, 'He may not remarry her.' . . ." (*m. Git.* 4.8 ab; *The Mishnah*, A New Translation by Jacob Neusner, 474).

55. "Another explanation: We will be glad and rejoice in Thee. We have learnt elsewhere: If a man has married a wife and lived with her ten years and she has not borne him a child, he is not at liberty to neglect the duty [of begetting children]. R. Idi said: It happened once that a woman in Sidon had lived ten years with her husband without bearing him a child. They came to R. Simeon b. Yohai and requested to be parted from one another. He said to them: I adjure you, just as you have always shared a festive board together, so do not part save with festivity. They took his advice and kept holiday and made a great feast and drank very freely. Feeling then in a good humor he said to her: 'My daughter, pick out any article you want in my house and take it with you to your father's house.' What did she do? When he was asleep she gave an order to her servants and handmaids to lift him up on the bed and take and carry him to her father's house. At midnight he awoke from his sleep, and when the effects of the wine passed from him he said: 'My daughter, where am I?' She replied: 'You are in my father's house.' 'And what am I doing in your father's house?' he said. She replied: did you not say to me last night, 'Take any article you like from my house and go to your father's house?' 'There is nothing in the world I care for more than you.' They again went to R. Simeon b. Yohai and he went and prayed for them, and they became fertile . . . ." (*Midrash Rabbah - The Song of Songs* I:30, *The Soncino Midrash Rabbah*, Soncino, 1983.)

"As many men, therefore, as marry virgins in ignorance of how will they will turn out as regards their prolificness, or the contrary, when after a long time they perceive, by their never having any children, that they are barren, and do not then put them away, are still worthy of pardon, being influenced by habit and familiarity, which are motives of great weight, and being also unable to break through the power of those ancient charms which by long habituation are stamped upon their souls." (Philo, *The Special Laws*, III 35, C. D. Yonge, trans. *The Works of Philo*, Electronic Edition.)

56. Also Instone-Brewer, *Divorce and Remarriage in the Bible*, 91-93.

Besides the above approach of marriage maintenance through the establishment of particular grounds for legitimate divorce action, another approach to marriage and divorce was well established during the first century AD in Jewish as well as in Greco-Roman societies. This is the so called an "any matter" divorce originated and defended by the school of Hillel resembled by divorce by separation practiced in the Greco-Roman world. The Jewish type of liberal divorce based on flexible divorce grounds was established through an interpretation of Deut 24:1. The Hillel school's interpreters understood the text in general and the phrase "*indecent matter*" (ערות דבר) in particular as providing not only grounds for divorce due to "indecency" but also as an open ground for divorce in case of "any matter." This interpretation found its opponents in the school of Shammai who interpreted the debatable phrase as "a matter of indecency" (ערות דבר) and within the context of Deut 24: 1 as referring to adultery or sexual immorality.[57]

> The School of Shammai say: A man should not divorce his wife unless he found in her a matter of indecency (דבר ערות) as it is said: *For he finds in her an indecent matter* (ערות דבר). And the School of Hillel say, Even if she spoiled his dish, since it says *For he finds in her an indecent matter* (ערות דבר).[58]

The grounds for divorce which the Hillelites suggested had become so broad that they might be considered not as actual grounds but as providing the possibility to formulate and execute one's desire to divorce. "R. Aqiba says, Even if he found someone else prettier than she, since it is said, And it shall be if she finds no favour in his eyes (Dt 24:1)."[59] This approach to divorce found a widespread acceptance in the Jewish community in the first century.[60] There are several reasons which propagated this attitude toward divorce. First, it did not require providing evidence to support a

---

57. Also Raymond F. Collins, "Marriage: New Testament," in *ABD* 4:569; and Instone-Brewer, *Divorce and Remarriage in the Bible*, 111.

58. *m. Gittin* 9.10ab, quoted in Instone-Brewer, *Divorce and Remarriage in the Bible*, 111.

59. *m. Gittin* 9.10 (*The Mishnah*, A New Translation by Jacob Neusner, 487).

60. "But if, proceeds the lawgiver, a woman having been divorced from her husband under any pretence whatever, ..." (Philo, *The Special Laws*, III 30, C. D. Yonge, trans. *The Works of Philo*); "He that desires to be divorced from his wife for any cause whatsoever (and many such causes happen among men), . . . " (Josephus, *The Antiquities of the Jews*, 4.253); Also Instone-Brewer, *Divorce and Remarriage in the Bible*, 115.

particular ground for the divorce action. Thus, it spared the family members from disgracing their image and especially saved the wife[61] from a shameful appearance in front of the court.[62] Second, since it required the return of the *ketubah* in any case, the community was not burdened by divorced women without financial support.[63] Finally, this type of divorce did not require a complex court procedure but was executed smoothly with the only engagement of settling the financial matters.[64]

Almost identical to the Jewish "any matter" divorce is the Greco-Roman divorce by separation or departure of the willing partner. The divorce procedure did not require either grounds, court involvement or any subsequent documents.[65] It is well summarized in the words of Emperor Alexander Severus (AD 223). "It was decided of old that marriages should

---

61. *b. Ketub.* 97b; Matt 1:19.

62. The following story shows that the man did not choose to go to court and argue for divorcing his wife on the grounds of material or emotional neglect even though he had the right to do it but decided to return her *ketubah* and spare them both from the shame. "I will make him a help ('EZER) against him (KENEGDO) 3: if he is fortunate, she is a help; if not, she is against him. R. Joshua b. Nehemiah said: If a man is fortunate, she is like the wife of Hananiah b. Hakinai; if not, she is like the wife of R. Jose the Galilean. R. Jose the Galilean had a bad wife; she was his sister's daughter, and used to put him to shame. His disciples said to him: 'Master, divorce this woman, for she does not act as benefits your honour.' 'Her dowry is too great for me, and I cannot afford to divorce her,' was his reply. . . . When they finished he said to him: 'Master, abandon this woman, for she does not treat you with proper respect.' ' Sir,' he replied, 'her dowry is too great for me and I cannot divorce her.' 'We [your pupils],' said the other, 'will apportion her dowry among ourselves, so you can divorce her.' And they did so for him; they apportioned her dowry and had her divorced from him, and made him marry another and better wife. . . ." (*Midrash Rabbah - Genesis* XVII:3, trans. D. Mandel, *The Soncino Midrash Rabbah*, Soncino, 1983, Davka Corporation's Judaic Classics Library, Version IIf by David Kantrowitz. Institute for Computers in Jewish Life. Davka Corporation & Judaica, 1999.)

63. Keith F. Nickle, *The Collection: A Study in Paul's Strategy* (London: SCM, 1966), 93–94, quoted in Instone-Brewer, *Divorce and Remarriage in the Bible*, 114.

64. *m. Sanh.* 1.1, 3. Also Instone-Brewer, *Divorce and Remarriage in the Bible*, 115–17.

65. Cicero encountered a case in which the husband left his pregnant wife and married another and after a short time died. Both women had babies and it was difficult to establish who was the legitimate son. Hence Cicero, knowing that it was not important for the husband to inform his wife when divorcing her or leave her any document related to the divorce, considers that in such cases a document would have been helpful in regard to the establishment of the exact heir. (*De Oratore* 1,40.183; Alfredo M. Rabello, "Divorce of Jews in the Roman Empire," in *The Jewish Law Annual*, ed. B. S. Jackson [Leiden: Brill, 1981] 4:80, quoted in Instone-Brewer, *Divorce and Remarriage in the Bible*, 73, 74.)

be free. Hence, it is settled that an agreement not to divorce is not valid and neither is a promise to pay a penalty on divorce."[66] Hence, reasons for the divorce action were not of any significance.[67] Both partners were free to leave the marriage at any time according to their desire.[68] The following petition of a husband complaining that his wife stole his property depicts very well the act of divorce through departure.

> To the governor Alexandrus from Tryphon son of Dionysius of the city of Oxyrhynchus. I married Demetrous the daughter of Heraclides and I supported her in a manner that exceeded my resources. She became dissatisfied with our marriage and eventually went off and they (In a fragment of another papyrus, POxy 315, dated AD 37, Tryphon complains that Demetrous and her mother assaulted his pregnant wife) took of property belonging to me, a list of which is appended. Accordingly I ask that she be brought before you so that she can get the punishment she deserves and return my property to me. Without prejudice to any other charges

---

66. Justinian, *Codex* 8.38.2. trans. T. Honore, in *Women's Life in Greece and Rome*, eds. Mary R. Lefkowitz and Maureen B. Fant, 2nd ed. (London: Duckworth, 1992), 112.

67. "... There was also the harsh marital severity of Gaius Sulpicius Gallus. He divorced his wife because he had caught her outdoors with her head uncovered: a stiff penalty, but not without a certain logic.... Quintus Antistius Ventus felt no differently when he divorced his wife because he had seen her in public having a private conversation with a common freedwoman. For, moved not by an actual crime but, so to speak by the birth and nourishment of one, he punished her before the crime could be committed, so that he might prevent the deed's being done at all, rather than punish it afterwards.... Publius Sempronius Sophus who disgraced his wife with divorce merely because she dared attend the games without his knowledge...." (Valerius Maximus, *Memorable Deeds and Sayings* 6.3.9-12, in *Women's Life in Greece and Rome*, trans. Lefkowitz and Fant, 96.)

68. Some boundaries for divorce initiation might have existed. "(1) Marriage is dissolved by divorce, death, captivity, or by any other kind of servitude which may happen to be imposed upon either of the parties. (3) It is not a true or actual divorce unless there is the intention to establish a perpetual parting of their ways. Therefore, whatever is done or said in the heat of anger is not valid, unless the determination becomes apparent by the parties persevering in their intention, and hence where a message of repudiation is sent in the heat of anger and the wife returns in a short time, she is not held to have divorced her husband." (*Digest* 24.2.1, 3. L. [Paul, *Edict*, book 35], in *Women's Life in Greece and Rome*, trans. Lefkowitz and Fant, 115.) Augustus' legislation also establishes some control with the demand on divorce notification and the presence of witnesses. (David G. Hunter, ed. and trans., *Marriage in the Early Church* [Eugene, OR: Wipf and Stock, 2001] 7.)

that I have made or will make against her. The articles she carried off . . . are worth 40 drachmas.[69]

The difference between the Jewish "any matter" divorce and Greco-Roman divorce by separation might be the requirement of a document in the case of the Jewish divorce for the purpose of providing a possibility for the wife to subsequently remarry.[70] Due to the strong social assumption for subsequent remarriage in a case of the Greco-Roman divorce which has been even expressed in a form of legislation,[71] and the higher extent of women's freedom, the irregularity in issuing a divorce certificate was not an obstacle for the subsequent remarriage of the divorcee.[72] Another possible dissimilarity might be related to the extent of the wife's freedom to initiate divorce. The wife in the Greco-Roman society was on an equal position with the husband in terms of the power to divorce. The Jewish woman might be considered as having a lower position to the husband in relation to that power.[73] However, some texts suggest that women were able to enact divorce through the rabbinic court and to be treated as an equal, on the grounds of the marriage contract, with the man in the matter of divorce initiation.[74] The wife's authority to initiate divorce and to issue a divorce certificate is acknowledged by some documents.[75] This role of the

---

69. *Oxyrhynchus Papyrus* 282. G, in *Women's Life in Greece and Rome*, trans. Lefkowitz and Fant, 92, 93.

70. *m. Gittin* 9:3 – "The text of the writ of divorce [is as follows]: 'Lo, you are permitted to any man.' R. Judah says, '[In Aramaic]: Let this be from me your writ of divorce, letter of dismissal, and deed of liberation, that you may marry anyone you want.'" (*The Mishnah*, A New Translation by Jacob Neusner, 485.)

71. *Lex Julia*, 18 BC. (see Dio Cassius, *History of Rome* 54.16.1–2, in *Women's Life in Greece and Rome*, trans. Lefkowitz and Fant, 103.)

72. David Instone-Brewer, *Divorce and Remarriage in the 1st and 21st Century* (Cambridge: Grove, 2001), section 3–1 [online], Available at http://www.tyndale.cam.ac.uk/Brewer/PPages/121/, Accessed on 8 September 2004.

73. "They said to him [to Yohanan b. Nuri], The man who divorces his wife is not equivalent to a woman who receives a divorce. For a woman goes forth willingly or unwillingly. But a man puts his wife away only willingly." (*m. Yebamot* 14.11, m, n; *The Mishnah*, A New Translation by Jacob Neusner, 370.)

74. *m. Arak.* 5.6; *m. Git.* 9.8; *t. Ketub.* 12.3; *m. Ketub.* 7.10, (Also Instone-Brewer, *Divorce and Remarriage in the Bible*, 86, 87). This has been a normal practice in the Karaite communities. (Judith Olszowy-Schlanger, *Karaite Marriage Documents from the Cairo Geniza* [Leiden: Brill, 1998] 126.)

75. "On the 20th of Sivan, year 3 of Israel's freedom. In the name of Simon bar Kosibar, the Nasi of Israel . . . I do not have . . . I, Shelamzion, daughter of Joseph Qebshan of Em

Jewish wife comes very close to the one exercised by the Greco-Roman wife.[76] Thus, a widespread form of divorce during the first century among Jewish and Greco-Roman communities was one which did not require the provision of specific grounds and as such did not relate to a failure of any of the parties in fulfillment of the contract stipulations. Against this liberal approach to marriage, divorce, and remarriage, the NT authors developed their argumentative stand.

On the one hand, Matthew (19: 3–12; 5: 31, 32) uses Jesus' teaching within the framework of his audience to object to such a liberal stand which required no grounds for terminating the marital union and initiating divorce and subsequent remarriage. The Pharisees' support of Hillel's position, (Matt 19:3), is criticized as a misinterpretation of Torah in general and Deut 24:1 in particular. Marriage should be understood from the holistic reading of Torah (Deut 24:1 and Gen 1:27; 2:24) as a lifelong union which may not be dissolved without particular lawful grounds. Divorce on "any matter" or without lawful grounds is illegal and leads to the adulterous state of potential remarriage for divorcees (Matt 19:9, 5:32). On the other hand, Mark (10:2–12), Luke (16:18), and Paul (1 Cor 7:10, 11, 12–14) use Jesus' teaching with respect to their readers to combat the licentious attitude toward marriage, divorce, and remarriage. Mark, dealing with the position of the woman in the divorce and remarriage acts, uses Jesus' teaching in its absolute and rigorous form in two directions: first, in order to prohibit the husband's liberal attitude toward divorce and remarriage which was abusive to the wife (10:11),[77] and second to condemn the wife's groundless divorce and subsequent remarriage

---

Gedi, with you, Eleazar son of Hananiah who had been the husband before this time, that this is from me to you a bill of divorce and release. . . . I do not have with you . . . Eleazar anything (I wish for?), as is my duty and remains upon me. I Shelamzion (accept) all that is written (in this document). Shelamzion present, lent her handwriting (?). Mattat son of Simon by her order . . . son of Simon, witness. Masbala, son of Simon, witness." (*Papyrus Se'elim* 13, trans. Tal Ilan, in Instone-Brewer, *Divorce and Remarriage in the Bible*, 88.) See also Philo, *Spec. Leg.* 3.30; Josephus, *Ant.* 15.259–60; 20.141–47; Instone-Brewer, *Divorce and Remarriage in the Bible*, 85–90.

76. Also Instone-Brewer, *Divorce and Remarriage in the Bible*, 191.

77. The argument is furnished through defining the phrase γυναῖκα αὐτοῦ as the antecedent of ἐπ' αὐτήν and understanding the promiscuous attitude of the husband to his wife in the Greco-Roman world. (see Antiphon, *Speeches* 1.13; Demosthenes, *Speeches* 51–61: *Apollodorus Against Neaera* 59.17; Aulus Gellius, *Avli Gelli Noctes Atticae*, 10, 23, 5; Also T. R. Martin, *An Overview of Classical Greek History from Homer to Alexander* [online].)

as adulterous (10:12).⁷⁸ Luke, combating such a liberal perspective on divorce based on the desire of subsequent remarriage uses Jesus' teaching shaping it in a particular syntactical construction⁷⁹ in order to point to the sinful marriage of Herod and Herodias⁸⁰ and the immoral attitude toward divorce among both Jews and Gentiles.⁸¹ Paul, facing the same attitude toward divorce and remarriage by some Corinthian Christian couples uses Jesus' teaching⁸² to prohibit them to divorce and remarry, (1 Cor 7:10, 11). He also argues against the desire of believers, part of mixed marriages, to use the liberal Greco-Roman divorce and depart from their unbelieving spouses for protecting their spirituality⁸³ (1 Cor 7: 12–14).⁸⁴ Paul views marriage as a lifelong union which should not be terminated without legitimate divorce grounds. Thus, the apostle follows closely the

78. This conclusion is substantiated by the fifth class conditional clause with an emphasis on its present generic nature and the common practice in the Greco-Roman culture of wives to divorce their husbands, (cf. 1 Cor 7:10, 13). See Gaius, *Institutes* 137a; Diodorus Siculus, *Library*, 12.18.1, XVIII; Also W. Hendriksen, *Mark*, 380; G. D. Fee, *The First Epistle to the Corinthians*, 294; Witherington III, *Conflict and Community in Corinth*, 171.

79. The syntactical nature of the saying (Luke 16:18a) determines a semantic notion of subordination which underlines the reason for divorce as that for subsequent remarriage. The second part of the text (16:18b) expresses the same notion but from the standpoint of the woman. (See D. B. Wallace, *Greek Grammar Beyond the Basics*, 667, f.2. For that function of the conjunction in the Patristic literature see Alber-Louis Descamps, *The New Testament Doctrine on Marriage*, 217–73, 347–63; Also J. Nolland, *Luke 9:21–18:34*, 819, 821, 822.)

80. It has been based on divorce with prearranged remarriage during the state of their former marriages. (See Josephus, *The Antiquities of the Jews*, 18.109–115. Also B. Witherington III, *Herodias*, 174–76; D. C. Braund, *Herod Antipas*, 160).

81. Their most common reason for divorce might be established as that of subsequent remarriage. (See Diodorus Siculus, *Library* 12.18.1.XVIII; M. Tullius Cicero, *Letters 1. Intro 20: The Letters to TERENTIA*, ed. Evelyn Shuckburgh [online], Available at http://perseus.csad.ox.ac.uk/cgi-bin/ptext?doc=Perseus:text:1999.02.0022&query=he ad%3d%2322, Accessed on 27 May 2001; idem, *Letters A 15.29*, ed. Evelyn Shuckburgh [online], Available at http://perseus.csad.ox.ac.uk/cgi-bin/ptext?lookup=Cic.+Att.+15.2 9, Accessed on 27 May 2001; *Mishnah, Sotah* 5:1; Halacha, 26, *Adultery - Sotah*. Also J. Nolland, *Luke 9:21–18:34*, 819; I. H. Marshall, *The Gospel of Luke*, 631.)

82. Cf. Mark 10:11, Matt 19:9 and Luke 16:16, Matt 5:32.

83. The Corinthians had a perception most likely shaped by a misunderstanding of Paul's previous letter that they should not have relations with unbelievers (5:9–11) and their ascetic understanding of life (7:1). Also Fee, *The First Epistle to the Corinthians*, 300; J. C. Laney, *Paul and the Permanence of Marriage in I Corinthians 7*, 286; Witherington III, *Conflict and Community in Corinth*, 178.

84. Also Instone-Brewer, *Divorce and Remarriage in the Bible*, 197–201.

contractual provision of stipulations according to the Jewish tradition based on Exod 21:10, 11 for establishing a strong marital union based on the mutual responsibility of the spouses for its maintenance and preservation.⁸⁵ Paul is using the same Jewish pattern of distinguishing the marital stipulations between material and emotional.

For Paul, the foundational emotional stipulation of every marriage is the obligation of the spouses to give each other their conjugal rights (1 Cor 7:1–9). The basis of the marital relationship is the mutual love of both spouses which finds its culmination and highest point of expression in physical love. The apostle is prompted to share this close Jewish understanding of marriage with the group of Corinthian believers who disregarded this marital obligation. He quotes their statement in order to facilitate a discussion which will clearly express his view which he believes is firmly based on Jesus' teaching. The Corinthian Christians offer to their teacher a statement by which they claimed that it is good for a married person not to have sexual intercourse (ἅπτεσθαι⁸⁶) with his or her spouse (1 Cor 7:1).⁸⁷ Paul disagrees completely arguing that marriage is main-

---

85. The following works recognize this connection: R. J. Rushdoony, *The Institutes of Biblical Law* (Phillipsburg, NJ: Presbyterian and Reformed, 1973) 403; William F. Luck, *Divorce and Remarriage: Recovering the Biblical View* (San Francisco: Harper and Row, 1987) 34–35; Otto A. Piper, *The Biblical View of Sex and Marriage* (London: James Nisbit, 1960) 31–32; Brain S. Rosner, *Paul, Scripture, and Ethics: A Study of 1 Corinthians 5–7* (Grand Rapids, MI: Baker, 1994) 159; Peter J. Tomson, *Paul and the Jewish Law: Halakha in the Letters of the Apostle to the Gentiles*. Compendia Rerum ludaicarum ad Novum Testamentum III.i (Minneapolis: Fortress, 1990) 107; D. Daube, *The New Testament and Rabbinic Judaism*, 365; N. Herz, "A Hebrew Word in Greek Disguise: I Cor. VII," *Expository Times* 7 (1895) 48, quoted in Instone-Brewer, *Divorce and Remarriage in the Bible*, 194.

86. The meaning of this word as "sexual intercourse" is well attested in the light of widespread euphemism, ἅπτω, referring to sexual intercourse in the literature of the first century AD and before. See Plato, *Laws* 8.840a, "οὔτε τίνος πώποτε γυναικὸς ἄπσατο οὐδ' αὐ παιδός." Plato. *Platonis Opera*, ed. John Burnet. Oxford University Press, 1903 [online], Available at http://www.perseus.tufts.edu/cgi-bin/ptext?lookup=Plat.+Laws +840a, Accessed on 28 October 2000; Gen 20:6, LXX: "ἕνεκεν τούτου οὐκ ἀφῆκά σε ἅψασθαι αὐτῆς;" Ruth 2:9, LXX: "ἰδοὺ ἐνετειλάμην τοῖς παιδαρίοις τοῦ μὴ ἅψασθαί σου;" Flavius Josephus, *Antiquitates Judaicae* 1.163: ". . . καὶ Θεάσασθαι σπουδάσας οἷος τε ὑν ἄπσαστηναι τύς Σάρρας." Flavius Josephus, *Antiquitates Judaicae*, ed. B. Niese [online]; See also Fee, *The First Epistle to the Corinthians*, 275; W. F. Orr and J. A. Walther, *I Corinthians*, 206.

87. I maintain the view that Paul quotes in v1b a phrase or general idea from the Corinthians' letter. If this verse is understood as Paul's introductory statement which expresses his belief it will create a contradiction with Paul's non-ascetic expressions in some

tained properly through the expression of spouses' love to each other in a sexual relationship. "The husband should give to his wife her conjugal rights, and likewise the wife to her husband," (1 Cor 7:3, RSV). He even goes further in his argument to make a direct connection with the law of the slave wife in Exod 21:10, presenting the marital bond between husband and wife established through conjugal relationship as the expression of the authority of the owner to the slave. Paul presents this as a mutual fulfillment. "For the wife does not rule over her own body, but the husband does; likewise the husband does not rule over his own body, but the wife does," (1 Cor 7:4, RSV). This obligation is so significant and crucial for the proper maintenance of marriage that the apostle provides only one proper reason for abstinence, restricted with two further limitations. "Do not refuse one another except perhaps by agreement for a season, that you may devote yourselves to prayer; but then come together again, lest Satan tempt you through lack of self-control" (1 Cor 7:5, RSV). Only for prayer are the spouses permitted to limit their conjugal relationship but only for a particular period of time and based on their mutual consent. This is once again a close resemblance to the rabbis' reason for abstaining from intercourse with one's spouse (*m. Ketub.* 5.6). The danger in case of the lack of fulfillment of this obligation in marriage is not only the possibility of a potential marital breakdown but a road to immorality and sin (1 Cor 7:2, 5). Paul is declaring marriage as the proper place for fulfillment of the sexual drive of both man and woman (1 Cor 7:9). The mutual fulfillment of conjugal rights between the spouses is to be based not on demand but on willing submission, as it is established in the marriage contract.[88]

Paul includes in his discussion about marital and celibate life (1 Cor 7:32–35) references to the material stipulations related to marriage maintenance. The nature of these stipulations might be defined as material due to the leading word for the argument μεριμνάω used in the present context (1 Cor 7:32, 33, 34). The word is used in Matthew 6:25–34 in the context of worldly affairs referring to "eating, drinking, and clothing." In the present passage it is placed in the context of worldly affairs in relation

---

of his letters (1 Cor 9:19–23; 10: 25–26, 29b–30; Rom 14; Eph 5:25–33; Col 2:20–21, 1 Tim 4:3). See also Fee, *The First Epistle to the Corinthians*, 276.

88. Also Instone-Brewer, *Divorce and Remarriage in the Bible*, 192–194.

to marriage (1 Cor 7:33, 34). However, here it is used in a positive way[89] being also used to refer to the affairs of the Lord (1 Cor 7:32, 34).[90] Hence, what Paul is referring to are the material stipulations of both spouses in the marriage. According to their contextually shaped role in marriage both husband and wife are obligated to support each other materially. This echoes the material obligations summarised in the legislation of Exod 21:10 of "food and clothing," which have been developed by Jewish interpreters to refer to the material stipulations of marriage and the material neglect as lawful grounds for divorce. Paul leads the discussion here to present the importance of the fulfillment of the material obligations of the spouses for the proper maintenance of marriage, ("but the married man is anxious [μεριμνάω] about worldly affairs [earthly responsibilities, NLT], how to please his wife" [1 Cor 7:33, RSV], ". . . but the married woman is anxious (μεριμνάω) about worldly affairs [earthly responsibilities, NLT], how to please her husband." [1 Cor 7:34, RSV]). The weight placed on this obligation in marriage is so great that it parallels the work of the Lord for the ones who are not married (". . . The unmarried man is anxious [μεριμνάω] about the affairs of the Lord, how to please the Lord" [1 Cor 7:32, RSV], ". . . And the unmarried woman or girl is anxious [μεριμνάω] about the affairs of the Lord, how to be holy in body and spirit . . ." [1 Cor 7:34, RSV]). Thus, for Paul the matter of material obligations in marriage is very serious and fundamental for the proper sustaining of every marital union. The apostle is concerned about the Lord's work, and especially in the present difficult context[91] (1 Cor 7: 26) of the Corinthian believers, it is better for those who are not married to stay as they are since the material obligations of marriage will consume their time and energy.[92] However, if they marry they do not sin, (1 Cor 7:28, 37) but they should be aware of the seriousness of their marital responsibilities

---

89. Also "17825: μεριμνάω," in *Friberg Greek Lexicon*, BibleWorks for Windows. Version 5.0. 020w, 2001.

90. Another positive usage of the word in Paul is 1 Cor 12:25. (Rudolf Bultmann, "Merimnáō, Promerimnáō, Mérimna," in *TDNT* 4:589–93.)

91. This might refer to the grain shortage or other material crises which had burdened the Corinthian society between 40–60 AD. (Bruce Winter, "Secular and Christian Responses to Corinthian Famines," *TynBul* 40 [1989]: 86–87, quoted in Instone-Brewer, *Divorce and Remarriage in the Bible*, 195.)

92. Also Instone-Brewer, *Divorce and Remarriage in the Bible*, 195–97.

before they make this step.⁹³ Paul emphasizes this when he argues for the preservation of marriage by believers when unbelievers are willing to do so (1 Cor 7:12–14). However, when the unbeliever wants to leave the marriage, such a significant failure of keeping ones marital obligations is established that Paul considers the believer free to divorce and remarry (1 Cor 7:15).

The full expression of the marital stipulations is depicted by the author of Ephesians through a comparison of Christian marriage with the symbolic presentation of the relationship between Christ and the church as matrimonial union. This portrait of the ideal marriage is grounded on the presentation of the marital union between Yahweh and Israel/Judah.⁹⁴ The picture depicted in Ezek 16:9–12, 16–19⁹⁵ presents Yahweh as the groom and Judah as the bride and narrates the fulfillment of the covenant stipulations of the groom according to the law in Exod 21:10–11. The detailed description of the groom's fulfillment of the marriage requirements shows the abundance of Yahweh's love and contrasts it with Judah's unfaithfulness and lack of fulfillment of her part of the marital stipulations. The picture depicted by the author of Ephesians is entirely positive and encourages both spouses to imitate the example of Christ as a groom in his relationship to the church his bride.

---

93. This is important in light of the Corinthians' problem that under the influence of Hellenistic dualism they valued more everything related to the sphere of spirituality than the matters related to the physical and material world (see 1 Cor 1:7; 4:7; 14:37). See also J. D. Tabor, *The Jewish Roman World of Jesus* [online]; Fee, *The First Epistle to the Corinthians*, 10, 11, 307; Hafemann, *Corinthians*, 174.

94. Also A. T. Lincoln, *Ephesians* (Dallas: Word, 2002).

95. "Then I bathed you with water and washed off the blood from you, and anointed you with oil. I clothed you with embroidered cloth and with sandals of fine leather; I bound you in fine linen and covered you with rich fabric. I adorned you with ornaments: I put bracelets on your arms, a chain on your neck, a ring on your nose, earrings in your ears, and a beautiful crown upon your head . . . . You took some of your garments, and made for yourself colorful shrines, and on them played the whore; nothing like this has ever been or ever shall be. You also took your beautiful jewels of my gold and my silver that I had given you, and made for yourself male images, and with them played the whore; and you took your embroidered garments to cover them, and set my oil and my incense before them. Also my bread that I gave you—I fed you with choice flour and oil and honey—you set it before them as a pleasing odor; and so it was, says the Lord GOD" (Ezek 16:9–12, 16–19, NRS).

> Husbands should love their wives, just as Christ loved the Church and sacrificed himself for her to make her holy by washing her in cleansing water with a form of words, so that when he took the Church to himself she would be glorious, with no speck or wrinkle or anything like that, but holy and faultless. In the same way, husbands must love their wives as they love their own bodies; for a man to love his wife is for him to love himself. A man never hates his own body, but he feeds it and looks after it; and that is the way Christ treats the Church, because we are parts of his Body. This is why a man leaves his father and mother and becomes attached to his wife, and the two become one flesh. This mystery has great significance, but I am applying it to Christ and the Church. To sum up: you also, each one of you, must love his wife as he loves himself; and let every wife respect her husband. (Eph 5:25–33, NJB)

The core of the whole discussion is the love of Christ to the church and the husband to the wife. The leading force of the argument is found in the groom's care of the bride.[96] The concept of care is based on an example of how man loves his own body and takes care of it by feeding[97] and cloth-

---

[96]. Francois Wessels remarks well the emphasis in the text (Eph 5:21–33) on the husband's obligations for material and emotional support to his wife as well as identifies the mutual sharing in these obligations by both spouses. However, even though he recognizes the roots of the passage in the marital ethics of Hellenistic Judaism, he fails to acknowledge the requirements of material and emotional support by the husband in both Jewish and Greco-Roman marriage traditions and contracts. (See Francois Wessels, "Exegesis and Proclamation: Ephesians 5:21–33," *Journal of Theology for Southern Africa* 67 [1989]: 69–75)

[97]. The word ἐκτρέφω is used in the present context (Eph 5:29) to refer to provision of food for nourishment during a considerable period of time. With the same meaning the word appears in the LXX (Gen 47:17) and in literature contemporary to the NT (Plutarch, *Lycurg.* 16, 4; PRyl. 178, 14 [I AD], in Catalogue of the Greek Papyri in the John Rylands Library, Manchester, Eng. I; II 1911–15) as well as in the NT (Matt 25:37) (See also J. P. Louw and E. A. Nida, eds., *Louw-Nida Greek-English Lexicon of the New Testament Based on Semantic Domains*, 2nd ed. [New York: United Bible Societies, 1988], [electronic edition], BibleWorks v. 5.0.020w, 2001; Timothy and Barbara Friberg, *Analytical Lexicon to the Greek New Testament*, 2000 edition. [electronic edition], BibleWorks v. 5.0.020w, 2001; Arndt, W., Gingrich, F. W., Danker and W. Bauer, *A Greek-English Lexicon of the New Testament and Other Early Christian Literature*. A translation and adaption of the fourth revised and augmented edition of *Walter Bauer's Griechisch-deutsches Worterbuch zu den Schrift en des Neuen Testaments und der ubrigen urchristlichen Literatur* [Chicago: University of Chicago Press, 1979], electronic edition by Logos Research Systems, 1996; Instone-Brewer, *Divorce and Remarriage in the Bible*, 229, 230.)

ing⁹⁸ it.⁹⁹ This same treatment is resembled by Christ's relationship to the church as husband. The picture is intensified with the reference to the church as Christ's body. The husband is exhorted to imitate the expressions of this love of Christ to the church toward his wife in the same way. The fundamental dynamics of marital relationship are depicted here on the basis of the law expressed in Exod 21:10 where the basic stipulations for the proper support in marriage are clearly stated.¹⁰⁰ The author leads the argument through the presentation of the first marital union which depicts the same covenantal dynamics with the expression of a new social allegiance which depends on love and support, (cf. Gen 2:24).¹⁰¹ The

---

98. The word, θάλπω, strictly speaking, refers to providing warmth and in its present context (Eph 5:29) as keeping the body warm most probably through the use of clothing. With that meaning the word is used in Classical Greek (*The Abridged Liddell-Scott Greek-English Lexicon*) as well as in Josephus, *The Antiquities of the Jews*, 7.343. This literal meaning of the word might also be expanded here in Eph 5:29 as referring to providing a constant care as mother for her children (1 Thess 2:7). (Also W. Bauer, *A Greek-English Lexicon of the New Testament*; J. P. Louw and E. A. Nida, eds., *Louw-Nida Greek-English Lexicon*; Timothy and Barbara Friberg, *Analytical Lexicon to the Greek New Testament*, 2000 edition. [electronic edition]; Instone-Brewer, *Divorce and Remarriage in the Bible*, 229, 230).

99. Also Instone-Brewer, *Divorce and Remarriage in the Bible*, 229, 230; R. Jamieson, A. R. Fausset, and David Brown, *A Commentary, Critical and Explanatory, on the Old and New Testaments* (Oak Harbor, WA: Logos Research Systems, 1997).

100. Also Instone-Brewer, *Divorce and Remarriage in the Bible*, 229, 230; Jamieson, Fausset, and Brown, *A Commentary, Critical and Explanatory, on the Old and New Testaments*. (electronic edition).

101. The phrase used in Eph 5:31 σάρκα μίαν is the same used by the authors of the LXX to translate the Hebrew phrase לְבָשָׂר אֶחָד (Gen 2:24). The latter suggests a three dimensional character of husband–wife relationship, i.e. social, domestic, and physical. (H. Blocher, *In the Beginning*, 106; H. C. Leupold, *Exposition of Genesis*, vol.1, 137; S. Zeisler, *What Is Marriage?* [online];) The husband is no more associated with his parents but with his wife. She is the object of his allegiance and to her he will express his love through material support and physical attraction and connection. (S. Bacchiocchi, *The Marriage Covenant* [online]) The establishment of the marital relationship goes through two steps of leaving one's parents (2:24a) and cleaving to one's spouse (2:24b), which resembles the picture of a covenant relationship. (See also Mal 2:14; Prov 2:17; S. Bacchiocchi, *The Marriage Covenant* [online]; Walter Brueggemann, *Genesis*, 47; W. J. Dumbrell, *Covenant and Creation*, 36; K. A. Mathews, *Genesis 1–11:26*, p. 222; J. M. Sprinkle, *Old Testament Perspectives on Divorce and Remarriage*. Electronic edition by Galaxie Software; J. E. Adams, *Marriage Divorce and Remarriage in the Bible*, 16, 17.) This is well expressed in the covenant relationship between Yahweh and Israel. This threefold character of marital union is reflected in Ex 21:10 in the form of three specific stipulations which establish the ground for a marital covenant relationship on the basis of a mutual obligation of the spouses for provision of food, clothing, and love (conjugal rights). This law has served

same connection between Exod 21:10 and Gen 2:24 with the purpose to express the nature of the marital union and to define its stipulations is made by Samaritan marriage contracts.[102]

> And he married her, 'and she became his wife' (Gen 24:67), excluded and withheld from every man apart from him. And he shall be her husband and shall treat her according to the manner with which women (are treated), as the Lord said through his servant Moses: 'He shall not diminish her food, her clothing, or her marital rights' (Ex 21:10). And he upholds her vows and her abstentions, or dissolves them. And towards him she is obliged to marital love; she shall listen to his words and not contradict him; 'and she shall be a fitting help for him' (Gen 2:18). But he should cleave to her as the Lord said: 'Therefore a man leaves his father and his mother, and cleaves to his wife, and from the two of them there becomes one flesh' (Gen 2:24, Samaritan Pent.). And this document was written, and the testimony of the witnesses shall be a perfect testimony.[103]

Even though the contract has an addition, ("she shall listen to his words and not contradict him"), which finds its roots in Samaritan theology as a whole, it shows the attempt of the Samaritans to come as close as possible to the Scriptural nature of marriage.[104] The husband's obligations and responsibilities are well defined and firmly based on Scripture. The wife's role in the marriage is also well defined scripturally. The document is following the general approach to refer primarily to the husband's stipulations so it does not engage in presentation of the wife's which are

---

to establish the three most basic stipulations of the Jewish marriage covenant in the Jewish Bible (Ps 132; Hos 2:3–13; Ezek 16:1–13), the Mishnah, and in latter Judaism as found in the marriage contracts in Geniza collection. (See *The Mishnah: Ketubot* 5:1–9, A New Translation by Jacob Neusner, 387–90; Jewish Marriage Contracts in *The Princeton Geniza Project* [online]; See also E. M. Yamauchi, *Cultural Aspects of Marriage in the Ancient World*, 245, 246.)

102. Even though the surviving contracts are from the sixteenth and eighteenth centuries AD, the general understanding is that the Samaritan tradition has remained unchanged. (Reinhard Pummer, *Samaritan Marriage Contracts and Deeds of Divorce*, vol. I. [Wiesbaden: Harrassowitz, 1993] 2; Instone-Brewer, *Divorce and Remarriage in the Bible*, 223)

103. R. Pummer, *Samaritan Marriage Contracts and Deeds of Divorce*, vol. I., p. 51.

104. Instone-Brewer, *Divorce and Remarriage in the Bible*, 224.

assumed according to cultural mores and in a mutual resemblance to the husband's.[105]

Another place where marital stipulations are clearly expressed according to Exod 21:10–11 with an attempt to communicate a close Scriptural concept of marriage are Karaite's marriage contracts.[106] The following are presentations of the husband's and wife's marriage obligations.

Husband's obligations:

> And I will dress, clothe, support, respect and esteem her and I will fulfil all her needs and desires to the best of my strength and possibilities. And I will be with her in truth, justice, love, and affection and I will not afflict her, act against her or oppress her and I will not diminish her food, clothes and sexual intercourse, like the children of Israel who feed, support, dress, clothe and esteem their pure wives, and do all they owe them in faithfulness and honesty. (n° 51)[107]

Wife's obligations:

> And this bride Rivqa accepted the words of our beloved and dear Elcazar, the groom, and wished to be married to him, to be his wife and companion in purity, holiness and awe, to obey, esteem, respect and help him, and to do in his house all that the pure daughters of Israel do in the house of their husbands, and to behave towards him in truth, justice, love, compassion, honesty and faith, to be under his dominion, and to have her desire directed towards him. (n° 26)[108]

While the husband's statement does clearly refer to the provision of "food, clothes and sexual intercourse," the wife's declaration makes this implicitly through reference to her domestic work and "her desire directed towards him." These two expressions of the fundamental marital stipulations parallel each other and provide the grounds for continuing proper maintenance of the marriage. The essential role of the stipulations for the proper execution of the marriage contract and the continuous efficient function-

---

105. Also Instone-Brewer, *Divorce and Remarriage in the Bible*, 223, 224.

106. Karaites might be considered "a back-to-Scripture movement" which began around the seventh century AD and whose writings date from the tenth to thirteenth centuries AD. (Instone-Brewer, *Divorce and Remarriage in the Bible*, 221.)

107. Olszowy-Schlanger, *Karaite Marriage Documents from the Cairo Geniza*, 186–87.

108. This is one of two closely related statements of the wife's obligations expressed through an agent. (Ibid., 205.)

ing of the marital union is well attested throughout Greco-Roman and Jewish marriage contracts contemporaneous to the NT.

Greco-Roman marriage and divorce papyri might be defined as a homogeneous group of documents which share close characteristics due to involvement of the most essential elements related to the matters of marriage and divorce and the customs connected with them. The most common features of the marriage and divorce papyri might be characterized as matters related to the location and the time frame of the agreement, financial matters regarding the dowry, matters regarding provision in the case of death, stipulations related to the behavior of the spouses in marriage, confirmation of the divorced wife's freedom to remarry, and assurance of the legitimacy of the contract through the signatures of the witnesses.[109] The following papyri are chosen as the clearest representations of Greco-Roman marriage and divorce agreements by scholars who have been engaged in extensive papyri research.[110] The texts offered in the following analysis, for the present discussions have been cleared from unnecessary details such as lists of properties, dates, and locations which are referred in the brackets. Also the names of the people involved have been replaced by abbreviations related to their gender (W for wife or bride, H for husband or groom, WM, WF, and WB for wife's mother, father, and brother).

The following Greco-Roman marriage contract underlines the usual Greco-Roman divorce by separation without specification of particular grounds and consideration of the role of the initiating party. However, the contract does refer to the condition of the spouses' relationship assuming fulfillment of their responsibilities and obligations whose neglect might have brought the change of the marital situation.

>   Marriage Contract, AD 66, Bacchias, Egypt
>   (GM66 = *P.Ryl.*II.154):
>
>   [Time, Place]. H acknowledges to WF that he has received from him as a dowry on his daughter W, who has previously been living

---

109. Instone-Brewer, *1 Corinthians 7 in the Light of the Graeco-Roman Marriage and Divorce Papyri* [online].

110. A. S. Hunt, C. C. Edgar, eds., *Select Papyri*, LCL 266, 282, 360 (Cambridge: Harvard University Press; London: Heinemann, 1959–70) v. 1. *Non-Literary Papyri: Private Affairs*; Instone-Brewer, *1 Corinthians 7 in the Light of the Graeco-Roman Marriage and Divorce Papyri* [online].

with H as his wife, [list of dowry], and as *parapherna*, [list of wife's personal belongings], and without valuation in usufruct and as a gift from the current year, [a field, described in detail]. Wherefore let the parties to the marriage, W and H, live together blamelessly as they have previously been doing, H conducting all the agricultural work of each year on [the field]. If a difference (διαφορᾶς) arise between them and they separate from each other ([χ]ωρίζονται ἀπ ἀλλήλων), whether H sends away (ἀποπέμποντος) W or she voluntarily leaves him (ἐκουσίω[ς ἀ]παλλασσομέν[η]ς [ἀ]π αὐτοῦ), [the field] shall belong to WF or, if he is no longer alive, to W. And H shall moreover return to her the aforesaid dowry and the *parapherna* in whatever state they may eventually be through wear, in the case of dismissal (ἀποπομπῆς) immediately, and in the case of her voluntarily departure (ἐκουσ[ίο]υ ἀπαλλαγῆς) within 30 days of demand. In whatever year of separation (χ]ωρ[ι]σμὸ[ν]) of the parties to the marriage takes place, the proceeds of the holding for the 12 months of the year of the divorce ([ἀ]ποπλοκῆς) shall be divided [more details]. To enforce the terms of the contract WF or, if he is no longer alive, W and those for her shall have the right of execution upon H and all his property as if by legal decision. The signatory is WF, H being illiterate.[111]

The introductory statements of the marriage certificate give the idea that it had been written later in the marriage and not at the time of its initiation. This was the practice when the initial marriage contract was offered verbally (γάμος ἄγραφος) and due to the appearance of the children and issues related to them as heirs or the increase of the value of the dowry involved, it became necessary to put the marriage agreement in a written form (γάμος ἔνγραφος). The contract suggests that the conditions of marriage so far have been acceptable for both husband and wife because of the designation of their behavior toward each as being without any blame. The statement constitutes a foundational assumption that the proper and continuous functioning of the marriage is based on the mutual fulfillment of the marriage stipulations. The following statement in the contract which suggests a break of a good relationship due to some unspecified

---

111. *P.Ryl*.II.154. The Duke Databank of Documentary Papyri [online], Available at http://www.perseus.tufts.edu/cgi-bin/ptext?doc=Perseus%3Aab0%3Apap%2CP.Ryl.&query=2%3A154, Accessed on 27 August 2004. Translation based on A. S. Hunt, *Select Papyri* 1:12–17, quoted in David Instone-Brewer, "1 Corinthians 7 in the Light of the Graeco-Roman Marriage and Divorce Papyri," *Tyndale Bulletin* 51.2 (2001) 103, 104; and Instone-Brewer, *1 Corinthians 7 in the Light of the Graeco-Roman Marriage and Divorce Papyri* [online].

differences confirms that the previous relationship had been based on the mutually accepted stipulations which had been violated and thus assumed a potential marital breakdown. From that point on the contract develops in narrating the consequences of the marital dissolution for both parties. The consequences do not depend on the guilt of any of the parties for the divorce. The dowry should be returned if either the wife is sent away or departs voluntarily. The only difference in the payment procedure is in terms of the period in which she needs to receive the dowry. However, the fact that the wife needs to receive the dowry immediately in case of dismissal might imply that the husband has failed to fulfill the marriage stipulations toward her and is required to return her dowry without delay.[112] Nevertheless, the contract is not interested in defining whether there is a guilty party but in providing a fair treatment of the financial belongings.

This approach to divorce without clear specification of any particular grounds based on the desire of one of the parties and through a simple departure has been under Paul's critique in dealing with such cases in the Corinthian church. In 1 Cor 7:10–15 Paul deals with 3 different cases of undertaking such a divorce action by one of the parties conditioned by the religious status of both partners. Thus, in his argumentation Paul is prohibiting divorce and remarriage on the basis of the tradition of Christ's teaching on these matters when both spouses are believers (vv10–11) and when the unbelieving party is willing to live with the believer (vv12–14). However, Paul allows divorce and remarriage of the believing party when the unbelieving party divorces (v15). The latter situation in light of rabbinic comprehension of such cases[113] and some Greco-Roman contracts, such as the following one, casts light on the grounds of Paul's argumenta-

---

112. "The adultery of a husband, if he is of age, is punished by requiring him to return the dowry at once, if it was to have been returned after a certain time; if his offence is less grave, it must be returned within six months . . . ." (Uplian, *Rules* 6.13, in *Women's Life in Greece and Rome*, trans. Lefkowitz and Fant, 116); See also Judith Evans Grubbs, *Law and Family in Late Antiquity: The Emperor Constantine's Marriage Legislation* (Oxford: Oxford University Press, 1999) 227.

113. Rabbinic discussions engaged in defining the necessary material support through a third party if the husband left for a period of time (*m. Ketub.* 5.8). The lack of establishing such material provision constituted grounds for divorce. However, if emotional support was not provided for over a month, even if material maintenance was supplied through a third party, divorce was prescribed due to emotional neglect (*m. Ketub.* 7.1). (Also Instone-Brewer, *Divorce and Remarriage in the Bible*, 110.)

tion as a violation of the marriage stipulations, which is a refusal of material and emotional support by the divorcing, deserting party.

The present contract employs several words which refer to the divorce action (χωρίζω,[114] ἀποπέμπω,[115] ἀπαλλάσσω,[116] ἀποπομπή,[117] ἀπαλλαγή,[118] and ἀποπλοκή[119]) without specific evident intention to provide different nuances for the sake of the argument. This underlines the usual Greco-Roman practice of divorce through separation and at the same time confirms that separation is treated as legal divorce in spite of the absence of any document. In relation to Paul who also utilizes several terms (χωρίζω,[120] 1 Cor 7:10, 11, 15; ἀφίημι,[121] 1 Cor 7:11, 12, 13) to refer to divorce actions, it is important to understand these words as referring to legal divorce in light of the contemporary context.[122]

The following marriage contract gives more weight to the foundational stipulations and their fulfillment with the related penalties in case of indifference by any of the spouses. This extensive treatment of the marriage stipulations underlines their importance for the Greco-Roman marriage contracts and casts light upon a tradition to summarize these stipulations in some of the contracts without diminishing their value for the marriage preservation. A usual summary might be the following: "Let the parties live together in a righteous marriage (γάμου δίκαια)."[123] The

---

114. To separate, to part, to divide (*Liddell and Scott's Greek-English Lexicon*, abridged edition [Oxford: Oxford University Press, 1979] 793.)

115. To send off or away, to dismiss (*Liddell and Scott's Greek-English Lexicon*, 91.)

116. To set free, to release, to depart, to go away, to cease (*Liddell and Scott's Greek-English Lexicon*, 76, 77.)

117. Sending away, getting rid of (*Liddell and Scott's Greek-English Lexicon*, 91.)

118. Deliverance, release, a removal, a going away, departure (*Liddell and Scott's Greek-English Lexicon*, 76.)

119. Chemical separation. (Instone-Brewer, *1 Corinthians 7 in the Light of the Graeco-Roman Marriage and Divorce Papyri* [online].)

120. Separate; pass. separate oneself, be separated (of divorce); leave, depart; be taken away. (Barclay M. Newman, Jr., ed. *A Concise Greek-English Dictionary of the New Testament* [United Bible Societies, 1971], electronic edition in BibleWorks for Windows v. 5.0.020w, BibleWorks, LLC, 2001.)

121. Leave; leave behind, forsake, neglect; let go, dismiss, divorce (B. M. Newman, Jr., ed. *A Concise Greek-English Dictionary of the New Testament*, [electronic edition]).

122. Instone-Brewer, *Divorce and Remarriage in the 1st and 21st Century*, section 1–2 [online].

123. Idem, *1 Corinthians 7 in the Light of the Graeco-Roman Marriage and Divorce Papyri* [online].

overall concern has been directed to complete support. The nature of the penalties given follows the usual model found not only in the Greco-Roman marriage contracts but also in their Jewish counterparts. The guilt of the husband is penalized by the return of the dowry with some extra payment and the guilt of the wife is charged with the losing of the dowry.

> Marriage Certificate, 92 BC, Tebtunis, Egypt
> (GM-92 = *P.Tebt.*I.104):

[Date, Place]. H acknowledges to W, having with her as guardian WB that he has received from her [money], the dowry for herself, W agreed upon with him. W shall live with H, obeying him (πειθαρχοῦσα αὐτοῦ) as a wife should (ὡς προσῆ[κό]ν ἐστιν) her husband, owning their property in common with him. H shall supply to W all necessaries (δέοντα π[ά]ντα) and clothing ([ἡμ]ατισμόν) and whatever is proper for a wedded wife, (τἆλλα ὅσα προσήκει γυναικὶ γαμετῆι) whether he is at home or abroad, according to their means (κατὰ δύναμιν). It shall not be lawful for H to bring in any other wife but W, nor to keep a concubine or boy, nor to have children by another women while W lives (ζώσ[η]σ), nor to live in another house over which W is not mistress, nor to eject or insult or ill-treat her, nor to alienate any of their property to W's disadvantage. If he is proved to be doing any of these things or does not supply her with necessaries (δέοντα) and clothing (ἱματισμόν) and the rest as stated, H shall forfeit forthwith to W the dowry [money]. In the same way it shall not be lawful for W to spend the night or day away from the house of H without H's consent or to have intercourse with another man or to dishonour the common household or to bring shame upon H in anything that causes a husband shame. If W wishes of her own will to separate (ἐκουσαβούλη[ται] ἀπαλλάσσεσθαι) from H, H shall repay her the bare dowry within ten days from the day it is demanded back. If he does not repay it as stated he shall forthwith forfeit the dowry he has received increased by one half. [Witnesses][124]

---

124. *P.Tebt.*I.104. The Duke Databank of Documentary Papyri. P.Tebt.: The Tebtunis Papyri [online], Available at http://www.perseus.tufts.edu/cgi-bin/ptext?doc=Perseus%3Aabo%3Apap%2CP.Tebt.&query=1%3A104, Accessed on 26 August 2004. Translation based on A. S. Hunt, *Select Papyri* 1:5–9, quoted in Instone-Brewer, *1 Corinthians 7 in the Light of the Graeco-Roman Marriage and Divorce Papyri*, 108 and idem, *1 Corinthians 7 in the Light of the Graeco-Roman Marriage and Divorce Papyri* [online].

The contract starts with establishing the financial aspect of marriage which will play significant role both for its guidance and for its maintenance materially and emotionally. The dowry is given to the young family, agreed upon by the husband, and executed by both spouses. The whole contract in its structural arrangement makes references to both husband and wife in relation to their mutual ownership of their property, the fulfillment of the marriage stipulations, and receiving of the penalties in case of their disregarding their obligations. The equal responsibility for fulfilling the stipulations of both spouses is found in the Jewish and Aramaic contracts. This manner of presentation of the marriage roles of both husband and wife is well attested in Paul's treatment of marriage issues. Paul refers to both husband and wife when discussing their obligations to each other in fulfilling the stipulation referring to conjugal rights (1 Cor 7:1-5). He also applies to both of them matters of material support in marriage (1 Cor 7:32-34). Arguing his point throughout the discussion related to marriage, divorce, and remarriage in 1 Cor 7, he addresses equally husband and wife.[125]

The present contract establishes the financial framework of marriage in order to bring out the core matter of consideration, the marriage stipulations. This might be interpreted as an attempt to further assure the fulfillment of the stipulations whose failure would bring financial penalty to the guilty party. The stipulations listed here might be categorized in two groups, positive and negative. The first group includes material and emotional support expressed as "all necessaries (δέοντα π[ά]ντα) and clothing ([ἡμ]ατισμόν) and whatever is proper for a wedded wife (τἆλλα ὅσα προσήκει γυναικὶ γαμετῆι)." The time for their fulfillment is established as constant while marriage still continues even when the husband is not present at home for a period of time. The wife's responsibilities are not explicitly mentioned here except the reference to obey the husband. But in light of the mutuality of presentation in the contract it might be expected that they are assumed according to the general expectations from the wife in the Greco-Roman family. The second group of stipulations is expressed negatively. It might be considered as a failure of fulfilling the

---

125. David Instone-Brewer, "1 Corinthians 7 in the Light of the Jewish Greek and Aramaic Marriage and Divorce Papyri," *Tyndale Bulletin* (2001) [online], Available at http://www.tyndale.cam.ac.uk/Brewer/MarriagePapyri/1Cor_7a.htm, Accessed on 26 August 2004.

stipulations specified in the first group,[126] but also a further elaboration of such a failure. The husband is expected to be faithful to his wife both emotionally and materially.[127] He is also required to treat the wife with all necessary respect and admiration.[128] In the same way the wife is expected to be faithful to her husband, to respect him and preserve the honor of his image in all her actions in the family and the society as whole.[129] If these stipulations are not fulfilled the marriage contract is terminated, and the marriage is ended with the execution of the penalties in relation to the guilty party which failed to fulfill the stipulations. The new state of divorce for both spouses is assured with the completion of financial matters. The divorce status of both parties is not further elaborated as defining the possibility for remarriage since such an action has been assumed in the contemporary society. The clause which might be understood as restricting the rights of the husband to remarry, providing the duration of time for fulfilling the marital stipulation, "while W lives," should be understood as limited to the context of marriage. The fulfillment of the marriage stipulations specified in the contract is expected only while the marriage exists. After the marriage has ended the marriage contract does not function anymore as a legal document to facilitate rules and obligations for the former spouses. The legal force in this new condition is given to the divorce certificate. References to such a clause appear in Paul's writings as well (Rom 7:2; 1 Cor 7:39). A close look at these passages show that Paul has used this clause in a similar way to refer to fulfillment of the marital obligations while the marriage exists. The married woman (ὕπανδρος γυνὴ) is charged with adultery if she "lives with another man while her husband is alive" (Rom 7:3, NRS). Marriage contract regulations are in force because the marital bond is unbroken. The intention of Paul here is to use an example with the binding force of the law of marriage. When marriage

---

126. "... does not supply her with necessaries (δέοντα) and clothing (ἱματισμόν) and the rest as stated, ..."

127. "It shall not be lawful for H to bring in any other wife but W, nor to keep a concubine or boy, nor to have children by another women while W lives (ζώσ[η]σ), nor to live in another house over which W is not mistress, ... nor to alienate any of their property to W's disadvantage."

128. "... nor to eject or insult or ill-treat her."

129. "In the same way it shall not be lawful for W to spend the night or day away from the house of H without H's consent or to have intercourse with another man or to dishonor the common household or to bring shame upon H in anything that causes a husband shame."

is established only the death of one of the partners might bring freedom to the other. Paul is not as concerned here with offering solutions to marriage problems and legitimizing grounds for divorce and remarriage as he is interested in giving a vivid example of Christian deliverance from the Law. This is accomplished only through the association of the believers with the death of Christ. Hence, Paul is taking the perspective of the marriage contract being in force to bind the spouses to a lifelong union which is not expected to be broken except through the death of one of the spouses.[130] The latter has been the usual expectation of the Jewish marriage contracts. Thus, any remarriage from this point of view is defined as adultery. However, this view of marriage does not exclude the possible dissolution of marriage through legitimate divorce on the grounds of a lack of fulfillment of the marriage stipulations.[131] The legitimacy of such a divorce brings the legitimacy of the subsequent remarriage which cannot be characterized as adultery. This argumentation is not foreign to Paul but it is not part of his intentions in this passage.[132] In the same way, leading his argumentation according to his main concern, Paul is using the clause in 1 Cor 7:39, 40 to establish his view about widows with a vivid expression of their rights to remarry anyone they wish only in the Lord. Hence, in such a context Paul is not interested to develop any argumentation about divorce and the subsequent remarriage of the divorcee. The widows are to look toward the possibility of remarriage without any concern of fulfilling levirate marriage or preserving their single status if they do not wish.[133]

There is a statement in the present contract which might seem to lead to the no grounds divorce through willing separation as practiced in the Greco-Roman society, "if W wishes of her own will to separate (ἐκουσαβούλη[ται] ἀπαλλάσσεσθαι) from H." However, in the context of

---

130. Also J. D. G. Dunn, *Romans 1–8*. WBC, vol. 38A (Dallas: Word, 2002), Nashville: Thomas Nelson. Libronix Digital Library System 2.0. 2000–2002.

131. Also Keener, *The IVP Bible Background Commentary: New Testament* (Downers Grove, IL: InterVarsity, 1993). Logos Research Systems, Libronix Digital Library System 2.0. 2000–2002.

132. Also Instone-Brewer, *Divorce and Remarriage in the Bible*, 209–12; Guy Duty, *Divorce and Remarriage* (Minneapolis, MN: Bethany Fellowship, 1967), 84–91, 136–37; S. Bacchiocchi, *The Marriage Covenant*, 189–90; W. W. Wiersbe, *The Bible Exposition Commentary* (Wheaton, IL: Victor, 1996, c1989). Logos Research Systems, Libronix Digital Library System 2.0. 2000–2002.

133. Instone-Brewer, *Divorce and Remarriage in the Bible*, 210, 211.

the whole contract and the following requirements of the returning of the dowry, it might be understood that the wife's desire to divorce has occurred due to the husband's fault.

The legal formulation of marital breakdown is well defined in the marriage contract with consequences for both parties. The attestation of the new social and material status of the former spouses is accomplished through a divorce deed. The main goal of that legal document was to acknowledge the dissolution of the marriage and the nullification of the marriage contract in order to provide confirmation of the freedom of the man and the woman from the marriage stipulations. The divorce deed is not intended to discuss the grounds for the marriage dissolution but to resolve the matters related to it.

> Divorce Deed, 13 BC, Alexandria, Egypt
> (GD-13 = BGU IV.1103):
>
> To the Protarchus, from W with her guardian WB and from H. W and H agree that they have separated from each other (κεχωρίσ[θ]αι ἀπ ἀλλήλων), severing their union which they had formed on the basis of an agreement made at [time and place]. W acknowledges that she has received from H by hand from his house the material which he received for dowry and [list of *parapherna*]. The agreement of marriage shall henceforth be null (ἄκυρον) and neither W nor other person acting for her shall take proceedings against H for restitution of the dowry, nor shall either party take proceedings against the other about cohabitation or any other matter whatsoever up to the present day, and hereafter it shall be allowable (ἐξεῖναι) both for W to marry another man and for H to marry another woman without either of them being answerable (ἀνυπευθύνοις). In addition to the agreement being valid, the one who transgresses it shall moreover be liable both to damages and to the prescribed fine. [Date].[134]

The divorce document begins and closes its content with the mutual agreement of both spouses about its content and the penalties related to eventual disregard of its legal force from any of the parties. The introduc-

---

134. BGU IV.1103. The Duke Databank of Documentary Papyri [online], Available at http://www.perseus.tufts.edu/cgi-bin/ptext?doc=Perseus%3Atext%3A1999.05.0001&layout=&loc=1103, Accessed on 28 August 2004. Translation based on A. S. Hunt, *Select Papyri* 1:22–25, quoted in Instone-Brewer, *1 Corinthians 7 in the Light of the Graeco-Roman Marriage and Divorce Papyri*, 112 and idem, *1 Corinthians 7 in the Light of the Graeco-Roman Marriage and Divorce Papyri* [online].

tory section provides reference to the existence of the marriage contract which has been properly established through the consent of both husband and wife to its stipulations. The end of the marriage however, leads one to the conclusion that the fulfillment of these stipulations has been disregarded by one or both of the parties. It is not the concern of the divorce certificate to analyze these grounds for the marriage breakdown. Furthermore, the former proper marriage agreement between the parties implies that all the financial matters related to proper marriage contract are well established. Thus, the financial status of both parties needs to be reestablished according to their new condition. The husband returns the dowry to the wife from his house whose quantity is acceptable for the wife. Hence, she agrees not to "take proceedings against H for restitution of the dowry." Further mentioning of the wife's agreement not to take any other proceedings against the H, such as cohabitation or any other matter, defines the divorce status of both spouses as completely disconnected from their previous status in marriage which carried the obligations defined by the marriage contract. The latter is completely null and has no legal bearings on either of the spouses. Another condition of their new status as divorcees is the freedom of both parties to remarry. These statements have not been required in terms of the cultural expectation for such an action but nevertheless have appeared as a traditional element of the divorce deeds. The present document states not only the mutual provision of the man and woman to remarry but also establishes the complete lack of accountability to each other in their further lives. Such a complete state of freedom is evident in Paul's argumentation to the believer who is divorced by the unbeliever (1 Cor 7:15). When the unbelieving party is willing to live with the believer Paul commands the Christian to sustain the marriage and not attempt divorce (1 Cor 7:12–14). However, the believer who is divorced by the unbeliever is released from Paul's command and his/her freedom to remarry is well established and clearly defined with no further obligations to the unbeliever.[135]

---

135. D. Atkinson, *To Have and to Hold*, 124; C. R. Swindoll, *Strike the Original Match*, 145–146, quoted in Laney, *Paul and the Permanence of Marriage in I Corinthians 7*, 288; Wiebe, *Divorce and Remarriage*, 137; J. E. Adams, *Marriage, Divorce and Remarriage*, 48, quoted in Laney, *Paul and the Permanence of Marriage in I Corinthians 7*, 287; Orr and Walther, *I Corinthians*, 214; Instone-Brewer, *Divorce and Remarriage in the Bible*, 201–203.

The content of the Latin marriage papyri has been defined as resembling closely the one of the Greek marriage papyri. The following is the most complete representative from the four papyri which have reached us today.

> Marriage Contract, AD 175, Philadelphia, Egypt
> (LM175 = ChLA.IV.249):
>
> WF gave his daughter W, a virgin, in marriage, according to the *Lex Julia* which was passed to govern marriage for the sake of producing children. H took her to wife and spoke to her about a dowry and she owes everything which follows in writing as the aforesaid dowry: [list] *parapherna*, [list]. Likewise H also said that he had taken possession of two of her father's fields . . .[136]

The portion left from the marriage contract does not allow a possibility for a holistic analysis but underlines the main aspects of the Latin marriage contracts. The main focus of the document is on the security of the marriage. This is established on two levels, one according to *Lex Julia* and the other through financial provision. The first level might be analyzed as coming closer to the appearance of "the Greek law" and "the law of Moses and the Judeans" in the Jewish Greek (P.Yadin.18) and Jewish Aramaic (P.Yad.10) marriage contracts. These references have been used in order to protect the marriage and ensure the fulfillment of the marital obligations of both parties. This same role of the law might be defined here in the Latin contract. The function of the *Lex Julia* for the present contract might be further understood through analysis of the main features of this legislation.[137]

The Emperor Augustus attempted to solve the social problems of adultery, low marriage and childbirth rates of the Roman society through legislating the *Lex Julia* (18 BC).[138] This law supported marriage and hav-

---

136. ChLA.IV.249 [online], Available at http://www.tyndale.cam.ac.uk/Brewer/MarriagePapyri/TableLM.htm, Accessed on 28 August 2004. Translation based on Instone-Brewer, *1 Corinthians 7 in the Light of the Graeco-Roman Marriage and Divorce Papyri*, 113 and idem, *1 Corinthians 7 in the Light of the Graeco-Roman Marriage and Divorce Papyri* [online].

137. Instone-Brewer, *1 Corinthians 7 in the Light of the Graeco-Roman Marriage and Divorce Papyri* [online].

138. The legislation of *Lex Julia* might be based on the understanding of the strong relationship between society and marriage. As Judith B. Perkins argues, the early Greek romances show such dependence. Marriage narrated in the form of a secure union based on the faithful devotional relationship between the spouses provided a stable social or-

ing children as a desirable and honorable act on the positive side and condemned adultery as crime against marriage on the negative side. Hence, rewards were given to those who welcomed the law by initiating marriage and having children.[139] Financial punishments were extended to those staying unmarried either bachelor, divorcee, or in widowhood.[140] Punishments for adultery were introduced for the adulterous party, either man or woman,[141] related to divorce,[142] exile, confiscation of property,[143] and under certain circumstances, even death.[144]

---

der and guaranteed a flourishing social future. "This focus on chastity in the romance inscribes an inherent endorsement of the prevailing social structures and their careful preservation, for chastity works to restrict the body to those socially approved and designated by the society and to preserve family and social arrangements. Its primary concern is with the proper passing on and allotment of property and social rights and privileges. Chastity is, in essence, one of society's most overt manifestations of its power over both nature and its members; it acts as the embodiment of social control. In the romance the function of chastity is to ensure the continuance of society as it exists." (See Judith B. Perkins, "This World or Another? The Intertextuality of the Greek Romances, the Apocryphal Acts and Apuleius' Metamorphoses," *Semeia* 80 [1997]: 251)

139. See also S. Treggiari, *Marriage and Family in Roman Society*, 150.

140. "[Augustus] assessed heavier taxes on unmarried men and women without husbands, and by contrast offered awards for marriage and childbearing. And since there were more males than females among the nobility, he permitted anyone who wished (except for senators) to marry freedwomen, and decreed that children of such marriages be legitimate." (Dio Cassius, *History of Rome* 54.16.1-2, in *Women's Life in Greece and Rome*, trans. Lefkowitz and Fant, 103.)

141. "The *lex Julia* relating to chastity forbids the two parties guilty of adultery, that is to say, the man and the woman, from being defendants on a charge of adultery at the same time, and in the same case, but they can both be prosecuted in succession." (Justinian, *Codex* 9.9.1, 8, in *Women's Life in Greece and Rome*, trans. Lefkowitz and Fant, 105.)

142. "After having killed the adulterer, the husband should at once dismiss his wife, and publicly declare within the next three days with what adulterer and in what place he found his wife." (Paul, *Opinions* 2.26.6) "It has been decided that a husband who does not at once dismiss his wife whom he has taken in adultery can be prosecuted as a pimp." (Paul, *Opinions* 2.25.8, in *Women's Life in Greece and Rome*, trans. Lefkowitz and Fant, 104.)

143. "It has been held that women convicted of adultery shall be punished with the loss of half of their dowry and a third of their goods, and by relegation to an island. The adulterer, however, shall be deprived of half his property, and shall also be punished by relegation to an island; provided the parties are exiled to different islands." (Paul, *Opinions* 2.26.14, in *Women's Life in Greece and Rome*, trans. Lefkowitz and Fant, 104.)

144. "If a son under paternal power, who is the father, should surprise his daughter in the act of adultery, while it is inferred from the words of the law that he cannot kill her, still, he ought to be permitted to do so." (Paul, *Opinions* 2.26.2, in *Women's Life in Greece*

It becomes clear that the law as mentioned in the introductory words of the Latin contract was intended to guarantee the fulfillment of the marriage stipulations by the husband and the wife. The two stipulations which might be clearly defined are related to husband and wife giving to each other their conjugal rights with the purpose of procreation, since the birth control methods were not well established, and preservation of their marital faithfulness. The mutual fulfillment of these stipulations guaranteed a preservation of the marriage contract and long lasting marriage. On the other hand, lack of their fulfillment resulted in divorce.[145]

Paul might have had the same intentions of underlining marital faithfulness while introducing the statements μιᾶς γυναικὸς ἄνδρα/ἀνήρ (1 Tim 3:2; Tit 1:6) and ἑνὸς ἀνδρὸς γυνή (1 Tim 5:9) in listing the requirements for church leaders and church assigned widows.[146] The importance

---

and Rome, trans. Lefkowitz and Fant, 104.)

145. Sterility was also a possible ground for divorce in the Roman society. A funeral eulogy, (Rome 1st century BC): "When you despaired of your ability to bear children and grieved over my childlessness, you became anxious lest by retaining you in marriage I might lose all hope of having children and be distressed for that reason. So you proposed a divorce outright and offered to yield our house free to another woman's fertility...." (ILS 8393, trans. E. Wistrand, in Women's Life in Greece and Rome, eds. Lefkowitz and Fant, 138).

146. Four different interpretations attempt to establish the intended meaning of the phrases μιᾶς γυναικὸς ἄνδρα (1 Tim 3:2), ἑνὸς ἀνδρὸς γυνή (1 Tim 5:9), and μιᾶς γυναικὸς ἀνήρ (Tit 1:6). The first suggests that the spouse under consideration should be married. However, it fails to consider the emphasis brought by the Greek text (μία). It disregards Paul's positive teaching on celibacy (1 Cor 7:17, 25–38) and makes him contradict himself, establishing a standard for overseers which neither he nor Timothy would fulfill. The second defines the phrase as prohibiting polygamy. Even though there might be grounds for this interpretation (potential presence of polygamy among Jews, Josephus, Ant. 17.1.2 and 14), it does not do justice for the widow since polyandry was not a contemporary practice neither for the community at large nor for Christians in particular. The third maintains a reference to a single marriage or prohibition of remarriage. Although this interpretation has carried some weight due to its acceptance by the early church (which might be due to some influences of Hellenistic asceticism and Montanism) it contradicts Paul's allowance of remarriage both in the closer context (1 Tim 5:14) and in his other writings (1 Cor 7:39; Rom 7:3). The fourth interprets the phrase as a reference to the spouse's frightfulness during the state of marriage. Hence, whether the spouse has been married more than once or widow, divorcee, or single before the marriage is not in view here. Paul intends to uphold the importance of the character of the church leaders as well as of those being under special church provision in light of the sexually promiscuous culture which had also impacted the church (2 Tim 3:6). This interpretation fits well in the context which states the qualifications of the leaders from a positive point of view. (Also Robert L. Saucy, "Husband of One Wife," Bibliotheca Sacra

of marital faithfulness for maintaining the marital union and establishing the proper social image of the marriage has been the apostle's concern in many of his discussions (Rom 7:3; 1 Cor 6:9; 1 Cor 7; 1 Tim 1:10). Here in the Pastoral Epistles he is especially interested in defining the image of the family which is guided and supported by the church leader. The latter should build such a marital relationship which is set as an example for the Christian community entrusted to him (1 Tim 3:5; 1 Tim 5:17). Thus, sexual faithfulness establishes a foundational characteristic of the marital relationship which requires the complete devotion of the spouses for its accomplishment and for the proper maintenance of the marriage.

The second level of securing the marriage has been depicted in the marriage contract through financial provisions. The dowry, well defined and agreed upon by the husband and the wife, facilitated the new economical status of the young family. The mutuality of its execution being well established in the agreement suggests the participation of both spouses in their mutual material support. These two levels of marriage provision required by the spouses might be paralleled on one side with the character of the stipulations found in the Greco-Roman marriage contracts and on the other side with the material and emotional provisions of the Jewish marriage contracts.

The form of the words and the style employed for the writing of Jewish marriage contracts during the first and second century Palestine have been determined by the language used, either Greek or Aramaic. Undertaking one or the other depended on the social concerns of the people involved.[147] However, in spite of the language employed, the main features of the written form of the contracts were established according to the Jewish marriage contracts with some parallels to the Greco-Roman marriage contracts. Only a few from the early 2nd century AD have reached us today. The first one to be considered is written in Greek.

---

131 [July-September 1974] 229–40; Sydney H. T. Page, "Marital Expectations of Church Leaders in the Pastoral Epistles," *Journal for the Study of the New Testament* 50 [1993]: 105–120; C. S. Keener, *. . . And Marries Another: Divorce and Remarriage in the Teaching of the New Testament*, 83–103; W. D. Mounce, *Pastoral Epistles*. WBC 46 (Dallas: Word, 2002). Electronic Edition by Libronix Digital Library System 2.0, 2002; Instone-Brewer, *Divorce and Remarriage in the Bible*, 227, 228; idem, *Divorce and Remarriage in the 1st and 21st Century*, section 3–6 [online].)

147. In some contexts, the Greek contract carried greater legal respectability.

Marriage Contract, AD 128, Petra (JM128 i.e. P.Yadin.18):

[Date, Place], WF gave over W, his very own daughter, a virgin, to H, for W at be a wedded wife to H for the partnership of marriage according to the laws, she bringing to him on account of bridal gift feminine adornment in silver and gold and clothing appraised by mutual agreement as they both say, to be worth 200 denarii of silver, which appraised value H acknowledged that he has received from her by hand forthwith from WF and that he owes to W together with another 300 denarii which he promised to give to her in addition to the sum of her aforesaid bridal gift (προσφορά), all accounted toward her dowry, pursuant to his undertaking of feeding and clothing both her and the children to come in accordance with Greek law (ἑλληνικῷ νόμῳ) upon H's good faith (πίστεως) and in peril and the security of all his possessions, both those which he now possesses in his said home village and here and all those which he may in addition validly acquire everywhere, in whatever manner W may choose, or whoever acts through her or for her may choose, to carry out the execution. H shall redeem this contract for W whenever she may demand it (ἀπαιτήσ[ει] from ἀπαιτέω to demand back) of him, in silver secured in due form, at his own expense interposing no objection. If not, he shall pay to her all the aforesaid denarii twofold, she having the right of execution, both from H and upon the possessions validly his, in whatever manner WW or whoever acts through her or for her may choose to carry out the execution. In good faith (πίστει) the formal question was asked and it was acknowledged in reply that this is thus rightly done.

I, WF, have given my daughter W, a virgin, in marriage to H, according to what is written above. WF wrote it.

I, H, acknowledge the debt of silver denarii, 500, the dowry of W according to what they wrote above. H wrote it.

I [name of scribe] wrote this.

[Witness signatures].[148]

---

148. P.Yadin.18 = P.Babatha.18 [online], Available at http://www.tyndale.cam.ac.uk/Brewer/MarriagePapyri/TableJM.htm, Accessed on 28 August 2004. Translation based on Naphtali Lewis, Yigael Yadin, and Jonas C. Greenfield, eds., *The Documents from the Bar Kokhba Period in the Cave of Letters: Greek Papyri* (Jerusalem: Israel Exploration Society: Hebrew University of Jerusalem: Shrine of the Book, 1989), 80, quoted in David Instone-Brewer, "1 Corinthians 7 in the Light of the Jewish Greek and Aramaic Marriage and Divorce Papyri," *Tyndale Bulletin* 52.2 (2001) 226–27 and idem, *1 Corinthians 7 in*

The most significant elements of the contract from which the rest depend are the stipulations established on the law and bound to the personal trustworthiness of the parties, here specifically written from the perspective of the groom. The stipulations mentioned in this contract are those of feeding and clothing. These usually appear in the Jewish contracts together with the one about conjugal rights which here is assumed due to the mentioning of the couple's children after the two stipulations. The regular performance of the stipulations is related to both the brideprice paid by the groom to the wife's family and the dowry paid by the wife's father to the new family. The former has been only theoretical here and is turned into a financial sum only in the case of divorce. The dowry is real and serves to support the family. Both of these are closely related to the preservation and fulfillment of the stipulations. A further guarantee for the daily completion of the stipulations during the lifetime of the spouses is given by the law, here referring to the Greek law. The usual Law which is referred to in the Jewish Aramaic and Hebrew marriage contracts is the Law of Moses and Israel. Next to the law, the personal faithfulness of the groom is considered as assurance for sustaining the marriage contract. The faithfulness of the spouses to the terms of the marriage contract appears to be a substantial element of the latter. This combination of law and faith for the purpose of facilitating security in the proper functioning of the marriage according to its stipulations, is not part of the Greco-Roman marriage contracts. The present Jewish contract guarantees the lifelong proper functioning of the marriage through the fulfillment of its stipulations, but also prescribes the breakdown of the latter in case of such failure. Here, only the manner in which divorce is defined, being initiated by the wife, has been influenced by the Greco-Roman contracts.[149]

Another type of expression of the Jewish marriage contract is in Aramaic. The contract still has some structural and minor content resemblances with the Greco-Roman marriage contracts such as involvement of matters of dowry, reference to the basic stipulations, and making provision in case of a change in the marital situation, but it appears to be more conservative in relation to the lifelong nature of marriage. While the overall understanding of the eventual change in the marriage situation of the usual Greco-Roman marriage contract refers predominantly

---

the Light of the Jewish Greek and Aramaic Marriage and Divorce Papyri [online].

149. Instone-Brewer, *1 Corinthians 7 in the Light of the Jewish Greek and Aramaic Marriage and Divorce Papyri* [online].

to divorce,[150] the Jewish marriage contracts view such a potential change in the form of the death of one of the partners, although not disregarding divorce as an option but minimizing it.

Marriage Contract, AD 126, Palestine (AM126 i.e. *P.Yad.*10):

> [Date][Place & names missing] . . . that you will be my wife according to the law of Moses and the Judeans and I will feed you and cloth you and I will bring you (into my house) by means of your *ketubah* and I owe you the sum of 400 denarii . . . together with the due amount of your food and your clothes and your bed, provision fitting for a free woman. [Some accidental duplication.] And if you are taken captive, I will redeem you, from my house and from my estate, and I will take you back as my wife, and I owe you your *ketubah* money . . . And if I go to my eternal home before you, male children which you will have by me will inherit your *ketubah* money, beyond their share with their brothers, female children shall dwell and be provided for from my house and from my estate until the time when they will be married. And if I go to my eternal home before you, you will dwell in my house and be provided for from my house and from my estate until the time that my heirs wish to give you your *ketubah* money. And whenever you tell me I will replace this document as is proper. [Signatures][151]

As in the case of the previous Jewish contract, here also the core of the contract rests on the fulfillment of the basic stipulations for the proper function of marriage. The contract relates the stipulations only to the groom due to his more significant financial involvement than that of the bride. However, equality in the fulfillment of the stipulations is well established through the numerous discussions in rabbinic case law. The stipulations which are clearly stated in the present marriage contract are the most fundamental requirements for the provision of food, cloth-

---

150. A funeral eulogy, (Rome, 1st cent. BC): "(27) Marriages as long as ours are rare, marriages that are ended by death and not broken by divorce. For we were fortunate enough to see our marriage last without disharmony for fully 40 years . . . ." (*ILS* 8393, trans. E. Wistrand, in *Women's Life in Greece and Rome*, eds. Lefkowitz and Fant, 136).

151. *P.Yadin.*10 [online], Available at http://www.tyndale.cam.ac.uk/Brewer/MarriagePapyri/TableAM.htm, Accessed on 28 August 2004, quoted in Yigael Yadin, Jonas C. Greenfield, and Ada Yardeni, "Babatha's *Ketubba*," *IEJ* 44 (1994) 75–101. Translation based on Y. Yadin, J. C. Greenfield, and A. Yardeni, *Babatha's Ketubba*, 75–101, quoted in Instone-Brewer, *1 Corinthians 7 in the Light of the Jewish Greek and Aramaic Marriage and Divorce Papyri*, 231 and idem, *1 Corinthians 7 in the Light of the Jewish Greek and Aramaic Marriage and Divorce Papyri* [online].

ing, and conjugal rights. The latter one is expressed through euphemistic references to the house of the groom and to the bed of the bride. The proper and constant fulfillment of these stipulations is secured through mentioning the Law as in the previous contract, but here the reference is to the Law of Moses and the Judeans.[152] This not only establishes the divine origin of the stipulations stated in Exod 20:10-11 but also refers to the stable social structures in which the marriage will exist. Marriage is assumed to continue until the death of one of the parties and in the case of this contract is related to the death of the groom. In this case provisions are made for the bride in terms of continuous material support until she is completely unattached to the husband's household with the returning of the *ketubah* to her. This approach of the marriage contract does not exclude the possibility of marital breakdown in case of a lack of fulfillment of the stipulations by one of the parties. The mentioning of the Law and the exact nature of the stipulations (Exod 20:10-11) provides resolutions in case of such a failure with the lost of the *ketubah* for the guilty party and freedom of the innocent party for independent life or remarriage. That might be understood as stated in the Jewish Aramaic divorce certificates. The following one is a clear example of a legitimate marital breakdown with the consequences for the husband and the wife and establishing the condition of the latter.

Divorce Deed, AD 72, Masada (AD72 i.e. *DJD*.II.19 = *P.Mur*.19):

[Date, Place] I H divorce and release of my own free will, today you W who had been my wife before this time. You are free on your part to go and become the wife of any Jewish man that you wish. This is for you a writ of release and a bill of divorce, [illegible portion]. And all ruined and damaged [. . .] to you will be restored and I will pay fourfold. And at any time that you ask me, I will replace for you this document, as is proper. [Signature of H][153]

---

152. This is even depicted with images of Moses, Aaron, and the two tables of the Law in some of the illuminated Jewish marriage contracts. (See Franz Landsberger, "Illuminated Marriage Contracts: With Special Reference to the Cincinnati *Ketubahs*," *Hebrew Union College Annual* 26 [1955] 526/24.)

153. *P.Mur*.19 [online], Available at http://www.tyndale.cam.ac.uk/Brewer/Marriage Papyri/TableAD2.htm, Accessed on 28 August 2004. Translation based on Roland deVaux, Jozef T. Milik and Pierre Benoit, *Discoveries in the Judaean Desert*, II: *Les grottes de Muraba'at* (Oxford, Clarendon 1961) 104-9 and Leone J. Archer, *Her Price Is Beyond Rubies: The Jewish Woman in Greco-Roman Palestine* (JSOTSup 60, Sheffield: Sheffield

The most significant element of the divorce certificate is defined as establishing the status of the wife as a free person with the right to remarry. It is argued that this has been the most important role of the divorce certificate for both Jewish and Greco-Roman societies.[154] Thus, the present divorce deed starts with defining the post marital condition of the wife as being completely free to go out of the present marriage and develop her life with the openness for remarriage. The present document includes a clear statement of its important role emphasizing its nature as writ of release and a bill of divorce. This more closely parallels the emancipation certificate in the early rabbinic traditions. Such a relation has not been established with the assumption that marriage is a state of slavery but is related to the foundational component for establishing the divorce certificate found in the law of the slave wife in Exod 20:10-11. This law combines both certificates in one, referring to the release of the slave from her service and the wife from her present marriage. The core statements of both certificates are clearly paralleled in the rabbinic literature.[155] In light of this usage Paul has also incorporated such language in his discussion of marriage, divorce, and remarriage. In the marriage context when defining one of the stipulations of the marriage covenant, (conjugal rights), for strengthening and preserving the marital bond Paul is implying the ownership of the partner's body in a very personal and intimate way (1 Cor 7:3-5). Paul is also referring to the marriage connection between husband and wife using the verb δέω (bind, tie, fetter, 1 Cor 7:27, 39; Rom 7:2) to establish it as that of a bond in order to stress its lifelong nature. However, at the same time he uses the language of release from slavery, terms such as ἀφίημι, (dismiss, release, 1 Cor 7:11-13), οὐ δεδούλωται, (not enslaved, from δουλόω enslave, make someone a slave, 1 Cor 7:15), and ἐλεύθερος, (free, 1 Cor 7:39; Rom 7:3), in order to show the legal

---

Academic, 1990) 298-99, as amended by Y. Yadin, J. C. Greenfield, and A. Yardeni, *Babatha's Ketubba*, 86, and in "Expedition D–the Cave of the Letters," *IEJ* 12 (1962) 227-57, p. 249, and by Tal Ilan in "Notes and Observations on a Newly Published Divorce Bill from the Judean Desert," *HTR* 89 (1996) 195-202, pp. 198-99, quoted in Instone-Brewer, *1 Corinthians 7 in the Light of the Jewish Greek and Aramaic Marriage and Divorce Papyri*, 237 and idem, *1 Corinthians 7 in the Light of the Jewish Greek and Aramaic Marriage and Divorce Papyri* [online].

154. Instone-Brewer, *1 Corinthians 7 in the Light of the Jewish Greek and Aramaic Marriage and Divorce Papyri* [online].

155. Certificate of emancipation: "Lo, you are a free girl, you belong to yourself"; divorce certificate: "Lo, you are permitted to (marry) any man."

termination of the marital bond and the initiation of the divorce state with its legal consequences for both parties related to the possibility of remarriage. This usage of slave terminology does not create a contradiction in terms of the expectancy of the marriage duration but shows that the lifelong nature of marriage is conditioned by the fulfillment of the marriage stipulations by both spouses. The present certificate of divorce suggests that there were reasons for the dissolution of the marriage. The fact that the husband is referring to the wife's condition as being degraded morally or financially within the marriage and his decisive answer for compensating this with a fourfold payment suggests the reason for the marriage breakdown and the existence of the divorce bill. There might have been lack of fulfillment of the stipulations of the marriage covenant on the side of the husband which led to the termination of the marriage and production of the divorce certificate. The compensation promised by the husband established a solid financial condition of the divorced wife. She might have considered either single life or remarriage. The latter was further limited by the inclusion of the religious afilliation of the possible partner. This is clearly resembled by Paul in his commendation related to the woman who is going to remarry, ". . . she is free to marry anyone she wishes, only in the Lord," (1 Cor 7:39, NRS).[156]

In conclusion, the NT expresses the view of marriage as a covenant relationship. It is developed in continuation of the OT concept of marriage covenant and firmly grounded in the marriage contracts of the contemporaneous culture. The twofold nature of the marriage covenant established through the fulfillment of some basic stipulations might be perceived from the NT texts. On the one hand, marriage is defined as a permanent union between husband and wife (Matt 19:6; Mark 10:9; Rom 7:2, 3). The perpetual nature of marriage is the core of the NT matrimonial teachings. The lifelong marital union is the very essence of marriage as established by God and echoed in the marriage contracts of the Jewish

---

156. Paul is using the wording of the usual divorce certificate to affirm the rights of widows to remarry. Perhaps here he is concerned to free the widow from the obligation to perform a levirate marriage. The same approach might be seen in the second century Jewish Greek Marriage contracts and in some of the rabbinic debates. The confirmation of the widow's rights using the words from the divorce certificate which are intended to confirm the freedom of a divorcee to remarry, give an assurance to the fact that there have been no doubts in the rights for remarriage of divorcees during NT times. (Also Instone-Brewer, *1 Corinthians 7 in the Light of the Jewish Greek and Aramaic Marriage and Divorce Papyri* [online].)

and Greco-Roman cultures. The preservation of the union throughout the lifetime of the spouses is defined with the specific covenant stipulations of marriage. The material and emotional commitment of the spouses to each other strengthens and protects the union from abuses, fruit of the sinful human nature. The fulfillment of the covenant stipulations defines the mutual obligation of the spouses for nourishing and preserving their lifelong union. Thus, all attempts for its destruction without justifiable lawful grounds have been condemned by the NT authors (Mark 10:11, 12; Matt 19:9; Luke 16:18; 1 Cor 7:10, 11, 12–14; Rom 7:3). The sinful channels of freely dissolving marriage covenants without any legitimate grounds of both Jewish and Greco-Roman societies have been argued against and firmly rejected by the NT authors. Groundless divorce and remarriage are destructive actions which negate the permanent nature of marriage. Against these the marriage covenant stipulations provide for clarity of the lifelong commitment of the spouses to their marriage.

On the other hand, the marriage covenant is vulnerable to sinful human actions and as such might be broken when its stipulations are not fulfilled by any one of the spouses. Various penalties have been established in the marriage contracts of both Jewish and Greco-Roman cultures to secure fulfillment of the covenant stipulations and prevent marital breakdown. However, when the severity of sinful human behavior extends all boundaries and endangers the dignity and life of a spouse, legitimate grounds for divorce and remarriage are provided. Hence, Matthew provides a channel for proper divorce and remarriage in the case of abuse of the spouse's conjugal faithfulness (Matt 19:9; 5:32). Paul also offers lawful grounds for both actions in the case of the spouse's refusal to perform the covenant stipulations (1 Cor 7:15, 16). The model for Christian marriage is defined as the relationship between Christ and his church, which permanent nature is clearly stated and vividly depicted through Christ's faithfulness in fulfilling his marital duties to his bride, the church (Eph 5:25–33).

five

The Context in Dogmatics

THE THEOLOGICAL CONCLUSION REACHED THROUGH THE INTEGRAtion of the exegetical results into the body of the canonical biblical literature using the concept of covenant marital relationship might be defined as a twofold concept which underlines the permanent nature of marriage prohibiting licentious divorce and remarriage and provides legitimate grounds for both actions in case of a failure of one of the parties to sustain the marital union. The latter might be elaborated as the intentional refusal of the spouse grounded upon his/her sinful intentions to fulfill the basic covenant stipulations of the marriage. This theological conclusion should be further established in the dogmatical context through its interrelation to the major Christian traditions. Hence, the matrimonial teachings of the Roman Catholic, Eastern Orthodox, and Protestant churches should be analyzed in relation to the previously formulated theological concept. The goal of this examination will be to establish a justifiable ecumenical[1] view of the NT teaching on divorce and remarriage and prepare the grounds for its further implementation in Christian communities and its social legislation within pluralistic context.

THE TEACHING OF THE ROMAN CATHOLIC CHURCH

The analysis of the Roman Catholic view of marriage is very essential task which contribution to the present work is defined of key importance due to the well established and defined Catholic teaching on matrimonial

---

1. It is the understanding of the present author that ecumenism should be defined as the mutual attempt of the major Christian traditions, i.e. Roman Catholic, Eastern Orthodox, and Protestant, to reach "a commonality in doctrine and in the life of faith." See Dietrich Ritschl, "Ecumenism," in *Dictionary of Mission: Theology, History, Perspectives*, eds. Karl Muller, et al. (Maryknoll, NY: Orbis, 1998) 120.

matters from historical, exegetical, theological, dogmatical, and pastoral perspective. This task, presents to the researcher various challenges in exploring the teaching of the church and the views of the Catholic theologians. Hence, in this presentation an attempt will be made to present the church position on the matrimonial matters through some of its most significant documents followed by an analysis of the important NT texts related to the matters of marriage, divorce, and remarriage as exegeted by a leading Catholic scholar and completed with the various matrimonial aspects as dealt with by different Catholic theologians.

The Catechism of the Catholic Church[2] formulates the Catholic view on matrimony in a holistic and detailed way giving a clear treatment of its various aspects and its boundaries related to the spouses behavior. Other important documents such as *Family, Marriage and "De Facto" Unions*,[3] *Letter to Families from Pope John Paul II*,[4] and the Apostolic Exhortation of Pope John Paul II, *Familiaris Consortio*[5] will also be used to contribute to the present discussion due to their crucial significance in relation to Catholic view of marriage.

The sacrament of matrimony is one of the seven sacraments of the church. The very covenant relationship of marriage between two Christians which is established as a sacrament by Christ is based on the mutual partnership between the spouses for a lifetime and is directed to the mutual edification of the spouses and their children (1601).[6] The very essence of this sacrament is designed by God to be a permanent reflection of the relationship between Christ and the church and as such to signify the sacrament of the New Covenant. This nature needs to be well

---

2. *Catechism of the Catholic Church*, Libreria Editrice Vaticana [online], Available at http://www.vatican.va/archive/ENG0015/_INDEX.HTM, Accessed on 17 September 2005.

3. Pontifical Council for the Family, *Family, Marriage and "De Facto" Unions*. Libreria Editrice Vaticana [online], Available at http://www.vatican.va/roman_curia/pontifical _councils/family/documents/rc_pc_family_doc_20001109_de-facto-unions_en.html, Accessed on 30 August 2005.

4. Pope John Paul II, *Letter to Families from Pope John Paul II*, (1994 – Year of the Family). Libreria Editrice Vaticana [online], Available at http://www.vatican.va/ holy_father/john_paul_ii/letters/documents/hf_jp-ii_let_02021994_families_en.html, Accessed on 29 August 2005.

5. Apostolic Exhortation of Pope John Paul II, *Familiaris Consortio* [online], Available at http://www.wf-f.org/FamCons.html, Accessed on 23 September 2004.

6. *Catechism of the Catholic Church* [online].

perceived by the couple preparing to celebrate the sacrament. "Baptized persons do not present themselves to the Church just to celebrate a feast with some special rites, but to contract a lifetime marriage which is a sacrament of the New Alliance."[7] Hence, the preparation of the young couple for contracting an indissoluble marriage covenant is very crucial and requires pastoral care which will lead both man and woman to personal formation through comprehension of the institution of marriage, its dynamics, nature, and virtues.[8]

Marriage plays a significant part of God's plan as it is presented in Scripture. It encompasses the whole history of human kind and its salvation being part of the creation of man as well as of man's salvation and participation of the Lord's future Kingdom (Rev 19:7, 9; cf. Gen 1:26–27). Scripture deals with the nature of marriage and its various dimensions including its vulnerability to the sinful human nature as well as its renewal in the new covenant relationship between Christ and the church (1602).[9] The covenant of marriage is grounded on the communion of conjugal love between man and woman which leads to their parenthood which nourishes and strengthens the covenant relationship between the spouses through the upbringing of their children.[10]

Marriage is created by God for the good of humankind. Marital union is designed to provide for man and woman a relationship which defines the complementary aspects of their genres and fulfills their unity through giving them procreative abilities (372).[11] The unity which formulates the relationship between husband and wife reflects the unity in God's being and designates the capacity of every human being as a person to form this communion of marriage and sustain it in truth and love.[12] The Trinitarian mystery which defines God's personality is imparted to marriage and family relationship through the image of God in man, formulating the communion and complementarity of both man and woman

---

7. Pontifical Council for the Family, *Family, Marriage and "De Facto" Unions*. Libreria Editrice Vaticana [online].

8. Ibid.

9. *Catechism of the Catholic Church* [online].

10. Pope John Paul II, *Letter to Families from Pope John Paul II*, (1994 – Year of the Family), 7. Libreria Editrice Vaticana [online].

11. *Catechism of the Catholic Church* [online].

12. Pope John Paul II, *Letter to Families from Pope John Paul II*, (1994 – Year of the Family), 8. Libreria Editrice Vaticana [online].

in their marital union which marks the whole of humanity, any community, and the society as a whole.[13] The very essence of marital union is indispensable part of the human nature bringing man and woman together for life filled with love deriving from and resembling God's love. This very characteristic of God's image in man forms the marital relationship as place for mutual commitment of the spouses to support and love each other serving God in overseeing his creation. Thus, the very nature of marriage is not only human but also reflects the character of its Creator which establishes it as permanent union of mutual and self-giving love (1603–1605).

The consequences from man's fall affect the matrimonial relationship between husband and wife due to the evil which affects both them and their environment (1606). The purity and perfection of marriage dynamics of the first marriage have been lost with the human fall. The vices of human sin distorted the relationship between husband and wife characterizing it with domination and lust. The joy and pleasure of fulfilling God's commandment to multiply and subdue the earth have been destructed with the pain in childbirth and the hardness of the human labor (1607). The marital relationship between the spouses being under the constant pressure of evil led to various failures of the commitment and devotion of husband and wife to each other in spite of their race, culture or nationality (1606). Only through God's grace the spouses may find healing from the effects of sin and accomplish God's intentions for the permanent marriage union (1608).[14] The church also plays a significant twofold role in regard to spouses who experience difficulties. On the one hand, the church is conveying the interpretation of the moral norm to the spouses in order to lead them to understanding and obeying the truth. On the other hand, the church is helping these couples who suffer various marital difficulties through perceiving well their situations from social and individual perspective offering assistance in the fulfillment of the moral norm.[15] The spouses will experience progressive fulfillment of the moral norm if they show willingness to obtain better knowledge of God's law and implement it in their daily decisions.[16]

---

13. Ibid., 6.
14. *Catechism of the Catholic Church* [online].
15. Apostolic Exhortation of Pope John Paul II, *Familiaris Consortio*, 33 [online].
16. Ibid., 34.

Marriage covenant relationship suffers from offenses such as adultery, divorce, polygamy, incest, and free unions (2400). Adultery is a sinful act of sexual relation with another person than one's spouse. It is condemned by God's Law, the prophets, the New Testament, and Christ himself (2380). Adultery is an act of infidelity to the marriage covenant which breaks the contract violating the spouse's rights and damaging the welfare of children (2381).

Divorce is the attempt of one or both of the spouses to break their marriage contract. Due to the indissoluble nature of a ratified and consummated marriage between two baptized Christians divorce is considered offensive to the natural law, the covenant of marriage, and the covenant of salvation which is signified through the sacramental nature of marriage. Acting against valid marriage through civil divorce and remarriage constitutes public and permanent adultery (2382, 2384). The act of divorce is offensive not only to the deserted spouse and children but to the order in society (2385). Only in cases when separation of the spouses is necessary due to the severe damage in their relationship or the civil divorce is the only way to secure the legal rights of the children divorce may be considered appropriate but not as terminating the bond of marriage (2383). The severity of divorce does not equalize the failure of the moral character of both spouses since there are some spouses who have been deserted in spite of their effort to preserve faithfully the indissoluble bond of the marriage covenant (2386).[17] The church needs to embrace these Christian spouses with love and understanding without creating any obstacle for their participation in the Eucharist and help them to remain faithful to the marital union, to forgive and eventually reconcile with their spouses.[18] For those divorced Christians who entered in new relationships and formalized them through civil institutions in spite of the validity of their marriages, the church extends its ministry embracing them as its members but restricts them from taking Eucharist and the sacrament of penance. The latter may be available only for those who continue their lives in complete continence. Marriage union is absolutely indissoluble and nothing should cast shadow of doubt in regard to this divine formulation.[19]

17. *Catechism of the Catholic Church* [online].
18. Apostolic Exhortation of Pope John Paul II, *Familiaris Consortio*, 83 [online].
19. Ibid., 84.

Polygamy is another offense against the nature of marriage which is designed by God to be an equal share of respect, conjugal love, and marital duties between one man and one woman (2387). Incest is another grave offense against marital relationship which should be established only between spouses who are not relatives (2388). Free unions such as concubinage, trial marriage, or any other form of rejection of marriage are considered serious offenses to the nature of marriage which requires complete and unreserved commitment of the spouses which is publicly recognized (2390, 2391).[20] Free unions are also called de facto unions.

De facto unions, all forms of sexually based cohabitation which are not valid marriages, endanger the institution of marriage and degrade its very nature and dimensions as established by God and narrated in his Holy Word. Any social or juridical justification of de facto unions will inevitable endanger the institution of marriage leading to its degradation and negatively impact the society as a whole. Civil recognition and equivalence of de facto unions with the institution of marriage destabilize the social structures offering equality, but expecting less social responsibilities in return from the parties in de facto unions. De facto unions may not be characterized with any of the essential elements of valid marital relationships such as spouses' commitment and mutual fidelity. The establishment of de facto unions is guided by the fundamental rejection of the institution of marriage by those couples who do not comprehend the nature of marital covenant relationship as the most excellent form of union which creates the ultimate framework for the spouses to express their complete personality and work toward their mutual wellbeing. The most foundational characteristic of de facto unions is the concept of "free love." This concept stays in a contrast with the substantial element of marital union, namely, the conjugal love between the spouses. Marital relationship based on the conjugal love between the spouses is in its very nature sacramentaly linked to their faith which is related to the salvation provided by Christ. On the other hand, de facto unions are entirely based on rationality which excludes the faith of the spouses. The institution of marriage cannot be considered as one of the many ways in which two people may enjoy sexual cohabitation and the upbringing of children. The very nature of marital union distinguishes it from any other form of union such as de facto unions due to its fundamental characteristics of

---

20. *Catechism of the Catholic Church* [online].

complementarity of the genders and the shared free will of the spouses for their complete and lifelong commitment to each other. The importance of marriage for the society as a whole is defined not only with the juridical, social, and economic value of the institution but also with the character of the family to create relational ties for mutual support between its parts and promote cultural, ethical, social, spiritual, and religious values for the benefit of its members. The solution for de facto unions is found in the careful analysis of their context and the financial, ideological, psychological, didactic, and various other reasons which have prompted these unions. Pastoral care needs to be offered with sensitivity toward the people who are a part of these unions and in relation to the differences in their motives. The covenant of marriage and its various dimensions which establish the ultimate framework for every marital relationship should be lived and witnessed by the spouses of valid marital unions. Finally, the social structures need to facilitate environment for stabilizing and promoting legal marital unions.[21] No society can maintain its proper functions if it compromises the institution of marriage and its true nature.[22] The social role of the family may be defined as procreative, educational, and political. Family has the potential given to it by the Creator to produce life and as such it is the generator of the human society. The family is based on communion between its members which is defined through sharing. This educational capacity of the family goes beyond its borders to become a powerful tool for transmitting knowledge in the society as whole. Family has a strong political role in the society to insure the capacity of social structures and laws for the safety and wellbeing of people.[23]

Marriage serves as an instrument for a remedy of human relationship which is affected by the fall. It does create an atmosphere where both spouses may serve each other and overcome the sinful tendencies of the flesh (1609). The institution of marriage developed its indissoluble characteristics under the Old Testament Law which did provide protection of the permanence of marriage and the wife's status in spite of the

---

21. Pontifical Council for the Family, *Family, Marriage and "De Facto" Unions*, Libreria Editrice Vaticana [online].

22. Pope John Paul II, *Letter to Families from Pope John Paul II*, (1994 – Year of the Family), 17, Libreria Editrice Vaticana [online].

23. Apostolic Exhortation of Pope John Paul II, *Familiaris Consortio*, 42, 43, 44 [online].

permission for divorce due to the "hardness of heart" (1610).[24] The character of marriage as an indissoluble union formulates the self-giving of the spouses to each other which fruit becomes the gift of a child.[25] God's covenant with Israel represents the model of loving and lasting marital relationship (1611).[26]

The bond of marriage defined through the conjugal love between husband and wife becomes the image of the covenant relationship between God and his people Israel in which God's faithfulness to his people sustains the permanent nature of the covenant in spite of the infidelity of his people expressed through their disobedience to his Law.[27] The marriage covenant between God and Israel has established the path for the new marriage covenant which became possible with the saving death of Jesus for the whole of humankind (1612). The significance of marriage during Jesus' life and ministry has been approved through his miraculous act during the wedding at Cana (1613). Marriage has been vindicated from the OT permission of divorce through the teaching of Jesus which confirmed its permanent nature through God's original intentions (1614). The indissolubility of marriage depicted clearly in the teaching of Jesus may not be perceived as an impossible to achieve union. For those spouses who commit themselves to follow the way of Jesus, his power and grace will equip them to fulfill his matrimonial standards (1615). The model for imitation of such a permanent union is the covenant between Christ and his church. This is the image which apostle Paul uses when he instructs the husbands to imitate the love of Christ (1616). It is this marriage covenant which believers enter through their baptism and nourish through their participation in the Eucharist, the upcoming wedding feast. Hence, every marriage between two baptized persons becomes a sign of grace due to its relation to the covenant of Christ and the church and as such "a true sacrament of the New Covenant." (1617).

The bond with Christ is foundational for every believer either married or in celibacy (1618). The ability to serve the Lord in any of these

---

24. *Catechism of the Catholic Church*, Libreria Editrice Vaticana [online], Available at http://www.vatican.va/archive/ENG0015/__P51.HTM, Accessed on 17 September 2005.

25. Pope John Paul II, *Letter to Families from Pope John Paul II*, (1994 – Year of the Family) 11, Libreria Editrice Vaticana [online].

26. *Catechism of the Catholic Church* [online].

27. Apostolic Exhortation of Pope John Paul II, *Familiaris Consortio*, 12 [online].

states is granted by Christ (1620). The virginity for the Kingdom of God communicates the centrality of the bond with Christ and the belonging of the institution of marriage to this present age (1619).

Marriage is celebrated by the Catholic believers during Holy Mass with their participation in the Eucharist. Through receiving Eucharist the spouses share their consent to give themselves to each other in the marriage covenant as Christ has sacrificed himself for the church and established eternal covenant with her (1621). Due to the sanctifying nature of marriage being expressed in its celebration it is advisable for the couple to prepare themselves for this act through receiving the sacrament of penance (1622). The celebration of marriage involves the public attestation of the spouses' mutual consent before the church and in the presence of the priests whose blessing validates the act (1623). The Holy Spirit who is the seal of the marriage covenant bestows his presence and love upon the couple during this celebration (1624).

Matrimonial consent ratifies the marriage covenant between baptized man and woman. The individual consent of every one of the parties defines their free will to contract marriage and confirms their freedom from any impediment of natural or ecclesiastical law (1625). The consent of the spouses is understood as the element which creates the marital bond since without consent no marriage can exist (1626). Through their free personal consent the spouses contract a marriage covenant according to God's laws which oblige them to treat and preserve their union as indissoluble (2364). The consent expresses the willingness of the spouses to commit themselves to each other and as such formulates "one flesh" union between them (1627).[28] Furthermore the personal consent of the spouses formulates their commitment to devote themselves for the common good of the spouse, children, and themselves which main aspects encompass concepts as mutual love, fidelity, honor, and permanence of the union.[29] The very nature of the consent is freedom without fear grounded on the individual will of the person (1628). If the consent is defected marriage may be null by the ecclesiastical tribunal making the couple free to marry again since their marriage has never existed (1629). The consent of the couple is given in the presence of a priest who validates the ecclesial reality of the marriage (1630). The importance of the ecclesiastical form

---

28. *Catechism of the Catholic Church* [online].

29. Pope John Paul II, *Letter to Families from Pope John Paul II*, (1994 – Year of the Family) 10, Libreria Editrice Vaticana [online].

of marriage derives from the liturgical nature of the sacrament of marriage, establishes the obligations of the spouses toward each other and their children within the ecclesial order of the church, formalizes marriage as part of the church life, and affirms the faithfulness of the spouses to their consent (1631). The importance of the personal consent of the spouses establishes a demand for developing the educational background of the spouses in this regard in their families and Christian communities (1632).

The religious differences between the spouses present difficulty in preserving the function of their marital union in a smooth and progressive way. The differences in spouses' religious convictions and understanding of the nature of marriage and its dynamics have strong impact upon their relationship and especially upon the education of their children (1633, 1634).[30] The importance of education is perceived in the communication of knowledge from parents to the child based on their mature humanity and the gift of freshness of humanity given from the child to the parents.[31] Mixed marriages between Catholic and a baptized non-Catholic or non-baptized person may not be defined as entirely impossible but they require special attention from the church and its leadership (1633, 1634). Hence, to initialize mixed marriage the spouses need to have the permission of ecclesiastical authority. The specific dispensation given for the establishing of this marriage validates the marriage and shows the awareness of the spouses with their obligations in regard to the nature of the union and makes clear the intentions of the Catholic party to the non-Catholic party to preserve the faith and ensure the baptism and education of their children in the Catholic Church (1635). Mixed marriages are exceedingly helped to provide the proper environment for the spouses' mutual commitment through the ecumenical dialog between different Christian communities (1636). The specific role of the Catholic spouses in marriages with non-baptized persons need to be underlined as facilitating conditions through their love and devotion for the conversion of their spouses to the Christian faith (1637).

There are two major effects which derive from a valid marriage, namely, perpetual bond and special sacrament (1638). The marriage bond which is established by God between two baptized Catholics through the

---

30. *Catechism of the Catholic Church* [online].

31. Pope John Paul II, *Letter to Families from Pope John Paul II*, (1994 – Year of the Family) 16, Libreria Editrice Vaticana [online].

exchange of their consent and the consummation of their union cannot be dissolved by any authority or power either religious or secular (1639, 1640). The sacrament of matrimony is defined and sustained through Christ's grace. This is foreshadowed in God's covenant with his people Israel. The covenantal faithfulness and love of Christ to his bride the church is shared by the spouses in the sacrament of matrimony. Through Christ's grace they are equipped with everything necessary to serve Christ and each other in the permanent union of marriage even in the midst of most difficult circumstances (1641, 1642).[32] The spouses being participants in the sacrament of marriage need to be a constant reminder to the church of Christ's salvific death on the cross fulfilling the threefold nature of every sacrament, namely, memorial, actuation and prophecy.

> As a memorial, the sacrament gives them the grace and duty of commemorating the great works of God and of bearing witness to them before their children. As actuation, it gives them the grace and duty of putting into practice in the present, towards each other and their children, the demands of a love which forgives and redeems. As prophecy, it gives them the grace and duty of living and bearing witness to the hope of the future encounter with Christ.[33]

The marital love is based on responsibilities and duties which being formulated in the fourth commandment, "Honor your father and your mother," establish the grounds for all the family relations which further define the whole of human civilization as "civilization of love." [34]

The nature of conjugal love in marriage is entirely based on the indissolubility of the union and the faithfulness between the two spouses and involves their entire devotion to each other not only physical but also spiritual as well as their openness to fertility (1643). This love of the spouses toward each other is nourished through their continuous dedication to the unity of marriage (1645) and their complete daily communion with each other and with Christ as well as through their faith and participation in the Eucharist (1644). The conjugal love of the spouses requires practicing the virtue of chastity (2349) as well as their complete and total faithfulness toward each other which permanent character formulates the

---

32. *Catechism of the Catholic Church* [online].

33. Apostolic Exhortation of Pope John Paul II, *Familiaris Consortio*, 13 [online].

34. Pope John Paul II, *Letter to Families from Pope John Paul II*, (1994 – Year of the Family) 15, Libreria Editrice Vaticana [online].

very essence of the union (1646). The most intimate expression of the conjugal love between the spouses is their sexuality through which they unite each other in a truly human way to experience joy and pleasure and also to share their permanent commitment to each other (2360, 2361, 2362). The fidelity of the spouses to their marriage covenant resembles the faithfulness of Christ to his covenant with the church which underlines the sacramental and indissoluble nature of their marriage (1647) as well as depicts the spouses as witnesses of this mystery to the world (2365). Due to the various difficult circumstances the permanence of the marital union may seem impossible to sustain but through sharing in God's love and grace and with the support of the ecclesial community the spouses receive the strength to sustain it (1648). However, when the tension in the relationship between the spouses becomes unbearable they may separate from each other through the church's permission but they cannot contract a new union since their bond is indissoluble. Hence, they need to remain open to reconciliation with each other (1649). Even if they divorce and contract a new union through civil authorities their new relationships cannot be recognized by the church as valid. In addition since they object God's law they are not allowed to participate in the Eucharist and to perform certain ecclesial responsibilities. They also cannot obtain the sacrament of penance unless they repent and dedicate their life to continence (1650). Ecclesial community, however, should allow these Christians to be part of the church communion and live their Christian faith daily raising their children accordingly (1651).

The most profound function of marital union and the essential role of marriage in regard to God's creation are the openness of the spouses to fertility which leads them to procreation of children and their upbringing (1652, also 2366–2372).[35] This desire for heirs springs from the creative will of God which formulates the genealogy of every person.[36] In the covenant of marriage both spouses give themselves to each other freely and accept each other fulfilling their union in this mutual sharing of their conjugal love and accept the gift of children from the "one flesh" union with its parental duties and obligations.[37] It is the parents' most important obligation to extend to their children their love and share with

---

35. *Catechism of the Catholic Church* [online].

36. Pope John Paul II, *Letter to Families from Pope John Paul II*, (1994 – Year of the Family) 9, Libreria Editrice Vaticana [online].

37. Ibid., 12.

them their moral, spiritual, and supernatural life (1653). This aspect of marital union which depicts the inner family relationships in which the participants, husband, wife, and their children become the carriers of God's way of life establishes the union as *Ecclesia domestica*, the domestic church, which role of serving the needs of its members as well as those of the people without families, defines its crucial importance for the ecclesial community and the society at large (1655, 1656, 1657, 1658). In this way also these married couples who have not been granted children by God find the entire fulfillment of their conjugal love through serving God and the people in need (1654).[38] The domestic church can maintain its nature and resist the pressure from social dynamics which intend to degrade it only through being part of the great mystery of the union between Christ and his bride, being itself the bride of Christ.[39]

In summary, in light of St. Paul's saying in Eph 5:25, 32 marriage is defined as a relationship between husband and wife which bears the mark of "a great mystery" due to its resemblance of the relationship between Christ and the church (1659). This relationship between the spouses is characterized as a covenant commitment which defines their life with mutual intimate love based on God's creation ordinances. The marriage covenant relationship is to provide a beneficial environment both for the couple and for its children. This covenant between two baptized spouses is established by Christ as a sacrament (1660). The sacramental nature of marriage furnishes such a relationship between the spouses being enlighten and empowered by the relationship between Christ and the church with sacrificial love and lifelong devotion that impacts the spouses' spiritual condition preparing them for the eternal life (1661).[40] It is according to God's creative will and Christ's renewing power of human heart to make the indissoluble nature of marriage a gift for the spouses to share their conjugal love in total fidelity and ensure the wellbeing of their children.[41] The entire commitment to the marriage covenant relationship is totally based on the personal consent of each of the spouses so that it may empower the personal choice for faithfulness and dedicated love (1662). The marriage institution being part of the body of Christ

38. *Catechism of the Catholic Church* [online].

39. Pope John Paul II, *Letter to Families from Pope John Paul II*, (1994 – Year of the Family), 19. Libreria Editrice Vaticana [online].

40. *Catechism of the Catholic Church* [online].

41. Apostolic Exhortation of Pope John Paul II, *Familiaris Consortio*, 20 [online].

and the society is to be established in a public liturgical setting in the church with the presence of priest, witnesses, and the whole congregation (1663). The boundaries in which the marriage covenant is to function according to God's ordinations are "unity, indissolubility, and openness of fertility (1664)." Beyond these boundaries which define the freedom of the couple to share their life in mutual commitment marriage is failing short form God's intentions. Hence, adultery, divorce, polygamy, incest, free unions, and refusal to fertility are actions against the holy matrimony and are incompatible with God's standards (1664). The act of remarriage for those who have ended their marriages with divorce establishes their impossibility to receive Eucharistic communion even though it does not place them outside of the church (1665). The remarried Christians are encouraged to live their lives in a Christian manner especially for the benefit of their children (1665). It is the secure relationship of the Christian marriage which constitutes the proper environment for raising the children (1666).[42]

One of the contemporary leading Catholic scholars offers an exegetical analysis of Jesus' logion on divorce as it is presented by the evangelists (Mark 10:2–12; Matt 5:32–34; 19:2–12; Luke 16:18) and Paul (7:10, 11; 12–16). Raymond F. Collins exegetes the passage of Mark 10:2–12 in light of the historical context of Jesus and Mark as well as in relation to its literary context and grammatical structure. He characterizes the saying of Jesus as a narrative with a literary character related to a conflict resolution. The conflict as appears in the narrative is between Jesus and Pharisees but also bears resolution to the questions of Jesus' disciples who are related to the Gentile-Christian community in Mark's context.[43] According to Collins the evangelist structures the narrative with presentation of two main scenes. The first one depicts the debate between Jewish authorities and Jesus. The second scene presents the dialog between Jesus and his disciples. The conflict between Pharisees and Jesus is described in a threefold manner. The first is led by Pharisees in regard to the matters of divorce according to the Torah. The challenging question of the religious leaders with the intention to test Jesus is referring to the legality of the man's freedom in the matters of divorce. Jesus' reply is constituted by a question referring to Moses' command which prompts the Pharisees'

---

42. *Catechism of the Catholic Church* [online].
43. R. F. Collins, *Sexual Ethics and the New Testament: Behavior and Belief*, 22–26.

reference to Deut 24:1 which is the key text in the contemporary debate referring to the grounds for divorce between the schools of Hillel and Shammai. However, Jesus does not consider this text as crucial to the issue of divorce as the Pharisees due to its misuse by those who guided by the hardness of their hearts dissolve their marriages for gratifying their sinful desires.[44] Second, Jesus using the rabbinic way of argumentation offers a more significant passage, Gen 1:27 and 2:24 to the debate due to its priority in appearance in the Scriptures. The creation of humankind by God in two genders is normative to the nature of marital union which is expressed through the language of joining both spouses to becoming one through their sexual union.[45] Third, Jesus concludes his argument with the Pharisees by diminishing the significance of their question with the seriousness of formulating God's intentions in human sexuality and marriage. This is presented in a way of a contrast. The human actions of divorce go in direct contradiction with God's intentions revealed in the creation of the first marriage.[46]

The second scene which Mark depicts refers to a new location which may be understood as bearing a reference to the Christian community in Mark's days. The discussion is led by the same topic but the audience is changed to Jesus' disciples. The disciples are following the Pharisees' inquiry but the answer given to them by Jesus tackles the issues in a different way. The discussion does not directly bear reference to the Torah since Mark's community constituted from Christians with Gentile background did not consider the Law bearing direct relevance to their life. Hence, Jesus continues the discussion in regard to God's intentions for marriage and the spouses' obligations for its preservation. The sense of mutuality is clearly defined as being determined due to the dimensions of the Gentile context. Both man and woman who act against God's intentions with initiating divorce and abandoning their spouse are judged with committing adultery through their subsequent remarriage. This bears indirect reference to the Pharisees' question giving an answer to the legality of divorce. Abandoning of one spouse through the act of divorce and remarriage is considered adultery which is a direct violation of the Law.[47]

44. Ibid., 26–27.
45. Ibid., 27.
46. Ibid., 27.
47. Ibid., 28–29.

An exegetical analysis of Matthew's second passage on divorce and remarriage (19:2–12) shows that the evangelist used the text from Mark and revised it according to his Jewish-Christian audience. The importance of the debate between the schools of Hillel and Sammaih receives a significant place in the debate between the Pharisees and Jesus. The question of the Pharisees from Mark's account which is edited by Matthew to bear relevance to the debate between these two Jewish schools is formulated as: what are exactly the legitimate lawful grounds for divorce? The approach of the Pharisees was guided by their intentions to establish Jesus' affiliation to one of their schools which defined the grounds of divorce differently. The school of Shammai limited all grounds of divorce to only that of adultery while the school of Hillel expanded the grounds to even finding a more pleasing wife by the man (*m. Git.* 9:10). Jesus led the discussion with a reference to God's intentions to marriage in the creation account which appeared not to be sufficient for the religious leaders who opposed this argument with the law from Deut 24:1. The counterargument of Jesus appears to formulate Moses' legislation as allowance based on God's wisdom (*mitzvot*) given to those who were not able to observe the strict demands of the Law.[48] Hence, the law did not command divorce but allowed it because of the hardness of heart of those who were not able to fulfill God's original intentions. The concrete answer of Jesus comes with an authoritative introductory statement to refute all grounds for divorce and remarriage except those on *porneia*, referring to general sexual misconduct. The exception which Matthew introduces to Mark's text has only one purpose firmly related to the particularity of the evangelist's context. It was demanded by "the patriarchal society of a Jewish Christian readership"[49] that the wife guilty of *porneia* was divorced. The permanence of marital union and the fulfillment of human sexuality only in marriage relationship is underlined by Matthew with Jesus' reference to every act of divorce and remarriage except on the grounds of *porneia* as constituting the sin of adultery.[50] The scene which refers to Jesus' disciples is developed by Matthew in the same location as Mark but here to express the possibility of the disciples to live a life according to Jesus' law on marriage, divorce, and remarriage. The affirming statement of Jesus offered

---

48. Ibid., 31.
49. Ibid., 32.
50. Ibid., 31.

to the disciples' pessimistic outlook on marriage defines God's grace as the empowering force behind the choice of status. God's grace will make the provision for those who are part of marital relationship to maintain them according to Jesus' law and will empower those who are dedicated to celibate life to live it in chastity.[51] Matthew's earlier account regarding the issues of divorce and remarriage (5:31–32) presents Jesus as interpreting the law of Deut 24:1. The authoritative interpretation of this *mitzvah* constitutes a twofold expansion of the tradition referring to illegal divorce and remarriage as adultery. First, due to the cultural expectations of remarriage of the divorced woman the man who divorces her is guilty of adultery forcing her into the new marriage. Second, anyone who marries a divorced woman is guilty of adultery. The exception offered by Matthew in his later account is presented here as well due to the same contextual reasons.[52]

Luke's presentation of Jesus' tradition on marriage, divorce, and remarriage (16:18) is without particular context related to these issues. The first part of the saying finds its parallels to Mark 10:11 and Matt 19:9 while the second part to Matt 5:32. Luke's version of the tradition comes closer to the original version of the saying which defines the acts of divorce and remarriage as adultery without allowing an exception.[53]

Paul deals with the matters of divorce and remarriage according to the particular situations encountered by the Corinthian Christians. In 1 Corinthians ch 7 the apostle instructs different groups of believers who found themselves in different situations in regard to their marital status. Paul approaches six different groups of believers, namely, those in Christian marriages (7:1–7), widows and widowers (7:8–9), those who wish to divorce (7:10–11), those in a "mixed marriage" (7:12–16), those who have not yet married (32–38), and finishes with the widow (39–40).[54] Two of these groups bear direct reference to Paul's understanding of Jesus' logion on divorce. The first group is constituted by Christians who are married but contemplating divorce (7:10–11). The order of approaching husband and wife giving priority to the wife suggests that Paul is dealing with situation occasioned both from the Greco-Roman context where

51. Ibid., 32.
52. Ibid., 33.
53. Ibid., 33, 34.
54. Ibid., 34.

women were free to initiate divorce and from the particular situation of the Christian community he addresses. Hence, the wife who wishes to divorce her husband is strongly admonished by the apostle not to separate. The emphasis on the permanent nature of marriage is so strong that Paul refers to the authority which the risen Lord has upon the Christian community. If the wife has reached the separation she is forbidden to remarry in order to provide grounds for reconciliation with her husband. The husband who contemplates divorce is also commanded on the grounds of Lord's authority not to divorce.[55] The permanent nature of marriage is the guiding force of Paul's argumentation with the next group as well, those of a "mixed marriage" (7:12–16). The literary and cultural contexts suggest that those were unique cases of families where only one of the spouses converted to Christianity. Paul defends the perpetual nature of marital union even under these arduous circumstances. The Christian spouses are given three major reasons to preserve their marriages with the non-Christian spouse. First, the concept of holiness is introduced signifying the state of the non-Christian spouse as becoming part of God's plan of salvation due to his marital relationship with the Christian spouse. The children of this marriage also share this holiness. Second, the concept of peace as related to marriage according to the Jewish tradition is to determine the desire of the Christian to preserve the marital union. Third, even the very salvation of the non-Christian spouse depends on the protection of the marriage since the presence of the Christian may be decisive in this regard.[56] Hence, even though in his articulation of Jesus' logion on divorce Paul does not define the actions of divorce and remarriage as adulterous as the evangelists depicted them, the apostle understands the importance of preserving the marital union by Christians who found themselves in various even difficult circumstances and argues convincingly for protecting the permanent nature of marriage.[57]

The core of the matrimonial teaching of the Roman Catholic Church is the permanent sacramental indissoluble nature of the marriage institution, which excludes the acts of divorce and remarriage for any reason and treats the breakdown of the canonically valid marriages as impossible, unless established on annulment grounds. The Roman

---

55. Ibid., 34, 35.
56. Ibid., 36.
57. Ibid., 37.

Catholic Church defines marriage as an institution (*matrimoniale familiareque institutum*).[58] Marriage is a covenant union (Canon 1055:1[59]) between man and woman established as a loving community for the purpose of helping the partners edify each other, accomplish their expectations from life, raise children, and help each other against sexual temptations (*remedium concupiscientiae*).[60] Marriage is viewed as one of the sacraments of the church (Canon 1055:2).[61] It is not a "ritualized" act expressed with a sacramental sign or special sacral gesture of the priest but a consecrated state which provides an atmosphere in which all the segments of healthy marital relationship are empowered with a redemptive potential for building the Kingdom of God.[62] Nevertheless, the special gesture represents a symbolic act which accompanied with related word proclaims the presence of God and instigates the response in faith by the parties.[63] The sacramental nature of marriage is firmly grounded in the mystical union between Christ and his church.[64] Thus,

---

58. D. O'Callaghan, *Marriage as Sacrament*, 102, 103. The second code of the canon law (1983) preserves the teaching of marriage as institution of the first code (1917), which has made it emphatically clear, but also incorporates a stronger concern about the individual. (Ladislas Orsy, SJ, *Marriage in Canon Law: Texts and Comments. Reflections and Questions* [Dublin: Fowler Wright, Leominster, 1988] 35, 37.)

59. "The matrimonial covenant, by which a man and a woman establish between themselves a consortium of the whole life, [which] by its very nature is ordered to the good of the spouses and to the procreation and education of children, has been raised by Christ the Lord to the dignity of a sacrament between baptized persons." (Canon 1055:1). The new code of the canon law presents marriage as a covenant but preserves the emphasis of the old law on the contractual nature of the union. (L. Orsy, SJ, *Marriage in Canon Law: Texts and Comments. Reflections and Questions*, 46, 47, 48.)

60. D. O'Callaghan, *Marriage as Sacrament*, 103; P. Čalić, *Brak u procijepu: oženjan-rastavljen-ponovno vjenčan*, 59, 61, 62.

61. L. Orsy, SJ, *Marriage in Canon Law: Texts and Comments. Reflections and Questions*, 54–58.

62. D. O'Callaghan, *Marriage as Sacrament*, 102, 103.

63. Edward J. Kilmartin, "When is Marriage a Sacrament," *Theological Studies* 34 (June 1973): 277–78.

64. "The sacrament of Matrimony signifies the union of Christ and the Church. It gives spouses the grace to love each other with the love with which Christ has loved his Church; the grace of the sacrament thus perfects the human love of the spouses, strengthens their indissoluble unity, and sanctifies them on the way to eternal life." (*Catechism of the Catholic Church*, 1661. Libreria Editrice Vaticana [online], Available at http://www.vatican.va/archive/ENG0015/__P51.HTM, Accessed on 25 September 2004, cf Council of Trent: DS 1799). L. Boff, *The Sacrament of Marriage*, 22, 23; R. M. Hogan, *John Paul II's New Vision of Human Sexuality, Marriage and Family Life* [online].

"every canonically valid marriage between two baptised persons is a sacrament, even if those persons are in no way influenced in their lives by their baptism, or do not know that they are baptised or attach no religious value at all to their marriage."[65] On the contrary, marriage which is contracted between non-baptised non-believers cannot be designated as a sacrament. The sacramentality of mixed marriages is supported and objected by different groups of scholars.[66] Disagreements extend even to the Christian and non-Christian marriages. Some of the Catholic theologians argue that marriage which lacks "love of charity" cannot be designated as a sacrament.[67] Others, to the contrary, designate every marriage as sacramental, even the marriages of non-Christians, due to the expression of God's union with mankind.[68]

The sacramental nature of marriage makes it indissoluble (Canon 1056[69]). Thus, the marital bond remains even when both parties fail to establish a healthy marital relationship and as a sacrament it provides a permanent ground for reactualization.[70] The indissoluble nature of marriage should be understood as two dimensional. On the one hand, it is the "moral obligation"[71] of the spouses to preserve the marital union. On the other hand, it defines the "nature of the bond" as extrinsically and intrinsically indissoluble.[72] In this respect the indissolubility might be further evaluated according to the nature of its impediments. Extrinsic indissolubility is formulated as the resistance of the marital bond in the face of an external force for marital breakdown. Intrinsic indissolubility refers to the protection of the bond from internal destructive forces. All marriages

---

65. Peter Huizing, "Canon Law and Broken Marriages," *Concilium* 7 (September 1973) 20.

66. Aug. Lehmkuhl, "Sacrament of Marriage," in *The Catholic Encyclopedia*, vol. IX, trans. Bobie Jo M. Bilz, CD-ROM edition, 2003, ed. Kevin Knight.

67. Philippe Delhaye, "The Development of the Medieval Church's Teaching on Marriage," *Concilium* 5/6 (May 1970): 85.

68. L. Boff, *The Sacrament of Marriage*, 26, 27.

69. "The essential properties of marriage are unity and indissolubility, which in Christian marriage, by reason of the sacrament, obtain a particular firmness." (Canon 1056) (L. Orsy, SJ, *Marriage in Canon Law: Texts and Comments. Reflections and Questions*, 58, 59.)

70. D. O'Callaghan, *Marriage as Sacrament*, 106.

71. L. Orsy, SJ, *Marriage in Canon Law: Texts and Comments. Reflections and Questions*, 58.

72. Ibid.

whether Christian or non-Christian are intended to be indissoluble as far as the moral obligation of the parties for their preservation is concerned. However, those marriages which are not consummated are losing the extrinsic indissolubility since they might be dissolved by the Roman Pontiff (Canon 1142). In addition, those marriages which have been established between non-Christians and suffer desertion by the non-baptized party after the baptism of the other party are under the force of both intrinsic and extrinsic dissolubility (Canon 1143:1).[73] Marriages indissoluble either intrinsically or extrinsically are those among baptized Christians which are ratified and consummated (Canon 1056 and 1141).[74] Even the act of adultery does not dissolve the marital bond and cannot be treated as proper grounds for divorce.[75] The Pauline privilege is important for some particular cases of unhealthy marriages, and it has been used as such in the history of the Roman Catholic Church,[76] but it may not be considered as legal imperative to the indissoluble nature of marriage.[77] However, some Catholic theologians recognize that the indissolubility of

73. Also ibid., 215.

74. Ibid., 58, 59, 212. However it is argued that the canon law does not limit the "sacred power" of the Catholic Church to dissolve even such marriages but just intends to express the church's desire to protect sacramental consummated marriages (ibid., 213).

75. "Propter adulterium alterius coniugum matrimonii vinculum non posse dissolvi." P. Fransen, *Divorce on the Ground of Adultery—The Council of Trent (1563)*, 95, 96. Matthew's exception clauses (5:32, 19:9) have been treated as separation of bed and board (ibid., 90).

76. Pauline privilege, an interpretation of 1 Cor 7:15 which permits divorce and remarriage for the Christian spouse who is deserted by the non-Christian one, has been used with different force as a remedy for unhealthy mixed marriages. Augustine, for example, allowed divorce but disallowed remarriage for the deserted Christian party. Theodore of Canterbury (690) insisted on complete dissolution of mixed marriages since the Council of Toledo (633) had already stated that divorce might be an useful tool for evangelism of the Jews who are married to Christians. Clement III (1191) used the Pauline privilege in the way Augustine did but applied it to the mixed marriages in which one of the spouses was still part of the Jewish or Muslim religion. Innocent III (1216) used the Pauline privilege in its full force allowing the believers deserted by the unbelieving party to divorce and remarry. Finally, the Roman curia used the Pauline privilege to allow both divorce and remarriage when there was a lack of signs for the conversion of the unbelieving party. (See P. Huizing, *Canon Law and Broken Marriages*, 14, 15.)

77. D. O'Callaghan, *Marriage as Sacrament*, 106, 107. It is argued that presently the Pauline privilege has lost completely its intended authority for dissolution of mixed marriages. It is interpreted just as a statement of the apostle that unhealthy mixed marriages do not provide an environment for the Christian party to live peacefully. (See P. Huizing, *Canon Law and Broken Marriages*, 19.)

marriage is not a "judicial law of absolute validity" but an ethical demand of Christ to his disciples.[78] The words of Christ, therefore, should be interpreted not only theoretically, but also in the light of their modification throughout the Christian tradition which applied them to particular situations taking in consideration the particular cultural background of the people involved and their fallen human nature. For that reason Catholic theologians maintain that not only the indissolubility of marriage should be taken into account in formulation of the canon law, but also the permission of divorce and remarriage allowed by Matthew (Matt 5:32; 19:9) and Paul (1 Cor 7:15) when dealing with sick marriages.[79] The church, however, recognizes the seriousness of some situations related to divorce and remarriage and empathises with its believers, who are victims of such situations, but cannot "institutionalise what Jesus refused to institutionalise: the law of faith is a single one–a monogamous and indissoluble sacramental marriage."[80] Thus, even in a case of adultery or desertion divorce is not allowed, but Matthew's exception clause and Pauline privilege are used to establish the grounds either for separation from bed and board (*divortium imperfectum*) of the adulterous party[81] or for marital annulment.[82] At times the Roman Catholic Church went so far to preserve the absolute indissolubility of marriage that it reckoned anyone who had been sexually active before the marriage or had had a former marriage before his/her baptism to be a bigamist.[83]

Although during its history the Roman Catholic Church used divorce and remarriage as a remedy for unhealthy marriages allowing them on different grounds,[84] due to its belief in the indissoluble nature

---

78. L. Boff, *The Sacrament of Marriage*, 29.

79. Paul Hoffmann, "Jesus' Saying About Divorce and Its Interpretation in the New Testament Tradition," *Concilium* 5/6 (May 1970) 64–66.

80. C. J. Snoek, *Marriage and the Institutionalisation of Sexual Relations*, 118.

81. Based primarily on the words of Paul in 1 Cor 7:11 that "if she does separate, let her remain unmarried or else be reconciled to her husband," (NRS) the practice of separation from bed and board is also applied in case of infidelity or heresy on the part of husband or wife. Aug. Lehmkuhl, "Divorce (in Moral Theology)," trans. Listya Sari Diyah, in *The Catholic Encyclopedia*, v.5 [online], Available at http://www.newadvent.org/cathen/05054c.htm, Accessed on 18 April 2001.

82. D. Armstrong and W. Klimon, *Dialogue: Annulment vs. Divorce* [online].

83. Korbinnian Ritzer, "Secular Law and the Western Church's Concept of Marriage," *Concilium* 5/6 (May 1970) 69.

84. Three reasons for proper divorce and remarriage might be identified: adultery

of marriage, the church prohibited divorce and remarriage for any reason.[85] However, since such a strict approach did not provide a channel for dealing with the cases of difficult marriages, the church created a tool for solving this problem with the annulment of marriages.[86] Hence, divorce appears to be substituted for with the act of marital annulment.[87] In this way the church attempted to protect its teaching of the indissolubility of sacramental marriages.[88] Annulment of the marital bond is possible to be established on either objective or subjective reasons. The former might be defined as prohibited blood-relations (*Sub Lege Custodiebamur Inclusi*) such as between brothers and sisters, uncles and aunts, great-uncles and great-aunts.[89] Further objective reason might be the lack of procreation

---

(The Council of Vannes [465]; The Council of Verberve [752]; Penitential of Theodore [7c]), disappearance of a spouse, (Gregory XIII [1585] allowed dissolution of marriages with provision for divorce and remarriage when one of the partners disappeared and could not be found for a fixed period of time), and in "favour of faith," (Pius XI [1924] granted dissolution of marriage and allowed remarriage for the divorced non-Catholics who wanted to become Catholics and marry a Catholic. Pius XII, John XXIII, and Paul VI allowed dissolution of marriages with provision for divorce and remarriage to Catholics whose spouses did not show interest in the Catholic faith). The last reason is also known as the Petrine privilege, since it relates to the authority of the Pope. See Yuri Koszarycz, *Divorce, Remarriage, and the Christian Tradition* [online], Available at http://www.mcauley.acu.edu.au/~yuri/ethics/Divorce.html, Accessed on 19 April 2001; P. Huizing, *Canon Law and Broken Marriages*, 15–18; R. Phillips, *Untying the Knot: A Short History of Divorce*, 8, 9.

85. N. Greinacher, *The Problem of Divorce and Remarriage*, 221–226. "A ratified and consummated marriage cannot be dissolved by any human power nor by any cause other than death." (Canon 1141) There is no legitimate cause for dissolubility apart from death. Even adultery cannot be a justified cause. (L. Orsy, SJ. *Marriage in Canon Law: Texts and Comments. Reflections and Questions*, 212.)

86. "An invalid marriage is called putative if it was celebrated in good faith at least by one party, until both become certain of its nullity." (Canon 1061:3); "Even if the previous marriage is invalid or dissolved for any reason, it is not therefore lawful to contract another one before the nullity or the dissolution of the previous one has been established legitimately and with certainty." (Canon 1085:2) (L. Orsy, SJ. *Marriage in Canon Law: Texts and Comments. Reflections and Questions*, 69, 112.)

87. *Divorce & Remarriage* [online]; Fr. B. Pinkston, *When A Marriage Fails* [online]. See also R. Phillips, *Untying the Knot: A Short History of Divorce*, 5.

88. Philip S. S. Keane, *Sexual Morality: A Catholic Perspective* (London: Philip Sullivan Keane and Gill and Macmillan, 1980), 142.

89. The Roman Catholic Church has been criticized by the Eastern Church for exercising acrobatic ingenuity in its efforts to annul marriages in order to allow divorce and remarriage even after a long period of marriage. See K. Ritzer, *Secular Law and the Western Church's Concept of Marriage*, 70–72.

ability (*Liberorum Quaerendorum Cause*) since one of the primary purposes of marriage is procreation of descendants.⁹⁰ In such a case both partners are allowed to remarry. Close to the previous reason is the lack of a marriage contract based on the mutual consent of the two parties (*Nuptias Non Concubitus, Sed Consensus Facit*).⁹¹ Defective consent includes a variety of reasons such as amentia (lack of adequate psychic maturity for undertaking marriage responsibilities), sexual anomalies (different kinds of sexual-psychic disorders, e.g. homosexuality, psychic impotence, insanity, nymphomania which hinder serious undertaking of conjugal obligations), morbus mentis (e.g. mental retardation), different mental disorders (e.g. schizophrenia), and perturbatio (e.g. drunkenness).⁹² In such instances even sexual intercourse cannot constitute a legal marriage.⁹³ In a case of subjective reasons the premarital correct intentions and ethical maturation of the spouses play a crucial role for binding marital agreement.⁹⁴ "All divorced Catholics are encouraged to apply for an Annulment even if they cannot see grounds for such an Annulment."⁹⁵ Finally, indissoluble marriage is very narrowly defined⁹⁶ and the validity of the marital bond very subjectively grounded⁹⁷ so that the possibility for annulment might always be applied if necessary. Hence,

90. Ibid., 72–73.

91. The importance of the marriage contract based on the mutual consent of the partners might be clearly seen in Pope Nicholas' declaration to Bulgars, who were young Christians, that without a marriage contract signed in agreement by both partners even the sexual intercourse cannot constitute a legal marriage. (See K. Ritzer, *Secular Law and the Western Church's Concept of Marriage*, 73–75)

92. See William LaDue, "The Expanding Limits of Lack of Due Discretion Cases," *Concilium* 7/9 (September 1973) 61–71.

93. See K. Ritzer, *Secular Law and the Western Church's Concept of Marriage*, 70–75.

94. Ladislas Orsy, "The Function of Ecclesial Decision: A Theological Evaluation of Marriage Tribunals," *Concilium* 7/9 (September 1973) 38.

95. Gwenda Callaghan, *Explaining What the Catholic Annulment Process Means and Does not Mean* [online], Available at http://www.aquinas-academy.syd.catholic.edu.au/editorial.htm, Accessed on 18 April 2001.

96. "Only a 'sacramental' marriage, that is, marriage between two baptised partners, is, after 'consummation,' that is, sexual intercourse between the two baptised partners, absolutely indissoluble. All other marriages are, subject to certain conditions, canonically dissoluble." (P. Huizing, *Canon Law and Broken Marriages*, 18.)

97. The Second Vatican Council included in the criteria for valid marriage the desires and the abilities of both parties to establish and preserve lasting personal relationships. (See P. Huizing, *Canon Law and Broken Marriages*, 18, 19.)

the Tribunals which analyze the validity of marriage consider as evidence toward its nullification even the parties' "intention to marry or the presence or absence of the knowledge required for a binding agreement."[98] Apart from church politics in relation to divorce and remarriage, baptised members of the church began terminating their marriages using secular courts. In such cases some Catholic theologians[99] plead for more flexible understanding by the church in relation to the indissolubility of the valid marriages[100] and for allowing these divorced believers to remarry in the church in a proper liturgical form.[101] However, the church does not respond positively to such an appeal even though it treats the remarried believers as proper members and under some circumstances allows them to participate in the Eucharist.[102] It becomes clear that the church's stand against divorce and remarriage did not stop or even decrease divorce and remarriage in Catholic countries and communities.[103]

The view of marriage as an indissoluble institution and the practice of nullification of marriages as a remedy for marriage breakdown have faced much criticism from some Catholic theologians. The indissolubility of marriage received the critique of being biblically inadequate and culturally irrelevant.[104] Hence, the biblical principal used by Jesus that the Law should be used for the well-being of the man, not vice versa, is applied as, "indissolubility was made for man, not man for indissolubility."[105] The nature of nullification as the only possible way of exercising

98. L. Orsy, *The Function of Ecclesial Decision: A Theological Evaluation of Marriage Tribunals*, 38.

99. See Klemens Richter, "The Liturgical Celebration of Marriage. The Problems raised by Changing Theological and Legal Views of Marriage," *Concilium* 7/8 (September 1973) 81–83.

100. Richter maintains that it is hard and even impossible to understand the nature of a broken valid marriage as indissoluble. (See ibid., 82.)

101. Richter argues that even when there is no evidence for nullification of the first marriage the church should allow divorced believers to remarry with a proper church wedding. (See ibid., 83.)

102. P. Čalić, *Brak u procijepu: oženjan-rastavljen-ponovno vjenčan*, 103, 110, 119; G. Callaghan, *Annulment Process. Remarriage in the Church: Pastoral Solutions. A Statement by the Board Members of the Association for the Rights of Catholics in the Church (ARCC)* [online].

103. J. Dominian, "Marital Breakdown," *Concilium* 7/9 (September 1973) 123–39.

104. See Giovanni Cereti, "Judges or Counsellors?" *Concilium* 7/9 (September 1973) 99.

105. Ibid., 100.

grace in relation to indissoluble sick marriages is exposed and criticized as being not only enormously flexible but also open to massive abuse.[106] Thus, the whole sacramental institution of marriage has been shaken since the broad grounds for nullification questioned the validity of every marriage.[107] "Probably a lot of very happy and healthy marriages could be considered as null, as non-marriages, if the criteria for true marital consent were applied to the beginnings of these now-successful marriages."[108] An escape from that complex situation is offered with a proposal for a more ecumenical understanding of marriage, divorce, and remarriage,[109] acceptance of the reality of the marital breakdown,[110] and a new approach to divorced and remarried believers.[111] The latter should be given the chance to repent, to undergo a suitable penance, and a new beginning.[112]

THE TEACHING OF THE EASTERN ORTHODOX CHURCH

The Eastern Orthodox Church defines marriage as an institution. It is based on the mutual consent of man and woman who are joined together in a covenant relationship with divine grace, which bound the first couple (Gen 1:28, 2:23–24), for the purpose of edifying each other and raising children.[113] The institution of holy matrimony is reaffirmed by Christ's

---

106. G. Cereti, *Judges or Counsellors*, 100, 101. See also Robert H. Vasoli, *What God Has Joined Together: The Annulment Crisis in American Catholicism* (Oxford: Oxford University Press, 1998).

107. G. Cereti, *Judges or Counsellors*, 103. Establishing the covenant nature of marriage as indissoluble does not lead Paul Palmer to preservation of marriage unions but to their further analysis for search of reasons for annulment. Hence, he embraces wholeheartedly grounds for annulment based on defective faith, defective love or lack of love, defective consent (obscure due to lack of freedom or physical, psychological, and emotional ability to enter the covenant relationship) during the time of marital initiation considering all of them as impediments to valid covenantal marriages and thus require annulment. (P. F. Palmer, *Christian Marriage: Contract or Covenant?* 664, 665.)

108. P. S. S. Keane, *Sexual Morality: A Catholic Perspective*, 142.

109. G. Cereti, *Judges or Counsellors*, 104, 105.

110. Ibid., 108.

111. Haring states that "the church is able to, and in my view should, bless a second but stable marriage rather than a doubtfully valid and hopelessly dead former marriage." Bernhard Haring, "Pastoral Word Among the Divorced and Invalidly Married," *Concilium* 5/6 (May 1970) 129, 130.

112. G. Cereti, *Judges or Counsellors*, 108, 109.

113. Fr. Ted, *What is the Orthodox Position on Divorce and Remarriage?* [online].

teaching (Matt 5:32; 19:4–6; Mark 10:5–9) and actions (John 2:1–11) and its nature is further explicated by Paul as a presentation of the mystical union between Christ and the church (Ephesians 5:32). The latter in its context (Eph 5:21–33) provides the most fundamental grounds for the Orthodox matrimonial doctrine, theology and practice. It formulates the very essence of marriage as sacrament articulated through the language of mystery. Theologically it expresses both notions of creation and covenant as realized by the salvific activity of Christ in his union with the church. Thus, in this very union husband and wife find themselves as parts of the body of Christ and, as such, sharers of the fullness of this relationship. The participation of both husband and wife in this perfect union between Christ and the church extends its dimensions in projecting this union in their own marital relationship. Thus, the ethical teaching of the church expects the ethical attributes of the relationship between Christ and the church to be precisely followed by the marital relationship between husband and wife.[114] Furthermore this description of the Apostle Paul intends to characterize the marriage as part of the Kingdom of God. Thus, it shares in the salvific nature of the Kingdom and offers a way for salvation of man. Humanity is created according to God's image and at the same time suffers the consequences of its sinful rejection of the Creator and lives under the power of sin in this world. However through Christ, whose human nature has received completeness and fulfillment through his divine nature, humanity is offered a way back to fulfillment of the divine image of its Creator. The believer becomes "one body" with Christ through the act of baptism and participation in the Eucharist. In this way man actualizes the image of God in himself and reaffirms his true humanity with all its divine potentials. This shared community with Christ is depicted as the mystery of marital union in the light of the Old Testament relation between God and his people. This communion is experienced in the Christian marriage between husband and wife. Thus, marriage becomes a ground for reaffirming one's true humanity as created by God, experiencing one's true potential within the atmosphere of joy and love of the Kingdom of God. As a contrast to the fallen human nature marriage as sacrament might be perceived as an ideal but more than that it reflects a communion with God and as such it goes beyond an abstract

---

114. William Basil Zion, *Eros and Transformation: Sexuality and Marriage—An Eastern Orthodox Perspective* (Lanham, MD: University Press of America, 1931) 39–45.

notion into the sphere of the Kingdom where it shares the presence of the Spirit. This divine presence does not suppress or manipulate human freedom, turning the mystery into a simple form of magic, but frees man from his sinfulness and empowers him for reaching the intended qualities of the image of God.[115] Thus, marriage is a divinely initiated and empowered permanent institution between two Christians which does not suffer obliteration of its human character, defined through all the spectrum of human emotions, thoughts, behavior, and actions. Its biblical regulations serve to encourage spouses' attitudes and actions for the preservation of the union.[116] Hence, the Orthodox teaching does not reduce the sacrament of marriage to a set of rules or legislative practices but expresses it as NT doctrine in its "absolute form."[117]

The church's tradition in the persons of the holy fathers testified a gradual progression toward this holy state of marriage.[118] Under the pressure of Gnostic, Montanist, and monastic movements, through the constant tension between the eschatologically nourished ideal of celibacy and the notion of marriage as sacramentally empowered union between man and woman, and through the process of maturation in the writings of the Fathers[119] the sacramental theology of marriage found its place in

---

115. John Meyendorff, *Marriage: An Orthodox Perspective* (USA: St. Vladimir's Seminary Press, 1975) 19–22.

116. J. Meyendorff, *Marriage: An Orthodox Perspective*, 52, 53.

117. Ibid., 19–22.

118. C. H. Demetry, *Catechism of the Eastern Orthodox Church* [online]; Sotirios, *Matrimony* [online].

119. Here an example might be given with the writings of St. Gregory of Nyssa and St. John Chrysostom related to the subjects of virginity and marriage. (W. B. Zion, *Eros and Transformation: Sexuality and Marriage—An Eastern Orthodox Perspective*, 61–85). Through a comparison of two quotations from the writings of St. John Chrysostom taken from different periods of his life it is clear that his perspective on marriage has developed from a negative to a positive one. Early work: "Do you perceive the origin of marriage? Why it seems to be necessary: It springs from disobedience, from a curse, from death. For where death is, there is marriage. When one does not exist, the other is not about. But virginity does not have this companion. It is always useful, always beautiful and blessed, both before and after death, before and after marriage." (John Chrysostom, *On Virginity* 14, 6, trans. Sally Rieger Shore, in *Studies in Women and Religion*, vol. 9 [New York and Toronto: Edwin Mellen, 1983], quoted in W. B. Zion, *Eros and Transformation: Sexuality and Marriage—An Eastern Orthodox Perspective*, 73.); Later work: "And if any persons have been hindered by marriage state, let them know that marriage is not the hindrance, but their purpose which made an ill use of marriage. Since it is not wine which makes drunkenness, but the evil purpose, and the using it beyond due measure.

the contemporary Orthodox Church.[120] Marriage is understood as an incarnate sacrament and as such it is viewed not just as a single ceremonial act but as a daily practising of the spiritual elements of the sacramental union.[121] Marriage is based on the mutual love of the spouses which produces both faithfulness and confidence in their relationship.[122] The institution of marriage is defined as a lifelong union which might reflect some aspects of indissolubility but not a justification of its absolute nature.[123] Even if the complete indissolubility of marriage is maintained as some Orthodox theologians attempt[124] the acceptance of marital break-

---

Use marriage with moderation, and thou shall be first in the kingdom . . . ." (St. John Chrysostom, *Homilies on the Epistle to the Hebrews.* 7.11., in *Post-Nicene Fathers of the Christian Church*, Series 1, vol.14, ed. Philip Schaff [Grand Rapids: Eerdmans, 1956], *Christian Classics Ethereal Library*, vol.2, CD-ROM, ed. Harry Plantinga [Wheaton, IL: Wheaton College, 1998].)

120. W. B. Zion, *Eros and Transformation: Sexuality and Marriage—An Eastern Orthodox Perspective*, 50–96.

121. M. Najim, *The Theology of the Orthodox Sacrament of Matrimony and Its Implications in our Family Life* [online].

122. Encyclical Letter of the Holy Synod of Bishops, *On Marriage* [online]; H.Van Der Wal, *Secular Law and The Eastern Church's Concept of Marriage*, 81.

123. John A. Hardon, *Divorce: Early Church vs. Eastern Orthodoxy* [online], Available at http://falcon.ic.net/~erasmus/RAZ332.HTM, Accessed on 20 April 2001; K. Richter, *The Liturgical Celebration of Marriage*, 81. For this reason no one who has been married more than once or married to a divorced woman or widow can be accepted as candidate for the priesthood office (Apostolic Canons 17 and 18). "He who has been twice married after baptism, or who has had a concubine, cannot become a bishop, priest or deacon, or a member of the clergy altogether (Apostolic Canon 17)." (See Encyclical Letter of the Holy Synod of Bishops, *On Marriage* [online]; J. Meyendorff, *Marriage: An Orthodox Perspective*, 121.) However Canon 48 of the Sixth Ecumenical Council stands against the indissolubility of marriage. (J. Meyendorff, *Marriage: An Orthodox Perspective*, 122.) Moreover there are numerous examples of ordination of priests who have been remarried after divorce or after death of a spouse. It has been argued that the legitimacy of these practices is established on the grounds of the decision issued by Pan-Orthodox council in 1923 which grants authority to local communities to decide the matter according to the particular circumstances. "The synod of the local churches are able, however, on the advice of the competent bishop, to permit the contracting of marriage to priest and deacons who request it." Hence, the church is able and should continue to modify its former contextually conditioned teachings according to the new situation, based on scholarly research and through the guidance of the Spirit. (Patrick Viscuso, "Concerning the Second Marriage of Priests," *Greek Orthodox Theological Review* 40/1–2 [Spr-Sum 1995] 201–11.)

124. "As a sacrament marriage is indissoluble since it is a sign of the Kingdom of God for whom a man and a woman are crowned in matrimony." (W. B. Zion, *Eros and Transformation: Sexuality and Marriage—An Eastern Orthodox Perspective*, 222.)

down by the Orthodox Church limits or even rejects its implications. The provision for divorce and remarriage in the matrimonial theology of the Orthodox Church makes this assertion difficult to sustain apart from defining it as notion in tension, paradox, and even contradiction. The attempted solution is provided in formulating the dichotomous character of Christian marriage. The divine disposition of marital union as expressed in the mystery of the bond between Christ and the church is indissoluble. Sinful human nature degrades the marital union and makes it dissoluble.[125] The force of the human failure to sustain the marital union expressed in such sins as adultery (Matt 5:32[126]) dissolves even what is indissoluble.[127] Numerous arguments are developed in order to maintain this relationship in conflict with the purpose to uphold the sanctity of the marriage in the church and justify its practice of divorce and remarriage.[128] However the concept of indissolubility is also negated by other orthodox theologians as being "abstract and legal notion"[129] which does not do justice to the nature of marriage as the ultimate model of union within the framework of the eschatological Kingdom dynamics and its church maintenance through pastoral "economy." It is this "ideal norm of an eternal union in the name of Christ" which has found its place in the canons and liturgy of the Orthodox Church, not the belief of indissolubility.[130] Marriage success does not depend entirely upon the efforts of the husband and wife but on God's blessings and promises.[131] The sacramental nature of marriage provides an environment in which God's saving grace is bestowed on the couple with the purpose to empower them for a lifestyle appropriate for the Kingdom of God in general and the family in particular. In this way of strong relation to the eternal Kingdom of God the marriage union reflects not only a lifelong duration but an eternal bond. However, the nature of divine grace does include the exercise of human freedom. Thus, if the notion of indissolubility is perceived as the

---

125. W. B. Zion, *Eros and Transformation: Sexuality and Marriage—An Eastern Orthodox Perspective*, 221–226.

126. J. Meyendorff, *Marriage: An Orthodox Perspective*, 15.

127. Timothy Ware, *The Orthodox Church* (Harmondsworth: Penguin, 1993), 295.

128. W. B. Zion, *Eros and Transformation: Sexuality and Marriage—An Eastern Orthodox Perspective*, 221–226.

129. J. Meyendorff, *Marriage: An Orthodox Perspective*, 51.

130. Ibid.

131. C. H. Demetry, *Orthodox Creed* [online].

norm of the sacramental nature of marriage it needs to be conditioned through human freedom. The divine gift of freedom is a foundational element of Christian marriage and is not suppressed by the ideal norm of union but encouraged toward its fulfillment. This establishes both the possibility of fulfillment and the realization of human freedom in reaching God's ideal and the vulnerability of the marital bond to human failure and marital breakdown.[132] Hence, due to sinful human nature and its constant failure to achieve God's standards for life, the church accepts the marital breakdown as a real fact, and though it condemns the sin, the church loves and attempts to help the sinners by giving them a second chance. Even when improper divorce and remarriage have been established by the believers, the church offers forgiveness after the sincere repentance of the couple.[133] However the church's ceremonial practices related to the second and third marriages reflect the breakdown of the first marriage, in a way removing some joyful elements from the ceremonies.[134]

The marriage is official only after a performance of the holy ceremony by an authorized Clergyman according to the ecclesiastical ceremony of marriage during which the marital vows are exchanged by the bride and groom. The significance of the ceremony and the solemnity of the marital union are underlined by the required premarital counseling and preparation of the couple.[135] Truly sacramental marriage may be established only among believers part of the Orthodox Church. This is deeply rooted in the relationship of marriage to baptism and Eucharist traced in the history of the Orthodox Church.[136] Marriage is unavoidably connected with the Eucharist. The true marriage is established only in relation to and in the atmosphere of Eucharist participation. The parallel is clearly established between a believer's body as the temple of God and the integration of the believer into the body of Christ through the

---

132. J. Meyendorff, *Marriage: An Orthodox Perspective*, 60, 61.

133. C. H. Demetry, *Orthodox Creed* [online].

134. J. Meyendorff, *Marriage: An Orthodox Perspective*, 50, 51.

135. This process starts from choosing the proper partner whose characteristics should match the church standards and it includes symposia for wedding preparation and family guidance with professional counselors and the church workers. See M. Najim, *The Theology of the Orthodox Sacrament of Matrimony and Its Implications in our Family Life* [online].

136. Also Aliuvlaadis C. Calivas, "Marriage: The Sacrament of Love and Communion," *Greek Orthodox Theological Review* 40 (Fall-Winter 1995) 251.

Eucharist. In the context of marriage this is the mystery of the formation of "one flesh" union between the husband and wife being sealed by the Holy Spirit's presence in both of them and their sharing in the body of Christ through participation in the Eucharist. The mystery of marriage also resembles the sacrament of baptism as being part of the liturgy and experiencing its completion in the Eucharist. The most explicit NT allusion to these three sacraments is found in the story of the marriage in Cana (John 2:1–11). The transformation of the water into wine in the presence of Christ depicts vividly the picture of the believer's life being transformed, passing through the experience of baptism and Eucharist. Thus, marriage is understood not only as earthly union between two human beings but also as a salvation mystery of human participation in the Kingdom of God which encompasses eternity. Here the role of a bridge between the two dimensions of life is performed by the priest as minister of both the marriage and the Eucharist. This relation between marriage and Eucharist is clearly stated in the writings of the church fathers, Tertullian (*To His Wife* II.8:6–9) and Ignatius (*To Polycarp* 5:2).[137] Thus, marriage as a substantial experience of the real unity beyond the external form and structure of worldly marriages can be experienced only in Christian marriage. It is in this relationship between the spouses where the empowering love of Christ might be embodied through their devotional life to him and to each other. In the context of the fragmented sinful world Christian marriage provides an environment for the spouses to experience the new life in Christ in a deep and profound way of unity with the Creator and "the original oneness of the creation."[138] The true marriage is the one between Christians inaugurated within the church. Thus, in the face of impediments such as difference in religion, relationship by blood, marriage, spiritual relationships created through baptism, or by legal adoption marriage cannot be validated.[139] Marriage which is not performed in the Orthodox Church, e.g. any other church or in a civil ceremony, is not valid.[140] Mixed marriages are

---

137. J. Meyendorff, *Marriage: An Orthodox Perspective*, 22–26.

138. A. C. Calivas, *Marriage: The Sacrament of Love and Communion*, 262.

139. C. H. Demetry, *Catechism of the Eastern Orthodox Church* [online]. Sotirios, *Matrimony* [online].

140. H. Van Der Wal, *Secular Law and The Eastern Church's Concept of Marriage*, 82.

prohibited[141] apart from the ones between Orthodox and non-Orthodox Christians.[142] The latter are tolerated because of the hope that since the heterodox partner desires this unity and does not oppose but supports the convictions of the Orthodox party, later in the course of marriage he/she will embrace completely the Orthodox faith.[143]

The Eastern Orthodox Church insists on the permanence of the marital union but still allows divorce and subsequent remarriage because of the paradoxical nature of the biblical teaching on these matters and "compassionate concern for human weakness."[144] The church is against divorce in general since Jesus abrogated its practice, but in particular it maintains that "Jesus did not prohibit all divorces."[145] Hence, divorce is not a rule but an exception since the church does not dissolve dead marriages[146] but just acknowledges their condition as such and, acting in mercy, allows the victims of such marriages to divorce and remarry.[147] The teaching of the majority of the church fathers is understood, although

---

141. "An orthodox man is not permitted to marry an heretical woman, nor an orthodox woman to be joined to an heretical man. But if anything of this kind appear to have been done by any, we require them to consider the marriage null, and that the marriage be dissolved . . . ." (Sixth Ecumenical Council, Canon 72, quoted in J. Meyendorff, *Marriage: An Orthodox Perspective*, 118).

142. Excluded are these non-Orthodox Christians who do not recognize baptism in the name of the Holy Trinity. Encyclical Letter of the Holy Synod of Bishops, *On Marriage* [online].

143. Ibid.

144. "Divorce may be allowed when avenues for reconciliation have been exhausted." (C. H. Demetry, *Orthodox Creed* [online].) See also Fr. Ted, *What is the Orthodox Position on Divorce and Remarriage?* [online].

145. S. S. Harakas, *The Orthodox Church: 455 Questions and Answers*, 107; Orthodox Church in America Tenth All-American Council, *Synodal Affirmations on Marriage, Family, Sexuality, and the Sanctity of Life* [online].

146. Three major types of marital death might be identified, moral, psychological, and political. The reasons for moral death are related to the ceasing of love between the parties due to the different kinds of moral abuse such as incest, murder, violence, homosexual activities etc. A psychologically dead marriage has one of the parties under a certain psychological condition which is unbearable to the other party. The political death of marriage appears when one of the parties is withheld from the other due to political reasons like imprisonment or going for a political career. See G. Callaghan, *Annulment Process. Remarriage in the Church: Pastoral Solutions. A Statement by the Board Members of the Association for the Rights of Catholics in the Church (ARCC)* [online].

147. Ibid.

quite controversially by their interpreters,[148] as maintaining negative attitude against all remarriages even after widowhood. However, some did not negate remarriage, and accepted divorce for valid reasons, maintaining positive attitudes toward some Christian reforms in the contemporary social legislation.[149]

> He who cannot keep continence after the death of his first wife or who has separated from his wife for a valid motive, as fornication, adultery, or another misdeed, if he takes another wife, or if the wife takes another husband, the divine word does not condemn him nor exclude him from the Church or the life; but she tolerates it rather on account of his weakness.[150]

The provision for divorce and remarriage in the Orthodox Church has gradually developed through the authoritative declarations of the Council of Laodicea (343–380 AD),[151] the Quinisext Council, the Council at Trullo (692 AD),[152] and the Council of Constantinople (920 AD).[153] The proper biblical grounds which may establish the legitimate

---

148. W. B. Zion, *Eros and Transformation: Sexuality and Marriage—An Eastern Orthodox Perspective*, 193–210.

149. J. Meyendorff, *Marriage: An Orthodox Perspective*, 62, 63.

150. St. Epiphanius of Cyprus, *Against Heresies*, 69, PG 41, col. 1024 C—1025 A, quoted in J. Meyendorff, *Marriage: An Orthodox Perspective*, 63.

151. Canon 1: "In conformity with ecclesiastical law we have decreed that communion must be given with forgiveness to those who entered legally and freely into a second marriage (without having contracted a clandestine marriage), but after an established period and once they have given themselves to prayer and fasting." (W. B. Zion, *Eros and Transformation: Sexuality and Marriage—An Eastern Orthodox Perspective*, 214).

152. "The right to remarry was not denied to the husband victimized by adultery or abandoned for no reason, according to Origen, Lactantius, Basil, or Chrysostom. They interpret Matthew's famous interpolation as support for this concession and like adultery or the death of a spouse . . . ." (W. B. Zion, *Eros and Transformation: Sexuality and Marriage—An Eastern Orthodox Perspective*, 214–15)

153. This council formulates the core of the Orthodox teaching of divorce and remarriage. Divorce and remarriage were allowed up to three times without punishment. This decision has been developed by Patriarch Alexius (1025–1043 AD) allowing divorce and remarriage of the innocent party on the grounds of unacceptable conduct, adultery, "madness, abortion, prenuptial unchastity on the part of the wife, unnatural vice on the part of the husband, implacable hatred on both sides, and apostasy from the Christian faith or entry into heresy." These grounds have been further expended after 1453 AD including unsustainable condition of a spouse, desertion, crime which has been publicly condemned, and mutual incompatibility or even consent which is approved by the Patriarch. (W. B. Zion, *Eros and Transformation: Sexuality and Marriage—An Eastern*

divorce and remarriage for some orthodox theologians remained only that of adultery.[154] Others, however, using as biblical support the passages of Matthew 5:32; 19:9 and 1 Cor 7:15 extend those grounds to sexual immorality, permanent insanity, desertion, forcing the spouse into prostitution, and endangering the life of the spouse.[155] When the crises in marital union begin, the priest makes every attempt to bring reconciliation to the two spouses, but if these attempts fail than he requests the Ecclesiastical Court to grant an ecclesiastical divorce. If the necessary grounds exist, the court allows divorce and subsequent remarriage. The latter might be extended to three times for any believer.[156] The fourth time, however, is forbidden.[157] This prohibition is not based on biblical or theological support but on the principle that more compromises lead to limitless compromises formulated in the form of Christian discipline.[158]

Therefore the Orthodox Church upholds the sanctity of Christian marriage, maintaining its sacramental nature as forming the ideal of permanent union and at the same time accepts marital breakdown and allows divorce and remarriage. This leads to emphasis on the spouses' responsibilities to sustain the union sparing no effort for its proper maintenance and rescue in the time of crises. If breakdown occurs, however, no hasty decision should be made for initiating second marital union.[159]

Orthodox Perspective, 219–20)

154. Sotirios, *Matrimony* [online].

155. Fr. Ted, *What is the Orthodox Position on Divorce and Remarriage?* [online].

156. The third marriage is allowed only if the person is under the age of 40 and does not have children from previous marriages. Encyclical Letter of the Holy Synod of Bishops, *On Marriage* [online]; H. Van Der Wal, *Secular Law and The Eastern Church's Concept of Marriage*, 81.

157. Greek Orthodox Archdiocese of America, *Divorces* [online], Available at http://www.goarch.org/search/oop/qfullhit.htw?CiWebHitsFile=%2Fgoa%2Fdetroit%2Fdivorces%2Ehtm&CiRestriction=divorce&CiBeginHilite=%3Cstrong+class%3DHit%3E&CiEndHilite=%3C%2Fstrong%3E&CiUserParam3=/search/query.asp&CiHiliteType=Full, Accessed on 21 April 2001; H. Van Der Wal, *Secular Law and The Eastern Church's Concept of Marriage*, 81; Encyclical Letter of the Holy Synod of Bishops, *On Marriage* [online].

158. The most famous president of fourth marriage in the History of the Orthodox Church is with Emperor Leo VI (886–912) which resulted in a church schism and a written ban of the fourth marriage by *Tome of Union* (920). (J. Meyendorff, *Marriage: An Orthodox Perspective*, 51, 52)

159. W. B. Zion, *Eros and Transformation: Sexuality and Marriage—An Eastern Orthodox Perspective*, 230–31.

On the other hand, the marriage theology of the church necessitates justification of the practice of divorce and remarriage. The grounds for such justification is substantiated through four reasons:

> (1) The tension between the ideals of the Kingdom of God and the fallen condition of our present life in history, (2) mercy extended by economy for saving the person or persons who have failed in their first marriage, (3) the non existence of the first marriage which had been bestowed upon an Orthodox Christian couple by the Church but which has disintegrated, (4) divorce and remarriage as the lesser of evils under the circumstances.[160]

THE TEACHING OF THE PROTESTANT CHURCHES

The analysis of the Protestant view of marriage, divorce, and remarriage is a difficult task which needs to take into consideration the diversity and the multiplicity of denominations which find their roots in the time of Reformation along with their theologies. The present exposition is developed from the viewpoint that there is both unity and diversity in the Protestant matrimonial teachings. The unity is based on the understanding that the mainline Protestant denominations[161] share a general view of marriage which finds its beginnings in the Continental and English reformation traditions.[162] The diversity is perceived on the level of various protestant scholars who have developed different theologies of marriage. The first part of the chapter will focus on the overall Protestant view of marriage, divorce, and remarriage.

Historically, the Protestant view of marriage laid down its foundations during the Reformation with two significant formulations of the marriage institution. First, Martin Luther defined the institution of marriage as formed at the time of creation and as such preceded the formation of both state and church.[163] Thus, two crucial dimensions of the nature of

---

160. Ibid., 226.

161. The following main denominations might be designated with this title: Lutheran, Episcopal, Presbyterian, Methodist, Baptist, Quakers, Congregationalists, United Christian churches, United Church of Christ, and United Church of Canada.

162. Wilson Yates, "The Protestant View of Marriage," *Journal of Ecumenical Studies* 22/1 (Wint 1985): 41.

163. In one of his sermons on the Ten Commandments Luther provides the following conclusion about the place of the institution of marriage in God's "order of creation":

marriage were established. The institution of marriage is part of the state and its dynamics and laws.[164] Hence, the nature of marriage lost its predominantly sacramental character[165] although it remained "a holy estate ordained by God."[166] Second, John Calvin and Martin Bucer defined the

---

"Therefore God blessed this institution above all others, and made everything on earth serve and spring from it, so that it might be well and amply provided for. It is not an exceptional estate, but the most universal and the noblest, pervading all Christendom, yea, extending through the whole world." (M. Luther, *Commentary on the Sixth Commandment*, quoted in Peter Coleman, *Christian Attitudes to Marriage: From Ancient Times to the Third Millennium*, ed. Michel Langford [London: SCM, 2004] 180-81). This reformulation of the institution of marriage has been started with the Catholic priest and Christian humanist Erasmus (1466-1536) who stated that: "Marriage was sanctioned by Christ at Cana. It is sanctioned by nature and condemned by heretics. It was instituted not by Moses or Solon, but by the Founder of the universe. For God said 'It is not good for man to be alone' and he created Eve, not out of mud, as in the case of Adam, but from his rib, that none should be closer and dearer than a wife. After the flood God told man 'to be fruitful and multiply.' Should not marriage be honoured above all the sacraments because it was the first to be instituted, and by God Himself. The other sacraments were established on earth, this one in paradise; the others as a remedy, this one as fellowship in felicity. The others were ordained for fallen nature, but this one for nature unspoiled. If human laws are revered how much more the law of marriage which we receive from him who gave us life?" (R. H. Bainton, *Erasmus of Christendom* [London: Collins, 1970] 20, quoted in P. Coleman, *Christian Attitudes to Marriage: From Ancient Times to the Third Millennium*, 178-79.)

164. W. Yates, *The Protestant View of Marriage*, 41.

165. Calvin offers a critique of the understanding the nature of marriage as a sacrament in the last chapter of his Institutes. "The last of all is Marriage, which, while all admit it to be an institution of God, no man ever saw to be a sacrament, until the time of Gregory. . . . They adduce the words of Paul, by which they say that the name of a sacrament is given to marriage, ... To treat Scripture thus is to confound heaven and earth. . . . The thing which misled them was the term sacrament. But, was it right that the whole Church should be punished for the ignorance of these men? . . . Marriage being thus recommended by the title of a sacrament, can it be anything but vertiginous levity afterwards to call it uncleanness, and pollution, and carnal defilement? How absurd is it to debar priests from a sacrament? . . . And, that they might not delude the Church in this matter merely, what a long series of errors, lies, frauds, and iniquities have they appended to one error? So that you may say they sought nothing, but a hiding-place for abominations when they converted marriage into a sacrament . . . ." (John Calvin, *Institutes of the Christian Religion*, trans. Henry Beveridge, book IV [London: Reinolde Wolfe & Richards Harison, 1561] XIX, 33-37. Electronic edition by Galaxie Software, 1999.); Also P. Coleman, *Christian Attitudes to Marriage: From Ancient Times to the Third Millennium*, 188, 189; John Witte Jr., *From Sacrament to Contract: Marriage, Religion, and Law in the Western Tradition*. The Family, Religion, and Culture, eds. Don S. Browning and Ian S. Evison (Louisville: Westminster John Knox, 1997) 79.

166. Timothy D. Lincoln, "Sacramental Marriage: A Possibility for Protestant Theol-

essence of marriage as covenant relationship.[167] This gave form and structure to the main Protestant view of marriage, divorce, and remarriage.[168]

The notion of covenant is formed entirely according to Scripture. The OT presents the relationship between God and his chosen people as covenant. This covenant is both envisioned as relationship between father and child and between husband and wife. The latter formed the understanding of marriage. The main characteristics of the covenant relationship between God and his people, i.e. love, faithfulness, trust and obedience, established the main characteristics of the marriage relationship. With the understanding of the NT view of marriage, Protestant thought formed the marriage covenant as relationship based on the mutual fulfillment of the spouses through experiencing companionship, love, and intimacy. This relationship is further characterised with permanency, stability, and faithfulness. The concept of a marriage covenant is formulated on the basis of six main streams in the Protestant theology of marriage and family. Five of these elements relate to the mutual commitment of the spouses for preservation of the marital bond through engagement in supporting and enriching both the partner and the marital relationship. The sixth element involves the parties' efforts to preserve the covenant in the face of marital breakdown and defines their freedom to undertake divorce and subsequent remarriage if the relationship collapses in spite of their efforts. The following sections will offer a summary of the six foundational characteristics of the marriage covenant.

First, one of the foundational aspects of the marriage covenant is related to the spouses' expectations and responsibilities to provide to each other the closest expression of mutual companionship.[169] This important element of marriage, stressed by Martin Luther and firmly incorporated into the Protestant theology of marriage by John Calvin and

---

ogy," *American Theological Library Association Summary of Proceedings* 49 (1995) 208; Also David L. Snuth, "Divorce and Remarriage: From the Early Church to John Wesley," *TrinJ* 11/2 (1990) 136–37.

167. W. Yates, *The Protestant View of marriage*, 41. Also J. Witte, Jr., *From Sacrament to Contract: Marriage, Religion, and Law in the Western Tradition*, 74–112; 149–53.

168. W. Yates, *The Protestant View of marriage*, 41. Also J. Witte, Jr., *From Sacrament to Contract: Marriage, Religion, and Law in the Western Tradition*, 109.

169. W. Yates, *The Protestant View of Marriage*, 43.

later confirmed by John Milton[170] and John Locke,[171] has received much attention in Protestant research and formed a concept whose depth and breadth affected every dimension of the marriage covenant relationship. Companionship has been initially understood as embracing the moral and spiritual aspects of sharing the life with the marriage partner. Protestant thought developed, giving place to the emotional dimension of companionship. The love between husband and wife provides an environment of romance and intimacy which enriches and stabilizes their covenant relationship. The concept of companionship reached a new level with the emphasis on its bodily expression. The intimacy between husband and wife achieves its culmination in the physical expression of their love. The role of sex in the covenant relationship has not been restricted any longer to the goal of procreation, but has become a crucial part of the companionship.[172] The sexual life of the spouses embraces not only their bodies but their whole personalities. Thus, the love of God has been understood as encompassing this very intimate sphere of the couple's relationship. The nature of companionship of the marriage covenant has received further attention to its intellectual and social dimensions. The marriage relationship is expected to meet the intellectual needs of the spouses as well as to provide support and facilitate their social engagements.[173]

Second, the marriage covenant relationship is to be characterised with virtues such as "honesty, trust, openness, and acceptance."[174] These four elements are expected to govern spouses' daily relationship. The dimension of honesty in the marriage encompasses the mutual devotion of the spouses to share the truth with each other in a moral and sensitive way which will honor their intellect, protect their image, and respect

---

170. Also D. L. Snuth, *Divorce and Remarriage: From The Early Church to John Wesley*, 140–41.

171. J. Witte, Jr., *From Sacrament to Contract: Marriage, Religion, and Law in the Western Tradition*, 186–93.

172. Also Greg W. Parsons, "Guidelines for Understanding and Utilizing the Song of Songs," *Bibliotheca Sacra* 156/624 (October 1999) 421.

173. W. Yates, *The Protestant View of Marriage*, 43–46.

174. W. Yates, *The Protestant View of Marriage*, 46. Also David Wegener, "Reflections on Marriage: Looking Back on Fifteen Years and the Lord's Design for Marriage in Genesis," *Journal for Biblical Manhood and Womanhood* 3/1 (March 1998). Electronic edition by Galaxie Software, 2002.

their personality.[175] The characteristic of trust is of vital importance to the marriage covenant. It stresses the marital fidelity of the spouses and embraces all aspects of their life. Trust becomes virtually the essence of every aspect of their relationship with God and with each other.[176] Openness is another crucial attribute of the marriage covenant which establishes mutual expression of the freedom to share even the deepest thoughts with the marriage partner.[177] This characteristic of the marriage relationship also requires the essential element of acceptance. The understanding of God's unconditional acceptance of the repenting sinner forms the Christian attitude between the spouses to accept each other within the frame of their limitations but always ready to offer forgiveness in the face of repentance.[178]

Third, the marriage covenant relationship provides an environment for the spouses to devote themselves to the embodiment of their Christian faith in attitude, communication and action toward each other, and towards family, church, and community. The most vivid illustration of the religious expression of marriage life is that of the Christian pilgrimage in this world. Both spouses are engaged in daily encounter with the difficult matters of life in the world of sin and death. This journey goes through various times whose nature requires the spouses' commitment to exercise their Christian faith in providing encouragement, support, and help to each other.[179] The family defines another aspect of the spouses' roles: that of parenthood. For Protestant marriage theology, procreation is not formulated as the goal of the covenant relationship. This poses no demand to the couple and preserves their freedom to formulate their own

---

175. W. Yates, *The Protestant View of Marriage*, 46–47.

176. Ibid., 47.

177. "Conceal not the state of your souls, nor hide your faults from one another. You are as one flesh, and should have one heart: and as it is most dangerous for a man to be unknown to himself, so it is very hurtful to husband or wife to be unknown to one another, in those cases wherein they have need of help." (Tim Beougher, "The Puritan View of Marriage: The Nature of the Husband/Wife Relationship in Puritan England as Taught and Experienced By a Representative Puritan Pastor, Richard Baxter," *Trinity Journal* 10/2 [1989] 140. Electronic edition by Galaxie Software, 1999.)

178. W. Yates, *The Protestant View of Marriage*, 48. Also "The St. Louis Statement on Human Sexuality: Reprinted with permission from Resource, a publication of Presbyterians for Renewal (March 1994)," *Evangelical Review of Theology* 19/1 (1995) 18, [electronic edition], Logos Library System, 2000.

179. W. Yates, *The Protestant View of Marriage*, 48. Also Richard A. Hunt, "Marriage as Dramatizing Theology," *Journal of Pastoral Care* 41/2 (1987) 123.

family goals. But for those who chose the role of parents, the covenant requires the investment of their faith into the life of their heirs. The faith of the spouses also necessitates their participation in the larger Christian community. The church provides an atmosphere of encouragement, worship, and discipleship for them. Christian marriage being part of the social structures formulates the position of the spouses in the society. Their stand in front of God and people offers possibility to share their faith in words and deeds and impact the society for the common good[180] of the community.[181]

Fourth, the marriage covenant is a union which requires the establishment of a holistic moral framework for the relationship. The four elements of "love, justice, freedom, and order"[182] might be defined as most essential for substantiating the moral expectations within the relationship. The spouses are to embrace each other with love, which must define every aspect of their relationship.[183] Love should not be exercised only as an obligation of the moral demands of marriage but also shared and experienced in all its aspects and nuances for the entire provision of the spouse with all the richness of the covenant relationship.[184] Justice is the fundamental demand of marriage covenant for the spouses' fulfillment of their obligations to each other and providing the proper environment for that fulfillment.[185] The model established by the Protestant scholarship is egalitarian marriage relationship in which spouses behave not according to stereotypes and prejudices but in freedom and respect for one's choice

---

180. Many of the reformers among whom Thomas Becon, Heinrich Bullinger and Martin Bucer stressed the importance of marriage for the common good of the society. Bucer even defined the very existence of the marital bond as socially conditioned, namely, "marriage must be maintained if it caters to the common good…but it must be dissolved if it detracts from the common good." (John Witte, Jr. "Anglican Marriage in the Making: Becon, Bullinger, and Bucer," in *the Contentious Triangle: Church, State and University*, eds. R. L. Petersen and C. A. Pater [Kirksville, MO: Thomas Jefferson University Press, 1999] 254.)

181. W. Yates, *The Protestant View of Marriage*, 48–50. Also A. Köstenberger, *Marriage and Family in the New Testament*, 253.

182. Ibid., 50.

183. Also J. Witte, Jr. *Anglican Marriage in the Making: Becon, Bullinger, and Bucer*, 257.

184. Ibid., 50–51.

185. Also *Baxter's Instructions for Maintaining Love in Marriage Condensed From "A Christian Directory," Works*, 1:431, quoted in T. Beougher, *The Puritan View of Marriage*, 158; Also T. Beougher, *The Puritan View of Marriage*, 139–45; 155–56.

and desire.[186] The principle of freedom is foundational for the marriage moral framework. This principle may be defined as the empowering of the individual to create, formulate, and act according to his/her own desire and personal choice. In the marriage covenant freedom is related to the attitude, behavior, and actions of the spouse toward the marriage partner, the marriage covenant, and himself/herself. In keeping this priority order freedom is protected from abuse.[187] The moral obligation of order is essential for the marriage covenant in two respects as providing stability and enabling development through flexibility to change.[188]

Fifth, the marriage covenant relationship requires provision of "boundaries or rules of behavior."[189] This characteristic refers to the spouses' agreement to formulate proper boundaries of their behavior in relation to every area of their marital and social life. Marriage relationship depends on the partners' commitment to this agreement. Marriage in all its dimensions, religious, physical, parental, economical, vocational, and social is entirely based on the success of the spouses to relate to each other within the mutually agreed boundaries. The formulated mutual behavior should be functional in a sense that the occurrence of eventual internal or external changes in the marriage is reflected in the adaptation of its boundaries. The importance of these rules of behavior for the successful maintenance of marriage and the accomplishment of its goals is enormous.[190]

Sixth, the breakdown of the marriage covenant should be recognized and accepted only when all the efforts for its renewal are exhausted. The marriage covenant relationship is established as a lifelong union between husband and wife. Hence, they should commit themselves to its preservation and nourishment. Even when the times of crises appear the spouses should put all their efforts to stabilize the relationship and if their resources are not enough they should look for help from the church and the appropriate social institutions.[191] The breakdown of the marriage

---

186. W. Yates, *The Protestant View of Marriage*, 51–52.

187. Ibid., 52.

188. Ibid.

189. Ibid.

190. Ibid., 52–53.

191. Also Daan Botha, "My Marriage Partner has Been Unfaithful—What Am I to Do?" *Orientation* 58–62 (December 1990–1991) 129.

covenant relationship is beyond repair when its inner life has gone out. Then the external legalization of the breakdown might take place through the act of divorce. Divorce is accepted as "morally responsible action" of the spouses in the light of the dissolution of the marriage covenant by the Protestant denominations.[192] The protestant tradition has always treated divorce on legitimate grounds and subsequent remarriage as scripturally formulated actions for marital breakdown. The most generally accepted legitimate grounds for divorce and subsequent remarriage have been that of adultery and desertion both strictly established on the basis of Scripture (Deut 24:1; Matt 5:31; 19:3-11; 1 Cor 7:10-16).[193] Throughout the development of the Protestant marriage tradition further legitimate grounds have been added by Luther ("hatred, anger, continuous conflict"[194]), Huldrych Zwingli ("sexually incapacitating illnesses, felonies, deception, and one spouse's serious threats against the life of the other spouse"[195]), Bucer (various[196]), Calvin ("impotence, extreme religious

---

192. W. Yates, *The Protestant View of Marriage*, 53.

193. C. Hodge, & A. Hodge, *Commentary on the Westminster Confession. The Confession of Faith: With Questions for Theological Students and Bible Classes* (Simpsonville SC: Christian Classics Foundation, 1996), [electronic edition based on the 1992 Banner of Truth reprint], (Logos Research Systems) Section 6 article 2.; D. L. Snuth, *Divorce and Remarriage: From the Early Church to John Wesley*, 140, 141; Also J. Witte, Jr., *From Sacrament to Contract: Marriage, Religion, and Law in the Western Tradition*, 68-69; H. G. Coiner, *Divorce and Remarriage: Toward Pastoral Practice*, 549. Even though it might be argued that the practices of divorce and subsequent remarriage have differed between the states being under the influence of Luther's and Calvin's matrimonial teachings due to the closer relationship between the state authorities and the theologians established by Calvin both Reformers agreed on the basic scripturally legitimate grounds on divorce and subsequent remarriage, namely, adultery and desertion. (T. A. Lacey, *Marriage in Church and State* [London: SPCK, 1947] 147-49; Also D. L. Snuth, *Divorce and Remarriage: From The Early Church To John Wesley*, 137-38.)

194. D. L. Snuth, *Divorce and Remarriage: From The Early Church to John Wesley*, 136.

195. J. Witte, Jr., *From Sacrament to Contract: Marriage, Religion, and Law in the Western Tradition*, 69.

196. "If the husband can prove the wife to be an adulteress, a witch, a murderess, to have bought or sold to slavery any one free born, to have violated sepulchers, committed sacrilege, favored thieves and robbers, desirous of feasting with strangers, the husband not willing, if she lodge forth without a just and probable cause, or frequent theaters and sights, he forbidding, if she be privy with those that plot against the State, or if she deals falsely, or offers blows [he may divorce her]. And if the wife can prove her husband guilty of any of those forenamed crimes, and [he] frequent the company of lewd women in her sight, or he beat her, she had the like liberty to quit herself, with this difference, that the

incompatibility"[197]), and Milton ("religious and carnal frustrations"[198]). Thus, the church recognizes divorce and is devoted to help the divorcees in reorganizing their lives and finding new beginnings.[199]

The diversity of the Protestant view of marriage, divorce, and remarriage is expressed through several theological stands of Protestant scholars in regard to these issues which stand in a complex unfinished debate which involves agreements and disagreements between them. The debate has been established on the grounds of four different viewpoints which cover the whole general range of protestant beliefs about the marital issues. Hence, a short survey of each view will prove helpful to establish the fourfold diversity in the protestant position.

Some Protestant theologians argue for the indissolubility of marriage and for no divorce and no remarriage for any reason.[200] Marriage is

---

man after divorce might forthwith marry again, the woman not till a year after, lest she might chance to have conceived." (Martin Bucer, *De Regno Christi*, 2/37; Martin Bucer, *De Regno Christi*, [1550], in *Martini Buceri Opera Latini*, ed. Francois Wendel [Paris: Presses Universitaires de France, 1955], vol. 25, quoted in J. Witte, Jr. *Anglican Marriage in the Making: Becon, Bullinger, and Bucer*, 255–56.)

197. D. L. Snuth, *Divorce and Remarriage: From The Early Church to John Wesley*, 137-38; David J. MacLeod, "The Problem of Divorce," *Emmaus Journal Volume 1/1* (1991) 146. Electronic edition by Galaxie Software, 1999). However some scholars insist that Calvin did not go beyond adultery and desertion as the only legitimate grounds for divorce and remarriage. (See J. Witte, Jr., *From Sacrament to Contract: Marriage, Religion, and Law in the Western Tradition*, 76, 85-87.)

198. J. Witte, Jr., *From Sacrament to Contract: Marriage, Religion, and Law in the Western Tradition*, 181. Most generally described religious frustration is "irreconcilable incompatibility" (ibid.), or "absence of true companionship" (W. Yates, *The Protestant view of Marriage*, 43) between the spouses. Carnal frustration might consist of "adultery, cruelty, desertion, drunkenness, incest, sloth, violent crime, or other pathos that destroys any prospects of intimacy with their spouse. . . . permanent impotence, frigidity, contagion, sterility, disfigurement, or similar permanent defect that precludes intercourse or conception." (J. Witte, Jr., *From Sacrament to Contract: Marriage, Religion, and Law in the Western Tradition*, 182.)

199. W. Yates, *The Protestant View of Marriage*, 53–54.

200. J. C. Laney, *No Divorce & No Remarriage*, 15–54. See also idem. *The Divorce Myth: A Biblical Examination of Divorce and Remarriage* (Minneapolis, MN: Bethany, 1981); idem, "Paul and the Permanence of Marriage in 1 Corinthians 7," *Journal of the Evangelical Theological Society* 25/3 (1982) 284–95. Electronic edition by Galaxie Software, 1998; idem, *Deuteronomy 24:1-4 and the Issue of Divorce*. Electronic edition by Galaxie Software; S. Wilcox, *The Restoration of Christian Marriage: A Call for Repentance and Reformation* [online]; C. C. Ryrie, *Biblical Teaching on Divorce and Remarriage*, 178–93; N. Smit, *Why May a Marriage not be Dissolved*, 111–117; H. G. Coiner, *Divorce and*

a permanent unto death institution established by God and the actions of divorce and remarriage constitute the sin of adultery. Marriage is defined as permanent and indissoluble as depicted in the creation account (Gen 2:24). The three concepts of "leaving,"[201] "cleaving,"[202] and "one flesh"[203] determine that nature. Marriage is a covenant relationship made on the basis of promises by the partners and in the presence of God and friends. Jesus' view of marriage is in full agreement with God's establishment of marriage in the creation. Hence, there are no proper grounds for divorce and remarriage and both of these actions are condemned as adultery by Jesus (Mark 10:11, 12; Luke 16:18). The so called exception clause, which appears in Matt 5:32 and 19:9, is related to incestuous Gentile marriages in Matthew's community[204] and cannot be used as biblical grounds for proper divorce and remarriage. Paul's view of marriage is in full agreement with Jesus' teaching on the matter. Paul's teaching is understood to prohibit divorce and remarriage for any reason (1 Cor 7:10, 11). The Pauline privilege is nothing more than a provision for the believer not to

---

Remarriage: Toward Pastoral Practice, 541–55; J. J. Kilgallen, *To What are the Matthean Exception-Texts (5,32 and 19,9) an Exception?* 102–5; David J. MacLeod, "The Problem of Divorce, Part 3: The Teaching of Jesus," *Emmaus Journal Volume* 3/1 (1994) 3–48. Electronic edition by Galaxie Software, 1999; Larry Christenson, *The Christian Family* (Minneapolis, MN: Bethany, 1970) 24–27; John Coblentz, *What the Bible Says about Marriage, Divorce, and Remarriage*, 2000 [online], Available at http://www.anabaptists.org/books/mdr/index.html#contents, Accessed on 24 January 2005.

201. It is basically the separation from the parents. The separation is not abandoning but simply leaving the original home of the partners in order to establish their own home and family.

202. The concept of cleaving is concerned with the lifelong attachment of the two partners in the marriage relationship. It is based on the unconditional love between the man and the woman.

203. The concept of "one flesh" expresses the physical aspect of marriage. This is the sexual aspect. Sexual intercourse provides the possibility for the two to become one in mystical, spiritual unity. The "one flesh" union is the climax of the marital relationship.

204. This view is based on three basic arguments. First, the exception clause cannot be treated as allowing divorce and remarriage for adultery due to diminishing the moral power of Jesus' teaching to that of the school of Shammai. Second, the meaning of πορνεία as incestuous marriage is well supported by its usage in Leviticus 18:6–18, 1 Cor 5:1, Acts 15:20, 29, and the Qumran literature and it is supported by the context of the incestuous marriage of Herod and Herodias. Third, the syntactical relation of the exception clause to the rest of the sentence presents an exception only to divorce but not to remarriage.

insist on the marriage when the unbeliever attempts to leave.[205] The solution for the believer in such cases is twofold, reconciliation or single life.

Some Protestant theologians believe in the indissolubility of marriage and that divorce in some sense is acceptable, but argue that the remarriage is prohibited as destroying God's design for marriage and constitutes the sin of adultery in violation of the seventh commandment.[206] Marriage is an indissoluble kingship institution. Its lifelong nature is designed by God and depicted in the creation account (Gen 1:27; 2:24). The two main characteristics of marital union establish this understanding. First, marriage is a covenant relationship based on two actions, "forsake" and "cleave," which determine the commitment of the spouses. In the sphere of marriage they represent the spouses' leaving of their parents and cleaving to each other in a covenant relationship. Second, marriage is a kinship relationship based on the understanding of a "one flesh" union between the partners. The latter is not primarily concerned with the consummation of the union sexually, but on the basis of the kinship formula presented in Gen 2:23, "bone and flesh," expresses a permanent kinship relationship. Both Jesus and Paul in their teachings agree completely underlining the indissoluble kinship nature of marriage, and recognising divorce as a failure of the guilty party, but not as dissolving the marital bond and thus condemning remarriage of both parties as adultery. Neither the exception

---

205. This understanding of Pauline privilege is based on establishing the meaning of δουλόω as the freedom of the rejected believer to maintain the marital bond, and the role of the context as insisting on reconciliation or single life.

206. W. A. Heth, *Divorce, but No Remarriage*, 73–129. See also W. A. Heth and G. J. Wenham, *Jesus and Divorce: The Problem with the Evangelical Consensus.*); W. A. Heth, *Why Remarriage is Wrong* [online], Available at http://www.christianitytoday.com/ct/2000/135/48.0.html, Accessed on 25 April 2001; idem, *Divorce and Remarriage: The Search for an Evangelical Hermeneutic*, 63–100; idem. "The Meaning of Divorce in Matthew 19:3–9," *Chruchman* 98/2 (1984) 136–152; idem, "Another Look at the Erasmian View of Divorce and Remarriage," *Journal of the Evangelical Theological Society* 25/3 (1982) 264–73. Electronic edition by Galaxie Software, 1998; idem, "Unmarried 'For the Sake of the Kingdom' (Matthew 19:12) in the Early Church Unmarried," *Grace Theological Journal* 8/1 (1987) 56–87. Electronic edition by Galaxie Software, 1999; D. Engelsma, *The Remarriage of the Guilty Party* [online]; Clinton D. Henry, *Perspective Paper on Marriage, Divorce, and Remarriage with Conclusions, Observations, Applications*, 2004 [online], Available at www.marriagedivorceremarriage.com, Accessed on 24 January 2005; Stephen W. Wilcox, *Restoration of Christian Marriage: A Call for Reformation*, 2004 [online], Available at www.MarriageDivorce.Com, Accessed on 24 January 2005.

clause of Matthew[207] nor Pauline privilege[208] might be understood as dissolving the marriage and allowing remarriage due to the kinship nature of marriage. Thus, the only solution for the divorced believer is reconciliation with the former spouse or the life of celibacy (Matt 19:12).[209]

Some Protestant theologians affirm the lifelong nature of marriage and allow divorce and remarriage only for adultery and desertion.[210] Marriage is designed by God to be a lasting relationship which might be dissolved and divorce and remarriage permitted for only two reasons, i.e. adultery and desertion. There is no biblical support for the indissolubility of the marital bond. Both the understanding of the "one flesh" union between husband and wife and Jesus' prohibition of divorce (Mark 10:9;

207. This understanding is established by six arguments. First, in the light of the early church practices and the Fathers' writings it might be argued that divorce and remarriage were actions prohibited during the first five centuries in the church. These practices remained in the Western church up to the sixteenth century when Erasmus' view was established and embraced by the Protestants. This view maintained that divorce and remarriage are permitted due to the obtaining of salvation only within the Catholic Church for those in non-Catholic marriages who divorce and remarry a Catholic party. Second, the exception clause is culturally limited to relate only to the expectations of the Jewish culture. Third, structurally the exception clause refers only to divorce but not to remarriage. Fourth, the context (Matt 19:9, 12) determines the exception clause as irrelevant for remarriage. Fifth, other evangelists do not mention an exception (Luke 16:18 and Mark 10:2–12). Sixth, Paul argues that the only reason for remarriage is the death of one of the spouses (Rom 7:2, 3).

208. This understanding is established by seven arguments. First, the early church fathers except Ambrosiaster supported it. Second, the meaning of the word δουλόω does not refer to the breaking of a legal marital bond. Third, Paul views marriage as indissoluble since he uses it as an image expressing the relationship between the church and Christ (Eph 5:31–32). Fourth, the context (1 Cor 7:10–16) insists on preserving the marriage. Fifth, the usage of the same word for "divorce" (χωρίζω) in v11 and v15 suggests that the same outcome needs to be preserved in both cases, namely reconciliation or celibacy. Sixth, the hope for salvation of the unbeliever should determine no remarriage desire of the believer. Seventh, Paul's principle related to the preservation of social status (vv17–24) underlines no remarriage interpretation.

209. The Eunuch passage is understood as referring to those faithful disciples who experienced divorce and for whom God provides the grace to live a single life.

210. T. R. Edgar, *Divorce & Remarriage for Adultery or Desertion*, 151–96. See also C. S. Keener, . . . *And Marries Another: Divorce and Remarriage in the Teaching of the New Testament*; idem, *Paul, Women & Wives: Marriage and Women's Ministry in the Letters of Paul* (Peabody: Hendrickson, 1992); idem, *Free to Remarry* [online]; J. MacArthur, *Divorce and Remarriage* [online]; J. K. Manful, *Divorce* [online]; T. S. Morton, *From Marriage to Remarriage: Has a Remarried Christian Committed an "Unpardonable Sin?"* [online]; D. J. Macleod, *The Problem of Divorce: the Teaching of Paul* [online]; J. D. Hoke, *Thinking Biblically About . . . Divorce & Remarriage: Matthew 19:1–10* [online].

Matt 19:6) signifying an indissoluble union might be defined as invalid assumptions. On the one hand, a "one flesh" relationship could not prove marriage as indissoluble, since it is also used to define a tentative sexual relationship (1 Cor 6:6). On the other hand, Jesus' prohibition of divorce does not emphasize the permanence of the marital bond but states an ethical imperative. Hence, what God has joined together might be separated only on the grounds established by God. These are clearly stated in the exception clause of Matthew (5:32; 19:9) and the privilege of Paul (1 Cor 7:15). The former is defined as a real[211] exception which requires[212] the actions of proper divorce and remarriage due to its grammatical[213] and syntactical[214] nature, and the meaning of πορνεία.[215] The latter as an interpretation of Jesus' teaching on divorce and remarriage by Paul in relation to the new situation of mixed marriages should be treated as provision for proper divorce and remarriage of the deserted believer.[216]

Some Protestant scholars maintain the lifelong nature of marriage, but accept divorce and remarriage for any reason.[217] God's ideal for mar-

---

211. The exception clause does not nullify or invalidate the marriage in the light of "betrothal unfaithfulness" or "incestuous marriages" since both the meaning of πορνεία and the context do not establish any grounds for such an interpretation.

212. The exception clause does not just allow divorce in case of adultery but in the light of the Jewish cultural mores it requires the removal of the adulterous party.

213. Due to the fact that the verse has only one subject which serves the clause concerning divorce and that concerning remarriage, the exception clause applies to both divorce and remarriage.

214. From its place in the sentence the exception clause defines both verbs of divorce and remarriage. To treat the exception clause as allowing divorce only when placed at the beginning of the sentence or as allowing remarriage only when placed at the end of the sentence does not do justice to the syntax.

215. The most probable meaning of the word according to the context is that of adultery. The more natural word for adultery μοιχεύω/μοιχεία is replaced with πορνεία since the former refers primarily to the husband's conduct and the latter to the wife's conduct. This also explains the usage of the two different terms with the same meaning in the same passage (Matt 5:32).

216. This conclusion is established on the basis of the meaning of χωρίζω as real divorce, the meaning of δουλόω as related to the freedom of the believer to remarry and the understanding of the context (1 Cor 7:10, 11) as supporting such an interpretation since it presupposes the exception clause of adultery.

217. L. Richards, *Divorce & Remarriage under a Variety of Circumstances*, 215–248. See also O. Hicks, *Bible Solutions to Divorce Problems* [online]; G. Codrington, *Marriage, Divorce and Remarriage in the Light of the Teaching of Jesus* [online]; Z. H. Merrill, *Marriage, Divorce, Remarriage: What Does the Bible Allow?* [online]; G. D. Collier, *Rethinking Jesus on Divorce* [online]; Dwight Hervey Small, *The Right to Remarry* (Old

riage is a permanent union of mutual support and enrichment between husband and wife. That ideal is to be followed by every couple and the potential for its fulfillment is given to every marriage. However part of every marriage is also sin, since humanity entered its realm after the first husband and wife failed God's standards of life. Hence, God has accommodated his ideal to fit the life of imperfect humanity. Due to the hardness of the human heart which brings about all unhealthy marital relations, e.g. mental, physical, and sexual abuse, extramarital sexual relationships, emotional, spiritual, and physical abandonment etc, divorce and remarriage are allowed as a cure for such marriages. However all divorces and remarriages are condemned as unsatisfactory for God's ideal and determined as sinful actions which require repentance. Even on the grounds of adultery divorce is considered sinful.[218] Nevertheless when divorce does not depend on the believer's action since the unbeliever leaves the marriage (the Pauline privilege, 1 Cor 7:15) it may not require repentance from the side of the innocent party. The final decision for divorce may be taken only by the spouses since both Moses[219] and Jesus[220] gave that responsibility to the couple. In addition the final decision for remarriage is taken by the divorced believer after he/she considers the potential to stay single related to God's gift of celibacy.

As a conclusion, a twofold dynamic might be defined as summarizing the matrimonial teachings of the major Christian traditions based on their inner unity and its tensions. Thus, all three Christian traditions attempt an establishment of a coherent view on marriage which intends to express the biblical teaching on the subject as interpreted through their particular church traditions and formulated in their dogmatical bodies.

Tappan, N.J.: Fleming H. Revell, 1977), 9–28; Bernard L. Ramm, *The Right, The Good and the Happy* (Waco: Word, 1971), 80–90; idem., "Survey of Church Views on Divorce," *Eternity* (June, 1976) 51, quoted in D. J. MacLeod, *The Problem of Divorce*, 155, 156.

218. The exception clause of Matthew (5:32; 19:9) might not be defined as exception for adultery for three basic reasons. First, if defined as such the exception clause will lower the high moral standard of Jesus' teaching. Second, God's attitude towards the adulterous spouse in the story of Hosea and his adulterous wife suggests that not divorce but reconciliation with forgiveness should be practiced in such cases. Third, the meaning of πορνεία cannot be clearly defined as adultery for which the word μοιχεία is used in the NT.

219. Even though there were ecclesiastical courts in Israel, Moses gave the responsibility for that decision into the hands of the husband (Deut 24:1).

220. Jesus condemned the Pharisees' legalistic attitude and actions which established the proper grounds for divorce (Mark 10:9; Matt 19:6).

Marriage is an institution which receives highly exalted status as God's creation and establishment. It is granted as a valuable and precious gift by the Creator to his most intimate creation, the man and the woman. It is for their fulfillment and realization in forming a union whose very nature resembles the most significant relationship in the universe, that between Christ and the church. This institution is nothing less than a covenant, intended to be permanent and indestructible. However, the institution of marriage experiences damage from human failure to protect it and sustain it. Thus, marriage breakdown in the light of the permanent nature of covenant creates tensions in the unity of the churches' matrimonial teachings if the permanence is defined as unconditional. If absolute indissolubility of the marriage covenant is perceived and defended, no solution to the marital breakdown may be provided. Hence, the Christian traditions struggle for the preservation of the unity of their teachings through facilitating channels for dealing with marital breakdown. Validating in this way such a solution for marital breakdown which will not destroy the permanence of the marriage covenant is to form grounds for preserving the unity within the matrimonial teachings of all three Christian traditions and establishing ecumenical unity among them. This is the task of the following chapter.

TOWARD AN ECUMENICAL VIEW

The analysis of the dogmatical context of the theological concept of divorce and remarriage presents grounds of continuity and discontinuity between the matrimonial teachings of the major Christian traditions. Underlining the former and solving the latter will provide a justifiable ecumenical view of the NT teaching on divorce and remarriage. The continuity between all Christian traditions is established by their understanding of marriage as a permanent covenant relationship between husband and wife.[221]

John Macquarrie formulates the result of his ecumenical research in *Christian Unity and Christian Diversity* that "all Christians, Catholic and

---

221. The participants in the Ecumenical Conversation in 1976, i.e. Catholic, Lutheran, and Reformed Christians, agreed that they have related views of marriage based on its understanding as covenant. ("The Theology of Marriage and the Problem of Mixed Marriages," paragraph 18, in *Growth in Agreement: Reports and Agreed Statements of Ecumenical Conversations on a World Level*, eds. Harding Meyer and Lukas Vischer [New York: Paulist, 1984] 286, quoted in T. D. Lincoln, *Sacramental Marriage: A Possibility for Protestant Theology*, 205.)

Protestant alike, are agreed that the Christian ideal of marriage is the lifelong monogamous union of the partners."[222] He argues that the prototype of all marriages is established in the creation account by God with the "one flesh" formulation of its nature. The latter presents a union between man and woman in which they have experienced "profound ontological transformation,"[223] which constitutes their relationship as a permanent bond. This nature of marriage is clearly referred to by Jesus (Mark 10:9).[224] The permanent nature of the union is based on the vow of the spouses to commit themselves to lifetime relationship characterised with the fulfillment of its obligations and responsibilities.[225] The lifelong marital union is further defined with its sexual consummation by the spouses. This is to be understood in its holistic form as deep mutual interconnectedness of the spouses formulated through a life of sexual belonging within the framework of daily devotion and companionship.[226] The sacrametality of the marital relationship formulates it as being empowered by divine grace to strengthen the spouses' lifelong commitment.[227]

The Roman Catholic view of marriage is characterised with the permanency of the marital union defined through its sacramental covenant nature. The institution of marriage is designed by God for the fulfillment of the diversity of two genders in the most perfect conditions of union which is defined through the communion and the conjugal love of the spouses. It is the unity of the very being of God which is reflected through the perfect unity between husband and wife in which they fulfill the image of their Creator. Thus, the very nature of marriage is not only human but also reflects the character of its Creator which establishes it as permanent union of mutual and self-giving love.[228] This union defines the whole of humanity, any community, and the society as a whole.[229] The permanency of marriage develops its characteristics under the Old Testament

---

222. John Macquarrie, *Christian Unity and Christian Diversity* (London: SCM, 1975) 79.

223. Ibid., 83.

224. Ibid., 83.

225. Ibid., 85.

226. Ibid., 86.

227. Ibid., 88.

228. *Catechism of the Catholic Church*, 1603–1605 [online].

229. Pope John Paul II, *Letter to Families from Pope John Paul II*, (1994 – Year of the Family), 6. Libreria Editrice Vaticana [online].

Law which defends the lifelong nature of marriage as well as the wife's marital status even in light of the impediments due to the "hardness of heart."[230] This perpetual bond of marriage affirmed through the conjugal love between the spouses reflects the covenant relationship between God and his people Israel in which God's faithfulness defines the permanent nature of the covenant in spite of the disloyalty of Israel.[231] This covenant relationship, on the other hand, foreshadows the covenant relationship between Christ and the church which according to the words of St. Paul in Eph 5:25, 32 is "a great mystery" transforming the relationship between husband and wife into a sacrament.[232] The essence of this sacrament is formulated by God to be a permanent reflection of the covenant between Christ and the church and as such to signify the sacrament of the New Covenant.[233] Thus, marriage of two baptized Catholics becomes a sign of grace and as such "a true sacrament of the New Covenant."[234] This covenant relationship between the spouses is based on their mutual partnership for a lifetime and is directed to the edification of the spouses and their children (Canon 1055:1[235]).[236] The relationship is firmly founded on the free matrimonial consent of the Christian spouses which obligates them to treat and preserve their union as permanent.[237] In the present society where various obstacles exist for sustaining the perpetual nature of marriage the only source of strength for the spouses is their sharing

---

230. *Catechism of the Catholic Church*, 1610 [online].

231. Apostolic Exhortation of Pope John Paul II, *Familiaris Consortio*, 12 [online].

232. *Catechism of the Catholic Church*, 1659, Libreria Editrice Vaticana [online], Available at http://www.vatican.va/archive/ENG0015/__P57.HTM, Accessed on 17 September 2005.

233. Pontifical Council for the Family, *Family, Marriage and "De Facto" Unions*. Libreria Editrice Vaticana [online].

234. *Catechism of the Catholic Church*, 1617, Libreria Editrice Vaticana [online], Available at http://www.vatican.va/archive/ENG0015/__P51.HTM, Accessed on 17 September 2005.

235. "The matrimonial covenant, by which a man and a woman establish between themselves a consortium of the whole life, [which] by its very nature is ordered to the good of the spouses and to the procreation and education of children, has been raised by Christ the Lord to the dignity of a sacrament between baptized persons."

236. *Catechism of the Catholic Church*, 1601 [online].

237. Ibid., 2364 [online].

in God's love and grace and being open to the support of the ecclesial community.[238]

The Eastern Orthodox Church view of marriage is defined by the permanent sacramental nature of the union. The sacramental nature of marriage is derived from the union between Christ and his church. Christ's love and faithfulness toward his bride the church reflecting in her treatment as his own body establishes the permanence and firmness of this bond.[239] This permanent commitment between husband and wife is signified in the liturgical celebration of marriage with the circular procession around the lectern in which the couple is led by the priest.[240] The sacrament of marriage embraces the purpose of the entire creation being established in the very beginning of the humankind and completed with its exaltation in Christ. The sacramentality of the bond further determines the closeness, unity, and equality in the relationship between husband, wife and their offspring since the family is viewed as reflecting the unity and equality of the relationship in the holy Trinity.[241] The social structures perceive family as their most basic unit but being empowered through God's grace and as a reflection of God's unity and completeness the family becomes a small church which needs to be nourished by the church in all its aspects.[242] This task of the church is accomplished through the help of God which reveals the nature of marriage as a mystery. It is only through God's assistance the church may lead the couple to developing their relationship to the biblical standards within the world of difficulties and sin.[243] Bearing these features of sacramentality and mystery marriage is perceived as a permanent union. The teaching of Christ affirmed this permanence of the union between husband and wife excluding any willingly taken action to dissolve it.[244] Marriage being a sacrament reflects the

---

238. Ibid., 1648 [online].

239. W. B. Zion, *Eros and Transformation: Sexuality and Marriage—An Eastern Orthodox Perspective*, 328.

240. J. Meyendorff, *Marriage: An Orthodox Perspective*, 45.

241. W. B. Zion, *Eros and Transformation: Sexuality and Marriage—An Eastern Orthodox Perspective*, 328.

242. Michael Pomazansky, *Orthodox Dogmatic Theology: A Concise Exposition*, trans. Hieromonk Seraphim Rose (Platina, CA: Saint Herman of Alaska Brotherhood, 1994) 301.

243. Pomazansky, *Orthodox Dogmatic Theology*, 302.

244. J. Meyendorff, *Marriage: An Orthodox Perspective*, 15.

Kingdom of God and as such affirms the permanency of the relationship between husband and wife.[245]

The Protestant view on the permanence of marriage is generally accepted by different protestant scholars and finds its roots in the covenant nature of marriage established by God in the creation of the first marriage and formulated by Jesus in his matrimonial teaching. J. C. Laney defines marriage as permanent institution established by God and depicted in the creation account (Gen 2:24). The fundamental importance for understanding of the nature of marital union as permanent is grounded on its formulation by God himself narrated in the creation account and presented by the evangelists in the teaching of Jesus (Matt 19:4–5).[246] This depicts marriage as based on three essential concepts, namely, "leaving," "cleaving," and "one flesh." Understanding of these three concepts leads Laney to affirm the lifelong nature of marriage. The "leaving" one's parents is the first step in the marriage. The separation from the parents does not constitute their abandoning but the establishment of a new relationship between the spouses with a bond which requires complete devotion and loyalty.[247] The second concept that of "cleaving" is subsequent to the first and defines the lifelong attachment of the two partners in a marriage relationship. The nature of this relationship is defined as resembling that of a covenant, union between two parties which requires their permanent commitment and loyalty to each other. It is based on the unconditional love between the man and the woman.[248] "The biblical concept of 'cleaving' suggests the idea of being 'superglued' together—bound inseparably by a commitment to a life-long relationship."[249] The third concept is that of "one flesh." It expresses the marital union through the sexual relationship between the two spouses. This aspect of marriage is the climax and the celebration of the permanent union extending to the spiritual unity of the spouses and to the physical expression of this unity in their children. Thus, marriage should be defined as a covenant relationship established between a man and a woman for their entire life to preserve their prom-

---

245. W. B. Zion, *Eros and Transformation: Sexuality and Marriage—An Eastern Orthodox Perspective*, 222.

246. Laney, *No Divorce & No Remarriage*, 16, 17.

247. Ibid., 17, 18.

248. Ibid., 18, 19.

249. Ibid., 18.

ises.[250] W. A. Heth agrees with J. C. Laney as well as with L. Richards who maintains that God's design for marriage is a permanent union.[251] Heth formulates the model of all marriages as being presented by Jesus' reference to God's establishment of the first marriage at the time of creation (Matt 19; Mark 10; Gen 2:24).[252] Marriage is a covenant relationship based on two fundamental concepts. First, the nature of marriage covenant is clearly expressed with the terminology of "leaving" and "cleaving." These two terms define a relationship which is based on mutual faithfulness and lifelong devotion of the spouses to each other. It bears a clear resemblance with the union between God and Israel.[253] Second, marriage is kinship relationship based on the understanding of "one flesh" union going beyond the sexual fulfillment of the marital union to express a permanent marital kinship relationship through the formula presented in Gen 2:23, "bone and flesh."[254]

The core of the discontinuity between the matrimonial teachings of the major Christian traditions could be defined as the understanding of the permanent nature of marriage as an indissoluble union even in light of such marital crises where the dignity and life of a spouse is endangered by the sinful actions and behavior of the other spouse. A probable solution to be proposed is to modify the indissoluble notion of marriage through analysis of the tensions it creates in the matrimonial matters and to incorporate its modified nature into the covenant concept of marriage. The analysis of the notion of indissolubility would endeavor to present fivefold ground of inadequateness of the concept related to the problems and tensions it creates in the matrimonial teachings and practices of the Catholic Church, its strongest supporter. The following five dimensions are examined: the tension in the understanding of the twofold nature of marriage; the problem of participation in the Eucharist of divorced and remarried Catholics; the problem with the juridical emphasis on the notion of consensus; the problem of the relationship between the sacramental nature of marriage, its indissolubility and the "living faith" of the

---

250. Ibid., 20, 21.
251. L. Richards, *Divorce and Remarriage Under a Variety of Circumstances*, 215.
252. W. A. Heth, *Divorce, but No Remarriage*, 74, 75.
253. Ibid., 75, 76.
254. Ibid., 76, 77.

parties contracting the union; and the tension between external tolerance and internal intolerance in the Catholic Church.

The problem with the nature of marriage is related to the understanding of the relationship between the two fundamental aspects of marriage namely, secular and religious. This relationship is understood by some Catholic scholars as dominated entirely by the religious aspect of marriage. They recognize that marriage has a secular dimension but that dimension is primarily related to the fact that marriage involves human beings and it exists in human society. However, all the dynamics of marriage should be entirely subjected to the divine and church laws.

Marriage is originated by God for man and woman for the purposes of the whole of creation. Thus, the nature of marriage is twofold, divine and human. Hence, it is subject to the divine law and assumes human resources for its realization. Also, it takes the free will of the spouses to initiate it and preserve it through fulfillment of their obligations and responsibilities and as such is defined through human law but its most essential elements remain subject only to divine law. Hence, human law has no authority over the marriage, which is defined by the divine law as monogamous, permanent, indissoluble by any cause except the natural death of either of the spouses. Nevertheless human society and culture have been operating with the general assumption that the institution of marriage is their creation and is to be subjected to their laws. Thus, under the influence of different philosophies, human society exercised various authoritative proceedings over the marriage nature, functions, and duration. Evolutionists defined and treated marriage as a natural instinct-based behavior of human beings for the purposes of procreation, sexual satisfaction, and mutual support and happiness. Socialists, following the same line of thought, treated marriages as important social units which needed to be entirely dependent on state guidance and control. Thus, the social dependence of marriage to different philosophical notions related to its character and nature formed it as an institution which has inferior moral value to the one intended by divine law and accepts further degradation of its nature into the forms of divorce or polygamy due to human failures.[255]

---

255. Selinger Jos, "Moral and Canonical Aspect of Marriage," trans. Douglas J. Potter, in *The Catholic Encyclopedia, Volume IX* [online Edition], ed. K. Knight, 2003 [online], Available at http://www.newadvent.org/cathen/09699a.htm, Accessed on 22 September 2004.

Christian marriage is established by Christ as being originated by the divine law as monogamous and indissoluble, whose nature is a sacrament conveying both sanctifying and sacramental grace. The nature of Christian marriage preserves the human element which constitutes it as a contract. Hence, marriage is both sacrament and contract. However marriage remains under the authority of the divine law and it is given under the guidance of the church to conduct its proper establishment, functioning, and moral character. Hence, the church accepts the divine definition of marriage as monogamous, an indissoluble sacrament, and guides it according to its moral and canon laws. Christian marriage is also in relation to the civil formulations of matrimonial matters. Thus, the church "respects the requirements of the State for the marriages of its citizens as long as those requirements are for the common good, and in keeping with the dignity and Divine purpose of marriage."[256] However the church preserves complete authority over the marriage, defining all its dimensions according to its laws. The only legally valid marriage which is by definition a sacrament may be established by two baptized Christians in a proper liturgical setting with the presence of a priest and witnesses. Thus, no civil marriage is defined as valid even between two baptized Christians and according to the requirements of the state. The nature of civil marriage is defined by the church as entirely financial. This understanding of marriage has been defined by some Catholic scholars as subject "to many serious problems, in connection both with the cause of ecumenism and with the Christian's loyalty as a citizen to the state."[257] These scholars maintain that the nature of marriage is "without qualification a secular reality, fully human and consequently subject to development and evolution."[258] Then the religious dimension of marriage is envisioned as incorporating this "total and human dimension."[259] Thus, marriage has become part of God's salvation and as such it has received its sacramental nature. On these grounds it might be argued that "every marriage, even civil marriage, is Christian—whether in the full sense, in the pre-Christian sense (marriage as having an orientation towards Christ), in the anonymously Christian sense, or even in the negatively Christian

---

256. S. Jos, *Moral and Canonical Aspect of Marriage* [online].

257. E. Schillebeeckx, *Marriage: Secular Reality and Saving Mystery. Marriage in the History of the Church*, vol.2, trans. N. D. Smith (London: Sheed and Ward, 1965), 195.

258. Ibid., 217.

259. Ibid.

sense (a deliberate denial of this Christian aspect of marriage)."[260] This understanding of marriage may be traced in the history of the church as its main teaching for the first eleven centuries.[261] Hence, Catholic scholars demand for new understanding of marriage in the light of the Thomas Aquinas' concept of marriage as historically and culturally grounded. This concept of marriage should reflect the changes in society and culture in a positive Christian manner. Many changes are defined as transforming the notion of marriage in contemporary society and culture. Marriage is understood on a more personal and communicational level as providing for care and companionship between the individuals. Sex and procreation have received new meanings with the invention of contraceptives and technologically assisted reproduction. The place of women in the society at large has influenced the understanding of marriage and family life. The formation of certain modern values related to social and public life has also marked the nature of marital life.[262] The establishment of new attitudes toward cohabitation[263] and divorce have relativized marriage further and accepted remarriage with approval.[264] Thus, the church is envisioned as being "in a transitional situation"[265] and as such expected to formulate its concept of marriage historically. Indeed this viewpoint is perceived to have grounds in documents such as *Gaudium et Spes* (Second Vatican Council, 1965), *Humanae Vitae* (1968), and *Familiaris Consortio* (1981) where marriage is understood as personal community in which love and faithfulness among the spouses prevail.[266] Furthermore the comparison between the definitions of marriage in the old (1917)[267] and the new code (1983)[268] of the canon law observes some elaborations

260. Ibid., 202.

261. Ibid., 204.

262. G. D. Coleman, *Divorce and Remarriage in the Catholic Church*, 14–16.

263. Karen Hurley, "New Perspectives on Christian Marriage," in *Keeping Up with Our Catholic Faith: Explaining Catholic Thinking Since Vatican II*, ed. Jack Wintz (Cincinnati: St. Anthony Messenger, 1975), 76, 77.

264. G. D. Coleman, *Divorce and Remarriage in the Catholic Church*, 14–16.

265. Ibid., 16.

266. Ibid.

267. "Matrimonial consent is an act of the will by which each party gives and accepts the perpetual and exclusive right over his or her body, for acts which are of themselves suitable for the generation of children." (Can. 1081:2), quoted in G. D. Coleman, *Divorce and Remarriage in the Catholic Church*, 18.

268. "The matrimonial covenant, by which a man and a woman establish between

of the nature of marriage by the new code in this direction.²⁶⁹ Marriage is defined as covenant union resulting from the personal willing self-giving of the spouses into the bond of marriage. The relationship between the husband and wife is defined by such attributes as love, mutuality, partnership, purposeful contribution for each others benefit and fulfillment of parenthood roles.²⁷⁰

The changes in the contemporary social and cultural situation of marriage, divorce, and remarriage, and the need for the church's redefinition of its doctrines related to these issues is seen through the statistical data. The result from different surveys produces the following picture:

> ... during the past fifteen years about a million Catholics have remarried with the Church's blessing. At the same time, about seventy-five percent of remarried Catholics live in presumably invalid second marriages. These divorced and remarried Catholics are not women and men who have rejected the Church's teaching on the permanence and indissolubility of marriage. They are not persons who promote divorce. They almost unanimously are people who profess a high regard for lifelong marriage and generally insist that they would never wish a divorce on anyone.²⁷¹

In this respect the position of the divorced and remarried ("outside the church") Catholic Christians in the church should be elaborated according to one of the most significant document discussing these matters, *Familiaris Consortio*.

An analysis of *Familiaris Consortio* (Community of the Family) which Pope John Paul II delivered to the 1980 Synod of Bishops and issued on 22 November 1981 provides four basic conclusions which express the main teaching of the document. First, the document clearly and unquestionably

---

themselves a partnership of the whole of life and which is ordered by its nature to the good of the spouses and the procreation and education of offspring, has been raised by Christ the Lord to the dignity of a sacrament between the baptized." (Can. 1055:1.); "Matrimonial consent is an act of the will by which a man and a woman mutually give and accept each other through an irrevocable covenant in order to establish marriage." (Can. 1057:2.) (*Code of Canon Law, Title VII, Marriage*. Libreria Editrice Vaticana [online], Available at http://www.vatican.va/archive/ENG1104/__P3V.HTM, Accessed on 23 September 2004.

269. Also L. Orsy, SJ, *Marriage in Canon Law: Texts and Comments. Reflections and Questions*, 37.

270. G. D. Coleman, *Divorce and Remarriage in the Catholic Church*, 19–21.

271. Ibid., 5.

provides the status of all Catholics who are divorced but not remarried as full members of the Catholic Church with no stigma of excommunication related to them and free participants in the Eucharist in unity with all the other members of the church in full rights, privileges, and responsibilities. Second, the document affirms the status of those Catholics who are divorced and remarried ("outside the church") as members of the Catholic Church who are not threatened with excommunication and as baptized believers sharing with the other members in all the aspects of the church life. Third, those Catholics who are divorced but remarried ("outside the church") are withheld from participating in the Eucharist due to the lack of complete recognition of the new marital union and protection of the previous marital bond by the church. The remarried believers are not prohibited the Eucharist because their condition is considered as sinful, but because there is an apparent contradiction between their two marriages, and also due to possible opposition by other Catholics if such permission is granted. Fourth, the document does not provide grounds for separation of these divorced and remarried Catholics ("outside the church") but even stresses the necessity for those couples to sustain the relationship due to various "serious pastoral reasons"[272] such as provision for the children. The church also underlines as the first responsibility of these believers to seek annulment of their previous marriage through the church's marriage tribunals. However if such annulment is not granted the church treats these families as "man and woman living together,"[273] until the contradiction from the previous marital union is resolved.[274] The document further depicts marriage as a covenant relationship between husband and wife which resembles the covenant between Christ and the church. The love of the husband to his wife is characterized by the expression of God's love finalized in the person of Jesus Christ. Marriage is seen as an active part in the structure of the church, even itself serving as a "domestic church."[275] The role of marriage within the church and outside the church is clearly defined as a contributor and facilitator of church growth.[276] This discussion leads to further and deeper consideration of the place of the divorced

---

272. Ibid., 11.

273. Ibid.

274. Ibid., 10, 11.

275. *Lumen Gentium*, no. 11. (Second Vatican Council), quoted in G. D. Coleman, *Divorce and Remarriage in the Catholic Church*, 17.

276. G. D. Coleman, *Divorce and Remarriage in the Catholic Church*, 18.

and remarried believers in the church in relation to their participation in the Eucharist.

The participation in the Eucharist of all Catholic believers is clearly defined by The Constitution on the Sacred Liturgy as "their right and duty by reason of their baptism."[277] Canon 897[278] underlines the importance of the Eucharist for all the members of the church "as both the sign of unity within the Church, as well as the source for unity in the Church."[279] The believers who are to be excluded from participation in the Eucharist are defined in the Canon 912[280]/915[281]. The latter states that those who should not participate in the Eucharist are either those excommunicated from the church or those who "obstinately persist and manifest grave sin."[282] However, Catholic divorced and remarried Christians are not considered excommunicated from the church. The Third Council of Baltimore (1884) with regard to its specific historical situation has pronounced the penalty of excommunication[283] for those baptized Catholics who have divorced and remarried using civil courts. However in May 1977 this penalty was

---

277. Constitution on the Sacred Liturgy, no. 14, quoted in G. D. Coleman, *Divorce and Remarriage in the Catholic Church*, 38.

278. "The most venerable sacrament is the blessed Eucharist, in which Christ the Lord himself is contained, offered and received, and by which the Church continually lives and grows. The Eucharistic sacrifice, the memorial of the death and resurrection of the Lord, in which the sacrifice of the cross is forever perpetuated, is the summit and source of all worship and Christian life. By means of it the unity of God's people is signified and brought about, and the building up of the body of Christ is perfected. The other sacraments and all the apostolic works of Christ are bound up with, and directed to, the blessed Eucharist." (G. D. Coleman, *Divorce and Remarriage in the Catholic Church*, 36)

279. Ibid., 37.

280. "Any baptized person who is not forbidden by law may and must be admitted to Holy Communion." (G. D. Coleman, *Divorce and Remarriage in the Catholic Church*, 37.)

281. "Those upon whom the penalty of excommunication or interdict has been imposed or declared, and others who obstinately persist and manifest grave sin, are not to be admitted to Holy Communion." (Ibid., 37.)

282. Ibid., 37.

283. "It is clearly evident that they are guilty of the gravest fault who petition the civil authority for a dissolution of marriage, or even worse, having obtained a civil divorce and without regard for the lawful bond, which in the sight of God and the Church still endures, attempt to enter another marriage. In order to curb such crimes, we enact the penalty of excommunication to be incurred automatically by those who, after obtaining a divorce, dare to attempt civil marriage." (G. D. Coleman, *Divorce and Remarriage in the Catholic Church*, 58–59.)

dropped by the American bishops with the approval of Rome.[284] This decision was based on the understanding that the overall motivation of those Catholics who divorce and remarry using civil courts is not against the church law but based on love to a new partner and providing a family atmosphere for the children. This declaration, in addition to removing the penalty of excommunication, formulates two further attitudes. First, that those Catholics who divorce and remarry through the civil courts do not perform these actions either against the church law or with the intention to leave the Catholic Church. Second, the Catholic Church "truly desires to encourage such people to make use of devotional, spiritual, charitable and pastoral activities of the Church that are permitted to them."[285] But Catholic divorced and remarried Christians are still not admitted to participate in the Eucharist for mainly three reasons. First, due to the fact that "their state and condition of life objectively contradict that union of love between Christ and the Church which is signified and effected by the Eucharist."[286] Second, the condition of life of these Christians "imperfectly symbolizes"[287] the unity established through the sacrament within the intrinsic nature of the church. Third, if the church gives its permission for participation in the Eucharist of these Christians the rest of its members will be morally deprived of their stand, which might prompt them to cause tensions within the church structures.[288] Thus, as it has been argued, if these Christians repent "for whatever contribution they have made to the breakdown of the first marriage, they may receive the Eucharist if they are willing to live a life of continence."[289] However this does not imply that those Christians are punished by the

---

284. The Chair of the Bishops' Committee on Canonical Affairs, Bishop Cletus O'Donnell, issues the statement. The following is just a short quotation from it: "After study and reflection, the bishops of the United States have concluded that the removal of this particular excommunication . . . can foster healing and reconciliation for many Catholics remarried after divorce . . . . This decision . . . is only a single step, but it offers encouragement and hope to disaffected or alienated Catholics . . . . For the future, thorough preparation for marriage and support for marriage and family life by the whole community of the Church are the only genuine solutions." (G. D. Coleman, *Divorce and Remarriage in the Catholic Church*, 62–63.)

285. Ibid., 64.

286. Apostolic Exhortation of Pope John Paul II, *Familiaris Consortio*, 84 [online].

287. G. D. Coleman, *Divorce and Remarriage in the Catholic Church*, 41.

288. Ibid.

289. Ibid., 37

church and are considered as living "in the state of subjective sin."[290] The statement of Pope John Paul II before the Synod of Bishops in Rome on October 25, 1980, bears such an implication, "divorced Catholics who are remarried are not to be considered separated from the Church . . . . By virtue of their baptism, they can and ought to participate in the life of the Church . . . ."[291] Furthermore there are some Catholic theologians[292] who maintain that divorced and remarried ("outside the church") Catholics may participate in the Eucharist if their situation reflects some specific characteristics. The condition of the previous marriage is evaluated as "irretrievably lost."[293] The official process of reconciliation is presently unattainable, "e.g., an annulment is not possible." There is clear evidence visible in the lives of those Christians that they intend to continue their church involvement. Finally, the present marriage shows stability and good progress in the relationship between the spouses.[294] It is argued that the argumentation and conclusions of these scholars do not diminish the concept of marital indissolubility, but take a different line of presenting it.[295] Its main development is structured around the understanding that the first marriage was entered into by both spouses with mutual consent for maintaining the marital union through the fulfillment of specific obligations for mutual support, commitment, and love. However, since due to religious and moral failure of the spouses to fulfill these responsibilities the relationship has been violated, the marriage can be considered dead. The segments constructing this argument are clearly based on the teaching of the Catholic Church. One of these segments is related to the basic church teaching about the end of marriage. "The Church teaches, and has always taught, that death alone can dissolve a ratified and consummated Christian marriage."[296] Thus, the authors' understanding of the nature of dissolubility is also in synchrony with the church teaching.

290. Ibid., 39.

291. Ibid., 1.

292. Some examples are: Charles M. Whelan, S.J., "Divorced Catholics," *America* 131 (1974) 363–65; James J. Young, ed., *Ministering to the Divorced Catholic* (New York: Paulist, 1979); James Provost, "Reconciliation of Catholics in Second Marriages," *Origins* 8 (1978–1979) 204–8, quoted in G. D. Coleman, *Divorce and Remarriage in the Catholic Church*, 41.

293. G. D. Coleman, *Divorce and Remarriage in the Catholic Church*, 36.

294. Ibid., 36.

295. Ibid., 42.

296. S. Jos, *Moral and Canonical Aspect of Marriage* [online].

The concept of the indissolubility of marriage affirmed by the Catholic Church is constructed historically on two grounds. First, it is formed through the patristic understanding of the concept as sacrament based on the spouses' promises, devotion, and personal commitment to the marital union. The indissolubility in this sense is constituted by the elements of the "task," whose fulfillment is dependent on the personal endeavor of the spouse to sustain the marital bond intact. Second, it is established on the scholastic (12th and 13th century) formulation of marriage as sacrament, entirely defined through the covenant relationship between Christ and his church, and including no human interference of any kind. Hence, once established, the indissolubility of the marital union is not dependent on any consequences from the actions of the spouses. It is further argued that both ideas are biblically affirmed, not mutually exclusive, and at the present time both defended and practiced by the Catholic Church.[297] However, the present discussion shows that these two natures of marital indissolubility provide grounds for disagreement among Catholic scholars. Thus, the authors under consideration stress the aspect of the nature of marital indissolubility which relates to the personal obligations of the spouses for its preservation. Finally, these scholars offer an interpretation of *Gaudium et Spes*, 48 which stresses the fact that marriage depicted as an institution, a covenant with a contractual nature and *communio*[298] is established and maintained through the personal devotion of the spouses to love, support, and partner each other on the lifelong journey.

> The intimate partnership of married life and love has been established by the Creator and qualified by His laws, and is rooted in the jugal covenant of irrevocable personal consent. Hence by that human act whereby spouses mutually bestow and accept each other a relationship arises which by divine will and in the eyes of society too is a lasting one. . . . Thus a man and a woman, who by their compact of conjugal love 'are no longer two, but one flesh' (Matt. 19:5), render mutual help and service to each other through an intimate union of their persons and of their actions. Through this union they experience the meaning of their oneness and attain to it with growing perfection day by day. . . . Christ the Lord . . .

---

297. E. Schillebeeckx, *Marriage: Secular Reality and Saving Mystery. Marriage in the Old and New Testaments*, vol.1, trans. N. D. Smith (London: Sheed and Ward, 1965), 203-4.

298. Mary Shivanandan, *Crossing the Threshold of Love: A New Vision of Marriage in the Light of John Paul II's Anthropology* (Edinburgh: T. & T. Clark, 1999) 82.

abides with them thereafter so that just as He loved the Church and handed Himself over on her behalf, the spouses may love each other with perpetual fidelity through mutual self-bestowal.... For this reason Christian spouses have a special sacrament by which they are fortified and receive a kind of consecration in the duties and dignity of their state. By virtue of this sacrament, as spouses fulfil their conjugal and family obligation, they are penetrated with the spirit of Christ, which suffuses their whole lives with faith, hope and charity. Thus they increasingly advance the perfection of their own personalities, as well as their mutual sanctification, and hence contribute jointly to the glory of God.... This the family will do by the mutual love of the spouses, by their generous fruitfulness, their solidarity and faithfulness, and by the loving way in which all members of the family assist one another.[299]

The main line of the argument developed in relation to the death[300] of the first marriage shows that the existence of the marital bond depends entirely on the mutual involvement of the spouses for its maintenance. When the sustaining effort of any of the spouses is diminished or extinguished due to the spouse's failure to accomplish the marriage covenant stipulations then the bond is ended. Hence, the new marriage does not enter into conflict with the still existing bond from the previous marriage since the bond "de facto no longer exists because it is irretrievably lost."[301]

> Indissolubility cannot mean that a first marriage continues to exist as a prohibition against a second marriage. Such a prohibition would leave indissolubility without any actual meaning; for it says

---

299. *Gaudium et Spes*, 48. Pastoral Constitution on the Church in the Modern World, Promulgated by His Holiness Pope Paul VI on December 7, 1965. Libreria Editrice Vaticana [online], Available at http://www.vatican.va/archive/hist_councils/ii_vatican_council/documents/vat-ii_cons_19651207_gaudium-et-spes_en.html, Accessed on 23 September 2004.

300. Three different kinds of marriage death are proposed. First moral death refers to marital demise which appears on the grounds of extinguishing of the spouses love because "such actions as incest, murder, violence, or betrayal can cause love to be changed into repulsion." Second, psychological death encompasses varieties of mental disorder which produce cessation of marital union. Third, political death takes place when one of the spouses either voluntarily deserts the marriage in preference to a political career or involuntarily is sentenced to prison for felony. (G. Callaghan, *Annulment Process. Remarriage in the Church: Pastoral Solutions. A Statement by the Board Members of the Association for the Rights of Catholics in the Church (ARCC)* [online].)

301. G. D. Coleman, *Divorce and Remarriage in the Catholic Church*, 43.

nothing, realistically speaking, about the first marriage in question. If that marriage has in fact completely broken down, then humanly speaking there is no more marriage; there is no longer anything to which 'indissolubility' or 'dissolubility' can be applied. Instead, there is only the reality of a radical failure, regardless of how one might assign guilt for it; there is the reality of an irrecoverably lost marriage.[302]

However the church is not ready to accept this argumentation, as becomes clear from the words of Pope Paul VI.

> . . . a marriage exists at the moment when the spouses express a juridically valid matrimonial consent. This consent is a will-act which establishes a contract (or a conjugal covenant, to use the phrase preferred today). In an indivisible moment of time it produces a juridical effect, namely, an existing marriage as a state

---

302. "Faced with this situation, a Christian can appeal to what Eastern theology calls *oikonomia* (an untranslatable Greek word that can perhaps best be understood as taking everything into account). The Eastern Church is sensitive about not tarnishing the ideal of marriage; it affirms that the intrinsic aim of marriage is an interpersonal relationship, but it also believes that Christians, as Paul says in this context, 'are called by God to freedom' (1 Cor 7:15). Now, the practice of Christian churches, especially those whose ecclesial nature is generally recognized, is for Catholics a source of theological information (*locus theologicus*) that can no longer be ignored. These churches, acting with an *oikonomia* that recognizes human failings, do not juridically veto people's desire to remarry, which they regard as a private decision of the two people concerned. This is clearly a pastoral interpretation of a practical problem for which there are models in the New Testament, although in a different cultural context than our own. If we want to be honest, we have to admit that the practice of *oikonomia* has come into existence in the Catholic church, although for the time being it has to remain underground because it conflicts with the code of canon law. This practice calls into question the legalism of the code, which attempts to safeguard the gospel but does so by translating it into strict legal language that can overstate the proper meaning of the evangelical ideal. We need to reflect on this new practice and on the growing appreciation among Catholics (though not in official circles) for a general Christian consensus with regard to a pastoral practice of recognizing and respecting divorced people's desire to remarry. In this spreading pastoral practice, there is a measure of truth coming to light, albeit indirectly." (Edward Schillebeeckx, "Christian Marriage and the Reality of Complete Marital Breakdown," in *Catholic Divorce: The Deception of Annulments*, eds. Pierre Hegy and Joseph Martos [London: Continuum, 2000] 97-98, quoted in Timothy J. Buckley, *What Binds Marriage? Roman Catholic Theology in Practice*. Revised and Expanded Edition [London: Continuum, 2002] 193, 194.) In light of Schillebeeckx's reasoning Timothy Buckley argues that "the time has come to set God's people free from the unnecessary burdens of refusing to consider the possibility of another union after complete marital breakdown and refusing Holy Communion to those caught up in what at present we regard as irregular unions." (T. J. Buckley, *What Binds Marriage? Roman Catholic Theology in Practice*, 194.)

of life. Once the moment is passed, the wills of the consenting partners have no power to affect the juridical reality they have brought into being. Consequently, once the consent has produced its juridical effect, it automatically becomes irrevocable and lacks power to destroy what it created.[303]

It is clear that the line of argumentation of the present declaration stresses the second dimension of the twofold nature of indissolubility. Once the marriage is initiated on the grounds of the personal consent of the parties which is inclusive to their mutual conjugal rights, the perpetual nature of the marital bond becomes independent from the actions of the parties and the marriage becomes indissoluble. However, due to the importance of participation in the Eucharist by all believers, and in the case of those Catholic Christians who are divorced and remarried outside the church, the matter is taken to further consideration by the internal forum of the church. This forum, which tackles the issues related to the individual spiritual health of the believer, works in synchrony with the external forum of the church, which deals with the matters related to the church law and juridical certitude.[304] Thus, the internal forum provides several grounds for participation of divorced and remarried Catholics in the Eucharist. First, for those mixed marriages in which the non-Catholic spouse is not willing to facilitate the blessing of the marriage in the Catholic Church with his personal presence, the marriage is healed (sanated) by the church, and the Catholic party is free to participate in the Eucharist. Second, those in irregular marriages who are not willing to separate for "pastoral reason, (e.g. care for the children)"[305] even though they perceive the validity of their previous marriages, are allowed to participate in the Eucharist if they continue to maintain their new marriage unions properly. Third, those in second marriages who are strongly convinced that their former marriages have not been valid and are unaware of their validity according to the church law are allowed to participate in the Eucharist on the ground of their "good faith."[306] Fourth, those who have not yet received annulment but are firmly grounded in their faith that their previous marriages have not been valid and their present marriages are the valid ones according

---

303. Pope Paul VI, *The Marriage Bond*, quoted in G. D. Coleman, *Divorce and Remarriage in the Catholic Church*, 40.
304. Ibid., 47, 56.
305. Ibid., 55.
306. Ibid., 48.

to church law are allowed to participate in the Eucharist.[307] However due to controversies related to the meaning and use of the internal forum[308] the situation of the divorced and remarried believers is not completely resolved, which leads the discussion to the problem with the juridical emphasis on the notion of consensus.

The question about the initiation aspect of marriage, or what constitutes marriage as marriage, is foundational for the discussion of indissolubility. It is argued that while Christ established marriage as an indissoluble union he did not explicate what is this essence of marriage which makes it a valid marriage.[309] The church in an attempt to provide a relevant answer for this question has combined two social and cultural notions of the essence of marriage, namely the Roman philosophical notion of consensus and the generally prevailing idea in human society that marriage is consummated through sexual intercourse.[310] Thus, the contractual nature of marriage and the inclusion of sexual intercourse in the mutual consent of the parties established the notion of the initial marital consent as the foundational characteristic of marriage formalization and validation. Due to this crucial role of consent to the existence of the marital bond, it becomes one of the most critical grounds for the marriage dissolubility. First, the consent of both parties needs to be clearly stated in such a format, and with such clarity that the willingness of the parties to enter the marriage is well understood by the performer of the marriage and its witnesses. The consent of one of the parties might be given in a written form but it is required to contain explicit language which leaves no doubts to the participants of the marriage initiation about the willingness of the party. Second, the consent must be given freely by both parties. Any obstacle to this freedom might make the consent defective and provide grounds for dissolubility of the contract. Fear might be an obstacle to the proper consent of a party if fear is threatening the will

---

307. G. D. Coleman, *Divorce and Remarriage in the Catholic Church*, 55, 56. Also Philip S. S. Keane, *Sexual Morality: A Catholic Perspective*, 146–48.

308. Some Catholic scholars consider the use of the internal forum only within its canonical boundaries (Canon 130 of the 1983 Code of Canon Law). Others understand it as dependent entirely on the individual's conscience. Even others criticize it as a temporal and inadequate solution. (See T. J. Buckley, *What Binds Marriage? Roman Catholic Theology in Practice*, 124, 133–34)

309. E. Schillebeeckx, *Marriage: Secular Reality and Saving Mystery: Marriage in the History of the Church*, vol.2, 207.

310. Ibid., 205, 206.

of the party to such a degree that it produces inner dissent, (see "Acta Apostolicæ Sedis", vol. II, nş 8, p. 348, 26 Feb., 1910). Third, consent must be given without any error by the giver to the other party. Both parties giving consent are required to possess the natural capacity for establishing the contract, formulating their willingness to initiate it, and sustaining the proper intention and determination related to it. The nature of the error might be related either to the person or to the quality of the person who contracts. If one of the parties is lacking such knowledge or being intentionally restricted to its access, the marriage can be dissolved if the plea of non-consent is proven valuable. Fourth, the contract with its nature and stipulations is independent of the will of the parties, which makes it corrupt and subject to dissolubility and nullity in a case of the parties' slightest intention to modify it. If any of the parties conditions the consent and the marriage through an implied or clearly stated condition which regards the future and is against the very nature of the marital contract the tribunal of conscience judges the marriage null. (Decretals, IV, tit. v, 7). Fifth, if an agreement is made between the contracting parties of such a nature as to go contrary to the matrimonial stipulations of both parties ("e. g., not to have more than one or two children, or not to have any children at all, until, in the judgment of the contracting parties, circumstances shall enable them to be provided for; or to divorce and marry someone else whenever they grow tired of each other"[311]) the marriage is nullified. Sixth, due to the dual nature of Christian marriage as sacrament and contract any consent or attempt which diminishes the sacramental nature of the contract nullifies the marriage.[312]

The focus on one element of marriage, even though so essential for marital substantiation, results in reducing the rest of the vital characteristics of marriage to expressing a kind of union which is completely dissoluble.[313] Furthermore, concentrating such an immense juridical value on the notion of consensus provides grounds for featuring a theology of marriage which is entirely "a juridical abstraction."[314] In addition, this diminishes the vast majority of other issues related to marriage dogmatics and especially to the practical side of marriage, which then yields a lack

311. S. Jos, *Moral and Canonical Aspect of Marriage* [online].
312. Ibid.
313. E. Schillebeeckx, *Marriage: Secular Reality and Saving Mystery: Marriage in the History of the Church*, vol.2, 209.
314. Ibid., 211.

of resources for empowering pastoral interaction in the various difficult pragmatic matrimonial matters.[315] Further impediments for an adequate pastoral ministry in the church are created due to the problem of the relationship between the sacramental nature of marriage, its indissolubility and the "living faith" of the parties contracting the union.

According to Canon 1055:2, "... a valid matrimonial contract cannot exist between the baptized without it being by that fact a sacrament."[316] The Catechism of the Catholic Church states this fact (1617) adding that the nature of this marriage is indissoluble. "Thus the marriage bond has been established by God himself in such a way that a marriage concluded and consummated between baptized persons can never be dissolved."[317] However, it is argued according to "the traditional teaching of the Church that there can be no automatic sacrament and there can be no sacrament without faith."[318] In this respect Pope John Paul II stresses the importance of faith for the parties who contract marriage.

> Christian spouses and parents are required to offer 'the obedience of faith.' They are called upon to welcome the word of the Lord which reveals to them the marvellous news-the Good News-of their conjugal and family life sanctified and made a source of sanctity by Christ Himself. Only in faith can they discover and admire with joyful gratitude the dignity to which God has deigned to raise marriage and the family, making them a sign and meeting place of the loving covenant between God and man, between Jesus Christ and His bride, the Church. . . . The celebration of the sacrament of marriage is the basic moment of the faith of the couple. This sacrament, in essence, is the proclamation in the Church of the Good News concerning married love. It is the word of God that 'reveals' and 'fulfils' the wise and loving plan of God for the married couple, giving them a mysterious and real share in the very love with which God Himself loves humanity. Since the sacramental celebration of marriage is itself a proclamation of the word of God, it must also be a 'profession of faith' within and with

---

315. Ibid.

316. *Code of Canon Law, Title VII, Marriage.* Libreria Editrice Vaticana [online]. Also G. D. Coleman, *Divorce and Remarriage in the Catholic Church*, 23.

317. *Catechism of the Catholic Church*, 1640, Libreria Editrice Vaticana [online], Available at http://www.vatican.va/archive/ENG0015/__P54.HTM, Accessed on 17 September 2005.

318. G. D. Coleman, *Divorce and Remarriage in the Catholic Church*, 23.

the Church, as a community of believers, on the part of all those who in different ways participate in its celebration.[319]

However, it is very difficult or even impossible to define what living faith means "in a juridical context."[320] Also, it appers insensitive to provide 'proof' for it since "such 'proof' can too easily destroy the meaning of grace within the sacrament of marriage."[321] The tension in the relationship between sacrament, indissolubility, and faith increases in the light of the conclusion of the International Theological Commission that "the personal faith of the contracting parties does not constitute the sacramentality of matrimony, but the absence of personal faith compromises the validity of the sacrament."[322] If the general principle is taken in consideration that "all human situations become 'sacramental' in the measure that they are grasped by faith,"[323] the sacrament of marriage should be considered in strong relation to the faith of the parties involved.[324] The logical line of this argument provides grounds for the claim that the difficulty in establishing the existence of "living faith" in the parties who contract marital union jeopardises the validation of their marriage as sacrament and its indissoluble nature. Thus, appears the phenomenon of "baptized non-believers" which establishes "a new theological problem and a grave pastoral dilemma"[325] for the Catholic Church. The tension around the indissolubility of Christian marriage is further intensified with the tension between external tolerance and internal intolerance in the Catholic Church on this issue.

It is argued that one of "the most complete and authoritative commentaries"[326] of Canon 1118 (Can. 1141) is that of Pope Pius XII made in 1941 in front of the members of the highest ecclesiastical marriage court in Roman Catholic Church (Sacred Roman Rota).

---

319. Apostolic Exhortation of Pope John Paul II, *Familiaris Consortio*, 51 [online].
320. G. D. Coleman, *Divorce and Remarriage in the Catholic Church*, 26.
321. Ibid.
322. Origins 8 (1977–1978), 235ff, quoted in G. D. Coleman, *Divorce and Remarriage in the Catholic Church*, 27.
323. E. J. Kilmartin, *When is Marriage a Sacrament*, 285.
324. Ibid., 285, 286.
325. G. D. Coleman, *Divorce and Remarriage in the Catholic Church*, 27.
326. J. M. Kuntz, *Is Marriage Indissoluble*, 333.

> It is superfluous before a juridical Tribunal such as yours, yet it is not irrelevant to Our discourse to recall, that a ratified and consummated marriage is by divine law indissoluble inasmuch as it is not able to be dissolved by any human power (Can. 1118); while other marriages, although intrinsically indissoluble, do not posses an absolute extrinsic indissolubility; but given certain necessary prerequisites can (in cases be it noted relatively very rare), besides the case of the Pauline Privilege, be dissolved by the Roman Pontiff in virtue of his ministerial power.... For the indissolubility or dissolubility of marriage the only norm and practice which can hold for the Church is that which God, the Author of nature and grace, has established. In this regard there are two passages of Sacred Scripture that in some manner indicate the limits within which the dissolution of the bond must remain, and that exclude both the laxity of today and the rigorism which is contrary to the divine will and command. One is: 'What God has joined together let no man put asunder.' (Matt. 19:6); that is to say, not man, but God can separate the married parties, and therefore there is no separating where God does not dissolve the bond. The other is 'A brother or sister is not under servitude; but God has called us in peace.' (I Cor. 7:15); that is to say, there is no longer any servitude or bond where God dissolves it and so permits the married person licitly to marry again. In every case the supreme norm according to which the Roman Pontiff uses his vicarious power to dissolve marriages is that same which We have adduced as the rule of the whole exercise of the judiciary power of the Church: that is to say, the salvation of souls. To the attainment of this end the common good of religious society, that of human relations in general, and the private benefits of individuals find due and proportionate consideration.[327]

The understanding of the Petrine privilege or the Privilege of faith and Pauline privilege should further illuminate the Pope's commentary on Canon 1118. Petrine privilege provides dissolution of marriages of two non-baptised Catholics when one of them is willing to marry a baptised Catholic without defining as prerequisite the baptism of the willing party. Pauline privilege, on the other hand, provides grounds for dissolution of marriages in which one of the parties becomes a baptised Christian. In both cases however, marriages have been initiated among the non-baptised parties prior to the appearance of the situation in which any of

---

327. Pope Pius XII, *Gia. per la terza volta*, allocution to the Sacred Roman Rota, 1941 A.A.S., vol 33 [1941] 424-25, translated and quoted by J. M. Kuntz, *Is Marriage Indissoluble*, 333-34.

the privileges may apply. In the light of these short references to the privileges and the commentary of canon law 1118 it is argued that "it seems that the Church has more power over the marriages of non-Christians that it does of Christians."[328] If further analysis is attempted it becomes clear that in the light of the reason for dissolution of non-Christian marriages as "the salvation of souls" the exercising of such authority by the church and the Pope becomes more relevant to the non-Christians than to the Christians. Thus, it is argued that "in some instances the Church and the Pope have more power to save the souls of non-Christians than of Christians."[329] Another example will further suffice the present conclusion. The Fathers of Vatican II, having the knowledge of the practices of Orthodox churches related to dissolution of ratified and consummated marriages using several explicit divorce grounds,[330] issued the Decree on Ecumenism which shows their attitude to these practices.

> From the earliest times, moreover, the Eastern Churches followed their own disciplines, sanctioned by the holy Fathers, by synods, even ecumenical councils. Far from being an obstacle to the Church's unity, such diversity of customs and observances only adds to her comliness, and contributes greatly to carrying out her mission, as has already been recalled. To remove any shadow of doubt, then, this sacred Synod solemnly declares that the Churches of the East, while keeping in mind the necessary unity of the whole Church, have the power to govern themselves according to their own disciplines, since these are better suited to the temperament of their faithful and better adapted to foster the good of souls. Although it has not always been honoured, the strict observance of this traditional principle is among the prerequisites for any restoration of unity.[331]

A positive attitude of approval is shown explicitly in this declaration which leads to two conclusions. First, Vatican II affirms that the Orthodox practices of the dissolution of ratified and consummated marriages "are better suited to the temperament of their faithful and better adapted

---

328. J. M. Kuntz, *Is Marriage Indissoluble*, 335.

329. Ibid., 335.

330. The Orthodox practices providing explicitly ten grounds for divorce and dissolution of marriage have been restated by encyclical letter of Bishop Jacobos on 16th of June 1966.

331. *The Decree of Ecumenism* 16. Vatican II, quoted in J. M. Kuntz, *Is Marriage Indissoluble*, 336.

to foster the good of souls." Second if the phrase "the good of souls" is understood to echo Pius XII's "salvation of souls," a higher concern is envisioned by the Catholic Church to Orthodox believers than to its own. Then a question is legitimately asked: "why cannot the Roman Catholic Church extend to her own members the same freedom that she permits to others?"[332] The answer is not provided, but deep concern is shown about those Catholic Christians who have been caught between the need for a practical solution for their intensified marital problems and the church's silence. "The solution would seem to be, for the 'good of souls' of Roman Catholics, to allow the dissolution of ratified and consummated marriages in the Roman Catholic Church."[333]

The indissoluble nature of marriage is further criticized by some Catholic scholars due to its social and cultural inadequacy, since it is irrelevant to the present pluralistic societies and rests on legalistic biblical grounds of interpretation.[334] Others insist on reduction of its judicial validity on behalf of its ethical demand.[335] Indeed, the future of indissolubility presently preserved by the church primarily related to the sacramental marriages (*ratum et consummatum*, marriage between baptized Christians in the proper liturgical setting and the presence of witnesses) is questionable in the light of the history of the Catholic Church's exercise of power to dissolve different kinds of marriages.[336]

One of the propositions for ecumenical solution of the indissolubility is that work should be done in "liberalizing of the concept of nullity so as to make the marriage discipline more compassionate."[337] In this way the marital union is evaluated as not been formed due to some impediment in its initial realization and thus the permanent marriage covenant as never constituted between the spouses.[338] However, the dangers of liberalizing the concept of marital annulment to the permanent character of marital union are more obvious than the attempt to protect the permanent nature

332. J. M. Kuntz, *Is Marriage Indissoluble*, 337.

333. Ibid.

334. G. Cereti, *Judges or Counsellors*, 99, 100.

335. L. Boff, *The Sacrament of Marriage*, 29.

336. John T. Noonan, *Power to Dissolve: Lawyers and Marriages in the Courts of the Roman Curia* (Cambridge: Belknap, 1972), quoted in Philip S. S. Keane, *Sexual Morality: A Catholic Perspective*, 143.

337. J. Macquarrie, *Christian Unity and Christian Diversity*, 89.

338. Ibid.

of marriage through restricting the grounds for divorce and remarriage only to the biblical model, those intentional failures of fulfillment of the marriage covenant stipulations. Therefore, the proposition of the present author is that the indissoluble nature of marriage should be modified as far as a place is provided for exceptional permission of divorce and remarriage on biblical grounds.[339] This is clearly expressed in the permanent nature of the covenant understanding of marriage which does establish marital union as a permanent relationship, but does not constitute it as indissoluble, due to the possible failure of one of the spouses to fulfill the required stipulations of the covenant grounded on sinful rebellious behavior which endangers the dignity and life of the other spouse.

Solving the problem of the indissolubility of marriage opens the possibility for those Christian denominations which practice annulment,[340] but prohibit divorce and remarriage, condemning them as evil,[341] to recognize marital breakdown on proper biblical grounds, and divorce and remarriage as legitimate solutions for sick marriages. This establishes the twofold exegetical and theological view of the NT teaching on divorce and remarriage as dogmatically valid and ecumenically relevant, offering a possibility to serve the purposes of the pragmatic task of the present work.

---

339. P. Hoffmann, *Jesus' Saying About Divorce and Its Interpretation in the New Testament Tradition*, 64–66.

340. This practice has been criticized by some Catholic scholars as an inadequate solution for sick marriages. See G. Cereti, *Judges or Counsellors*, 100, 101, 103.

341. This attitude has been considered as extreme by some Protestant scholars. See George Ensworth, Jr., "Notice the Divorced Among Us," *Christianity Today* 26 (May 21, 1982) 21.

six

Applying the Conclusions in a Pluralistic Context

THE CONCEPT OF MARRIAGE, DIVORCE, AND REMARRIAGE WHICH HAS been exegetically established through the analysis of the relevant NT texts, canonically defined through the concept of covenant in both OT and NT literature, and dogmatically formulated with an ecumenical proposal requires pragmatic attestation of its relevance for the Christian communities and the society at large. The nature of this task is established as fourfold. The first is devoted to the analysis of the contemporary context in relation to its social, cultural, religious, and philosophical dimensions. The second provides a formulation of the contemporary notion of marriage and examination of its inner dynamics. The third endeavors to apply the ecumenical proposal in all levels of the Christian communities. The fourth offers an example of the social relevance of the twofold concept of marriage, divorce, and remarriage. With the successful accomplishment of the pragmatic task the work will be led to its conclusion.

The most simplified definition of the contemporary context[1] is that of pluralism. Generally defined, pluralism maintains "that diversity is beneficial to society and that autonomy should be enjoyed by disparate functional or cultural groups within a society, including religious groups, trade unions, professional organizations, and ethnic minorities."[2] In its relation to assimilation, pluralism might be defined as the alternative to the resistance of a particular minority to assimilation by the predominant identity group of the society, so as to preserve its ethnic particularities.[3]

---

1. The present work will focus primarily on the Western countries and USA due to the transitional state of the post-communist eastern European countries.
2. "Pluralism," in *Encyclopædia Britannica*.
3. Ian Robertson, *Society: A Brief Introduction* (New York: Worth, 1989) 196–97.

In a pluralistic society, different ethnic groups preserving their cultural identity coexist with an equal share of social responsibilities.[4] Pluralism might also be understood as "incomplete assimilation," which includes different ethnic groups which have passed different levels of assimilation and have preserved their identity. The ethnic groups in the United States survived after passing through cultural,[5] structural,[6] and indentificational[7] assimilation. Thus, the United States is described as "a pluralistic society made up of diverse ethnic subcultures."[8]

Pluralism might be further related to three subjects which attempt to define its nature, empirical pluralism, cherished pluralism, and philosophical pluralism. The phenomenon of empirical pluralism[9] describes the kind of diversity within a culture which is primarily found in the Western countries. It refers to the varieties related to "race, value systems, heritage, language, culture, and religion."[10] The Western societies in general and the United States in particular maintain a strong empirical pluralism which defines their cultures and societies as characterized by predominant diversity versus a lower element of homogeneity. This affects life in these societies in all its aspects. On the one hand, it forms an environment in which freedom of belonging to a particular group and of expressing one's personal religious conviction is normative. Freedom of choice is also essential for defining one's values and norms. "Value systems embodied in styles of living are not right or wrong, true or false. They are matters of

---

4. Lewis A. Coser, et al., *Introduction to Sociology*, 2nd ed. (New York: Harcourt Brace Jovanovich, 1987) 255.

5. Prominent features of this stage are the adaptation of language, values, and customs of the predominant ethnic group. (L. A. Coser, et al., *Introduction to Sociology*, 261.)

6. At this level the ethnic minority enters into the institutions of the dominant group. (L. A. Coser, et al., *Introduction to Sociology*, 261.)

7. A long history of interethnic marriages brings the particular ethnic group to a level where it identifies itself with the predominant group. Due to this process many Americans define themselves as "100 percent American." (L. A. Coser, et al., *Introduction to Sociology*, 261.)

8. L. A. Coser, et al., *Introduction to Sociology*, 260–61. It is also argued that United States is "the most religiously diverse society in history." (Robertson, *Society*, 271.)

9. It is also referred to as sociocultural pluralism. (Gregor McLennan, *Pluralism* [Minneapolis: University of Minnesota Press, 1995] 6.)

10. D. A. Carson, *The Gagging of God: Christianity Confronts Pluralism* (Grand Rapids: Zondervan, 1996) 13.

personal choice."[11] On the other hand, such a society loses its stability and coherence. It also tends to empower its government with more authority for providing unity in laws and acceptable social behavior.[12] The main role in the formation of stability in the pluralistic society is played by the State's law. Although it is a subject of modifications and improvements, the State's law exercises control, facilitating and sustaining the structures of the customary law. It is only through the existence of the State's law that legal pluralism may be acknowledged and defined.[13]

Cultural pluralism, which might be described as a subcategory of empirical pluralism, defines culture as a diverse assembly of various identity groups which preserve their own culture and tradition within the frame of the overall national distinction.[14] In this society people from different cultural backgrounds are free to attain to their own lifestyle, expressing their cultural distinctiveness in a personal and unique way to the predominant culture. This cultural pluralism is believed to enrich society and promote freedom and identity awareness. Due to the ethical dimension of the nature of culture, its pluralistic expression requires supervision in preventing those cultural practices which might bring physical harm[15] to the other members of the society.[16] The predominant relativism in the pluralistic culture obscures any religious or ethical guidance.[17]

> In contrast to traditional societies, modern Western society leaves its members free, within very wide limits, to adopt and hold their own views about what is good and desirable, about what kind of life is to be admired, about what code of ethics should govern one's private life.[18]

Even religious guidance based on the interpretation of religious source might be further culturally distorted through the practices of its adher-

---

11. Lesslie Newbigin, *Foolishness to the Greeks: The Gospel and Western Culture* (Geneva: World Council of Churches, 1986) 17.

12. D. A. Carson, *The Gagging of God*, 14–17.

13. G. McLennan, *Pluralism*, 49.

14. Robertson, *Society*, 215.

15. An example might be given with the practice of cannibalism. (Newbigin, *The Gospel in a Pluralist Society* [Grand Rapids: Eerdmans, 1989] 185.)

16. Newbigin *The Gospel in a Pluralist Society*, 14.

17. Ibid., 186.

18. Idem, *Foolishness to the Greeks*, 16.

ents.¹⁹ Cultural pluralism is a stable characteristic in Western society in general and the United States in particular.²⁰

Empirical pluralism is understood as an advanced form of the development of social and cultural life which is to be deeply appreciated and highly assessed. That understanding of empirical pluralism leads to cherished pluralism, a category which unites those, mostly intellectuals, of the West who support and promote empirical pluralism in all spheres of life.²¹ Cherished pluralism makes a very strong argument by focusing on the benefits which empirical pluralism brings to every individual. The possibility of defining one's personal convictions and beliefs within a complexity of opinions has become a given opportunity to everyone. The presence of diversity in all levels of society has formulated the virtue of individual choice as a personal benefit to every member of that society.²² "Pluralism in the West signified the modern citizen's membership of overlapping groups, equal access to political goods, and a general consensus over values."²³

Philosophical pluralism²⁴ expresses the understanding held by various different approaches. Namely, that the search for objective truth is irrelevant since no philosophical, ideological, or religious statement has the authority to affirm its validity and reject the alternative position as false or invalid. This line of thinking has been developed through the new hermeneutic and, with the assistance of deconstruction theory, furnishes

---

19. The NT maintains the view of monogamous marriage union. The question might be raised which practice is closer to this Christian ethical norm, the serial monogamy of the Western culture or the polygamy of some of the African cultures. L. Newbing argues that the African model is closer since "at least acknowledges binding covenant obligations while the Western model dissolves them." (L. Newbing *The Gospel in a Pluralist Society*, 187.)

20. It is argued that the United States maintains one of the most advanced levels of cultural plurality. (Robertson, *Society*, 215.)

21. The defenders of pluralism are generally divided in two groups: those who exercise pluralistic attitude to the academic matters allowing diversity of opinions to be considered welcoming all as potential contributions to the discussed issue and those who defended doctrinal pluralism maintaining plurality but excluding any monism from the discussion. (G. McLennan, *Pluralism*, 75–76.)

22. D. A. Carson, *The Gagging of God*, 18–19.

23. G. McLennan, *Pluralism*, 41.

24. It is also discussed under the title of methodological pluralism. (G. McLennan, *Pluralism*, 6.)

the body of postmodernist philosophy.[25] The new hermeneutics have shifted the search for meaning from the subject matter under consideration to the individuality of the interpreter and his/her cultural setting. Deconstructionists defined all language and its comprehensible meaning as socially determined and historically conditioned. That provides the possibility for the interpreter to deconstruct the text in a free manner, validating this free interpretation through his social and cultural stand.[26] The influence of philosophical pluralism has extended not only to the spheres of academia but also to the everyday life of the common person. The pursuit of objective and universal truth has been abandoned in all spheres of life. The ethical guidance and life of the pluralistic society has been profoundly relativized. Ethically proper behavior now finds its source of guidance in contemporary influential, popular entertainment programs.[27]

Philosophical pluralism becomes the foundation of various forms of religious pluralism, whose foundational belief is that all religions contain the knowledge which is necessary to lead a human being to salvation.[28] Faith is understood as a matter of personal convictions and individual choice. The differences in various religions cannot be analyzed from the perspective of true or false but as "a different perception of the one truth."[29] Under the influence of this phenomenon, tolerance has modified its perspective. The object of tolerance has been changed from the people to their ideas. That ruled out the necessity of discussing different ideas since their value and validity have been generally accepted and confirmed. The object of intolerance has become the individual whose beliefs went beyond the generally accepted framework of "plausibility structures."[30] The latter, when referring to the dominance of one religion over the others, is not tolerated in the pluralistic society. The diversity of religious beliefs and practices may not be ruled out on the basis of stronger objective assertions of one religion, since the personal sincerity of the expression

---

25. Also G. McLennan, *Pluralism*, 76.
26. D. A. Carson, *The Gagging of God*, 19–22.
27. Ibid., 22–25.
28. Ibid., 26.
29. L. Newbing *The Gospel in a Pluralist Society*, 14.
30. D. A. Carson, *The Gagging of God*, 19–32.

of one's faith validates the religious belonging of the individual.[31] Thus, pluralism in all its dimensions facilitates a social, cultural, religious, and philosophical environment in which the institution of marriage receives new formulation.

The attitudes to marriage, socially framed and cultural defined, have changed drastically in the Western countries in general and the USA in particular over the length of one generation during the period between 1965 and 2004. The impact might be defined as a failure to understand marriage as a stable social institution.[32] The overall perception of marriage before 1960 formulated marriage as a lifelong union between husband and wife based on mutual support and loving commitment which provides a proper place for raising the family heirs. However, at the end of the second millennium, such a comprehension of marriage has become very rare, especially within the younger generation. The function of marriage as a social institution could be described as providing a proper framework in society at large, and facilitating a particular model of behavior for individuals and social groups in particular, in order to accomplish people's goals and satisfy their needs. Marriage as such might be defined as a fundamental part of every culture, empowering individuals with the means for a proper expression of human sexuality, satisfying the need for companionship, facilitating an environment for raising children, and providing channels for economic cooperation. Thus, the deinstitutionalization of marriage means that alternative ways within society and culture need to be provided for accomplishing the same individual and community goals, as well as satisfying people's needs.[33] That process characterizes the present stage of marriage in the Western world. The forces driving it might be attributed to different aspects of the social and cultural revolutions.

The sexual revolution, whose massive impact on culture and society may be seen since the mid-1960s, undermines marriage as an institution and as the normative context for sexual relationships between male and female. The new expression of sexuality demanded freedom in all its dimensions. No restriction should be applied to one's personal desire except the mutual consent of the partner. The establishment of new norms of

31. L. Newbing *The Gospel in a Pluralist Society*, 25, 26.
32. David P. Gushee, *Getting Marriage Right: Realistic Counsel for Saving and Strengthening Relationships* (Grand Rapids: Baker, 2004) 21–22.
33. Ibid., 24, 25.

sexual conduct has been overtaken by the media at large and promoted through various means, including that of pornography, and its main and most easily accessed source, the Internet. Thus, marriage lost its role of defining human sexual behavior, establishing its borders of proper expression, and condemning its failures. Marriage played no importance in the satisfaction of individual sexual needs and had no relevance in formalizing one's sexual partner. Free sexual relationships have become the norm and their various expressions provided individuals on all social levels with ways to satisfy their needs and accomplish their goals without any consequences. A crucial supportive role in this process has been played by establishing and developing artificial means for birth control.[34]

The possibility of preventing undesirable pregnancy might be approached from two perspectives. On the one hand, it might serve the needs of a married couple to prepare a proper environment for the child through organizing their emotional and financial resources in a given frame of time. On the other hand, the possibility to prevent pregnancy provides an opportunity for single individuals to engage in free sexual practices attempting escape from any consequences. This second approach to contraceptives undermines marriage and leads to a lack of understanding one's responsibilities related to sex and parenthood. This openness to the abuse of contraceptives has brought much initial opposition to their massive distribution. Most of this opposition has been overcome on two levels through the decision of the United States Supreme Court in 1965, which has allowed the use of contraceptives by married couples and, in 1972, by even unmarried individuals. The only opposition which has remained until the present is that of the Catholic Church, which regards the danger of abusing contraceptives as overwhelming their positive input to marriage.[35] The use of contraceptives outside the marital union has brought another problem, the possibility of undesirable pregnancy.

The liberation of sexual behavior and the availability of contraceptives for unmarried couples have created an environment for potential undesirable pregnancy which results either in abortion or in illegitimacy. The former has brought devaluing of the child's life for the benefit of the adult, due to the adult's lack of responsibility. The decision of the Supreme Court in *Roe v. Wade* for legalizing abortion on demand in 1973 has

---

34. Ibid., 26, 27.
35. Ibid., 27, 28.

confirmed this practice and its overall devastating results.[36] The latter refers to children being born to unwed mothers. The attempt to soften the description of this phenomenon with "out-of-wedlock birth" has not diminished its problematic nature.[37] A child being born outside the provisionary framework of marriage for protection and support is at risk of lacking these essential life components. Both the mother and the child in such a situation are faced with different financial difficulties and challenges which question even their survival.[38] Even further, this problem undermines the existence of marriage itself as the proper environment for raising a child.[39]

The development of new attitudes toward sex that accompanied the possibility of sex without pregnancy, and the resulting increase in the number of unwed mothers has in turn produced an alternative to marital social behavior, namely that of cohabitation.[40] The mutual decision by male and female to live together without providing the legal framework of their relationship according to the existing social system, with marriage as a social institution, has found many expressions related to its duration and nature. The main intentions of the couple entering into this relationship might be defined as an attempt to facilitate marital life without the legal framework of marriage. Both sides play family roles to some extent, enjoying sexual relationship and mutual provisions, but without the official recognition of their union with the expected obligations and responsibilities defined under the institution of marriage. Thus, cohabitation might be understood as an attempt of male and female to share their lives with all the pleasing outcomes but to avoid the expectations of mutual responsibilities coming with the formalization of the union through the marriage institution. However, this free relationship does not bring the expected results. It neither benefits the couple to reach the level of sharing

---

36. "The ensuing abortion revolution, in which for a time one out of every three American pregnancies ended in elective abortion (before 'settling down' to one out of four or five today), carries profound social consequences that extend well beyond the 'mere' killing of more than one million developing children a year." (Gushee, *Getting Marriage Right*, 28)

37. The statistics related to pregnancies of unmarried mothers are as follows: In 1960, 5 percent of all pregnancies; in 1970, 10.7 percent; in 1980, 18.4 percent; in 1990, 28 percent and in 1999, 33 percent. (Gushee, *Getting Marriage Right*, 29)

38. Also Robertson, *Society*, 256.

39. Gushee, *Getting Marriage Right*, 29, 30.

40. Also Robertson, *Society*, 259.

their lives as married partners nor prepares them for an eventual marriage. It is obvious that a relationship which has not been formalized with public recognition of the spouses' consent for fulfillment of their marital duties and legalized through the proper social institutions would not require either emotional or material devotion of the spouses to the union.[41] Thus, in spite of high expectations, such unions suffer much violence, exploitation, and negligence, with a high rate of sexual and physical abuse including even the death of children from previous relationships. Studies have shown that cohabitation does not usually lead to marriage, and its temporary nature does not prove beneficial to the couple in any respect. What it offers are grounds for more frequent sexual practices outside of marriage, which lead to more unexpected and undesired pregnancies, more children exposed to abuse and lack of a supportive environment, more possibility for financial, moral, and physical mistreatment, and more frustration and disappointment of the involved parties.[42] The problem of cohabitation extends beyond its actual practice to the whole attitude of those involved toward marriage and divorce. Couples who cohabit with the purpose of evaluating a partner and the environment created by him/her for establishing an eventual marital relationship understand marriage as a temporal solution until they find a better partner, and accept divorce easily.[43] Research shows that the divorce rate is higher among those who have cohabited before marriage than those who have married without cohabitation.[44] The formation of this attitude in the cohabiting couples is also shown through the temporary nature of the cohabiting itself, no more than 2 years.[45] However in spite of these negative results the West has discarded marriage and embraced cohabitation.[46]

---

41. James Q. Wilson, *The Marriage Problem* (New York: HarperCollins, 2002) 38, 39.

42. Gushee, *Getting Marriage Right*, 30–32; Wilson, *The Marriage Problem*, 3–7.

43. Wilson, *The Marriage Problem*, 6.

44. The statistics show that in Sweden the divorce rate is 80 present higher among those who have cohabited before marriage than those who have begun with marriage on the first place. (Wilson, *The Marriage Problem*, 5, 6, 198.)

45. Wilson, *The Marriage Problem*, 39.

46. In Sweden one-third of all couples of marriage age cohabit instead of marrying. In the Western world in general and in countries such as England, France, and United States half or more of all marriages have been proceeded by cohabitation. (Wilson, *The Marriage Problem*, 3, 4.)

Another revolutionary innovation which has contributed to the deinstitutionalizing of marriage, is technologically assisted reproduction (AR). After the first successful birth of a baby from a tube in 1978, several AR techniques have been developed to produce such a result. The help offered to unfertile married couples through this medical advance has been enormous.[47] However, the practice has prompted difficult ethical questions, challenged the understanding of parenthood, social family roles, and utterly undermined the institution of marriage. One of the main concerns has been related to the "legal ownership (custody?) of viable frozen embryos."[48] Another problem has emerged due to the openness of AR to any individual who is able to afford it financially. Thus, giving birth to children through this method has not been limited to married couples. This further destroys the relations between sexual intercourse, marriage, and parenthood, and challenges the institution of marriage as the proper environment for raising children.[49] A further concern has pointed to the understanding of family roles and their social implications. A child being born through the procedures involved in AR appears to have several "parents," namely "sperm donor, egg donor, gestational mother, contracting father, and contracting mother," without taking into consideration those who may appear through eventual divorce and remarriage. This requires a fundamental redefinition of family and social roles, one which affects both the marriage institution and societal structures.[50]

The institution of marriage has been further destabilized through the new legal and cultural grounds occupied by the supporters of homosexuality.[51] The challenge to marriage arose with the change to understanding homosexuality as a behavior which does not require treatment.[52] This has

---

47. Gushee, *Getting Marriage Right*, 32.

48. Steven L. Nock, James D. Wright, and Laura Sanchez, "America's Divorce Problem," *Society* 36/4 (1999) 46.

49. Gushee, *Getting Marriage Right*, 32.

50. "Shared understandings of social roles, role relationships, and associated behavioural expectations are the glue that holds societies together and we should therefore be cautious about fundamental re-definitions of these most basic adult roles." (Nock, Wright, and Sanchez, "America's Divorce Problem," 46.)

51. Also Robertson, *Society*, 260.

52. The understanding of homosexuality as psychological disorder which has been common prior to mid-1970s has been changed with the removing it from the list of disorders in 1973 by the American Psychiatric Association. (Gushee, *Getting Marriage Right*, 33.)

established the foundation for further development of gay rights, both in relation to popularizing the attitude toward homosexual partnership and even to legalizing marital union among such individuals. On the one hand, this has led to promiscuous behavior in changing partners over a period of time, thus expanding the sexual revolution on homosexual grounds. On the other hand, it has further undermined the social understanding of the nature of marriage as union between male and female which is consummated through sexual intercourse and results in giving birth and raising children. This conservative social view of marriage is constantly challenged by the continuous efforts of the homosexual community to legalize marriage for its members using even marriage-supportive[53] claims.[54]

The change of the attitude toward divorce has caused an enormous effect on the institution of marriage. While prior to 1960 divorce was considered as a rare exceptional provision for a marital malfunction,[55] gradually it has developed to a routine way of resolving marital dissatisfaction.[56] One of the main reasons for that change may be attributed to the passing of "no-fault" divorce laws in many European countries as well as the United States during the 1960s.[57] The facts provided from the statistics (by the year 2001 almost every second marriage ends in divorce) show that divorce has become a social institution by itself, paralleling that of marriage. The understanding of the nature and the function of this institution has stood in opposition to that of marriage. Divorce has not been treated anymore as an exceptional possibility, but as a possible opportunity. The formal exception in the society and culture has been established as a normative practice and proper behavior. In their search for a better

---

53. Here is the usual form of the argument posed by homosexuals toward their opposition: "We press for marriage because we, like you, value the stability of lasting romantic commitments. In a society that devalues such commitments at every turn, we are your allies, not your enemies. Grant us the right to marry, and let us join you in defense of marriage as an institution." (Gushee, *Getting Marriage Right*, 33.); Also Tonya Jameson, "Gay Unions Aren't Enemy of Marriage; Heterosexuals and Hollywood do Far More to Undermine it," *The Charlotte Observer*, 27 July 2003.

54. Gushee, *Getting Marriage Right*, 33, 34.

55. While in California in the mid-1960s the grounds for divorce were adultery, cruelty, and desertion in New York the only ground for divorce, legalized in 1787 by Alexander Hamilton, was adultery. (Wilson, *The Marriage Problem*, 162.)

56. Gushee, *Getting Marriage Right*, 34.

57. Wilson, *The Marriage Problem*, 19

partner, spouses have passed from marriage through divorce and remarriage numerous times to initiate a phenomenon called serial monogamy. Research shows that those new marriages are even less stable and usually end with divorce. Those who have chosen cohabitation instead of marriage do not progress better, but even further destabilize the institution of marriage. Society and culture have faced a new dimension of family life where many relations have been formed on the basis of marriages and remarriages. That has moved the process of the deinstitutionalizing of marriage one step further.[58]

The marriage institution has been further challenged, and its values and norms blurred, through the widely-spread and well-established consumer attitude in the culture and the society at large. Consumer thinking is grounded on the individual drive for psychological and therapeutic fulfillment and stability. From the historical point of view this attitude has been formed through a combination of the "human potential movement"[59] (1970s) whose main goal has been individual personal growth and the formation of thinking based on market values (1980s and 1990s) which propagated the striving for one's best satisfaction in spite of failures and losses. The relationship between traders and customers has been established through advertisements which intend to capture not only the thoughts and the heart of the latter but to appeal to one's feelings. The product must be sold and at the same time provide a place for the next one. The customer is to be compelled to strive for the best. The goal of the process is the satisfaction of the consumer's needs. However, the needs are always present and never satisfied. The constant struggle from product to product disregards loyalty and promotes quality and value. Thus, the society and culture with their values and norms are filtrated through this consumer attitude. Marriage relationships become evaluated through the prism of such attitudes of the marriage partners. The spouse is looking at his/her marriage from the perspective of personal satisfaction and achievements. The thinking is that of a business, formed in the evaluation of the amount of one's investments and their results. Faithfulness is not a highly valued virtue of the relationship because of the possibility and openness for a better mate. If one's personal satisfaction is not fulfilled, marriage ties can be destroyed and a new partner with a promising better

---

58. Gushee, *Getting Marriage Right*, 34, 35.
59. William J. Doherty, *Take Back Your Marriage* (New York: Guilford, 2001) 27.

approach can be found. Here is how a marriage and family therapist with 25 years of practice defines the consumer marriage.

> Mid-twentieth-century marriage, which featured high expectations for personal satisfaction, mutated into consumer marriage, with the same high psychological expectations but now spiced with a sense of entitlement and impermanence. The chief value of consumer marriage is making sure that one's needs are being met and that one's options are always open.[60]

The result of the consumer attitude to marriage is the unnecessary divorce. The reasons for this divorce are not formulated on the basis of lack of fulfillment of the spouse's responsibilities but are more sensually characterized.[61] The measure for one's marital happiness is defined on the basis of a fluid and flexible scheme based on one's feelings and formed through a consumer value system. The relationship appears to function only through the evaluation of the spouse's performance, without consideration for one's personal involvement. Hence, divorce has turned from being the last choice for a solution to being the first opportunity to escape, instead of looking for possibilities for improving the relationship. Small and insignificant problems in the marriage have become deep and significant failures of conduct and abuse due to the reluctance of spouses to engage in facilitating a possibility for change and to feeding one's striving for a better companion. Thus, the very reasons which have established the grounds for divorce have become a constant approval of one's desire to leave the relationship and look for a new one, indifferent to the constant marital failure.[62]

The place of the institution of marriage in the present society and culture throughout the developed world[63] has been overtaken by the new patterns of behavior, norms, and value systems which have replaced mar-

---

60. Doherty, *Take Back Your Marriage*, 34.

61. The following reasons have been collected by Doherty through his therapy consultations. "The relationship was not working for me anymore;" "Our needs were just too different;" "I was not happy;" "We just grew apart;" "I grew and he did not;" "She has changed too much;" "I deserve more;" "We are not the same people we were when we got married;" "After the children left home, there was nothing left;" "The relationship became stale;" "My husband was a nice guy, but boring;" "We had no real intimacy. What kind of role model is that for the kids?" (Ibid., 35–36.)

62. Ibid., 14–17, 26–47.

63. Gushee, *Getting Marriage Right*, 36.

riage structures and have attempted to satisfy the needs of the individuals and the society as a whole. However, the results are devastating. The practices of free sex resulted in illegitimacy and a high number of venereal diseases.[64] Cohabitation with the use of contraceptives has attempted to provide security in expressions of free sexual conduct and provisional training for the eventual marriage but instead it has produced more illegitimacy, disappointment, and a higher divorce rate. The methods of technologically assisted reproduction and the gay rights reforms have further confused the model of marital relationships and parenthood. And finally, the consumer attitude toward marriage and the flexible attitude toward divorce have made the marriage institution a temporary provision for companionship until a better option appears. The notion of marriage as lifelong, covenantal union has been drastically changed surrendering to the challenges of a pluralistic culture and society.[65] Another serious challenge to the permanent character of marriage has been defined since the early 1970s as a serious threat to the inner structures of marital union, the relationship between the spouses. Domestic violence has been always an accompanying problem of the marital relationship, but its escalation against women has brought the issue to the surface of social concern, and has become a focus of intensive scholarly research.[66]

Domestic violence or intimate partner violence might be defined as behavior of the perpetrator toward an intimate partner which causes physical, sexual, emotional, economic or spiritual harm "including acts of physical aggression, sexual coercion, psychological abuse and controlling behaviors."[67] It involves former or current spouses or partners. In the majority of cases of intimate partner violence, women are the victims and men are the perpetrators although the reverse is also possible.[68] The studies of man as a victim of intimate partner violence have not been well developed worldwide, but in the United States abuse of men is 5 times

---

64. Also Robertson, *Society*, 152–53.

65. Also Wilson, *The Marriage Problem*, 41.

66. Marina Ajduković, "Određenje i oblici nasilja u obitelji," u *Nasilje nad ženom u obitelji*," uredile: Marina Ajduković i Gordana Pavleković (Zagreb: društvo za psihološku pomoć, 2000) 11.

67. Hugh Waters, et al., *The Economic Dimensions of Interpersonal Violence* (Geneva: Department of Injuries and Violence Prevention, World Health Organization, 2004) 3.

68. Ibid., 3.

less than that of women.[69] Although this might be attributed to the insufficient data due to the male reservation in reporting the cases, it is clear that women suffer much more abuse than men.[70] The National Crime Victimization Survey (NCVS) confirms the fact that males also suffer abuse, but in a significantly lower percent.[71]

A general survey of 42 nations around the world reveals that "intimate partner violence is a widespread phenomenon with devastating consequences for families, communities, and societies in all parts of the world."[72] NCVS in one of its most complete and revealing studies[73] shows that 5 million females in the United States have suffered different forms of abuse. The research demonstrates that in 75% of the cases the offender has been alone, and in almost half of these cases (29%) he has been an intimate partner, either former or current husband or boyfriend. Another survey reveals almost the same percentage (22%)[74] including also such countries as Canada (29%), Egypt (34%),[75] and León, Nicaragua, (27%). However, this percentage increases when related to currently married women in South Korea (38%), and the West Bank and Gaza (53%).[76] In

69. Emily F. Rothman, Alexander Butchart, Magdalena Cerda, *Intervening with Perpetrators of Intimate Partner Violence: A Global Perspective* (Geneva: World Health Organization, 2003) 1.

70. Aimee K. Cassidey-Shaw, *Family Abuse and the Bible* (Binghamton: Haworth Pastoral Press, 2002) 53.

71. Ibid., 51–52.

72. E. F. Rothman, A. Butchart, M. Cerda, *Intervening with Perpetrators of Intimate Partner Violence*, 1.

73. The study has covered 50000 households and 100000 individuals in the United States for the period of 1992–1993. (Ronet Bachman and Linda Saltzman, "Violence Against Women: Estimates from the Redesigned Survey," Bureau of Justice Statistics: Special Report (August, 1995), quoted in Cassidey-Shaw, *Family Abuse and the Bible*, 51–54.

74. Tjaden, N. Thoennes, *Full Report of the Prevalence, Incidence, and Consequences of Violence Against Women: Findings From the National Violence Against Women Survey* (Washington, DC: National Institute of Justice, Office of Justice Programs, 2000), quoted in H. Waters, et al., *The Economic Dimensions of Interpersonal Violence*, 17.

75. F. El-Zanaty, et al., Egypt Demographic and Health Survey (Calverton, MD: Macro International, 1996), quoted in H. Waters, et al., *The Economic Dimensions of Interpersonal Violence*, 17.

76. E. Krug, et al., eds. *World Report on Violence and Health* (Geneva: World Health Organization, 2002), quoted in H. Waters, et al., *The Economic Dimensions of Interpersonal Violence*, 17. The analysis of UNICEF in 1994 shows that domestic violence against women in the countries under transition (including Croatia, Bulgaria and Romania)

Hackney in the United Kingdom one of every nine women suffers domestic violence.[77] The NCVS continues the analysis showing that from 500 000 reported sexual assaults, in more than a half of the cases (250 000) the sexual abuse has been committed by an intimate partner.[78] Furthermore, from those who have experienced different kinds of assault, 52% sustained injuries and 41% required medical intervention.[79] The results of the Uniform Crime Reports in 1992 show that around 30% of all female homicides have been committed by an intimate partner.[80] The average percentage worldwide for women abused by an intimate partner is calculated to be over 80% of all cases of violence, and from all cases of female homicides 45% have died from the hands of their intimate partner.[81] These results demonstrate that violence is more prevalent among those who are in a close relationship. The victims of domestic violence, predominantly women, suffer disastrous consequences which affect not only their physical and mental health, injuring them for a long period of time but even causing death to many of them. However, many of them continue to stay in the abusive relationship under the fear imposed on them by the threats of the offenders against their life if they attempt to leave. This is clear from the report of the NCVS which shows that "the victimization rate of women separated from their husbands is about three times higher than that of divorced women, and twenty five times higher than that of married women."[82] In addition, the National Violence Against Women Survey concludes that 50% of female victims of stalking are threatened by their intimate partners and 80% of these women have been physically assaulted.[83] There are numerous other reasons which prevent the women victims of domestic violence from leaving the relation-

---

undergoes a constant growth. (M. Ajduković, *Određenje i oblici nasilja u obitelji*, 13.)

77. E. Stanko, et al., *Counting the Costs: Estimating the Impact of Domestic Violence in the London Borough of Hackney* (London: Hackney Safer Cities and the Children's Society, 1998), quoted H. Waters, et al., *The Economic Dimensions of Interpersonal Violence*, 17.

78. Cassidey-Shaw, *Family Abuse and the Bible*, 53.

79. Ibid., 54.

80. Ibid.

81. Gordana Pavleković, Marina Ajduković, Maja Mamula, "Nasilje nad ženom u obitelji: osobni, obiteljski ili javnozdravstveni problem?" u *Nasilje nad ženom u obitelji*, uredile: Marina Ajduković i Gordana Pavleković (Zagreb: društvo za psihološku pomoć, 2000), 24.

82. Cassidey-Shaw, *Family Abuse and the Bible*, 55.

83. Ibid., 56.

ship. Some of them might be economical, parental, salvific, obligatory, low self-esteem, denial, shame, isolation, justification of the man's family role,[84] and deep loving devotion.[85]

Domestic violence is a problem which affects Christian households as well. The violence in these relationships extends to new religious dimensions of misusing the language, the meaning, and the authority of the Bible. A survey conducted among 5 700 Protestant pastors shows the reason why many sincere Christian wives continue obediently to endure suffering and to stay in an abusive marriage. The spiritual counselors of these women have manipulated their consciousness and spiritual devotion, perverting the biblical truth.[86] From the group surveyed, 93% rejected divorce as an option for the wife victim of domestic abuse by the husband. Another 72% would even insist that the wife continue physically to be part of the relationship, 26% promised her that submission to the violent husband would bring her God's deliverance and another 25% even judged her lack of obedience to the husband as the cause of the abuse. The opinion of the majority of the church leaders was that "it is better for a woman to tolerate some level of violence in the home–even though it is not God's perfect will–than to seek separation that might end in divorce."[87] The extent of damage from domestic violence affects not only the society as whole but every household and even every individual in particular. If danger is to be expected from those who are supposed to provide the strongest support and intimate friendship, then security and peace become unobtainable conditions in family life.[88]

---

84. Here are the words of an abused wife: "My husband slaps me, has sex with me against my will and I have to conform. Before being interviewed I did not really think about this. I thought this is only natural. This is the right way a husband behaves" (Woman interviewed in Bangladesh). (WHO, *Multi-Country Study on Women's Health and Domestic Violence Against Women* [Geneva: World Health Organization, 2002] 10.)

85. Maja Mamula & Marina Ajduković, "Dinamika zlostavljanja unutar obitelji," u *Nasilje nad ženom u obitelji*, uredile: Marina Ajduković i Gordana Pavleković (Zagreb: društvo za psihološku pomoć, 2000), 86; Also Rober J. Ackerman and Susan E. Pickering, *Before It's Too Late: Helping Women in Controlling or Abusive Relationships* (Deerfield Beach: Health Communications, 1995) 29–50.

86. J. R. Beck also considers the counseling help given to the victims of domestic violence by their clergy as useless and inapplicable to their situations. (J. R. Beck, *Theology for the Healthy Family*, 219.)

87. Cassidey-Shaw, *Family Abuse and the Bible*, 55.

88. Ibid., 54, 55.

The attempt to categorize the domestic violence or abuse by intimate partner on a scale from less to more severe does not do justice to the damage which it does to the victim. The consequences of verbal abuse can be as damaging to the health of the person as those from physical abuse. Thus, the following categorization of violence does not intend to minimize its devastating effects but to identify its different expressions.[89] Domestic violence[90] might be discussed under five topics, namely, physical abuse, emotional abuse, sexual abuse, economic control/abuse, and spiritual abuse.[91]

Physical abuse is a form of violent behavior which endangers the physical health of the individual. Not only the actual physical injury is considered abusive but also the threat from such physical harm should be included under the same category.[92] Fifty surveys of thirty-six nations around the world with an average of seven to two thousand participants per year provided the information that ten to fifty percent of the women suffered physical abuse by an intimate partner during their lifetimes.[93] Other research underlines the fact that the widely spread understanding in different societies and cultures is that physical abuse of women is highly tolerable.[94] Such a social tolerance toward domestic violence is not a surprise in the light of the widespread use of violence in different spheres of our society and its constant presentation by media and internet.[95] Physical abuse represents the highest percentage of domestic

89. Ibid., 59.

90. Also M. Ajduković, *Određenje i oblici nasilja u obitelji*, 11.

91. As a result of 50 surveys of 36 nations around the world with average of 7–2000 participants per year the following percentage is provided for each of different kinds of violence caused by intimate partner. All the participants of the survey defined physical abuse as intimate partner violence then 91% include emotional abuse, 89% include sexual abuse, 71% include economic control/abuse, 4% include spiritual abuse. (E. F. Rothman, A. Butchart, M. Cerda, *Intervening with Perpetrators of Intimate Partner Violence*, 11, 12.)

92. Cassidey-Shaw, *Family Abuse and the Bible*, 62–66.

93. E. F. Rothman, A. Butchart, M. Cerda, *Intervening with Perpetrators of Intimate Partner Violence*, 1.

94. N. Pečnik, *Nasilje u ljubavnim vezama mladića i djevojaka i stavovi prema fizičkom zlostavljanju žena*. Diplomski rad. (Zagreb: Odsjek za psihologiju, Filozofski fakultet, 1990), citirano u Mariana Ajduković, et al., "Nasilje u partnerskim odnosima," u *Nasilje nad ženom u obitelji*, uredile: Marina Ajduković i Gordana Pavleković (Zagreb: društvo za psihološku pomoć, 2000), 58.

95. Also M. Ajduković, *Određenje i oblici nasilja u obitelji*, 12, 13.

violence. The women in most of the cases are mistreated physically by their intimate partner at home where they should experience peace, joy and the satisfaction of intimate relationship. Instead of security at home, women experience physical violence in all its dimensions. The perpetrator might direct his physically abusive attitude toward the victim, expressing it through gesture, voice, vivid action or through destroying her possessions. He might also threaten her physical health and even her life, whether verbally or through showing a weapon. The actual violent physical contact might be performed with different tools or weapons or with bare hands. The consequences for the victim are tremendous. In addition to the psychological pressure and fear produced by the threats, any part of her body is vulnerable to the injuries inflicted by the physical actions of the perpetrator.[96] Research conducted in Atlanta shows "that an estimated 5.3 million incidents of intimate partner violence occur each year among USA women age 18 and older – resulting in nearly 2 million injuries, more than 550 000 of which required medical attention."[97] The gravity of the physical consequences for the women who are victims of physical abuse is further underlined by the fact that they are three times more vulnerable to sickness, and the period of their illness is longer than the women who have not experienced physical abuse.[98] Also, a survey done in 1998 shows that in the United States "women who are victims of intimate partner violence have 1.6 times higher estimated medical costs compared to other women."[99] If surveys are consulted which estimate the costs for medical treatment of women victims of violence in general and of abuse by an intimate partner in particular, the same devastating results will be observed. In Canada for the year 2002 the direct medical costs for treat-

---

96. Maja Mamula, Gordana Pavleković, "Tjelesni, psihički i socijalni znakovi zlostavljanja žene u obitelji," u *Nasilje nad ženom u obitelji*, uredile: Marina Ajduković i Gordana Pavleković (Zagreb: društvo za psihološku pomoć, 2000) 103.

97. Centers for Disease Control and Prevention (CDC), *Costs of Intimate Partner Violence Against Women in the United States* (Atlanta, GA: National Center for Injury Prevention and Control, 2003), quoted in H. Waters, et al., *The Economic Dimensions of Interpersonal Violence*, 21.

98. C. Kirkwood, *Leaving Abusive Partners* (London: Sage, 1997), quoted in Maja Mamula, "Zdravstvenene i psihološke posljedice spolnog nasilja nad ženama," u *Nasilje nad ženom u obitelji*, uredile: Marina Ajduković i Gordana Pavleković (Zagreb: društvo za psihološku pomoć, 2000), 93.

99. Y. C. Ulrich, et al., "Medical Care Utilization Patterns in Women with Diagnosed Domestic Violence," *American Journal of Preventative Medicine* 24 (2003) 9–15, quoted in H. Waters, et al., *The Economic Dimensions of Interpersonal Violence*, 21.

ment of women victims of violence has been $1.1 billion.[100] The medical cost per patient who is a victim of intimate partner violence and other violence in Kingston Public Hospital in Jamaica during 1993 was $709.[101] The picture in different states in the USA shows the same devastating results. In Washington State for the year 2000, the average compensation given to women victims of violence for mental health treatment has been around $3087.[102] The health plan of Minnesota during 1999 shows that "the intimate partner violence victims had an annual average of $4341 of health care costs, or $2120 more on average than other women in the plan."[103] The estimates of these costs for medical treatment of physical injuries caused by an intimate partner show the damage caused by physical violence not only to the victims but to the society as a whole. Physical domestic violence is constantly accompanied by psychological and emotional abuse.[104]

Emotional abuse is such a behavior which intends to destabilize the intimate partner emotionally. Different patterns of behavior may be used by the perpetrator, with the intent to impose on the victim a sense of guilt or mental disorder. Jealousy might become a ground for constant psychological terror or threats, projecting a sense of insecurity and guilt upon the victim. Men, especially in religious circles, tend to assume leading positions in the family which may turn to abusive use of power and authority toward the wife. The husband playing a dominant, tyrannical role in everyday domestic matters turns the wife into the silent performer of a slave role.[105] Each of the partners might also misuse intimate information with the purpose to offend the other. Verbal abuse might also be con-

---

100. H. Waters, et al., *The Economic Dimensions of Interpersonal Violence*, 19.

101. A. Mansingh & P. Ramphal, "The Nature of Interpersonal Violence in Jamaica," *West Indian Medical Journal* 42 (1993) 53–56, quoted in H. Waters, et al., *The Economic Dimensions of Interpersonal Violence*, 20.

102. M. New, L. Berliner, "Mental Health Service Utilization by Victims of Crime," *Journal of Traumatic Stress* 13 (2000) 693–707, quoted in H. Waters, et al., *The Economic Dimensions of Interpersonal Violence*, 21.

103. C. Wisner, et al., "Intimate Partner Violence Against Women: Do Victims Cost Health Plans More?" *The Journal of Family Practice* 48 (1999) 439–43, quoted in H. Waters, et al., *The Economic Dimensions of Interpersonal Violence*, 21.

104. H. Waters, et al., *The Economic Dimensions of Interpersonal Violence*, 17.

105. Also Marina Ajduković, et al., "Nasilje u partnerskim odnosima," u *Nasilje nad ženom u obitelji*, uredile: Marina Ajduković i Gordana Pavleković (Zagreb: društvo za psihološku pomoć, 2000), 57.

sidered as part of emotional abuse. Constant offensive language creates an emotional pressure which degrades the partner. Insensitive comments related to the partner's weaknesses might also be used to offend and humiliate her. Various languages of curses inflict deep long term damages in the mental health of the partner.[106] The verbal offenses might also include different sexual aspects which cross the border from emotional abuse to sexual abuse.[107]

Sexual violence is a wide spread problem infecting all cultures, countries, ethnic and religious groups, and the society in all its levels. Researching sexual violence is difficult, and the results do not show the complete picture due to obstacles in the communication of information from the victim to the investigator based on lack of trust, fear, and in the case of male victims, gender presuppositions.[108] Surveys conducted in small communities on national and international levels show that women are the most vulnerable group even though men and children suffer sexual abuse as well. The frequency and the depth of occurrence of sexual violence in the society is a fact which is very alarming and distressing. It touches almost every individual, whether directly or indirectly. The picture is devastating, "one woman in every five has suffered an attempted or completed rape by an intimate partner during her lifetime and up to one-third of women describe their first sexual experience as being forced."[109] The victims of sexual violence are usually female and their offenders are male, most of the time either a former or present intimate partner.[110] This expressed as a percentage is 83% of all cases of sexual abuse from which 20% is done by boyfriends and 33% by husbands or cohabitation partners.[111] Sexual abuse might be divided into three types according to the behavior of the perpetrator, i.e. nonverbal, verbal, and physical. The

---

106. Cassidey-Shaw, *Family Abuse and the Bible*, 59–62.

107. Also M. Mamula, *Zdravstvenene i psihološke posljedice spolnog nasilja nad ženama*, 94.

108. WHO, *Guidelines for Medico-Legal Care of Victims of Sexual Violence*, 9.

109. Ibid., 6.

110. "Population based studies of abuse by intimate partners indicate that between 6% and 46% of women report that they have experienced attempted or completed forced sex by an intimate partner or ex-partner at some time in their lives. Rape and domestic violence account for an estimated 5–16% of healthy years of life lost to women of reproductive age." (WHO, *Guidelines for Medico-Legal Care of Victims of Sexual Violence*, 8–9.)

111. M. Mamula, *Zdravstvenene i psihološke posljedice spolnog nasilja nad ženama*, 96.

nonverbal sexual abuse might be described as the varieties of signs, gestures, and offerings of explicit sexual materials by the offender with the purpose to impose sexual intercourse on the victim. Verbal sexual abuse relates to those kinds of verbal expressions and suggestions which treat the person as a sexual object and imply a desire for sexual intercourse. Finally, physical sexual abuse focuses on actions of the perpetrator which include the body of the victim, from pinching and caressing to the use of force for performing sexual intercourse.[112]

The victims of sexual violence endure long lasting physical, psychological, and spiritual damage. Physically, they suffer various consequences such as "unwanted pregnancy, unsafe abortion, sexually transmitted infections (STIs) including human immunodeficiency virus/acquired immunodeficiency syndrome (HIV/AIDS), sexual dysfunction, infertility, pelvic pain and pelvic inflammatory disease, urinary tract infections and even death."[113] Their mental health is distorted with various disorders which affect their life in the short and long term.[114] Even spiritually they might carry a burden of guilt[115] or experience the adoption of risky sexual behaviors.[116] The main causes of sexual violence are not the craving desire for sexual satisfaction of the perpetrator but his intent to dominate the victim, to show authority and demonstrate power.[117] "Although sexuality and aggression are involved in all forms of sexual violence, sex is merely the medium used to express various types of non-sexual feelings such as

---

112. Ibid., 94.

113. World Health Organization, *Guidelines for Medico-Legal Care of Victims of Sexual Violence* (Geneva: World Health Organization 2003) 12.

114. Also M. Mamula, *Zdravstvenene i psihološke posljedice spolnog nasilja nad ženama*, 97. Some general psychological traumas: "rape trauma syndrome, post-traumatic stress disorder, depression, social phobias (especially in marital or date rape victims), anxiety, increased substance use or abuse and suicidal behaviour." Some long-term psychological traumas: "chronic headaches, fatigue, sleep disturbances (i.e. nightmares, flashbacks), recurrent nausea, eating disorders, menstrual pain, sexual difficulties." (WHO, *Guidelines for Medico-Legal Care of Victims of Sexual Violence*, 13, 14.)

115. Shirley Gillett, "No Church to Call Home," in *Women Abuse, and the Bible: How Scripture Can be Used to Hurt or Heal*, eds. Catherine Clark Kroeger and James R. Beck (Grand Rapids: Baker, 1996) 107.

116. WHO, *Guidelines for Medico-Legal Care of Victims of Sexual Violence*, 1.

117. WHO, *Guidelines for Medico-Legal Care of Victims of Sexual Violence*, 9; Also James R. Beck, "Theology for the Healthy Family," in *Women, Abuse, and the Bible: How Scripture Can be Used to Hurt or Heal*, eds. Catherine Clark Kroeger and James R. Beck (Grand Rapids: Baker, 1996) 218.

anger and hostility towards women, as well as a need to control, dominate and assert power over them."[118] One further consequence of sexual abuse might be directed to economical crises due to the woman's inability to continue her work and career.[119] This leads to the next expression of domestic violence, that of economic abuse.

Economic control/abuse can summarize all the actions of the perpetrator which relate to material mistreatment of the intimate partner, mistreatment which results in her lack of fundamental resources for life.[120] This abuse may start with lack of support and extend to financial robbery. The violator may use different methods to abuse his partner. Strong financial control over the mutual funds and the personal funds of the wife might result in a failure of the husband to satisfy her material needs. The financial responsibilities toward the mutual needs of the couple might be imposed on the victim and she might be oppressed with constant work and lack of resources to sustain life. The abuser might refuse to work and indulge himself in a lifestyle which consumes all the financial resources of the couple, which causes suffering of the female partner. He might even prohibit her from attending work for different reasons, which also causes her financial damage.[121] The offender might also damage in various ways the property of the victim.[122] Economic abuse in contemporary families takes different shapes, but the consequences of all of them are devastating and life threatening to the victim.[123]

Spiritual abuse is an intentional use of religious teachings based on misinterpretation of a religious source of authority with the purpose of demoralizing the victim, infiltrating her thinking and conscience, and developing an atmosphere for the constant infliction of violence without blame. Even though this form of abuse does not find its necessary

---

118. WHO, *Guidelines for Medico-Legal Care of Victims of Sexual Violence*, 10.

119. Also M. Mamula, *Zdravstvenene i psihološke posljedice spolnog nasilja nad ženama*, 94.

120. Also M. Ajduković, et al., *Nasilje u partnerskim odnosima*, 58.

121. "A second study in Queensland (Australia, 1998) included indirect costs related to women's lost wages due to absenteeism from work, resulting in an estimated $546 million annually." (H. Waters, et al., *The Economic Dimensions of Interpersonal Violence*, 19.)

122. "A 1991 study of 40 women in Tasmania calculated $8117 in direct costs and an additional $19023 in indirect costs—mostly replacement of damaged property—per woman." (H. Waters, et al., *The Economic Dimensions of Interpersonal Violence*, 19.)

123. Also Cassidey-Shaw, *Family Abuse and the Bible*, 60.

recognition and treatment in the overall debate of domestic violence it is one of the most manipulative and dangerous forms because it attempts to disguise itself behind the religious language, traditions, and rituals.[124] Spiritual abuse might be found in various religious groups and communities but due to such a vast area to consider, I will concentrate only on the Christian types of spiritual abuse. Four basic expressions may be identified as forming an abusive behavior based on intentional misuse of some biblical teachings. They relate to dominance in the relationship, imposition of inferiority, spiritualizing of involuntary suffering, and obligatory instant forgiveness.

Domination in the relationship of a couple is frequently pursued by the male partner. Different biblical teachings are used in order to facilitate a rigid patriarchal pattern of communication in which the woman submits to the husband's dominance. The behavior of the husband following this pattern is based on imposition of power and authority upon the wife in all spheres of the marital relationship and family life. The wife is expected to obey and submit to the will and the actions of the husband unconditionally in spite of their effect upon her and the family as a whole. The image of God is used as a facilitator of the male's dominance and as a support for such behavior as well as for imposing fear and guilt on the victim. This creates an environment of total control in which the whole range of domestic abuse might be exercised by the perpetrator with the expectation of the complete submission of the victim and her reluctance to look for a solution.[125]

The imposition of the inferiority form of abusive religious thinking defines the woman as incapable of moral judgment and as such dependent on the male figure for spiritual and moral control. This inferior position of the woman has been developed through the argumentative line that she has become the channel of male and human failure to sin. Thus, she is to be morally and spiritually subordinate to the husband's ethical judgments and decisions. Such a line of reasoning prepares the grounds for various types of abuse due to the implied inability of the wife to evaluate the nature of the husband's behavior. The woman's moral inferiority to

---

124. Ibid., 66.

125. Also Carolyn Holderread Heggen, "Religious Beliefs and Abuse," in *Women, Abuse, and the Bible*, eds. Catherine Clark Kroeger and James R. Beck (Grand Rapids: Baker, 1996) 16–19.

the husband has been well grounded on the misuse of the Bible to justify that position.

> Women are more often led into spiritual error than men. That is the reason God commanded her not to usurp authority over man, so she can be protected by him, from false doctrine. The Scriptures say woman must ignore her feelings about the will of God and do what her husband says. She is to obey her husband as if he were God Himself. She can be as certain of God's will, when her husband speaks, as if God had spoken audibly from Heaven![126]

The elevated spiritual image of the woman according to this spiritual abuse depicts her as "submissive in the home; gentle and soft spoken; lets spouse make decisions; dependent; passive; finds identity through spouse; withholds criticism."[127] The image which appears characterizes an intimate female partner who is underpowered and unresisting any kind of abuse by the male partner.[128]

The abusive concept defined as spiritualizing of involuntary suffering refers to forming an attitude of toleration toward suffering in the female victims, justified on religious grounds. All suffering might be characterized as displeasing and contrary to human nature. However, suffering which is intentionally undertaken on purpose to serve a higher cause might be considered as a spiritual virtue which deserves praise. But suffering which has been involuntarily inflicted on a victim by an abusive partner should always be judged as moral failure and sin. Women who have become victims of violent partners and suffer the consequences of such a relationship should not be encouraged to continue enduring abusive actions for the accomplishment of a high spiritual goal. The encouraging statements of some leaders to the victims of abusive relationships promising spiritual salvation of the abuser if the victim submits to his violence should be characterized as fundamentally wrong and biblically misleading. Such an attitude not only endangers the woman's life but also does not take measures for restricting the violent behavior of the man and in such a way promotes both suffering and violence.[129] Thus, no suffering caused by violence, abuse or mistreatment of one spouse by the other in

---

126. C. H. Heggen, *Religious Beliefs and Abuse*, 19.
127. Ibid., 23.
128. Ibid., 19–22.
129. Also ibid., 22–24.

the marital relationship is justifiable. There are failures from the proper marital relationship between the spouses which may cause suffering of any of them. These need to be approached with sincere repentance by the guilty spouse and forgiveness of the one who suffered. However constant infliction of suffering and chronic violence by one of the spouses to the other should not be tolerated and suffering should not be endured. This kind of relationship should be ended, the marriage covenant should be dissolved and divorce should be obtained.[130]

The obligatory instant forgiveness required from the victims of abuse in spite of the attitude of the violator is another ground for spiritual abuse. The victim of domestic violence has been forced to forgive either by her spiritual leaders, church community, or the perpetrator who has exercised spiritual control over her. Christian teaching on repentance and forgiveness is fundamental for the Christian faith and for the soundness of a Christian's relations both in the community and in the family. However, forgiveness cannot be treated either as unconscious automatic action of the victim to the perpetrator nor as an excuse for further imposition of violence by the offender. Christian forgiveness should be inspirited by God's love and mercy and should be based on the independent choice and convictions of the individual. It should not be rushed by superficial religious obligations but developed through a period of personal spiritual and physical restoration after the abuse. The violent behavior of the perpetrator should not be encouraged through quick forgiveness and reconciliation but condemned and he should be led to sincere repentance and change of conduct. Only in this way the circle of domestic violence can be broken and victim and offender reconciled.[131]

> While the Christian community must continue to uphold the sacredness of the marital covenant, the church must struggle to understand the permissive will of God in instances where the marriage covenant has already been broken by violence and abuse. The importance of marital permanence must not be elevated above the sanctity of individual personhood and safety. We dare not overlook nor minimize the destructive evils of battery and abuse because of our high regard for the permanence of marriage.[132]

---

130. Also Gushee, *Getting Marriage Right*, 147–67.
131. C. H. Heggen, *Religious Beliefs and Abuse*, 24–27.
132. Ibid., 26.

Domestic violence is never just an individual act of abuse but always constitutes a process.[133] Once the process is initiated it requires taking serious steps for its termination. After the initial act of violence, men will continue terrorizing their intimate partners if there is no negative impact upon them. Usually the intensity of the process of domestic violence grows with time. The process might be divided into three phases forming a circle which determines the relationship between the spouses for an unlimited period of time. The first phase defines the relationship as progressively tense, and characterizes the behavior of the husband as increasingly resentful toward the wife who, anticipating the upcoming violence, attempts to prevent it with a behavior absorbing the tension. The second phase is the time of violent aggression toward the wife expressed in varieties of ways through which the husband releases his anger accumulated during the first phase. The wife passes through a time of shock, unbelief, and denial of the behavior of the husband. Due to this condition the wife usually does not look for help except rarely in the cases of physical injury[134] and does not attempt to leave the relationship. The third phase is the time when the husband's behavior experiences outward change. He passes through remorse excusing his actions on the basis of different issues related to his work, condition (involving alcohol), and the family situation (finances, children). The wife accepts the change with the hope for final termination of the violence in the relationship. However the

---

133. From all victims of domestic abuse, 72% defines it as a long lasting violence and 52% confirms that it is occurring on daily basis. (G. Pavleković, M. Ajduković, M. Mamula, *Nasilje nad ženom u obitelji: osobni, obiteljski ili javnozdravstveni problem?* 24.)

134. A survey shows (1992–1995) that from all the women victims of domestic violence 28% suffer serious physical injuries but only 5% to 9.5% report it to the police. (B. A. Elliot and M. M. P. Johnson, "Domestic Violence in a Primary Care Setting: Patterns and Prevalence," *Archives of Family Medicine* 4 (1995) 113–19; L. K. Hamburger, G. D. Saunders and M. Hovey, "Prevalence of Domestic Violence in Community Practice and Rate of Physician Inquiry," *Family Medicine* 24 (1992) 283–87; A. G. Walch and W. E. Broadhead, "Prevalence of Lifetime Sexual Victimization Among Female Patients," *Journal of Family Practice* 35 (1992) 511–16, quoted in G. Pavleković, M. Ajduković, M. Mamula, *Nasilje nad ženom u obitelji: osobni, obiteljski ili javnozdravstveni problem?* 25.) Another survey demonstrates that every 10th woman requesting help from emergency medical services is victim of domestic violence. (J. Abbott, et al., "Domestic Violence Against Women. Incidence and Prevalence in an Emergency Department Population," *Journal of American Medical Association* 273 (1995) 1763–67, quoted in G. Pavleković, M. Ajduković, M. Mamula, *Nasilje nad ženom u obitelji: osobni, obiteljski ili javnozdravstveni problem?* 25.)

process of violence continues leading to the first phase.¹³⁵ Breaking the circle of domestic violence requires undertaking a serious action to terminate this abusive relationship. This is well formulated in the covenant structure of marital union. When there is a serious failure of fulfilling the covenant stipulations by one of the spouses and the attempts for restoring the relationship are exhausted the other spouse is free to divorce. Thus, the contemporary crumbling notion of the permanent institution of marriage and the escalation of violence in its inner structures demand the application of the twofold covenant understanding of marital union both in Christian communities and in society as a whole.

The covenant concept of marriage has been established as exegetically grounded, theologically compatible, and dogmatically justifiable which leads to undertaking some concrete steps to its integration through the previously proposed ecumenical formulation in the Christian communities within the complex pluralistic framework of our societies. Hence, the two dimensions of the concept should be allowed to shape all Christian teaching, preaching, counseling, actions, and attitudes in relation to each of the four levels of Christian communities, i.e. unmarried, married, divorced, and remarried. On the one hand, the permanent covenant nature of marriage should evoke strong and persistent teaching of marriage as a lifelong union which requires a significant amount of effort and time in order to select one's spouse. Thus, all relationships outside the Christian faith and even outside one's Christian tradition¹³⁶ should be discouraged whenever possible due to the significant risk of marital breakdown in mixed marriages.¹³⁷ Premarital counseling and marriage preparation

---

135. M. Mamula, M. Ajduković, *Dinamika zlostavljanja unutar obitelji*, 83.

136. "Difference of confession between the spouses does not constitute an insurmountable obstacle for marriage, when they succeed in placing in common what they have received from their respective communities, and learn from each other the way in which each lives in fidelity to Christ. But the difficulties of mixed marriages must not be underestimated. They arise from the fact that the separation of Christians has not yet been overcome. The spouses risk experiencing the tragedy of Christian disunity even in the heart of their own home. Disparity of cult can further aggravate these difficulties. Differences about faith and the very notion of marriage, but also different religious mentalities, can become sources of tension in marriage, especially as regards the education of children. The temptation to religious indifference can then arise." (*Catechism of the Catholic Church*, 1634, Libreria Editrice Vaticana [online], Available at http://www.vatican.va/archive/ENG0015/__P53.HTM, Accessed on 17 September 2005.)

137. See Tertullian, *To His Wife* II.4; Also A. R. G. Deasley, *Marriage & Divorce in the Bible and the Church*, 190; Otto E. Sohn, "The Church and Mixed Marriage," *Concordia*

courses should be offered for those who are considering marriage.¹³⁸ Believers who are going through marriage crises should be counselled in such a way as to consider all the possible ways of preserving the marital union.¹³⁹ The ones who are in the process of divorce, or are divorced on unbiblical grounds, should be encouraged to look for reconciliation with their spouses until all the possibilities are exhausted.¹⁴⁰ For the remarried, all their effort should be given to understand and live their marriages as permanent covenant unions, which should be preserved, sustained, and nourished until the death of one of the spouses. On the other hand, the exceptional permission for legitimate divorce and remarriage on proper biblical grounds should shape the attitude of the unmarried and married Christians from all hierarchical levels towards those who are divorced and/or remarried in a positive manner.¹⁴¹ All those who have experienced divorce should not be treated as second class Christians.¹⁴² They should be allowed to work through the process of grief and helped to recover.¹⁴³ Those who have brought about an unbiblical divorce should be led to repentance, discipline, and restoration, giving them the freedom to decide their future marital status, i.e. celibacy or remarriage.¹⁴⁴ Those who conducted a proper biblical divorce should be allowed to continue their

---

Theological Monthly 34/9 (1963) 519–26.

138. An Ecumenically developed Christian declaration on marriage was issued on November 14, 2000 in Washington, DC with the purpose to raise the community marriage standards encouraging the churches to organize programs for premarital and marital counseling and education. ("An Ecumenical Marriage Strategy," *Christian Century* 117/33 [November 22–29, 2000] 1211.)

139. Also Thomas Needman, "How Not to Fail Hurting Couples," *Christianity Today* (December 14, 1992) [online], Available at http://www.christianityonline.com/ct/2000/135/49.0.html, Accessed on 2 September 2000; Everett Worthingon, *I Care About Your Marriage* (Chicago: Moody, 1994) 51.

140. Also Edward G. Dobson, *What the Bible Really Says about Marriage, Divorce and Remarriage* (Old Tappan: Fleming H. Revell, 1986) 91, 161.

141. Also David Instone-Brewer, *Divorce and Remarriage in the Church: Biblical Solutions for Pastoral Realities* (Carlisle, Cumbria: Paternoster, 2003), DRC 94 [online], Available at http://www.tyndale.cam.ac.uk/Brewer/PPages/DRC/, Accessed on 2 September 2004.

142. Also Michel A. Braun, *Should Divorced People be Treated Like . . . Second-Class Christians? A New Approach to the Dilemma of Divorced People in the Church* (Downers Grove, IL: InterVarsity, 1989).

143. Also See G. Ensworth, Jr., *Notice the Divorced Among Us*, 22.

144. Also G. Cereti, *Judges or Counsellors*, 108, 109.

services or to exercise their gifts in any area of Christian ministry.¹⁴⁵ They should be granted freedom to consider the possibility of a life of celibacy related to the presence of such a χάρισμα in their lives or remarriage. The latter should be performed in the same way as the first marriage with all solemnity and happiness in the rituals. Finally, in order to fulfill the Lord's expectations of being a church "without a spot or wrinkle or anything of the kind" (Eph 5:27, NRS) at the time of his return, Christians of any kind should firmly integrate the concept of marriage covenant which defines the NT teaching on divorce and remarriage into their personal belief systems and into the church catechisms. This concept of marriage, divorce, and remarriage should modify the contemporary loose view about them widespread in our societies and contribute to reformulation of their marriage law systems.

The concept of marriage covenant as being defined exegetically, theologically, dogmatically, and pragmatically in relation to the Christian communities allows its integration into the marriage law of our societies. The most vivid example of such implementation is the incorporation of the covenant marriage passage into the law systems of the states of Louisiana (1997)¹⁴⁶ and Arizona (1998)¹⁴⁷. The roots of this "systematic reform of the marriage law regime"¹⁴⁸ might be found in the arguments of different scholars related to strengthening the commitments of the spouses to the marital union,¹⁴⁹ the legislative proposal for covenant mar-

---

145. Also Stanley A. Ellisen, *Divorce and Remarriage in the Church* (Grand Rapids: Zondervan, 1980), 77–89; A. R. G. Deasley, *Marriage & Divorce in the Bible and the Church*, 179–82.

146. For the covenant marriage law in Louisiana see *New Louisiana Covenant Marriage Law Regular Session, 1997*, House Bill No. 756 [Louisiana], Part VII. Covenant Marriage [online], Available at http://patriot.net/~crouch/cov/index.html, Accessed on 20 September 2004.

147. For the covenant marriage law in Arizona see *Arizona Covenant Marriage Law of 1998*. Arizona 43rd Legislature—Second Regular Session. Senate Bill 1133, Passed by both houses and Approved by the Governor May 21, 1998 [online], Available at http://www.divorcereform.org/ari.html, Accessed on 20 September 2004.

148. David P. Gushee, "The Divorce Epidemic: Evaluating Policy Options That Can Reduce Divorce," in *Christians and Politics Beyond the Culture Wars*, ed. David P. Gushee (Grand Rapids: Baker, 2000) 158–59.

149. Elizabeth S. Scott, "Rational Decision-making about Marriage and Divorce," *Virginia Law Review* 76 (1990); Etzioni, "How to Make Marriage Matter," *Time*, September 6, 1993, 76, quoted in D. P. Gushee, *The Divorce Epidemic*, 158; and Christopher Wolfe, "The Marriage of Your Choice," *First Things* 50 (February 1995) 37–41.

riage in the state of Florida (1990),[150] the Washington state bill restricting "no-fault" divorce (1995)[151] and other contributions related to the notion of covenant marriage.[152] The passage of the marriage law which was introduced on 15 August 1997 in Louisiana and is presently still in force is defined as covenant marriage.[153] The nature of marriage established according to the covenant marriage law is a lifelong union between husband and wife which can be dissolved only on particular grounds. The divorce grounds are constituted by a failure of one of the spouses to the covenant stipulations including adultery, imprisonment for a felony, desertion, physical or sexual abuse of the spouse or a child of any of the spouses, and living separately for more than two years without reconciliation.[154] The formalization of the marital union requires fulfillment of three conditions, namely, a declaration recited by the parties, a premarital counseling affidavit with a notarized attestation of the counselor, and a witness' attestation. The latter requires the presence of a witness or witnesses who solemnly confirm the legitimacy of the spouses' declaration

150. Covenant Marriage Bill HR 1585.

151. "SB 5532 - Authorizes two persons of the opposite sex to enter into a written marriage contract providing that the marital relationship will not be dissolved except upon a showing by a preponderance of the evidence by one party of the fault of the other party that constitutes grounds for dissolution." (House Committee on Law & Justice, *Marriage Contracts Restricting No-Fault Divorce—Washington State Bill* [online], Available at http://patriot.net/~crouch/wash/index.html, Accessed on 20 September 2004.)

152. See *History of the Idea of Covenant Marriage* [online], Available at http://www.divorcereform.org/cov.html, Accessed on 20 September 2004.

153. Summary of the covenant marriage law introduced in 2001 as informative document to be offered to the prospective spouses by license-issuing officer is as follows: "The summary of covenant marriage law shall emphasize that premarital counseling is mandatory at which time the necessary documents consisting of the declaration of intent and the affidavit and attestation of the counselor shall be executed, that the couple agrees to take all reasonable steps to preserve their marriage if marital difficulties arise, including marriage counseling, that divorce in a covenant marriage is restricted to fault by a spouse and living separate and apart for two years as provided in R.S. 9:307, and that divorce under the general marriage law of this state differs significantly." (Louisiana House Bill No.234. Section 1. R.S. 9:237.C. Enacted 22 June 2001 [online], Available at http://www.divorcereform.org/la01.html. Accessed on 20 September 2004.)

154. *New Louisiana Covenant Marriage Law*, Regular Session, 1997, House Bill No. 756, Section 4. R.S. 9:307.A. [online], Available at http://patriot.net/~crouch/cov/index.html, Accessed on 20 September 2004; Gushee, *The Divorce Epidemic*, 159; idem, *Getting Marriage Right*, 220, 221; Also Nock, Wright, and Sanchez, "America's Divorce Problem," 43.

and the marriage certificate. The premarital counseling affidavit is issued after the potential spouses have passed through a process of counseling conducted by either a clergyperson or counselor. The counseling sessions should have covered material related to the nature of covenant marriage as lifelong union and the obligations of the parties related to it including understanding of their responsibility for marital counseling in case of crises and the legal grounds for divorce. The counselor's attestation is either part of the affidavit, or attached to it, confirming that all main dimensions of the covenant union are well defined to the parties and that all the terms and conditions of the covenant marriage explicitly stated in the manual provided by the state attorney general's office law are clarified to them. The final requirement for initiation of the marital union includes a declaration recited by both man and woman which states their understanding of the covenant marriage, the obligations and responsibilities it confirms upon them, and their consent to fulfill them. Without the following declaration the couple could not obtain a marriage license.

> We do solemnly declare that marriage is a covenant between a man and a woman who agree to live together as husband and wife for so long as they both may live. We have chosen each other carefully and disclosed to one another everything which could adversely affect the decision to enter into this marriage. We have received premarital counseling on the nature, purposes, and responsibilities of marriage. We have read the Covenant Marriage Act, and we understand that a Covenant Marriage is for life. If we experience martial difficulties, we commit ourselves to take all reasonable efforts to preserve our marriage, including marital counseling.
>
> With full knowledge of what this commitment means, we do hereby declare that our marriage will be bound by Louisiana law on Covenant Marriages and we promise to love, honour, and care for one another as husband and wife for the rest of our lives.[155]

This declaration clearly states the nature of the marriage as covenantal union. The legal initiation of the marriage covenant conveyed upon the couple the responsibility to preserve the covenant relationship and in the case of failure to undertake marital counseling. If the counseling proves unsuccessful and divorced is to be undertaken then proof for justifying

155. *New Louisiana Covenant Marriage Law.* Regular Session, 1997, House Bill No.756. Section 3. Part VII.273.A.(1) [online], Available at http://patriot.net/~crouch/cov/index.html, Accessed on 20 September 2004. Also quoted in Gushee, *The Divorce Epidemic*, 159; idem, *Getting Marriage Right*, 220.

the legitimate grounds for divorce should be provided. The only legitimate dissolution of the marriage covenant could be sustained on the grounds of adultery, imprisonment, desertion, abuse or long separation without reconciliation.[156]

This legislation of covenant marriage has faced two major critiques. On the one hand, it has been defined as religiously discriminative since it integrates specific religious and moral convictions into the law.[157] On the other hand, it has been characterised as insufficient for significant social change due to its existence next to an alternative marriage law which nature is defined by "no-fault" divorce opportunity.[158] However these two critical observations may not be treated as serious oppositions to the law since they neutralise each other. The covenant marriage law offered as an alternative to the already existing marriage law provides both the possibility for choice according to one's moral and religious values and convictions and legalizes a marriage union defined as a lifelong institution which allows no easy divorce.[159] The value of this law has been further confirmed by it being considered in another twenty states.[160] In addition,

---

156. *New Louisiana Covenant Marriage Law*, Regular Session, 1997, House Bill No. 756, Section 4. R.S. 9:307.A. [online]; also Gushee, *The Divorce Epidemic*, 159; Nock, Wright, and Sanchez, "America's Divorce Problem," 43; Wilson, *The Marriage Problem*, 213.

157. Also Wilson, *The Marriage Problem*, 213; Joe Cook, "No to Covenant Marriage," *World & I* 13/1 (1998) 302.

158. Gushee, *The Divorce Epidemic*, 160; idem, *Getting Marriage Right*, 221, 222.

159. Two main differences might be defined between the new covenant marriage law and the conventional contract of marriage with "no-fault" divorce option. The latter offers a reasonable easy initiation of the marriage. The former requires the parties to pass through a process of premarital counseling before obtaining the marriage license. The result of this process is the formation of stable understanding the nature of the spouses' commitment to the lifelong union as well as expectancy of their obligations to sustain this union with sufficient efforts to prevent breakdowns with further counseling. The second difference refers to the grounds for divorce. The conventional marriage law offers easy "no-fault" grounds for divorce which provide in different states a framework of time ranging from 6 to 18 months in which spouses may initiate divorce with no consequences. The covenant marriage, on the other hand, establishes firm grounds for divorce related to spouse's failure to adultery, a felony, physical or sexual abuse, desertion or long period (2 years) separation without reconciliation. (Also Benedict Carey, "Is Divorce too Easy?" *Health* 13/7 [1999] 122.)

160. Nock, Wright, and Sanchez, "America's Divorce Problem," 43. For the covenant marriage legislation in the other States see *Covenant Marriage Legislation* [online], Available at http://www.divorcereform.org/cov.html, Accessed on 20 September 2004.

a high percentage of formerly married couples used the opportunity given by the covenant marriage law to convert their marriages.[161] Covenant marriage has faced not only strong support but also serious opposition from different social, religious, and intellectual groups.[162] However the predominant concern of those who opposed it has been triggered either by its restrictions on the personal freedom of the spouse to terminate the marriage, such as exists in the standard "no-fault" divorce law, or because of a lack of understanding of its present applications and its long term consequences.[163] More recent studies show that the general attitude toward the covenant marriage legislation is positive and supportive.[164] Thus, the covenant marriage law has brought the society and the individual to a new level of understanding of marriage which necessitates a decision for sustaining or refusing the marriage virtues of lifelong love, support, and provision between the spouses.

> Right now, every day, thousands of couples all over the country vow to 'love and honour' one another 'until death do us part.' The wedding vow itself is intended to stress the permanence of the commitment being made. Many may think, but none utter, 'or until something better comes along,' and yet that seems to have become the tacit understanding, the unspoken rider in every marriage contract under the no-fault divorce regime. But some people actually mean what they say during their wedding ceremony, fully intending their marital commitment to be permanent, and two

---

161. Also D. P. Gushee, *The Divorce Epidemic*, 161.

162. For an overview of different opinions see Nock, Wright, and Sanchez, "America's Divorce Problem," 44–52.

163. Also Nock, Wright, and Sanchez, "America's Divorce Problem," 45–52; Margaret F. Brinig, "Economics, Law, and Covenant Marriage," *Gender Issues* 16/1–2 (1998) 4.

164. Survey of the attitudes toward divorce and covenant marriage among adults in the states of Louisiana and Arizona, which have covenant marriage law already operating for several years and in Minnesota which does not offer covenant marriage but considers such legislation reported the following results: "Overall, most people in our study are positive about covenant marriage and its components. The less religious, more liberal, and those with less traditional gender ideologies were less supportive, although generally not opposing covenant marriage. In sum, our research provides some evidence that there is broad support for modest initiatives of the type incorporated into covenant marriage legislation, at least among the residents of the states surveyed." (Alan J. Hawkins, Steven L. Nock, Julia C. Wilson, Laura Sanchez, and James D. Wright, "Attitudes about Covenant Marriage and Divorce: Policy Implications from a Three-State Comparison," *Family Relations* 51 [2002] 169, 173.)

states (with more soon to follow) have now given their citizens a legal mechanism to affirm that intention, publicly and legally.[165]

Therefore the covenant concept of marriage which emphasizes the permanent nature of marriage and allows divorce and remarriage only on exceptional grounds of a spouse's failure to fulfill the marriage covenant stipulations, a concept which has been biblically formulated and dogmatically validated is established as a valuable solution for reforming the notion of marriage and resolving its inter tensions in our pluralistic societies and cultures. The concept articulated in the ecumenical proposal has shown adequacy and appropriateness in serving the needs of church communities at all their levels. Moreover, its nature and dynamics demonstrate social relevance and legislative applicability. Hence, the NT teaching on divorce and remarriage expressed through the concept of covenant not only substantiates theoretical stability but also demonstrates pragmatic relevance.

---

165. Nock, Wright, and Sanchez, "America's Divorce Problem," 52.

seven

Conclusion

THE FOCUS OF THE PRESENT RESEARCH HAS BEEN TO GIVE A FRESH answer to the divorce and remarriage dilemma from a NT perspective. The necessity for such an endeavor was established on the grounds of the continued increase of marriage breakdown in the changing Christian communities within complex pluralistic societies and the inadequacy and multiplicity of Christians' answers to the fundamental question: "May Christians legitimately divorce and remarry and on what grounds?" The attempts of the theologians to give an answer to this question have been defined not only as methodologically, exegetically, ecumenically, and practically inadequate, but also their theories have been established as enormously diverse to offer a reliable and coherent formulation of the NT teaching on marriage, divorce, and remarriage. The answer provided by the present author attempts to resolve the tensions and inadequacies of the scholars' views and at the same time to preserve their continuity leading to an ecumenical solution. Hence, a working hypothesis of this work has been proposed with a covenant concept of marriage, which emphasizes the permanence of marital union and also makes an exceptional provision for divorce and remarriage on the grounds of the lack of fulfillment of the covenant stipulations by a spouse.

The thesis received its methodological formulation in a modified fourfold enterprise for the development of NT ethical argumentation, argumentation expressed in the descriptive, synthetic, hermeneutical, and pragmatic tasks. This then required five areas of research. First, the proper contextual grounds for the analysis of the NT texts and holistic canonical environment for the NT conclusions had to be established through formulation of the OT perspective on marriage covenant with its fundamental characteristics as related to the nature of marriage, divorce, and remarriage. Second, exegetical analyses had to be provided of all the relevant passages in relation to the subject using a compilation of the historical-critical and narrative-critical methods for biblical analysis. Third, synthetical analysis of the NT canonical literature had to be attempted, establishing its contribution to the subject with the input from the previously established OT perspective through the unifying concept of the marriage covenant. Fourth, dogmatical analysis had to be undertaken of the main Christian traditions (Catholic, Orthodox, and Protestant) in regard to their view of marriage, divorce, and remarriage, with an attempt to establish an ecumenical understanding of these issues. Fifth, pragmatical implementation of the thesis had to be provided through an analysis of the contemporary pluralistic context in relation to the subject of marriage and through applications of the thesis' twofold nature in both Christian communities and the larger society within its legislative system. The fulfillment of all these levels of analysis establishes four conclusions which substantiate the main thesis of the present work, resolve the divorce and remarriage dilemma created by the scholars' multiple theories, and answer the main question posed in the introduction.

First, through a thorough exegetical analysis of the five most relevant NT passages (Mark 10:2–12; Matt 5:31, 32; 19:3–12; Luke 16:18; and 1 Cor 7:12–16), a twofold concept was established as the presentation of Jesus' teaching on divorce and remarriage through the editorial work of the NT authors. Expressed in the most rigorous form, being part of the controversy material in the narrative format of the gospels, the twofold concept articulates the illegitimate actions of divorce and remarriage as strongly prohibited due to the permanent nature of marriage and presents their legitimate form, defined on the grounds of sexual misconduct and desertion, as clearly, but only exceptionally permitted. Hence, Mark's presentation of Jesus' saying in its present unexceptional form (10:10–12) based on his endeavor to critique the liberal position of women in the divorce and remarriage situations of the Greco-Roman world, poses no contradiction to Matthew's understanding of the saying (Matt 19:9; 5:32) when he introduces an exception clause and as such makes a provision for proper divorce and remarriage in a case of πορνεία because of the impossibility of living with an adulterous partner for his Jewish-Christian audience. Luke's formulation of Jesus' teaching on divorce and remarriage (16:18) places no opposition to Matthew's articulation since its absolute and unexceptional form is preserved with the purpose to fight divorce and remarriage on the basis of prearranged divorce plans for subsequent remarriage in the light of Herod and Herodias' case. Paul's usage of Jesus' tradition on the issues of divorce and remarriage provides further grounds for establishing the unity and coherence of the presentations of Mark, Matthew, and Luke. The apostle uses the rigid form of the tradition to prohibit remarriage in a case of divorce (1 Cor 7:10–11) when a similar situation to Mark's women divorce liberty, and Luke's defective remarriage attitude appears, but articulates the exception tradition allowing divorce and remarriage when the context of mixed marriages requires a moderate approach to the deserted Christian spouse (1 Cor 7:15, 16). The concept of marriage, divorce, and remarriage expressed through the presentation of Jesus' teaching by the evangelists and Paul defines marriage as a permanent union and strictly prohibits divorce and remarriage except on limited exceptional grounds based on a spouse's intentional failure to fulfill the marriage responsibilities.

Second, the theological contribution of the whole corpus of the canonical biblical literature in understanding the nature of marriage as a covenant union has underlined and further elaborated the exegetical conclusions. The holistic OT and NT views of marriage are that of a covenant relationship (Mal 2:10–16; Prov 2:17) whose nature is established in the creation account of the first family (Gen 2:24). The understanding of the marriage covenant in both the OT and NT corpuses and in their contemporary contexts, including marriage covenantal and contractual agreements in ANE, Greco-Roman, and extrabiblical Jewish literature, establishes its twofold character. Marriage covenant forms a permanent relationship between husband and wife based on their mutual fulfillment of some specific stipulations (Matt 19:6; Mark 10:9; Rom 7:2, 3). Every attempt to break the covenant relationship is condemned and prohibited (Deut 22:13–19; 28–29; Mal 2:10–16; Mark 10:11, 12; Matt 19:9; Luke 16:18; 1 Cor 7:10, 11, 12–14). However, it is vulnerable to disruption and dissolution when there is a lack of fulfillment of its stipulations by one of the parties (Exod 21:10–11; Ezek 9:9; 16:15–26; Jer 3:8–10; 5:11; Hos 8:14). This failure of maintaining the marriage covenant relationship is resolved for the innocent party with the permission of divorce and remarriage. Both Matthew and Paul address such situations when dealing with a spouse's conjugal unfaithfulness (Matt 19:9; 5:32) and a spouse's refusal to perform the covenant stipulations through departure (1 Cor 7:15, 16). The most explicit example of the dynamics of marriage covenant is offered in both Testaments with the relationship between God and Israel in the OT (Hos 2:15; Jer 2:2; Ezek 16:3) and Christ and the church in the NT (Eph 5:31, 32).

Third, the analysis of the dogmatical context has established both continuity and discontinuity between the matrimonial teachings of the major Christian traditions. The continuity is envisioned as an attempt to provide a coherent view on marriage which intends to express the biblical, historical, and dogmatical teachings on the subject. Hence, the marriage institution created and formulated by God for the goodness of his creation and the realisation of his image in the unity of man and woman has received highly exalted status in the churches' matrimonial teachings. Marriage is defined as a covenant relationship and the spectrum of its characteristics is expressed in the relationship between God and Israel and Christ and the church. It is this unity between divine and human which formulates marriage permanency, and for some of the Christian traditions makes it even absolutely indissoluble. When this indissolubility is applied on a human level the marriage covenant relationship comes under question due to human failures to preserve it. Thus, the discontinuity between the Christian traditions is formulated as their attempts to resolve the problem of marital breakdowns in the light of marriage absolute indissolubility. Resolving this discontinuity opened a possibility for establishing a dogmatically coherent and ecumenically relevant view of marriage, divorce, and remarriage. The resolution has been provided through systematic analysis following an argumentative critique of the scholars within the tradition which appears to be the strongest defender of absolute indissolubility. Hence, the evaluation of some of the tensions created in its matrimonial teaching through the concept of absolute indissolubility has been used to show the need for modification of the concept of indissolubility to the extent that provision be made for divorce and remarriage on legitimate biblical grounds. With such a resolution, intrinsic and extrinsic unity is attempted in the matrimonial traditions which suffer tensions between marital breakdown and marriage indissolubility by formulating the nature of marriage covenant concept as permanent but not indissoluble, providing an exceptional solution through divorce and remarriage in a case of spouse's failure to fulfill the covenant stipulations. The ecumenical understanding of marriage as covenant emphasizes its permanence which is deeply grounded in the agreement of all Christian traditions and at the same time resolves their disagreements with proposing modification of the view of indissolubility through allowing exceptional grounds for divorce and remarriage in cases when the lack of fulfillment of the marriage covenant stipulations endangers the moral dignity and life of the spouse. This defines the twofold exegetical and theological view of the NT teaching on divorce and remarriage as dogmatically valid and ecumenically justifiable.

Fourth, the pragmatic task necessitated the implementation of the biblical, theological, dogmatical, and ecumenical covenant concept of marriage, divorce, and remarriage. The successful accomplishment of this task required analysis of the context, the contemporary notion of marriage, and its inner dynamics. The results from this analysis established the need for redefining the notion of marriage in relation to its deinstitutionalized nature and providing solution for its inner tensions. Hence, the concept of the marriage covenant with its permanence and exceptional provision of divorce and remarriage in the light of a spouse's failure to fulfill the covenant obligations offered both a formulation of the proper permanent notion of the marriage institution and a solution for the victims of domestic abuse. This firmly justified the concept's applicability in the contemporary context. Furthermore, the formulation of the concept in the ecumenical proposal proved its practical value through facilitating guidance for all levels of the Christian communities. The pragmatic actualisation of the marriage covenant concept on the social legislative level also has been shown through real life examples in the law systems of the states of Louisiana (1997) and Arizona (1998).

Finally, the fundamental question "May Christians legitimately divorce and remarry and on what grounds?" which instigated the present research requires a simple and adequate answer which provides theoretical stability and demonstrates pragmatic relevance. The answer is integrated in the covenant concept of marriage. Christian marriage is a permanent union which requires the commitment of both spouses for its maintenance through fulfillment of its stipulations. The failure of the fulfillment of the latter provides legitimate grounds for divorce and remarriage of the innocent party. Hence, the answer is positive with defining the legitimate grounds as any intentional failure of fulfillment of the marriage covenant stipulations. However, the focus of all marriages must be the permanency of the relationships which demands the efforts of both spouses. Any shift of this focus would endanger the very nature of the covenant. This establishes the possibility for defining the answer as ecumenically justifiable making the emphasis on the agreement about the permanent nature of marriage between all Christian matrimonial traditions and leading to a proposition of resolving their disagreement through modifying their understanding of the indissolubility of marriage. Finally, the challenging task of proper handling of the concept of marriage covenant remains for all who are willing to accept it as the most satisfactory presentation of the NT teaching on divorce and remarriage.

Bibliography

Abbott, J., et al., "Domestic Violence Against Women. Incidence and Prevalence in an Emergency Department Population." *Journal of American Medical Association* 273 (1995) 1763–67.
Achtemeier, Paul J. "Mark, Gospel of." In *ABD* 4:541–57.
Ackerman, Rober J. and Susan E. Pickering. *Before It's Too Late: Helping Women in Controlling or Abusive Relationships*. Deerfield Beach: Health Communications, 1995.
Adams, Bert N. "Ethical Issues Facing the Contemporary Family." *RevExp* 75 (1978) 105–14.
Adams, Jay E. *Marriage Divorce and Remarriage in the Bible*. Grand Rapids: Baker, 1980.
Aeschylus. *Suppliant Women*. Edited by Herbert Weir Smyth. [online]. Available at http://www.perseus.tufts.edu/cgi-bin/ptext?lookup=Aesch.+Supp.+141. Accessed on 29 October 2000.
Ajduković, Marina, et al., "Nasilje u partnerskim odnosima." U *Nasilje nad ženom u obitelji*. Uredile: Marina Ajduković i Gordana Pavleković, 57–67. Zagreb: društvo za psihološku pomoć, 2000.
Ajduković, Marina. "Određenje i oblici nasilja u obitelji." U *Nasilje nad ženom u obitelji*. Uredile: Marina Ajduković i Gordana Pavleković, 11–15. Zagreb: društvo za psihološku pomoć, 2000.
Akkadian-Hittite Treaty. Edited by Daniel Bellissimo. [online]. Available at http://ccat.sas.upenn.edu/~humm/Topics/Contracts/treato1.html. Accessed on 26 November 2000.
Aland, Kurt and Barbara, editors. *Critical Apparatuses of NA^{26}*. Munster/Westphalia: Deutsche Bibelgesellschaft, 1993.
Albright, W. F., and C. S. Mann. *Matthew: Introduction, Translation, and Notes*. AB 26. Garden City, NY: Doubleday, 1971.
Alexander, Ralph H. "Marriage." In *Evangelical Dictionary of Biblical Theology*. Edited by Walter A. Elwell. Grand Rapids: Baker, 1998.
———. "Divorce." In *Evangelical Dictionary of Biblical Theology*. Edited by Walter A. Elwell. Grand Rapids: Baker, 1998.
Allam, Schafik. *Everyday Life in Ancient Egypt*. Egypt: Prism, 1985.
Allen, Joseph J. "Practical Issues of Sexuality." *SVSQ* 27 (1983) 39–51.
Allison, Dale C. "Divorce, Celibacy and Joseph (Matthew 1:18–25 and 19:1–12)." *JSNT* 49 (1993) 3–10.
———. "The Structure of the Sermon on the Mount." *JBL* 106 (1987) 423–45.
Alonso-Schökel, Luis. "Sapiential and Covenant Themes in Genesis 2–3." *ThDig* 13/1 (1965) 3–10.

Anderson, Hugh. *The Gospel of Mark*. NCBC. Grand Rapids: Eerdmans, 1981.

Anthony, Michael J. "The Relationship Between Marital Satisfaction and Religious Maturity." *Religious Education* 88 (1993) 97–108.

Antiphon. *Speeches*. Edited by K. J. Maidment. [online]. Available at http://perseus.csad.ox.ac.uk/cgi-bin/ptext?lookup=Antiph.+1+13. Accessed on 21 December 2000.

Apostolic Exhortation of Pope John Paul II. *Familiaris Consortio*. [online]. Available at http://www.wf-f.org/FamCons.html. Accessed on 23 September 2004.

Aramaic Papyri from Elephantine. Translated by H. L. Ginsberg. [online]. Available at http://ccat.sas.upenn.edu/~humm/Topics/Contracts/marrio1.html#M1Mo. Accessed on 26 November 2000.

Aristarchos, Maurakis. *Law of Marriage and Divorce in the Church of England and the Church of Greece in Recent Times (1850–1980) with Its Theological Implications*. Athens, Greece: Historical Publications, S. D. Basilopoulos, 1992.

Arizona Covenant Marriage Law of 1998. Arizona 43rd Legislature–Second Regular Session. Senate Bill 1133, Passed by Both Houses and Approved by the Governor 21 May 1998. [online]. Available at http://www.divorcereform.org/ari.html. Accessed on 20 September 2004.

Armerding, Carl. "The Marriage in Cana." *BibSac* 118 (1961) 320–26.

Armstrong, Dave and William Klimon. *Dialogue: Annulment vs. Divorce*. [online]. Available at http://ic.net/~erasmus/RAZ150.HTM. Accessed on 19 April 2001.

Arndt, William. *A Greek-English Lexicon of the New Testament and Other Early Christian Literature* [computer file]: a translation and adaption of the fourth revised and augmented edition of Walter Bauer's Griechisch-deutsches Worterbuch zu den Schriften des Neuen Testaments und der ubrigen urchristlichen Literatur by William F. Arndt and F. Wilbur Gingrich. – electronic ed. of the 2nd ed., rev. and augmented. Chicago: University of Chicago Press, c1979; Published in electronic form by Logos Research Systems, 1996.

Arnold, William V. "Preach on Marriage and Divorce, Pastor." *JP* 7/2 (1984) 2–6.

Arnold, William V., Dicie McKie Baird, Joan Trigg Langan, and Elizabeth Blakemore Vaughan, *Divorce: Prevention or Survival. A Practical Manual*. Philadelphia: Westminster, 1977.

Atkinson, David. *To Have and to Hold*. Grand Rapids: Eerdmans, 1979.

———. "A Response: Comments on the Article by Gordon Wenham." *Churchman* 95/2 (1981) 162–63.

Augustin, St. Aurelius. *Our Lord's Sermon on the Mount*. In *Nicene and Post-Nicene Fathers*. Edited by Philip Schaff. Series 1. Vol.6. *Christian Classics Ethereal Library*. Vol.2. CD-ROM. Edited by Harry Plantinga. Wheaton, IL: Wheaton College, 1998.

Bacchiocchi, Samuele. *The Marriage Covenant: A Biblical Study on Marriage, Divorce, and Remarriage*. Berrien Springs, MI: Biblical Perspectives, 1991.

———. *The Marriage Covenant: A Biblical Study on Marriage, Divorce, and Remarriage*. [online]. Available at http://www2.andrews.edu/~samuele/books/marriage/1.html. Accessed on 18 November 2000.

Bachman, Ronet, and Linda Saltzman. "Violence Against Women: Estimates from the Redesigned Survey." *Bureau of Justice Statistics: Special Report* (August, 1995).

Bailey, Sherwin Derrick. *The Mystery of Love Marriage*. New York: Harper, 1952.

Baird, William. "Biblical Criticism: New Testament Criticism." In *ABD* 1:730–36.

Balch, David L. "1 Cor 7:32–35 and Stoic Debates About Marriage, Anxiety, and Distraction." *JBL* 102 (1983) 429–39.

Banks, Robert. "Matthew's Understanding of the Law: Authenticity and Interpretations in Matthew 5:17-20." *JBL* 93 (1974) 226-42.
Barber, J. Cyril. "Marriage, Divorce, and Remarriage: A Review of the Relevant Religious Literature, 1973-1983." *Journal of Psychology and Theology* 12/3 (1984) 170-77.
Barclay, John. Review of *Jesus and Divorce*, by W. A. Heth and G. J. Wenham. In *EvQ* 58 (1986) 362-63.
Barclay, William. *The Letters to the Corinthians*. Philadelphia: Westminster, 1954.
Barclay-Newman Greek Dictionary in BibleWorks for Windows 95/NT v.4.0.025e [0]. Logos Development Corporation, 1996.
Barnabas. *The Epistle of Barnabas*. In *Ante-Nicene Fathers: Translations of The Writings of the Fathers Down to A.D. 325*. Edited by Alexander Roberts and James Donaldson. Vol.1. *Christian Classics Ethereal Library*. Vol.2. CD-ROM. Edited by Harry Plantinga. Wheaton, IL: Wheaton College, 1998.
Barnette, Henlee H. "Coarchy: Partnership and Equality in Man-Woman Relationships." *RevExp* 75 (1978) 20-25.
Barré, Michael L. "To Marry or to Burn: *Pyrousthai* in I Cor 7:9." *CBQ* 36 (1974) 193-202.
Barrett, C. K. *A Commentary on the First Epistle to the Corinthians*. Harper's New Testament Commentary. New York: Harper & Row, 1968.
Barth, Gerhard. "Matthew's Understanding of the Law." In *Tradition and Interpretation in Matthew*, 58-158. New Testament Library. Philadelphia: Westminster, 1976.
Barth, Karl. *Church Dogmatics*. Vol. III/1: *The Doctrine of Creation*. Edited by G. W. Bromiley and T. F. Torrance. Translated by J. W. Edwards, O. Bussey, and Harold Knight. Edinburgh: T. & T. Clark, 1958.
Barton, S. C. "Family." In *DJG*, 225-29.
Basil. *Letter 188: To Amphilochius, Concerning the Canons 9*. In *Early Church Fathers: Nicene and Post-Nicene Fathers*. Edited by Philip Schaff and Henry Wace. Series II. Vol.VIII. *Christian Classics Ethereal Library*. Vol. 2. CD-ROM. Edited by Harry Plantinga. Wheaton, IL: Wheaton College, 1998.
Batto, Bernard F. "The Institution of Marriage in Genesis 2 and in Atrahasis" *CBQ* 62 (2000) 621-31.
———. Review of *Battered Love*, by Renita J. Weems. In *CBQ* 59 (1997) 362-63.
Bauer, David R. "The Major Characters of Matthew's Story." *Int* 46 (1992) 357-67.
Bauer, Walter. *A Greek-English Lexicon of the New Testament and Other Early Christian Literature*. Translated by William F. Arndt and F. Wilbur Gingrich. Chicago: University of Chicago Press, 1957.
Baugh, S. M. "Marriage and Family in Ancient Greek Society." In *MFBW*, 103-31.
Bauman, Philip J. "Marital Intimacy and Spiritual Well-Being." *JPC* 52 (1998) 133-45.
Baumann, Gerlinde. *Love and Violence: Marriage as Metaphor for the Relationship between Yhwh and Israel in the Prophetic Books*. Translated by Linda M. Maloney. Collegeville, MN: Liturgical, 2003.
Baumert, Norbert. *Woman and Man in Paul: Overcoming a Misunderstanding*. Translated by Patrick Madigan and Linda M. Maloney. Collegeville, MN: Liturgical, 1996.
Baxter's Instructions for Maintaining Love in Marriage Condensed From. "A Christian Directory." Works, 1:431. Quoted in Tim Beougher, "The Puritan View of Marriage: The Nature of the Husband/Wife Relationship in Puritan England as Taught and Experienced by a Representative Puritan Pastor, Richard Baxter." *TJ* 10/2 (1989) 158. Electronic Edition by Galaxie Software, 1999.

Beck, James R. "Theology for the Healthy Family." In *Women Abuse, and the Bible: How Scripture Can Be Used to Hurt or Heal.* Edited by Catherine Clark Kroeger and James R. Beck, 216-31. Grand Rapids: Baker, 1996.

Becker, U. "Hard, Hardened." In *NIDNTT* 2:156.

Beeson, Trevor. "British Debate Remarriage in Church." *ChrCent* 95 (July 1978) 681-82.

———. "Love over Law." *ChrCent* 87 (June 1970) 748.

———. "A Welcome Report. Marriage, Divorce and the Church, Church of England." *ChrCent* 88 (April 1971) 517-18.

Beeston, A. F. L. "One Flesh." *VT* 36 (1986) 115-17.

Behm, Johannes. "Καρδία among the Greeks." In *TDNT* 3 (1964) 3:608-9.

———. "Σκληροκαρδία." In *TDNT* 3 (1964) 3:613-14.

Beougher, Tim. "The Puritan View of Marriage: The Nature of the Husband/Wife Relationship in Puritan England as Taught and Experienced by a Representative Puritan Pastor, Richard Baxter." *TJ* 10/2 (1989) 131-160. Electronic Edition by Galaxie Software, 1999.

BGU IV.1101. The Duke Databank of Documentary Papyri. [online]. Available at http://www.perseus.tufts.edu/cgi-bin/ptext?doc=Perseus%3Atext%3A1999.05.0001&layout=&loc=1101. Accessed on 22 August 2000.

BGU IV.1102. The Duke Databank of Documentary Papyri. [online]. Available at http://www.perseus.tufts.edu/cgi-bin/ptext?doc=Perseus%3Atext%3A1999.05.0001&layout=&loc=1102. Accessed on 22 August 2000.

BGU IV.1103. The Duke Databank of Documentary Papyri. [online]. Available at http://www.perseus.tufts.edu/cgi-bin/ptext?doc=Perseus%3Atext%3A1999.05.0001&layout=&loc=1103. Accessed on 28 August 2004.

BibleWorks for Windows. Version 4.0.026e (4000). Cambridge, MA: Lotus Development Corporation, 1998.

BibleWorks for Windows. Version 5.0.020w, BibleWorks, LLC, 2001.

BibleWorks for Windows. Windows 98/XP Release. Version 6.0.005y, BibleWorks, LLC, 2003.

BibleWorks Greek New Testament Morphology (BNM). Morphology database is the result of a collaborative effort between Michael Bushell (BibleWorks) and two scholars Jean-Noel Aletti, SJ, Professor of New Testament Exegesis at the Pontifical Biblical Institute, in Rome and Andrzej Gieniusz, CR, Doctor in Sacra Scriptura, BibleWorks LLC, 1999-2001.

Biblia Hebraica Stuttgartensia (BHS) [or WTT] (Hebrew Bible, Masoretic Text or Hebrew Old Testament). Fourth Corrected Edition. Edited by K. Elliger and W. Rudoph. Stuttgart: Deutsche Bibelgesellschaft (German Bible Society), 1966, 1977, 1983, 1990.

Biblia Sacra Iuxta Vulgatam Versionem, Vulgate Latin Bible (VUL). Edited by R. Weber, B. Fischer, J. Gribomont, H.F.D. Sparks, and W. Thiele [at Beuron and Tuebingen]. Stuttgart: Deutsche Bibelgesellschaft (German Bible Society), 1969, 1975, 1983.

Bildstein, Walter. "The Joint Working Group: Instrument of Dissent and Metanoia: a Discussion of the Issue of Mixed Marriage." *JES* 23 (1986) 107-12.

Blass, F., and A. Debrunner. *A Greek Grammar of the New Testament and Other Early Christian Literature.* Translated by Robert W. Funk. Chicago: University of Chicago Press, 1961.

Blocher, Henri. *In the Beginning: The Opening Chapters of Genesis.* Translated by David G. Preston. Downers Grove, IL: InterVarsity, 1984.

Block, Daniel I. "Marriage and Family in Ancient Israel." In *MFBW*, 33–102.
Blomberg, Craig L. "Form Criticism." In *DJG*, 243–49.
———. "Marriage, Divorce, Remarriage, and Celibacy: An Exegesis of Matthew 19:3-12." *TJ* 11 (1990) 162–97.
———. *Matthew: An Exegetical and Theological Exposition of Holy Scripture*. The New American Commentary 22. Nashville: Broadman, 1992.
Bock, Darrell L. "Form Criticism." In *NTCI*, 174–96.
Boff, Leonardo. "The Sacrament of Marriage." *Concilium* 7/9 (September 1973) 22–33.
Borchert, Gerald L. "1 Corinthians 7:15 and the Church's Historic Misunderstanding of Divorce and Remarriage." *RevExp* 96 (1999) 125–29.
Borelli, M. Jane. "Sexuality in the Ancient World." *Religious Studies Review* 20 (July 1994) 182–87.
Borland, James A. "Women in the Life and Teaching of Jesus." In *Recovering Biblical Manhood and Womanhood: A Response to Evangelical Feminism*. Edited by John Pipers and Wayne Grudem, 105–16. Wheaton, IL: Crossway, 1991.
Borresen, Kari Elisabeth. "Women and Men in the Creation Narratives and in the Church." *Concilium* 146 (June 1981) 62–69.
Botha, Daan. "My Marriage Partner has been Unfaithful-What Am I to Do?" *Orientation* 58–62 (December 1990–1991) 122–130.
Botman, H. Russell. "Exegesis and Proclamation–1 Corinthians 7:29–31: 'To Live . . . as if it Were Not.'" *Journal of Theology for Southern Africa* 65 (December 1988) 73–79.
Bradshaw, Robert I. *Covenant*. [online]. Available at http://www.robibrad.demon.co.uk/covenant.htm. Accessed on 16 June 2001.
Brandon, S. G. F. *Creation Legends of the Ancient Near East*. Manchester: Hodder and Stoughton, 1963.
Braun, Michel A. *Should Divorced People be Treated Like . . . Second-Class Christians? A New Approach to the Dilemma of Divorced People in the Church*. Downers Grove, IL: InterVarsity, 1989.
Braund, David C. "Herod Antipas." In *ABD* 3:160. New York: Doubleday, 1992.
Brinig, Margaret F. "Economics, Law, and Covenant Marriage." *Gender Issues* 16/1–2 (Winter/Spring 98) 4.
Bromiley, Geoffrey W. "Divorce: Historical Survey." In *The New International Standard Bible Encyclopedia*. Edited by James Orr. Grand Rapids: Eerdmans, 1979.
Brooke, Christopher N. L. *The Medieval Idea of Marriage*. Oxford: Oxford University Press, 1989.
Brooks, James A., and Carlton L. Winbery. *Syntax of New Testament Greek*. Lanham, MD: University Press of America, 1979.
Brown, C. "Χωρίζω." In *NIDNTT*.
Brown, Raymond E. *The Birth of the Messiah: A Commentary on the Infancy Narratives in Matthew and Luke*. The Anchor Bible Reference Library. New York: Doubleday, 1993.
Bruce, F. F. *1 and 2 Corinthians*. New Century Bible Series. Greenwood: Attic, 1971.
Brueggemann, Walter. *Genesis*. IBC. Atlanta: John Knox, 1982.
Brundage, James A. Review of *Putting Asunder*, by Roderick Phillips. In *CH* 59 (March 1990) 104–6.
———. *Law, Sex, and Christian Society in Medieval Europe*. Chicago: University of Chicago Press, 1987.

Brunec, Michael. "Tertio de clausulis divortii Mt 5, 32 et 19, 9." *Verbum domini* 27 (1949) 3–16.
Bucer, Martin. *De Regno Christi*, [1550]. In *Martini Buceri Opera Latini*. Vol. 25. Edited by Francois Wendel. Paris: Presses Universitaires de France, 1955.
Buchanan, John M. "Talking About Marriage." *ChrCent* 117 (December 2000) 1291.
Buckley, Timothy J. *What Binds Marriage? Roman Catholic Theology in Practice*. Rev. ed. London: Continuum, 2002.
Buijs, Joseph A., editor. *Christian Marriage Today: Growth or Breakdown?* Interdisciplinary Essays. Lewiston, NY: Mellen, 1985.
Bultmann, Rudolf. "Merimnáō, Promerimnáō, Mérimna." In *TDNT* 4:589–93.
———. *Form Criticism: Two Essays on New Testament Research*. Translated by F. C. Grant. New York: Harper, 1962.
Burge, Gary M. "You're Divorced-Can You Remarry?" [online]. Available at cteditor@christianitytoday.com. Accessed on 30 June 2000.
Burns, C. *Divorce and Remarriage*. [online]. Available at http://www.utdallas.edu/~michaelh/christian/message/divorce.html. Accessed on 7 December 2000.
Bush, John C., and Patrick R. Cooney, editors. *Interchurch Families: Resources for Ecumenical Hope. Catholic/Reformed Dialogue in the United States*. Louisville: Geneva, 2002.
Bush, Trudy Bloser. "Happily Married with Children." *ChrCent* 113 (January 1996) 109–12.
Bustanoby, Andre. "When Wedlock Becomes Deadlock: Biblical Teaching on Divorce, Part I." *ChrTo* 19 (June 1975) 918–20.
———. "When Wedlock Becomes Deadlock: Biblical Teaching on Divorce, Part II." *ChrTo* 19 (June 1975) 1013–14.
Butler, Sara. Review of *Ecumenical Marriage and Remarriage: Gifts and Challenges to the Churches*, by Michael Lawler. In *JES* 29 (1992) 269–70.
Butting, Klara. "Pauline Variations on Genesis 2.24: Speaking of the Body of Christ in the Context of the Discussion of Lifestyles." Translated by McNeil Brian. *JSNT* 79 (2000) 79–90.
Buxbaum, Robert E. "When Pastors Divorce: A New Approach to Congregational Healing." *JPC* 49 (1995) 173–86.
Byrne, Brendan. "Sinning Against One's Own Body: Paul's Understanding of the Sexual Relationship in 1 Corinthians 6:18." *CBQ* 45 (1983) 608–16.
Byron, Brian. "1 Cor 7:10–15: a Basis for Future Catholic Discipline on Marriage and Divorce?" *TS* 34 (1973) 429–445.
Cahill, Lisa Sowle. "Sexual Ethics, Marriage, and Divorce." *TS* 47 (1986) 102–17.
———. "The Ethical Implications of the Sermon on the Mount." *Int* 41 (1987) 144–56.
———. *Between the Sexes: Foundations for a Christian Ethics of Sexuality*. Philadelphia: Fortress, 1985.
———. *Sex, Gender and Christian Ethics*. Cambridge: Cambridge University Press, 1996.
Čalić, Petar. *Brak u procijepu: oženjan-rastavljen-ponovno vjenčan*. Zagreb: Glas Koncila, 1995.
Calivas, Aliuvlaadis C. "Marriage: The Sacrament of Love and Communion." *GOTR* 40 (1995) 247–76.

Callaghan, Gwenda. *Annulment Process. Remarriage in the Church: Pastoral Solutions. A Statement by the Board Members of the Association for the Rights of Catholics in the Church (ARCC)*. [online]. Available at http://astro.temple.edu/~arcc/marriage.htm. Accessed on 19 April 2001.

———. *Explaining What the Catholic Annulment Process Means and Does not Mean*. [online]. Available at http://www.aquinas-academy.syd.catholic.edu.au/editorial.htm. Accessed on 19 April 2001.

Callahan, Sidney. "A Psychological Perspective. Marriage and the Religions." *JES* 22 (1985) 103–7.

Calvin, John. *Institutes of the Christian Religion*. Translated by Henry Beveridge. London: Reinolde Wolfe & Richards Harison, 1561. Electronic Edition by Galaxie Software, 1999.

Campbell, Ken M., editor. *Marriage and Family in the Biblical World*. Downers Grove, IL: InterVarsity, 2003.

Cantwell, Yager L. "A Matrimonial Trial Lawyer Responds." *JES* 22 (1985) 112–19.

Capper, LeRoy S. "The *Imago Dei* and Its Implications for Order in the Church." Πρεσβυτέριον: *A Journal of the Eldership* 11/1 (1985) 21–33.

Carey, Benedict. "Is Divorce Too Easy?" *Health* 13/7 (1999) 122.

Carlson, Eric Josef. *Marriage and the English Reformation*. Oxford: Blackwell, 1994.

Carmody, Denise Lardner. "Marriage in Roman Catholicism." *JES* 28–40.

———. "Women in Modern Judaism." *Horizons* 11 (1984) 28–41.

Carson, D. A. *Matthew*. EBC 8. Grand Rapids: Zondervan, 1984.

———. "Redaction Criticism: On the Legitimacy and Illegitimacy of a Literary Tool." In *Scripture and Truth*. Edited by D. A. Carson and John D. Woodbridge, 119–42. Leicester: InterVarsity, 1983.

———. *The Gagging of God: Christianity Confronts Pluralism*. Grand Rapids: Zondervan, 1996.

Carter, Warren. *Matthew: Storyteller, Interpreter, Evangelist*. Peabody, MA: Hendrickson, 1996.

Cassiday-Shaw, Aimee K. *Family Abuse and the Bible: The Scriptural Perspective*. Binghamton: Haworth, 2002.

Cassin, Elena. *Une Querelle de Famille. Studies on the Civilization and Culture of Nuzi and the Hurrians*. In Honor of Ernest R. Lacheman. Edited by M. A. Morrison and D. I. Owen. Winona Lake, IN: Eisenbrauns, 1981.

Cassius, Dio. *Roman History VII, Books 56–60*. Translated by Earnest Cary and Herbert B. Foster. LCL 175. Cambridge: Harvard University Press, 1924.

———. *History of Rome 54.16.1–2*. Translated by Mary R. Lefkowitz and Maureen B. Fant. [online]. Available at http://www.uky.edu/ArtsSciences/Classics/wlgr/wlgr-romanlegal120.html. Accessed on 14 October 2000.

———. *History of Rome 54.16.1–2*. In *Women's Life in Greece and Rome: A Source Book in Translation*. 2nd ed. Translated by Mary R. Lefkowitz and Maureen B. Fant. Baltimore: Johns Hopkins University Press, 1992.

Catchpole, David R. "Tradition History." In *New Testament Interpretation: Essays on Principles and Methods*. Edited by I. Howard Marshall, 165–80. Exeter: Paternoster, 1977.

Catechism of the Catholic Church. Libreria Editrice Vaticana. [online]. Available at http://www.vatican.va/archive/ENG0015/_INDEX.HTM. Accessed on 17 September 2005.

Catechism of the Catholic Church: Part 3, Life in Christ. Section 2, The Ten Commandments. Chapter 2, "You Shall Love Your Neighbour as Yourself." Article 6, The 6th Commandment. [online]. Available at http://www.scborromeo.org/ccc/p3s2c2a6.htm. Accessed on 19 April 2001.

Catechism of the Catholic Church. London: Chapman, 1994.

Centres for Disease Control and Prevention (CDC). *Costs of Intimate Partner Violence Against Women in the United States.* Atlanta: National Center for Injury Prevention and Control, 2003.

Cereti, Giovanni. "Judges or Counsellors?" *Concilium* 7/9 (1973) 98–110.

Chapman, David W. "Marriage and Family in Second Temple Judaism." In *MFBW*, 183–239.

Chapman, Gary. *Hope for the Separated: Wounded Marriages Can be Healed.* Chicago: Moody, 1982.

Chirban, John T. "Psychological Stressors in Mixed Marriages." *GOTR* 40 (1995) 322–37.

ChLA.IV.249. [online]. Available at http://www.tyndale.cam.ac.uk/Brewer/Marriage Papyri/TableLM.htm. Accessed on 28 August 2004. Translation based on David Instone-Brewer, "1 Corinthians 7 in the Light of the Graeco-Roman Marriage and Divorce Papyri." *TynBul* 51.2 (2001) 113 and David Instone-Brewer, "1 Corinthians 7 in the Light of the Graeco-Roman Marriage and Divorce Papyri." *TynBul* (2001). [online]. Available at http://www.tyndale.cam.ac.uk/Brewer/MarriagePapyri/1Cor_7a.htm. Accessed on 26 August 2004.

Cholij, Roman. *Clerical Celibacy in East and West.* Leominster: Fowler-Wright, 1988.

Christakis, Christos B. Review of *Law of Marriage and Divorce in the Church of England and the Church of Greece in Recent Times (1850–1980) with Its Theological Implications*, by Maurakis Aristarchos. In *GOTR* 41 (1996) 94–95.

Christenson, Larry. *The Christian Family.* Minneapolis: Bethany, 1970.

Chrysostomos. *The Orthodox Family.* [online]. Available at http://orthodoxinfo.com/praxis/orthodox_family.htm. Accessed on 22 April 2001.

Chrysostom, St. John. *Homilies on the Epistle to the Hebrews.* 7.11. *Post-Nicene Fathers of the Christian Church.* Series 1. Volume 14. Edited by Philip Schaff. Grand Rapids: Eerdmans, 1956. *Christian Classics Ethereal Library.* Vol.2. CD-ROM. Edited by Harry Plantinga. Wheaton, IL: Wheaton College, 1998.

———. *On Virginity* 14, 6. Translated by Sally Rieger Shore. In *Studies in Women and Religion.* Vol. 9. New York and Toronto: Edwin Mellen, 1983. Quouted in William Basil Zion, *Eros and Transformation: Sexuality and Marriage—An Eastern Orthodox Perspective.* 73. Lanham, MD: University Press of America, 1931.

Cicero, M. Tullius. *Letters 1. Intro 20: The Letters to TERENTIA.* Edited by Evelyn Shuckburgh. [online]. Available at http://perseus.csad.ox.ac.uk/cgi-bin/ptext?doc=Perseus:text:1999.02.0022&query=head%3d%2322. Accessed on 27 May 2001.

———. *Letters A 15.29.* Edited by Evelyn Shuckburgh. [online]. Available at http://perseus.csad.ox.ac.uk/cgi-bin/ptext?lookup=Cic.+Att.+15.29. Accessed on 27 May 2001.

Clement of Rome. *The First Epistle of Clement to the Corinthians.* In *Ante-Nicene Fathers: Translations of The Writings of the Fathers Down to A.D. 325.* Edited by Alexander Roberts and James Donaldson. Vol. 1. *Christian Classics Ethereal Library.* Vol. 2. CD-ROM. Edited by Harry Plantinga. Wheaton, IL: Wheaton College, 1998.

Clement of Alexandria. *From the Books of the Hypotyposes* 6.14. [online]. Available at http://www.ccel.org/fathers2/ANF-02/anf02-77.htm#P10243_2869382. Accessed on 14 March 2001.

Clendenin, Daniel B. Review of *Divorce and Remarriage: Four Christian Views*. Edited by H. Wayne House. In *JETS* 35 (1992) 559–60.

Coates, Robert B. "A Ministry of Mediation: The Divorce Settlement." *JPC* 37 (1983) 265–75.

Coblentz, John. *What the Bible Says about Marriage, Divorce, and Remarriage*, 2000. [online]. Available at http://www.anabaptists.org/books/mdr/index.html#contents. Accessed on 24 January 2005.

Code of Canon Law, Title VII, Marriage. Libreria Editrice Vaticana. [online]. Available at http://www.vatican.va/archive/ENG1104/__P3V.HTM. Accessed on 23 September 2004.

Codrington, Graeme. *Marriage, Divorce and Remarriage in the Light of the Teaching of Jesus*. [online]. Available at http://www.youth.co.za/papers/divorce.htm. Accessed on 25 April 2001.

Coe, Bufford W. *John Wesley and Marriage*. Bethlehem, PA: Lehigh University Press, 1996.

Coiner, Harry G. "Divorce and Remarriage: Toward Pastoral Practice." *CTM* 34 (1963) 541–55.

Coleman, Gerald D. *Divorce and Remarriage in the Catholic Church*. Mahwah, NJ: Paulist, 1988.

Coleman, Peter. *Christian Attitudes to Marriage: From Ancient Times to the Third Millennium*. Edited by Michel Langford. London: SCM, 2004.

Collier, Gary D. "Rethinking Jesus on Divorce." [online]. Available at http://www.rq.acu.edu/Volume_037/rq03702collier.htm. Accessed on 25 April 2001.

Collins, John C. "The (Intelligible) Masoretic Text of Malachi 2:16: or, How Does God Feel About Divorce?" *Presbyterion* 20/1 (1994) 36–40.

Collins, John J. Review of *Marriage as a Covenant*, by Gordon Paul Hugenberger. In *JBL* 114 (1995) 306–8.

Collins, Raymond F. *Sexual Ethics and the New Testament: Behavior and Belief*. New York: Crossroad, 2000.

———. "Marriage: New Testament." In *ABD* 4:569–72.

"Confidence in Marriage on the Decline." *ChrCent* 116 (July 28–August 4 1999) 738.

Congdon, Roger D. "Did Jesus Sustain the Law in Matthew 5?" *BibSac* 135/538 (1978) 118–26.

Constantelos, Demetrios J. "Marriage and Celibacy of the Clergy in the Orthodox Church." *Concilium* 8 (October 1972) 30–31.

———. "Marriage in the Greek Orthodox Church." *JES* 22 (1985) 21–27.

———. "Mixed Marriage in Historical Perspective." *GOTR* 40 (1995) 277–85.

Conzelmann, Hans. *1 Corinthians: A Commentary on the First Epistle to the Corinthians*. Hermeneia. Translated by James W. Leitch. Philadelphia: Fortress, 1975.

Coodling, Richard A. and Cheryl Smith. "Clergy Divorce: A Survey of Issues and Emerging Ecclesiastical Structures." *JPC* 37/4 (1983) 277–91.

Cook, Joe. "No to Covenant Marriage." *World & I* 13/1 (1998) 302.

Cornes, Andrew. *Divorce and Remarriage: Biblical Principles and Pastoral Practice*. Grand Rapids: Eerdmans, 1993.

Coser, Lewis A., et al., *Introduction to Sociology*. 2nd ed. New York: Harcourt Brace Jovanovich, 1987.

Couch, Mal. "The Importance of the Book of Matthew." *CTJ* 3 (1999) 219–28.

Countryman, William L. *Dirt Greed and Sex: Sexual Ethics in the New Testament and Their Implications for Today*. Minneapolis: Fortress, 1989.

Covenant Marriage Legislation: Current Covenant Marriage Laws. [online]. Available at http://www.divorcereform.org/cov.html. Accessed on 20 September 2004.

Cowan, Rachel B. "Jewish-Christian Marriages: Shall I Officiate?" *Cross Currents* 40/1 (1990) 34–40.

Craigie, P. C. *The Book of Deuteronomy*. The New International Commentary on the Old Testament. Grand Rapids: Eerdmans, 1976.

Crosmer, Arthur J. "Marriage, a Type of God's Relationship to His People." *CTM* 27 (1956) 370–82.

Cross, L. B. "The Teaching of Jesus on Divorce and Remarriage." *The Modern Churchman* 1 (October 1957–April 1958) 18–32.

Dart, John. "Ecumenical Wobbling: the NCC Reversal on Marriage." *ChrCent* 117 (13 December 2000) 1292–94.

Daube, David. *The New Testament and Rabbinic Judaism*. New York: Arno, 1973.

Davids, Peter H. "Tradition Criticism." In *DJG*, 831–34.

Davies, Jon, and Gerard Loughlin. *Sex These Days: Essay on Theology, Sexuality and Society*. Sheffield: Sheffield Academic, 1997.

Davies, W. D., and Dale C. Allison. *The Gospel according to Saint Matthew*. Vol. 1. ICC. Edinburgh: T. & T. Clark, 1988.

———. *The Gospel according to Saint Matthew*. Vol. 2. ICC. Edinburgh: T. & T. Clark, 1991.

———. *The Gospel according to Saint Matthew*. Vol. 3. Edinburgh: T. & T. Clark, 1991.

Dawes, Gregory W. "But if You Can Gain Your Freedom (1 Corinthians 7:17–24)" *CBQ* 52 (1990) 681–97.

The Dead Sea Scrolls Translated: 11QTemple. Translated by Florentino Garcia Martinez. Netherlands: Copyright Bruce and Kenneth Zuckerman, 1992. In *Dead See Scrolls Electronic Reference Library*, v 5.3. Provo, Utah: Brigam Young University; Leiden: Brill, 1999.

The Dead Sea Scrolls Translated: The Damascus Document. Translated by Wilfred G. E. Watson. Netherlands: Copyright Bruce and Kenneth Zuckerman, 1992. In *Dead See Scrolls Electronic Reference Library*, v 5.3. Provo, Utah: Brigam Young University; Leiden: Brill, 1999.

The Dead Sea Scrolls Translated: Wisdom Poems. Translated by R. Eisenman and M. Wise. Netherlands: Copyright Bruce and Kenneth Zuckerman, 1992. In *Dead See Scrolls Electronic Reference Library*, v 5.3. Provo, Utah: Brigam Young University; Leiden: Brill, 1999.

Deasley, Alex R. G. *Marriage and Divorce in the Bible and the Church*. Kansas City: Beacon Hill, 2000.

Delhaye, Philippe. "The Development of the Medieval Church's Teaching on Marriage." *Concilium* 5/6 (May 1970) 83–88.

Demetry, Constas H. "Orthodox Creed." [online]. Available at http://www.bible.ca/cr-Orthodox.htm. Accessed on 21 April 2001.

———. *Catechism of the Eastern Orthodox Church*. [online]. Available at http://www.christusrex.org/www1/CDHN/catechis.html. Accessed on 21 April 2001.

Deming, Will. *Paul on Marriage and Celibacy: The Hellenistic Background of 1 Corinthians 7*. Society for New Testament Studies Monograph Series 83. Cambridge: Cambridge University Press, 1995.

Demosthenes. *Speeches 51–61: Apollodorus Against Neaera*. Translated by A. T. Murray, Norman W. DeWitt, and Norman J. DeWitt. [online]. Available at http://perseus.csad.ox.ac.uk/cgi-bin/ptext?lookup=Dem.+59+17. Accessed on 21 December 2000.

DeRoche, Michael. "Israel's 'Two Evils' in Jeremiah 2:13." *VT* 31 (1981) 369–71.

Descamps, Alber-Louis. "The New Testament Doctrine on Marriage." In *Contemporary Perspectives on Christian Marriage*. Edited by R. Malone and J. R. Connery, 217–73, 347–63. Chicago: Loyola University Press, 1984.

Dever, John P. "Marriage." In *The New International Dictionary of the Christian Church*. Edited by J. D. Douglas. Grand Rapids: Zondervan, 1978.

Dicks, Henry. *Marital Tensions: Clinical Studies Towards a Psychological Theory of Interaction*. London: Routledge and Kegan Paul, 1967.

Divorce and Remarriage. [online]. Available at http://www.catholic.com/answers/tracts/_divorce.htm. Accessed on 02 November 2000.

Divorce and Remarriage An Exegetical Study: A Report of the Commission on Theology and Church Relations of the Lutheran Church—Missouri Synod. November 1987. [online]. Available at http://www.iclnet.org/pub/resources/text/wittenberg/mosynod/web/divrem-2.html. Accessed on 25 April 2001.

"Divorce Becomes Legal in Ireland." *ChrCent* 114 (May 1997) 445–46.

"Divorce Culture." *ChrCent* 117 (November 2000) 1101.

Dixon, John W. "Blessing Divorce." *ChrCent* 102 (April 1985) 358.

Dobson, Edward G. *What the Bible Really Says about Marriage, Divorce and Remarriage*. Old Tappan, NJ: Revell, 1986.

Doherty, William J. *Take Back Your Marriage: Sticking Together in a World That Pulls Us Apart*. New York: Guilford, 2001.

Dominian, Jack, and Hugh Montefiore. *God, Sex and Love: An Exercise in Ecumenical Ethics*. London: SCM, 1989.

Dominian, Jack. *Marital Breakdown*. Harmondsworth: Penguin, 1968.

———. "Marital Breakdown." *Concilium* 7/9 (1973) 123–39.

———. *Marriage Faith and Love*. London: Darton, Longman and Todd, 1981.

Dora, Peter P. "Mutual Care and Commitment: A Ministry to Ecumenical Families." *JES* 16 (1979) 629–42.

The Douay-Rheims 1899 American Edition (DRA). Very literal translation of the Latin Vulgate. Public Domain.

Down, M. J. "The Sayings of Jesus About Marriage and Divorce." *Expository Times* 95 (1984) 332–33.

Draper, Jonathan A. "The Genesis and Narrative Thrust of the Paraenesis in the Sermon on the Mount." *JSNT* 75 (1999) 25–48.

Driedger, Leo, Michael Yoder, and Peter Sawatzky. "Divorce among Mennonites: Evidence of Family Breakdown." *The Mennonite Quarterly Review* 59 (1985) 367–82.

Driver, S. R. *Deuteronomy*. ICC. Edinburgh: T. & T. Clark, 1986.

Droleskey, Thomas. *One Thing Leads to Another*. [online]. Available at http://www.ewtn.com/library/ISSUES/ONETHING.TXT. Accessed on 19 April 2001.

Dulau, Pierre. "Pauline Privilege: Is it Promulgated in the First Epistle to the Corinthians." *CBQ* 13 (1951) 146–52.

Dumbrell, W. J. *Covenant and Creation: A Theology of the Old Testament Covenants*. Grand Rapids: Baker, 1984.

Dunn, James D. G. *Romans 1–8*. WBC 38A. Dallas: Word, 2002.

Dupont, Jacques Dom. *Marriage et Divorce dans L'evangile: Matthieu 19, 3–12 et parallèles*. Bruges: Abbaye De Saint-Andre/Desclee De Brouwer, 1959.

Duty, Guy. *Divorce and Remarriage*. Minneapolis: Bethany Fellowship, 1967.

Eastern Orthodox-Roman Catholic Consultation. "An Agreed Statement on the Sanctity of Marriage." *GOTR* 23 (1978) 318–22.

Eckel, Paul T. "Mark 10:1–16." *Int* 42 (1988) 285–91.

"An Ecumenical Marriage Strategy." *ChrCent* 117/33 (November 2000) 1211.

Edgar, Robert W. "NCC Chief Backtracks." *ChrCent* 117/34 (December 2000) 1264–1265.

Edgar, Thomas R. "Divorce and Remarriage for Adultery or Desertion." In *Divorce and Remarriage: Four Christian Views*. Edited by H. Wayne House. Downers Grove, IL: InterVarsity, 1990.

———. "Response to Divorce, But No Remarriage" by William A. Heth. In *Divorce and Remarriage: Four Christian Views*. Edited by H. Wayne House. 133–143. Downers Grove, IL: InterVarsity, 1990.

———. "Response to No Divorce and No Remarriage." by J. Carl Laney, In *Divorce and Remarriage: Four Christian Views*. Edited by H. Wayne House. 61–66. Downers Grove, IL: InterVarsity, 1990.

Ehrlich, Rudolf J. "The Indissolubility of Marriage as a Theological Problem." *Scottish Journal of Theology* 23 (1970) 291–311.

Eichhorst, William R. "Ezra's Ethics on Intermarriage and Divorce." *GTJ* 10/3 (1969) 17–27.

Elder, Robert J. "The Theology of Marriage Encounter." *ChrCent* 96 (June 1979) 672–74.

Elliot, B. A., and M. M. P. Johnson. "Domestic violence in a Primary Care Setting: Patterns and Prevalence." *Archives of Family Medicine* 4 (1995) 113–19.

Elliott, J. K. "Paul's Teaching on Marriage in I Corinthians: Some Problems Considered." *NTS* 19 (1972–1973) 219–25.

Ellisen, Stanley A. *Divorce and Remarriage in the Church*. Grand Rapids: Zondervan, 1980.

El-Zanaty, F., et al., *Egypt Demographic and Health Survey*. Calverton, MD: Macro International, 1996.

Emerson, James G. Jr. *Divorce, the Church, and Remarriage*. Philadelphia: Westminster, 1961.

Emmet, C. W. "Marriage." In *Dictionary of the Bible*. Edited by James Hastings and John A. Selbil. New York: Hendrickson, 1989.

Encyclical Letter of the Holy Synod of Bishops. *On Marriage*. [online]. Available at http://www.holy-trinity.org/morality/synod-marriage.html. Accessed on 21 April 2001.

Engelsma, David. *The Remarriage of the Guilty Party*. [online]. Available at http://www.rsglh.org/remarriage_of_the_guilty_party.htm. Accessed on 25 April 2001.

The English Bible in Basic English 1949/1964 (BBE). ASCII version Copyright © 1988–1997 by the Online Bible Foundation and Woodside Fellowship of Ontario, Canada. Licensed from the Institute for Creation Research. Printed in 1965 by Cambridge Press in England.

The English Darby Bible 1884/1890 (DBY). A literal translation by John Nelson Darby (1800–1882), ASCII version Copyright © 1988–1997 by the Online Bible Foundation and Woodside Fellowship of Ontario, Canada.

The English Noah Webster Bible 1833 (WEB), The Holy Bible, Containing the Old and New Testaments, in the Common Version, with Amendments of the language by Noah Webster, LL.D., ASCII version Copyright © 1988–1997 by the Online Bible Foundation and Woodside Fellowship of Ontario, Canada. Licensed from the Institute for Creation Research.

The English Revised 1833 Webster Update 1995 (RWB) with Pierce's Englishman's-Strong's Numbering System, ASCII version Copyright © 1988–1997 by the Online Bible Foundation and Woodside Fellowship of Ontario, Canada. Licensed from the Institute for Creation Research.

The English Translation of the Septuagint Version of the Old Testament (LXE). Translated by Sir Lancelot C. L. Brenton, (1844, 1851). London: Bagster, 1988.

The English Young's Literal Translation of the Holy Bible 1862/1887/1898 (YLT) by J. N. Young, ASCII version Copyright © 1988–1997 by the Online Bible Foundation and Woodside Fellowship of Ontario, Canada.

Ensworth Jr., George. "Notice the Divorced Among Us." *ChrTo* 26 (May 1982) 20–22.

Erickson, John H. "The Council in Trullo: Issues Relating to the Marriage of Clergy." *GOTR* 40 (Spring-Summer 1995) 183–199.

Ernst, Theodore. "Not by Law but by Love: Divorce and Co-Parenting." *ChrCent* 97 (October 1980) 933.

Etzioni. "How to Make Marriage Matter." *Time*, September 6, 1993, 76.

Euripides. *Helen*. Edited by Gilbert Murray. [online]. Available at http://www.perseus.tufts.edu/cgi-bin/ptext?lookup=Eur.+Hel.+666. Accessed on 29 October 2000.

———. *Iphigenia in Tauris*. Edited by Robert Potter. [online]. Available at http://www.perseus.tufts.edu/cgi-bin/ptext?lookup=Eur.+IT+203. Accessed on 29 October 2000.

———. *Andromache*. Edited by David Kovacs. [online]. Available at http://perseus.csad.ox.ac.uk/cgi-bin/ptext?lookup=Eur.+Andr.+957. Accessed on 02 December 2000.

Evans, Craig A. "Luke 16:1–18 and the Deuteronomy Hypothesis." In *Luke and Scripture: The Function of Sacred Tradition in Luke-Acts*. Craig A. Evans and James A. Sanders. Minneapolis: Fortress, 1993.

Evdokimov, Paul. *The Sacrament of Love: The Nuptial Mystery in the Light of the Orthodox Tradition*. Translated by Anthony P. Gythiel and Victoria Steadman. Crestwood: St Vladimir's Seminary Press, 1985.

Falardeau, Ernest R. "Mutual Recognition of Baptism and Pastoral Care of Interchurch Marriages." *JES* 28 (1991) 63–73.

"Family Values, Christian Values: A Roundtable Discussion." *ChrCent* 113 (January 1996) 104–8.

Farley, Margaret A. "The Church and the Family: An Ethical Task." *Horizons* 10 (September 1983) 50–71.

Fee, Gordon D. "1 Corinthians 7:1 in the NIV." *JETS* 23 (1980) 308–314.

———. *New Testament Exegesis: A Handbook for Students and Pastors*. Rev. Ed. Louisville: Westminster John Knox, 1993.

———. *The First Epistle to the Corinthians*. NICNT. Edited by F. F. Bruce. Grand Rapids: Eerdmans, 1987.

Feinberg, Charles Lee. "The Image of God." *BibSac* 129/515 (1972) 235–46.

Ferguson, Everett. *Backgrounds of Early Christianity*. Grand Rapids: Eerdmans, 1993.

Ferm, Deane W. Review of *Putting Asunder*, by Phillips, Roderick. In *ChrCent* 25 (January 1989) 87–88.

Field, David. "Talking Points: The Divorce Debate-Where Are We Now?" *Themelios* 8/3 (1983) 26–31.

Filbeck, David. "Abuse in Marriage." *Missiology* 2 (1974) 225–35.

Filson, Floyd V. *The Gospel according to St. Matthew*. BNTC. London: A. & C. Black, 1975.

Findikyan, Michael. "Old Testament Readings in the Liturgy of Matrimony of the Armenian Apostolic Orthodox Church." *SVSQ* 33 (1989) 86–96.

Findlay, G. G. "St. Paul's First Epistle to the Corinthians." In *The Expositor's Greek Testament*. Edited by W. Robertso Nicoll. Vol. 2. Grand Rapids: Eerdmans, 1979.

Finney, Michael R. *A Biblical View of Divorce and Remarriage*. [online]. Available at http://www-personal.si.umich.edu/~rlm/gifs/gotopbtn.gif. Accessed on 30 June 2000.

Fitzmyer, Joseph A. "The Matthean Divorce Texts and Some New Palestinian Evidence." *TS* 37 (1976) 197–226.

———. *The Gospel according to Luke X–XXIV*. AB 28A. New York: Doubleday, 1985.

Fleming, Thomas V. "Christ and Divorce." *TS* 24 (March 1963) 106–20.

Foster, Michael Smith. *How Can a Marriage be Declared Null?* [online]. Available at http://www.rcab.org/marriage7.html#MARRIAGE%20FIRST. Accessed on 19 April 2001.

Fowler, Robert M. *Let the Reader Understand: Reader-Response Criticism and the Gospel of Mark*. Minneapolis: Fortress, 1991.

Frame, John M. "Men and Women in the Image of God." In *Recovering Biblical Manhood and Womanhood: A Response to Evangelical Feminism*. Edited by John Pipers and Wayne Grudem. Wheaton, IL: Crossway, 1991.

France, R. T. *Matthew: Evangelist and Teacher*. Grand Rapids: Zondervan, 1989.

Fransen, Piet. "Divorce on the Ground of Adultery-The Council of Trent (1563)." *Concilium* 5/6 (May 1970) 89–100.

Frazer, Elizabeth, Jennifer Hornsby, and Sabina Lovibond. *Ethics: A Feminist Reader*. Oxford: Blackwell, 1992.

Frei, Hans. "Apologetics, Criticism, and the Loss of Narrative Interpretation." In *Why Narrative? Readings in Narrative Theology*. Edited by Stanley Hauerwas and L. Gregory Jones. 45–64. Grand Rapids: Eerdmans, 1989.

Friberg, Timothy and Barbara. *Analytical Lexicon to the Greek New Testament*, 2000 edition. [electronic edition], BibleWorks v.5.0.020w, 2001.

"Friendly Divorce." *ChrCent* 103/30 (October 1986) 881–82.

Fuchs, Eric. *Sexual Desire and Love: Origins and History of the Christian Ethic of Sexuality and Marriage*. Translated by Marsha Daigle. Cambridge: James Clarke, 1983.

Fuerth, Patrick W. "Anglican-Roman Catholic Colloquium on Marriage." *JES* 17 (1980) 759–60.

Fuller, Russell. Review of . . . *And Marries Another: Divorce and Remarriage in the Teaching of the New Testament*, by Craig S. Keener. In *JETS* 38:2 (June 1995) 278–292. Electronic Edition by Galaxie Software, 1998.

Furnish, Victor Paul. "Belonging to Christ: A Paradigm for Ethics in First Corinthians." *Int* 44 (1990) 145–57.

Gaius. *Institutes*. Translated by Gordon and Robinson. [online]. Available at http://www.stoa.org/diotima/anthology/wlgr/wlgr-romanlegal132.shtml. Accessed on 25 December 2000.

———. *Institutes*. Translated by Gordon and Robinson. L. In *Women's Life in Greece and Rome*. Edited by Mary R. Lefkowitz and Maureen B. Fant. [online]. Available at http://www.stoa.org/diotima/anthology/wlgr/wlgr-romanlegal132.shtml. Accessed on 24 December 2004.

Garafalo, Robert C. "Habits of the Hearth: Co-dependence and Sacramental Marriage." *Worship* 65 (1991) 38–49.

Garland, David E., editor. "First Corinthians." *RevExp* 80 (1983) 313–425.

———. "A Biblical View of Divorce." *RevExp* 84 (1987) 419–32.

———. "The Christian's Posture Toward Marriage and Celibacy: 1 Corinthians 7." *RevExp* 80 (1983) 351–62.

———. *Reading Matthew: A Literary and Theological Commentary of the First Gospel*. New York: Crossroad, 1993.

Garland, Diana S. Richmond. "Divorce and the Church." *RevExp* 92 (1995) 419–34.

Garrard, James, editor. *Sex and the Christian Tradition*. Third Millennium. Edited by Jeremy Morris. London: MPG, 1999.

Gaudium et Spes, 48. Pastoral Constitution on the Church in the Modern World, Promulgated by His Holiness Pope Paul VI on December 7, 1965. Libreria Editrice Vaticana. [online]. Available at http://www.vatican.va/archive/hist_councils/ii_vatican_council/documents/vat-ii_cons_19651207_gaudium-et-spes_en.html. Accessed on 23 September 2004.

Geldard, Mark. "Jesus' Teaching on Divorce." *Churchman* 92 (1978) 134–43.

Geller, Markham J. "New Sources for the Origins of the Rabbinic Ketubah." *HUCA* 49 (1978) 227–45.

Gellius, Aulus. *Avli Gelli Noctes Atticae*. [online]. Available at http://www.gmu.edu/departments/fld/CLASSICS/gellius10.html#23m. Accessed on 19 March 2001.

———. *Attic Nights*. In *Women's Life in Greece and Rome*. Translated by Mary R. Lefkowitz and Maureen B. Fant. [online]. Available at http://www.stoa.org/diotima/anthology/wlgr/wlgr-romanlegal111.shtml, Accessed on 24 December 2004.

Genesis Rabbah: The Judaic Commentary to the Book of Genesis. A New American Translation. Vol.1. Translated by Jacob Neusner. Atlanta: Scholars, 1985.

Genné, William H. "Sex, Marriage and Family: An Update from Amsterdam." *JES* 16 (1979) 154–60.

Gibson, Colin S. *Dissolving Wedlock*. London: Routledge, 1994.

Gill, Robin, editor. *The Cambridge Companion to Christian Ethics*. Cambridge: Cambridge University Press, 2001.

Gillett, Shirley. "No Church to Call Home." In *Women, Abuse, and the Bible: How Scripture Can be Used to Hurt or Heal*. Edited by Catherine Clark Kroeger and James R. Beck, 106–14. Grand Rapids: Baker, 1996.

Gillingham, Susan E. *One Bible, Many Voices: Different Approaches to the Biblical Studies*. London: SPCK, 1998.

Gillman, John. Review of *Not Like the Gentiles*, by O. Larry Yarbrough. In *CBQ* 49 (1987) 164–65.

Glaser, John W. "Commands–Counsels: a Pauline teaching?" *TS* 31 (1970) 275–87.

Glasscock, Ed. "'The Husband of One Wife' Requirement in 1 Timothy 3:2." *BibSac* 140 (1983) 244–58.

Glasser, H. Paul, and Lois N. Glasser, editors. *Families in Crisis*. Readers in Social Problems. London: Harper & Row, 1970.

Glazier-McDonald, Beth. "Intermarriage, Divorce, and the Bat'-el Nekar: Insights Into Mal 2:10–16." *JBL* 106 (1987) 603–11.

Glenny, W. Edward. "1 Corinthians 7:29–31 and the Teaching of Continence in *The Acts of Paul and Thecla*." *GTJ* 11 (1990) 54–90.

GNM Morphology in BibleWorks for Windows 95/NT v.4.0.025e [o]. Logos Development Corporation, 1996.

Godet, Frederic Louis. *Commentary on First Corinthians*. Grand Rapids: Kregel, 1977.

———. *The Gospel of St. Luke*. Vol. 2. ICC. Edinburgh: T. & T. Clark, 1957.

Goldenberg, Robert. "Shammai, School of." In *ABD* 5:1158.

Goldingay, John. "The Old Testament and Christian Faith: Jesus and the Old Testament in Matthew 1–5, Part 1." *Themelios* 8/1 (1982) 4–10.

———. "The Old Testament and Christian Faith: Jesus and the Old Testament in Matthew 1–5, Part 2." *Themelios* 8/2 (1983) 5–12.

Gooch, Paul W. "Authority and Justification in Theological Ethics: A Study in 1 Corinthians 7." *JRE* 11 (1983) 62–74.

Goodling, Richard, and Cheryl A. Smith, "Clergy Divorce: A Survey of Issues and Emerging Ecclesiastical Structures." *JPC* 37 (1983) 277–91.

Gordis, Robert. "Hosea's Marriage and Message: A New Approach." *HUCA* 25 (1954) 9–35.

Gordon, Cyrus H. "Erēbu Marriage." In *Studies on the Civilization and Culture of Nuzi and the Hurrians*. Edited by M. A. Morrison and D. I. Owen, 155–160. Winona Lake, IN: Eisenbrauns, 1981.

Gordon, Lorni Heyman, and Morris Gordon. "A Format for an Ethical and Emotional Divorce." *JPC* 38 (1984) 288–93.

Gordon, Robert P. Review of *Marriage as a Covenant*, by Gordon Paul Hugenberger. In *VT* 46 (1996) 413–14.

Goslin, Thomas S. "Divorce, Spanish Style." *ChrCent* 98 (September 1981) 908–10.

Gould, Ezra P. *Critical and Exegetical Commentary on the Gospel according to St. Mark*. ICC. Edinburgh: T. & T. Clark, 1969.

Grabowski, John S. Review of *What Binds Marriage*, by Timothy J. Buckley. In *Worship* 73 (1999) 75–77.

Granqvist, Hilma. *Marriage Conditions in a Palestinian Village II*. Societas Scientarum Fennica, Commentationes Humanarum Litterarum, VI. Helsingfors: Centraltryckeriet, 1935.

Gratsias, Emmanuel. "The Effect of Mixed Marriage on the Parish." *GOTR* 40 (1995) 365–70.

The Greek New Testament (GNT). Edited by Kurt Aland, Matthew Black, Carlo M. Martini, Bruce M. Metzger, and Allen Wikgren, in cooperation with the Institute for New Testament Textual Research, Münster/Westphalia, Fourth Edition (with exactly the same text as the Nestle-Aland 27th Edition of the Greek New Testament). Stuttgart: United Bible Societies (UBS), (1966, 1968, 1975) and Deutsche Bibelgesellschaft (German Bible Society), (1993, 1994).

Greek Orthodox Archdiocese of America. *Divorces*. [online]. Available at http://www.goarch.org/search/oop/qfullhit.htw?CiWebHitsFile=%2Fgoa%2Fdetroit%2Fdivorces%2Ehtm&CiRestriction=divorce&CiBeginHilite=%3Cstrong+class%3DHit%3E&CiEndHilite=%3C%2Fstrong%3E&CiUserParam3=/search/query.asp&CiHiliteType=Full. Accessed on 21 April 2001.

Green, Barbara. "Jesus' Teaching on Divorce in the Gospel of Mark." *JSNT* 38 (1990) 67–75.
Green, Joel B., Scot McKnight, and I. Howard Marshall, editors. *Dictionary of Jesus and the Gospels*. Downers Grove, IL: InterVarsity, 1992
Greenberg, Blu. "Marriage in the Jewish Tradition." *JES* 22/1 (1985) 3–20.
Greenberg, Moshe. *Ezekiel 1–20*. AB 22. Garden City, NY: Doubleday, 1983.
Greengus, Samuel. "Bridewealth in Sumerian Sources." *HUCA* 61 (1990) 25–88.
Greinacher, Norbert. "The Problem of Divorce and Remarriage." *ThDig* 35/3 (1988) 221–26.
Grelot, Pierre. "The Human Couple in Scripture." *ThDig* 14/2 (1966) 137–42.
Grenz, Stanley J. "Theological Foundations for Male-Female Relationships." *JETS* 41 (1998) 615–30.
Griffith, Marie. "Wifely Submission: The SBC Resolution." *ChrCent* 115 (July 1998) 636–38.
Grosheide, F. W. *Commentary on the First Epistle to the Corinthians: The English Text with Introduction, Exposition and Notes*. Grand Rapids: Eerdmans, 1953.
Grosz, Katarzyna. "Dowry and Brideprice in Nuzi." In *Studies on the Civlization and Culture of Nuzi and the Hurrians*. Edited by M. A. Morrison and D. I. Owen, 161–82. Winona Lake, IN: Eisenbrauns, 1981.
Groves-Wheeler Westminster Morphology and Lemma Database (WTM, JDP). Chestnut Hill (Philadelphia) Westminster Theological Seminary, 1991–1992 (Release 1), 1994 (Release 2), 1996–2000 (Release 3), and 2001 (Release 3.5).
Grubbs, Judith Evans. *Law and Family in Late Antiquity: The Emperor Constantine's Marriage Legislation*. Oxford: Oxford University Press, 1999.
Guelich, Robert A. *Mark 1–8:26*. WBC 34A. Dallas: Word, 1989.
———. "Mark, Gospel of." In *DJG*, 512–25.
Gundry, Robert H. *Mark: A Commentary on His Apology for the Cross*. Grand Rapids: Eerdmans, 1993.
Guroian, Vigen. "Family and Christian Virtue in a Post-Christendom World: Reflections on the Ecclesial Vision of John Chrysostom." *SVSQ* 35 (1991) 327–50.
Gushee, David P. "The Divorce Epidemic: Evaluating Policy Options That Can Reduce Divorce." In *Christians and Politics Beyond the Culture Wars: An Agenda for Engagement*. Edited by David P. Gushee, 143–64. Grand Rapids: Baker, 2000.
———. *Getting Marriage Right: Realistic Counsel for Saving and Strengthening Relationships*. Grand Rapids: Baker, 2004.
Guthrie, Donald. "New Testament Study Helps: Mark's Gospel." In *Theology Website*. [online]. Available at http://www.theologywebsite.com/nt/mark.shtml. Accessed on 13 March 2001.
Hafemann, S. J. "Corinthians, Letters to the." In *DPHL*, 164–79.
Hagner, Donald A. "The New Testament, History, and the Historical-Critical Method." In *NTCI*, 72–96.
———. *Matthew 1–13*. WBC 33A. Dallas: Word, 1993.
———. *Matthew 14–28*. WBC 33B. Dallas: Word, 1995.
Halacha. *Women-Nashim, 22, Procreation*. [online]. Available at http://www.torah.org/learning/halacha-overview/chapter22.html. Accessed on 19 October 2000.
Halacha, 26. *Adultery-Sotah*. [online]. Available at http://www.torah.org/learning/halacha-overview/chapter26.html?print=1. Accessed on 18 October 2000.

Halacha, 23. *Divorce–Geirushin*. [online]. Available at http://www.torah.org/learning/halacha-overview/chapter23.html. Accessed on 03 December 2000.

Hamar, Paul A. *The Book of First Corinthians*. The Radiant Commentary of the New Testament. Springfiled: Gospel, 1980.

Hamburger, L. K., G. D. Saunders, and M. Hovey, "Prevalence of Domestic Violence in Community Practice and Rate of Physician Inquiry." *Family Medicine* 24 (1992) 283–87.

Hamilton, Victor P. "Marriage: Old Testament and Ancient Near East." In *ABD* 4:559–69.

Hammurabi's Code of Laws. Translated by L. W. King. [online]. Available at http://www.fordham.edu/halsall/ancient/hamcode.html#text. Accessed on 26 November 2000.

Harakas, Stanley S. "Emerging Ecumenical Families." *GOTR* 40/3–4 (1995) 346–63.

———. *The Orthodox Church: 455 Questions and Answers*. Minneapolis: Light & Life, 1987.

Haran, Manaham. *Midrashic and Literal Exegesis and the Critical Method in Biblical Research*. Studies in Bible. Jerusalem: Magnes, 1986.

Hardon, John A. *Divorce: Early Church vs. Eastern Orthodoxy*. [online]. Available at http://falcon.ic.net/~erasmus/RAZ332.HTM. Accessed on 20 April 2001.

Hare, Douglas R. A. *Matthew*. IBC. Louisville: John Knox, 1993.

Haring, Bernhard. "Pastoral Work Among the Divorced and Invalidly Married." *Concilium* 5/6 (1970) 123–30.

Harris, M. J. "Χωρίζω." In *NIDNTT*.

Harrison, R. K., B. K. Waltke, D. Guthrie, and G. D. Fee, *Biblical Criticism: Historical, Literary and Textual*. Grand Rapids: Zondervan, 1978.

Hart, Mark D. "Reconciliation of Body and Soul: Gregory of Nyssa's Deeper Theology of Marriage." *TS* 51 (1990) 450–78.

Hart, Nicky. *When Marriage Ends: A Study in Status Passage*. London: Tavistock, 1976.

Hauck, Friedrich. "Μοιχεύω." In *TDNT* 4 (1967) 729–35.

Hauerwas, Stanley. "Sex and Politics: Bertrand Russell and 'Human Sexuality.'" *ChrCent* 95 (April 1978) 417–22.

Hawkins, Alan J., Steven L. Nock, Julia C. Wilson, Laura Sanchez, and James D. Wright. "Attitudes about Covenant Marriage and Divorce: Policy Implications From a Three-State Comparison," *Family Relations* 51 (2002) 166–75.

Hawthorne, G. F. "Marriage and Divorce, Adultery and Incest." In *DPHL*, 594–601.

Hays, Richard B. "Scripture-Shaped Community: The Problem of Method in New Testament Ethics." *Int* 44 (1990) 42–55.

———. "The Church as a Scripture-Shaped Community: The Problem of Method in New Testament Ethics." *Evangelical Review of Theology* 18 (1994) 234–46.

———. *The Moral Vision of the New Testament: Community, Cross, New Creation. A Contemporary Introduction to the New Testament Ethics*. New York: HarperSanFrancisco, 1996.

———. *Echoes of Scripture in the Letters of Paul*. London: Yale University Press, 1989.

Heaney-Hunter, JoAnn C. "Gregory the Theologian: An Enlightened View of Marriage." *GOTR* 39 (1994) 227–41.

Heggen, Carolyn Holderread. "Religious Beliefs and Abuse." In *Women, Abuse, and the Bible: How Scripture Can be Used to Hurt or Heal*. Edited by Catherine Clark Kroeger and James R. Beck. 15–27. Grand Rapids: Baker, 1996.

Heijke, Jan P. "The Church's Pronouncements on Marriage: the African Contribution at the Synod in Rome (1980)." *Mission Studies* 2/1 (1985) 110.

Heil, John Paul. *The Gospel of Mark as a Model for Action: A Reader-Response Commentary.* New York: Paulist, 1992.

Helmer, Ringgren. *Israelite Religion.* Translated by David E. Green. Philadelphia: Fortress, 1966.

Hendricks, Hans Jurgens. "Juridical Aspects of the Marriage Metaphor in Hosea and Jeremiah." D. Lit. diss. University of Stcllenhosch, South Africa, nd. 1974.

Hendricks, Howard G. "Preparing Young People for Christian Marriage." *BibSac* 128 (1971) 245–62.

Hendriksen, William. *The Gospel of Mark.* New Testament Commentary. Edinburgh: The Banner of Truth Trust, 1976.

———. *The Gospel of Luke.* Grand Rapids: Baker, 1978.

———. *Matthew.* New Testament Commentary. Edinburgh: The Banner of Truth Trust, 1989.

Henry, Clinton D. *Perspective Paper on Marriage, Divorce, and Remarriage with Conclusions, Observations, Applications,* 2004. [online]. Available at www.marriagedivorceremarriage.com. Accessed on 24 January 2005.

Herodotus. *The Histories.* [online]. Available at http://perseus.csad.ox.ac.uk/cgi-bin/ptext?lookup=Hdt.+5.39.1. Accessed on 02 December 2000.

Herron Jr., Robert W. "Mark's Jesus on Divorce: Mark 10:1–12 Reconsidered." *JETS* 25 (1982) 274–83.

Hess, Ann L. "Catholics and Protestants in a UCC Church." *ChrCent* 107 (April 1990) 401–2.

Heth, William A. "Another Look at the Erasmian View of Divorce and Remarriage." *JETS* 25 (1982) 264–273.

———. "Divorce and Remarriage: The Search for an Evangelical Hermeneutic." *TJ* 16 (1995) 63–100.

———. "Divorce, but No Remarriage." In *Divorce and Remarriage: Four Christians Views.* Edited by H. Wayne House, 79–104. Downers Grove, IL: InterVarsity, 1990.

———. "Response to Divorce and Remarriage for Adultery or Desertion." by Thomas R. Edgar. In *Divorce and Remarriage: Four Christian Views.* Edited by H. Wayne House. 203–9. Downers Grove, IL: InterVarsity, 1990.

———. "The Changing Basis for Permitting Remarriage after Divorce for Adultery: The Influence of R. H. Charles." *TJ* 11 (1990) 144–161.

———. "The Meaning of Divorce in Matthew 19:3–9." *Chruchman* 98/2 (1984) 136–52.

———. "Unmarried 'For the Sake of the Kingdom' (Matthew 19:12) in the Early Church Unmarried." *GTJ* 8/1 (1987) 56–87.

———. *Why Remarriage Is Wrong.* [online]. Available at http://www.christianitytoday.com/ct/2000/135/48.o.html. Accessed on 25 April 2001.

———, and Gordon J. Wenham. *Jesus and Divorce: The Problem with the Evangelical Consensus.* London: Hodder and Stoughton, 1984.

Hetherington, Mavis E. and John Kelly. *For Better or For Worse: Divorce Reconsidered.* New York: Norton, 2002.

Hickey, James L. "Christian Ecumenical Marriages: A Major Pastoral Concern." *JES* 7 (1970) 707–20.

Hicks, Olan. *Bible Solutions to Divorce Problems.* [online]. Available at http://www.theophilus.org/divorce.html. Accessed on 25 April 2001.

Hiebert, D. Edmond. *An Introduction to the Pauline Epistles.* Chicago: Moody, 1954.

Hill, David. *The Gospel of Matthew.* NCBC. Grand Rapids: Eerdmans, 1972.

Hillers, Delbert R. *Covenant: The History of a Biblical Idea.* Maryland: Johns Hopkins, 1969.

Himes, Kenneth R., and James A. Coriden. "Pastoral Care of the Divorced and Remarried." *TS* 57 (1996) 97-123.

History of the Idea of Covenant Marriage. [online]. Available at http://www.divorcereform .org/cov.html. Accessed on 20 September 2004.

Hix, Douglas W. "Preaching and the Family Crisis." *JP* 17/4 (1994) 9-13.

Hodge, C., and A. Hodge. *Commentary on the Westminster Confession. The Confession of Faith: With Questions for Theological Students and Bible Classes.* Simpsonville SC: Christian Classics Foundation, 1996. [electronic edition based on the 1992 Banner of Truth reprint]. Logos Research Systems.

Hodge, Charles. *An Exposition of 1 and 2 Corinthians.* Wilmington, Delaware: Sovereign Grace, 1972.

Hoffmann, Paul. "Jesus' Saying about Divorce and Its Interpretation in the New Testament Tradition." *Concilium* 5/6 (1970) 51-88.

Hogan, Richard M. *John Paul II's New Vision of Human Sexuality, Marriage and Family Life.* [online]. Available at http://nfpoutreach.org/Hogan_New_Vision_marriage. htm. Accessed on 19 April 2001.

Hoge, Dean R. "Sociological Research on Interfaith Marriage in America." *GOTR* 40 (1995) 299-312.

Hoke, J. David. *Thinking Biblically About . . . Divorce and Remarriage: Matthew 19:1-10.* [online]. Available at http://www.horizonsnet.org/sermons/tba04.html. Accessed on 25 April 2001.

Holmes, Michael W. "The Text of the Matthean Divorce Passages: A Comment on the Appeal to Harmonization in Textual Decisions." *JBL* 109 (1990) 651-64.

Holmes, Paul A. "A Catechumenate for Marriage: Presacramental Preparation as Pilgrimage." *Journal of Ritual Studies* 6 (1992) 93-113.

The Holy Bible, American Standard Version, 1901 (ASV). Similar to the English Revised Version of 1881-1885, both being based upon the Hebrew Masoretic text for the OT and upon the Westcott-Hort Greek text for the NT. The machine readable database Copyright © 1988 by the Ellis Enterprises, CompuBible Concordance Study System by NASSCO, Lubbock, TX.

The Holy Bible, Revised Standard Version, 1952 (RSV). The authorized revision of the American Standard Version of 1901, Copyright © 1946, 1952, 1973 by the Division of Christian Education of the National Council of Churches of Christ in the United States of America.

Homer. *The Iliad.* Edited by Samuel Butler. [online]. Available at http://www.perseus.tufts. edu/cgi-bin/ptext?lookup=Hom.+Il.+3.1. Accessed on 29 October 2000.

Hooker, Morna D. *The Gospel according to Saint Mark.* BNTC. Peabody, MA: Hendrickson, 1991.

Hopkins, Paul E. "Families in Process." *JPC* 42 (1988) 329-37.

Horst, Friedrich. "Face to Face: The Biblical Doctrine of the Image of God." *Int* 4 (1950) 259-70.

House Committee on Law and Justice. *Marriage Contracts Restricting No-Fault Divorce - Washington State Bill.* [online]. Available at http://patriot.net/~crouch/wash/index. html, Accessed on 20 September 2004.

Howell Jr., Don N. "Pauline Eschatological Dualism and Its Resulting Tensions." *TJ* 14 (1993) 3–24.

Huehnergard, John. "Biblical Notes on Some New Akkadian Texts from Emar (Syria)." *CBQ* 47 (1985) 428–34.

Hugenberger, Gordon Paul. *Marriage as a Covenant: A Study of Biblical Law and Ethics Governing Marriage Developed from the Perspective of Malachi*. New York: Brill, 1994.

Hughes, Edward. "Reflections on Mixed Marriage in the Context of Parish Ministry." *GOTR* 40 (1995) 371–76.

Huizing, Peter. "Canon Law and Broken Marriages." *Concilium* 7 (September 1973) 13–21.

Hunt, A. S., C. C. Edgar, editors. *Select Papyri*, Loeb Classical Library; no. 266, 282, 360. Cambridge, MA: Harvard University Press; London: Heinemann, 1959–70. Vol.I. *Non-Literary Papyri: Private Affairs*.

Hunt, Richard A. "Marriage as Dramatizing Theology." *JPC* 41 (1987) 119–31.

Hunter, David G. *Marriage in the Early Church*. Translated and edited by David G. Hunter. 1992. Reprint, Eugene, OR: Wipf and Stock, 2001.

Hurley, Karen. "New Perspectives on Christian Marriage." In *Living Our Faith After the Changes: Explaining Catholic Thinking Since Vatican II*. 75–87. Edited by Jack Wintz. Cinncinnati: St. Anthony Messenger, 1977.

Hurtado, Larry W. *Mark*. New International Biblical Commentary. Peabody, MA: Hendrickson, 1993.

Ide, Arthur Frederick. *Marriage, Divorce, Remarriage, Woman and the Bible*. Garland, TX: Tangelwuld, 1995.

Ilan, Tal. "The Provocative Approach Once Again: A Response to Adiel Schremer." *HTR* 2 (1998) 203–4.

ILS 8393. Translated by E. Wistrand. In *Women's Life in Greece and Rome: A Source Book in Translation*, 2nd ed. Edited by Mary R. Lefkowitz and Maureen B. Fant. Baltimore: Johns Hopkins University Press, 1992.

Ingram, Martin. *Church Courts, Sex and Marriage in England, 1570–1640*. Cambridge: Cambridge University Press, 1987.

Instone-Brewer, David. "1 Corinthians 7 in the Light of the Graeco-Roman Marriage and Divorce Papyri." *TynBul* 51.2 (2001) 101–16.

———. "1 Corinthians 7 in the Light of the Jewish Greek and Aramaic Marriage and Divorce Papyri." *TynBul* 52.2 (2001) 225–43.

———. "Biblical Divorce and Remarriage: Short Article on Jesus' Teaching on Divorce." [online]. Available at http://www.tyndale.cam.ac.uk/brewer/index.html. Accessed on 30 June 2000.

———. "Jesus' Old Testament Basis for Monogamy." In *The Old Testament in the New Testament: Essays in Honour of J.L.North*. Edited by Steve Moyise, JNTS Supp 189. Sheffield: Sheffield Academic Press, 2000. 75–105. [online]. Available at http://www.tyndale.cam.ac.uk/Tyndale/PDF%20files/Monogamy.pdf. Accessed on 2 September 2004, pp.1–24.

———. "Jewish Women Divorcing Their Husbands in Early Judaism: The Background to Papyrus Se'elim 13." *HTR* 92 (1999) 349–57.

———. "Three Weddings and a Divorce: God's Covenant with Israel, Judah and the Church." [online]. Available at http://www.tyndale.cam.ac.uk/brewer/3Weddings.htm. Accessed on 30 June 2000.

———. *Biblical Divorce and Remarriage: The Jewish Background to the New Testament Teaching on Divorce*, ch.2 & 3. [online]. Available at http://www.tyndale.cam.ac.uk/brewer/Academic/Chap_02.htm. Accessed on 26 November 2000.

———. *Divorce and Remarriage in the 1st and 21st Century*. Cambridge: Grove, 2001. [online]. Available at http://www.tyndale.cam.ac.uk/Brewer/PPages/121/. Accessed on 2 September 2004.

———. *Divorce and Remarriage in the Bible: The Social and Literary Context*. Cambridge: Eerdmans, 2002.

———. *Divorce and Remarriage in the Church: Biblical Solutions for Pastoral Realities*. Carlisle, Cumbria: Paternoster, 2003. [online]. Available at http://www.tyndale.cam.ac.uk/Brewer/PPages/DRC/. Accessed on 2 September 2004.

Irenaeus. *Against Heresies*. [online]. Available at http://www.ccel.org/fathers2/ANF-01/anf01-60.htm#P7297_1937859. Accessed on 14 March 2001.

Irvin, Charles E., and Steven J. Raica. *On Marriage and Annulments in the Roman Catholic Church*. [online]. Available at http://www.rc.net/lansing/st_mary/essays/annulment.html. Accessed on 19 April 2001.

Isaeus. *Speeches*. [online]. Available at http://perseus.csad.ox.ac.uk/cgi-bin/ptext?lookup=Isaeus+8+35. Accessed on 02 December 2000.

Isaksson, Abel. *Marriage and Ministry in the New Temple: A Study with Special Reference to Matt 19:13–12 and 1 Cor 11:3–16*. Lund: Gleerup Lund, 1965.

Isocrates. *Speeches and Letters*. Edited by George Norlin. [online]. Available at http://perseus.csad.ox.ac.uk/cgi-bin/ptext?lookup=Isoc.+12+76. Accessed on 4 December 2000.

Jackson, Roger. *God's Ideal in Marriage*. [online]. Available at http://www.bible-infonet.org/ff/articles/marriage_divorce/107_11_01.htm. Accessed on 03 November 2000.

Jameson, Tonya. "Gay Unions Aren't Enemy of Marriage; Heterosexuals and Hollywood do Far More to Undermine it." *The Charlotte Observer*, 27 July 2003.

Jamieson, R., A. R. Fausset, and David Brown. *A Commentary, Critical and Explanatory, on the Old and New Testaments*. Oak Harbor, WA: Logos Research Systems, 1997. Libronix Digital Library System 2.0. 2000–2002.

Janzen, David. "The Meaning of *Porneia* in Matthew 5:32 and 19:9: An Approach from the Study of Ancient Near Eastern Culture." *JSNT* 80 (2000) 66–80.

Jennings, Theodore W. "Theological Perspectives on Sexuality." *The JPC* 33 (1979) 3–16.

Jeremias, J. "War Pls. Witwer?" *Zeitschrift für die neutestamentliche Wissenschaft* 25 (1926) 310–12.

Johannes, P. Louw and Eugene A. Nida, editors. *Greek-English Lexicon of the New Testament: Based on Semantic Domains*. New York: United Bible Societies, 1989.

———, editors. *Louw-Nida Greek-English Lexicon of the New Testament Based on Semantic Domains*. 2nd ed. New York: United Bible Societies, 1988.

Johansen, John H. "The Prophet Hosea: His Marriage and Message." *JETS* 14 (1971) 179–84.

Johnson, Arthur M. "San Francisco Bay Area A/RC Conference on Marriage." *JES* 16 (1979) 824–26.

Joncas, J. Michael. "Solemnizing the Mystery of Wedded Love: Nuptial Blessings in the Ordo Celebrandi Matrimonium 1991." *Worship* 70 (1996) 210–37.

Jones, David Clyde. "A Note on the LXX of Malachi 2:16." *JBL* 109 (1990) 683–85.

———. "Malachi on Divorce." *Presbyterion* 15/1 (1989) 16–22.

Jones, Eric F. "Clergy Beliefs, Preparation, and Practice in Premarital Counselling." *JPC* 48 (1994) 181–86.

Jordan, Mark D. *The Ethics of Sex.* New Dimensions to Religious Ethics. Oxford: Blackwell, 2002.

Josephus, Flavius. *Antiquitates Judaicae.* Edited by B. Niese. [online]. Available at http://www.perseus.tufts.edu/cgi-bin/ptext?lookup=J.+AJ+1.161. Accessed on 28 October 2000.

———. *Antiquities of the Jews.* Edited by William Whiston. [online]. Available at http://www.perseus.tufts.edu/cgi-bin/ptext?lookup=J.+AJ+18.109. Accessed on 20 January 2001.

———. "The Antiquities of the Jews." In *The Works of Josephus* [computer file]: complete and unabridged/ translated by William Whiston – electronic ed. of the new updated ed. – Peabody: Hendrickson, 1996, c1987. Oak Harbor, WA: Logos Research Systems, 1997.

———. "The Life of Flavius Josephus." In *The Works of Josephus.* Translated by William Whiston. Peabody, MA: Hendrickson, 1987.

———. "Against Apion." In *The Works of Josephus.* Translated by William Whiston. Peabody, MA: Hendrickson, 1987.

"Joseph and Aseneth." Translated by David Cook. In *The Apocryphal Old Testament.* Edited by H. F. D. Sparks, 473–503. Oxford: Oxford University Press, 1984. [online]. Available at http://www.bham.ac.uk/theology/goodacre/aseneth/translat.htm. [9/7/2004 12:01:10 PM]. Accessed on 22 December 2004.

Justinian, *Codex* 8.38.2. Translated by T. Honore. In *Women's Life in Greece and Rome: A Source Book in Translation.* Edited by Mary R. Lefkowitz and Maureen B. Fant, 2nd ed. Baltimore: Johns Hopkins University Press, 1992.

Justin Martyr. *1 Apology.* In *Ante-Nicene Fathers: Translations of The Writings of the Fathers Down to A.D. 325.* Edited by Alexander Roberts and James Donaldson. Vol. 1 and Vol. 2. *Christian Classics Ethereal Library.* Vol. 2. CD-ROM. Edited by Harry Plantinga. Wheaton, IL: Wheaton College, 1998.

Kalland, Earl S. Deuteronomy. *EBC.* Grand Rapids: Zondervan, 1999.

Kalluveettil, Paul. *Declaration and Covenant A Comprehensive Review of Covenant Formulae from the Old Testament and the Ancient Near East.* Rome: Biblical Institute Press, 1982.

Kampen, John. "A Reexamination of the Relationship Between Matthew 5:21–48 and the Dead Sea Scrolls." In *SBL Seminar Papers* (1990) 51–54.

Karmiris, John "Concerning the Sacraments." In *Eastern Orthodox Theology: A Contemporary Reader.* Edited by Daniel B. Clendenin. 21–31. Grand Rapids: Baker, 1995.

Kasper, Walter. *Theology of Christian Marriage.* London: Burns & Oates, 1980.

Keane, Philip S. S. *Sexual Morality: A Catholic Perspective.* London: Philip Sullivan Keane and Gill and Macmillan, 1977, 1980.

Keener, Craig S. . . . *And Marries Another: Divorce and Remarriage in the Teaching of the New Testament.* Peabody, MA: Hendrickson, 1991.

———. *Paul, Women and Wives: Marriage and Women's Ministry in the Letters of Paul.* Peabody: Hendrickson, 1992.

———. *The IVP Bible Background Commentary* (New Testament). Downers Grove, IL: InterVarsity, 1993.

———. *Free to Remarry.* [online]. Available at http://www.christianitytoday.com/ct/2000/135/48.0.html. Accessed on 25 April, 2001.

Kelleher, Stephen J. *Divorce and Remarriage for Catholics?* Garden City, NY: Doubleday, 1973.

Kelly, Kevin T. *New Directions in Sexual Ethics: Moral Theology and the Challenge of Aids*. London: Chapman, 1998.

Kelly, William. *Pope Gregory II on Divorce and Remarriage: A Canonical-Historical Investigation of the Letter Desiderabilem Mihi, with Special Reference to the Response Quod Proposuisti*. S.J. Analecta Gregoriana 2003. Rome: Gregorian University, 1976.

Kenkel, W. F. "Divorce." In *New Catholic Encyclopedia*. Edited by C. Joseph Nuesse, et al. Washington, DC: The Catholic University of America, 1967.

Kenslea, Timothy J. "Mixed Marriages: Faith and Family." *ChrCent* 95 (September 20 1978) 862–63.

Khodre, George. "Great Mystery: Reflections on the Meaning of Marriage." *SVSQ* 8/1 (1964) 31–37.

Kilgallen, John J. "To What are the Matthean Exception-Texts (5,32 and 19,9) an Exception?" *Bib* 61 (1980) 102–5.

Kilmartin, Edward J. "When is Marriage a Sacrament." *TS* 34 (1973) 275–86.

Kim, S. "Jesus, Sayings of." In *DPHL*, 474–92.

King, Philip J. Review of *Mariage et divorce dans l'évangile*, by Jacques Dupont. In *TS* 22 (1961) 466–67.

Kingdon, Robert M. *Adultery and Divorce in Calvin's Geneva*. Cambridge: Harvard University Press, 1995.

Kingsbury, Jack Dean. "The Place, Structure, and Meaning of the Sermon on the Mount within Matthew." *Int* 41 (1987) 131–43.

———. "The Plot of Matthew's Story." *Int* 46 (1992) 347–56.

———. *Matthew as Story*. 2nd ed. Philadelphia: Fortress, 1988.

Kirk, Kenneth E. *Marriage and Divorce*. London: Hodder and Stoughton, 1948.

Kirkwood, C. *Leaving Abusive Partners*. London: Sage, 1997.

Kline, Meredith G. *The Structure of Biblical Authority*. 2nd ed. Grand Rapids: Eerdmans, 1975.

Knight, George W. III. "Husbands and Wives as Analogues of Christ and the Church: Ephesians 5:21–33 and Colossians 3:18–19." In *Recovering Biblical Manhood and Womanhood: A Response to Evangelical Feminism*. Edited by John Pipers and Wayne Grudem, 161–75. Wheaton, IL: Crossway, 1991.

Knutson, Galen C. "Toward a Common Theology of Marriage." *Worship* 73 (1999) 125–39.

Koch, Dietrich-Alex. "Source Criticism (New Testament)." In *ABD* 6:165–71.

Köstenberger, Andreas. "Marriage and Family in the New Testament." In *MFBW*, 240–84.

Koszarycz, Yuri. *Divorce, Remarriage, and the Christian Tradition*. [online]. Available at http://www.mcauley.acu.edu.au/~yuri/ethics/Divorce.html. Accessed on 19 April 2001.

———. *Sexual Morality and the Catholic Tradition*. [online]. Available at http://www.mcauley.acu.edu.au/~yuri/ethics/sex.html. Accessed on 19 April 2001.

Kroeger, Catherine Clark, and Nancy Nason-Clark. *No Place for Abuse: Biblical and Practical Resources to Counteract Domestic Violence*. Downers Grove, IL: InterVarsity, 2001.

Krommydas, Nicholas. "Pastoral Response to Intra-Christian Marriages: An Orthodox Perspective." *GOTR* 40 (1995) 339–46.

Krug, E., et al., editors. *World Report on Violence and Health*. Geneva: World Health Organization, 2002.

Kruger, Gert. "Marrying a Divorced Person." *Orientation* 58–62 (1990–1991) 62–67.

Kubo, Sakae. "I Corinthians VII. 16: Optimistic or Pessimistic?" *NTS* 24 (1978) 539–44.

Kugleman, Richard. "1 Cor. 7:36–38." *CBQ* 10 (1948) 63–71.

Kümmel, Werner George. *Introduction to the New Testament*. Translated by Howard Clark Kee, 17th ed. Nashville: Abingdon, 1975.

Kuntz, J. M. "Is Marriage Indissoluble." *JES* 7 (1970) 333–37.

Lacey, T. A. *Marriage in Church and State*. London: SPCK, 1947.

LaDue, William. "The Expanding Limits of Lack of Due Discretion Cases." *Concilium* 7/9 (1973) 61–71.

Landsberger, Franz. "Illuminated Marriage Contracts: With Special Reference to the Cincinnati Ketubahs." *HUCA* 26 (1955) 503–42.

Lane, Belden C. "Two Schools of Desire: Nature and Marriage in Seventeenth-Century Puritanism." *CH* 69 (2000) 372–402.

Lane, Christopher. *PHYΞ ΗΑΠΑΞ*. [online]. Available at http://home1.gte.net/zzyzlane/write/poetry/rhapax06.html. Accessed on 21 December 2000.

Lane, William L. *The Gospel of Mark*. NICNT. Grand Rapids: Eerdmans, 1974.

Laney, J. Carl. "Deuteronomy 24:1–4 and the Issue of Divorce." *BibSac* 149/593 (1992) 4–16.

———. "No Divorce and No Remarriage." In *Divorce and Remarriage: Four Christians Views*. Edited by H. Wayne House, 15–54. Downers Grove, IL: InterVarsity, 1990.

———. "Paul and the Permanence of Marriage in 1 Corinthians 7." *JETS* 25 (1982) 284–95.

———. "Response to Divorce and Remarriage for Adultery or Desertion." by Thomas R. Edgar. In *Divorce and Remarriage: Four Christian Views*. Edited by H. Wayne House, 195–202. Downers Grove, IL: InterVarsity, 1990.

———. Review of *Divorce and Remarriage: Recovering the Biblical View*, by William F. Luck. In *JETS* 32 (1989) 251–52.

———. Review of *Jesus and Divorce*, by William A. Heth and Gordon J. Wenham. In *JETS* 30 (1987) 94–95.

———. *The Divorce Myth: A Biblical Examination of Divorce and Remarriage*. Minneapolis: Bethany, 1981.

Laughery, G. J. "Paul: Anti-marriage? Anti-sex? Ascetic? A Dialogue with 1 Corinthians 7:1–40." *EvQ* 69 (1997) 109–28.

Lawler, Michael G. "Faith, Contract, and Sacrament in Christian Marriage: A Theological Approach." *TS* 52 (1991) 712–31.

———. "The Mutual Love and Personal Faith of the Spouses as the Matrix of the Sacrament of Marriage." *Worship* 65 (1991) 339–61.

———. Review of *From Sacrament to Contract: Marriage, Religion, and Law in the Western Tradition*, by John Witte. In *TS* 60 (1999) 180–81.

———. *Ecumenical Marriage and Remarriage: Gifts and Challenges to the Churches*. Mystic, CT: Twenty Third Publications, 1990.

Lawler, Michael G., Gail S. Risch, Lisa A. Riley. "Church Experience of Interchurch and Same-Church Couples." *Family Ministry* 13 (1999) 36–46.

Lawler, Ronald, Joseph M. Boyle Jr., and William E. May. *Catholic Sexual Ethics: A Summary, Explanation, and Defence*. Indiana: Our Sunday Visitor, 1985.

Lawton, Robert B. "Genesis 2:24: Trite or Tragic?" *JBL* 105 (1986) 97–98.

Lazor, Paul. "A Review of Pastoral Guidelines on Holy Matrimony in the Orthodox Church in America." *SVSQ* 26/3 (1982) 173–83.

Legrand, Lucien. "Celibacy: Death and Sacrifice." *ThDig* 11/2 (1963) 114–18.

Lehmkuhl, Aug. "Divorce (in Moral Theology)." Translated by Listya Sari Diyah. In *The Catholic Encyclopedia*, v.V. [online]. Available at http://www.newadvent.org/cathen/05054c.htm. Accessed on 18 April 2001.

Lenski, R. C. H. *The Interpretation of I and II Corinthians*. Minneapolis: Augsburg, 1937.

———. *The Interpretation of St. Mark's Gospel*. Minneapolis: Augsburg, 1961.

———. The Interpretation of St. Matthew's Gospel. Minneapolis: Augsburg, 1943.

Leonard, Bill J. "Celibacy as a Christian Lifestyle in the History of the Church." *RevExp* 74 (1977) 21–32.

Lepper, John. "Implications From my Corner: If We Build it, Will They Come?" *JFM* 15/4 (2001) 29–30.

Lesko, Barbara. *Women's Earliest Records From Ancient Egypt and Western Asia Proceedings of the Conference on Women in the Ancient Near East. Brown University, Providence Rhode Island November 5-7, 1987*. Atlanta: Scholars, 1989.

Letham, Robert. Review of *Divorce and Remarriage: Biblical Principles and Pastoral Practice*, by Andrew Cornes. In *Westminster Theological Journal* 57 (1995) 273–75.

Leupold, H. C. *Exposition of Genesis*. Vol.1. Grand Rapids: Baker, 1942.

Levitt, Laura S. "Covenant or Contract? Marriage as Theology." *Cross Currents* 48 (1998) 169–84.

L'Huillier, Peter, Bp. "Novella 89 of Leo the Wise on Marriage: An Insight into Its Theoretical and Practical Impact." *GOTR* 32 (1987) 153–62.

———. "The Indissolubility of Marriage in Orthodox Law and Practice." *SVSQ* 32 (1988) 199–221.

Liddell and Scott's Greek-English Lexicon. Abridged ed. Oxford: Oxford University Press, 1979.

Lincoln, A. T. *Ephesians*. WBC 42. Dallas: Word, 2002. Nashville: Thomas Nelson. Libronix Digital Library System 2.0. 2000–2002.

Lincoln, Timothy D. "Sacramental Marriage: A Possibility for Protestant Theology." *American Theological Library Association Summary of Proceedings* 49 (1995) 205–16.

Litfin, A Duane. "Biblical View of the Marital Roles: Seeking a Balance." *BibSac* 133 (1976) 330–37.

Lloyd-Jones, D. Martyn. *Studies in the Sermon on the Mount*. Grand Rapids: Eerdmans, 1993.

Lochet, Abbe Louis. "The Ends of Marriage." *ThDig* 1/1 (1953) 21–27.

Long, Thomas G. "Something Old, Something New: Rethinking the Marriage Service." *JP* 9/3 (1986) 14–21.

Louisiana House Bill No.234. Section 1. R.S. 9:237.C. Enacted 22 June 2001. [online]. Available at http://www.divorcereform.org/la01.html. Accessed on 20 September 2004.

Louw-Nida Lexicon in BibleWorks for Windows 95/NT v.4.0.025e [o]. Lotus Development Corporation, 1996.

Luck, William F. *Divorce and Remarriage: Recovering the Biblical View.* San Francisco: Harper & Row, 1987.

———. Review of *The Divorce Myth: A Biblical Examination of Divorce and Remarriage*, by J. Carl Laney. In *JETS* 26 (1983) 469–501.

Lull, Timothy F. "Ecumenical Marriage: Pastoral Problem or Opportunity?" *JES* 16 (1979) 643–50.

Lutting, Bettie. "I Have Lost All Feeling for My Marriage Partner-Should I Get a Divorce." *Orientation* 58–62 (December 1990–1991) 117–22.

Luz, Ulrich. *The Theology of the Gospel of Matthew.* Translated by J. Bradford Robinson. New Testament Theology. Cambridge: Cambridge University Press, 1995.

LXX Septuaginta (LXT) (Old Greek Jewish Scriptures). Edited by Alfred Rahlfs. Stuttgart: Württembergische Bibelanstalt / Deutsche Bibelgesellschaft (German Bible Society), 1935.

Lynch, J. E. "Mixed Marriages in the Aftermath of 'Matrimonia Mixta.'" *JES* 11/4 (1974) 637–59.

———. Review of *Pope Gregory II on Divorce and Remarriage: A Canonical-Historical Investigation of the Letter Desiderabilem Mihi, with Special Reference to the Response Quod Proposuisti*, by William Kelly. In *TS* 38 (1977) 795–97.

Lysias. *Speeches.* In *Lysias* with an English translation by W. R. M. Lamb. LCL. Cambridge: Harvard University Press; London: William Heinemann, 1930. [online]. Available at http://www.perseus.tufts.edu/cgi-bin/ptext?lookup=Lys.+2+69. Accessed on 29 October 2000.

MacArthur, John. *Divorce and Remarriage.* [online]. Available at http://www.webzonecom.com/ccn/bible-s/divorce.txtm. Accessed on 25 April 2001.

MacLeod, David J. "The Problem of Divorce." *Emmaus Journal* 1/1 (1991) 138–57.

———. "The Problem of Divorce, Part 3: The Teaching of Jesus." *Emmaus Journal* 3/1 (1994) 3–48.

———. *The Problem of Divorce: The Teaching of Paul.* [online]. Available at http://www.emmaus.edu/ej_div.html. Accessed on 25 April 2001.

Macquarrie, John. *Christian Unity and Christian Diversity.* London: SCM, 1975.

Mahoney, Aidan. "New Look at the Divorce Clauses in Mt 5:32 and 19:9." *CBQ* 30 (1968) 29–38.

Malick, David. *An Introduction to the Gospel of Mark.* [online]. Available at http://www.bible.org/docs/nt/books/mar/mrk_intr.htm. Accessed on 14 March 2001.

Maller, Allen S. "Reducing the Risks of Divorce: A Responsibility of Religious Educators." *Religious Education* 87 (1992) 471–78.

Mamula, Maja, and Gordana Pavleković. "Tjelesni, psihički i socijalni znakovi zlostavljanja žene u obitelji." U *Nasilje nad ženom u obitelji.* Uredile: Marina Ajduković i Gordana Pavlekovič, 103–5. Zagreb: društvo za psihološku pomoć, 2000.

Mamula, Maja, and Marina Ajduković. "Dinamika zlostavljanja unutar obitelji." U *Nasilje nad ženom u obitelji.* Uredile: Marina Ajduković i Gordana Pavleković. 81–87. Zagreb: društvo za psihološku pomoć, 2000.

Mamula, Maja. "Zdravstvenene i psihološke posljedice spolnog nasilja nad ženama." U *Nasilje nad ženom u obitelji.* Uredile: Marina Ajduković i Gordana Pavleković, 93–101. Zagreb: društvo za psihološku pomoć, 2000.

Manful, J. K. *Divorce.* [online]. Available at http://home.freeuk.net/otchereh/divorce.htm. Accessed on 25 April 2001.

Mann, C. S. *Mark.* AB 27. Garden City, NY: Doubleday, 1986.

Mann, Jacob. "Rabbinic Studies in the Synoptic Gospels." *HUCA* 1 (1924) 323–55.

Mansingh, A., and P. Ramphal. "The Nature of Interpersonal Violence in Jamaica." *West Indian Medical Journal* 42 (1993) 53–56.

Mare, W. Harold. *I Corinthians*. EBC 10. Grand Rapids: Zondervan, 1976.

Marriage and the Church's Task: The Report of the General Synod Marriage Commission. London: CIO, 1978.

"Marriage Breakdown." *ChrCent* 87 (December 1970) 1528.

Marriage Contract of a Former Slave Girl Who is Subject to Paramoné, 420 B.C. Translated by H. L. Ginsberg. [online]. Available at http://ccat.sas.upenn.edu/~humm/Topics/Contracts/marri05.html. Accessed on 25 November 2000.

Marriage and Divorce Papyri of the Ancient Greek, Roman and Jewish World: A Collection of Papyri from 4th C BCE to 4th C CE. D. Instone-Brewer 2000. [online]. http://www.tyndale.cam.ac.uk/Brewer/MarriagePapyri/Index.html. Accessed on 2 September 2004.

"Marriage Requirements." *ChrCent* 103/19 (June 1986) 545–46.

"Married Catholic Priests." *ChrCent* 107/14 (1990) 1057.

"A Married Roman Catholic Priest." *ChrCent* 104 (November 1987) 1056–1057.

Marshall, Christopher D. *Faith as a Theme in Mark's Narrative*. Cambridge: Cambridge University Press, 1989.

Marshall, Howard. *The Gospel of Luke: A Commentary on the Greek Text*. NIGTC. Exeter: Paternoster, 1978.

———. *Understanding the New Testament: Mark*. London: Scripture Union, 1978.

———. "Divorce." In *NIDNTT*.

———. "Ἀπολύω." In *NIDNTT*.

———. "Historical Criticism." In *New Testament Interpretation: Essays on Principles and Methods*. Edited by I. Howard Marshall, 126–136. Exeter: Paternoster, 1977.

Marterns, Elmer A. *God's Design: A Focus on Old Testament Theology*. Grand Rapids: Baker, 1981.

Martin, Dale B. Review of *The Moral Vision of the New Testament: A Contemporary Introduction to New Testament Ethics*, by Richard B. Hays. In *JBL* 117 (1998) 358–60.

Martin, James D. "Forensic Background to Jeremiah 3:1." *VT* 19 (1969) 82–92.

Martin, Ralph. *Mark: Evangelist and Theologian*. Contemporary Evangelical Perspectives. Grand Rapids: Zondervan, 1973.

Martin, Thomas R. *An Overview of Classical Greek History from Homer to Alexander*. [online]. Available at http://perseus.csad.ox.ac.uk/cgi-bin/ptext?doc=Perseus:text:1999.04.0009:head%3D%23197. Accessed on 21 December 2000.

Martinez, German. "Marriage as Worship: a Theological Analogy." *Worship* 62 (July 1988) 332–53.

———. "The Newly Revised Roman Rite for Celebrating Marriage." *Worship* 69 (1995) 127–42.

Martos, Joseph. "A New Conceptual Context for the Sacramentality of Marriage." *Horizons* 22 (1995) 214–36.

Mathews, Kenneth A. *Genesis 1–11:26*. The New American Commentary: An Exegetical and Theological Exposition of the Holy Scripture NIV Text. Nashville: Broadman & Holman, 1996.

"Matrimonia Mixta: Mixed Blessing." *ChrCent* 87 (May 1970) 588–89.

Matthews, Victor H. "Marriage and Family in the Ancient Near East." In *MFBW*, 1–32.

Maximus, Valerius. *Memorable Deeds and Sayings*. In *Women's Life in Greece and Rome*. Translated by Mary R. Lefkowitz and Maureen B. Fant. [online]. Available at http://www.stoa.org/diotima/anthology/wlgr/wlgr-romanlegal109.shtml. Accessed on 24 December 2004.

———. *Memorable Deeds and Sayings*. In *Women's Life in Greece and Rome: A Source Book in Translation*. 2nd ed. Translated by Mary R. Lefkowitz and Maureen B. Fant. Baltimore: Johns Hopkins University Press, 1992.

McCarthy, David Matzko. *Sex and Love in the Home: A Theology of the Household*. London: SCM, 2001.

McCarthy, Dennis J. *Old Testament Covenant: A Survey of Current Opinions*. Oxford: Blackwell, 1973.

———. *Treaty and Covenant: A Study in Form in the Ancient Oriental Documents and in the Old Testament*. Rev. ed. Analecta Biblica 21. Rome: Biblical Institute Press, 1978.

McCormick, Richard A. "Notes on Moral theology: 1979." *TS* 41 (1980) 98–150.

———. "Notes on Moral Theology: 1981." *TS* 43 (1982) 69–124.

———. "Notes on Moral Theology: Divorce and Remarriage, April–September 1971." *TS* 33 (1972) 91–100.

———. "Notes on Moral Theology: Divorce and Remarriage, April–September 1974." *TS* 36 (1975) 100–17.

———. "Notes on Moral Theology: Pastoral Problems." *TS* 27 (1966) 620–29.

———. "Notes on Moral Theology: Theology and Divorce, April–September 1970." *TS* 32 (1971) 107–22.

McDaniel, Charles Gene. "Children in Divorce Cases: The Wisdom of Solomon Challenged." *ChrCent* 89 (February 1972) 202–4.

McDonagh, Enda. "Man and Woman Are in the Image of God and We Are All Brothers and Sisters in Christ." *Concilium* 130 (1979) 115–24.

McFadden, Dennis E. "Just What did Jesus Say About Divorce?" *ChrTo* 25 (November 1981) 46–47.

McKelway, Alexander J. "Perichoretic Possibilities in Barth's Doctrine of Male and Female." *The Princeton Seminary Bulletin* 7/3 (1986) 231–43.

McKenzie, John L. "The Gospel according to Matthew." In *The Jerome Biblical Commentary*. Edited by Raymond E. Brown, S. S. et.al. Vol.2., The New Testament and Topical Articles, 62–114. Norwich: Fletcher & Son, 1977.

———. "The Literary Characteristics of Genesis 2–3." *ThDig* 6/1 (1958) 19–24.

McKnight, Edgar V. "Presuppositions in New Testament Study." In *Hearing the New Testament: Strategies for Interpretation*. Edited by Joel B. Green. 278–301. Grand Rapids: Eerdmans, 1995.

McKnight, Scot. "Matthew, Gospel of." In *DJG*, 526–41.

———. "Source Criticism." In *NTCI*, 136–72.

McLennan, Gregor. *Pluralism*. Minneapolis: University of Minnesota Press, 1995.

McManus, Frederick R. "The Council in Trullo: A Roman Catholic Perspective." *GOTR* 40 (1995) 79–96.

McRae, William J. "The Church's Role in Marriage Enrichment." *BibSac* 144 (July-September 1987) 330–39.

Meeks, Wayne A. *The Origins of Christian Morality, The First Two Centuries*. New Haven: Yale University Press, 1993.

Meier, John P. "Matthew, Gospel of." In *ABD* 4:622–41.

Meilaender, Gilbert. "Love Abides: The Posture of Faithfulness." *ChrCent* 117 (October 2000) 990–91.

Mendenhall, G. E. "Covenant." In *IDB* 1 (1962) 717.

Merz, Annette. "Why Did the Pure Bride of Christ (2 Cor. 11.2) Become a Wedded Wife (Eph. 5:22–33)? Theses About the Intertextual Transformation of an Ecclesiological Metaphor." Translated by Brian McNeil. *JSNT* 79 (2000) 131–47.

Meyendorff, John. *Marriage: An Orthodox Perspective*. New York: St. Vladimir's Seminary Press, 1975.

Meyer, Harding and Lukas Vischer, editors. "The Theology of Marriage and the Problem of Mixed Marriages." Paragraph 18. In *Growth in Agreement: Reports and Agreed Statements of Ecumenical Conversations on a World Level*, 286. New York: Paulist, 1984. Quoted in Timothy D. Lincoln, "Sacramental Marriage: A Possibility for Protestant Theology." *American Theological Library Association Summary of Proceedings* 49 (1995) 205.

Meyer, Lauree Hersch and Graydon F. Snyder. "Sexuality: Its Social Reality and Theological Understanding in 1 Corinthians 7." In *SBL Seminar Papers* 19 (1980) 359–70.

Meyers, Carol. "Procreation, Production, and Protection: Male-Female Balance in Early Israel." *Journal of the American Academy of Religion* 51 (1983) 569–95.

Midrash Rabbah—Genesis XVII:3. Translated by D. Mandel. *The Soncino Midrash Rabbah*. Soncino, 1983, Davka Corporation's Judaic Classics Library. Version IIf by David Kantrowitz. Institute for Computers in Jewish Life. Davka Corporation & Judaica, 1999.

Midrash Rabbah—The Song of Songs I:30. *The Soncino Midrash Rabbah*, Soncino, 1983. Davka Corporation's Judaic Classics Library. Version IIf. English Translation by D. Mandel. Brooklyn: Judaica, 1983.

Mileant, Alexander. *The Orthodox Church: Some Contemporary Moral Questions*. [online]. Available at http://www.fatheralexander.org/booklets/english/catechism_ext.htm. Accessed on 22 April 2001.

Milgrom, Jacob. *Cult and Conscience: The Asham and the Priestly Doctrine of Repentance*. Leiden: Brill, 1976.

Millar, J. G. "The Ethics of Deuteronomy: An Exegetical and Theological Study." *TynBul* 46 (1995) 389–92.

Miller, Kevin E. "The Nuptial Eschatology of Revelation 19–22." *CBQ* 60 (1998) 301–18.

Milligan, George. *Selections From the Greek Papyri: Edited with Translations and Notes*. Chicago: Ares, 1910.

Mindlin, M., M. J. Geller, and J. E. Wansbrough, editors. *Figurative Language in the Ancient Near East*. London: School of Oriental and African Studies, 1987.

The Mishnah. A New Translation by Jacob Neusner. New Haven: Yale University Press, 1988.

Moiser, Jeremy. "A Reassessment of Paul's View of Marriage with Reference to 1 Cor 7." *JSNT* 18 (1983) 103–22.

Molldrem, Mark J. "A Hermeneutic of Pastoral Care and the Law/Gospel Paradigm Applied to the Divorce Texts of Scripture." *Int* 45 (1991) 43–54.

Moloney, Francis J. "Matthew 19:3–12 and Celibacy: A Redactional and Form Critical Study." *JSNT* 2 (1979) 42–60.

Monti, Joseph. *Arguing about Sex: The Rhetoric of Christian Sexual Morality*. Albany: State University of New York, 1995.

Moo, D. J. "Law." In *DJG*, 450–61.

Moore, Trevor Wyatt. "The Ecumenical Then." *ChrCent* 88 (February 1971) 192–93.
Morgan, Richard Lyon. "A Ritual of Remarriage." *JPC* 37 (1983) 292–301.
Morton, Timothy S. *From Marriage to Remarriage: Has a Remarried Christian Committed an "Unpardonable Sin?"* [online]. Available at http://members.citynet.net/morton/marriage.htm. Accessed on 25 April 2001.
Moulton, James Hope and George Millgan. *The Vocabulary of the Greek Testament. Illustrated from the Papyri and Other Non-Literary Sources*. 1930. Reprint, Grand Rapids: Eerdmans, 1985.
Mulder, John M. Review of *From Sacrament to Contract: Marriage, Religion, and Law in the Western Tradition*, by John Witte Jr. In *JFM* 12 (1998) 68–69.
Munro, Joyce Huth. "The Family: Cradle of Spiritual Development." *RevExp* 75 (1978) 45–55.
Murphy-O'Connor, Jerome. "Essenes in Palestine." *Biblical Archaeologist* 40 (1977) 100–24.
———. "Sex and Logic in 1 Corinthians 11:2–16." *CBQ* 42 (1980) 482–500.
———. "The Corinth that Saint Paul Saw." *Biblical Archaeologist* 47 (1984) 147–59.
———. "The Divorced Woman in 1 Cor 7:10–11." *JBL* 100 (1981) 601–6.
Murray, John. "Divorce." *Westminster Theological Journal* 11 (1949) 105–22.
Myers, Allen C. "Marriage." In *The Eerdmans Bible Dictionary*. Edited by Allen C. Myers. Grand Rapids, MI: Eerdmans, 1975.
Najim, Michel. *The Theology of the Orthodox Sacrament of Matrimony and Its Implications in our Family Life*. [online]. Available at http://www.antiochian.org/theology/theology_of_the_orthodox_marriage.htm. Accessed on 22 April 2001.
National Conference of Catholic Bishops Standing Conference of Oriental Orthodox Churches. *Oriental Orthodox-Roman Catholic Interchurch Marriage*. Washington, DC: United States Catholic Conference, 1995.
Needman, Thomas. "How Not to Fail Hurting Couples." *ChrTo* (December 14, 1992). [online]. Available at http://www.christianityonline.com/ct/2000/135/49.0.html. Accessed on 2 September 2000.
Nelson, James B. *Embodiment: An Approach to Sexuality and Christian Theology*. Minneapolis: Augsburg, 1978.
Nemoy, Leon. "Two Controversial Points in the Karaite Law of Incest." *HUCA* 49 (1978) 247–65.
Neuer, Werner. *Man and Woman: In Christian Perspective*. Wheaton, IL: Crossway, 1991.
Neufeld, E. *Ancient Hebrew Marriage Laws. With Special References to General Semitic Laws and Customs*. London: Longmans, Green, 1944.
The New American Standard Bible, NASB (NAS[1977] and NAU[1995]), Copyright © by The Lockman Foundation, 1960–1995.
The New International Version 1984 (NIV). "Quotations designated (NIV) are from THE HOLY BIBLE: NEW INTERNATIONAL VERSION®. NIV®. Copyright © 1973–1984 by International Bible Society. Used by permission of Zondervan. All rights reserved."
The New Jerusalem Bible (NJB), with Deutero-Canon. Garden City, NY: Doubleday, 1985.
The New King James Version (NKJV, NKJ). Thomas Nelson, 1982.
New Louisiana Covenant Marriage Law Regular Session, 1997, House Bill No. 756 [Louisiana], Part VII. Covenant Marriage. [online]. Available at http://patriot.net/~crouch/cov/index.html. Accessed on 20 September 2004.

New Louisiana Covenant Marriage Law. Regular Session, 1997, House Bill No. 756, Section 4. R.S. 9:307.A. [online]. Available at http://patriot.net/~crouch/cov/index.html, Accessed on 20 September 2004.

New Louisiana Covenant Marriage Law. Regular Session, 1997, House Bill No.756. Section 3. Part VII.273.A.(1). [online]. Available at http://patriot.net/~crouch/cov/index.html, Accessed on 20 September 2004.

The New Revised Standard Version of the Bible (NRSV, NRS). The Scripture quotations contained herein are from the New Revised Standard Version (NRSV) of the Bible, Copyrighted 1989 by the Division of Christian Education of the National Council of the Churches of Christ in the United States of America, and are used by permission. BibleWorks™ includes the various NRSV OT Apocryphal-Deutero-Canonical books.

New, M. L. Berliner. "Mental Health Service Utilization by Victims of Crime," *Journal of Traumatic Stress* 13 (2000) 693–707.

Newbigin, Lesslie. *Foolishness to the Greeks: The Gospel and Western Culture.* Geneva: World Council of Churches, 1986.

———. *The Gospel in a Pluralist Society.* Grand Rapids: Eerdmans, 1989.

Newman, Barclay M. Jr., editor. *A Concise Greek-English Dictionary of the New Testament.* United Bible Societies, 1971.

Newman, Louis. "The Work of David Weiss Halivni: A Source-Critical Commentary to *b Yebamot* 87b." *Semeia* 27 (1983) 93–101.

Nichols, J. Randall. "Rethinking Some Aspects of Ministry to the Divorced: A Theological Retake." *JPC* 42 (1988) 101–15.

Nicholson, Ernest W. *God and His People: Covenant and Theology in the Old Testament.* Oxford: Clarendon, 1986.

"No Benefit of Clergy." *ChrCent* 100/9 (1983) 1010.

Nock, Steven L., James D. Wright, and Laura Sanchez, "America's Divorce Problem." *Society* 36/4 (1999) 43–52.

Nolland, John. "The Gospel Prohibition of Divorce: Tradition History and Meaning." *JSNT* 58 (1995) 19–35.

———. *Luke 9:21–18:34.* WBC 35B. Dallas: Word, 1993.

Noonan, John T. "Indissolubility of Marriage and Natural Law." *ThDig* 19/1 (1971) 9–14.

———. *Power to Dissolve: Lawyers and Marriages in the Courts of the Roman Curia.* Cambridge, MA: Belknap of Harvard University Press, 1972.

North, R. "Flesh, Covering, and Response, Ex. XXI:10." *VT* 5 (1955) 204–206.

NovT Graece (BNT), Nestle-Aland 27th Edition. Stuttgart: Deutsch Bibelgesellschaft, 1993.

Oates, Wayne E. "The Psychosocial Dynamics of Family Living." *RevExp* 75 (1978) 3–174.

O'Brien, John A. "Why Priests Marry: The Roman Clergy's Cry for Optional Celibacy Deserves Support From all People of Good Will." *ChrCent* 87 (April 1970) 415–19.

O'Callaghan, Denis. "Marriage as Sacrament." *Concilium* 5/6 (1970) 101–10.

Oden, Thomas C., & Christopher A. Hall, editors. *Mark.* Ancient Christian Commentary on Scripture. New Testament II. Downers Grove, IL: InterVarsity, 1998.

O'Doherty, Eamonn. Review of *Mariage et divorce dans l'évangile*, by Jacques Dupont. In *CBQ* 22 (1960) 343–45.

O'Donovan, Oliver. "Transsexualism and Christian Marriage." *JRE* 11 (1983) 135–62.

Olsen, V. Norskov. Review of *Jesus and Divorce: The Problem with the Evangelical Consensus*, by William A. Heth and Gordon J. Wenham. In *ChrTo* 29 (December 13, 1985) 43–44.

———. *The New Testament Logia on Divorce: A Study of Their Interpretation from Erasmus to Milton*. Tübingen: Mohr/Siebeck, 1971.

Olshewsky, Thomas M. "A Christian Understanding of Divorce." *JRE* 7 (1979) 117–38.

Olszowy-Schlanger, Judith. *Karaite Marriage Documents From the Cairo Geniza: Legal Tradition and Community Life in Mediaeval Egypt and Palestine*. Leiden: Brill, 1998.

Oppenheimer, Helen. *The Marriage Bond*. Leighton, Buzzard: Faith, 1976.

O'Rourke, John J. "Does the New Testament Condemn Sexual Intercourse Outside Marriage?" *TS* 37/3 (1976) 478–79.

———. "Hypotheses Regarding 1 Corinthians 7:36–38." *CBQ* 20 (1958) 292–98.

Orr, William F., and James Arthur Walther. *I Corinthians*. AB 32. Garden City, NY: Doubleday, 1976.

Orsy, Ladislas. "Faith, Sacrament, Contract, and Christian Marriage: Disputed Questions." *TS* 43 (1982) 379–98.

———. "Relief in Difficult Marriage Cases." *ThDig* 19/1 (1971) 13–22.

———. "The Function of Ecclesial Decision: A Theological Evaluation of Marriage Tribunals." *Concilium* 7/9 (1973) 34–46.

———. *Marriage in Canon Law: Texts and Comments, Reflections and Questions*. Wilmington, DE: Glazier, 1986.

Orthodox Church in America Tenth All-American Council. *Synodal Affirmations On Marriage, Family, Sexuality, and the Sanctity of Life*. [online]. Available at http://www.oca.org/pages/ocaadmin/documents/All-American-Council/10-Miami-1992/Synodal-Affirmations.html. Accessed on 22 April 2001.

Osborne, Grant R. "Preaching the Gospels: Methodology and Contextualization." *JETS* 27 (1984) 27–42.

———. "Round Four: The Redaction Debate Continues." *JETS* 28 (1985) 399–411.

———. "The Evangelical and Redaction Criticism: Critique and Methodology." *JETS* 22 (1979) 306–23.

———. "Hermeneutics/Interpreting Paul." In *DPHL*, 388a–97b.

———. "Redaction Criticism." In *DJG*, 662–69.

———. "Redaction Criticism." In *NTCI*, 188–224.

O'Shea, William J. "Marriage and Divorce: The Biblical Evidence." *ThDig* 19/1 (1971) 4–8.

Otten, Willemien. "Augustine on Marriage, Monasticism, and the Community of the Church." *TS* 59 (1998) 385–405.

Owings, Timothy L. "John 2:1–11." *RevExp* 85 (1988) 533–37.

Oxyrhynchus Papyrus 282. G. In *Women's Life in Greece and Rome: A Source Book in Translation*. 2nd ed. Translated by Mary R. Lefkowitz and Maureen B. Fant. Baltimore: Johns Hopkins University Press, 1992.

Ozment, Steven. "Marriage and the Ministry in the Protestant Churches." *Concilium* 8 (October 1972) 39–56.

Padgett, Alan. "Feminism in First Corinthians: A Dialogue With Elisabeth Schussler Fiorenza." *The Evangelical Quarterly* 8 (1986) 121–32.

Page, Sydney H. T. "Marital Expectations of Church Leaders in the Pastoral Epistles." *JSNT* 50 (1993) 105–20.

Palmer, Paul F. "Christian Marriage: Contract or Covenant?" *TS* 33 (1972) 617–65.

Pamphilus, Eusebius. *The Church History of Eusebius* 6.25.4. In *Nicene and Post-Nicene Fathers*. Edited by Philip Schaff and Henry Wace. Series II. Vol.I. *Christian Classics Ethereal Library*. Vol.2. CD-ROM. Edited by Harry Plantinga. Wheaton, IL: Wheaton College, 1998.

Parsons, Greg W. "Guidelines for Understanding and Utilizing the Song of Songs." *BibSac* 156/624 (1999) 399–422.

Patrinacos, Nicon D. "Sacramental Character of Marriage." *GOTR* 1 (1955) 118–32.

Patsavos, Lewis J. "A Canonical Response to Intra-Christian and Inter-religious Marriages." *GOTR* 40 (1995) 287–98.

———. "Mixed Marriages and the Canonical Tradition of the Orthodox Church." *GOTR* 23 (1978) 243–56.

Paul. *Opinions L*. Translated by Mary R. Lefkowitz and Maureen B. Fant. [online]. Available at http://www.uky.edu/ArtsSciences/Classics/wlgr/wlgr-romanlegal120.html. Accessed on 16 October 2000.

———. *Opinions*. In *Women's Life in Greece and Rome: A Source Book in Translation*, 2nd ed. Translated by Mary R. Lefkowitz and Maureen B. Fant. Baltimore: Johns Hopkins University Press, 1992.

Pavleković, Gordana, Marina Ajduković, and Maja Mamula. "Nasilje nad ženom u obitelji: osobni, obiteljski ili javnozdravstveni problem?" U *Nasilje nad ženom u obitelji*." Uredile: Marina Ajduković i Gordana Pavleković, 17–28. Zagreb: društvo za psihološku pomoć, 2000.

Payer, Pierre J. *The Bridling of Desire: Views of Sex in the Later Middle Ages*. Toronto: University of Toronto Press, 1993.

Pečnik, N. *Nasilje u ljubavnim vezama mladića i djevojaka i stavovi prema fizičkom zlostavljanju žena*. Diplomski rad. Zagreb: Odsjek za psihologiju, Filozofski fakultet, 1990. Citirano u Mariana Ajduković, et al., "Nasilje u partnerskim odnosima," u *Nasilje nad ženom u obitelji*. Uredile: Marina Ajduković i Gordana Pavleković, 57–67. Zagreb: društvo za psihološku pomoć, 2000.

Pelser, Gert. Review of *Paul on Marriage and Celibacy: The Hellenistic Background of 1 Corinthians 7*, by Will Deming. In *CBQ* 58 (1996) 544–45.

Pentecost, J. D. Review of *The Divorce Myth: A Biblical Examination of Divorce and Remarriage*, by J. Carl Laney. In *BibSac* 139/553 (1982) 85.

Perkins, Judith B. "This World or Another? The Intertextuality of the Greek Romances, the Apocryphal Acts and Apuleius' Metamorphoses." *Semeia* 80 (1997) 247–60.

Pestman, P. W. *Marriage and Matrimonial Property in Ancient Egypt: A Contribution to Establishing the Legal Position of the Woman*. Leiden: Brill, 1961.

Peters, G. W. *Divorce and Remarriage*. Chicago: Moody, 1972.

Petersen, Norman R. *Semeia 16: Perspectives on Mark's Gospel*. [online]. Available at http://shemesh.scholar.emory.edu:6336/dynaweb/Semeia/Semeia_16/@Generic__BookView. Accessed on 23 October 1999.

Phillips, Anthony. "Another Look at Adultery." *JSOT* 20 (1981) 3–25.

Phillips, Roderick. *Putting Asunder: A History of Divorce in Western Society*. Cambridge: Cambridge University Press, 1988.

———. *Untying the Knot: A Short History of Divorce*. Cambridge: Cambridge University Press, 1991.

Philo. *The Special Laws*. Translated by C. D. Yonge. New updated ed. Peabody, MA: Hendrickson, 1993.

Phipps, William E. "Jesus on Marriage and the Afterlife." *ChrCent* 102 (April 1985) 327–28.

Pichon, Christophe. "La prohibition des mariages mixtes par Néhémie (XII 23–31)." *VT* 47 (1997) 168–99.

Pinkston, Fr. Bob. "When A Marriage Fails." [online]. Available at http://www.rc.net/org/paulist/cicdoc6.htm. Accessed on 02 November 2000.

Piper, John. "The Authority and Meaning of the Christian Canon: A Response to Gerald Sheppard on Canon Criticism." *JETS* 19 (1976) 92.

Pitkin, Barbara. Review of *Marriage and Divorce in the Thought of Martin Bucer*, by Herman J. Selderhuis. In *CH* 69/4 (December 2000) 894–96.

Plato. *Plato in Twelve Volumes.* Vols. 10 & 11. Translated by R. G. Bury. Cambridge, MA: Harvard University Press; London: William Heinemann, 1967, 1968. [online]. Available at http://www.perseus.tufts.edu/cgi-bin/ptext?lookup=Plat.+Laws+774a. Accessed on 29 October 2000.

———. *Platonis Opera.* Edited by John Burnet. Oxford University Press. 1903. [online]. Available at http://www.perseus.tufts.edu/cgi-bin/ptext?lookup=Plat.+Laws+840a. Accessed on 28 October 2000.

Plummer, Alfred. *An Exegetical Commentary on the Gospel according to S. Matthew.* Grand Rapids: Eerdmans, 1956.

"Pluralism." In *Encyclopædia Britannica*, (electorinic editon). Ultimate Reference Suite DVD, Encyclopædia Britannica, 2004.

Plutarch. *Lives.* Translated by Bernadotte Perrin. [online]. Available at http://www.perseus.tufts.edu/cgi-bin/ptext?lookup=Plut.+Lys.+30.1. Accessed on 16 October 2000.

———. *Lives: Alcibiades.* In *Plutarch's Lives.* Translated by Bernadotte Perrin [Cambridge, MA: Harvard University Press, 1914]. [online]. Available at http://www.perseus.tufts.edu/cgi-bin/ptext?lookup=Plut.+Alc.+8.1. Accessed on 23 December 2004.

———. *Moralia.* Translated by R. Warner. G. In *Women's Life in Greece and Rome.* Edited by Mary R. Lefkowitz and Maureen B. Fant. [online]. Available at http://www.stoa.org/diotima/anthology/wlgr/wlgr-privatelife242.shtml. Accessed on 24 December 2004.

P.Mur.19. [online]. Available at http://www.tyndale.cam.ac.uk/Brewer/MarriagePapyri/TableAD2.htm. Accessed on 28 August 2004. Translation based on Roland de Vaux, Jozef T. Milik and Pierre Benoit, *Discoveries in the Judaean Desert*, II: *Les grottes de Muraba'at*, 104–109. Oxford, Clarendon 1961, and Leone J. Archer, *Her Price Is Beyond Rubies: The Jewish Woman in Greco-Roman Palestine*, 298–299. JSOTSup 60, Sheffield: Sheffield Academic Press, 1990. As amended by Yigael Yadin, Jonas C. Greenfield, and Ada Yardeni, "Babatha's *Ketubba*." *IEJ* 44 (1994) 86, and in "Expedition D–the Cave of the Letters." *IEJ* 12 (1962) 227–57, p. 249, and by Tal Ilan in "Notes and Observations on a Newly Published Divorce Bill from the Judean Desert." *HTR* 89 (1996) 195–202 [198–99]. Quoted in David Instone-Brewer, "1 Corinthians 7 in the Light of the Jewish Greek and Aramaic Marriage and Divorce Papyri." *Tyndale Bulletin* 52.2 (2001) 237 and David Instone-Brewer, "1 Corinthians 7 in the Light of the Jewish Greek and Aramaic Marriage and Divorce Papyri." *Tyndale Bulletin* (2001). [online]. Available at http://www.tyndale.cam.ac.uk/Brewer/MarriagePapyri/1Cor_7b.htm, Accessed on 26 August 2004.

Pomazansky, Michael. *Orthodox Dogmatic Theology: A Concise Exposition*, trans. Hieromonk Seraphim Rose. Platina, CA: Saint Herman of Alaska Brotherhood, 1994.

Pontifical Council for the Family. *Family, Marriage and "De Facto" Unions*. Libreria Editrice Vaticana. [online]. Available at http://www.vatican.va/roman_curia/pontifical_councils/family/documents/rc_pc_family_doc_20001109_de-facto-unions_en.html. Accessed on 30 August 2005.

Pope John Paul II. *Letter to Families from Pope John Paul II*. (1994 – Year of the Family). Libreria Editrice Vaticana. [online]. Available at http://www.vatican.va/holy_father/john_paul_ii/letters/documents/hf_jp-ii_let_02021994_families_en.html. Accessed on 29 August 2005.

Porter, Stanley E. and Paul Buchanan. "On the Logical Structure of Matt 19:9." *JETS* 34 (1991) 336–41.

Posey, Lawton W. "Before God and These Witnesses." *ChrCent* 95 (May 1978) 526–27.

Potts, Kenneth. "Martin Buber's 'Healing Dialogue' in Marital Therapy: A Case Study." *JPC* 48 (1994) 325–38.

Powell, Mark Allan. "Narrative Criticism." In *Hearing the New Testament: Strategies for Interpretation*. Edited by Joel B. Green, 239–55. Grand Rapids: Eerdmans, 1995.

———. "Toward a Narrative-Critical Understanding of Matthew." *Int* 45 (1992) 341–46.

———. "Toward a Narrative-Critical Understanding of Mark." *Int* 47 (1993) 341–46.

———. *What is Narrative Criticism?* Guides to Biblical Scholarship. Minneapolis: Fortress, 1990.

Powers, B. Ward. *Marriage and Divorce: The New Testament Teaching*. Petersham: Jordan, 1987.

The Princeton Geniza Project. [online]. Available at http://www.princeton.edu/~geniza/. Accessed on 19 November 2000.

Price, Elizabeth. "Sexual Misunderstanding: The True Cause of the Magisterium's Ban on Contraception." *Cross Currents* 30 (1980) 27–37.

Prince, Gerald. "Narratology." In *The Cambridge History of Literary Criticism: From Formalism to Poststructuralism*. Edited by Raman Selden, 8:110–30. Cambridge: Cambridge University Press, 1995.

P.Ryl.II.154. The Duke Databank of Documentary Papyri. [online]. Available at http://www.perseus.tufts.edu/cgi-bin/ptext?doc=Perseus%3Abo%3Apap%2CP.Ryl.&query=2%3A154. Accessed on 27 August 2004. Translation based on A. S. Hunt, C. C. Edgar, editors, *Select Papyri*, Loeb Classical Library; no. 266, 282, 360. Cambridge, MA: Harvard University Press; London: Heinemann, 1959–70, v.I. *Non-Literary Papyri: Private Affairs*, pp. 12–17. Quoted in David Instone-Brewer, "1 Corinthians 7 in the Light of the Graeco-Roman Marriage and Divorce Papyri." *TynBul* 51.2 (2001) 103, 104 and David Instone-Brewer, "1 Corinthians 7 in the Light of the Graeco-Roman Marriage and Divorce Papyri." *TynBul* (2001). [online]. Available at http://www.tyndale.cam.ac.uk/Brewer/MarriagePapyri/1Cor_7a.htm. Accessed on 26 August 2004.

P.Tebt.I.104. The Duke Databank of Documentary Papyri. P.Tebt.: The Tebtunis Papyri. [online]. Available at http://www.perseus.tufts.edu/cgi-bin/ptext?doc=Perseus%3Abo%3Apap%2CP.Tebt.&query=1%3A104. Accessed on 26 August 2004. Translation based on A. S. Hunt, C. C. Edgar, editors, *Select Papyri*, Loeb Classical Library; no. 266, 282, 360. Cambridge, MA: Harvard University Press; London: Heinemann, 1959–70, v.I. *Non-Literary Papyri: Private Affairs*, pp. 5–9. Quoted in David Instone-Brewer, "1 Corinthians 7 in the Light of the Graeco-Roman Marriage and Divorce Papyri." *TynBul* 51.2 (2001) 108 and David Instone-Brewer, "1 Corinthians 7 in the Light of the Graeco-Roman Marriage and Divorce Papyri." *TynBul* (2001). [online].

Available at http://www.tyndale.cam.ac.uk/Brewer/MarriagePapyri/1Cor_7a.htm. Accessed on 26 August 2004.

Pummer, Reinhard. *Samaritan Marriage Contracts and Deeds of Divorce.* Vol. 1. Wiesbaden: Harrassowitz, 1993.

———. *Samaritan Marriage Contracts and Deeds of Divorce.* Volume II. With the collaboration of Abraham Tal 1997. Wiesbaden: Otto Harrassowitz, 1993.

P.Yadin.10. [online]. Available at http://www.tyndale.cam.ac.uk/Brewer/MarriagePapyri/TableAM.htm. Accessed on 28 August 2004. Quoted in Yigael Yadin, Jonas C. Greenfield, and Ada Yardeni, "Babatha's Ketubba." *IEJ* 44 (1994) 75–101. Translation based on Yigael Yadin, Jonas C. Greenfield, and Ada Yardeni, "Babatha's Ketubba." *IEJ* 44 (1994) 75–101. Quoted in David Instone-Brewer, "1 Corinthians 7 in the Light of the Jewish Greek and Aramaic Marriage and Divorce Papyri." *TynBul* 52.2 (2001) 231 and David Instone-Brewer, "1 Corinthians 7 in the Light of the Jewish Greek and Aramaic Marriage and Divorce Papyri." *TynBul* (2001). [online]. Available at http://www.tyndale.cam.ac.uk/Brewer/MarriagePapyri/1Cor_7b.htm. Accessed on 26 August 2004.

P.Yadin.18 = P.Babatha.18. [online]. Available at http://www.tyndale.cam.ac.uk/Brewer/MarriagePapyri/TableJM.htm. Accessed on 28 August 2004. Translation based on Naphtali Lewis, Yigael Yadin, and Jonas C. Greenfield, editors, *The Documents from the Bar Kokhba Period in the Cave of Letters: Greek Papyri,* 80. Jerusalem: Israel Exploration Society: Hebrew University of Jerusalem: Shrine of the Book, 1989. Quoted in David Instone-Brewer, "1 Corinthians 7 in the Light of the Jewish Greek and Aramaic Marriage and Divorce Papyri." *TynBul* 52.2 (2001) 226–227 and David Instone-Brewer, "1 Corinthians 7 in the Light of the Jewish Greek and Aramaic Marriage and Divorce Papyri." *TynBul* (2001). [online]. Available at http://www.tyndale.cam.ac.uk/Brewer/MarriagePapyri/1Cor_7b.htm. Accessed on 26 August 2004.

Quesnell, Quentin. "Made Themselves Eunuchs for the Kingdom of Heaven (Mt 19:12)." *CBQ* 30 (1968) 335–58.

Rabinowitz, Jacob J. "The 'Great Sin' in Ancient Egyptian Marriage Contracts." *Journal of Near Eastern Studies* 18 (1959) 73.

Ragland, Jack. Review of *Marriage After Modernity,* by Adrian Thatcher. In *JFM* 15/4 (2001) 62–63.

Rallis, Irene Kerasote. "Nuptial Imagery in the Book of Hosea: Israel as the Bride of Yahweh." *SVSQ* 34 (1990) 197–219.

Rambam. "List of 613 Mitzvot." In *Halakhah.* Edited by Tracey R Rich. [online]. Available at http://www.jewfaq.org/613.htm. Accessed on 08 October 2000.

Ramm, Bernard L. "Survey of Church Views on Divorce." *Eternity* (June 1976) 51. Quoted in David J. MacLeod, "The Problem of Divorce." *Emmaus Journal Volume* 1/1 (1991) 156. Electronic Edition by Galaxie Software, 1999.

———. *The Right, The Good and the Happy.* Waco: Word, 1971. Quoted in David J. MacLeod, "The Problem of Divorce." *Emmaus Journal Volume* 1/1 (1991) 156. Electronic Edition by Galaxie Software, 1999.

Ramsaran, Rollin A. "More Than an Opinion: Paul's Rhetorical Maxim in First Corinthians 7:25–26." *CBQ* 57 (1995) 531–41.

Ramsey, Paul. "Biblical Norm of Righteousness." *Int* 24 (1970) 419–29.

———. "Human Sexuality in the History of Redemption." *JRE* 16 (1988) 56–86.

Ranke-Heinemann, Uta. *Eunuchs for Heaven: The Catholic Church and Sexuality*. Translated by John Browniohn. London: Andre Deutsch, 1990.
Reardon, Ruth. "Mixed Marriages: The Cost of Eucharistic Division." *Ecumenical Review* 44 (1992) 65–72.
Reibstein, Janet and Martin Richards. *Sexual Arrangements: Marriage and Affairs*. London: Heinemann, 1992.
Reisser, H. "Discipline, Prudence, Immorality, Prostitute." In *NIDNTT*.
"Remarriage of Divorced in Church of England." *ChrCent* 117 (February 2000) 175–76.
Rengstorf. "Δουλόω, καταδουλόω." In *Theological Dictionary of the New Testament*. Edited by Gerhard Kittel. Vol.II. Translated by Geoffrey W. Bromiley. Grand Rapids: Eerdmans, 1965.
Resnick, Irven M. "Marriage in Medieval Culture: Consent Theory and the Case of Joseph and Mary." *CH* 69/2 (June 2000) 350–371.
Reynolds, Philip Lyndon. *Marriage in the Western Church: The Christianization of Marriage During the Patristic and Early Medieval Periods*. Boston: Brill, 2001.
Rich, Tracey R, editor. *Marriage: The Marital Relationship*. [online]. Available at http://www.jewfaq.org/marriage.htm#Relationship;. Accessed on 08 October 2000.
———. *Divorce: Inequality of the Sexes*. [online]. Available at http://www.jewfaq.org/divorce.htm. Accessed on 08 October 2000.
Richards, Larry. "Divorce and Remarriage Under a Variety of Circumstances." In *Divorce and Remarriage: Four Christians Views*. Edited by H. Wayne House. Downers Grove, IL: InterVarsity, 1990.
Richardson, Peter. "Judgment in Sexual Matters in 1 Corinthians 6:1–11." *NovT* 25 (1983) 37–58.
Richter, Klemens. "The Liturgical Celebration of Marriage. The Problems Raised by Changing Theological and Legal Views of Marriage." *Concilium* 7/8 (September 1973) 81–83.
Rich, Tracey R., editor. *Divorce: Inequality of the Sexes*. [online]. Available at http://www.jewfaq.org/divorce.htm. Accessed on 08 October 2000.
Ricoeur, Paul. "The Narrative Function." In *Semeia 13: The Poetics of Faith: Essays Offered to Amos Niven Wilder Part 2*. [online]. Available at http://shemesh.scholar.emory.edu:6336/dynaweb/Semeia/Semeia_13/@Generic__BookView, Accessed on 23 October 1999.
Riley, Patrick G. *Civilizing Sex: On Chastity and the Common Good*. Edinburgh: T. & T. Clark, 2000.
Risch, Gail S. "The First Five Years of Marriage: Resources and Programs for Ministry." *JFM* 15/4 (2001) 22–28.
"Rising to the Occasion." *ChrCent* 111 (February 1994) 159–60.
Ritschl, Dietrich. "Ecumenism." In *Dictionary of Mission: Theology, History, Perspectives*. Edited by Karl Muller, et al., 120–130. New York: Orbis, 1998.
Ritzer, Korbinnian. "Secular Law and the Western Church's Concept of Marriage." *Concilium* 5/6 (1970) 67–75.
Robbins, Vernon K. "Form Criticism: New Testament." In *ABD* 2:841–44.
Roberts, William P. Review of *Divorce and Remarriage in the Catholic Church*, by Gerald D. Coleman. In *Horizons* 17 (1990) 158–59.
Robertson, Acrhibald, and Alfred Plummer. *The First Epistle of St. Paul to the Corinthians*. ICC. Edinburgh: T. & T. Clark, 1911.
Robertson, Ian. *Society: A Brief Introduction*. New York: Worth, 1989.

Rock, Stanley A. "Marriage, Ministry and the Families that Shaped Us." *JFM* 13 (1999) 25–36.
Rogers, William H. "Marriage Enrichment Conferences for the Local Church." *RevExp* 75 (1978) 25–43.
Rohrbaugh, Richard L. "The Social Location of the Markan Audience." *Int* 47 (1993) 380–95.
Rolfe, David J. "Preparing the Previously Married for Second Marriage." *JPC* 39 (1985) 110–26.
Rosner, Brian S. *Paul, Scripture, and Ethics: A Study of 1 Corinthians 5–7*. Grand Rapids: Baker, 1994.
Ross, Susan A. "The Aesthetic and the Sacramental." *Worship* 59 (1985) 2–17.
Roth, Martha T. *Babylonian Marriage Agreements 7th–3rd Centuries B.C.* Neukirchen-Vluyn: Neukirchener, 1989.
Rothman, Emily F., Alexander Butchart, Magdalena Cerda, *Intervening with Perpetrators of Intimate Partner Violence: A Global Perspective*. Geneva: World Health Organization, 2003.
Rousseau, Richard W. "The Vatican and Mixed Marriages." *ChrCent* 87 (August 1970) 963–70.
Rowatt, G. Wade. "Divorce: an Open Perspective for the Church." *RevExp* 74 (1977) 51–61.
———. "Managing Conflict in the Christian Family." *RevExp* 75 (1978) 57–66.
Rubio, Julie Hanlon. Review of *Marriage After Modernity*, by Adrian Thatcher. In *TS* 61 (2000) 783–85.
Ryrie, Charles C. "Biblical Teaching on Divorce and Remarriage." *GTJ* 3 (1982) 178–93.
S, M. A. "Divorce." In *Encyclopedia of Early Christianity*. Edited by Everett Ferguson. New York: Garland, 1988.
Sabourin, Leopold S.J. *The Gospel according to St. Matthew*. Vol. 2. Bandra: St. Paul, 1982.
Sailhamer, John H. "Genesis." In *EBC* 2. Grand Rapids: Zondervan, 1999.
———. *The Pentateuch as Narrative: A Biblical-Theological Commentary*. Grand Rapids: Zondervan, 1992.
Sandholm, Gayle L. "The Changing Face of Marriage and Extramarital Relationships." *JPC* 43 (1989) 249–58.
Sarna, Nahum M. *Genesis*. The JPS Torah Commentary. Jerusalem: The Jewish Publication Society, 1989.
Saucy, Robert L. "Husband of One Wife." *BibSac* 131 (1974) 229–40.
Scanzoni, John. "Family: Crisis or Change?" *ChrCent* 98 (August 1981) 794–99.
Schaper, Donna. "Marriage: the Impossible Commitment?" *ChrCent* 96 (June 1979) 669–72.
Schatkin, Margaret S. "Divorce." In *Encyclopedia of Early Christianity*. Edited by Everett Ferguson. New York: Garland, 1977.
Schick, Ludwig. "Marriage and Celibacy for the Sake of the Kingdom of Heaven." *ThDig* 36/2 (1989) 135–40.
Schillebeeckx, E. "Christian Marriage and the Reality of Complete Marital Breakdown." In *Catholic Divorce: The Deception of Annulments*. Edited by Pierre Hegy and Joseph Martos, 97–98. London: Continuum, 2000.
———. *Marriage: Secular Reality and Saving Mystery: Marriage in the Old and New Testaments*. Vol. 1. Translated by N. D. Smith. London: Sheed and Ward, 1965.

———. *Marriage: Secular Reality and Saving Mystery: Marriage in the History of the Church.* Vol. 2. Translated by N. D. Smith. London: Sheed and Ward, 1965.

Schmeiser, James A. "Marriage: New Alternatives." *Worship* 55 (1981) 23–34.

Schmidt, Karl Ludwig, and Martin Anton Schmidt. "Σκληρότης." In *TDNT* 5 (1964) 1028.

Schremer, Adiel. "Divorce in Papyrus Se'elim 13 Once Again: A Reply to Tal Ilan." *HTR* 91 (1998) 191–202.

Schroeder, C. Paul. "The Mystery of Love: Paradigms of Marital Authority and Submission in the Writings of St John Chrysostom." *SVSQ* 44 (2000) 143–68.

Schroeder, Christoph. "'A Love Song:' Psalm 45 in the Light of Ancient Near Eastern Marriage Texts." *CBQ* 58 (1996) 417–32.

Schwartz-Salant, Nathan. "For Better or For Worse." *Living Pulpit* 1/4 (1992) 20–21.

Scott, Elizabeth S. "Rational Decision-making about Marriage and Divorce." *Virginia Law Review* 76 (1990).

Scott, J. Julius Jr. "The Synoptic Gospels." In *EBC*. Grand Rapids: Zondervan, 1999.

Scott, Kieran, and Michael Warren. *Perspectives on Marriage: A Reader.* Oxford: Oxford University Press, 2001.

Scourby, Alice. "The Orthodox Church and Intra-Christian Marriages." *GOTR* 40 (1995) 313–19.

Seboldt, Roland H. "Spiritual Marriage in the Early Church: A Suggested Interpretation of 1 Cor 7:36–38." *CTM* (February 1959) 103–19.

———. "Spiritual Marriage in the Early Church: A Suggested Interpretation of 1 Cor 7:36–38. (Continued)." *CTM* (March 1959) 176–89.

Selderhuis, Herman J. *Marriage and Divorce in the Thought of Martin Bucer.* Translated by John Vriend and Lyle D. Bierma. Sixteenth Century Essays and Studies 48. Kirksville, MO: Truman State University Press, 1999.

Selms, A.van. *Marriage and Family Life in Ugaritic Literature.* Pretoria Oriental Series 1. London: Luzac, 1954.

Senior, Donald. *What Are They Saying about Matthew?* New York: Paulist, 1983.

Sheed, F. J. *Nullity of Marriage.* Rev. ed. New York: Sheed & Ward, 1959.

The Shepherd of Hermas. In *Ante-Nicene Fathers: Translations of The Writings of the Fathers Down to A.D. 325.* Edited by Alexander Roberts and James Donaldson. Vol. 2. Grand Rapids: Eerdmans, 1973. Christian Classics Ethereal Library. Vol. 2. CD-ROM. Edited by Harry Plantinga. Wheaton, IL: Wheaton College, 1998.

Sheppard, Gerald. "Canon Criticism: The Proposal of Brevard Childs and an Assessment for Evangelical Hermeneutics." *Studia Biblica et Theologica* (October 1974) 10.

Sherrard, Philip. *Christianity and Eros: Essays on the Theme of Sexual Love.* London: SPCK, 1976.

Shideler, Mary McDermott. "An Amicable Divorce." *ChrCent* 88 (May 1971) 553–55.

———. "Are Sanity and Sanctity at Odds: The Range of Permissible Variation in Ethical Behaviour." *ChrCent* 89 (October 1972) 1004–7.

Shivanandan, Mary. *Crossing the Threshold of Love: A New Vision of Marriage in the Light of John Paul II's Anthropology.* Edinburgh: T. & T. Clark, 1999.

Shriver, Donald W., Jr. Review of *From Sacrament to Contract: Marriage, Religion, and Law in the Western Tradition,* by John, Jr. Witte. In *ChrCent* 115 (December 1998) 1191–92.

Siculus, Diodorus. *Library*. Translated by C. H. Oldfather. [online]. Available at http://perseus.csad.ox.ac.uk/cgi-bin/ptext?lookup=Diod.+12.18.1. Accessed on 21 December 2000.
Silva, Moises. "Has the Church Misread the Bible?" In *Foundations of Contemporary Interpretation*. Edited by Moises Silva, 25-27. Grand Rapids: Zondervan, 1996.
Sim, David C. "The Gospel of Matthew and the Gentiles." *JSNT* 57 (1995) 19-48.
Sinks, Robert F. "Theology of Divorce." *ChrCent* 94 (April 1977) 376-79.
Slack, Kenneth. "Remarriage in Church: An Issue for Anglicans." *ChrCent* 102 (January 1985) 38-39.
———. "Remarriage in the Church." *ChrCent* 100 (September 1983) 767-68.
———. "Remarriage: Still an Explosive Anglican Issue." *ChrCent* 101 (February 1984) 159-61.
Small, Dwight Hervey. *The Right to Remarry*. Old Tappan, NJ: Revell, 1977.
Smit, Neels. "Why May a Marriage not be Dissolved." *Orientation* 58-62 (December 1990-1991) 111-17.
Smith, W. Robertson. *Kinship and Marriage in Early Arabia*. With Additional Notes by the Author and by Ignaz Goldziher. Edited by Stanley A. Cook. London: A. & C. Black, 1993.
Smith, Barry D. *The Gospel of Mark: Introduction and Outline*. [online]. Available at http://www.abu.nb.ca/courses/NTIntro/Mark.htm. Accessed on 13 March 2001.
Smith, C. *Divorce and Remarriage*. [online]. Available at http://members.aol.com/cbsmith/TheWord.html. Accessed on 8 December 2000.
Smith, David. *Divorce and Remarriage in Church History*. [online]. Available at http://www.providence.mb.ca/didcurar.htm. Accessed on 8 December 2000.
Smoke, Jim. *Growing through Divorce, with Working Guide*. Eugene, OR: Harvest, 1986.
Snodgrass, Klyne R. "Matthew's Understanding of the Law." *Int* 46 (1992) 368-78.
Snoek, C. Jaime. "Marriage and the Institutionalisation of Sexual Relations." *Concilium* 5/6 (1970) 111-22.
Snuth, David L. "Divorce and Remarriage: From the Early Church to John Wesley." *TrinJ* 11/2 (1990) 131-42.
Sohn, Otto E. "The Church and Mixed Marriage." *CTM* 34/9 (1963) 517-40.
Sophocles. *Oedipus Tyrannus*. Edited by Sir Richard Jebb. [online]. Available at http://www.perseus.tufts.edu/cgi-bin/ptext?lookup=Soph.+OT+1212. Accessed on 29 October 2000.
Sorg, T. "Heart." In *NIDNTT*.
Sotirios. "Matrimony." In *Orthodox Catechism: Basic Teachings of the Orthodox Faith*. [online]. Available at http://www.gocanada.org/Catechism/catmatri.htm. Accessed on 21 April 2001.
Soulen, Richard N. "Marriage and Divorce: A Problem in New Testament Interpretation." *Int* 23 (1969) 439-50.
———. Review of *Divorce and Remarriage: Recovering the Biblical View*, by William F. Luck. In *Theology Today* 45 (1988) 263-64.
Spencer, Aida Besancon. "Literary Criticism." In *NTCI*, 225-51.
Spong, John S., Bp. "Can the Church Bless Divorce." *ChrCent* 101 (November 1984) 1126-27.
Springer, Robert H. "Notes on Moral Theology: Marriage and Divorce, July-December 1967." *TS* 29 (1968) 297-300.

Sprinkle, Joe M. "Old Testament Perspectives on Divorce and Remarriage." *JETS* 40 (1997) 530–51.

"The St. Louis Statement on Human Sexuality: Reprinted with permission from Resource, a publication of Presbyterians for Renewal (March 1994)." In *Evangelical Review of Theology* 19/1 (January 1995) 8–42.

Stackhouse, Max L. "Living the Tensions: Christians and Divorce." *ChrCent* 114 (August 1997) 685–86.

Stagg, Frank. "Biblical Perspectives on the Single Person." *RevExp* 74 (1977) 5–19.

Stählin, Gustav. "Χήρα." In *TDNT* 9 (1974) 440–65.

———. "Φίλος." In *TDNT* 9 (1974) 113–71.

Stallard, Mike. "An Essay on Liberal Hermeneutics." *CTJ* 3/10 (1999) 290–304.

Stanko, E., et al., *Counting the Costs: Estimating the Impact of Domestic Violence in the London Borough of Hackney*. London: Hackney Safer Cities and the Children's Society, 1998.

Stanley-Stevens, Christopher and Leslie Stanley-Stevens. "A Reconciling Approach to the Divorce Dilemma." *JPC* 46 (1992) 373–81.

Stanton, Graham N. "The Communities of Matthew." *Int* 46 (1992) 379–91.

Stauffer, Ethelbert. "Γαμέω, γάμος." In *TDNT* 1 (1964) 648–56.

Stegemann, Wolfgang. "Paul and the Sexual Mentality of His World." *Biblical Theology Bulletin* 23 (1993) 161–66.

Stein, Robert H. "Is it Lawful for a Man to Divorce His Wife?" *JETS* 22 (1979) 116–23.

———. "Redaction Criticism (NT)." In *ABD* 5:647–50.

———. "Synoptic Problem." In *DJG*, 787–92.

———. "What is Redaktionsgeschichte?" *JBL* 88 (1969) 45–56.

———. *Gospel and Tradition: Studies on Redaction Criticism of the Synoptic Gospels*. Grand Rapids: Baker, 1991.

Steinberg, Naomi. "Alliance or Descent: The Function of Marriage in Genesis." *JSOT* 51 (1991) 45–55.

Stephanopoulos, Robert G. "Marriage and Family in Ecumenical Perspective." *SVSQ* 25 (1981) 21–34.

Stewart, William Charles. *The Minister as Marriage Counsellor*. Nashville: Abingdon, 1961.

Stitzinger, Michael F. "Genesis 1–3 and the Male/Female Role Relationship." *GTJ* 2 (1981) 23–44.

Stone, Ira F. "The Precarious Ties That Bind Us: Sotah 2a." *Cross Currents* 51/2 (2001) 273–87.

Strabo. *Geography*. Edited by H. L. Jones. [online]. Available at http://perseus.csad.ox.ac.uk/cgi-bin/ptext?lookup=Strab.+8.6.1. Accessed on 21 December 2000.

Strauss, Mark L. Review of *Paul, Scripture, and Ethics: A Study of 1 Corinthians 5–7*, by Brian S. Rosner. In *JETS* 38 (1995) 292–93.

Strong, John T. Review of *Marriage as a Covenant*, by Gordon Paul Hugenberger. In *CBQ* 57 (1995) 557–59.

Stuart, Elizabeth, and Adrian Thatcher, editors. *Christian Perspectives on Sexuality and Gender*. Grand Rapids: Eerdmans, 1996.

Stylianopoulos, Theodore G. "The Indissolubility of Marriage, in the New Testament: Principle and Practice." *GOTR* 34 (1989) 335–45.

———. "Toward a Theology of Marriage in the Orthodox Church." *GOTR* 22 (1977) 249–83.

Suetonius. *Life of Augustus*. Translated by Mary R. Lefkowitz and Maureen B. Fant. [online]. Available at: http://www.uky.edu/ArtsSciences/Classics/wlgr/wlgr-romanlegal120.html. Accessed on 14 October 2000.

Sunderland, Edwin. "The Pastoral Care of Ecumenical Marriages—the Episcopal Perspective." *JES* 16 (1979) 619–28.

Sunukjian, D. R. Review of *Jesus and Divorce: The Problem with the Evangelical Consensus*, by William A. Heth and Gordon J. Wenham. In *BibSac* 142/568 (1985) 375–76.

Swindoll, C. R. *Strike the Original Match*. Portland: Multnomah, 1970. Quoted in J. Carl Laney, "Paul and the Permanence of Marriage in 1 Corinthians 7." *JETS* 25 (1982) 288.

Talbert, Charles H. "Are There Biblical Norms for Christian Marriage?" *JFM* 15 (2001) 16–27.

Talmud—Mas. Gittin 57a. The Sonico Talmud, 1973. Davka Corporation's Judaic Classics Library, Version IIf, by David Kantrowitz. Institute for Computers in Jewish Life. Davka Corporation & Judaica, 1999.

Talmud—Mas. Kethuboth. The Soncino Talmud, 1973. Davka Corporation's Judaic Classics Library. Version IIf by David Kantrowitz. Institute for Computers in Jewish Life. Davka Corporation & Judaica, 1999.

Tannehill, Robert C. *The Gospel of Mark as Narrative Christology*. [online]. Available at http://shemesh.scholar.emory.edu:6336/dynaweb/Semeia/Semeia_16/@Generic__BookView. Accessed on 23 October 1999.

———. *The Narrative Unity of Luke-Acts: A Literary Interpretation*. Vol. 1. Philadelphia: Fortress, 1991.

Tasker, R. V. G. *Matthew: An Introduction and Commentary*. Tyndale New Testament Commentaries. London: Tyndale, 1961.

Taylor, Vincent. *The Gospel according to St Mark*. London: Macmillan, 1966.

Tebtunis Papyrus I 104. G. In *Women's Life in Greece and Rome*. Translated by Mary R. Lefkowitz and Maureen B. Fant. [online]. Available at http://www.stoa.org/diotima/anthology/wlgr/wlgr-greeklegal101.shtml. Accessed on 24 December 2004.

Ted. *What is the Orthodox Position on Divorce and Remarriage?* [online]. Available at http://www.beliefnet.com/story/15/story_1595_1.html. Accessed on 21 April 2001.

Tegels, Aelred. "An Ecumenical Rite of Marriage." *Worship* 59 (1985) 444–47.

Terrien, Samuel. *Till the Heart Sings: A Biblical Theology of Manhood and Womanhood*. Philadelphia: Fortress, 1985.

Tertullian. *Exhortation to Chastity*. Translated by S. Thelwall. In *Ante-Nicene Fathers: Translations of The Writings of the Fathers Down to A.D. 325*. Edited by Alexander Roberts and James Donaldson. Vol.4. *Christian Classics Ethereal Library*. Vol. 2. CD-ROM. Edited by Harry Plantinga. Wheaton, IL: Wheaton College, 1998.

———. *To His Wife*. Translated by S. Thelwall. In *Ante-Nicene Fathers: Translations of The Writings of the Fathers Down to A.D. 325*. Edited by Alexander Roberts and James Donaldson. Vol.4. *Christian Classics Ethereal Library*. Vol.2. CD-ROM. Edited by Harry Plantinga. Wheaton, IL: Wheaton College, 1998.

———. *Treatises on Marriage and Remarriage. To His Wife. An Exhortation to Chastity. Monogamy*. Translated by William P. Le Saint. London: Longmans, Green, 1951.

Thatcher, Adrian. *Living Together and Christian Ethics*. New Studies in Christian Ethics. Cambridge: Cambridge University Press, 2002.

———. *Marriage after Modernity: Christian Marriage in Postmodern Times*. Sheffield: Sheffield Academic, 1999.

Thiel, Josef Franz. "The Institution of Marriage: An Anthropological Perspective." *Concilium* 5/6 (May 1970) 13–24.

Thielicke, Helmut. *The Ethics of Sex*. Translated by John W. Doberstein. New York: Fortress, 1964.

Thiselton, Anthony C. *The First Epistle to the Corinthians*. NIGTC. Grand Rapids: Eerdmans, 2000.

Thomas, Frank N. "Competency-Based Relationship Counseling: The Necessity of Goal Setting and Counsellor Flexibility in Efficient and Effective Couples Counseling." *JPC* 53 (1999) 87–99.

Thomas, John L. "Family, Sex, and Marriage in a Contraceptive Culture." *TS* 35 (1974) 134–53.

Thomas, Kenneth J. "Torah Citations in the Synoptics." *New Testament Studies* 24 (1977) 85–96.

Thomas, Robert L. "The 'Jesus Crisis:' What is It?" In *The Jesus Crisis*. Grand Rapids: Kregel, 1998. Quoted in Mike Stallard, "An Essay on Liberal Hermeneutics." *CTJ* 3/10 (December 1999) 290–303.

Thompson, David A. *Counseling and Divorce, Resources for Christian Counseling*. Dallas: Word, 1989.

Thompson, Thomas L. "Catholic View on Divorce." *JES* 6/1 (1969) 53–67.

Thornes, Barbara and Jean Collard. *Who Divorces?* London: Routledge & Kegan Paul, 1979.

Thornton, Edward E. "Raising God-Consciousness in the Family." *RevExp* 75 (1978) 75–88.

Tjaden, N. Thoennes. *Full Report of the Prevalence, Incidence, and Consequences of Violence Against Women: Findings From the National Violence Against Women Survey*. Washington, DC: National Institute of Justice, Office of Justice Programs, 2000. Quoted in Hugh Waters, et al., *The Economic Dimensions of Interpersonal Violence*, 17. Geneva: Department of Injuries and Violence Prevention, World Health Organization, 2004.

Tosato, Angelo. "On Genesis 2:24." *CBQ* 52 (1990) 389–409.

———. "The Law of Leviticus 18:18: a Reexamination." *CBQ* 46 (1984) 199–214.

Toussaint, S. D. Review of *Divorce and Remarriage*, by Guy Duty. In *BibSac* 125/499 (July 1968) 275. Electronic Edition by Galaxie Software, 1999.

Transliterated BHS Hebrew Old Testament. Database by Matthew Anstey. CCAT Michigan-Claremont-Westminster electronic database, 2001.

Treggiari, Susan. "Marriage and Family in Roman Society." In *MFBW*, 132–82.

Trible, Phyllis. *God and the Rhetoric of Sexuality*. OBT. Philadelphia: Fortress, 1978.

Tucker, Karen B. Westerfield. Review of *John Wesley and Marriage*, by Bufford W. Coe. In *Worship* 71 (1997) 358–59.

Tuckett, C. M. "1 Corinthians and Q." *JBL* 102 (1983) 607–19.

Turner, David L. Review of *New Testament Exegesis: A Handbook for Students and Pastors*, by Gordon D. Fee. In *GTJ* 6 (1985) 126–29.

TWOT Hebrew Lexicon. In *BibleWorks for Windows*. Version 4.0.026e [4000]. Cambridge, MA: Lotus Development Corporation, 1998.

Ulrich, Y. C., et al., "Medical Care Utilization Patterns in Women with Diagnosed Domestic Violence." *American Journal of Preventative Medicine* 24 (2003) 9–15.

Uplian. *Rules* 6.13. In *Women's Life in Greece and Rome: A Source Book in Translation*. 2nd ed. Translated by Mary R. Lefkowitz and Maureen B. Fant. Baltimore: Johns Hopkins University Press, 1992.
Vaccari, Alberto. "Divorce in the Gospels." *ThDig* 5/1 (1957) 31–33.
Van Arnold, William. "Marriage in and out of Favour." *JP* 1/3 (1978) 53–55.
Van Der Wal, Hicolass. "Secular Law and The Eastern Church's Concept of Marriage." *Concilium* 5/6 (1970) 76–82.
Van, Leeuwen, and Mary Stewart. "Deconstructing the Culture of Divorce." *ChrCent* 114 (August 1997) 690–93.
Vanier, Jean. *Man and Woman He Made Them*. London: Darton, Longman and Todd, 1985.
Vasoli, Robert H. *What God Has Joined Together: The Annulment Crisis in American Catholicism*. Oxford: Oxford University Press, 1998.
Vaux, Roland de. *Ancient Israel: Its Life and Institutions*. Translated by John McHugh. London: Darton, Longman and Todd, 1962.
Vawter, Bruce. "Divorce and the New Testament." *CBQ* 39 (1977) 528–42.
———. "Divorce Clauses in Matthew 5:32 and 19:9." *CBQ* 16 (1954) 155–67.
Venter, Cassie. "What is God's Intention with Marriage." *Orientation* 58–62 (December 1990–1991) 98–100.
Verhey, Allen. "The Holy Bible and Sanctified Sexuality: An Evangelical Approach to Scripture and Sexual Ethics." *Int* 49 (1995) 31–45.
Verkhovskoy, Serge S. "Creation of Man and the Establishment of the Family in the Light of the Book of Genesis." *SVSQ* 8 (1964) 5–30.
Vidal, Marciano. "The Object of Consensus." *Concilium* 7/9 (September 1973) 88–97.
Viscuso, Patrick. "Concerning the Second Marriage of Priests." *GOTR* 40 (1995) 201–11.
———. "Late Byzantine Canonical Views on the Dissolution of Marriage." *GOTR* 44 (1999) 273–90.
———. "Marriage Between Christians and Non-Christians: Orthodox and Roman Catholic Perspectives." *JES* 31 (1994) 269–78.
———. "Marriage Between Orthodox and Non-Orthodox: A Canonical Study." *GOTR* 40 (1995) 229–46.
———. "Orthodox-Catholic Unity and the Revised Code of Eastern Canon Law." *JES* 27 (1990) 108–115.
———. "The Formation of Marriage in Late Byzantium." *SVSQ* 35 (1991) 309–325.
Vondenberger, Victoria. *Catholics, Marriage and Divorce: Real People, Real Questions*. Cincinnati: St. Anthony Messenger, 2004.
Vos, Betty. "Practicing a Love Ethic for all Families." *ChrCent* 108/13 (1991) 1060–1062.
Waanders, David D. "Ethical Reflections on the Differentiation of Self in Marriage." *JPC* 41 (1987) 100–110.
Wakeman, M. K. "Sacred Marriage." *JSOT* 22 (1982) 21–31.
Walch, A. G. and W. E. Broadhead. "Prevalence of Lifetime Sexual Victimization Among Female Patients." *Journal of Family Practice* 35 (1992) 511–16.
Wall, John. "Marriage Today: Sacramental or Utilitarian?" *ChrCent* 117/30 (January 2000) 1120–21.
Wallace, Daniel B. *Greek Grammar Beyond the Basics: An Exegetical Syntax of the New Testament*. Grand Rapids: Zondervan, 1996.
———. *Mark: Introduction, Argument, and Outline*. [online]. Available at http://www.bible.org/docs/soapbox/markotl.htm. Accessed on 14 March 2001.

Wallis. "Dābhaq." In *Theological Dictionary of the Old Testament*. Edited by G. Johannes Bofferweck and Helmer Ringgren. Translated by John T. Willis, Geoffrey W. Bromiley, and David E. Green. Vol.3. Grand Rapids: Eerdmans, 1978.

Walsh, Efthalia Makris. "Saint Gregory the Theologian's Use of the Abraham and Sarah Tradition in Relation to Marriage." *GOTR* 39 (1994) 211–26.

Walvoord, John F. "Interpreting Prophecy Today. Part 3: The New Testament Doctrine of the Kingdom." *BibSac* 139/555 (1982) 205–14.

Wangerin, Walter. "On Mourning the Death of a Marriage: It Should not Be; But if Death Occurs, We Need to Know How to Grieve." *ChrTo* 28 (May 1984) 20–23.

Ware, Timothy. *The Orthodox Church*. Harmondsworth: Penguin, 1993.

Waters, Hugh, et al., *The Economic Dimensions of Interpersonal Violence*. Geneva: Department of Injuries and Violence Prevention, World Health Organization, 2004.

Watson, Francis. "Biblical Criticism and Interpretation 2: New Testament." In *The Blackwell Encyclopaedia of Modern Christian Thought*. Edited by Alister E. McGrath, 41–50. Oxford: Basel Blackwell, 1993.

Webb, William J. "Unequally Yoked Together with Unbelievers Part 2: What Is the Unequal Yoke (ἑτεροζυγοῦντες) in 2 Corinthians 6:14? " *BibSac*. Electronic Edition by Galaxie Software, 1999.

Weems, Renita J. "Gomer: Victim of Violence or Victim of Metaphor?" *Semeia* 47 (1989) 87–104.

———. *Battered Love: Marriage, Sex and Violence in the Hebrew Prophets*. Overtures to Biblical Theology. Edited by Walter Brueggemann, et al. Minneapolis: Fortress, 1995.

Wegener, David. "Reflections on Marriage: Looking Back on Fifteen Years and the Lord's Design for Marriage in Genesis." *Journal for Biblical Manhood and Womanhood Volume* 3/1 (March 1998). Electronic Edition by Galaxie Software, 2002.

Wenham, Gordon J. "*Betûlah*, a Girl of Marriageable Age." *VT* 22 (1972) 326–48.

———. "Matthew and Divorce: an Old Crux Revisited." *JSNT* 22 (1984) 95–107.

———. "May Divorced Christians Remarry?" *Churchman* 95/2 (1981) 150–61.

———. "The Restoration of Marriage Reconsidered." *Journal of Jewish Studies* 30 (1979) 36–40.

———. "The Syntax of Matthew 19:9." *JSNT* 28 (1986) 17–23.

———. *Genesis 1–15*. WBC 1A. Dallas: Word, 1998.

Wenham, Gordon J., and William E. Heth. *Jesus and Divorce*. Updated ed. Waynesboro: Paternoster, 2002.

Wenham, John. *Redacting Matthew, Mark and Luke: A Fresh Assault on the Synoptic Problem*. Downers Grove, IL: InterVarsity, 1992.

Wessel, Walter W. "Mark." In *EBC*. Grand Rapids: Zondervan, 1999.

Wessels, Francois. "Exegesis and Proclamation: Ephesians 5:21–33." *Journal of Theology for Southern Africa* 67 (1989) 67–75.

Westbrook, Raymond. "The Prohibition on Restoration of Marriage in Deuteronomy 24:1–4." In *Studies in Bible* 31. Edited by Sara Japhet, 387–405. Jerusalem: Magnes, 1986.

Westermarck, Edward. *The Future of Marriage in Western Civilisation*. New York: Books for Libraries, 1970.

What Does the Bible Teach: The Divine Permission. [online]. Available at http://www.gospelcom.net/rbc/ds/q0806/point1.html. Accessed on 20 November 2000.

Where We Stand on Jewish Marriage. [online]. Available at http://www.fishponds.freeserve.co.uk/where_we_stand/marriage.html. Accessed on 6 October 2000.

White, Ernest. "Biblical Principles for Modern Family Living." *RevExp* 75 (1978) 5–18.

———. Review of *To Have and to Hold*, by David J. Atkinson. In *RevExp* 80 (1983) 644–45.

Whittaker's Revised BDB. In *BibleWorks for Windows*. Version 4.0.026e [4000]. Cambridge, MA: Lotus Development Corporation, 1998.

WHO. *Multi-Country Study on Women's Health and Domestic Violence Against Women*. Geneva: World Health Organization, 2002.

Wiebe, P. H. "Jesus' Divorce Exception." *JETS* 32 (1989) 328–35.

———. "The New Testament on Divorce and Remarriage: Some Logical Implications." *JETS* 24 (1981) 137.

Wiersbe, W. W. *The Bible Exposition Commentary*. Wheaton, IL: Victor, 1996, c1989. Logos Research Systems, Libronix Digital Library System 2.0. 2000–2002.

Wiesner-Hanks, Merry E. *Christianity and Sexuality in the Early Modern World: Regulating Desire, Reforming Practice*. London: Routledge, 2000.

Wiethaus, Ulrike. "Sexuality, Gender, and the Body in Late Medieval Women's Spirituality: Cases from Germany and the Netherlands." *Journal of Feminist Studies in Religion* 7 (1991) 35–52.

Wilcox, Stephen W. *Restoration of Christian Marriage: A Call for Reformation*, 2004. [online]. Available at www.MarriageDivorce.Com. Accessed on 24 January 2005.

———. *The Restoration of Christian Marriage: A Call for Repentance and Reformation*. [online]. Available at http://www.mastershelp.com/wwwboard/divorceforum/messages/35.html. Accessed on 25 April 2001.

Wilfong, Marsha M. "Genesis 2:18–24." *Int* 42 (1988) 58–63.

Williamson, Lamar. *Mark*. IBC. Louisville: Westminster John Knox, 1983.

Willimon, William H. "Marriage: The Impossible Commitment." *ChrCent* 96 (June 1979) 669–74.

———. "The People We're Stuck With." *ChrCent* 107 (October 1990) 924–25.

———. "The Risk of Divorce." *ChrCent* 96 (June 1979) 666–69.

Wilson, Douglas. *Reforming Marriage*. Moscow: Canon, 1995.

Wilson, James Q. *The Marriage Problem: How Our Culture Has Weakened Families*. New York: HarperCollins, 2002.

Wilson, Patricia. Review of *Divorce and Remarriage for Catholics*, by Stephen J. Kelleher. In *ChrCent* 91 (February 1974) 241–42.

Wingenbach, Gregory Charles. "Improvement in Orthodox/Roman Catholic Relations: Issues of Marriage and Family Life." *SVSQ* 35 (1991) 359–79.

Wintz, Jack, editor. *Living Our Faith After the Changes: Explaining Catholic Thinking Since Vatican II*. USA: St. Anthony Messenger, 1977.

Wisner, C., et al., "Intimate Partner Violence Against Women: Do Victims Cost Health Plans More?" *The Journal of Family Practice* 48 (1999) 439–443. Quoted in Hugh Waters, et al., *The Economic Dimensions of Interpersonal Violence*, 21. Geneva: Department of Injuries and Violence Prevention, World Health Organization, 2004.

Witherington, Ben III. "Herodias." In *ABD* 3:174–76.

———. "Matthew 5:32 and 19:9—Exception or Exceptional Situation?" *NTS* 31 (1985) 571–76.

———. *Conflict and Community in Corinth: A Socio-Rhetorical Commentary on 1 and 2 Corinthians*. Grand Rapids: Eerdmans, 1995.

———. *The Paul Quest: The Renewed Search for the Jew of Tarsus.* Downers Grove, IL: InterVarsity, 1998.

———. *Paul's Narrative Thought World: The Tapestry of Tragedy and Triumph.* Louisville: Westminster John Knox, 1994.

Witmer, John A. Review of *. . . And Marries Another*, by Craig S. Keener. In *BibSac* 151 (1994) 250.

Witte Jr., John. "Consulting a Living Tradition: Christian Heritage of Marriage and Family." *ChrCent* 113/13 (1996) 1108–11.

———. *From Sacrament to Contract: Marriage, Religion, and Law in the Western Tradition.* The Family, Religion, and Culture. Louisville: Westminster John Knox, 1997.

———. "Anglican Marriage in the Making: Becon, Bullinger, and Bucer." In the *Contentious Triangle: Church, State and University.* Edited by R. L. Petersen and C. A. Pater, 241–59. Kirksville, MO: Thomas Jefferson University Press, 1999.

Wojtyla, Karol (Pope John Paul II). *Love and Responsibility.* Translated by H. T. Willetts. San Francisco: Ignatius, 1981.

Wolfe, Christopher. "The Marriage of Your Choice." *First Things* 50 (1995) 37–41.

Wolff, Hans Walter. *Anthropology of the Old Testament.* Translated by Margaret Kohl. Philadelphia: Fortress, 1974.

Wood, Susan. "The Marriage of Baptized Nonbelievers: Faith, Contract, and Sacrament." *TS* 48 (1987) 279–301.

World Health Organization. *Guidelines for Medico-Legal Care of Victims of Sexual Violence.* Geneva: World Health Organization 2003.

Worthingon, Everett. *I Care About Your Marriage.* Chicago: Moody, 1994.

Wright, David F. "Woman Before and After the Fall: A Comparison of Luther's and Calvin's Interpretation of Genesis 1–3." *Churchman* 98/2 (1984) 126–35.

Wurster, David F. C. "Marriage: Crucible for Growth." *JPC* 37 (1983) 253–63.

Yadin, Yigael, Jonas C. Greenfield, and Ada Yardeni. "Babatha's *Ketubba.*" *IEJ* 44 (1994) 75–101.

Yamauchi, Edwin M. "Cultural Aspects of Marriage in the Ancient World." *BibSac* 135/539 (1978) 241–51.

Yarbrough, Larry O. *Not Like the Gentiles: Marriage Rules in the Letters of Paul.* Atlanta: Scholars, 1985.

Yaron, R. "The Restoration of Marriage." *Journal of Jewish Studies* 17 (1966) 1–11.

Yates, Wilson. "The Protestant View of Marriage." *JES* 22 (1985) 41–54.

Yonge, C. D., trans. *The Works of Philo: Complete and Unabridged.* Peabody: Hendrickson, 1996. Electronic Edition by Libronix Digital Library System 2.0, 2002.

Young, Richard A. Review of *The Moral Vision of the New Testament*, by Richard B. Hays. In *JETS* 42 (1999) 136–38.

Young, Sharon L. "Ending Marriage, Keeping Faith: A New Guide Through the Spiritual Journey of Divorce." *JPC* 51 (1997) 125–26.

Zeisler, Steve. *What is Marriage?* [online]. Available at http://www.pbc.org/dp/zeisler/4556.html. Accessed on 19 November 2000.

Zenith, Harris Merrill. *Marriage, Divorce, Remarriage: What Does the Bible Allow?* [online]. Available at http://www.bloomington.in.us/~lgthscac/marriagedivorce.htm#marriage,%20divorce,%20remarriage:%20what%20does%20the%20bible%20allow? Accessed on 25 April 2001.

Zerwick, Maximilian. *Biblical Greek.* Eng. ed. Rome: Scripta Pontificii Instituti Biblici, 1963.

Zion, William Basil. *Eros and Transformation: Sexuality and Marriage - An Eastern Orthodox Perspective.* Lanham, MD: University Press of America, 1931.

www.ingramcontent.com/pod-product-compliance
Lightning Source LLC
Chambersburg PA
CBHW071229290426
44108CB00013B/1339